Betty Goes Vegan

Betty Goes Vegan

ANNIE & DAN SHANNON

500 Classic Recipes for the Modern Family

GRAND CENTRAL
Life & Style
NEW YORK · BOSTON

· ·

Grand Central Publishing
Hachette Book Group
237 Park Avenue
New York, NY 10017
www.HachetteBookGroup.com

Printed in the United States of America

QMA

First Edition: February 2013

10 9 8 7 6 5 4 3 2 1

Grand Central Publishing is a division of Hachette Book Group, Inc.

The Grand Central Publishing name and logo is a trademark of Hachette Book Group, Inc.

The Hachette Speakers Bureau provides a wide range of authors for speaking events.
To find out more, go to www.hachettespeakersbureau.com or call (866) 376-6591.

The publisher is not responsible for websites (or their content) that are not owned by the publisher.

· ·

Library of Congress Cataloging-in-Publication Data

Shannon, Annie.
 Betty goes vegan : 500 classic recipes for the modern family / by Annie and Dan Shannon. — 1st ed.
  p. cm.
 Includes index.
 ISBN 978-1-4555-0933-1 (hardcover) ISBN 978-1-4555-1720-6 (ebook) 1. Vegan cooking. I. Shannon, Dan. II. Title.
 TX837.S46172 2013
 641.5'636—dc23
                    2012025857

For the lobsters

CONTENTS

INTRODUCTION

At first, it was a charming movie that seemed tailor-made for me. A devoted, vintage clothing–wearing amateur foodie with a loyal and patient husband cooking her way through Julia Child's *Mastering the Art of French Cooking*. Just a normal person with a normal kitchen who hated her job and had hoped for more by this point in her life. She even wore pearls in the kitchen—one of my own personal dreams. Of course, in my dreams those pearls are fake. On the surface, I felt like I'd found someone a lot like me. But as you can imagine, Julie Powell lost me when she killed the lobster.

From the moment they showed her walking through the farmers' market choosing the doomed crustaceans, right up to when she finally overcame her "fear" and threw them *alive* into a pot of boiling water, I kept waiting for her to have a change of heart. I thought she would succumb to her conscience—she even admitted that she knew it was wrong—but she never did. It was at that moment I realized that Julie and I were not so alike after all. I just couldn't stop thinking about the celebrated Lobster Killer and how there needed to be a humane alternative.

Contrary to some stereotypes, vegans are just as passionate about cooking and eating as any meat-eating foodie. After years of working at the largest animal-advocacy organizations on the planet and meeting thousands of vegans from all over the world, I can say with complete confidence that no one loves food the way vegans do. We think about it constantly. We read labels with Christmas-morning eagerness, searching for those deal-breaker words: whey, egg whites, skim milk protein, and casein. We sit around talking about food like the gals on *Sex and the City* talk about orgasms. We send emails to our friends and family telling them about new products and restaurants with a passion that can only be compared to Beatlemania.

So when my husband, Dan, and I decided to start our own cookbook cook-through on our blog, we had an equally impassioned goal in mind: we wanted to show that you can make anything vegan and that no animal ever needs to be force-fed, confined to a crate or a cage, or boiled alive, or to endure any of the other nightmares animals face to satisfy our culinary desires.

But any good campaigner knows you can't just tell people that. The proof is in the vegan pudding. You need to show people that *any* recipe can be veganized, and you need to prove the result can be even more delicious than the original. This meant we needed to show people how to use vegan products like mock meats and cheeses to their full potential. I used to ignore products like soy cheese and fake meats because when I first went vegan, technology hadn't quite caught up with demand, and those early versions weren't really right yet. Like many vegans, I also spent years avoiding ingredients like nutritional yeast and agave nectar because I didn't know how to use them correctly. But these days, there are outstanding vegan products and ingredients available in every grocery store, and all folks need is a little inspiration and guidance on how to reimagine compassionate and often healthier versions of their all-time favorite dishes.

Once we had a clear idea of what we wanted to do and how we were going to do it, Dan and I drove to every bookstore in southern Virginia. We begrudgingly agreed that Julia's historic book wasn't the right fit. Julia really did revolutionize how Americans looked at cooking and mainstreamed French cuisine—but sadly *Mastering the Art of French Cooking*, with all its beef-flavored Jell-O molds and frightening organ-based dishes, wasn't going to inspire the kinds of recipes we needed to create to achieve our goal.

We flipped through more cookbooks than I can remember, but there was one that stood out: a bright red binder decorated like Bavarian gingerbread. It was the original 1950s edition of *Betty Crocker's Picture Cook Book*. This book was for someone just like me, in (nonleather) saddle shoes and black-rimmed glasses, aspiring to one day wear (faux) pearls in the kitchen. But I had to put it back. The goal was to show that *anything* could be vegan—and this edition lacked any real international dishes and included recipes like Broiled Grapefruit and Herring-Appleteasers, which aren't exactly in fashion with the modern family. We decided to compromise, going with the 2010 edition of the *Betty Crocker Cookbook*, which had more than just pork chops, meat loafs, and Jell-O molds. This would be the perfect outline for family-friendly vegan recipes and for showcasing the tips and tricks we'd picked up over the years for "veganizing" recipes.

See, it had to be Betty. The Betty Crocker brand has a well-deserved reputation for teaching amateur American chefs how to get the most out of products and ingredients that they might not have otherwise used. Betty Crocker would be the perfect inspiration for showing people you really can turn anything vegan once you know the tricks.

Since the day we walked out of the bookstore with our own copy of Big Red, I have fallen in love with Betty Crocker. This project has not only encouraged me to make some outrageous casseroles and use all of the crazy kitchen gadgets I hoard, but also gives me an opportunity to share with others how easy a vegan lifestyle can be.

And that, kids, is how the Betty Crocker Project was born!

For more than two years, Dan and I shared our lives, discoveries, tips, tricks, and secrets with the loyal readers of our blog at MeetTheShannons.net—as well as all of those hidden lurkers, Twitter followers, and Facebook fans. This book takes the Betty Crocker Project one step further. It's more than just a collection of recipes we created out of admiration for Betty Crocker and several hundred other recipes that will help any vegan or not-yet-vegan cook like a gourmet chef. There are instructions for equipping your vegan kitchen with all the products and gadgets you need to cook these and other vegan recipes; tips and tricks for making the transition to a vegan lifestyle and making it stick; reflections on what we've learned about Betty Crocker and her place in a modern, vegan-friendly world; and much more. Basically, it's your all-in-one guide to becoming a cook like Betty Crocker that pays homage to her and the all-American superwoman she was created to represent, while celebrating vegan cuisine.

We've always said that we can make anything vegan. Now we can say we've proved it! Thank you, Lobster Killer, for inspiring a project that I suspect you would absolutely hate.

WHO IS BETTY, ANYWAY?

Any women's studies major can tell you that for generations, the history of women has been recorded in quilts and on recipe cards and kept alive through oral traditions. So it's kind of refreshing to actually have a documented origin story for one of the most famous female faces in culinary history … even if she's not a real person.

Betty Crocker was "born" in Minneapolis, Minnesota, in 1921 to the all-male staff of Gold Medal. She would later come to be known as "the First Lady of Food," but in the beginning she was just a branding campaign. Ultimately she would become one of the most successful branding campaigns of all time. The character was named "Crocker" after William G.

Crocker, a retired director at Washburn Crosby, the parent company of Gold Medal, which would become General Mills. "Betty" was just the obvious choice.

Bettys have always been pleasant, cheery, all-American gals. They're that perfect combination of friendly and sexy, flashing garters and patooties like Grable, Boop, and Page. They're the cutie-pies of neighborhood potlucks, with pterodactyl casseroles and fresh-baked cookies, like Rubble and Cooper (you know, Veronica's archrival). They're mysterious like Davis. They're hilarious like White. And now they're vegan.

"Betty Crocker" is an avatar for a uniquely American style of womanhood, and this book is for all those ladies courageously trying to live up to that expectation: those superhuman women who can cook tofu scramble for breakfast, get the kids off to school, bake vegan cupcakes for the office potluck, get the customer report submitted on time, chair the PTA meeting, pick the kids up from practice, and serve a nutritious three-course vegan dinner around an impeccably set table—all while wearing pearls and a smile. We're the ones who see birthdays as an opportunity to bake towers of eggless cupcakes with better-than-buttercream frosting to show how much we care. We're the ones who know deep down that there's always a way to make a compassionate and delicious version of any dish. Betty Crocker represents everyone who ever looked at her kitchen and said, "You will not defeat me!" And now you can be like Betty Crocker too.

❋ ❋ ❋

Chapter One
BETTY'S VEGAN KITCHEN

Six days after my thirty-sixth birthday, I was up before dawn to drink coffee and settle in to my day of work in my pajamas, like I did every morning. Thirty-five was the year I tried to find a new job but didn't. Thirty-five was the year most of my friends moved to other cities all over the world. Thirty-five was the year we tried to have a baby but didn't. But thirty-five was also the year we threw ourselves into an ambitious project that was getting more attention than I had ever imagined possible.

Our little blog had been featured in *Maclean's* and on Jezebel.com and a bunch of other websites. The *Virginian-Pilot* had even done a human-interest story about us that was on the cover of the food section. We were getting emails from literary agents and publishers who wanted to work with us. I kept hearing that things in our lives were about to change ... but yet there I was, up before dawn, sitting down at my computer to watch hours of horrific animal-abuse footage online and trying to track down the IP addresses of the people who uploaded it so I could pester YouTube and the proper authorities and hopefully bring people to justice.

My career as an activist was a far cry from where it had been a few years previously, when I traveled around the world advocating for fur-free fashion. I went to New York, Paris, and London for Fashion Weeks and worked with celebrities and famous designers. I wore nice clothes! But I'd traded in those days for domestic bliss with the love of my life and my best friend—and a new job that was decidedly less glamorous. It was hard watching my friends and former peers in the movement moving past me professionally, but in the end I knew that I was truly happy for the first time in my life.

This brings us back to my life as an online cruelty caseworker ... but first I needed to type up "Come & Get It! Our Top 15 Favorite Vegan Recipes for Picnic & BBQ Season!" for the blog. Dan had already left for work at his own busy, important, glamorous job in the animal rights movement—and it was just me and the cats, writing our blog post for the day. If it were any other day, this would be the best half hour I'd have until Dan came home that night. But it wasn't any other day.

On May 27, 2011, I logged on to Blogger and noticed that five thousand people had visited our blog that morning. That wasn't *that* weird for us ... after we'd posted for the day and we had our lunchtime traffic rush. But it was really early, and the little bar on our analytics page was still rising. So I followed the link back to where all this traffic was coming from.

There we were, listed second in the "What We're Reading" section of the *New York Times Diner's Journal* blog. The next half hour is still a little bit of a blur. I know I sent Dan an email and asked him to log on to chat. Then I believe our chat went like this:

DAN: Good morning!
ME: http://dinersjournal.blogs.nytimes. com/2011/05/27/what-were-reading-192/
DAN: Holy s--t!

From there, a lot of things happened quickly. We got connected with a lovely, amazing literary agent. She hooked us up with a clever, supportive publisher. We signed a book deal. I quit my job. And just like that, I was a Really Real Professional Writer Person, working on a cookbook that was going to help make it easier for people to become and stay vegan. This was the career

I always wanted—something that made the world a better place for animals, didn't give me nightmares or break my heart every day, and made me feel like I had something unique and valuable to contribute to the world. And I didn't have to give up finally being happy to get it.

But even before all this, being inspired by the icon that is Betty Crocker did more than just give me a creative outlet. It gave me a way to explore and share with the world more than twenty years of vegan cooking, culinary adventures, and experiments. I wasn't classically trained in Paris like Julia Child. Dan and I were just two normal people who are madly in love and who started an ambitious cooking project while working demanding full-time jobs and had a test kitchen about the size of a bathtub. We aren't millionaires, and we have only so much room in our fridge and pantry—so we have to shop and cook smart. You're probably no different.

You don't want to invest a lot of time and money hunting down rare and exotic ingredients, and then use them only once. This book uses a lot of the same ingredients for a wide variety of recipes, so if you're newly vegan and investing in these products for the first time, you'll end up with a fully functioning pantry, rather than a kitchen cluttered with one-hit wonders. This chapter highlights some of the basic ingredients and tools every person who wants to cook like Betty Crocker needs to not just make the recipes in this book, but also quickly whip up any creative five-course vegan meal.

THE PANTRY

These are some of the basic ingredients you'll be using; others can be found in "A Field Guide to Mock Meats" on page 157, "The Evolution of Vegan Cheese" on page 189, "Egg Replacers" on page 323, "Thanksgiving" on page 442, and a few other spots throughout the book.

If you're not fortunate enough to live near a Whole Foods, Trader Joe's, or decent health food store, you can always order these things online. Oftentimes you can even buy them in bulk and save on shipping. It's also nice to support local vegan businesses, such as Food Fight! in Portland, Oregon, and Pangea Vegan Store in Rockville, Maryland, so Google their websites if you need to order any of these ingredients online.

All the ingredients we use in this book are, of course, vegan. But there are two things to keep in mind. One: some products come in different varieties, like Bisquick mix; there are vegan and nonvegan versions; we obviously recommend using the vegan versions. Two: sometimes products change their formulations, and something that used to be vegan isn't anymore. The day that happens is a tragic day. So just make sure to double-check the label if you're buying something for the first time.

Agar-Agar I hesitate to tell you that this wonder-product is made from seaweed—but it is. So if you're worried I'm pushing Frankenfoods on you, well, this one isn't one of them. It's a vegan "gelatin" that, once you get the hang of it, will make you believe in miracles.

Agave Nectar I'll be the first to admit that one of the most frustrating parts of being vegan is trying to make products with weird and icky names sound as delicious as they are (read: Tofurky). Agave nectar is not one of those. To me, agave nectar sounds like something British hummingbirds enjoy with their tea. This natural sweetener actually comes from Mexican cacti and is one of our favorite ways to replace both honey and sugar.

Almond Milk I love it in coffee, smoothies, and baked goods. It's not as easy to bake with and doesn't behave quite like soy milk, but once you get the hang of it, it's a great way to diversify your diet.

Applesauce Whether you love chickens or you're just trying to eat healthier, replacing eggs with applesauce is a great way to do both. We use it in our recipes as much as possible because it's an ingredient you can find in every grocery store. Heck, you can find it at some gas stations. So no matter where you live, vegan baking is possible.

Arrowroot This might sound like something from a witch's brew, but really it's a wonderful light powder used for thickening a sauce or for binding in baked goods.

Better Than Bouillon Not all of these bouillons are vegan, but they do have a faux beef and faux chicken broth that are. They also are fat-, MSG-, and GMO-free and contain a third less sodium than other bouillons. We can't recommend this product enough and suggest you locate a jar of it as soon as you finish reading this.

Bisquick Mix Yes, several Bisquick mix varieties are vegan, and they'll save you time and money. At this point I'm going to refer you to the incredibly well-written story behind Bisquick mix, "We've Got a Mix for That," on page 317.

Bragg's Liquid Aminos What is this brown number that looks and tastes quite a bit like soy sauce? It's a liquid protein concentrate, derived from healthy non-GMO soybeans, that contains the sixteen naturally occurring essential and nonessential amino acids. We use it all the time to replace salt and to add a rich "beefy" flavor to soups, sauces, and just about everything. Cows all over the world want you to combine this with liquid smoke and a Gardein veggie burger and serve it to your not-yet-vegan friends and family ASAP.

Coconut Milk Using coconut milk to replace heavy cream is one of the oldest tricks in the vegan-baking playbook and still one of the very best.

Earth Balance There are a lot of vegan "buttery" spreads and shortenings to choose from, but Earth Balance is hands down our favorite. Their margarine is the best, both for baking and on toast. It won't just make you forget about butter, it'll make you wonder why it even exists to begin with! For those who are trying to avoid palm oil because of the deforestation and the hunting of orangutans, Earth Balance should not be a problem. Thirty percent of their palm oil comes from Brazil, where orangutans are not native and the Brazilian palm industry does not adversely impact their well-being. The remaining 70 percent of their palm oil comes from peninsular Malaysia, which is also not a native orangutan habitat, from farmers who are all members of the Roundtable on Sustainable Palm Oil (RSPO). I encourage you to check out their website to learn more about this group, which is working to bring sustainable and animal-friendly farming back into this industry.

Ener-G Egg Replacer This combination of starches and leavening agents can be used instead of eggs to bind your baked goods. We often use it in a recipe in its original powder form, rather than mixing it with water per the instructions on the package.

Flaxseeds They don't just contain protein and fiber. Flaxseeds are one of the richest sources of alpha-linolenic acid, an omega-3 fatty acid that protects against heart disease and stroke. Flaxseeds are also great for replacing eggs in baked goods. You'll want to buy your flaxseeds whole and grind them into a fine powder in a coffee grinder.

Liquid Smoke Once you've had mock meat cooked with liquid smoke, you'll never go back. Most liquid smoke isn't a synthetic chemical city; it's made by liquefying the flavor of real wood smoke using steam.

Miso A lot of us have had it as soup, but it can also make a great sauce or marinade. There are several different kinds. Maybe I'm crazy, but it was fun figuring out which one I like best. Enjoy your taste testing!

Nutritional Yeast This will quickly become one of your favorite pantry items despite its terrible name. These nutty and savory flakes can add a "cheesy" flavor to almost anything and are a great source of B vitamins (something vegans need to make sure we get enough of).

Seaweed or Sea Kelp Dried sea vegetables such as nori, dulse, and wakame have a unique sea-salty flavor or brininess that when added to a sauce, soup, or marinade can help replace seafood in your diet. They're also excellent sources of iron and vitamin C.

Silk Soy Coffee Creamer This a creamier, thicker version of soy milk that you can use to replace heavier creams when you want to avoid any trace of coconut flavor or when you're cooking for someone with allergies.

Tahini This sauce is made from ground sesame seeds and has a lovely nutty flavor that you're going to fall in love with, both as a condiment and as an ingredient.

Tony Chachere's Creole Seasoning Julia Child was convinced that she must be secretly French because of her innate love for the food and culture. This is how I feel about Cajun and Creole food. I adore veganizing it all, and although personally I like to create my own spice blends, Tony Chachere's products offer a way to skip several steps, save a few dollars, and add kick by the teaspoon.

Vegan Worcestershire Sauce Worcestershire sauce is one of the world's most beloved cooking ingredients, but sadly it contains anchovies in its original form. There are a few fish-free versions of this popular sauce on the market today that you can use in your sauces and stews, including the Wizard's and Annie's (no relation).

Vegenaise Invented in the seventies, Vegenaise is one of the founding fathers of vegan products. It can replace mayonnaise in any recipe, sandwich, or burger. I've heard a lot of people say that even though they never liked real mayo, they can't get enough Vegenaise.

WHERE DO THEY GET THOSE WONDERFUL TOYS?

This is our collection of all-star kitchen tools that have recurring roles throughout this book, and a few random gadgets you might have been wondering about. We've included some tips for how to use and care for some of these old friends. There might even be a few new friends in here that you could give a good home.

Blender I'm pretty sure we all know that blenders liquefy and mix ingredients. They're the star of any margarita party or fast-paced morning. Every day, my husband makes me a smoothie while he watches *The Daily Show* from the night before on his laptop. To learn more about this, check out "The Smoothie Renaissance" on page 50. Even the best blenders aren't terribly expensive and are well worth the money. It's an investment in a multipurpose tool that can even take the place of a full-fledged food processor.

Bread Knife A bread knife has a serrated blade that's ideal for cutting through bagels and bread crusts. You'll get a much cleaner slice with a bread knife than with any other, and you won't end up shredding your bread or looking at a pile of crumbs when you're done.

Casserole Dish This covered or uncovered cookware is great for baking and serving food straight from the oven. These dishes can be made of glass or oven-safe ceramics. We have a few different kinds and have used each and every one of them. If you like lasagnas, enchiladas, and macaroni and cheese, you need a casserole dish.

Cast-Iron Grill Pan Imagine a cast-iron skillet with raised ridges to create grill marks on vegetables, tofu, and mock meat. We use ours all the time, and not just because it's pretty—well, mostly because it's pretty—but also because unlike those meatier eaters, vegans don't have to worry about draining saturated fat from their mock meats.

Cast-Iron Skillet We use our cast-iron skillet every day for everything. I've used it to make tofu scramble and veggie burgers. I've even baked a cake in it. The key is having a well-seasoned skillet; once you reach the point where your foods glide right off, you'll never go back to those Teflon monstrosities again. A well-seasoned cast-iron pan will only get better with age and will last a lifetime. If you don't own a cast-iron skillet, it's well worth the time and money to invest in one. If you've had bad experiences with cast-iron skillets in the past, it probably came down to one of two things: you were cooking at a heat that was too high or your skillet wasn't seasoned yet.

Not sure how to season your skillet? It's actually a pretty easy, but long-term, project. You're creating a coating of baked-on oil that will act like a nonstick surface and protect your skillet from getting rusted or messing up your favorite food. Between each use preheat the oven too 400°F, rub a little olive oil on your skillet in a thin coating, and let it soak in a little. If your skillet is glistening, you've used too much. Bake your skillet for 5 minutes. Turn your oven off and let your skillet cool in the oven. Do this the first five times you use your skillet. If your skillet smokes, that's okay. You also might notice that your skillet is discolored, but it will only stay like that until you start using it regularly. The more you use your skillet, the more your seasoning will bake in and create that smooth surface you're hoping for.

Chef's Knife There's a saying that a chef is only as good as her knife. Some prefer a lighter knife that flits through the air like the sword of Inigo Montoya avenging his father. Others like to wield their knives like a Viking pillaging the shores. Which is best for you is something you have to figure out for yourself. What I can tell you is when you stock your kitchen, make sure you have a good chef's knife. They're typically around 9 inches long, with a curved side for rocking the blade while you chop. The other side is a flat ridge, so you can place your hand there to guide your cuts or use the dull side to move food around on your cutting board without damaging the blade.

Dutch Oven This huge lidded pot that holds a few quarts of soup will soon become your favorite go-to pot. I won't bore you to death with the history of Dutch ovens no matter how fascinating I may find it, but I will say this about these modern-day cauldrons: if you take care of them, they will last forever. We have an enameled Dutch oven, which does have some downsides. For example, you shouldn't use it for deep-frying. But the upside is that you don't need to season an enameled Dutch oven like you do a cast-iron skillet.

Electric Mixer Once upon a time, I was a woman who randomly fought back against technology. I loved carbonated water, long-lasting lipstick, and flying in airplanes—but when it came to investing in an electric handheld mixer, I never saw the point, especially since I had Dan and a variety of medieval instruments including potato mashers and whisks to blend my frostings, batters, and doughs. Who needed electricity and lightning-fast speed when I had good old-fashioned manpower?

Well, as it turns out, I did. Once I opened our home to this little modern wonder, our lives—and our cupcakes—were forever changed. Our mixer has multiple speeds and attachments and is so versatile I use it for everything. I can't recommend enough getting one with dough hook attachments. That dough is sticky stuff, and if you use any other attachment, it'll crawl right up into your little friend and make a huge mess. Baking your own bread can be one of the most gratifying moments in a chef's life, and this tool will help make that happen!

TWO MEASURING CUPS

It might sound a little simple, or maybe even silly. But having two different measuring cups—one for wet ingredients and one for dry—will save you a lot of time and mess. We've all been there: we pour the sugar into a measuring cup that had oil in it, and then we can't get all the sugar out. It's annoying, and washing the cups between ingredients doesn't solve the problem either. You can get a good glass measuring cup for around five dollars, and it's well worth having a second so as to not fuss around with goopy, gross, contaminated ingredients.

Flavor Injector This is probably the craziest looking of all the toys. Okay, it's a giant syringe that might give you nightmares. It's made for people who aren't happy just eating meat—they need to inject things into the meat. But I love my reappropriated flavor injector. We originally got it to make our Vegan Fried Eggs (see page 23), but since then we've gotten all Paula Deeny with it and injected marinades into To-furkys and A.1. steak sauce into veggie burgers. It's taken our mock meat dishes to a whole new level.

Food Processor I owe my love of food processors to my college roommate Libbe. She had this little handheld number we used to make walnut pesto about once a week. When she moved out and took it with her, I found it hard to go back to prepping things by hand. When I became a proper person with my own kitchen, I invested in a real, grown-up-size food processor and started pureeing and shredding like a crazed food tornado. We made vegan ricotta for manicottis. We shredded potatoes for latkes and hash browns without tearing up our knuckles. We made vegan cheesecakes, all kinds of sauces, and pie fillings. What can't a food processor do? Algebra. That's it.

Frosting Gun/Cookie Press Think about all those little clues that give away an amateur chef: cookies that aren't perfectly smooth and round, cupcakes topped with lopsided clumps of frosting. Investing in a good frosting gun can turn any baked treat into the polished vision that you imagined. It will take practice to get those high peaks of frosting, but in the end you actually get more than just an aesthetic boost to your food. Properly formed cookies bake better, and you'll be able to do even fancier things, like fill pastries and make your own birthday cake sugar rosettes. If I had to boil it down to two words: game changer.

Graters I've had my grater for so long, I'm not sure I can even tell you where it came from. If I had to guess, I'd say our grater is more than ten years old and has lived in St. Louis, Seattle, Atlanta, D.C., Norfolk, and now New York City. I'd also guess that a month hasn't gone by when I haven't used it in one way or another for soups, salads, or my personal favorite—grating citrus peel! They call it "zest" for a reason, ya know. We use grated citrus peel a lot and think that once you start, you will too.

Immersion Blender My friend Anjali is a talented chef and incredibly crafty. At her wedding, while we were setting up all the wonderful DIY details she had spent a year perfecting, I heard my fun but sort of quiet friend actually squeal, "Soup!" She had just opened an early wedding present from her sister—an immersion blender. These handy portable blenders liquefy and mix ingredients inside the pot your soup or sauce is cooking in—while it cooks! No more ladling soup into your food processor or blender to puree; fewer mixing bowls and tools to clean. Some of them are powerful enough to grind coffee or chop ingredients such as parsley and garlic. My only word of warning: if your Dutch oven or soup pot is enameled, be careful to not nick or scratch the inside.

Mandoline No, we're not talking about the little Italian guitar-like instruments you hear on Belle and Sebastian albums. These incredibly sharp and slightly dangerous tools can shred and slice any firm vegetable, fruit, or vegan cheese (or fingers) into uniformly sized and shaped pieces in a ridiculously short amount of time. We love making our own potato chips and recommend investing in a mandoline if you do too.

Paring Knife While the chef's knife might get all the glory, it's the brave little paring knife that does a lot of your dirty work. This small knife will core apples, pull seeds out of avocados, cut gross brown spots off potatoes and bananas, and perform all kinds of other mundane but important tasks.

Pastry Blender This crazy thing might look more like a gladiator weapon, but this kitchen tool has probably been around since there were gladiators. You can use this tool to mix solid fat (shortening or margarine) into flour to make batters and dough for breads and pastries. Though many people just use food processors now for this, I really prefer using the handheld pastry blender—there aren't as many things to clean up afterward.

Pizza Stone If geeky food had a mascot, it would be pizza: "cheesy," cheap, delivered to your door or pulled out of the freezer. You'd be hard-pressed to find a food that requires less interaction with other people and yet provides so much deliciousness. But whether you're defrosting a cheat pizza or making one from scratch, you need a pizza stone. This flat piece of stone or ceramic evenly distributes heat to pizzas and other baked goods in a way that mimics those brick or masonry ovens you see in pizzerias. The porous nature of a pizza stone absorbs excess moisture in your dough and gives you a crisp crust—and when you're dealing with vegan cheese, it's really important to have your oven as dry as it can be.

Rice Cooker Has there ever been a more polarizing kitchen tool? For some, the stovetop method of 2 cups water to 1 cup rice is so magical that the mere mention of owning a rice cooker is like suggesting you fry doughnuts in a microwave. But there are secret tricks to making perfect stovetop rice, and that alone has been enough to discourage people from even trying. I mean, there's a whole section of the grocery store full of instant rice so that people don't have to even attempt the stovetop method. The bad news is that instant rice is pretty processed stuff, and not nearly as good for you as the real thing.

That's where the rice cooker comes in. It'll cut down your prep time for a meal by giving you one less step to worry about. Just follow the instructions that come with it, add the correct ratio of water to rice, put the lid on, and flip a switch. It'll let you know when your rice is done, and if you plan it right, you'll have fresh rice ready just as your vegetables are tender or your taco shells are crisp.

Silicone Bakeware This miracle bakeware comes in bright, cheery colors; is nonstick without using shortening, oils, or sprays; and is safe for the oven and freezer. Of course nothing is perfect, and you really need to read the instructions that come with it to see how hot your new friends can get and how best to clean them.

Springform Pan This round, deep pan looks more steampunk than June Cleaver and is one of the cleverest little soldiers in our arsenal. It's made of a disk and a removable ring that clamp together to create your new favorite cheesecake pan. After your dessert has set, just release the side and gently remove it to reveal your masterpiece.

Waffle Iron There are a lot of different waffle irons out there. Some are intended for children's food and make cute animals and heart shapes. Some are downright ladylike, with their tight hospital corners and little wells for syrup. I can't stress enough that when it comes to investing in a waffle iron, you need to make sure it has a nonstick surface. It doesn't just make preparing the waffles easier; it makes cleaning up afterward much faster. It's up to you to figure out what kind of waffles you want in your life, but trust me when I say this: everyone loves waffles.

Whoopie Pie Pan You don't need a whoopie pie pan to make whoopie pies, but it helps. Having one of these inexpensive pans will help guarantee that you end up with an even amount of equally sized cookies to build your pies.

Wok Before I fell in love with my cast-iron skillet, there was our faithful wok. Now, that may seem odd, since most people use their woks only for stir-frying. But with a little research, you can find tips on how to use your wok for steaming, deep-frying, braising, stewing, smoking, even making sauces.

But being a superwoman in life and in the kitchen is more than just having the right pans and a shopping list. It's about finding a sustainable way to live a more compassionate life. That's why in this book, we have recipes for all skill levels and for a variety of different lifestyles. Some recipes take a lot of prep and maybe a little practice, but most are actually pretty easy and quick. If you can use a blender and boil water, you can make a lot of these recipes. You really can. Just don't forget the most important part—have fun! Whether you're going meatless only one day a week or are a lifelong vegan, being vegan doesn't have to be a chore or involve sacrifice. These recipes will help you enjoy dishes you grew up with while making a lifestyle choice that's not just better for you but better for the environment and of course the animals.

❋ ❋ ❋

Chapter Two

BREAKFAST AND BRUNCH

The ancient Romans had a toast that went something like this: *aut viam inveniam aut faciam.*

It means "I will either find a way or make one." I think it's a motto that any long-term vegan can relate to. Sometimes it takes a little creativity and effort to replace a beloved dish with something healthier and animal-free, but once you do, it really is a victory for everyone involved. Breakfast can often be the greatest challenge due to school buses, long showers, and alarm clocks with snooze buttons. In the end it's always worth it to start your day with smoked tempeh rather than bacon. Choosing to start your day with a diet that's better for you, the environment, and of course the animals, is never a bad idea.

THE VEGAN ANSWER TO EGGS

Ab ovo usque ad mala... [*]

For many people, "breakfast" means "eggs." So for many vegans, breakfast ends up meaning Clif bars, leftover Chinese food, or a tall soy hazelnut latte—which is a shame. It's a fundamental law of physical science, on par with $E = mc^2$ and the Pythagorean theorem, that breakfast food is the best food.[**] When it comes to the Right Breakfast, the sum of the square roots of hash browns and fakin' bacon is equal to the square root of the remaining side (see what I did there?). Or something like that. The point I'm trying to make here is that everyone should eat breakfast—both because it's good for you and because it's delicious. And as a vegan, you shouldn't let eggs' traditional tyranny over the morning meal keep you down. Eggs can take our lives...but they cannot take our breakfast!

Not to get all "where do you get your protein" on you or anything, but the key to a nutritious breakfast is, well, protein. Hence the tyranny of eggs. A protein-centered meal is easy to digest and gives your body energy to keep you running all morning. It'll help keep you focused and alert. Carbs don't give you that same boost—they're harder to digest and make your body do more work in the morning, when you're already trying to feed the cats and take a shower and get ready for work and just check Facebook for like five minutes if the goddarn computer would just start already oh my God this thing takes forever I'm gonna throw it out the window maybe I shouldn't have drunk all that coffee with just a bagel in my stomach. So while it's tempting to just go the bagel route for your vegan breakfast every morning, something with more protein will help start your day on a more pleasant note. And there are plenty of vegan protein options to choose from.

In the Shannon household, our breakfast every weekday morning consists of a fruit smoothie, often made with soy protein powder. It takes five minutes to make, is light but still hearty, gives us a check mark in the fruits and veggies category right off the bat, and provides a great energy boost to start the day. But if smoothies aren't your thing, we've got a ton of recipes for tofu scrambles, soy sausage, and other protein-packed breakfasts that'll start your day off right. Or, if you're looking for more of a weekend treat to surprise that special someone who may or may not still be in bed at ten after staying up all night playing computer games, we've got pancakes and crepes and waffles that'll go great with that tall soy hazelnut latte—which, while it shouldn't be a substitute for breakfast, does balance the morning equation nicely.

[*] Latin for "from the egg to the apples" which appears in Horace's *Satire 1*.
[**] Not actually a fundamental law.

VEGAN FRIED EGGS

Oh, classic fried egg…with your runny yolk for dipping toast in and your crispy edges. I'm over you. I don't need you or your cholesterol or potential salmonella. Now vegans can enjoy this American breakfast staple—either alone or as an ingredient in a number of other recipes in this book.

MAKES 4 SERVINGS

½ cup Cheezy Sauce (page 286)

1 (14-ounce) package firm tofu, drained and cut into 4 rectangular pieces (we recommend using the brands Nasoya or Trader Joe's)

2 to 3 tablespoons olive oil

Crushed pink Himalayan salt and crushed black peppercorns

Dash of paprika

First, make your Cheezy Sauce. It should take about 20 minutes.

With warm water, rinse your flavor injector (see "Where Do They Get Those Wonderful Toys?" on page 18 to read more about flavor injectors). Fill the injector with Cheezy Sauce. Slowly stick the injector into the center of one of the short sides of one tofu rectangle. Make sure it doesn't go in too far and pierce the opposite side. You want the tip of the injector to be at the center of your tofu piece. Then—this is key—very gently move the tofu back and forth. Don't move the needle; it'll tear a hole in the outside of the tofu. But if you slowly rock the tofu back and forth, it creates a pocket inside the tofu, while keeping the injection site as small as possible.

Fill the tofu pieces with no more than 1 tablespoon each of the Cheezy Sauce. Go very slowly to make sure the tofu doesn't burst, and stop when you see a lump start to form in the center. This is kind of tricky, so don't get discouraged. Some tofu brands are more solid and crack more easily than others. Some just work better. We suggest using Nasoya or Trader Joe's. The key is to very slowly fill your tofu eggs and stop when you start to feel the tofu expand.

In your amazing cast-iron skillet or frying pan, heat the olive oil. Once it's hot, gently place the "eggs" in the skillet with the lump side up. Fry with that side up until you can see the edges begin to brown. Then gently flip the tofu with a spatula. Fry until you see that side's edges begin to brown as well. Do this a few times, until the "egg" has crispy light brown edges.

Sprinkle with salt and pepper to taste and a dash of paprika. Serve hot with your favorite vegan bacon and potatoes…and maybe call a friend and brag a bit about how much you rocked breakfast.

NO-HUEVOS RANCHEROS

This recipe is an easy yet impressive spread for Sunday brunch. It's not quite breakfast, it's not quite lunch, but it comes with a slice of cantaloupe at the end.

MAKES 4 SERVINGS

Olive oil

Dash of liquid smoke

1 (12-ounce) package soyrizo

½ red onion, diced

½ green bell pepper, diced

4 (6-inch) vegan corn tortillas (read the labels—some have pork fat in them)

4 Vegan Fried Eggs (page 23)

1 batch Dan's Guacamole (page 432)

2 cups pico de gallo

8 to 12 tablespoons shredded Daiya vegan cheddar cheese or your favorite vegan cheese

Cilantro and sliced black olives for tossing on top

In your cast-iron skillet or frying pan, heat 2 tablespoons olive oil and a dash of liquid smoke over medium heat. Toss the soyrizo, onion, and green pepper in the oil. Stir a few times, but mostly just be patient, letting the soyrizo brown until the edges are crispy and the vegetables cook until they are tender. Remove from the frying pan and set aside in a large bowl.

In the same skillet, add another tablespoon of olive oil and another dash of liquid smoke. Then, one at a time, fry the corn tortillas. Flip and fry them until they're golden and crispy on both sides, and stiff like chips. Drain out as much oil as you can from each tortilla when you remove it from the skillet, leaving the oil in the pan for the next step. Place the fried tortillas on a plate with a paper towel to soak up any excess oil.

While the soyrizo and tortillas are frying, prepare your Vegan Fried Eggs. Use the same warm skillet with another dash of olive oil to fry your vegan eggs. This is a good time to make the guacamole and pico de gallo.

Once your vegan eggs are golden brown and have crispy edges, put together your Huevos Rancheros. For each serving, place your components in this order from the bottom up: 1 crispy tortilla, 1 Vegan Fried Egg, one-quarter of the soyrizo and veggies, 2 to 3 tablespoons vegan cheddar, one-quarter of the guacamole, and one-quarter of the pico de gallo. Sprinkle with cilantro and black olives and serve.

¡Buen provecho!

GRAND VEGAN BREAKFAST

Also known as the "great English breakfast" and the "full breakfast," this British tradition is known throughout the world as "the breakfast that stopped a million hearts." It's a combination of pretty much every classic breakfast food that you can fry—primarily made up of several different animals and rarely including anything green. I mean, we don't count the garnishes, right? But we changed all that when we leveled up this classic British Isles feast. It's still primarily protein, and we still wouldn't suggest you eat like this every day, but if you ever find yourself up early watching a royal wedding or enjoying some *Doctor Who*…it might be fun to make this notorious meal.

MAKES 4 SERVINGS

1 batch Newfangled Baked Beans (page 228; you'll want to make this the night before and reheat it on the stovetop)

4 Vegan Fried Eggs (page 23)

1 cup Lightlife Gimme Lean vegan breakfast sausage, defrosted

Olive oil cooking spray

2 Yukon Gold potatoes, diced very small

¼ red onion, diced very small

¼ green bell pepper, diced very small

2 dashes of liquid smoke

1 tablespoon chopped fresh parsley

3 to 4 slices vegan bacon or smoked tempeh

¼ cup sliced white mushrooms

1 large beefsteak tomato, cut into wedges

1 teaspoon Bragg's liquid aminos

2 slices whole wheat toast

2 teaspoons chopped fresh chives

Crushed pink Himalayan salt and crushed black peppercorns

Margarine, marmalade, and jam for your toast

Preheat the oven to 250°F. This is where you'll keep your breakfast components warm while you prepare your breakfast, so if your oven runs hot you may want to turn it down to 200°F.

First things first, you need to prepare all the elements. Things are going to move pretty quickly once you get going. Make the Cheezy Sauce for your "yolk" and make the desired number of sausage patties using the Gimme Lean sausage. Set all these aside, but keep them handy.

Next, make your Vegan Fried Eggs. I like to keep the extra Cheezy Sauce from the recipe warm to dip my toast in, but you may also want to inject a little more "yolk" into your egg if any leaks out before you're done cooking. Once your fried "eggs" are done, put them in a glass lasagna dish that's been sprayed with a light coating of olive oil. Put them in the oven to stay warm while you fry up the rest of breakfast.

In a saucepan, reheat your Newfangled Baked Beans over medium heat. Be sure to keep the pan covered so your sauce doesn't get sticky. Stir your pot frequently, and once the beans begin to bubble, reduce the heat to a simmer.

In a large mixing bowl, toss the diced potatoes, onion, and bell pepper.

Recoat your hot cast-iron skillet or frying pan with olive oil cooking spray and toss in a dash of liquid smoke. Toss in your diced vegetable mix and spray another coating of olive oil cooking spray over the top. Let the vegetables brown for a bit while you prepare your other skillet.

Yes, I said "other skillet." There are a lot of fried foods going on here. Take another cast-iron skillet if you have it, or just a regular skillet, spray it with olive oil cooking spray, and toss in a dash of liquid smoke. We recommend using a skillet with ridges if you can; it'll give you those lovely grill lines. Heat your new skillet over medium heat.

Now go back and revisit your diced vegetables. With your metal spatula, mix and toss the diced vegetables to make sure they're cooking evenly. Once the potatoes are tender, remove the skillet from the heat. The smaller they're diced, the faster they'll cook. Once the potatoes are tender, mix in the parsley and move the diced vegetable hash to the warming dish in the oven with the vegan eggs. Try to keep the vegetables and "eggs" in separate piles.

Once your new skillet is warm, you're going to crowd the vegan sausage patties, vegan bacon, mushrooms, and tomato in there. If that's not all going to fit, first put the vegan sausage patties in the center; then make a pile of mushrooms on one side and put the tomato wedges on another. Lay the bacon strips over the top. Drizzle ½ teaspoon of Bragg's over the tomatoes and ½ teaspoon over the mushrooms. Brown on one side for 1 to 2 minutes, or until the edges start to brown. Then flip your breakfast wonderland with a metal spatula so that the other side browns. You'll have plenty of time to get those crispy edges.

Your tomatoes and mushrooms might be done before your sausage patties and vegan bacon. If that happens, move them to your warming dish in the oven with your vegan eggs. Try to keep the tomatoes and mushrooms in two neat separate piles. Once the sausage patties are done, move them to the warming dish too. Your vegan bacon will already be cooked, but if you like nice, crispy edges, let your vegan bacon fry for 30 seconds on each side in the hot skillet. While your vegan bacon fries, toss some slices of whole wheat bread in the toaster.

You're now ready to build your grand English breakfast!

Put two Vegan Fried Eggs on your plate, then a pile of hash, followed by a separate pile of baked beans. Now fill any gaps on your plate with vegan sausage patties and tomatoes. If there are any open spaces, fit those mushrooms in there, or just lay them over the top. Do the same with your vegan bacon and toast. Sprinkle a few pinches of fresh chives over the top of your Vegan Fried Eggs, and maybe some salt and pepper if you're into that. Don't forget your margarine, marmalade, or jam to dress up your toast.

You'll probably be tempted to enjoy this feast with a cup of coffee, but if you really want to get your Brit on, we suggest brewing up a pot of Earl Grey or English Breakfast tea.

#1 BREAKFAST SANDWICH

One morning, while I was watching *Star Trek: The Next Generation* and enjoying a cup of Earl Grey with our cat Agatha, I had a revelation. As you may know, Captain Picard refers to First Officer Riker as "Number One." And Agatha is my number one. She listens well, gives good counsel when I need it, and can always be counted on. Similarly, this recipe is the number one of vegan breakfasts—completely reliable. Even the pickiest of eaters will enjoy this breakfast sandwich.

MAKES 4 SERVINGS

4 Vegan Fried Eggs (page 23)

1 whole wheat baguette

3 tablespoons olive oil

3 tablespoons shredded Daiya vegan cheddar or your favorite vegan cheese

4 slices vegan bacon or smoked tempeh

½ cup raw kale

¼ teaspoon red pepper flakes

1 clove garlic, minced

1 Roma tomato, sliced

Crushed pink Himalayan salt and crushed black peppercorns

Dash of hot sauce, optional

Preheat the oven to 350°F.

Make your Vegan Fried Eggs and set them aside on a plate, covered with foil to keep them warm and moist. Slice your baguette horizontally in half. Brush your top half with 2 tablespoons of the olive oil and sprinkle your vegan cheese evenly over the bottom half. Place your baguette into the oven on the rack faceup and allow to lightly toast for no more than 5 minutes. Once your baguette is toasted and your vegan cheese is melted, remove the baguette from the oven.

While your baguette is toasting, make the vegan bacon and kale. In your extraordinary cast-iron skillet, heat the remaining 1 tablespoon olive oil over medium heat. Once your skillet is warm, place the slices of vegan bacon in the skillet to brown. Once they start to get slightly crispy, toss the kale, red pepper flakes, and garlic over the top of the vegan bacon and cook for less than a minute. Once the vegan bacon is browned and crispy, use a spatula to flip and mix the kale and crispy vegan bacon a few times so that the kale gets covered in the warm olive oil.

Place your Vegan Fried Eggs on the "cheesy" half of your baguette. Then place the vegan bacon and sliced tomatoes in an even layer over the vegan eggs. Pile the garlicky kale over the vegan bacon. Using a serrated bread knife, slice the baguette sandwich into 4 pieces so that each sandwich has a Vegan Fried Egg in it. Add salt, pepper, and hot sauce (if desired) to taste.

Awesome day—engage!

TURKISH VEGAN EGGS

We've probably all had this breakfast before but had no idea that it was known in some circles by such an exotic name. It's a combination of vegan eggs, peppers, and all types of wonderful warm spices in one dish you can enjoy on a morning when the ordinary needs a little extra.

MAKES 4 SERVINGS

¼ cup vegan plain yogurt

2 tablespoons vegan sour cream

2 teaspoons lemon peel, grated

1 tablespoon lemon juice

½ teaspoon crushed black peppercorns

½ teaspoon Bragg's liquid aminos

3 cloves garlic, minced

3 small shallots, thinly sliced

1 red bell pepper, thinly sliced

½ green bell pepper, thinly sliced

½ orange bell pepper, thinly sliced

¼ cup fresh baby spinach leaves

1 (14-ounce) can diced tomatoes

2 teaspoons agave nectar

1 chipotle pepper, diced

1 teaspoon adobo sauce (the red sauce your chipotle pepper comes in)

1 teaspoon smoked paprika

Dash of liquid smoke

4 Vegan Fried Eggs (page 23)

2 tablespoons olive oil

3 tablespoons chopped fresh parsley

In a small bowl, mix the yogurt, sour cream, lemon peel, lemon juice, black pepper, Bragg's, and 2 cloves of the garlic. Cover the bowl with foil and put it in the fridge to chill out while you prepare the rest of your breakfast.

Toss your shallots and peppers in a medium bowl with your spinach. In another small bowl, with a large spoon, mix the diced tomatoes with the agave nectar, chipotle pepper, adobo sauce, smoked paprika, liquid smoke, and the remaining 1 clove garlic. Pour the tomato mixture over the fresh vegetable mixture and use a large spoon to blend it in. Cover and put in the fridge to chill with the yogurt sauce while you make the vegan eggs.

Make the Vegan Fried Eggs. Keep the extra Cheezy Sauce warm to serve on the side. Before you get to the frying step of the recipe, put the prepared vegan eggs aside and get the vegetable mixture from the fridge.

Heat the olive oil in your always-handy cast-iron skillet or frying pan over medium heat. Pour the vegetable mixture into the skillet and use a metal spatula to mix the vegetables around a bit so they will cook evenly. Once the peppers start to get tender, use a metal spatula to open up small pockets to place the prepared vegan eggs into the skillet. You'll want to place the vegan eggs in the skillet one at a time, and don't worry if you have to move some of the peppers over the vegan eggs. They'll still cook.

Once it's time to flip the vegan eggs, dig them out one at a time and flip them. While you're doing that, you're going to be moving the peppers around too. Try to get the ones that were on top of the vegan eggs onto the skillet surface so they can brown a little. After about 1 minute, remove the skillet from the heat.

While the vegan eggs cool, take the yogurt sauce from the fridge. Use an electric handheld mixer and blend the yogurt sauce until it's creamy.

Serve in bowls with the vegan eggs lying on top of the vegetable mix and with some yogurt sauce and fresh parsley on top.

DENVER OMELET

After years and years of scrambling my tofu, I get pretty excited about new ways of making "eggs" for breakfast. Just the idea of a French-style or fold-over omelet puts a big smile on my face. These aren't the easiest recipes to make, but they bring the "shock and awe" and are very filling. You may want to have them for brunch, actually, because you won't need a second meal after this. A mile-high breakfast!

MAKES 2 LARGE OR 4 SMALL SERVINGS

FILLING

Olive oil cooking spray

Dash of liquid smoke

1 green bell pepper, diced

½ red onion, diced

¾ cup diced vegan ham, smoked tempeh, or Hickory Smoked Tofurky Deli Slices

½ cup shredded Daiya vegan cheddar cheese or your favorite vegan cheese

½ cup shredded smoked cheddar Sheese

Diced fresh chives for topping

Freshly ground lemon pepper

OMELET

1 (14-ounce) package tofu

1 tablespoon soy coffee creamer

2 tablespoons nutritional yeast

1 tablespoon cornstarch

½ teaspoon onion powder

¼ teaspoon cumin

¼ teaspoon miso paste

¼ teaspoon turmeric

½ teaspoon Bragg's liquid aminos

¼ teaspoon paprika

Crushed pink Himalayan salt and crushed peppercorns, optional

Freshly ground lemon pepper

2 to 3 tablespoons margarine per omelet

First prepare the filling. Spray your cast-iron skillet or frying pan with a light coating of olive oil, toss in a dash of liquid smoke, and place over medium heat. Then toss in the bell pepper, red onion, and vegan meat. Fry until the vegan meat browns and the vegetables are tender. Move the vegetables and vegan meat mixture from the skillet into a large bowl and set the skillet aside. Keep whatever oil is left over from the vegetables and vegan meat in the skillet for a little extra flavor.

Begin preparing the omelet. In a food processor, blend the tofu, soy coffee creamer, nutritional yeast, cornstarch, onion powder, cumin, miso paste, turmeric, Bragg's, and paprika until you get a smooth paste. Here's where you can taste the blend to see if you want salt or pepper. I tossed a pinch of lemon pepper into one of the omelets at this step and really liked it.

Next, melt 1 to 2 tablespoons of the margarine over medium heat in the same skillet you used for the vegetables and vegan meat. Now separate your tofu blend into two equal portions. Once the skillet is warm and the margarine is melted, pour one portion of the tofu blend into the center of the skillet and spread it out like a nice even pancake. You have to move pretty fast so that your omelet doesn't form lumps. If you don't move fast enough, you can always use a spatula to spread it out evenly. Watch for bubbles and cracks. If you get a bubble, try and gently pop it with a fork. Cracks can be smoothed over with uncooked tofu blend.

Let the tofu blend fry for 5 to 8 minutes. During that time, use your spatula to keep loosening the edges. Once the edges begin to get brown and crispy, gently use your spatula to lift and check the progress of the omelet. You want the omelet to be golden and crispy, so make sure you can see that beginning to happen before you toss in your fillings. Don't worry if the center is still a little soft. Make an even layer of half the vegetable and vegan meat filling on one half of the omelet; then top with a layer of half the vegan cheddar and Sheese. Cook for another 2 minutes to let your vegan cheese and Sheese melt a little and heat the vegetables and vegan meat. Keep an eye on your edges to make sure they don't burn.

Preheat the oven to 200°F.

Now here's where it gets tricky. Seriously. Take your spatula and flip the empty side of the omelet over the side with the fillings. Very gently move your omelet to the plate by turning your skillet and slowly sliding the omelet out, using your spatula to guide and control it.

Keep the first omelet warm in the oven while you make the second one with the other half of your ingredients.

To serve, just toss some fresh chives and pepper on top.

This makes 2 pretty huge omelets, or you could always split them into 4 smaller ones.

✳ ✳ ✳

Here are few other combos you can try if you're not a Denver fan. Just replace the filling in the omelet above with the ingredients below.

GREEK OMELET

My big fat Greek breakfast!

MAKES 2 TO 4 SERVINGS

Denver Omelet without the filling (page 29)

¼ cup raw baby spinach leaves

3 cherry tomatoes, quartered

¼ cup kalamata olives, pitted and drained

1 teaspoon fresh oregano leaves

Handful of fresh basil leaves

1 Roma tomato, sliced

½ cup shredded Daiya vegan mozzarella cheese or your favorite vegan cheese

2 tablespoons vegan feta cheese

¼ teaspoon crushed black peppercorns

Red pepper flakes to sprinkle over the top

Now, unlike the filling for the Denver Omelet, you don't need to cook the filling for your Greek Omelet. Prepare your first omelet using the ingredients and instructions from the Denver Omelet on page 29. In a large bowl, using a spoon, mix the spinach, cherry tomatoes, olives, oregano, basil, Roma tomato, vegan cheeses, and black pepper. Pile half your filling into your first omelet while it cooks. Repeat the process with your second omelet. Sprinkle red pepper flakes over the top before serving.

SOUTHWESTERN OMELET

Technically Colorado is part of the Southwest, so there's some regional overlap here with the Denver Omelet…but I think you get the distinction.

MAKES 2 TO 4 SERVINGS

Olive oil cooking spray

1 (14-ounce) can black beans, drained and rinsed

½ green bell pepper, sliced

½ red bell pepper, sliced

½ teaspoon cumin

Denver Omelet without the filling (page 29)

1 Roma tomato, sliced

1 ripe avocado, peeled, pitted, and sliced

4 tablespoons sliced black olives, pitted and drained

½ cup shredded Daiya vegan pepperjack cheese or your favorite vegan cheese

1 batch Salsa Verde (page 433)

Spray a light coating of olive oil cooking spray over your cast-iron skillet or frying pan and heat it over medium heat. Once your skillet is warm, toss in the black beans and peppers and sprinkle your cumin over the top. Once your vegetables are tender, move them to a warm plate. Prepare your first omelet using the ingredients and instructions from the Denver Omelet on page 29.

Once your omelet is cooked, pile half the cooked vegetables, tomato, avocado, olives, vegan cheese, and Salsa Verde into the omelet before folding it over. Then transfer to your plate.

Repeat the whole thing all over again with the second omelet.

BENEDICT OMELET

This omelet will never betray you.

MAKES 2 TO 4 SERVINGS

Olive oil cooking spray

Dash of liquid smoke

8 vegan bacon strips or smoked tempeh

¼ cup sliced white mushrooms

Denver Omelet without the filling (page 29)

1 ripe avocado, peeled, pitted, and sliced

1 Roma tomato, sliced

⅓ cup raw baby spinach leaves

1 batch Vegan Hollandaise Sauce (page 290)

Paprika

Spray your cast-iron skillet or frying pan with a light coating of olive oil, toss in a dash of liquid smoke, and heat over medium heat. Fry up the vegan bacon strips and mushrooms until the edges are crispy. Remove them from the skillet.

Prepare your omelets one at a time using the ingredients and instructions in the Denver Omelet on page 29. Put half the vegan meat, mushrooms, avocado, tomato, and spinach in each omelet as you cook it. When you serve your omelet, pour a little Vegan Hollandaise Sauce over the top and dash some paprika over that.

The Tofu Scramble Tradition

What can we say about tofu scramble that hasn't been said before? It's a vegan tradition, a staple in the vegan diet that we've all relied on and enjoyed. It's so versatile, you can enjoy it mixed with veggies or alone on toast. But like many dishes, it's just as easy to make it wonderful as it is to make it completely awful. Tofu scramble walks a thin line between revolutionary experience and cautionary tale. So here are a few tips to ensure your tofu scramble is season four *Simpsons*, not season fourteen.

Make sure your tofu is completely drained of the water it's packaged in. You can do this a few ways beyond just squeezing. Wrap the tofu in paper towels and place it in the fridge for 2 hours. Or place a paper towel under the tofu and something heavy on top for a half hour, to gently press the moisture out. You can also take tofu that has already been squeezed and freeze it overnight. Then in the morning when you defrost it, even more water will drain out.

When breaking up the tofu, never mash it into a paste; you want medium to fine crumbles.

The tofu will crumble even more when you toss it while cooking, so start with pieces a tiny bit smaller than bite-size.

Unlike with eggs, you can test your tofu scramble for taste before cooking it—so monitor and adjust the flavor before committing to the cooked dish.

When cooking your tofu scramble with vegetables, remember that they'll release moisture into the scramble and also take longer to cook than the tofu. So it's a good idea to cook the vegetables first, and then mix the tofu in, especially for larger pieces of vegetables. Broccoli is an exception to this rule; the delicate little flowers at the top can singe easily.

When the tofu is cooking, don't be afraid to just let it sit. You want your scramble to be light golden brown and evenly cooked, which means you only need to toss and mix it a few times. If you're constantly mixing your scramble in the skillet, it'll never really get those crispy edges that you want. Mushy tofu scramble is the runny scrambled eggs of vegan breakfast.

THE SCRAMBLES

POTATO, TEMPEH, AND TOFU SCRAMBLE

This recipe takes about 10 minutes and is so easy you can make it on a weekday before school or work. Throw in some toast points and huge cups of coffee, and you're pretty much set for a perfect morning. We made this on a lazy Sunday morning when we wanted to remain lazy. The baby birds were flying all around the holly trees in the courtyard of our apartment building, and the squirrels were sunning themselves on the window ledges. We watched them, talked about how the Celtics were doing in the playoffs, and enjoyed the simple things in life … like this recipe.

MAKES 2 TO 4 SERVINGS

2 to 3 tablespoons olive oil, plus more as needed

6 small red potatoes, cubed

6 pieces vegan bacon or smoked tempeh

Dash of liquid smoke

1 (14-ounce) package firm tofu, drained

¼ cup nutritional yeast

1½ teaspoons cumin

1 teaspoon dried basil

1 teaspoon thyme

1 teaspoon paprika

1 teaspoon Bragg's liquid aminos

¼ teaspoon turmeric

½ red bell pepper, sliced

4 medium green onions, chopped

In your loyal cast-iron skillet or frying pan, heat the olive oil over medium heat.

Heat salted water to a boil in a large stockpot. Add the potatoes and cover the pot. Remove the potatoes once they're tender.

Fry the vegan bacon until it reaches the desired crispiness. When you remove your vegan bacon from the skillet, place it on top of some paper towels to soak up the oil. When the bacon has drained and cooled enough to handle, cut into strips small enough to sprinkle over your scramble.

Add a dash of liquid smoke to the olive oil in the skillet. Add the potatoes and fry. Let them start to get crispy on one side before flipping.

In a large bowl, mash the tofu, and then mix in the nutritional yeast, cumin, basil, thyme, paprika, Bragg's, and turmeric. Normally I wouldn't tell you to mash the tofu, but we're re-creating liquid eggs and coating the vegetables with the tofu mix, so it's okay if it's pasty.

Before the potatoes reach the desired crispiness, pour the tofu mixture over the potatoes and add the red peppers. Mix in the skillet until the vegetables are covered. You may need to add a tiny bit more oil, but not more than 1 teaspoon. Cook for a few minutes, and flip your tofu occasionally. Add the green onions to the mix.

You're now cooking off the moisture from the tofu and the vegetables. Once your scramble reaches the desired texture, remove it from the skillet and sprinkle the vegan bacon on top.

VEGAN SHRIMP AND SCALLION SCRAMBLE

I'll admit, this might not sound like a combination you would love, but back in 2007, I saw a recipe for scrambled eggs and shrimp and was intrigued. I mean, after years and years of the classic breakfast combos, I saw an opportunity here to make something unique. This scramble incorporates Asian flavors and vegetables into a dish that is unique and delicious.

MAKES 2 TO 4 SERVINGS

6 small red potatoes, cubed

1 (14-ounce) package firm tofu, drained

¼ cup nutritional yeast

1½ teaspoons cumin

1 tablespoon finely chopped fresh cilantro, plus additional cilantro leaves for garnish

1 teaspoon grated lemon peel

1 teaspoon finely chopped lemongrass

1 teaspoon paprika

1 teaspoon Bragg's liquid aminos

¼ teaspoon turmeric

2 to 3 tablespoons olive oil, plus more as needed

2 dashes of liquid smoke

5 pieces vegan shrimp, defrosted (we recommend using 8 to 10 May Wah shrimp balls cut in half)

½ red bell pepper, sliced

6 green onions, chopped

Sriracha sauce for topping

Lime wedges

Heat salted water to a boil in a large pot. Once the water starts to boil, add the potatoes and cover the pot. Boil until the potatoes are tender.

In a large bowl, mash the tofu with a pastry blender and then mix in the nutritional yeast, cumin, chopped cilantro, lemon peel, lemongrass, paprika, Bragg's, and turmeric. Normally we'd advocate against mashing your tofu in a scramble, but we're re-creating liquid eggs and coating the vegan shrimp and vegetables with the tofu mix, so it's okay if it's pasty.

In your handy wok, heat the olive oil and 1 dash of liquid smoke over a high heat. Roll your wok with your wrist a few times to mix your oil and liquid smoke.

Once your wok is hot, toss in the vegan shrimp and roll your wrist a few times to coat the vegan shrimp in hot oil. Toss in the potatoes and the other dash of liquid smoke. You're going to stir-fry your mix; you want the vegan shrimp and potatoes to cook evenly and to have crispy edges.

Before your mix reaches the desired crispiness, pour the tofu mixture over the vegan shrimp and potatoes and add the red bell peppers. Mix the ingredients in the wok until the vegan shrimp and vegetables are coated. You may need to add a tiny bit more oil, but not more than 1 teaspoon. Let the mixture cook, and flip the tofu occasionally. Add the green onions to the mix.

Cook off the moisture from the tofu and the vegetables. Once the mixture has reached the desired texture, remove the scramble from the wok and sprinkle fresh cilantro leaves over the top. Serve hot with Sriracha sauce and lime wedges.

BREAKFAST TACOS

In America, we seem obsessed with revamping breakfast. We make sandwiches with mini-pancakes instead of bread, and French toast sticks you can eat with your hands. So a breakfast taco wasn't that odd a concept for us. I feel like I've seen them before. This was one of the first recipes we made in the Betty Crocker Project. We made it for brinner (breakfast for dinner) since we were both working beyond full-time jobs at the time and it was a quick recipe to look forward to at the end of a pretty hectic day.

MAKES 6 TACOS

1 tablespoon olive oil

½ teaspoon garlic powder

2 teaspoons cumin

1 teaspoon paprika

¼ teaspoon crushed black peppercorns

1 (14-ounce) package firm tofu, drained

2 tablespoons nutritional yeast

2 pinches of turmeric

½ cup shredded Daiya vegan cheddar cheese or your favorite vegan cheese

6 taco shells

1 ripe avocado, sliced

¼ cup chopped red bell peppers

⅓ cup fresh cilantro, chopped

1 (16-ounce) jar of your favorite salsa

Heat the olive oil over medium heat in a cast-iron skillet or frying pan. Add the garlic powder, cumin, paprika, and black pepper to the oil and mix. In a bowl, crumble—don't mash—the tofu, and stir in the nutritional yeast and turmeric. Put the tofu in your hot skillet, stirring occasionally and flipping the tofu mixture to keep it from sticking. Cook until it reaches the desired texture and moistness. Mix in the vegan cheese so that it can melt a bit before serving.

Heat the taco shells as directed on the package. Spoon the tofu mixture into the heated shells, and top with avocado, red bell pepper, cilantro, and salsa.

VIVA LA SUNDAY MORNING SANDWICH

This Mexican breakfast sandwich, a cup of coffee, and your favorite conversation partner is all you need to have a *buena mañana*. It adds a bit of spiciness to your normal breakfast sandwich while maintaining that down-home goodness of scrambled tofu on toast.

MAKES 2 TO 4 SANDWICHES

2 tablespoons olive oil

1 (12-ounce) package soyrizo

½ red onion, diced

1 (14-ounce) package extrafirm tofu (drained and pressed)

2 teaspoons cumin

1 teaspoon oregano

2 tablespoons nutritional yeast

1 teaspoon paprika

½ teaspoon turmeric

1 red bell pepper, sliced

1 green bell pepper, sliced

1 yellow bell pepper, sliced

1 cup shredded Daiya vegan cheddar cheese or your favorite vegan cheese

4 to 8 slices of whole wheat bread

Hot sauce, guacamole, and pico de gallo for topping

Fresh cilantro, chopped

In your favorite cast-iron skillet or frying pan, heat 1 tablespoon of the olive oil over medium heat. Once the skillet is warm, toss in the soyrizo and red onion. Cook, turning occasionally with a spatula, until the edges begin to brown and get crispy.

In a mixing bowl, use a fork to break the tofu into bite-size pieces. Don't mash it to the point that it gets pasty. Add the cumin, oregano, nutritional yeast, paprika, and turmeric, and mix thoroughly.

Add the tofu mixture and the remaining tablespoon of olive oil to the soyrizo and onion in the skillet. Fry until the moistness starts to disappear and the tofu turns yellow and takes on a firm texture. Flip and mix your tofu and soyrizo a few times to make sure they cook evenly. Add the peppers and continue to cook until the tofu and soyrizo are lightly browned and the peppers are tender. The peppers will add more moisture to the scramble.

Once you like the texture and tenderness of your scramble, pull your skillet from the heat and mix in the vegan cheese. Now toast your whole wheat bread.

Once you have your toast, build your sandwiches. Between those lovely slices of toast, pile a good amount of scrambled tofu and peppers. Top with hot sauce, guacamole, and pico de gallo, and sprinkle with cilantro before serving. *¡Disfruta!*

BANANAS FOSTER WAFFLES

Bananas Foster is a rich dessert of bananas and ice cream that's often served flambé-style—that means on fire—for a little flair. We do *not* recommend setting these waffles on fire. It will not achieve the same effect. Just serve them straight from the waffle iron and watch your family's faces light up naturally.

MAKES 4 TO 6 SERVINGS

WAFFLES
1 cup whole wheat pastry flour
1 tablespoon baking powder
½ teaspoon ground cinnamon
⅛ teaspoon crushed pink Himalayan salt
1 tablespoon brown sugar

1 cup soy milk, plus more as needed
1 ½ tablespoons olive oil

BANANAS FOSTER TOPPING
½ cup margarine
⅓ cup brown sugar

½ teaspoon ground cinnamon
¼ teaspoon grated nutmeg
¾ cup maple syrup
¼ teaspoon agave nectar
1 tablespoon rum or rum extract
4 ripe bananas, sliced

Plug your waffle iron in and let it heat up, following any instructions it came with, because not all waffle irons are created equal.

Preheat the oven to 200°F.

In your favorite mixing bowl, whisk together the flour, baking powder, cinnamon, and salt.

In another bowl, blend the brown sugar, soy milk, and olive oil with an electric handheld mixer using the whisk attachments. Once it's smooth, pour the sugar mixture into the flour mixture and blend with your electric handheld mixer using the whisk attachments until the batter is smooth and lump-free. It should take at least 2 minutes. This is really important, so don't rush your batter. If your batter is a little thick, blend in more soy milk, 1 tablespoon at a time, until it's just right.

Use a ladle to pour your batter into the waffle iron.

Make your waffles one at a time. To keep them warm, put the finished waffles in a glass lasagna dish in the oven. The oven will also keep your waffles from getting soggy while you make the rest.

Make your topping while your waffles are cooking.

In your favorite saucepan, melt the margarine over medium heat. Once it's melted, whisk in the brown sugar, cinnamon, nutmeg, maple syrup, agave nectar, and rum until smooth. Once the mixture begins to bubble, reduce the heat to a simmer and drop in the slices of banana. Use a large spoon to mix the bananas into the syrup. Once the bananas are tender, remove the saucepan from the heat and allow it to thicken.

Once your waffles are made and your topping has cooled and thickened, it's time to build your perfect morning treat by ladling the warm, sticky, sweet topping over your waffles.

BAKED VEGAN CHICKEN AND EASY WAFFLES

When I lived in Atlanta, there seemed to be signs everywhere for chicken and waffles "shacks." I mean, even Motown legend Gladys Knight had a chain of them, and they seemed to be in every strip mall. At first I assumed they served waffles in the morning and fried chicken at night. Imagine my northern-girl surprise when I learned that this heart attack–inducing combination was actually a staple in soul food cuisine. It seemed strange to me, but is it really that much weirder than having a side of fried bacon or sausage with waffles or pancakes? It's savory, oily meat with a sweet, bready treat. So I came around.

When I was putting together a menu for a vegan soul food dinner party, I started thinking of ways to veganize this classic dish while also making it a bit healthier—but I didn't have a proper waffle iron to pull it off. Forty dollars later, there we were enjoying Baked Vegan Chicken and Easy Waffles. I have to admit that this northern girl has fallen in love with this southern combo.

MAKES 2 TO 4 SERVINGS

BAKED VEGAN CHICKEN
2 cups vegan chicken, defrosted (we recommend Gardein Chick'n Scallopini)

Olive oil cooking spray

¼ cup beer (we use Brooklyn Brewery's Pumpkin Ale, but I think any ale would be great)

Dash of liquid smoke

½ teaspoon Louisiana hot sauce

1 cup vegan Bisquick mix

1½ teaspoons Tony Chachere's Creole seasoning

EASY WAFFLES
2 cups vegan Bisquick mix

1½ cups soy milk

1 tablespoon applesauce

2 tablespoons olive oil

2 teaspoons vanilla extract

Dash of ground cinnamon

Dash of crushed pink Himalayan salt

"BUTTERY" SYRUP
½ cup margarine

2 cups maple syrup

Preheat the oven to 375°F. Cut your vegan chicken into strips or nuggets. Line a cookie sheet with foil and spray it with olive oil.

In a small bowl, mix the beer, liquid smoke, and hot sauce. In another small bowl, combine the vegan Bisquick mix and the Creole seasoning. Using one hand, put your vegan chicken in the beer bowl and flip it a few times to make sure it gets completely covered. Then, using the same hand, drop the vegan chicken into the bowl with the Bisquick mixture. Now using your other hand, flip the vegan chicken in the Bisquick mixture to get an even coating. You're using separate hands to help prevent contamination of the bowls.

After you've coated each piece of vegan chicken, place it on the cookie sheet. Spray an even coating of olive oil cooking spray over the coated vegan chicken—enough that it's no longer powdery looking. Once the vegan chicken is coated, bake for 10 to 15 minutes, until it is light golden brown and crispy.

While the vegan chicken is baking, make the waffles. Preheat your waffle iron using the manufacturer's instructions. In a large mixing bowl, blend all the waffle ingredients using an electric handheld mixer until smooth. Because some waffle irons are bigger than others, you'll want to follow the instructions that came with yours to determine how much batter you should use for each waffle. We use ½ cup of batter for each waffle. Make all your waffles.

To make the "Buttery" Syrup, in a saucepan heat the margarine and maple syrup over medium heat until the margarine melts and is incorporated with the syrup. Remove from the heat.

Serve the baked vegan chicken and waffles warm, with the waffles at the bottom, the baked vegan chicken on top, and the syrup drizzled over everything.

SPICED APPLE WAFFLES

Every waffle iron is different, so it's hard to say how many waffles this will make, or how long it'll take for each waffle to cook. You should refer to your waffle iron's instruction manual to get the best waffles possible. And remember—sticking together is what good waffles do.

MAKES 2 TO 4 SERVINGS

2 cups whole wheat flour

1 teaspoon vanilla extract

1 tablespoon brown sugar

2 tablespoons applesauce

1 teaspoon ground cinnamon

4 teaspoons baking powder

½ cup margarine, melted

1¾ cups soy milk

¼ teaspoon crushed pink Himalayan salt

Margarine and maple syrup for topping

Heat your waffle iron and prep for cooking per the instruction manual.

In a large bowl, blend the flour, vanilla, brown sugar, applesauce, cinnamon, baking powder, margarine, soy milk, and salt with an electric hand mixer until smooth. I recommend turning the bowl a little to get the batter a bit fluffier.

Following the directions that come with your waffle iron, pour the correct amount of batter onto the center of the heated waffle iron and close the lid.

Bake for about 5 minutes, or until the steaming stops. Carefully remove the waffle and serve immediately with margarine and maple syrup.

WHOLE WHEAT BANANA AND CHOCOLATE CHIP PANCAKES

The weekend we made these, most of the United States was buried in snow. We felt it was our patriotic duty to share this recipe with the world, so that snowed-in vegans everywhere could enjoy a fancy brunch in the comfort of their own home in their slippers and pj's. I hope that it worked out. It sure did for us.

MAKES 2 TO 4 LARGE SERVINGS

1 ripe banana, mashed

½ cup whole wheat flour

½ cup all-purpose flour

¾ cup soy milk

1 tablespoon sugar

2 tablespoons olive oil or hazelnut oil

3 teaspoons baking powder

¼ teaspoon crushed pink Himalayan salt

⅓ cup vegan chocolate chips

Olive oil cooking spray

In a mixing bowl, blend the banana, flours, soy milk, sugar, oil, baking powder, and salt for 2 minutes using an electric handheld mixer. You want the mix to be completely blended and without any clumps. Fold the vegan chocolate chips in with a large spoon until they're evenly mixed into the batter.

Heat your always-loyal cast-iron skillet or frying pan over medium heat. Once your skillet is hot, spray with olive oil cooking spray, then ladle on the batter.

Your batter will start to cook as soon as it hits the skillet, so try to make the pancakes the desired size and shape. Let your pancakes cook until they begin to bubble slightly and the edges begin to look puffed and dry. Then flip and cook the other side. Flip a few more times until golden brown. Serve with your favorite syrup or berries and smile. I mean, you have chocolate chip banana pancakes…what's not to smile about?

BREAKFAST ALL-STARS

Everyone has a favorite special breakfast, for those lazy Saturday mornings when the day is ripe with possibility, no one needs to rush out the door for work or school, and you can bask in the luxury of a quiet morning with a delicious meal. Whether it's a rare moment alone in the breakfast nook, an opportunity for the whole family to relax together, or a weekly brunch with girlfriends, special breakfast is always an important occasion.

When I think of special breakfast, I always think of those first mornings I spent with Dan in the apartment we ended up sharing together. Dan would get up early and make me pancakes, and then we'd enjoy them together with a cup of coffee and a great conversation.

In hindsight there was nothing particularly special about those pancakes (other than that pancakes are always amazing)—it was the love with which they were made that made them stand out. So maybe special breakfast isn't about the specialness of the recipe—maybe it's about the specialness of the moment.

Maybe. It's a cute story. But all the same, everyone should still be able to bring the thunder with a go-to special breakfast recipe. Maybe it'll help impress a new temporary houseguest, or just get a house full of screaming children to sit around the same table for twenty minutes. Either way, these recipes will ensure that special breakfasts remain special—on top of the quality of the company.

BLUEBERRY BANANA BREAD PANCAKES

A combination of two famous breakfast favorites, this is like a DC/Marvel crossover. However, unlike the actual DC/Marvel crossovers, this combination actually accentuates the high points of both parties, creating a whole that is greater than the sum of its parts—rather than just a pandering attempt to sell us silly comics. It's got all the fluffy decadence of banana bread, combined with the wholesome goodness of pancakes. What could be better?

MAKES 2 TO 4 SERVINGS

1 ripe banana, mashed into a paste

1 cup whole wheat flour

¾ cup soy milk

1 tablespoon sugar

2 tablespoons olive oil

¼ cup crushed walnuts

3 tablespoons baking powder

¼ teaspoon crushed pink Himalayan salt

⅓ cup fresh blueberries

Olive oil cooking spray

Margarine and your favorite syrup for serving

Heat your griddle, cast-iron skillet, or frying pan over medium heat.

In a medium bowl, blend the banana, flour, soy milk, sugar, oil, walnuts, baking powder, and salt. Once your batter is smooth, fold in the blueberries with a large spoon.

Lightly spray the pan with olive oil cooking spray before making each pancake. When forming pancakes, use less than ¼ cup of batter for each. Cook each pancake on one side until bubbly on top and puffed up and dry around the edges. Then flip and cook the other side.

Serve with margarine and your favorite syrup.

BISCUITS WITH SOYSAGE GRAVY

Can I get a hell yeah?

MAKES 1 DOZEN BISCUITS AND A WHOLE LOT OF GRAVY

BISCUITS

2 cups all-purpose flour, plus extra for flouring surfaces

1 tablespoon sugar

3 teaspoons baking powder

1 teaspoon crushed pink Himalayan salt

½ cup vegetable shortening

¾ cup almond milk

SOYSAGE GRAVY

Olive oil cooking spray

1 cup Lightlife Gimme Lean vegan sausage, Match vegan meat sausage, or your favorite vegan sausage

½ cup whole wheat flour

2 cups nutritional yeast

2 tablespoons olive oil

4 cups vegetable broth

2 tablespoons Bragg's liquid aminos

3 teaspoons poultry seasoning (most poultry seasonings are vegan, but some aren't, be sure to read the label)

2 teaspoons onion powder

1 teaspoon garlic powder

¼ teaspoon celery seed

3 tablespoons chopped fresh parsley

¼ teaspoon crushed black peppercorns

Preheat the oven to 450°F.

In a bowl, mix the flour, sugar, baking powder, and salt. Mix the shortening into the flour mixture using a pastry blender until the mixture becomes fine crumbs. Mix in the almond milk with a handheld mixer until the dough is smooth but very sticky.

Place the dough on a large, flat, floured surface. Knead gently a few times and then, using a floured rolling pin, roll the dough out to ½-inch thick. Using a biscuit cutter or the top of a pint glass, cut out biscuits and place them on an ungreased cookie sheet about an inch apart. Bake for 10 to 15 minutes, until the tops are golden brown. Immediately place them on a wire rack to cool.

While they're baking, prepare your gravy.

Spray your dearest cast-iron skillet or frying pan with olive oil cooking spray and heat on medium. Once the oil begins to warm, add small clumps of vegan sausage to the oil and let it brown. Be sure to flip the clumps a few times, letting them crumble until bite-size.

In a saucepan, toast the flour and nutritional yeast in the olive oil until they begin to brown. Whisk in the vegetable broth until the mixture is smooth and creamy. Then whisk in the Bragg's, poultry seasoning, onion powder, garlic powder, celery seed, parsley, and black pepper and simmer. Once the gravy begins to bubble and the vegan sausage has crispy edges, pour the gravy into your cast-iron skillet and gently mix.

Serve the biscuits hot with gravy over the top, and serve any extra gravy on the side for those folks who'll want a little more.

MONTE CRISTO POCKETS

The Monte Cristo is a fancy name for a fried ham-and-cheese sandwich. This is what Americans have done to France's croque-monsieur, or "Sir Crunch." The variations on this sandwich seem endless. In Houston, you can get a Monte Cristo made with Texas toast. In California, you can find it made with smoked turkey. And you can find Monte Cristos made with French toast instead of regular bread on brunch menus all over the country.

Our version combines the architecture of an empanada with a melty cheese center and smoked Tofurky. Dust with a little powdered sugar if you want to re-create the real diner experience.

MAKES 4 TO 6 POCKETS

CRUST
1 cup all-purpose flour
¼ teaspoon crushed pink Himalayan salt
⅓ cup vegetable shortening
3 tablespoons cold water
Olive oil cooking spray

2 tablespoons margarine
3 tablespoons almond milk

FILLING
1 (5.5-ounce) package Hickory Smoked Tofurky Deli Slices, separated

¾ cup shredded Daiya vegan cheddar cheese or your favorite vegan cheese
1 teaspoon nutritional yeast
1 teaspoon olive oil
Dash of liquid smoke

In a large mixing bowl, whisk together the flour and salt. Using a pastry blender, cut in the shortening until the mixture is crumbly. Sprinkle with the cold water 1 tablespoon at a time, and mix with an electric hand-held mixer until the dough forms. Form your dough into a patty, wrap in plastic wrap, and refrigerate for 30 minutes.

Preheat the oven to 450°F. Spray an unlined cookie sheet with olive oil.

In another mixing bowl, mix the Tofurky, vegan cheese, nutritional yeast, olive oil, and liquid smoke with a wooden spoon until the nutritional yeast and olive oil make a light paste that covers the Tofurky pieces.

On a floured surface, roll out the dough until it is ⅛ inch thick. Using a biscuit cutter or the top of a pint glass, cut your dough into 4-inch round disks. Reroll any scraps, and cut one more disk out of the extra. For each pocket, spoon 2 tablespoons of filling into the center of the disk. Moisten your fingers with water, trace along the edges, then fold the dough over. Use your wet fingers to seal the edges completely. Press a fork very gently along the edges to seal in the filling. Melt the margarine and whisk it together with the almond milk. Brush the top of each pocket lightly with the almond milk mixture and place on your cookie sheet 2 inches apart.

Bake for 20 to 25 minutes, until golden brown. Don't freak out if any of the almond milk burns on the cookie sheet—it doesn't mean your pockets have burned.

LA PETIT FRENCH TOAST

"Breakfast" in French is *petit déjeuner*, or "little lunch." How cute is that? This "little lunch" is mini French toasts made from baguette slices, rather than whole pieces of bread. Perfect for little eaters and Francophiles alike.

MAKES 2 TO 4 SERVINGS

¾ cup vanilla soy milk

1 tablespoon sugar

¼ teaspoon vanilla extract

⅛ teaspoon crushed pink Himalayan salt

2 tablespoons nutritional yeast

¼ teaspoon Ener-G egg replacer—just the powder, not prepared like the package instructs

Olive oil cooking spray

1 baguette, sliced into 1-inch slices

Margarine and maple syrup for topping

In a bowl with high sides, mix the soy milk, sugar, vanilla, salt, nutritional yeast, and egg replacer powder with an electric handheld mixer.

Spray a light coating of olive oil cooking spray over your cast-iron skillet and heat over medium heat. Preheat the oven to 200°F.

Dip the baguette slices into the soy milk mixture, making sure to get an even coating but not so much that the bread gets soggy. Place the baguette slices in the skillet one at a time. Brown until the edges are crispy; then flip and brown the other side.

After removing the baguette slices from skillet, put them on an oven-safe plate in the oven to keep warm. Serve warm with margarine and maple syrup.

HAWAIIAN TOAST

Say "aloha" to your morning with this delicious twist on classic French toast. The pineapple and coconut are complementary flavors to the sweetness of the toast itself, adding an extra layer of flavor depth to this decadent breakfast treat.

MAKES 2 TO 4 SERVINGS

½ cup coconut milk from a can, blended

¼ cup pineapple juice

1 tablespoon brown sugar

¼ teaspoon vanilla extract

⅛ teaspoon crushed pink Himalayan salt

2 tablespoons nutritional yeast

¼ teaspoon Ener-G egg replacer—just the powder, not prepared like the package instructs

Olive oil cooking spray

1 baguette, sliced into 1-inch slices

Crushed pineapple and shredded coconut for topping

In a bowl with high sides, mix the coconut milk, pineapple juice, brown sugar, vanilla, salt, nutritional yeast, and egg replacer powder with an electric handheld mixer.

Spray a light coating of olive oil cooking spray on your cast-iron skillet or frying pan, and heat over medium heat. Preheat the oven to 200°F.

Dip the baguette slices into the coconut milk mixture, making sure to get an even coating, but not so much that the bread gets soggy. Place the baguette slices in the skillet one at a time. Brown until the edges are crispy; then flip and brown the other side.

Remove the baguette slices from the skillet and place them on an oven-safe plate in the oven to keep warm. Serve warm with crushed pineapple and shredded coconut over the top.

CREPES

I have a long-standing love affair with France. It's strictly a platonic thing that encourages me to take long flights across the Atlantic from time to time. When I can't, I take my own little French stay-cations in our apartment, where I watch movies with subtitles and wear fancy hats. To Americans, crepes are a fancy breakfast item you pay an extra dollar for at IHOP (well, not to vegans; those bros have eggs in them). But if you go to Paris, one thing you can't miss is the adorable crepe carts set up throughout the city. You can spot their striped umbrellas and long lines a block away (or huge, weather-warped, handwritten signs if you happen to be walking through a less affluent area). I'd love to tell you these crepes are just like those, but those crepes have eggs and lard in them, so I've had to pass. These crepes are vegan, and although I can't tell you they're good for you, they are healthier than their egg-ridden comrades, ridiculously easy, and *délicieux!* *Faisons des crêpes!*

MAKES 2 TO 4 SERVINGS

1 ½ cups all-purpose flour

1 tablespoon granulated sugar

½ teaspoon baking powder

½ teaspoon crushed pink Himalayan salt

2 cups soy milk

2 tablespoons margarine, plus more for cooking

½ teaspoon vanilla extract

2 tablespoons applesauce

Berries, applesauce, jelly, peanut butter, or your favorite other crepe filling

Powdered sugar to sprinkle over the top

In a bowl and using an electric handheld mixer with whisk attachments, mix the flour, sugar, baking powder, salt, and soy milk until smooth. Then add the margarine, vanilla, and applesauce. Blend for 2 to 3 minutes with the bowl tilted, so the batter gets really smooth and creamy.

Lightly "butter" your *préféré* cast-iron skillet or frying pan with margarine and heat at a medium temperature until bubbly. You'll need to do this before you cook each crepe, so keep that margarine out.

For each crepe, pour ⅓ cup batter into the skillet. Immediately rotate the skillet with your wrist until a

thin layer of batter covers the bottom. Cook until you start to see light brown around the edges. Run a wide spatula along the edge to loosen; flip and cook the other side until light brown. Remove from heat and repeat with the rest of the batter.

Stack the crepes on a plate with pieces of wax paper between them; keep covered. When you're ready to serve, you can go two routes. You can fill them and roll them up like a cigar, or you can just fold them over, all Food Network Canada–style. Sprinkle powdered sugar over the crepes just before serving.

BEIGNETS

Now, we've never eaten at the famous Cafe Du Monde in New Orleans. Their beignets aren't vegan, but they do look tasty. It really is a shame they don't offer a vegan-friendly version of this old-school New Orleans favorite, because we would have eaten a dozen every morning we were in New Orleans for our honeymoon, while drinking barrels of café au (soy) lait and reading our travel books. But that's part of what makes this recipe so awesome. It's vegan, and you can make several dozen for the price of a single fancy coffee in the French Quarter. And let's be honest: New Orleans is a pretty liberal place, but they don't usually let you hang out in their cafés barefoot in your pajamas. You can do that while you eat these.

You're going to need to let your dough chill out overnight — so you'll want to start these li'l darlings the night before.

MAKES 1 TO 2 DOZEN BEIGNETS, DEPENDING ON HOW LARGE YOU CUT THEM

- 1 cup vanilla soy milk
- 2 tablespoons brown sugar
- 2 tablespoons margarine
- ½ package active dry yeast
- ½ teaspoon crushed pink Himalayan salt
- ¾ teaspoon grated nutmeg
- 1½ cups all-purpose flour, plus more to flour your surfaces
- 1 tablespoon Ener-G egg replacer—just the powder, not prepared as instructed on the package
- 1 tablespoon applesauce
- 3 to 4 cups olive oil
- Powdered sugar for topping

In a small saucepan, heat the soy milk over a medium heat until it begins to steam. Stir in the sugar and margarine; then turn the heat down to a simmer. Once the margarine is melted and completely incorporated, remove from the heat and cool to room temperature.

In a large bowl, combine the soy milk mixture with the yeast, salt, nutmeg, and flour. Stir in the egg replacer powder and applesauce with a large spoon, and then blend with an electric handheld mixer for about 2 minutes, until the batter becomes smooth. The batter is very sticky, so watch your mixer; the batter can creep right up into your mixer before you know it. Cover the batter with foil and allow it to chill in the fridge overnight.

The next morning, gently knead the batter on a heavily floured surface, and roll it out to a little less than ½ inch thick with a floured rolling pin. Cut into triangles or squares or a mixture of the two. We tried different sizes and types of triangles to see if one was better than another, and they were all equally awesome, so I'll let you decide.

Lay cut, raw beignets out on a piece of wax paper and cover with a fabric napkin or towel. Let them chill and rise in the fridge for another 30 minutes.

Fill your largest stewpot or Dutch oven with the olive oil, until halfway full. I know that seems like a lot, but you can get a big bottle of nonorganic olive oil for five dollars, and we used half of one of those bottles for this recipe. Heat your oil at a high temperature until it starts to bubble.

Once your oil is hot, place the beignets in one at time. Fry for 30 to 45 seconds on each side, or until they turn a golden brown. Use a slotted spoon to remove them, and place them on a plate with a paper towel to soak up the extra oil. Once they're cool—but not cold—dump a ton of powdered sugar on them and *laissez les bon temps rouler!*

CRUMPETS

This English breakfast treat looks similar to a pancake, but don't be fooled—it's more savory than sweet. But it's still a bloody great snack for breakfast and high tea alike.

MAKES A DOZEN CRUMPETS

1 (¼-ounce) package active dry yeast

3 cups warm water

3½ cups all-purpose flour

½ cup whole wheat flour

2 tablespoons baking powder

1½ teaspoons sugar

1½ teaspoons crushed pink Himalayan salt

Olive oil cooking spray

Margarine and your favorite jam for serving

In a small bowl, mix the yeast in the warm water until it dissolves.

In a large bowl, whisk together the flours, baking powder, sugar, and salt until blended. Add the dissolved yeast to the flour mixture and blend with an electric handheld mixer using dough hooks. Cover with foil and set aside in a warm spot while you heat your skillet.

Spray your favorite cast-iron skillet or frying pan with olive oil cooking spray, and heat over medium heat. Once the oil is hot, use a biscuit cutter as a form and ladle the batter in until the form is half-full. Press gently on the biscuit cutter to keep the batter from escaping while you fill it. Be sure and wear an oven mit to protect your hand.

Allow the crumpets to cook on the skillet for approximately 10 minutes, or until the surface is covered with bubbles and holes. Remove the biscuit cutter and put a lid on the skillet for 1 to 2 minutes to allow the tops of the crumpets to cook. Move the crumpets from the skillet to a wire rack to cool once the tops are fully baked.

If you have more than one biscuit cutter, you can cook more than one at a time; but be careful—it's challenging.

Once your crumpets have cooled and are easy to handle, serve with margarine and your favorite jam—and of course a pot of Earl Grey.

STRAWBERRY AND CREAM QUINOA PORRIDGE

This protein-packed breakfast dish is sort of an unconventional take on oatmeal, and guaranteed to start your day off right.

MAKES 2 SERVINGS

1 cup quinoa

2⅓ cups almond milk or vanilla soy milk

½ teaspoon vanilla extract

3 tablespoons brown sugar

1 cup sliced fresh strawberries

Read the instructions on your quinoa package to see if your brand needs to be presoaked or rinsed the night before. Prep if you need to.

In your favorite little saucepan, bring your almond milk and vanilla to a boil over medium heat. Add the quinoa, cover, and turn the heat down to a simmer. Remove from the heat after the quinoa has absorbed half the almond milk, 15 to 20 minutes.

Stir in the sugar. Put the top back on, return to the heat, and simmer for another 5 to 7 minutes. Remove from the heat.

Serve warm with slices of strawberry on top.

ALMOND CHAI

If you're not a coffee drinker—or even if you are—you might be looking for a delicious new beverage to start your day off right. We're big coffee drinkers in the Shannon house, but that doesn't mean we don't appreciate a little variety. Try as you might, you cannot live on caffeine alone. This sweet, spicy treat has been a coffeehouse staple for years. Now you can make this decadent drink right in the comfort of your own home. It's perfect for those who prefer to get their caffeine from tea instead of coffee but still want the creamy goodness of a latte.

MAKES 2 TO 4 SERVINGS

2 cups water

5 bags Darjeeling tea

2 cups almond milk

2 whole cloves, crushed

4 whole black peppercorns, crushed

Pinch of ground cinnamon

3 teaspoons agave nectar

In a saucepan, heat the water to a rapid boil and then reduce to a simmer. Add the tea bags and simmer for 5 minutes. Remove and discard the tea bags.

Stir in the almond milk, cloves, peppercorns, and cinnamon. Heat to a boil, but remove from the heat before the pot boils over. Stir in the agave nectar and then pour through a strainer into mugs.

MEXICAN HOT CHOCOLATE MOCHA

Chocolate with chili pepper. Could there be anything better? The combination of flavor-hot and temperature-hot will blast through even the coldest of winter chills.

MAKES 2 SERVINGS

3 ounces unsweetened baking chocolate (this should be 3 squares)

1½ cups water

2 tablespoons agave nectar

2 tablespoons brown sugar (you may want to add a pinch or two more if you like your drinks really sweet)

⅛ teaspoon chili powder

Dash of crushed pink Himalayan salt

1 shot espresso

4½ cups almond milk

In a saucepan, heat the chocolate and water over a medium heat, stirring constantly with a whisk, until the chocolate is melted and the mixture is smooth.

Whisk in the agave nectar, brown sugar, chili powder, and salt. Reduce the heat to a simmer and let sit for about 1 minute. Then whisk in the shot of espresso and almond milk. Continue whisking the mixture and let it sit on the heat until it begins to bubble.

Pour into two large mugs and maybe add some of Whipped Coconut Cream from page 403!

VITAMIN C COMMITTEE

Vitamin C is good for you. Everyone can agree on that. This beverage basically takes every source of vitamin C out there and combines it all into one mega-cocktail that's as delicious as it is healthy. Drink one of these every day if you feel like you're coming down with a cold.

MAKES 2 TO 4 SERVINGS

½ cup pink grapefruit juice

¾ cup orange juice

¼ cup lime juice

1 orange, peeled, segments pulled apart

½ cup pomegranate or cranberry juice

Blend the grapefruit, orange, and lime juices and the orange segments in a blender until smooth. Place ¼ cup ice in each of two pint glasses, and pour half the blended juice in each. Pour ¼ cup of pomegranate juice into each glass; this should make a lovely "sunrise" as the red juice settles at the bottom and the lighter orange juice rises. You'll want to remix the juice in your glass a few times while drinking.

SHANNON SMOOTHIE

Warning: This smoothie is supereasy and really good and may improve your mornings by an estimated 80 percent. We often use fresh cherries in this recipe, but to be honest, I like using frozen cherries because you get more juice and don't have to take out the pits yourself.

MAKES 2 SERVINGS

2 ripe bananas

3 cups soy milk

½ cup cherries, pitted

2 ripe pears, cored and sliced (I like to leave the skin on)

½ cup frozen blackberries, defrosted

1 tablespoon lemon or pomegranate juice

½ cup silken tofu or ½ cup vegan vanilla yogurt

Toss all the ingredients in a blender, making sure to get as much juice from your fruits as possible. Blend until smooth. Serve fresh in pint glasses.

ELVIS SMOOTHIE

All hail the King! The king of nutty, sweet, and protein-rich smoothies, that is.

MAKES 2 SERVINGS

2 ripe bananas

1½ tablespoons chunky peanut butter

3⅓ cups vanilla almond milk

2½ teaspoons ground flaxseed

1 teaspoon maple syrup

1 tablespoon apple juice

Toss all the ingredients in your blender. Puree until smooth and creamy.

THE SMOOTHIE RENAISSANCE

During the Renaissance, Western civilization dragged itself out of the Dark Ages by refocusing on two things that had been more or less lost in Europe since the fall of the Roman Empire—arts and sciences. This reconnection with the arts and sciences reversed centuries of societal decline and transformed a backwater peninsula sticking awkwardly off of Asia into the world powerhouse that it would become. Of course, in the Middle East and China, people had been continuing their advancements in these pursuits this whole time … but that's another story.

Making a good smoothie is both an art and a science—and can help rescue you from the Dark Ages of breakfast. The art is in the combination of fruit flavors and pretty colors that make smoothies so delicious and fun; the science is in maximizing the limited time in the morning and in crafting a complete, nutritious breakfast that'll give you everything you need to rebuild Western civilization … er, get you through your busy day. Here are the key ingredients for your own smoothie Renaissance:

BANANAS. The backbone of a good smoothie, bananas will give your smoothie that nice thick texture and hold all of the other ingredients together. You want your bananas to be just ripe: if they're underripe, they won't blend up as well and your smoothie will have sort of a chalky taste to it; if they're overripe, like you would use for baking, the smoothie will have sort of a runny, oily consistency. One banana per serving is a good rule of thumb.

SWEET FRUIT. If you use the right fruit, you won't need to add any sugar or other sweeteners to your smoothie—many berries are plenty sweet on their own. Strawberries and blueberries are your classic smoothie fruits, but peaches, mangos, pineapples, and many others are great to experiment with.

TART FRUIT. Complementing your sweet fruits with something tart will give your smoothie a more complex flavor. Raspberries are the go-to tart smoothie berry, but pomegranates, acai berries, and citrus fruits or juices will also do the job.

PROTEIN. Protein is an important part of a healthy breakfast, so try to get some in your smoothie. An easy way to do this is by adding some soy milk to your smoothie—this will also give it a creamier taste and consistency, which you might like or not, depending on your palate. There are many vegan protein powders out there that come with or without a flavor—we like Trader Joe's soy protein powder.

EXTRA NUTRITION. The great thing about fruit smoothies is that their strong flavors are pretty hard to break through—so you can add all sorts of goodies to your smoothie without altering the flavor much or at all. Green leafy vegetables like spinach or kale may seem out of place in a fruit smoothie—but throw a few leaves into your next one and see if you can even tell they're in there. We've also been known to add some flaxseed oil to our smoothies for omega-3s. Many different supplements can be thrown into a smoothie to level up its nutritional value—so experiment and see!

Chapter Three

LUNCH

Perhaps nowhere have our changing American lives affected our culinary habits more than in our lunches. Once upon a time, lunch was the focal point of the daily meal calendar, a time for the woman the iconic Betty Crocker represented to enjoy some time with her family. Now it's something that she "grabs" as an afterthought—if she even has the thought at all—in between doing a million other things. This, we believe, is a grave injustice—and one that we're here to rectify. ¡Viva la revo-luncheon!

In our early, preindustrial, agrarian society, the largest meal was consumed midday, as a break from toiling in the fields and to fuel up for the rest of the day's labor. As the economy, and many people's daily lives, shifted away from field labor and toward artisanal work performed away from the home, men would still often return home for a midday meal with their families. However, as many agrarian societies urban-ized, and work took place farther and farther from the home, men began bringing their own portable meals to work with them, leaving women to have lunch either alone or with small groups of other women in their social circle—a precursor to those epic *Sex and the City* lunches, perhaps?

Once women entered the workforce en masse as well, everyone was eating quick meals designed more for convenience than deliciousness—meaning the traditional version of the midday meal had faded into the annals of history (for working people, at least). And, as with most major shifts in societal norms, there isn't much chance of recovering it. But that doesn't mean that today's superwoman can't still enjoy a delicious and nutritious lunch that'd make those agrarian Betty Crocker emulators jealous—even if she can't lounge around in fancy Manhattan bistros for hours like Carrie Bradshaw and her pals.

✳ ✳ ✳

SOUPS

Some food historians believe that soup was one of the first true signs of human civilization. Sure, you had your farming of grains and building of homes—but it seems undeniable that shortly after that first guy discovered the benefits of fire, he put a pot of soup over it and invited his buddies over to the cave for a potluck. Sounds like civilization to me.

Soup is an easy-to-make lunch that you can prepare in large quantities and then freeze, so you can enjoy it over a long period of time. You can bring it to work in a thermos or have it stocked up in your freezer for quick dinners when you have to work late. So it'll help you deal with modern civilization too.

BEEFLESS STEW

This stew is the perfect fall lunch, and it makes a lot, so you can have leftovers for a few days. It's hearty, has warm flavors without being too spicy, and brings a nice, rustic charm that makes me wish the leaves outside were red and orange. Like regular old "meaty" stew, this stew is even better the next day. The onion and "beefy" flavors really come out after the stew sits for a bit, so I suggest not eating it all in one meal. You'll see what I mean the next day. I was genuinely sad to see the bottom of my bowl the first night, but the next day it was like saying good-bye to a friend. And because I'm impatient, the best part for me is that you can get the same flavor from this stew in an hour that it would take you four hours to achieve with a "meaty" stew.

MAKES 5 TO 6 BOWLS OF STEW

Olive oil cooking spray

8 red potatoes, cut into pieces about the size of your vegan beef

1 (8-ounce) bag baby carrots

1 (9-ounce) bag Gardein beefless tips or vegan beef seitan

1 red onion, sliced

1 cup frozen peas

1 (14.5-ounce) can diced tomatoes

2 cups Better Than Bouillon vegetable broth, made per the instructions on the package

1 (8-ounce) can tomato sauce

⅓ cup nutritional yeast or whole wheat flour (the whole wheat flour will make the stew thicker; we like more broth, so we went with the nutritional yeast)

2 tablespoons vegan Worcestershire sauce

2 teaspoons Bragg's liquid aminos

1 teaspoon agave nectar

1 teaspoon olive oil

1 teaspoon marjoram leaves

1½ teaspoons thyme leaves

1½ teaspoons onion powder

½ teaspoon celery seed

1 teaspoon Tony Chachere's Creole seasoning

Crushed black peppercorns

Preheat the oven to 325°F.

Spray a glass baking dish with olive oil cooking spray. Place the potatoes in the dish skin-side down. Add the baby carrots in one layer, then the vegan beef, and finally the sliced onion. Spray the ingredients with more olive oil cooking spray. Bake uncovered for 30 minutes, or until the onions and vegan beef are brown. After you remove the dish from the oven, place the vegan beef and onions into a bowl and the potatoes and carrots into a Dutch oven or large stewpot with a cover.

Mix the peas, tomatoes, broth, tomato sauce, nutritional yeast, vegan Worcestershire sauce, Bragg's, agave nectar, olive oil, and herbs and spices into the vegetables in the Dutch oven, keeping the vegan beef and onions separate for now. Stir a few times to make sure the herbs are mixed in. Put the Dutch oven into the oven with the lid on and let the vegetable mixture simmer for 30 minutes, checking it and stirring once. Remove from the oven and taste. This is when you can check to see if your vegetables are tender, and add more Bragg's or pepper if the mixture is too bland for your taste. We added a few dashes of black pepper and put the Dutch oven back in for another 10 minutes because our potatoes weren't right yet. Once the seasonings are to your liking, mix in the onions, place the Dutch oven on the stovetop, and simmer for 10 minutes over medium heat.

Separate the vegan beef into however many servings you're planning on. To serve, put one serving of vegan beef into a soup bowl, and then ladle the stew over it. This will reheat your vegan beef and keep it from getting mushy in the broth.

Store any leftover stew and vegan beef separately.

5-BEAN CHILI

This is the recipe for our family chili. I'm pretty sure every vegan family has one, so I hope you'll still give ours a chance—because it's really good. We can't recommend enough baking up some Cheezy Jalapeño Corn Bread (page 327) to go with it!

MAKES 5 TO 6 BOWLS

2 cups Better Than Bouillon vegan beef broth, made per the instructions on the package (you may want to add another ½ cup if you don't like your chili thick)

1 (14-ounce) can garbanzo beans, drained and rinsed

1 (14-ounce) can black beans, drained and rinsed

1 (14-ounce) can kidney beans, drained and rinsed

1 (14-ounce) can pinto beans, drained and rinsed

½ cup dry lentils

1 (14-ounce) can corn, drained

1 green bell pepper, diced

1 red onion, diced

2 cloves garlic, minced

1 (28-ounce) can Mexican-flavored diced tomatoes

2 tablespoons chili powder

1½ teaspoons cumin

1 teaspoon Bragg's liquid aminos

½ teaspoon oregano

Dash of liquid smoke

1 teaspoon onion powder

1 teaspoon olive oil

Shredded Daiya vegan cheddar cheese or your favorite vegan cheese to sprinkle over the top

Add the broth, beans and lentils, vegetables, seasonings and oil to your slow cooker and set it on low heat. Cover and cook for 5 to 6 hours, stirring occasionally.

If you don't have a slow cooker, you can use a large stewpot and cook, covered, over medium heat for 5 to 6 hours. Be sure to stir the chili often. The beans are more likely to stick to the sides in a stewpot.

When you serve—sprinkle with vegan cheese and don't forget your corn bread.

WHITE CHILI

I admit I'm partial to lime juice, so that might be why I've fallen in love with this chili. But it's also possible that this chili takes beans and broth to a new place in their relationship. Hard to say... who can explain love?

MAKES 4 TO 5 BOWLS

1 red onion, diced

4 cloves garlic, minced

2 tablespoons olive oil

2 cups white wine

5 cups Better Than Bouillon vegetable broth, made per the instructions on the package

4 tablespoons lime juice

4 tablespoons chopped fresh cilantro

3 teaspoons cumin

1 teaspoon onion powder

1 teaspoon lemon pepper

1 teaspoon dried oregano

¾ teaspoon hot sauce

½ teaspoon Bragg's liquid aminos

1 cup frozen whole-kernel corn

1 (15-ounce) can garbanzo beans, drained and rinsed

1 (15-ounce) can butter beans, drained and rinsed

1 (15-ounce) can cannellini beans, drained and rinsed

1 cup frozen peas

1 cup frozen green beans

3 stalks celery, chopped

Vegan Parmesan for topping

Bread for dipping and eating with your soup

In a huge soup pot with a lid or a Dutch oven, cook the red onion, garlic, and olive oil over medium heat until the onions are tender.

Add the wine, broth, lime juice, seasonings, and vegetables. Cover and heat to a boil. Reduce heat to a simmer. Remove the cover and simmer for 20 minutes. Serve with vegan Parmesan and your favorite bread.

SHORTCUT GUMBO

I do declare! I like my gumbo rouxy and so spicy it'll make you smack your mama.*

MAKES 6 TO 8 SERVINGS

2 tablespoons olive oil

Dash of liquid smoke

1 (14-ounce) package Tofurky Italian sausages, Field Roast Italian sausages, or your favorite vegan sausages, cut into coins

1 (14-ounce) can artichoke hearts, drained and quartered

2 cups vegan shrimp (we recommend May Wah shrimp balls, but you can also substitute seitan or your favorite vegan chicken)

Dash of beer (we suggest a pale ale)

¼ cup margarine

2 medium red onions, sliced

1 green bell pepper, diced

3 cloves garlic, minced

2 tablespoons whole wheat flour

3½ cups Better Than Bouillon vegan beef broth, made per the instructions on the package

½ teaspoon Louisiana hot sauce

½ teaspoon Bragg's liquid aminos

¼ teaspoon crushed black peppercorns

1 teaspoon Tony Chachere's Creole seasoning

¼ teaspoon thyme

2 dried bay leaves

½ cup frozen cut okra

3 celery stalks, diced

1 (28-ounce) can diced tomatoes

¼ cup chopped fresh parsley

3 cups cooked brown rice

In your *cher* cast-iron skillet or frying pan, heat the olive oil and liquid smoke over medium heat. Once the oil is hot, add the vegan sausage, artichoke hearts, vegan shrimp, and beer. Stir occasionally and simmer until the vegan sausage begins to brown. With a slotted spoon, remove the vegan sausage and vegan shrimp from the skillet and set them aside.

Add the margarine to the skillet and let it melt. Toss in the red onions, green bell pepper, and garlic and cook for 5 minutes, or until your vegetables are tender. Remove the vegetables from the skillet and set

aside. Gradually stir the flour into the cast-iron skillet. Cook over medium heat until the flour mixture begins to bubble. Add the broth, hot sauce, Bragg's, pepper, Creole seasoning, thyme, bay leaves, and vegetables, and simmer for 10 to 15 minutes.

To serve, spoon the cooked vegan shrimp, vegan sausage, and vegetables over your cooked rice. Then use a ladle to fill the rest of your bowl with soup. Sprinkle a little parsley over the top. Mix it all up in your bowl before you eat; you may want to invest in some dipping bread too. Not that we're telling you what to do or anything.

---

* This is just a saying. The Shannons do not condone or endorse mama smacking.

FRESH LEMON AND ASPARAGUS SOUP

When professional chefs make soup, there are several key factors. All the vegetables should be cut into a uniform size, and the broth should be poured through a china-cap strainer more than once. So I feel like I'm showing my amateur status by posting this as a "soup." See, I could have strained this soup into a fine light broth, but then it would lose a lot of the asparagus…and isn't that the star of asparagus soup? I thought about calling it a chowder, but "Asparagus Chowder" didn't exactly sing to me. So soup it is. And what a soup! I recommend making this recipe in the spring, when there's still a lot of great asparagus available in grocery stores and farmers' markets.

MAKES 6 TO 8 BOWLS

1 pound fresh asparagus spears

2 medium shallots, thinly sliced

3 tablespoons olive oil, plus more for sautéing

1 (15-ounce) can cannellini beans, drained and rinsed

2 cups Better Than Bouillon vegan chicken broth, made per the instructions on the package

3 stalks celery, diced

1 (14-ounce) can artichoke hearts, drained

½ cup white wine or apple juice

½ teaspoon cumin

1 teaspoon onion powder

½ teaspoon crushed black peppercorns

1½ teaspoons Bragg's liquid aminos

1 tablespoon fresh thyme leaves

2 teaspoons fresh lemon zest

1 tablespoon fresh lemon juice

Shredded smoked cheddar Sheese or vegan Parmesan to sprinkle over the top

Sauté the asparagus and shallots in olive oil.

Once the asparagus and shallots are tender, set a few spears of asparagus aside to garnish your soup. Put the rest of the asparagus and shallots in a food processor or blender with 3 tablespoons of the olive oil. Blend until smooth. Add the cannellini beans and blend until smooth again. This should take about a minute and a half.

In a large soup pot or Dutch oven, heat the bouillon, celery, artichoke hearts, and white wine over medium heat. Once the mixture begins to boil, add the asparagus blend, and stir. Then add the cumin, onion powder, black pepper, Bragg's, and thyme. Cover and simmer for 5 minutes on low heat, stirring occasionally.

After 5 minutes, remove from the heat and stir in the lemon zest and lemon juice. Serve hot, with your saved asparagus tips fanned out over the top as garnish and grated vegan cheese sprinkled over that.

SHŌYU RAMEN BOWLS
FEATURING THE VEGAN HARD-BOILED EGG

Real Japanese ramen is more than noodles. It has beautiful, colorful vegetables and flavorful broth in countless variations. Needless to say, when you make this traditional dish vegan, it's pretty much heaven. Adding little touches like the Vegan Hard-Boiled Egg will take your ramen out of the dorm room and into those big-city noodle shops where the menus are in Hiragana and the mock meat selection is so impressive you wonder why anyone in Japan eats meat at all.

MAKES 4 LARGE BOWLS

VEGAN HARD-BOILED EGG

1 (14-ounce) package extrafirm tofu, drained and pressed

3 tablespoons nutritional yeast

1 teaspoon cumin

½ teaspoon onion powder

¼ teaspoon turmeric

¼ teaspoon Tony Chachere's Creole seasoning

1 tablespoon olive oil for cooking

SHŌYU RAMEN BOWLS

2 tablespoons olive oil

2 cups vegan chicken, diced (we recommend Gardein Chick'n Scallopini)

6 cups Better Than Bouillon vegetable broth, made per the instructions on the package

4 cloves garlic, minced

¼ cup white wine or Chinese rice wine

2 tablespoons lime juice

2 tablespoons Bragg's liquid aminos

¼ cup shredded carrots

1 (15-ounce) can baby corn, drained

1 (8-ounce) can sliced water chestnuts, drained

¼ cup fresh pea pods

¼ teaspoon minced fresh ginger

1 (8-ounce) package Chinese misua wheat noodles

40 to 48 baby bok choy leaves (10 to 12 per bowl)

1 sheet nori, cut into strips

Chopped green onion and black sesame seeds to sprinkle over the top

Preheat the oven to 300°F.

To make the Vegan Hard-Boiled Eggs, cut the block of tofu into 4 rectangular pieces. With your 1-teaspoon measuring spoon, scoop a half-circle cup out of each piece of tofu. These cups are what you are going to fill with your "yolk," so make sure they aren't too shallow, but also not so deep that they make your "eggs" fall apart. Then, with a soupspoon, gently cut the corners off your rectangular "eggs" to create lopsided oval or egg shapes.

Put the tofu pieces you scooped out of and cut off your "eggs" in a small bowl. Mash the tofu pieces into a paste with a fork, and mix in the nutritional yeast, cumin, onion powder, turmeric, and Creole seasoning to make your "yolk." Then, with your soupspoon, fill the cups you made in the "eggs" with the "yolk" mix. You're going to have some "yolk" left over, so it's okay to overfill the "eggs."

Coat a glass baking dish with olive oil. Place the "eggs" in the baking dish and into the oven for 10 minutes. Remove from the oven and set aside to put into your soup once they're cool enough to pick up with your hands.

Next prepare the ramen bowls. In your international superstar wok, heat the olive oil over medium heat. Then fry up your vegan chicken until it's crispy and brown. You want a thick "skin" to form on the outside of the vegan chicken so it won't get spongy in the broth. Set aside and cool in the wok.

In a large soup pot, heat the bouillon, garlic, white wine, lime juice, Bragg's, and carrots to a boil. Add the baby corn and water chestnuts. Boil for 1 minute. Now add the pea pods, ginger, and noodles and boil for another minute. The noodles should cook pretty fast, but read your package to see what the manufacturer suggests for cooking time. Once the noodles are tender, add the baby bok choy leaves and remove the pot from the heat.

To serve, first distribute the noodles, vegetables, and broth among 4 bowls; then mix in pieces of the vegan chicken. Gently place 1 vegan egg on top of each bowl and sprinkle with slices of nori, green onions, and sesame seeds.

どうぞめしあがれ!

THE ULTIMATE CORN CHOWDER EXPERIENCE

We both frakking love corn and potatoes. I mean, of course we do. We're American. Who doesn't love corn and potatoes? Our society has been fattening us up on French fries and corn syrup since we were little eaters. That's why we tried to do something different with this classic soup, which is paired with sandwiches in cafeterias all over this grand nation of ours. We added protein and extra veggies, making this a whole meal in a bowl—a wonderful, filling meal you could bring to lunch all week because it reheats so well.

MAKES 6 TO 8 BOWLS

½ red onion, diced

2 tablespoons olive oil

6 red potatoes, cubed and boiled until tender (I like to leave my skins on, but that's your call)

1 (15-ounce) can creamed corn

1 cup frozen corn

½ cup frozen peas

½ cup frozen green beans

1 (15-ounce) can garbanzo beans, drained and rinsed

3 tablespoons Bragg's liquid aminos

1 cup frozen hash browns, thawed

1 cup soy milk

1 cup Better Than Bouillon vegetable broth, made per the instructions on the package

½ teaspoon vegan Worcestershire sauce

2 tablespoons nutritional yeast

1 teaspoon lemon pepper (add more if you like your soup with a kick)

1 teaspoon dried rosemary, crushed

1½ teaspoons onion powder

Fresh parsley and vegan bacon bits to toss on top

Place the onions and olive oil in a large soup pot or Dutch oven and cook over medium heat, stirring occasionally. Once the onions become tender, add the potatoes, vegetables, beans, Bragg's, hash browns, soy milk, broth, vegan Worcestershire sauce, nutritional yeast, lemon pepper, rosemary, and onion powder, mixing thoroughly. When the soup begins to boil, cover the pot and lower the heat to a simmer for 20 to 30 minutes, stirring occasionally. You'll know the soup is done when the hash browns have begun to disintegrate.

Serve with fresh parsley and vegan bacon bits sprinkled on top.

I don't like to tell people what to do...but eat this with some sourdough bread. Just do it. No time for questions. You have soup to eat!

BEER AND CHEESE SOUP

Beer and cheese soup may sound a bit odd to some, but in reality it's pretty tasty stuff. It has all the key flavors of French onion soup: rich, savory, "beefy" broth with vegan cheese mixed in. We suggest getting some toasted bread for dipping in your soup and cleaning your bowl. If you consider your heart to be full of adventure and a love of beer, this soup is a must-try!

MAKES 4 TO 6 BOWLS

2 tablespoons margarine

1 medium red onion, chopped

4 stalks celery, chopped

2 tablespoons flour

¼ cup nutritional yeast

½ teaspoon lemon pepper

1 (12-ounce) bottle beer (we used brown ale, but any dark beer will work)

2 cups Better Than Bouillon vegetable broth, made per the instructions on the package

1 teaspoon olive oil

1 tablespoon Bragg's liquid aminos

Dash of liquid smoke

1 teaspoon dried thyme

2 cups shredded Daiya vegan cheddar cheese or your favorite vegan cheese

Paprika

Baguette for dipping in your soup

In a large soup pot or 2-quart saucepan, melt the margarine over medium heat. Once the margarine is melted, toss in the onion and celery and stir to evenly coat the vegetables with the melted margarine. Let them cook until they're tender.

Stir the flour, half the nutritional yeast, and the lemon pepper into your melted margarine. It will make a smooth paste; watch out for clumps. You can break them up by gently pressing them against the side of the pot. Stir in the beer, broth, olive oil, Bragg's, liquid smoke, and thyme. Heat to a boil, boil for 1 minute, then taste. If it's too salty, add water 1 tablespoon at a time. If it needs more salt, add more Bragg's 1 teaspoon at a time.

Gradually stir in the vegan cheese. Reduce the heat to a simmer. Keep checking, and remove from the heat once your vegan cheese melts. Serve with a dash of paprika over the top and some bread to dip in it.

CHICKEN AND WILD RICE SOUP

When I first posted this recipe to our blog, it was prime cold season. All over Facebook, statuses were littered with stuffy heads, runny noses, and sore throats. Many of us grew up eating chicken noodle soup in these times of crisis, but after I went vegan, that tradition fell by the wayside because I couldn't find a vegan chicken product that didn't get spongy in soup. But with advancements in food technology have come vegan chicken products that can safely be used in comforting chicken noodle soup. I prefer wild rice to noodles, but there's a substitution note in the recipe if you're more the conventional type. This recipe is very simple, so you can make it for yourself if your mom, partner, or whoever isn't available. Or you can be an angel and make it for that special someone in your life when he or she isn't feeling well.

MAKES 4 TO 6 BOWLS

2 cups vegan chicken, defrosted (we recommend Gardein Chick'n Scallopini)

2 tablespoons olive oil

1 cup cooked wild rice*

5 cups Better Than Bouillon vegetable broth, made per the instructions on the package

1 cup sliced carrots (coins)

1 cup sliced celery

1 red onion, chopped

1 cup frozen peas

1 teaspoon onion powder

1 teaspoon dried oregano

1 teaspoon dried thyme

2 dried bay leaves

½ teaspoon celery seed

Dash of crushed black peppercorns

Preheat the oven to 350°F.

In a glass baking dish, toss the vegan chicken and olive oil until your vegan chicken is completely coated. Bake for 10 to 15 minutes, flipping once to make sure it cooks evenly. Once the vegan chicken is brown and crispy, remove from the oven and cool.

In a large soup pot or Dutch oven, heat the remaining ingredients over medium heat until they boil. Reduce the heat to a simmer.

To serve, slice or chop the vegan chicken, and then divide into 4 to 6 portions. Fill each soup bowl three-quarters of the way with soup, then toss one portion of vegan chicken on top.

---

* For traditional chicken noodle soup, replace the wild rice with 1 cup uncooked broken vegan fettuccine or medium-size pasta. Be sure to check the label for eggs; a lot of fettuccine contains eggs.

SOUTH AMERICAN CORN AND QUINOA SUMMER STEW

Have I ever told you I can read minds?* Right now, you're thinking this: South American? That's pretty general. There's a wide range of distinct cultures in South America. How authentic is this recipe? Well, I was trying to find a chilled soup during a particularly merciless heat wave and kept stumbling across soups from South America that sounded delicious, like *canja de galinha*, which is a Portuguese/Brazilian soup made with chicken and lemon. We also had this package of quinoa our friend brought back from Peru that was begging for a special project. So I collected what I liked about all of these soups and made this hybrid. Viva summer stew!

MAKES 4 TO 6 BOWLS

- 1½ pounds red potatoes, cubed
- 1 cup mixed whole string beans,
- 6 cups Better Than Bouillon vegan chicken broth, made per the instructions on the package
- 2 large corncobs, broken in half
- 1 tablespoon olive oil
- 1 zucchini, sliced
- 3 tablespoons diced fresh cilantro
- 1 tablespoon cumin
- 1 red bell pepper, diced
- ½ cup lemon or lime juice
- ⅓ cup quinoa, uncooked
- 1 tablespoon beer (I suggest an India Pale Ale, or ginger ale if you're not into alcohol)
- 4 cloves garlic, minced
- ¼ teaspoon crushed black peppercorns
- ½ teaspoon hot sauce
- Fresh lemon or lime slices

In the largest soup pot you can find, throw in all the ingredients except the lemon slices, and simmer over medium heat for about 1 hour. You want your vegetables to be tender but still crisp, so remove your pot from the heat when your vegetables are ready, even if it hasn't been an hour.

Let the stew sit and cool to room temperature, which may take another hour. You can also put it in the fridge to chill more quickly. Serve at room temperature with a slice of fresh lemon, which you can smash into the soup with your spoon when you begin to eat.

You may want to serve this stew with extra napkins too. You're supposed to eat the corn off the cob with your hands, and that can get a little messy. But if you love corn, you won't even notice.

---

* I actually can't read minds.

MINESTRONE

Minestrone is as common on Italian dinner tables as pasta. Some say that minestrone predates Rome's conquering of the Italian peninsula in the second century BCE, but back then it was made with spelt, not pasta, because Marco Polo hadn't yet gone on his adventures.* Besides being a nutritious and healthy dish that predates the republic, it's easy to take for granted, because it's often already vegan. But minestrone is an easy dinner that pretty much makes itself. All you need is a slow cooker and some patience; even Betty Crocker can't rush happiness. This soup takes about a half hour to prep for and about 6 hours to make. We like ours with Easy Olive Oil Garlic Toast (see page 271).

MAKES 6 TO 8 BOWLS

- 1 (28-ounce) can stewed tomatoes with basil
- 5 cups Better Than Bouillon vegetable broth, made per the instructions on the package
- 2 tablespoons Bragg's liquid aminos
- 1 cup raw kale, chopped
- ½ red onion, finely chopped
- ⅓ cup red wine
- 1 (15-ounce) can kidney beans, drained and rinsed
- 1 (15-ounce) can cannellini beans, drained and rinsed
- 1 large zucchini, sliced
- 3 celery stalks, chopped
- ½ cup baby carrots
- ¾ cup frozen green beans
- 3 cloves garlic, minced
- 2 tablespoons fresh basil, chopped
- 2 teaspoons dried oregano
- ¼ teaspoon dried thyme leaves
- 2 bay leaves
- 1 teaspoon celery seed
- 1 cup small vegan pasta (such as mini shells or macaroni)
- 1 tablespoon olive oil
- Crushed pink Himalayan salt and crushed black peppercorns
- Smoked cheddar Sheese or vegan Parmesan for sprinkling

Toss the tomatoes, broth, Bragg's, kale, onion, wine, beans, zucchini, celery, carrots, green beans, garlic, basil, oregano, thyme, bay leaves, and celery seed in the slow cooker and set it to high. Every 45 minutes while the vegetables cook down, stir your soup to keep the vegetables on top from drying out, and break up your tomatoes by pressing them against the side of your slow cooker. Do this for about 5½ hours. Once your carrots are tender, add the pasta. Cook for 10 to 15 minutes, or until your pasta is tender. Add salt and pepper to taste.

To serve, fill your bowl with soup and grate smoked cheddar Sheese or sprinkle vegan Parmesan over the top.

GARLIC, PORTOBELLO MUSHROOM, AND KALE SOUP

There are a few truths in this wild universe of ours. One, kittens are cute. Two, a rainy afternoon is a good time to catch up on your novel reading (and writing). And three, this soup is easy and delicious while being different enough to make it special. Even the most inexperienced chefs can make this soup.

MAKES 4 TO 6 BOWLS

---

* Some actually don't credit ol' Marco for bringing pasta to Europe. They claim it was brought by Turkish traders before the birth of Christ and shared throughout the Roman Empire.

¾ cup cubed red potatoes

½ red onion, diced very small

3 cloves garlic, minced

¼ cup diced fresh celery

1 large carrot, sliced

1 (15-ounce) can cannellini beans, drained and rinsed

6 cups Better Than Bouillon vegetable broth, made per the instructions on the package

Dash of Liquid smoke

¼ teaspoon celery seed

1½ teaspoons Italian seasoning

1 tablespoon Bragg's liquid aminos

1 tablespoon chopped fresh parsley

1 tablespoon olive oil

1 cup raw baby kale

½ cup sliced baby portobello mushrooms

⅓ cup frozen peas

¼ cup cooked wild rice

French-fried onions to sprinkle over the top

Toss all the ingredients except the wild rice and French-fried onions in a slow cooker on the highest setting or a large stewpot and heat over a medium heat.

Cook for 2 to 3 hours, or until the carrots are tender. Before you serve, mix in the wild rice. Sprinkle French-fried onions over the top.

GREEK LEMON SOUP

In Greece, there is an amazing lemon-and-egg combo called avgolemono. People eat it as a sauce over dolmas and artichokes, or just as a soup with pieces of chicken. I like to combine both versions and make a bright vegan soup, perfect for that time of year when it looks like spring outside but is still freezing. I like to serve it with the Pesto Chicken and Vegetable Sandwich (page 86).

MAKES 4 TO 6 BOWLS

6 cups Better Than Bouillon vegan chicken broth, made per the instructions on the package

⅓ cup orzo

2 teaspoons nutritional yeast

¼ teaspoon turmeric

⅓ cup lemon juice

¼ teaspoon lemon zest

Pinch of fresh thyme leaves

1 clove garlic, minced

½ teaspoon crushed black peppercorns, plus additional as needed

1 (15-ounce) can garbanzo beans, drained and rinsed

1 (14-ounce) can artichoke hearts, drained

Crushed pink Himalayan salt

1 lemon, sliced

Chopped fresh parsley for garnish

In a large pot, bring the broth to a boil on a high heat, and then add the orzo. Cook until tender, stirring occasionally. Turn the heat down to a simmer. With a whisk, blend in the nutritional yeast and turmeric. Once the nutritional yeast dissolves, add the lemon juice and zest, thyme, garlic, black pepper, beans, and artichoke hearts. Cover and simmer for 10 minutes. Now taste test your soup to see if it needs any salt or pepper. Add what you need a little at a time.

Serve warm with a slice of lemon and some fresh parsley on top. Before you eat, take your spoon and press the lemon slice into the soup. The fresh lemon pulp will add a nice kick!

1-HOUR BOEUF-LESS BOURGUIGNON STEW WITH HERB DUMPLINGS

Julia Child described boeuf bourguignon as "certainly one of the most delicious beef dishes concocted by man." It's hard to not hear Julia's unique voice in your head as you prepare this classic French dish, which has not only been made more compassionate and healthy, but also can be made in 1 hour. The original "meaty" dish takes more than 10 hours and requires a lot of prep work. This stew is actually pretty light for how flavorful and rustic it is. My favorite part is the dumplings on top, which have convinced me that everything is a little better with a dumpling on top.

MAKES 6 SERVINGS

BOEUF BOURGUIGNON

1 (9-ounce) bag Gardein beefless tips or beef seitan

1 large red onion, ½ sliced into rings, the other ½ diced

4 carrots, sliced into coins

3 stalks celery, chopped

1 (14.5-ounce) can diced tomatoes

1 cup sliced white mushrooms

¾ cup fresh spinach

1 cup frozen peas

1 cup frozen green beans

1 cup red wine or apple cider

2 tablespoons olive oil

3 teaspoons Bragg's liquid aminos

1 teaspoon dried thyme leaves

½ teaspoon onion powder

½ teaspoon ground mustard seed

½ teaspoon celery seed

½ teaspoon crushed black peppercorns

¼ cup chopped fresh parsley

½ cup Better Than Bouillon vegan beef broth, made per the instructions on the package

2 tablespoons whole wheat flour

Pinch of nutritional yeast

Crushed pink Himalayan salt and crushed black peppercorns

HERB DUMPLINGS

1½ cups vegan Bisquick mix

¼ teaspoon dried sage leaves, crumbled

½ teaspoon dried thyme leaves

½ cup soy milk

Preheat the oven to 400°F.

Place the vegan beef in a glass baking dish. Cover with a layer of red onion slices. Bake the vegan beef and red onion for around 10 minutes, or until both are golden brown and tender. A brothy liquid will form in the bottom of the baking dish; you'll use this in the next step of the recipe.

While the vegan beef is baking, start the rest of your stew. In a large soup pot, combine the remaining stew ingredients, and heat over medium heat, stirring occasionally. When the stew begins to boil, cover and reduce the heat to a simmer, stirring occasionally. Pour the liquid from the glass baking dish into the stew but don't add the vegan beef and onions yet. Stir until mixed in.

Taste your stew and add more Bragg's or pepper to taste.

Let the stew simmer for 30 to 40 minutes. Remove from the heat when the vegetables are tender. The carrots are the key—it's a judgment call on how tender you like them. Keep in mind that you will also bake the stew for another 5 to 8 minutes later in the recipe.

While the stew simmers, make the dumplings. In a large bowl, combine the Bisquick mix, sage, and thyme thoroughly with a whisk; then pour in the soy milk. Stir it all together with an electric handheld mixer until blended.

Once your vegetables are the desired tenderness, pour the stew into a large casserole dish or Dutch oven. Place a layer of baked red onion slices on top, and then a layer of vegan beef. You're making a net with the red onion to keep the vegan beef from sinking into the stew. Then, using a soupspoon, drop spoonfuls of dough on top to make your dumplings.

If you've turned off your oven, you're going to need to preheat it back to 400 F. Bake uncovered for 5 to 8 minutes, or until your dumplings are golden brown and you can remove a toothpick from them cleanly. If you run out of dumplings before you run out of stew, don't worry—you can always use the dumpling recipe again to bake up extras in less than 10 minutes.

MINESTRA MARITATA—ITALIAN WEDDING SOUP

When we were planning our wedding, a handful of things may have made me a tiny bit bridezilla-y. At the top of my completely reasonable and rational list of what was required for a perfect wedding was vegan Italian wedding soup. That one request ended up shaping the entire menu for our reception. Ironically, Italian wedding soup is actually more of an Italian-American tradition that in the Old Country has very little to do with making a lifelong commitment. The soup we know in the States as Italian wedding soup is actually called *minestra maritata*—or married soup—because of the "marrying" of meat and green vegetables in one soup. Either way you look at it, this soup is a delicious tradition that will make any day you have it the happiest day of your life.

MAKES 4 TO 6 SERVINGS

Olive oil cooking spray

2 cups Lightlife Gimme Lean vegan ground beef or Match vegan ground beef

6 cups Better Than Bouillon vegan beef broth, made per the instructions on the package

2 cloves garlic, minced

¼ cup fresh basil leaves

2 teaspoons Bragg's liquid aminos

2 cups fresh spinach

1 zucchini, sliced

1 (14.5-ounce) can diced tomatoes

2 stalks celery, diced

½ red onion, diced

2 teaspoons olive oil

1 tablespoon red wine

½ teaspoon oregano

Crushed pink Himalayan salt and crushed black peppercorns

1 cup small shell pasta

Vegan Parmesan for topping

Preheat the oven to 400°F.

Spray a glass baking dish with olive oil cooking spray. Form your meatballs using the vegan ground beef, using no more than one tablespoon per meatball. Place them in the glass baking dish so they aren't touching. Spray another coating of olive oil cooking spray over the top when done.

Bake the meatballs until they're brown and slightly crispy on the outside. It shouldn't take more than 30 minutes.

While the meatballs are baking, add the broth, garlic, basil, Bragg's, vegetables, olive oil, wine, oregano, and salt and pepper to taste to a large stewpot and bring to a boil over high heat. When the soup begins to boil, add the pasta shells and cover the pot. After 10 minutes, turn the heat down to a simmer. Once the zucchini and pasta shells are tender, taste test your soup to see if it needs any more salt or pepper. Add what you need and get ready to eat!

To serve your soup, fill 4 to 6 bowls three-quarters of the way with soup; then top with a few meatballs and a few dashes of vegan Parmesan.

SOPA DE FRIJOLES NEGROS

This soup made me think a lot about our friend Cassandra, who is in Cuba going to medical school. This soup is smoky and spicy in all the right ways, just like her. I wish everyone had a Cassandra. You're going to need to soak your beans overnight for this recipe. So you'll want to start it the night before you want to serve it.

MAKES 6 TO 8 BOWLS

1 pound dried black beans, rinsed and soaked overnight

2 tablespoons olive oil

½ red onion, diced

5½ cups Better Than Bouillon vegetable broth, made per the instructions on the package

Dash of liquid smoke

¼ cup rum or apple juice

1 bay leaf

1 tablespoon cumin

1¼ teaspoons oregano

5 cloves garlic, minced

1 green bell pepper, diced

1 large tomato, diced

½ cup frozen corn

3 teaspoons Bragg's liquid aminos

Pinch of turmeric

Pinch of paprika

Pinch of cayenne pepper

Hot sauce, optional

1 ripe sliced avocado, sliced green onions, and vegan bacon bits or crumbled smoked tempeh for garnish

In a large soup pot, heat the olive oil over medium heat. Cook the red onion in the heated oil for about 5 minutes, or until the onion is tender, stirring occasionally.

Stir in the beans, broth, liquid smoke, rum, bay leaf, cumin, oregano, garlic, vegetables, Bragg's, turmeric, paprika, and cayenne pepper and heat to a boil. Let the soup boil for 3 to 4 minutes. Reduce the heat to a simmer and cover the pot. Let the soup simmer for 2 hours.

After 2 hours, continue simmering, checking regularly until the beans are tender. Remove from the heat. If you find that the soup is getting too salty, add water 1 tablespoon at a time to adjust the flavor. If it gets too bland, add Bragg's 1 teaspoon at a time. You can also add a dash or two of hot sauce if you're feeling *caliente*.

To serve, top with avocado slices, green onions, and bacon bits.

VEGGIE LOVERS' PIZZA SOUP

When we first saw pizza soup, I admit that we wrote it off as one of the recipes we were dreading. We were being biased and unfair. We never even read the recipe, and there we were making jokes about how bowls of melted cheese shouldn't really be called "soup." But this soup isn't anything like what we thought. It's actually a flavorful and unique vegetable soup with some melted cheese and toast on top. It's delicious, and the bell peppers, mushrooms, and basil make it pretty and colorful as well.

MAKES 4 TO 6 BOWLS

2 tablespoons olive oil

½ red onion, diced

1 green bell pepper, diced

1 red bell pepper, diced

3 cloves garlic, minced

1 bottle of your favorite pale ale or pilsner

2 cups Better Than Bouillon vegan beef broth, made per the instructions on the package

1 (14.5-ounce) can diced tomatoes

3 tablespoons Bragg's liquid aminos

¼ cup fresh basil, whole leaf or lightly chopped

¼ cup chopped fresh spinach

½ cup sliced fresh white mushrooms

1½ teaspoons Italian seasoning

1 teaspoon fennel seed

¼ teaspoon onion powder

1 (15-ounce) can kidney beans, drained and rinsed

1 (15-ounce) can cannellini beans, drained and rinsed

1 to 1½ cups shredded Daiya vegan mozzarella or your favorite vegan cheese (¼ cup per bowl)

4 to 6 slices toasted French bread

Vegan Parmesan, red pepper flakes, and dried oregano to sprinkle over the top

In a soup pot or Dutch oven, heat the olive oil over medium heat. Once the oil is warm, toss in the red onion, bell peppers, and garlic. Stir occasionally, cooking until the red onion is tender. Then stir in the ale, broth, tomatoes, and Bragg's until blended.

Stir in the basil, spinach, mushrooms, Italian seasoning, fennel seed, onion powder, and beans. Heat to a boil. Reduce the heat to low, cover, and simmer for around 10 minutes. Stir occasionally.

Turn on the broiler or set the oven to broil.

Pour your soup into oven-safe bowls. Sprinkle a little vegan cheese over the soup, place a slice of toast on top, and sprinkle more vegan cheese on the toast. Then sprinkle on some vegan Parmesan. Broil the soups for 30 to 90 seconds. I recommend checking on them every 30 seconds and removing them once the vegan cheese melts and the Vegan Parmesan begins to brown.

Sprinkle some red pepper flakes and dried oregano over the top, like a pizza, and serve. I know some of you love some ranch dressing with your pizza. If you go that way, we have a recipe for Vegan Ranch Dressing (page 110) that you can use.

16-BEAN, LEEK, AND KIELBASA SOUP

Someone needs to say it. SyFy Channel's vampire and werewolf movie marathon was a little too heavy on the werewolves and had a significant lack of vampires. That's not to say it wasn't still completely wonderful. I mean, who doesn't love a good monster movie? But sometimes a gal needs more dialogue during the big, bad death scene than most werewolf movies allow…and less icky transformation scenes and poorly made muzzle faces. So what do the Shannons make for dinner when there's this level of distraction? We pull out the slow cooker, let 'er rip, and return to debating which movie has better werewolves, taking into account origin stories, transformation scenes, and CGI cheating, of course.

MAKES 6 TO 8 BOWLS

1 (20-ounce) package 15-bean soup (a package of assorted dried beans you can find in the soup section of your local grocery store)

6 cups Better Than Bouillon vegetable broth, made per the instructions on the package

4 carrots, diced

4 stalks celery, diced

½ red onion, diced

2 teaspoons olive oil, plus more for cooking

1 tablespoon red wine

1 tablespoon Bragg's liquid aminos

2 dashes of liquid smoke, plus more for cooking

1 teaspoon thyme

½ teaspoon crushed black peppercorns

½ teaspoon celery seed

½ teaspoon Tony Chachere's Creole seasoning

1 teaspoon onion powder

1 clove garlic, minced

1 leek, sliced

1 cup frozen green beans

1 (14.5-ounce) can diced tomatoes

⅓ cup beer

1 (14-ounce) package Tofurky kielbasa sausages or Field Roast's Smoked Apple and Sage Sausages, cut into coins

French-fried onions for topping

SLOW COOKER INSTRUCTIONS

In the slow cooker, combine the beans, broth, carrots, celery, onion, 2 teaspoons of the olive oil, wine, Bragg's, 2 dashes of the liquid smoke, thyme, black pepper, celery seed, Creole seasoning, onion powder, and garlic. Cover and cook on the lowest setting for 8 to 10 hours, stirring occasionally, until the beans are tender. Once the beans are tender, stir in the leek, green beans, and tomatoes. Cover and start cooking your vegan sausages.

STEWPOT INSTRUCTIONS

In your largest stewpot, mix the beans, broth, carrots, celery, onion, 2 teaspoons of the olive oil, wine, Bragg's, 2 dashes of the liquid smoke, thyme, black pepper, celery seed, Creole seasoning, onion powder, and garlic. Cover and cook over medium heat for 6 to 8 hours, stirring occasionally, until the beans are tender. Then stir in the leek, green beans, and diced tomatoes. Cover and start cooking your vegan sausages.

❊ ❊ ❊

Whether you used the slow cooker or the stewpot, the next step should be the same: In your hunky cast-iron skillet, heat 2 tablespoons of olive oil, the beer, and a dash of liquid smoke over medium heat. Toss your vegan sausage in the skillet once the liquid is warm. Brown your vegan sausage until the beer has cooked off and the edges are crispy.

You'll know your soup is ready when the green beans are tender and warm. To serve, fill your soup bowls and then drop 3 to 4 coins of sausage into each serving, sprinkling some French-fried onions over the top.

SPRING ONION RAMEN

This is an easier but equally lovely version of Shōyu Ramen Bowls (page 59).

MAKES 4 TO 6 LARGE BOWLS

3 tablespoons sesame oil

1 large sweet onion, sliced very thinly (we suggest using a Walla Walla Sweet Onion)

2 cups fresh pea pods

1 carrot, shredded

6 cups Better Than Bouillon vegetable broth, made per the instructions on the package

1 tablespoon Bragg's liquid aminos

15 to 20 green onions, sliced (you'll want a little extra to sprinkle over the top)

¾ teaspoon hot sauce

1½ teaspoons ginger paste

1 (8-ounce) package Chinese misua wheat noodles

1 cup baby bok choy leaves

Black sesame seeds, French-fried onions, and if you're feeling fancy, a Vegan Hard-Boiled Egg (page 59)

In your international superstar wok, heat the sesame oil over medium heat. Once the oil is hot, toss in the sweet onion and stir-fry until the onion begins to turn translucent. Then toss in the pea pods and carrots. Stir-fry for another minute.

In a large soup pot, heat the broth, Bragg's, 1¼ cups of the green onions, the hot sauce, and the ginger paste. Stir with a slotted spoon until the ginger paste dissolves into the soup. Then add the onion mixture and turn the heat up to a boil. Let the soup boil for 1 minute. Add the noodles and boil for another minute. The noodles should cook pretty quickly, but read your package for suggested cooking time. Once the noodles are tender, add the baby bok choy leaves and remove the pot from the heat.

To serve, fill your bowl with noodles and vegetables; then garnish with black sesame seeds and French-fried onions. You can level up your ramen pretty quickly by adding a Vegan Hard-Boiled Egg or two.

ファンシーパンツになる勇敢さ!

BEEFLESS AND BARLEY SOUP

When I realized I'd have to come up a vegan beef and barley soup for this book, the ten-year-old in me smiled and said, "You owe me this for all those spelling tests I worked so hard on, which you promptly forgot about once you discovered spell check." [Ed. note: true story]

When I was a little eater, I loved beef with barley soup from a can. My dad would make it for me when he was left in charge, and he always served it with cheddar Goldfish crackers. I can say with no hesitation that this soup is much better than anything you could get from a can. Don't forget to pick up some Eco-Planet Non-Dairy Cheddar Crackers—they're pretty close to those smirky little "cheesy" Goldfish. The recipe below has stewpot and slow cooker versions.

MAKES 4 TO 6 SERVINGS

1 red bell pepper, chopped

1 red onion, chopped

⅔ cup frozen green beans

⅔ cup frozen corn

⅔ cup frozen peas

⅔ cup sliced white mushrooms

⅔ cup pearled barley, uncooked

5 cups Better Than Bouillon vegan beef broth, made per the instructions on the package

3 tablespoons Bragg's liquid aminos

1 teaspoon dried thyme

1 teaspoon onion powder

1 tablespoon diced fresh parsley

½ teaspoon dried oregano

1 (14.5-ounce) can diced tomatoes, Italian flavor with garlic and basil

2 tablespoons olive oil

1 (9-ounce) package Gardein beefless tips, or 9 ounces beef seitan

SLOW COOKER INSTRUCTIONS

In a 4- to 5-quart slow cooker, mix the red pepper, half the red onion, frozen vegetables, mushrooms, barley, broth, Bragg's, thyme, onion powder, parsley, oregano, tomatoes, and olive oil. Cover and cook on low heat for 8 to 8½ hours, until the barley is tender.

STEWPOT INSTRUCTIONS

In a large stewpot, mix the pepper, half the red onion, and the frozen vegetables, mushrooms, barley, broth, Bragg's, thyme, onion powder, parsley, oregano, tomatoes, and olive oil. Cover and simmer over low to medium heat for 9 hours, until the barley is tender, stirring the pot occasionally.

❋ ❋ ❋

Whether you used the slow cooker or the stewpot, the next steps should be the same:

Preheat the oven to 400°F. 15 to 20 minutes before you're ready to serve.

In a glass baking dish, place the vegan beef and cover it with a layer of the remaining red onion. Bake for around 10 minutes, until both are golden brown and tender.

To serve, fill your bowls with soup, and then add the roasted red onion and vegan beef. Enjoy!

If you have leftovers, store the vegan beef separately from the soup so it doesn't get soggy.

CURRY AND WILD RICE SOUP

This is one of those soups that people expect in a vegan cookbook. It's easy, just the right amount of hot and deliciously spicy, and good for you. All-around awesome. No cookbook, vegan or otherwise, is complete without it.

MAKES 4 TO 6 BOWLS

1 tablespoon olive oil

1 tablespoon all-purpose flour

4 cups Better Than Bouillon vegetable broth, made per the instructions on the package

3½ teaspoons garam masala curry powder

½ cup coconut milk

½ cup frozen peas

2 cups cooked wild rice

1 cup raw broccoli florets

1 red bell pepper, sliced

1 teaspoon crushed black peppercorns

5 large fresh basil leaves, chopped

1 teaspoon lemon zest

2 teaspoons lemon juice

In a large stewpot or Dutch oven, heat the olive oil over medium heat until warm. Use a whisk to blend in the flour. Once the flour and oil have made a paste, add the broth and continue to whisk your soup until the flour has blended in. Add the curry powder and coconut milk and continue to whisk until the curry powder has blended into the soup.

Toss in the peas, wild rice, broccoli florets, and bell pepper and simmer until the vegetables are tender. With a large wooden spoon, mix in the black pepper, basil leaves, lemon zest, and lemon juice.

Serve warm and often.

SMOKY WINTER VEGETABLE BISQUE

Bisques are French soups originally made with crustaceans that were too beat-up to be sold in the market. Over the years, the term has also been used to describe cream-based vegetable soups. Sometimes the term means both. So, not traditionally the most vegan-friendly soups on the block. This bisque has vegan Worcestershire sauce to add a subtle savory/fishy flavor, and some vegan sour cream and blended garbanzo beans to create the "creamy" effect. This is also a great recipe to bring for lunch, because it's very filling and goes perfectly with toasted slices of Whole Wheat Sunflower Herb Bread (see page 320).

MAKES 4 TO 6 BOWLS

2 parsnips, cubed

1 large turnip, cubed

3 large sweet potatoes, cubed

1 large rutabaga, cubed

1 raw beet, cubed

2 large carrots, sliced

⅓ cup olive oil

3 cups Better Than Bouillon vegetable broth, made per the instructions on the package

1 cup white wine

1 teaspoon vegan Worcestershire sauce

2 teaspoons Bragg's liquid aminos

2 dashes of liquid smoke

4 cloves garlic, minced

1 teaspoon onion powder

1 teaspoon fresh thyme leaves

¼ teaspoon dill weed

1½ teaspoons rubbed sage

1 (15-ounce) can garbanzo beans, drained and rinsed

⅓ cup vegan sour cream

1 tablespoon almond milk

Vegan bacon bits or crumbled smoked tempeh to sprinkle over the top

Smoked chili oil to drizzle over the top, optional

Preheat the oven to 400°F.

In a large mixing bowl, toss the parsnips, turnip, sweet potatoes, rutabaga, beet, and carrots with olive oil until they are completely covered. In a shallow glass baking dish, spread the vegetables in an even layer. Bake for 10 to 15 minutes, or until the vegetables are tender.

While the vegetables are baking, fill your largest stewpot with the broth, wine, vegan Worcestershire sauce, Bragg's, liquid smoke, garlic, onion powder, thyme, dill weed, and sage. Heat at the highest heat until the pot begins to boil. Then add the baked vegetables and garbanzo beans. Boil for another 3 minutes. The vegetables will begin to dissolve into the broth. Remove from the heat and let sit for 1 minute.

Add the vegan sour cream and almond milk and puree with an immersion blender in the pot, or in a food processor or blender, until your bisque is smooth and creamy.

Serve with vegan bacon bits sprinkled over the top and a drizzle of smoked chili oil. The oil is optional but adds a kick and a little extra flavor to your snowy-time soup.

SIESTA TACO SOUP

Betty Crocker cookbooks generally refer to Mexican recipes as "fiesta" whatever-it-is. Since we made our taco soup in the slow cooker, it only seemed right to throw the "siesta" in there—sleepy little soup that it is. I actually kind of like those "fiestas," though. They're just the perfect level of campy for Betty Crocker. They remind me of something Betty Draper would serve to her kids during a break in her chain smoking. I'm not sure why that appeals to me, but in a weird way it totally does. We didn't add some of the traditional taco toppings, like sour cream and avocados, this time but maybe you should…I would skip the lettuce, though.

MAKES 4 TO 6 SERVINGS

1 (28-ounce) can fire-roasted diced tomatoes

2 cups Better Than Bouillon vegetable broth, made per the instructions on the package

1 (15-ounce) can black beans, drained and rinsed

1 (15-ounce) can kidney beans, drained and rinsed

1 (15-ounce) can lentils, drained and rinsed

1 red onion, very thinly diced

2 cloves garlic, minced

1 to 2 fresh jalapeños, sliced (the more you add, the spicier the soup will be)

1 yellow bell pepper, diced into large pieces

2 teaspoons chili powder

1 teaspoon onion powder

2½ teaspoons cumin

¼ teaspoon paprika

1 teaspoon oregano

2 teaspoons Bragg's liquid aminos

Dash of liquid smoke

Crushed pink Himalayan salt and crushed back peppercorns

1 tablespoon hot sauce (add a few dashes more if you want take up the spice a notch)

2 to 3 cups tortilla chips (½ cup per bowl of soup), broken up a bit but not crushed

1 to 1½ cups shredded Daiya vegan cheddar cheese or your favorite vegan cheese (¼ cup per bowl of soup)

Sliced black olives and chopped fresh cilantro for garnish

Toss the tomatoes, broth, beans, lentils, onion, garlic, jalapeños, bell pepper, chili and onion powders, cumin, paprika, oregano, Bragg's, and liquid smoke into your faithful little slow cooker and mix. Fire up your slow cooker to high and cook for 2 hours. Then taste test the soup and add salt, pepper, and hot sauce until you like the flavor. Cover the slow cooker back up and cook for another hour.

Preheat the oven to 400°F.

You're going to know your soup is ready when you taste test it and your heart does a little two-step—and when your onion has dissolved. Fill oven-safe bowls three-quarters of the way with your new favorite soup, then sprinkle tortilla chips and vegan cheese over the top and bake until the vegan cheese gets all melty, 1 to 2 minutes. Remove from the oven using mitts—your bowls are going to be hot. Let your bowls cool for about 15 minutes, or until you can handle them without burning yourself. Then sprinkle olives and cilantro—or really whatever your favorite taco topping is— over the top and serve warm.

FRENCH ONION SOUP

Once upon a time, there was a very tall woman with an oddly lovable voice who brought French cooking to the servantless American cook. We all know the story of how Julia Child came to master the art of French cooking, but what we may not know is that several dishes we find in almost every U.S. restaurant were made popular due to the influence of this culinary Amazon. One of these is French onion soup, or in French, *soupe à l'oignon*.

This soup is dark and savory in a "beefy" way that is hard to forget. The flavor actually comes from the caramelized onions, which makes the soup easy to veganize. The hard part is getting the layer of vegan cheese to melt and brown just right. It is possible, though, so don't skip that step. You'll be happy you were brave enough to reach for the stars.

MAKES 4 TO 6 SERVINGS

CROUTON AND BROILED VEGAN CHEESE TOPPING

4 to 12 (½-inch-thick) baguette slices (1 to 2 per serving)

⅓ to ½ cup olive oil

1⅓ to 3 cups shredded Daiya vegan mozzarella cheese or your favorite vegan cheese (⅓ to ½ cup per bowl)

4 to 6 teaspoons vegan Parmesan cheese (1 teaspoon per bowl)

ONION SOUP

2 tablespoons margarine

5 red onions, sliced (the thinner the better)

6 cups Better Than Bouillon vegan beef broth, made per the instructions on the package

¼ teaspoon crushed black peppercorns

½ teaspoon fresh thyme leaves

2 bay leaves

1 tablespoon sherry or dry white wine (you can use flat ginger ale if you don't do alcohol)

1 teaspoon Bragg's liquid aminos

1 clove garlic, minced

Preheat the oven to 400°F.

Brush both sides of your baguette slices with olive oil and place them on a cookie sheet lined with foil. Bake for 5 minutes; then flip the baguette slices and bake for another 5 to 10 minutes, until toasted and golden brown. You want to make sure they are completely toasted so they don't become soggy in your soup later. Make your soup while you bake your croutons.

In a Dutch oven or large soup pot, melt the margarine over medium heat. Once the margarine is liquefied, toss in the sliced onion and mix with the margarine until the onions are completely coated. Cook uncovered for 10 to 15 minutes, until the onions begin to turn a light golden brown and become translucent. Turn down your heat if the onions start getting crispy edges.

Once the onions have caramelized, add the broth, black pepper, thyme, bay leaves, sherry, Bragg's, and garlic. Cover and increase the heat to high. Once the soup begins to boil, reduce the heat and simmer for 15 more minutes.

Turn on the broiler or set the oven to broil.

Fill 4 to 6 oven-safe bowls or large ramekins three-quarters of the way with onion soup. Place 1 to 2 croutons on top of the soup, depending on how big your bowls are, and top with an even layer of vegan cheese.

Broil with the vegan cheese about 5 inches from the flame for about 1 minute—just long enough to melt. Then sprinkle an even layer of vegan Parmesan over the melted vegan cheese. Return the soup under the broiler and broil for around another minute, removing when the top is a light golden brown. Be sure to watch the soup the whole time it is under the broiler to make sure it doesn't catch fire.

HOT AND SOUR SHIITAKE MUSHROOM MISO SOUP

In college in Olympia, Washington, I was lucky enough to have a roommate whom I adored more than I probably ever told her I did. I don't always get along with women, so to live with one whom I liked this much meant a lot to me. The point of this story is that she loved the hot and sour soup in Olympia. When she left town over the summer to work on Block Island on the East Coast, we worked together on a plan to help ease her through her withdrawal. It involved several secondhand plastic thermoses from children's long-lost lunch boxes and overnight shipping. Don't worry, it got there in time, and she survived the summer. Whenever I think of hot and sour soup, I think of the weeks of prep and testing that went into that mission, and how I look forward to meeting up with Libbe again someday over some great Pacific Northwest Asian food.

MAKES 4 TO 6 SERVINGS

3 tablespoons miso paste

4 cups water

⅓ cup rice vinegar

3 tablespoons Bragg's liquid aminos

3 tablespoons sherry

2 teaspoons ginger paste

2 cloves garlic, minced

3 teaspoons Sriracha sauce

1 teaspoon crushed black peppercorns

½ teaspoon sesame oil

7 to 8 shiitake mushrooms, sliced

3 carrots, sliced

1 (8-ounce) can sliced bamboo shoots

1 cup whole baby bok choy leaves

1 (14-ounce) package extrafirm tofu, cubed

2 teaspoons lemon juice

2 teaspoons chopped fresh cilantro

1 tablespoon sliced green onion

In a large stewpot, mix the miso, water, rice vinegar, Bragg's, and sherry until the miso dissolves. Heat to a boil over high heat. Once the mixture begins to boil, turn the heat down to a simmer and add the ginger paste, garlic, Sriracha sauce, black pepper, sesame oil, shiitake mushrooms, carrots, bamboo shoots, bok choy leaves tofu, and lemon juice and simmer for 5 minutes. Stir occasionally to make sure the ginger dissolves. Your soup is ready when the mushrooms are tender. Toss in the cilantro and green onion and serve to your oldest and dearest.

CREAM OF BROCCOLI SOUP

Cream of broccoli/mushroom/whatever soups have always seemed a little weird to me. Not to get all technical or grammar-nerdy or gross on you, but broccoli can't produce cream—only mammals can do that (sorry, I know, gross). So really it should be cream *and* broccoli soup—right? *Right?* Ahem. Either way, this soup is simple, delicious, and hearty—perfect for a cold winter's day.

MAKES 4 TO 6 BOWLS

½ cup margarine

1 red onion, thinly sliced

3 stalks celery, sliced

½ cup whole wheat flour

5 cups miso soup, made per the instructions on the package

1 (15-ounce) can cannellini beans, rinsed and drained

2 tablespoons Bragg's liquid aminos

¼ cup white wine

2 cloves garlic, minced

1 teaspoon onion powder

Pinch of turmeric

1 cup nutritional yeast

1½ cups broccoli florets

½ teaspoon smoked paprika

4 to 6 tablespoons shredded Daiya vegan cheddar cheese or your favorite vegan cheese (1 tablespoon per bowl)

2 dashes of liquid smoke

Crushed pink Himalayan salt and crushed black peppercorns to taste

Vegan bacon bits for garnish

In a Dutch oven or large soup pot, heat the margarine over medium heat until melted. Toss in the onion and celery. Use a metal spatula to mix the vegetables until coated with the melted margarine. Toss in the flour and continue to mix until the flour is blended into the margarine.

Add the miso soup, beans, Bragg's, white wine, garlic, onion powder, and turmeric and use a wooden spoon to blend the flour mixture into the miso soup. Cover and simmer for 3 minutes.

Slowly pour in the nutritional yeast and blend with a whisk until smooth. Add the broccoli florets, smoked paprika, vegan cheese, and liquid smoke, and stir your soup with a wooden spoon. Cover and simmer for 5 to 10 minutes. Once the broccoli is tender, pour the soup into a blender or food processor and blend until smooth. Pour the soup back into the Dutch oven or soup pot and heat back up to a simmer.

Before serving, give your soup a taste test and add any needed salt and pepper. Sprinkle vegan bacon bits over the top to add a little awesome.

HEARTY NEW ENGLAND CHOWDER

This recipe uses the classic vegan trick of replacing clams with oyster mushrooms, like we did when we made Linguine and Vegan Clam Sauce (page 199). But even though the "clams" are wonderful, the real stars of this recipe are the artichokes and potatoes. The slight "fishy" flavor is really nice and represents what I remember when I think of this wintery favorite. I must stress that you'll want some crackers or bread to get every last drop of this chowder. This is a clean-your-bowl situation.

MAKES 4 TO 6 BOWLS

2 tablespoons olive oil

Dash of liquid smoke

1 large red onion, diced

¾ cup sliced oyster mushrooms

1 tablespoon white wine

1 teaspoon fresh thyme

3 stalks celery, diced

2 russet potatoes, baked and cubed

1 cup Better Than Bouillon vegetable broth, made per the instructions on the package

1 teaspoon onion powder

½ teaspoon dill weed

½ teaspoon celery seed

1 teaspoon crushed black peppercorns, plus more as needed

1 teaspoon vegan Worcestershire sauce

1 (14-ounce) can artichoke hearts, drained

½ teaspoon sea kelp or seaweed granules

1 tablespoon chopped fresh parsley

1 cup soy milk

1 tablespoon Bragg's liquid aminos

Crushed pink Himalayan salt and crushed black peppercorns to taste

In a large soup pot or Dutch oven, heat the olive oil and liquid smoke over medium heat. Toss in the red onion and oyster mushrooms once the oil gets warm. Cook, stirring occasionally.

Once the onion is tender, toss the white wine, thyme, celery, and baked potatoes into the pot and gently mix. Simmer for 2 to 3 minutes, until the potatoes start to break down a little. Then stir in the broth, onion powder, dill weed, celery seed, 1 teaspoon of the black pepper, and the vegan Worcestershire sauce with a wooden spoon. Once the chowder begins to boil, stir in the artichoke hearts, sea kelp, fresh parsley, soy milk, and Bragg's.

Simmer another 5 to 7 minutes. Give your chowder another taste test and add any needed salt or pepper. Once the soy milk thickens, remove the soup from heat and enjoy with a good book, cup of tea, and some crackers!

CREOLE-SPICED BUTTERNUT SQUASH AND SWEET POTATO SOUP

This hearty soup has a thick, rich, creamy flavor, without relying on cream or cheese—vegan or otherwise. It's a nice, healthy recipe that tastes like something you should feel bad about eating. It'll also freeze well—so you can enjoy the fruits of your labor all week long.

MAKES 4 LARGE SERVINGS

- 1 butternut squash, peeled, seeded, and cubed
- 1 cup diced carrots
- 2 leeks, thinly sliced
- 1 sweet potato, cubed
- 5 cups Better Than Bouillon vegan chicken broth, made per the instructions on the package

- 1 tablespoon Tony Chachere's Creole seasoning
- 2 dashes of liquid smoke
- 1 teaspoon crushed black peppercorns (you'll want more to sprinkle over the top)
- 2 teaspoons Louisiana hot sauce

- 1 tablespoon dry white wine
- 2 teaspoons lemon juice
- 1 teaspoon cumin
- 2 cloves garlic, minced
- 2 tablespoons olive oil
- Dry-roasted pepitas to sprinkle over the top

Toss all the ingredients except the pepitas into a large soup pot or Dutch oven and heat to a boil. Cover and reduce the heat to a simmer. Simmer for 20 to 30 minutes, or until all the vegetables are extremely tender.

Now, if you have an immersion blender, you can use it to puree your soup, but if you are using an enameled Dutch oven you may not want to do that, because immersion blenders can chip your Dutch oven coating.

Instead, you can puree your soup in batches in a regular blender.

Serve with black pepper and pepitas sprinkled over the top and large French-style faux-cheese-crusted croutons (Crouton and Broiled Vegan Cheese Topping, page 75).

This recipe makes several large bowls of soup...but don't be afraid—prepare for glory! No surrender! That is vegan law! No vegan soup shall be spared!

How the Betty Crocker Project Made Me a Slow Cooker Believer

For years I had aunts, roommates, and loved ones of all kinds try to get me excited about Crock-Pots and slow cookers. There was the economic argument: by using a slow cooker I could switch from canned to dry beans and save five dollars a year on my grocery bills! There was the time-management argument: by tossing in all my ingredients in the morning and letting them simmer all day, I could come home to a bucket of hot soup and very few dishes! But a combination of oppositional defiant disorder and a belief that slow cookers were for hippies and grandmas made me dig in my heels and refuse.

But the Betty Crocker Project on our blog changed all that—because for the first time I had to use one. I mean, I could have used my beautiful blue Dutch oven to make these dishes, but it was the readers who commented, Tweeted, and emailed their requests for vegan versions of the more difficult slow cooker recipes that really pushed me over the edge. Apparently the world was full of vegan slow cookers, and I needed one. Shortly after this realization, Dan got me a very fancy slow cooker for Christmas/Hanukkah, and a new chapter in our lives as vegans began.

Soups and chilies were easy; lentils and exotic saucy dishes too. Lasagna and beefless briskets were a bit harder, but completely doable. But even that didn't win me over ... until I found myself living in Brooklyn during the historic "Heat Dome" of 2011. I still needed to cook for our blog and this book, but even going near the stove felt op-

pressive. But I could plug in the slow cooker and make pasta sauce, brownies, and delicious dishes without turning my home/office into an oven. It only took one day for me to understand why Betty Crocker calls slow cookers "one of the best-kept time-saving secrets of mealtime preparation."

Now I can't imagine life without it. If you're new to slow cookers, here are a few tips to help get you started:

- Although it might seem like a good way to "season" a soup or sauce, never cook seitan or any mock meat in a liquid recipe—even in a slow cooker. For the best results, brown your mock meats in a cast-iron skillet with some olive oil cooking spray; then add them to your dishes as you serve them. This will keep your mock meat from losing its flavor and becoming spongy.

- Watch your liquids both going in and coming out of your slow cooker. Slow cookers don't allow for evaporation while they cook, so watch out for frozen and some fresh vegetables releasing water into your soups and sauces and diluting your flavors.

- Not all slow cookers are the same: the "high" setting on one is "nuclear" on another. Keep that in mind when experimenting with a new recipe. I know checking on a dish regularly takes away from the convenience of a slow cooker, but it could make a huge difference in how your recipe turns out.

SANDWICHES

Funny thing about sandwiches...I feel weird calling them "recipes." I mean, are they really recipes, or are they more combinations of food items with a dash of cooking and condiment tips? Either way, they're crucial to an epic lunch. So let's continue...

TOFURKY REUBEN

Like a lot of Bettys, I'm a simple woman. I love my husband and my cats. I love Patsy Cline and a nice tall glass of iced tea. I love walking through Manhattan in red shoes in the rain. And I love Reuben sandwiches. I mean, it's a sandwich that includes both sauerkraut and rye bread...brilliant. But even the happiest cowboy sings a sad song. When it comes to Reubens, for me that sad song is the Thousand Island dressing. Even when I wasn't vegan that stuff skeeved me out. So needless to say, when I made my own vegan version, I was pleasantly surprised when I loved it! I don't think I'll be dumping it on any salads anytime soon, but I do promise that from this moment on, all my Reubens will include this tasty condiment. This recipe makes one good-size sandwich.

MAKES 1 SANDWICH

2 slices marbled rye bread

2 tablespoons Bragg's liquid aminos

6 to 8 slices Peppered Tofurky Deli Slices, separated

3 to 5 slices smoked cheddar Sheese or Daiya vegan Havarti cheese wedge

2 tablespoons Thousand Island Dressing (page 107)

Sauerkraut (it's your call how much you want to add; my Reubens are around 40 percent sauerkraut)

Preheat the oven to 250°F.

Place the rye bread in the oven to dry out a little and help keep it from getting soggy.

Put the Bragg's in a shallow bowl and dip the Tofurky in it, to give it a corned beef–pastrami flavor.

Take the rye bread out of the oven. Stack one slice with all the Tofurky, then all the vegan cheese slices on top of that. Put both slices of rye bread back in the oven.

Turn the oven up to 350°F. Remove the bread from the oven in about 5 minutes, when it is the desired toastiness and the vegan cheese is melted.

Put Thousand Island Dressing and sauerkraut on the slice with no Tofurky. Put the slices together. You now have a vegan version of one the greatest deli sandwiches ever!

BAKED BLACK PEPPER TOFU REUBEN

The road to happiness is paved with olive oil, liquid smoke, and tofu. For a different take on this deli classic, you can always use baked tofu to add a little something special. During the years when mock meat technology was catching up to my dreams, this was the recipe I used to re-create one of my very favorite sandwiches in the world.

MAKES 2 SANDWICHES

½ teaspoon crushed black peppercorns

1 tablespoon plus 2 teaspoons olive oil

1 tablespoon plus 2 teaspoons lemon juice

Dash of liquid smoke

1 clove garlic, minced

1 tablespoon plus 1 teaspoon Bragg's liquid aminos

½ (14-ounce) package extrafirm tofu, cut into strips

4 slices marbled rye bread

4 to 6 tablespoons Thousand Island Dressing (page 107)

6 to 8 slices smoked cheddar Sheese or Daiya vegan Havarti cheese wedge

Sauerkraut (it's your call how much you want to add; my Reubens are around 40 percent sauerkraut)

In a shallow dish, combine the black pepper, olive oil, lemon juice, liquid smoke, garlic and Bragg's. Cut your tofu into strips that are as even as possible, so when they're baking they all bake evenly. Marinate your tofu slices in the oil and pepper mixture for 1 hour.

Preheat the oven to 400°F.

Cover a cookie sheet with foil and place your marinated tofu slices on the foil about an inch apart. Reserve your leftover marinade. Bake the tofu for 20 minutes; then flip and bake for another 20 minutes, until crispy and golden brown. When ready, remove from the oven and cool until you can touch them. Once you can comfortably touch your baked tofu, divide the pieces into two equal portions. This is a good time to toast your bread and make your Thousand Island Dressing.

Turn the heat on the oven down to 250°F.

Put the bread in the oven to dry out and slightly toast, to help keep it from getting soggy.

Immediately after taking your bread out of the oven, dip your baked tofu into the leftover marinade before placing it in an even layer onto two of the pieces of bread. Then place vegan cheese slices on top of the baked tofu. Put all 4 slices of bread back in the oven.

Turn the oven up to 350°F. Remove the bread from the oven in about 5 minutes, when the bread is golden brown and the vegan cheese is melted.

Put Thousand Island dressing and sauerkraut on the bread with no tofu slices. Put those slices together with the tofu and cheese slices, and you've just made yourself some sandwiches that will make you believe in love again.

THE MVP AVOCADO SANDWICH

I won't lie: if there were a Sandwich Hall of Fame, this fella would be in there all Heismanning it up. If there were a Little Miss Sandwich Pageant, this sandwich would be singing "The Impossible Dream" while twirling flaming batons and ending all its sentences with a wink. If there were a Fellowship of the Sandwich, this sandwich would be infiltrating Mordor. I'm glad no one was around to see me eat this epic creation, though, because to be honest, this little guy is messy. I looked a tiny bit like the Swamp Thing after I was done eating it. I had a green avocado beard, but it was worth it! I think you'll agree.

MAKES 4 SANDWICHES

1 loaf artisan sourdough baguette
½ cup Fresh Herb Vinaigrette
(page 108)

4 to 6 slices Tofutti American slices or 1 cup shredded Daiya vegan cheddar cheese

2 large ripe avocados, pitted, peeled, and sliced

½ fresh lemon

Lemon pepper

Turn on the broiler or set the oven to broil.

Cut the baguette horizontally in half. Drizzle the vinaigrette over the top half of the baguette. Spread vegan cheese over the bottom slice; if you're using Tofutti slices, you'll want to cut them in half. Place both baguette halves on your beloved pizza stone, so that the dressing and vegan cheese are top-up and can melt onto the bread. Broil for 5 minutes, until the bread gets a golden crispy edge and the vegan cheese is melted. Remove from oven.

Spread slices of avocado over the melted vegan cheese. Squeeze the lemon half over the avocado slices. Sprinkle the desired amount of lemon pepper over the avocados. Then close and cut the loaf into 4 pieces.

Please use your sandwich influence for good rather than evil.

BOURBON STREET VEGAN CHICKEN PO'BOY

On our honeymoon in New Orleans, we stayed in a hotel right off of Bourbon Street. We're early birds, so while everyone else was partying the night away on Bourbon, we'd long since gone to bed, only to then be up and walking around at the wee hour of 8 a.m. like proper old married people. Bourbon Street at 8 a.m. looks like a frat house after a keg party, only if the frat house were a main thoroughfare through a major American city. There was literally no one else around for blocks, so we got to stroll through the picturesque French Quarter all by ourselves every morning. It was a perfect honeymoon—except when Dan came down with West Nile virus or some horrible thing that laid him up in bed for two days feverishly reading *Interview with the Vampire* for the millionth time. In conclusion, this vegan chicken recipe has all the spice and flavor of our Bourbon Street honeymoon, with none of the influenza.

MAKES 4 SANDWICHES

2 to 3 tablespoons olive oil

2 cups vegan chicken, defrosted (we recommend Gardein Chick'n Scallopini)

¼ cup bourbon

1 cup ketchup

1 tablespoons vegan Worcestershire sauce

2 tablespoons Bragg's liquid aminos

1 tablespoon brown sugar

2 tablespoons garlic powder

¼ teaspoon yellow mustard

2 tablespoons pomegranate juice

2 teaspoons applesauce

Dash of Louisiana hot sauce

Dash of liquid smoke

1 batch Creole Veganaise (page 288)

1 loaf French bread, split horizontally but not sliced in half

Romaine lettuce leaves (most po'boys use iceberg, but I just can't endorse that)

4 to 6 slices tomato

1 slice red onion, broken into rings

Pickles or various pickled things, like okra or peppers

Dijon mustard or A.1. steak sauce, optional

Heat 2 to 3 tablespoons of the olive oil in your favorite cast-iron skillet or frying pan over medium heat. Toss in the vegan chicken to brown a little on each side.

In a large bowl, mix the bourbon, ketchup, vegan Worcestershire sauce, Bragg's, brown sugar, garlic powder, yellow mustard, pomegranate juice, applesauce, hot sauce, and liquid smoke with an electric handheld mixer with whisk attachments. Make sure that the mixture is smooth and that you like the taste. If it's too hot, add more ketchup; if it isn't hot enough, add more hot sauce.

Spread the Creole Veganaise over both sides of the French bread evenly. You probably won't use the entire batch, but use as much as you like.

Dip your vegan chicken into the bourbon sauce. Cover it evenly on both sides; then toss it into the skillet. Flip it a few times, really keeping an eye on it. The bourbon sauce will cook onto the vegan chicken in a thick coating. Take the vegan chicken out of the skillet and put it straight into your po'boy. You'll want to drizzle any extra bourbon sauce over the vegan chicken. Just trust me.

Pile the lettuce, tomatoes, onion rings, and pickles onto your sandwich, and add either Dijon mustard or A.1. steak sauce if you like that kind of thing. I'm a devoted A.1. steak sauce fan myself.

Slice your loaf of French bread into 4 equal pieces.

DRESSED CREOLE VEGAN SHRIMP PO'BOY

Here's how you know that vegan shrimp is a great replica of the real deal: Dan hates it. No joke. Before he was vegan, he always disliked shrimp—both because of its oceany, salty, briny flavor and because of shrimps' unmistakable resemblance to insects. And now Dan hates vegan shrimp, because its taste and texture are too similar to real shrimp's. So if you love real shrimp, you'll love this recipe. If not, well, there are plenty of other recipes in this book for you to choose from.

MAKES 4 SANDWICHES

3 to 4 tablespoons olive oil

2 tablespoons beer

1 to 2 tablespoons Tony Chachere's Creole seasoning

1 teaspoon lemon pepper

2 teaspoons lemon juice

Dash of liquid smoke

1 to 2 cups vegan shrimp, defrosted (we recommend May Wah shrimp balls cut in half)

1 batch Creole Veganaise (page 288)

1 loaf French bread, spilt horizontally but not sliced in half

Dashes of Louisiana hot sauce, optional

Romaine lettuce leaves (most po'boys use iceberg, but that's not okay)

4 to 6 slices of tomato

Slice red onion, broken into rings

Pickles or various pickled things like peppers or green beans

Dijon mustard or A.1. steak sauce, optional

Heat your olive oil over medium heat in your friendly neighborhood cast-iron skillet or frying pan.

In a large bowl, blend the beer, Creole seasoning, lemon pepper, lemon juice, and liquid smoke with an electric handheld mixer with whisk attachments. Add the defrosted vegan shrimp to the bowl and toss. Make sure to get a heavy even coating.

Once the oil is hot, toss in the spicy vegan shrimp and fry 'em up!

Spread the Creole Veganaise evenly over both sides of the French bread. You won't use the entire batch,

but use as much as you like. Once the vegan shrimp has crispy edges, use a slotted spoon to pull them out of the skillet and place them on the bread. Toss a few dashes of hot sauce over the vegan shrimp if you like your food very spicy.

Pile the lettuce, tomato, onion rings, and pickles onto your sandwich and add either Dijon mustard or A.1. steak sauce if you like that kind of thing. I'm a devoted A.1. steak sauce fan myself.

Slice your loaf of French bread into 4 equal portions.

FRENCH DIP SANDWICH

This sandwich makes me feel like dancing around to a Brigitte Bardot pop song all yé-yé-girl-style. Our take on this exquisite sandwich includes portobello mushrooms and a lot of passionate, savory flavor.

MAKES 2 SANDWICHES

2 tablespoons olive oil

Dash of Bragg's liquid aminos

2 large portobello caps, sliced

2 cloves garlic, minced

Dash of dried rosemary

Dash of dried thyme

Dash of crushed black peppercorns

1 package Oven Roasted Tofurky Deli Slices, separated

½ baguette, sliced horizontally

1 cup Better Than Bouillon vegan beef broth, made per the instructions on the package

In your *aimé* cast-iron skillet or frying pan, heat the olive oil and Bragg's over medium heat. Once the oil is warm, add the sliced portobello, garlic, rosemary, thyme, and black pepper. Let the mushrooms simmer a bit while you stir occasionally. Once the mushrooms are tender, add the Tofurky slices and toss. Make sure that all the ingredients get blended and coated evenly.

Preheat the oven to 300°F. and slightly toast the bread in the oven. In a saucepan, prepare the broth, which will be the *jus.*

Once the mushrooms and Tofurky are tender, warm, and juicy, you're ready to make up your sandwich. All you have to do is pile your mushroom and Tofurky slices onto your bread and slice the bread in half with a serrated knife. Serve with the *jus* in a ramekin on the side to dip your sandwich in.

Bon appétit!

PESTO CHICKEN AND VEGETABLE SANDWICH

This is an easy and impressive way to level up your vegan chicken sandwiches. I recommend pairing this one with the Greek Lemon Soup on page 65.

MAKES 4 SANDWICHES

2 cups vegan chicken, defrosted (we recommend Gardein Chick'n Scallopini)

3 Roma tomatoes, sliced

2 zucchinis, sliced to about the same thickness as your vegan chicken

⅓ cup sliced white mushrooms

⅓ cup kalamata olives, pitted

2 tablespoons raw pine nuts

⅔ cup Super Green Basil Pesto (page 284)

2 teaspoons olive oil

1 clove garlic, minced

Crushed pink Himalayan salt and crushed black peppercorns to taste

4 hoagie rolls

Preheat the oven to 375°F.

Toss all the ingredients except the hoagie rolls in a large mixing bowl until the vegetables and vegan chicken are completely covered with the pesto mixture. Divide the mixture into 4 equal portions and put each portion on a separate 18 x 12-inch sheet of foil.

Fold the foil over the mixture and seal the edges tightly; then place the foil packets in the oven so that the seals are facing up. Bake for 15 to 20 minutes, checking for doneness 10 minutes in. Not all the vegan chicken products cook at the same rate, due to thickness and consistency. You'll know it's done when the vegan chicken has golden brown edges and the zucchini is tender.

Once your packets are ready, fill the hoagie rolls to make your sandwich. Each packet will make one sandwich.

You should really invest in some peperoncini, pickles, or olives to go with your sandwiches. Or, if you're an overachiever, all three.

SLOPPY JOELS

Just as with brownies, every vegan has their favorite sloppy joes recipe. Over the years, I've had tasty vegan sloppy joes made with everything from textured vegetable protein to jackfruit. While I wasn't too in love with the eggplant version (Amanda, if you're reading this, I'm sorry), my all-time favorite is made with tempeh. I debated using that version here—but one of the most important missions of this book is to teach people how to use vegan products in new and interesting ways. Not every vegan has had a tempeh sloppy joe before, but you can find them in restaurants all over the country. So we opted for using vegan ground beef instead, which really does have the perfect texture and flavor for this recipe. But the great thing about this recipe is that you can substitute the "beef" part of it with tempeh or Boca crumbles or jackfruit or whatever. It's your call.

MAKES 4 SANDWICHES

2 cups Match vegan ground beef, Lightlife Gimme Lean vegan ground beef, or tempeh

Olive oil for cooking

½ large red onion, diced

½ green bell pepper, diced

⅓ cup celery, diced

1 small tomato, diced

1 tablespoon Bragg's liquid aminos

Dash of liquid smoke

½ teaspoon onion powder

1 cup ketchup*

1½ teaspoons vegan Worcestershire sauce

⅛ teaspoon crushed black pepper

6 whole wheat hamburger buns, toasted

In your brave little cast-iron skillet or frying pan, cook the vegan beef in 2 tablespoons of olive oil over medium heat. Once you start to see slightly crispy edges on the vegan beef, toss in the onion, bell pepper, celery, and tomato and continue to cook over medium heat. You may want to add another teaspoon of olive oil if you see the vegetables sticking. Once the vegan beef is brown and the vegetables begin to get tender, add the Bragg's, liquid smoke, onion powder, ketchup, vegan Worcestershire sauce, and black pepper. Simmer for 5 to 10 minutes, stirring occasionally, until the vegetables are the desired tenderness.

Fill the hamburger buns with the sloppy joe mix and get out a bib…because these guys are just as messy as they are delicious.

---

* I strongly suggest going organic and high-quality with the ketchup: less sugar, fillers, food coloring, and cheap vinegar.

VEGAN BACON RANCH AND CHICKEN PITA

Smoky vegan bacon, avocado, spinach, roasted chicken, and ranch dressing...you complete me.

MAKES 4 PITAS

2 cups vegan chicken (we recommend Lightlife Smart Strips, Chick'n)

Olive oil cooking spray

8 slices vegan bacon or smoked tempeh

6 to 8 whole wheat pitas

1 ripe avocado, sliced

½ cup raw baby spinach

1 Roma tomato, sliced

⅓ cup fresh sprouts

½ cup Vegan Ranch Dressing (page 110)

4 tablespoons sunflower seeds

If you want to take this to work or school, make your vegan chicken and Vegan Ranch Dressing the night before you want to make your sandwiches.

Preheat the oven to 400°F.

Put the vegan chicken in a glass baking dish and spray with an even coating of olive oil cooking spray. Using a spoon, flip the vegan chicken a few times until completely covered with the olive oil. Place the vegan bacon over the top of the vegan chicken. Bake for 15 to 20 minutes. Remove from the oven when the vegan chicken and bacon are golden brown and crispy on the edges. Cover and refrigerate overnight.

When you're ready to make your sandwiches, gently break up the vegan bacon into bite-size pieces. Slightly heat the pitas using the directions on their package so they are soft enough to fill. Fill each pita with equal portions of vegan chicken, vegan bacon, avocado, spinach, tomato, and sprouts; then drizzle with Vegan Ranch Dressing. Sprinkle some sunflower seeds over the top.

GIRLFRIEND'S MOCK CHICKEN SALAD BAGELWICH

For years, I made vats of vegan chicken salad for just about every occasion. Huge bowls of our original recipe of savory vegan chicken, crunchy celery, bright lemon juice, spicy black pepper, and Vegenaise were enjoyed at baby showers and potlucks. The recipe remained constant through friends falling in love, breaking up, and moving away; through vegan chicken products changing their ingredients so they weren't vegan anymore; through different (some unfortunate) hair colors and styles. This recipe was something we could count on, like the rising sun and Dan's devotion to the Red Sox. But the Betty Crocker Project inspired me to make this salad into something exceptional, rather than just reliable. But I guess ultimately that's what Betty Crocker does…gets all of us to break out of our comfortable little ruts and reach our full potential.

MAKES 4 TO 6 SANDWICHES

2 tablespoons olive oil	¼ teaspoon lemon pepper	2 stalks celery, chopped
Dash of liquid smoke	2½ tablespoons lemon juice	½ large red onion, chopped
2 cups vegan chicken, defrosted (we recommend Gardein Chick'n Scallopini)	3 tablespoons nutritional yeast	Crushed pink Himalayan salt and crushed black peppercorns
½ cup Grapeseed Vegenaise	2 pinches of celery seed	4 to 6 toasted bagels
	¼ cup chopped parsley	

Cook the vegan chicken the night before you plan to serve.

Heat the olive oil and liquid smoke in your favorite cast-iron skillet or frying pan over medium heat. Once your oil is hot, toss the vegan chicken in and cook until browned and crispy. Remove the vegan chicken from the skillet and place on a plate with a paper towel on it. Once the vegan chicken has cooled enough that you can touch it, chop it into small chunks, place in an airtight container, and refrigerate overnight.

The next day, mix the chilled vegan chicken with the Vegenaise, lemon pepper, lemon juice, nutritional yeast, celery seed, parsley, celery, and onion in a large bowl. Add salt and pepper to taste. Toast your bagels. Serve the vegan chicken salad on a bagel with lettuce, spinach, sprouts, tomatoes, pickles, mustard…whatever sandwich goodies you like.

What's also great about this salad is that you don't need bread to eat it. You can eat it by itself or on a bed of lettuce…get creative and reach your own full potential!

NIÇOISE TOFU EGG SALAD SANDWICH

Niçoise salad is one of those French dishes made famous in the United States by Julia Child. Prior to that leggy dame convincing us we could be just as fancy as those French folks, this odd salad made exclusively with raw vegetables was even more obscure than it is now. Since the sixties, this salad has been re-created so many times that it's often nothing at all like what those fine folks in Nice consider their signature salad. This sandwich obviously falls into that category. I like to think that we captured a lot of the spirit of the Niçoise salad in this sandwich, but it's funny since most people have never heard of a Niçoise salad—so who's to say if we went off road with this one. Yes, that last sentence is to be read in Julia's singsongy voice.

You'll want to make the vegan diced eggs in this recipe the night before.

MAKES 4 SANDWICHES

½ (14-ounce) package extrafirm tofu, drained and pressed

2 tablespoons nutritional yeast

¼ teaspoon cumin

¼ teaspoon onion powder

⅛ teaspoon turmeric

⅛ teaspoon Tony Chachere's Creole seasoning

1 baguette, split horizontally

½ cup Fresh Herb Vinaigrette (page 108)

4 Roma tomatoes, sliced

1 large green bell pepper, sliced

½ large red onion, sliced and broken into rings

1 (14-ounce) can quartered artichoke hearts, drained

¼ cup kalamata olives, pitted

¾ cup shredded Daiya vegan mozzarella cheese or your favorite vegan cheese

4 dashes of smoked paprika (1 per sandwich)

In a large bowl, break up the tofu into small chunks with a fork. You don't want it to be a paste, but more like bite-size pieces. Use a large spoon to mix in the nutritional yeast, cumin, onion powder, turmeric, and Creole seasoning with your tofu. Cover and refrigerate overnight. This is your vegan diced egg.

The next day, preheat the oven to 375°F.

Open the baguette and brush both sides with Fresh Herb Vinaigrette. You'll have some dressing left over. Toast your sandwich in the oven with the split side up until the edges begin to brown.

Fill your baguette with an even layer of vegan diced egg. Then layer on the tomatoes, bell pepper, onion rings, artichoke hearts, and olives. Sprinkle an even layer of vegan cheese over the top. Put the sandwich back into the oven and bake for another 10 to 15 minutes, or until the vegan cheese melts.

Drizzle the remaining Fresh Herb Vinaigrette over the top of the melted vegan cheese. Cut the baguette into 4 equal portions, then add a dash of smoked paprika to each sandwich.

SPICY PEANUT SAUCE TOFU WRAP

This recipe seems like something you'd order in the café of a yoga studio in LA—and, I don't know, maybe it is. A lot of Bettys enjoy yoga—me, not so much. What I do enjoy is a dish with bold flavors and a subtle kick that just happens to be healthy without really tasting like it. That's what we've got here.

MAKES 4 TO 6 WRAPS

¾ cup chopped raw broccoli florets

⅓ cup shredded carrots

1 red bell pepper, sliced thin

1 (11-ounce) can bamboo shoots, julienned

4 green onions, chopped

4 tablespoons chopped fresh cilantro

¼ cup drained pineapple pieces

¼ cup warm water (you may need more if your sauce gets too thick, see note)

2 teaspoons sesame oil

2 tablespoons rice vinegar

4 tablespoons Bragg's liquid aminos

¾ teaspoon ginger paste

½ teaspoon cumin

1 teaspoon lime juice

1 teaspoon Sriracha sauce

¼ cup creamy peanut butter

1 (14-ounce) package extrafirm tofu, drained and cut into strips

Olive oil cooking spray

4 to 6 whole wheat tortillas

¼ cup dry-roasted peanuts

In a large bowl, mix the broccoli, carrots, bell pepper, bamboo shoots, green onions, cilantro, and pineapple. Cover and refrigerate for 2 to 3 hours. This is your veggie mix.

In a saucepan, heat the water, sesame oil, rice vinegar, Bragg's, ginger paste, cumin, lime juice, and Sriracha sauce to a boil. Add the peanut butter and reduce your heat to a simmer. Use a whisk to blend in the peanut butter. Now, the more "natural" your peanut butter, the more oily your peanut butter will be, because it'll have less filler. If your peanut sauce is too thick because of fillers, add more water a tablespoon at a time until you like the consistency. Keep whisking your sauce over low heat until it is smooth and creamy but not pasty. Once it's done, remove it from the heat. While you make your peanut sauce, you can bake your tofu.

Preheat the oven to 400°F.

Place the cut tofu in a glass baking dish and spray with olive oil cooking spray. Flip the tofu and spray on another layer of olive oil. Bake for 10 to 15 minutes, until the tofu is golden brown.

Reduce the heat to 250°F. After a few minutes, toss the whole wheat tortillas in the oven to warm. You want them to get warm enough that they are pliable but not toasted. Once the tortillas are soft, remove them from the oven.

To make your wraps, use a slotted spoon to place a scoop of veggie mix and a portion of tofu in the center of your tortilla. Drizzle Sriracha-peanut sauce over the top. Sprinkle some dry-roasted peanuts over each wrap before gently folding up the bottom of the tortilla and then the sides. Leave the top open so you can see the tofu and vegetables.

This recipe should make 4 to 6 wraps, depending on how big your tortillas are and how ambitiously you fill them. If you're a real overachiever, you might wrap your wrap with foil to help keep it together.

Happy eating!

LEMON PEPPER TOFU BAGEL SANDWICH

Baking up a batch of this tofu on Sunday night can give you sandwich fixings (or salad toppings) that will last you all week, and save you loads of money on those overpriced rice bowls and undercooked veggie burgers at lunch counters. Recipes like this are a busy woman's best friend.

MAKES 4 TO 6 SANDWICHES

1 cup lemon juice

1 teaspoon grated lemon peel

2 teaspoons crushed black peppercorns

2 teaspoons tahini dressing

1½ teaspoons Bragg's liquid aminos

2 (14-ounce) packages extrafirm tofu, drained and cut into strips

Olive oil cooking spray

4 to 6 whole wheat bagels

Tomato slices, baby spinach leaves, red onion slices, and dill pickle chips for toppings

In a shallow dish, whisk together the lemon juice, lemon peel, black pepper, tahini, and Bragg's. Put the tofu in the shallow dish and use a ladle to cover it completely with the marinade. Let sit for 20 minutes.

Preheat the oven to 400°F.

Spray a large lasagna dish with olive oil cooking spray; then place the tofu strips in the dish so that they don't touch. Use a soupspoon to pour a little marinade over the top. Bake for 20 minutes; then flip the tofu and spray the dish with an even layer of cooking spray again, and spoon any extra marinade over the top. Bake for another 20 to 30 minutes, until the tofu is golden brown.

Toast your bagels and make up your sandwiches with tomato, baby spinach, red onion, and pickle chips, or your favorite toppings.

SPICY EGGLESS SALAD SANDWICH

We've had a lot of different eggless salad sandwiches over the years, some much better than others. It's an easy thing to mess up. But I think this salad has the right amount of kick from the Creole seasoning and good flavor from the nutritional yeast and tahini. It makes a nice sandwich when you pair it with some whole wheat bread... they're like BFFs. I'm sure if they weren't food, they'd buy each other little broken-heart lockets and talk about boys over soy mochas.

MAKES 4 PRETTY BIG SANDWICHES

1 16-ounce package extrafirm tofu, drained and pressed

⅓ cup Grapeseed Vegenaise

2 stalks celery, diced

¼ red onion, diced

¼ cup diced raw kale

2 tablespoons chopped fresh parsley

2 green onions, chopped

4 tablespoons nutritional yeast

½ teaspoon cumin

½ teaspoon onion powder

¼ teaspoon turmeric

¼ teaspoon celery seed

2 pinches of paprika

¼ teaspoon Tony Chachere's Creole seasoning

¼ teaspoon tahini dressing

2 teaspoons Dijon mustard

2 teaspoons pickle relish

8 slices whole wheat bread

In a large mixing bowl, gently mash the tofu. You want to have bite-size pieces, so be careful to not mash the tofu into paste. Stir in the Vegenaise, celery, red onion, kale, parsley, and green onions.

In another bowl, blend the nutritional yeast, cumin, onion powder, turmeric, celery seed, paprika, and Creole seasoning. Once your spices are mixed, blend in the ta-hini, Dijon mustard, and pickle relish using a whisk. Then gently mix your tahini blend into your tofu-vegetable blend. Cover with foil and put in the fridge for 3 hours. Toast your bread, spread with the eggless salad, and serve.

Years of scientific studies and research have proven that every time an eggless salad sandwich is served on toasted wheat bread, with pickles, an angel gets his wings.

BÁNH MÌ CHAY

The original bánh mì sandwiches are the product of the French colonization of Vietnam. They're usually made with a wide variety of pork products on small baguettes. I've never been to Vietnam, so I can only tell you what vegan bánh mì sandwiches are like in San Francisco and Seattle. I love them, with their lightly seasoned mock meat and vegetables. It's a special sandwich that you can't find just anywhere. Ours are made with a whole wheat baguette and a unique combination of vegetables that have a nice texture and crunch.

MAKES 4 SANDWICHES

¼ teaspoon five-spice powder

1 teaspoon rice vinegar

2 teaspoons Bragg's liquid aminos

2 teaspoons lime juice

2 teaspoons chili-infused oil or olive oil

¼ teaspoon ginger paste

1 teaspoon apple juice

2 cups vegan chicken, cut into bite-size pieces

1 package extrafirm tofu, thinly sliced lengthwise

½ cup julienned daikon radish

1 (11-ounce) can water chestnuts, diced

½ cup shredded carrots

1 cucumber, sliced

1 whole wheat baguette, split lengthwise

½ cup fresh cilantro

Sriracha sauce or Asian hot sauce to drizzle over the top

In a large bowl, whisk together the five-spice powder, rice vinegar, Bragg's, lime juice, chili-infused oil, ginger paste, and apple juice. Put the vegan chicken, tofu, daikon, water chestnuts, carrots, and cucumber into a glass lasagna dish and pour the marinade over the top. Let the vegan chicken and vegetable mixture sit for 1 hour. Using a fork, fill the baguette with the vegan chicken and vegetable mixture. Sprinkle cilantro over the top; then slice into 4 equal portions. Drizzle a little Sriracha sauce over the top and enjoy!

Ăn ngon nhé!

CAPRESE CHICKEN PITA

Peek into any bistro or deli near the park in Bensonhurst and you'll find Caprese salad on the menu. This salad is ridiculously easy to make, and it's the simple nature of it that makes it brilliant. I mean, is there anything more lovely than fresh basil? That's not a theoretical question. The correct answer is "no." We used Caprese salad as the base for a pita sandwich that's fancy enough for a tea party or baby shower, but Brooklyn enough for any blue-collar vegan.

You're going to want to prepare your chicken the night before you plan to eat these sandwiches.

MAKES 4 TO 6 SANDWICHES

2 cups vegan chicken, defrosted

Olive oil cooking spray

¾ cup fresh basil leaves

3 Roma tomatoes, sliced

1 cup shredded Daiya vegan mozzarella cheese or your favorite vegan cheese

1½ teaspoons capers

4 to 6 whole wheat pitas

Crushed black peppercorns

Preheat the oven to 400°F.

Put the vegan chicken in a glass baking dish and spray with an even coating of olive oil cooking spray. Use a spoon to flip your vegan chicken a few times to make sure it gets completely covered. Bake for 15 to 20 minutes. Remove from the oven when your vegan chicken is golden brown and crispy on the edges. Cover and refrigerate overnight.

The next day, gently toss together your basil, tomatoes, vegan cheese, and capers. Make sure you're gentle so that you don't crush your tomatoes. This is a Caprese salad.

To make your sandwiches, slightly heat the pitas so they are soft enough to fill. Fill each pita with equal portions of chicken and Caprese salad. Sprinkle a little black pepper over the top.

You're done. I told you it was ridiculously easy.

MOROCCAN SPICE CHICKEN WRAP

This wrap is a combination of savory and sweet and awesome-sauce. I would never go so far as to say that this is an actual Moroccan dish, but it combines a lot of what makes traditional Moroccan food great. I compare it to that made-for-TV movie *Ewoks: The Battle for Endor*. I mean, it had adorable Ewoks and lovable, mustachioed Wilford Brimley. Ten-year-old me freaking loved this movie. I loved the tree-house sets and one-sided conversations with the Ewoks. Just typing this now, I can feel my pulse rise. If I have to be honest with myself, it's actually extremely tangentially connected to the Star Wars universe. But it was enough for me to fall madly in love with it. This wrap is a lot like that.

MAKES 4 TO 6 WRAPS

2 teaspoons paprika

¼ teaspoon crushed black peppercorns

½ teaspoon crushed pink Himalayan salt

¾ teaspoon cumin

¼ teaspoon turmeric

¼ teaspoon allspice

¼ teaspoon ground cinnamon

¼ teaspoon ground cardamom

1 tablespoon olive oil

2 cups vegan chicken, defrosted (we suggest using Gardein Chick'n Scallopini)

1 zucchini, thinly sliced

¼ cup hummus

4 to 6 whole wheat tortillas

1 mango, cubed

4 tablespoons fresh cilantro leaves

4 to 6 lemon wedges

Preheat the oven to 400°F.

Put the paprika, pepper, salt, cumin, turmeric, allspice, cinnamon, and cardamom in a sealable plastic freezer bag, seal the bag carefully, and shake to mix.

Pour the olive oil in a shallow bowl. One piece at a time, dip the vegan chicken into the oil and flip it a few times to make sure it gets completely covered. Then toss the vegan chicken into the spice bag and shake until the vegan chicken is completely covered. Place your coated vegan chicken in a glass baking dish in an even layer. The more vegan chicken you coat, the more oil will get into your spices, so by the time you get to the last pieces, you might have to press the spices into your vegan chicken through the bag rather than shake.

Once all the vegan chicken is covered, place the zucchini slices over the vegan chicken, and then bake for 10 minutes, or until your zucchini is tender.

While the vegan chicken bakes, prepare your wraps. Spread hummus on each tortilla. When your vegan chicken and zucchini are done, place them on the tortillas in even portions. Spoon on the fresh mango and sprinkle the cilantro over that. Squeeze a lemon wedge over the top.

To wrap a wrap, fold up the bottom third of each tortilla. Then fold in the sides on the right and left of that to form a cone shape. The top of your wrap should be open, so you can see inside your wrap.

This wrap is a little juicy, so you may want to wrap your wrap in foil to help keep all the deliciousness in there.

ROASTED VEGAN CHICKEN GYRO

We've all seen it. We go in for our favorite falafel, and rotating around on a pike is a slab of mystery meat, dripping with stuff and looking a little haggard. Yet the line to get a warm pita full of this slow-cooked sliced lamb is long and uncompromising. Why? Well, I have a theory that it's really the tzatziki sauce that people love. Everyone loves that mellow yogurt-based sauce, with all its clean flavors of dill and cucumber. We make a vegan version a few times a year, and it's usually gone in about an hour. There's a secret magic infused in this combination of cool and creamy that will make you crave it nightly. Seriously. Don't be surprised if the next cat we adopt is named Tzatziki.* I recommend picking up some fancy olives and making a nice Tabbouleh (page 225) to go with your gyro.

MAKES 4 TO 6 SANDWICHES

1 tablespoon margarine

1 teaspoon paprika

2 teaspoons Bragg's liquid aminos

3 cloves garlic, minced

1 teaspoon oregano

1 teaspoon hot sauce (you might want a little more to dash over the top)

2 cups vegan chicken, defrosted (we suggest using Gardein Chick'n Scallopini)

4 to 6 lafahs or pocketless pitas

½ red onion, sliced

1 cucumber, sliced

1 Roma tomato, sliced

¾ cup Vegan Tzatziki Sauce (page 289)

Preheat the oven to 450°F.

Melt the margarine in a small saucepan. Once it is liquefied, used a spoon to mix in the paprika, Bragg's, garlic, oregano, and hot sauce. Cut the vegan chicken into strips or silver dollar–size chunks if it comes in one large piece. Thread the vegan chicken onto metal skewers; then place the skewers over a glass baking dish that is shorter than the skewers, so that the vegan chicken is raised and not touching the bottom of the dish. The skewers should look like a rotisserie spit. Brush the skewers with the margarine-garlic mixture, rotating them a few times to get melted margarine all over in an even coating. Be sure to get inside any folds or nooks. Bake for 10 to 15 minutes, or until the vegan chicken is golden brown. While the vegan chicken is roasting, brush it with the melted margarine to keep it from drying out.

Right before you're ready to take your vegan chicken out of the oven, put your pita bread in the oven for about 30 seconds. This should warm the bread long enough to make it soft.

Immediately remove the vegan chicken from the skewers directly into the pitas. You want to include the few drops of flavored oil that come off the skewer. Toss onion, cucumber, and Roma tomatoes into your pita; then drizzle Vegan Tzatziki Sauce over the top. Fold your pita, and you're ready to enjoy one of the most popular sandwiches on the planet (according to Wikipedia).

---

* Don't steal my baby name.

SALADS

There's an outdated stereotype that vegans live on salads alone. It's a silly notion that dates back to the days before you could have a vegan pizza delivered to your house, and when tofu could only be found in Chinatown. We may appreciate a good salad more than our omnivorous colleagues, but I'd bet that has more to do with our enhanced appreciation for food than with any particular affinity for salads. See, there's a funny thing that happens when you go vegan. It's like your sense of taste levels up, and you appreciate everything you eat a little bit more. Think about it. That means at least two hours of your day just got a lot better.

In this section we've veganized some of the most high-profile salads in the canon, salads that have graced the menus of restaurants around the world for decades. Most are complete meals in a bowl, and all of them are so much better than those iceberg monstrosities you can pick up in a cafeteria or drive-through. These are the salads you're looking for.

A KINDER AND GENTLER CHICKEN CAESAR SALAD

Little known fact: the original Caesar salad actually didn't have any little bits of anchovies in it. The only fishy flavor was from the Worcestershire sauce. Legend has it that Caesar Cardini invented the salad in his restaurant in Tijuana, during Prohibition, when his supplies were low. Since then, it's become a staple at restaurants around the world. Most versions include an anchovy paste or pieces of anchovies to make the salad fancier. Many also add grilled chicken breast or raw eggs to make the dish more substantial. Our recipe makes four salads that use vegan Worcestershire sauce, nutritional yeast, and mock meat to take Caesar salad to a whole new place...a kinder, gentler place, where all the little fish and birds are free and safe.

MAKES 4 SALADS

1 tablespoon olive oil

Dash of liquid smoke

1 cup vegan chicken, defrosted (we suggest using Gardein Chick'n Scallopini)

2 hearts of romaine lettuce, chopped

½ cup French-fried onions

2 tablespoons sunflower seeds

1⅓ cups Caesar Salad Dressing (page 106)

4 tablespoons grated smoked cheddar Sheese or Daiya vegan Havarti cheese wedge

In a cast-iron skillet or frying pan, heat the olive oil and liquid smoke over medium heat. Once the oil is hot, add the vegan chicken. Cook until the vegan chicken is evenly browned. Remove from the heat and slice into strips. Separate into 4 equal portions.

In a large bowl, toss the romaine lettuce, French-fried onions, sunflower seeds, and Caesar Salad Dressing. Separate the salad into 4 equal portions, then put a portion of vegan chicken on top of each. Grate some vegan cheese over the top.

GREEK SALAD

The very first night of the Betty Crocker Project, we started with Chicken Tetrazzini and my personal favorite salad: Greek. Let's face it—is there anything better than lemony olive oil dressing, kalamata olives, and hot peperoncini? You can even find vegan feta cheese at your local food co-op or Whole Foods. We also added garbanzo beans and avocado, because who wouldn't want more of them? So really, the question isn't why haven't you been eating vegan Greek salad this whole time…it's why aren't you eating it right now?

MAKES 4 SALADS

2 hearts of romaine lettuce, chopped

½ cup raw baby spinach leaves

½ large red onion, thinly sliced

¾ cup whole kalamata olives, pitted

2 Roma tomatoes, sliced

1 large cucumber, sliced

3 tablespoons French-fried onions

¾ cup vegan feta or extrafirm tofu, cubed

¾ cup peperoncini, drained

1 ripe avocado, sliced

1 (15-ounce) can garbanzo beans, drained and rinsed

1⅔ to 2 cups Greek Dressing (page 108)

Toss all your ingredients except the Greek Dressing in a large bowl and divide into 4 equal portions.

Serve the dressing on the side.

TACO SALAD

The night I wrote the blog post about this salad, I had planned on writing this whole thing about how there are a lot of Americans who don't eat proper Mexican food, citing examples like the caulking guns they use at Taco Bell to serve their bean and guacamole pastes, their strange octagon-shaped taco sandwiches, and of course the role they play in the evil axis that is Yum! brands. But let's be honest—taco salad isn't really proper Mexican food. It's more like Mexican-inspired—but that's not to say this isn't delicious! So now as I type this book out while I watch *Dexter* with a cat on my lap, I think I need to skip the rant about America's need to experience real Mexican food. Let's just focus on this Mexican-ish recipe instead.

MAKES 4 SALADS

- 4 cups vegetable oil
- 4 (10-inch) flour tortilla shells
- 3 tablespoons olive oil
- 2 dashes of liquid smoke
- 1 tablespoon Texas Pete hot sauce
- 2 cups Lightlife Gimme Lean vegan ground beef, Match vegan ground beef, crumbled tempeh, or Tofurky ground burger, defrosted
- ½ large red onion, diced
- 1 (15-ounce) can kidney beans, drained and rinsed (keep the can)
- ½ teaspoon Bragg's liquid aminos
- ¼ teaspoon cayenne pepper
- ¼ teaspoon garlic powder
- ¼ teaspoon poultry seasoning (most are vegan, but you need to read the label to make sure)
- ¼ teaspoon cumin
- 1 head romaine lettuce, chopped into bite-size pieces
- 1 cup shredded Daiya vegan cheddar cheese or your favorite vegan cheese
- ⅔ cup sliced black olives
- 1 ripe avocado, sliced
- Vegan sour cream, salsa, chopped green onions, and chopped cilantro for toppings

Start by making your tortilla shell bowls.

Remove the label and both ends from your empty kidney bean can.

In a 3-quart saucepan, heat the vegetable oil to a boil. Carefully place 1 tortilla atop the boiling oil in the pan. With long-handled tongs, place the kidney bean can in the middle of the tortilla and very slowly and gently push the tortilla into the oil. Count to 5; then remove the can. If the tortilla hasn't set into a flower-shaped cup, replace the can and hold for another 5 seconds. Remove the can and continue to fry the tortilla for 1 to 2 minutes longer, turning frequently until crisp and golden brown.

Carefully remove the tortilla shell using the tongs and place on a paper towel on a plate to soak up excess oil. Let cool and repeat with the other tortillas.

In your hardworking cast-iron skillet or frying pan, heat the olive oil over medium heat. Stir in the liquid smoke and hot sauce. Add the defrosted vegan ground beef, diced red onion, and kidney beans; then mix in the Bragg's, cayenne pepper, garlic powder, poultry seasoning, and cumin. Make sure everything gets mixed thoroughly and gets an even coating. It should take around 10 minutes for the mixture to finish cooking, but different types of vegan ground beef have different cooking times. Remove from the heat once the vegan ground beef is browned and the onions are caramelized. Let the vegan beef mixture cool before serving. If you serve it warm, the vegan beef will wilt your lettuce.

Once your shells and vegan beef reach room temperature, you can build your salads! Put your lettuce in the tortilla shells as a base and add the vegan beef mixture. Sprinkle on the vegan cheese, olives, and avocado, and then add the vegan sour cream, salsa, green onions, and cilantro, or whatever fixings you want… It's your party!

VEGAN BACON AND SPINACH SALAD FEATURING THE VEGAN HARD-BOILED EGG

"The Shannon Family Album" is one of our favorite segments on our blog. Over the years, we've been lucky enough to meet some of the most amazing animal advocates on the planet. Technology like Facebook has made it easier than ever for vegans all over the world to connect, learn from each other, and build a strong online community that's promoting a more compassionate world for animals on a scale never before seen. One of those outstanding advocates is a lovely lady named Jasmin Singer. You may know her as half the talented and dedicated duo at Our Hen House—a website that helps people find their own way to change the world for animals. We were honored to have her join "The Shannon Family Album" by testing out this recipe. This salad is one of those mischievous dishes that looks extremely impressive and more complicated than it really is. Even the most inexperienced chefs can pull this off and bring some shock and awe.

MAKES 4 TO 6 SERVINGS

1 batch Vegan Hard-Boiled Eggs (page 59)

VEGAN BACON AND SPINACH SALAD

6 pieces vegan bacon or smoked tempeh

3 tablespoons olive oil

2 dashes of liquid smoke

5 green onions, chopped

2 tablespoons diced fresh parsley

¼ teaspoon lemon pepper

Pinch of celery seed

2 teaspoons Bragg's liquid aminos

3 tablespoons white wine

1 clove garlic, minced

¼ teaspoon agave nectar

2 tablespoons white wine vinegar

2 tablespoons lemon juice

4 to 6 cups fresh baby spinach leaves

Make your Vegan Hard-Boiled Egg first using the recipe on page 59. Preheat the oven to 300°F.

To make the salad, in your delightful little cast-iron skillet or frying pan, cook the vegan bacon in 2 tablespoons of the olive oil with a dash of liquid smoke over medium heat. Once it's crispy, remove it from the skillet and set aside. You want the oil on the fake bacon, so you don't want to put it on a paper towel like many of us just automatically do when we make bacon—even the vegan kind. Chop the vegan bacon into bite-size pieces.

Add the remaining 1 tablespoon olive oil and another dash of liquid smoke to the warm skillet and take the heat down to low. We're re-creating bacon fat. I know that sounds gross, but I feel I should be honest. Plus it's not really bacon fat so it's not really gross. We're going for the smoky flavor so many people love about bacon but don't realize that's what they actually like rather than the pig meat.

Once your oil is warm and smoky, add the green onions, parsley, lemon pepper, celery seed, Bragg's, white wine, garlic, and agave nectar to your skillet. Heat until the green onions become tender. Then add the white wine vinegar and lemon juice. Remove from the heat. Now you have your dressing!

Put the spinach in a large bowl. Pour warm salad dressing over your spinach and toss your salad to coat. Place the "eggs" around the bowl, and sprinkle vegan bacon pieces over the top of the salad. Serve immediately, so it doesn't wilt too much.

When you eat it, make sure you get a lot of dressing on your "eggs," because they taste almost poetic together.

COBB SALAD

Before the Lobster Killer scene of *Julie and Julia* that sparked this project, I had fallen in love with Amy Adams's portrayal of Julie Powell. I could relate to her in ways I'm still embarrassed to admit. At that time in my life, I was watching my husband, friends, and peers move past me professionally at a rate that made me cry in the shower from time to time. The Cobb salad scene in particular hit me really hard: watching her politely ask about the projects her friends were working on, and playfully joke with a serious table, well…I'd had my share of dinner parties monopolized by discussions of projects I wasn't working on. So I wanted to save this recipe for the finale week of the Betty Crocker Project, but then something amazing happened…we got a book deal. Just like in the movie! So I needed to make it sooner. You can serve this recipe at your next dinner party, regardless of how content you are with your current station in life.

You'll want to prepare the vegan diced eggs, vegan bacon, and vegan chicken the night before you're going to serve your salad.

MAKES 4 TO 6 SERVINGS

- 1 cup vegan chicken, defrosted, diced (we suggest using Gardein Chick'n Scallopini)
- Olive oil cooking spray
- 8 slices vegan bacon or smoked tempeh, diced
- ½ (14-ounce) package extrafirm tofu, drained and pressed
- 2 tablespoons nutritional yeast
- ¼ teaspoon cumin
- ¼ teaspoon onion powder
- ⅛ teaspoon turmeric
- ⅛ teaspoon Tony Chachere's Creole seasoning
- 2 hearts of romaine lettuce, chopped
- ½ bunch watercress, chopped
- 2 ripe avocados, cubed
- 1 (5.5-ounce) package Hickory Smoked Tofurky Deli Slices, separated and cut into strips
- ½ red onion, diced
- 6 stalks celery, diced
- ½ cup cubed blue cheese–flavored Sheese or your favorite vegan cheese
- 2 Roma tomatoes, sliced
- 2 tablespoons chopped fresh chives
- 1 batch Dijon Vinaigrette (page 109)

Preheat the oven to 400°F.

Put the vegan chicken in a glass baking dish and spray with an even coating of olive oil cooking spray. Use a spoon to flip the vegan chicken a few times to make sure it gets completely covered. Place the vegan bacon over the top. Bake for 15 to 20 minutes. Remove from the oven when the vegan chicken and vegan bacon are golden brown and crispy on the edges. Cover and refrigerate overnight.

Make your "vegan diced egg" in a large bowl. With a fork, break up the tofu into small chunks. You don't want it to be a paste, but more like bite-size pieces. Use a large spoon to mix the nutritional yeast, cumin, onion powder, turmeric, and Creole seasoning with the tofu. Cover and refrigerate overnight.

Right before you're ready to make your salad, chop your chilled vegan chicken and vegan bacon into bite-size pieces.

To make your salad, fill a huge salad bowl with a layer of romaine and watercress. Then layer the following ingredients in rows across the top: avocados, vegan bacon, vegan chicken, Tofurky slices, red onion, vegan diced eggs, celery, vegan cheese, and tomatoes. Sprinkle with chives. Serve with Dijon Vinaigrette on the side.

ITALIAN CHOPPED SALAD

Salads can be hard to mess up and easy to take for granted. This is one of those salads you may never have tried before and didn't know you wanted to. Yes, this is the Mr. Right Salad that will complete you.

MAKES 4 TO 6 SERVINGS

3 tablespoons olive oil

Dash of liquid smoke

1 cup vegan chicken, defrosted (we suggest using Gardein Chick'n Scallopini)

3 tablespoons raw pine nuts

8 to 10 pieces of crumbled smoked tempeh or Lightlife Smart Deli vegan pepperoni

6 cups chopped romaine lettuce

1 cup fresh whole basil leaves

1 large beefsteak or heirloom tomato, chopped into big chunks

2 cucumbers, chopped into big chunks

¼ large red onion, chopped

1 (15-ounce) can cannellini beans, drained and rinsed

1 (15-ounce) can quartered artichoke hearts, drained

Handful of kalamata olives, Sicilian green olives, and peperoncini

1 batch Fresh Herb Vinaigrette (page 108)

Make the Fresh Herb Vinaigrette the night before you make your salad.

In your handy cast-iron skillet or frying pan, heat the olive oil and a dash of liquid smoke over medium heat. Fry up the vegan chicken, pine nuts, and tempeh till they reach the desired crispiness. Set aside to cool on a plate with a paper towel to soak up oil.

Once the vegan chicken, pine nuts, and tempeh are cooled, chop them up. Place them in a bowl with the lettuce, basil, tomato, cucumbers, onion, beans, artichoke hearts, olives, and peperoncini, and toss. Pour as much vinaigrette as you want over it and serve family-style!

MANDARIN VEGAN CHICKEN SALAD

This was one of the first salads I ever made for the Betty Crocker Project. At the time, I gave Betty Crocker a hard time on the blog for adding sugar to a salad. I mean, I'm okay adding sugar to a cookie or a doughnut. It's a cookie. Or a doughnut. It's in their nature to be sweet. But salads are our friends. If you can't trust a salad to do right by you… who can you trust? That's why we skipped the candied almonds and kept them raw. Partner it with our Toasted Sesame Dressing (page 109).

MAKES ABOUT 4 SALADS

1 tablespoon sesame oil

2 cups vegan chicken (we suggest using Lightlife Smart Strips, Chik'n)

1 can water chestnuts, chopped

2 tablespoons Bragg's liquid aminos

¼ cup raw almond slices

2 hearts of romaine lettuce, chopped

½ cup baby spinach leaves

3 stalks celery, chopped

2 green onions, chopped

¼ cup shredded carrots

1 (11-ounce) can mandarin orange slices, drained

2 tablespoons chow mein noodles (make sure to read your labels to check that your brand is vegan)

1 batch Toasted Sesame Dressing (page 109)

Heat the sesame oil in your cast-iron skillet or frying pan on a medium heat. Once the oil is hot, add the vegan chicken and stir occasionally. Once the vegan chicken starts to brown, add the water chestnuts and Bragg's and keep tossing the mixture so that the hot oil and Bragg's cover the vegan chicken and water chestnuts. Once the mixture is fully cooked and has golden brown edges, pull it off the heat and set aside on a separate plate to cool.

Wipe your cast-iron skillet with a cloth towel to get any excess oil or crumbs out of it. It's okay if a light film of oil remains. Toss the almond slices into the warm skillet and lightly brown them over low heat. You'll know they're done when the edges are a soft brown. Set them aside to cool in the skillet.

In a large bowl, mix the lettuce, spinach, celery, green onions, carrots, mandarin oranges, chow mein noodles, and vegan chicken by gently tossing them all together. Then toss the toasted almonds on top and serve the dressing on the side.

AVOCADO AND SMOKED SHEESE SALAD

This might not be the healthiest salad ever made, but it's so delicious, and when partnered with the Toasted Walnut Dressing (page 107), it's packed with those omega-3s vegans need. But I admit I love it because it tastes great. I love it like Captain Kirk loves women with big hair.

MAKES 2 SERVINGS

2 cups chopped romaine lettuce

⅓ cup cubed smoked cheddar Sheese or Daiya vegan Havarti cheese wedge

1 ripe avocado, sliced

⅓ cup baby carrots

⅓ cup kalamata olives, pitted

1 batch Toasted Walnut Dressing (page 107)

Raw sunflower seeds, dried cranberries, and vegan bacon bits to sprinkle over the top

Toss the lettuce, vegan cheese, avocado, carrots, and olives in a large bowl with the Toasted Walnut Dressing. Sprinkle on the sunflower seeds, dried cranberries, and vegan bacon bits, and serve family-style.

THANKSGIVING SALAD

This is the salad I make the most often. It gets huge fast and becomes a feast all its own, and I make it year-round. This recipe makes 4 salads, so you can share it with your loved ones in the spirit of Thanksgiving.

MAKES 4 TO 6 SERVINGS

3 hearts of romaine lettuce, chopped

½ cup baby spinach leaves

1 (5.5-ounce) package Tofurky Deli Slices, separated and sliced into strips

¼ cup baby carrots

¼ cup whole black olives (the kind you stick on your fingers)

¼ cup sliced celery

½ cup croutons (read your labels to make sure they are vegan)

4 tablespoons dried cranberries

4 tablespoons raw almond slivers

¼ cup French-fried onions

4 tablespoons raw pumpkin seeds

1 batch Fresh Herb Vinaigrette (page 108)

In a large mixing bowl, toss the romaine, spinach, Tofurky, carrots, olives, celery, and croutons. Divide the salad into 4 equal portions; then top with equal portions of the dried cranberries, almonds, French-fried onions, and pumpkin seeds. Serve your Fresh Herb Vinaigrette on the side family-style.

MEDITERRANEAN SALAD

Prior to the Betty Crocker Project, you could have said our vegan "diet" was pretty Mediterranean. We're all about eating whole grains and legumes when we can. We use primarily olive oil, and we may have polished off more than one bottle of red wine with dinner from time to time. This salad reflects what the Shannons are really eating when we aren't making Baked Vegan Chicken and Waffles (page 38) and baking cupcakes. It's flavorful, using fruit and herbs in a way that really appeals to my Mediterranean roots. Serve family-style to really get that Mediterranean feel.

MAKES 4 TO 6 SERVINGS

4 cups baby spinach leaves

¼ cup fresh whole basil leaves

2 large navel oranges, peeled, cleaned, and segmented

1 large red bell pepper, sliced

1 cucumber, sliced

4 tablespoons kalamata olives, pitted

½ cup seedless red grapes, cut in half

4 tablespoons pomegranate seeds

1 (15-ounce) can cannellini beans

2 tablespoons julienned sun-dried tomatoes

6 peperoncini

1 batch Greek Dressing (page 108)

In a large serving bowl, toss the spinach, basil, oranges, bell pepper, and cucumber. Sprinkle the olives, grapes, pomegranate seeds, beans, and tomatoes over the top. Serve the peperoncini and dressing on the side.

SESAME VEGAN CHICKEN SLAW

The day I made this slaw for the first time, I woke up with the echo of a dream and a lingering wisdom: "Don't let your boat turn into Charlie Brown." What does it mean? I have no idea. But I do know that this salad is a quick lunch that has sunny mandarin oranges and crunchy ramen bits and is salty and sweet all at the same time. In less than 15 minutes you can be eating this slaw and enjoying ramen in a whole new way.

MAKES 4 TO 6 SERVINGS

2 tablespoons sesame oil

2 cups vegan chicken, defrosted, diced (we suggest using Gardein Chick'n Scallopini)

2 tablespoons margarine

1 (3-ounce) package oriental-flavored ramen (read your label to make sure your brand is vegan)

2 tablespoons sesame seeds

¼ cup agave nectar

¼ cup rice vinegar

½ teaspoon tamari

1 teaspoon ginger paste

¼ teaspoon crushed black peppercorns

¼ cup dry-roasted peanuts

4 green onions, chopped

2 cups broccoli slaw mix

1 (10-ounce) can mandarin orange segments, drained

2 tablespoons chopped fresh cilantro

4 to 8 lime wedges

In your favorite cast-iron skillet or frying pan, heat 1 tablespoon of the sesame oil over medium heat. Once the oil is hot, toss in the vegan chicken and cook until the edges are browned and slightly crispy. Remove from heat.

In the same skillet, melt the margarine into any leftover sesame oil over medium heat. Once the margarine is melted, whisk in the ramen flavor packet. Then break the ramen noodles over the skillet into bite-size pieces. Use a metal spatula to blend the noodles into the melted margarine. Cook the noodles for no longer than a minute; then mix in the sesame seeds. Toss and cook for another minute. Don't let the noodles burn or brown too much—you want to remove them from the heat once they are slightly golden.

In a large bowl, whisk together the agave nectar, rice vinegar, tamari, ginger paste, remaining 1 tablespoon sesame oil, and black pepper. Add the cooked noodles, vegan chicken, peanuts, green onions, broccoli slaw mix, mandarin oranges, and cilantro and toss. Serve immediately with the lime wedges on the side.

DRESSINGS AND VINAIGRETTES

Salads are a great and easy way to add raw vegetables to your life, but most of us don't enjoy a naked salad. Unfortunately, it can be hard to find a prepackaged salad dressing that doesn't use a lot of sugar, corn syrup, or unhealthy oils. That's why we suggest investing in a five-dollar glass salad dressing bottle with a cap that seals so you can shake it. That one bottle is one of the most popular items in our whole kitchen—always out on a counter, encouraging us to snack on some baby carrots or add a side salad to our dinner.

We tried to make dressings that had both unique flavors and good ingredients. That's why we use olive oil instead of soybean and canola oil like most store-bought dressings. Olive oil has more monounsaturated fats (the good ones) and fewer omega-6 fats (the bad ones)—and if all those studies of the Mediterranean diet can be believed, that's why there's an association between olive oil intake and a decreased risk of heart disease. It also means that you can't store your homemade dressing in the fridge, because olive oil becomes a solid when it gets cold. We store ours on the counter next to the knives, but we do our best to finish a bottle in 24 to 36 hours so it doesn't sit there for long.

In this section you'll find the dressings that go with our classic salads, but these recipes can do much more than just complement—they can encourage you to make your own signature salads and hopefully eat more vegetables.

CAESAR SALAD DRESSING

This is one of my favorite salad dressings ever. In fact, it has convinced us to never again buy a bottle of salad dressing. Sorry, Paul Newman. We had a nice run, but this was what we've been searching for in your cleverly labeled bottles all these years. Don't worry; we can still be friends. Until we find a way to make our own Newman-O's.

....

1 clove garlic, minced	1 teaspoon vegan Worcestershire sauce	½ teaspoon lemon pepper
⅓ cup olive oil	¼ teaspoon Bragg's liquid aminos	1 tablespoon nutritional yeast
3 tablespoons lemon juice	2 pinches of ground mustard seeds	

....

Toss all the ingredients in a tight container, shake, and drizzle over a bed of your favorite salad stuff. Our Kinder and Gentler Caesar Salad can be found on page 97 if you want to be proper and serve this with the expected fixings.

TOASTED WALNUT DRESSING

If avocado had a soul mate, it would be this dressing.

⅓ cup raw walnuts, crushed

⅓ cup olive oil

2 tablespoons lemon juice

1 tablespoon red wine vinegar

¼ teaspoon capers, drained

1 clove garlic, minced

¼ teaspoon vegan Parmesan

¼ teaspoon dried rosemary, crushed

Dash of crushed black peppercorns

Toast the walnuts in a cast-iron skillet or frying pan over medium heat for around 5 minutes, until golden brown. Put all the ingredients, including the toasted walnuts, in an airtight container and shake. Shake before each time you use it.

TOMATO-LIME VINAIGRETTE

Tomatoes and limes—not just for Mexican food anymore! This dressing works for just about any veggie combination.

½ cup spicy tomato and vegetable
   juice cocktail

¼ cup olive oil

¼ teaspoon hot sauce

¼ cup lime juice

3 tablespoons Bragg's liquid aminos

2 teaspoon crushed black peppercorns

3 cloves garlic, minced

1 teaspoon cumin

Put all your dressing ingredients in an airtight container and shake until blended.

THOUSAND ISLAND DRESSING

I'm not sure I'd put this dressing on a salad, personally, but you need it for a proper Tofurky Reuben sandwich (page 81). Sometimes it's the details that really matter. When it comes to Reubens, this is very true; without the Thousand Island Dressing, you're just eating a sandwich. But with this dressing, you're part of delicatessen history!

1 cup Vegenaise

1 tablespoon diced fresh parsley

2 tablespoons sweet pickle relish

2 tablespoons Texas Pete Hot Sauce

1 teaspoon diced red onion

½ teaspoon paprika

2 tablespoon nutritional yeast

In a small bowl, mix all ingredients. Store tightly covered in the fridge until you're ready to serve.

GREEK DRESSING

Χόβερκράφτ μου είναι γεμάτο χέλια!*

¼ cup olive oil	½ teaspoon sugar	¼ teaspoon Bragg's liquid aminos
2 tablespoons lemon juice	1½ teaspoons Dijon mustard	¼ teaspoon lemon pepper

Put all the ingredients in a tightly covered container and shake well.

AGAVE DIJON DRESSING

Dan makes the best Agave Dijon Dressing in the world. It's great on salads and over vegan chicken. Just typing this up is making me fall in love with him a little bit more.

½ cup olive oil	¼ teaspoon grated lemon peel	1 clove garlic, minced
⅓ cup agave nectar	1 tablespoon Dijon mustard	1 teaspoon chopped fresh chives
⅓ cup lemon juice	½ teaspoon dark beer	

In a mixing bowl, blend all the ingredients with an electric handheld mixer until smooth. This is a thick salad dressing, so you'll want to serve it with a soup ladle rather than pouring it into your salad dressing bottle.

FRESH HERB VINAIGRETTE

No matter how fancy you like your salads, everyone needs a fresh herb vinaigrette recipe.

⅓ cup olive oil	1 tablespoon chopped fresh oregano leaves	¼ teaspoon Bragg's liquid aminos
¼ cup red wine vinegar	1 teaspoon fresh thyme leaves	1 teaspoon lemon juice
2 tablespoons chopped fresh basil leaves	1 teaspoon sugar	1 clove garlic, minced
		¼ teaspoon crushed black peppercorns

Place all the vinaigrette ingredients in a tight container and shake well.

---

* It means, "My hovercraft is full of eels." I don't speak Greek.

TOASTED SESAME DRESSING

When Dan and I lived in Norfolk, we used to go to a Japanese restaurant named Kotobuki for vegan lobster and avocado rolls that came with unremarkable salads topped with an exceptional sesame salad dressing. I mean, that dressing is so good I've seen people drink it. We loved it so much that we once bribed our waitress to sell us a jelly jar of the stuff to take home. That was before we came up with our own recipe. We live in New York now but can revisit those early years whenever we want with some homemade sushi and this salad dressing recipe.

1 tablespoon plus 2 teaspoons raw sesame seeds

⅓ cup rice vinegar

¼ cup olive oil

1 tablespoon sesame oil

3 tablespoons Bragg's liquid aminos

2 tablespoons apple juice

1 teaspoon ginger paste

Dash of hot sauce

Toast the sesame seeds in a cast-iron skillet or frying pan over medium heat. Using a metal spatula, continually mix the seeds while they are being toasted so that they heat evenly and don't burn. It shouldn't take more than 5 minutes to get them to a soft golden brown.

Put all the ingredients in an airtight container and shake to mix. Shake your dressing before each time you serve to keep your sesame seeds from clumping together.

DIJON VINAIGRETTE

This dressing goes great with a fancy Cobb Salad (page 101), some baby carrots, and everything in between. I love it drizzled over steamed asparagus.

5 tablespoons olive oil

4 tablespoons red wine vinegar

4 tablespoons lemon juice

2 teaspoons grated lemon peel

3 teaspoons Dijon mustard

3 teaspoons vegan Worcestershire sauce

3 cloves garlic, minced

1 teaspoon Bragg's liquid aminos

1 teaspoon crushed black peppercorns

⅛ teaspoon agave nectar

½ teaspoon celery seed

½ teaspoon mustard seed, crushed

Put all the ingredients in a tightly covered container and shake well.

VEGAN RANCH DRESSING

I was never a big ranch-dressing lover before I went vegan. I didn't grow up dipping my pizza or hot wings in it. There were no ranch-dressing fountains at parties I went to. Then one day I discovered Nasoya vegan dressings—and I may have gone a little ranch-crazy. I made dips, sandwiches, and fancy mashed potatoes. I was the most popular gal in town at potlucks and parties. People I knew (vegan or not) were always trying to scam a few bites of my lunches, and hinting at ranch-dressing dips they wanted me to bring on road trips. I thought those days were over when Nasoya discontinued that line of products. But then I started the Betty Crocker Project. This recipe won me over to the Cult of Ranch. I would sign over all my financial wealth to this dressing if it asked. We've made amazing mashed potatoes with it and dipped vegan hot wings and pizzas in it. I think the only thing wrong with this dressing is that I don't have enough things to dip in it and drizzle it over.

½ cup Vegenaise	1 teaspoon lemon zest	½ teaspoon onion powder
½ cup vegan sour cream	1 teaspoon tahini	Pinch of celery seed
¼ cup firm tofu	2 teaspoons nutritional yeast	1 teaspoon fresh dill weed
1 teaspoon fresh parsley, diced	1 ½ teaspoons Bragg's liquid aminos	¼ teaspoon crushed black peppercorns
1 ½ teaspoons dried minced onions	2 cloves garlic, minced	Pinch of ground mustard seeds

Put all your ingredients in your favorite food processor and blend until smooth.

SMOKED PAPRIKA FRENCH DRESSING

French dressing is one of those culinary terms that could mean a number of different things. Some store-bought brands taste like ketchup, in my opinion. But there's also a more savory version that reminds me of a mystery sauce we had over falafels in Budapest. Hungarians know their paprika, and I think it was our visit to this country that developed my healthy respect for this seasoning, which is often either skipped or just used for color. I recommend investing in good smoked paprika for this dressing because it will make a difference.

1 cup olive oil	1 teaspoon prepared yellow mustard	¼ teaspoon garlic powder
¼ cup apple cider vinegar	1 teaspoon smoked paprika	¼ teaspoon celery seed
¼ cup lemon juice	⅛ teaspoon liquid smoke	½ teaspoon agave nectar
2 teaspoons vegan Worcestershire sauce		

Put all the ingredients in a tightly covered container and shake well.

PASTA, BEAN, AND FRUIT SALADS

Many classic salads of this kind are already vegan, and many more are nearly there. But just because this genre of recipes is traditionally vegan-friendly, that doesn't mean we can't enjoy them. Since they're generally served cold and are easy to prepare at home, transport, and serve, these recipes make good lunches to bring to work. They also make large quantities, so you can make a big batch on Sunday and have lunch for a few days. They're also great for potlucks!

VEGAN CHICKEN AND THYME PASTA SALAD

This is a really nice recipe. There's no scorching spiciness, no rich and creamy fake cheese, no hot kitchen afterward—nothing to put a dent in a perfect summer afternoon. This recipe just makes you feel good about spending your Saturday with loved ones and gets along with everyone: Triscuits, iced tea, whatever.

MAKES 4 TO 6 SERVINGS

3 cups cooked whole wheat penne

2 to 3 cups vegan chicken, cooked and diced

2 cups red grapes, cut in half

3 stalks celery, sliced

⅓ cup diced red onion

3 tablespoons olive oil

3 tablespoons fresh thyme

1¼ cups Vegenaise

1 tablespoon agave nectar

1 tablespoon Dijon mustard

2 teaspoons Bragg's liquid aminos

2 tablespoons nutritional yeast

Pinch of celery seed

¼ teaspoon crushed black peppercorns

1 cup raw walnuts, crushed

Vegan Parmesan to sprinkle over the top

Put your cooked penne and vegan chicken in separate covered bowls in the fridge to chill for 2 hours.

In a huge bowl, mix the penne, vegan chicken, grapes, celery, and onion.

In a much smaller bowl, mix the olive oil and thyme. Let that sit for about 15 minutes. Once you can get a faint herbal scent from the oil mixture, pour it over your pasta mixture and toss until completely blended.

In a medium bowl, mix the Vegenaise, agave nectar, Dijon mustard, Bragg's, nutritional yeast, celery seed, and black pepper with an electric handheld mixer until smooth. Pour over your pasta mix and toss until completely blended. Cover and refrigerate for 2 hours. Right before you serve the salad, mix in your walnuts, and sprinkle each bowl with some vegan Parmesan.

Doesn't that sound nice?

3-BEAN SALAD

Is there anything more fun than a Shannon road trip? Really, who doesn't like sing-alongs to the Beastie Boys in the family truckster and hitting the road with your best friend? We attended a coed baby shower near Lexington, Virginia, one weekend in 2010, and we made the most of it and paid a visit to Thomas Jefferson's Monticello. So when we were planning the food for our trip, it seemed only right to bring some traditional American favorites. Of course, the *Betty Crocker Cookbook* has more of these than you can imagine. Pages and pages of them actually...and then *eureka!*—3-Bean Salad! Who doesn't love that? So we hit the road with Tofurky sandwiches, brownies, potato chips, and 3-Bean Salad!

MAKES 4 TO 6 SERVINGS

1 cup Fresh Herb Vinaigrette (page 108)

1 (14-ounce) can green beans, drained

1 (14-ounce) can wax beans, drained

1 (14-ounce) can kidney beans, rinsed and drained

4 medium green onions, chopped

¼ cup chopped fresh parsley

5 stalks celery, chopped

1 tablespoon sugar

2 tablespoons nutritional yeast

3 cloves garlic, minced

Make your Fresh Herb Vinaigrette.

In a bowl, mix all of your ingredients with your Fresh Herb Vinaigrette gently with a large slotted spoon until completely blended. Cover and place in the fridge for 3 hours. Visit your salad to stir a few times while it chills out. Once your sugar dissolves, you're ready to pack up your salad and hit the road!

PEPPER AND LIME GAZPACHO PASTA SALAD

Gazpacho is a classic Iberian vegetable soup traditionally served cold in the summertime. We've taken those classic tomato, onion, and garlic flavors and made them into a pasta salad—also traditionally served cold in the summertime. It's like these two dishes have been secret soul mates this whole time without realizing it...just like Dan and me.*

MAKES 4 TO 6 SERVINGS

1 package rotelli or wheel pasta

3 large Roma tomatoes, diced

1 red bell pepper, diced

1 yellow bell pepper, diced

1 green bell pepper, diced

1 large cucumber, sliced into coins

6 green onions, chopped

½ red onion, diced

¼ cup Spanish olives, pitted and drained

½ cup chopped fresh cilantro

½ cup raw baby spinach leaves

2 celery stalks, diced

2 tablespoons roasted sunflower seeds

1 ripe avocado, peeled, pitted, and diced

1 green Anaheim chili, seeded and diced

1 batch Tomato-Lime Vinaigrette (page 107)

*Gross.

Cook and drain the pasta as directed on the package. Then put your pasta in a mixing bowl, cover with foil, and put in the fridge to chill out for 15 minutes.

Once your pasta is cool, add all the remaining salad ingredients except your Tomato-Lime Vinaigrette and toss until completely blended. Pour the desired amount of Tomato-Lime Vinaigrette over the top and toss again. Serve immediately with Easy Olive Oil Garlic Toast (page 271).

SPINACH WALDORF SALAD

The Waldorf salad was unsurprisingly created at the Waldorf-Astoria hotel in New York City. It seems a little questionable when you look at the ingredients list—apples and mayonnaise? really?—but is actually quite flavorful and delicious.

MAKES 4 TO 6 SERVINGS

½ cup vegan plain yogurt

2 tablespoons Vegenaise

4 tablespoons chopped fresh parsley

2 teaspoons agave nectar

2 tablespoons grated lemon peel

2 pinches of celery seed

1 teaspoon crushed black peppercorns

½ cup raw walnuts, chopped

2 large firm Gala apples, cored and sliced thin

3 celery stalks, chopped

2 tablespoons dried cranberries

1 cup seedless red grapes, cut in half

3 tablespoons lemon juice

4 cups fresh baby spinach leaves

In a small mixing bowl, whisk together your yogurt, Vegenaise, parsley, agave nectar, lemon peel, celery seed, and black pepper.

In another, much larger bowl, toss the walnuts, apples, celery, cranberries, grapes, and lemon juice. Once your fruit is mixed, use a slotted spoon to mix in your yogurt dressing. Cover your bowl with foil and refrigerate for not longer than 10 minutes.

Serve chilled and tossed with your spinach. Sadly, this salad doesn't really keep, so you might want to share with friends.

HEIRLOOM TOMATO, BASIL, AND SHEESE SALAD

This is a classic Italian salad recipe made fancier by using heirloom tomatoes—the fancy-pants indie rock stars of the vegetable world that provide a wide variety of color, texture, and flavor to any recipe.

MAKES 4 TO 6 SERVINGS

5 to 8 heirloom tomatoes in a variety of colors and sizes (around 3 pounds)

1 (8-ounce) package smoked cheddar Sheese

4 tablespoons red wine vinegar

1 teaspoon brown sugar

¾ cup olive oil

1 tablespoon Bragg's liquid aminos

2 teaspoons crushed black peppercorns

2 cloves garlic, minced

1 tablespoon lemon juice

¼ cup fresh basil leaves

2 tablespoons chopped fresh parsley

Cut the tomatoes into 1/2-inch slices or thin wedges. Slice your Sheese into 1/2-inch slices also.

In your always-handy mixing bowl, whisk together the vinegar, brown sugar, and olive oil until thoroughly blended. Then whisk in the Bragg's, black pepper, garlic, and lemon juice.

Now it's time to build your salad! On a pretty serving platter, layer your different colored tomato slices with your Sheese. Sprinkle with basil leaves and parsley, and drizzle with the olive oil dressing. Serve immediately and keep chilled if you can.

CLASSIC DELI POTATO SALAD

Everyone should have a deli-style potato salad recipe—for BBQs and potlucks and to enjoy with your Baked Black Pepper Tofu Reubens (page 82).

MAKES 4 TO 6 SERVINGS

6 medium-size red potatoes

3 to 4 stalks celery, chopped

½ red onion, diced

1¼ cups Vegenaise

1 tablespoon cider vinegar

2 tablespoons yellow mustard

1 teaspoon Bragg's liquid aminos

¼ teaspoon lemon pepper

¼ teaspoon lemon juice

Pinch of celery seed

¼ teaspoon dried dill weed

1 tablespoon chopped fresh parsley

2 tablespoons nutritional yeast

Place the potatoes in a 3-quart pot. Add enough water to cover your potatoes. Cover the pot and heat to boiling. Cook covered for around half an hour. With a slotted spoon, check on the potatoes regularly. Remove your potatoes when they're soft and tender, but before they get mushy.

Once the potatoes are cool enough to handle, cut them into cubes. Toss them in a bowl with your celery and red onions. Let cool.

In a large bowl, mix the Vegenaise, vinegar, mustard, Bragg's, lemon pepper, lemon juice, celery seed, dill weed, parsley, and nutritional yeast. Use a whisk to make sure the mixture is smooth. Once your potatoes and vegetables reach room temperature, mix in the Vegenaise mixture and toss.

Cover and refrigerate for 4 hours. Make sure you serve it chilled … Vegenaise is awesome until it gets warm.

GERMAN POTATO SALAD

I'm not German, but I love Oktoberfests! What's not to love? Polka dancing, pretzels, cheap random imported beers, sauerkraut, beer brats (vegan, of course), and all kinds of other awesomeness. When we were in Budapest, we hid out from a biblical thunderstorm in a German-fest tent (not an Oktoberfest, but it had the same vibe) and watched some pretty amazing accordion-accompanied karaoke. Of course, in Budapest around May Day, festivals aren't hard to find, but it was one of the best nights we had there during one of the best weeks ever. In America, we're used to our potato salad chilled and with more mayo than potato, but in Germany there is a very popular dish called Kartoffelsalat that is actually a potato salad served warm and with bacon. Ours is of course pig-free, but it was intended to capture the spirit of that original dish. Are you ready to start Deutsching it up? Can I get a *"Hölle ja!"* right now?

MAKES 4 TO 6 SERVINGS

8 to 10 small red potatoes, quartered

2 tablespoons olive oil

3 dashes of liquid smoke

½ large red onion, diced

1 tablespoon whole wheat flour

1 teaspoon sugar

½ teaspoon onion powder

1 tablespoon Bragg's liquid aminos

½ teaspoon celery seed

½ teaspoon Dijon mustard (if you want it spicy)

1 teaspoon nutritional yeast

¼ cup dry white wine

1 tablespoon water

½ teaspoon apple cider vinegar

1 tablespoon fresh thyme leaves

⅓ cup raw baby spinach leaves

¼ cup vegan bacon bits

Crushed pink Himalayan salt and crushed black peppercorns

Boil your potatoes till they are tender. Drain and let cool a bit while you make the rest of the dish. It will help firm them up a little before they go in the salad.

Heat the olive oil and liquid smoke in your *geliebt* cast-iron skillet or frying pan over medium heat. Once your oil is hot, toss in the onions and cook until they begin to get tender. Then add the flour, sugar, onion powder, Bragg's, celery seed, Dijon mustard, and nutritional yeast and mix with a spatula until blended.

Add the potatoes and cook, while flipping and mixing occasionally. You want to get an even coating on your potatoes. Be careful so your potatoes don't fall apart.

Add the wine, water, vinegar, thyme, and spinach. Continue to cook while flipping and mixing occasionally. When your liquid is about halfway cooked off, add your vegan bacon bits. Continue to cook until the liquid cooks away enough to make a light sauce.

Give your salad a taste test and toss in a little salt and pepper to your liking!

CURRY VEGAN CHICKEN AND POTATO SALAD

If this salad were in the Olympics, it would be the triple axel, triple toe loop that would have brought the 1980s Eastern European judge to tears. We combined two summertime favorites, chicken salad and potato salad, and added a warm seasoning twist to these classic and often overlooked chilled dishes. We're taking this "side" out of the shadow of those showy pies and veggie burger headliners; just like how *Star Trek: The Next Generation* began as a spin-off of a wildly popular cult classic, but with some tweaks here and there came into its own, and some would argue is superior to the original. You know what I mean... Don't act like you're too cool for *Star Trek*.

MAKES 4 TO 6 SERVINGS

2 cups vegan chicken, defrosted (we recommend Gardein Chick'n Scallopini)

1½ pounds small new potatoes, cubed

2 tablespoons olive oil

2 cloves garlic, minced

1¾ cups Vegenaise

3 stalks celery, diced

½ cup diced red onion

½ cup frozen peas

⅓ cup julienned carrots

¼ cup chopped fresh cilantro

2 teaspoons curry powder

¼ teaspoon cayenne chili powder

½ teaspoon garlic powder

¼ teaspoon onion powder

¼ teaspoon crushed pink Himalayan salt

½ teaspoon poultry seasoning (there are many brands that are vegan; you just need to read some labels)

¼ teaspoon lemon juice

½ teaspoon cumin

¼ teaspoon crushed black peppercorns

1 (14-ounce) can garbanzo beans, drained and rinsed

Smoked paprika to sprinkle over the top

Preheat the oven to 400°F.

In a shallow glass baking dish, toss your vegan chicken, potatoes, and olive oil until the vegan chicken and the potatoes are evenly coated. Bake for 20 minutes, or until your vegan chicken and potatoes are a light golden brown and have a light, crispy crust. Cover with foil and put in the fridge to chill for 30 minutes.

While your vegan chicken and potatoes are chilling, mix the garlic, Vegenaise, celery, onion, peas, carrots, cilantro, curry powder chili powder, garlic powder, onion powder, salt, poultry seasoning, lemon juice, cumin, black pepper, and garbanzo beans in a large bowl, and let them chill for 10 minutes to help blend the flavors.

Then toss your vegan chicken and potatoes into your Vegenaise–garbanzo beans mixture and put it back into the fridge for another 30 minutes.

Sprinkle some smoked paprika over the top and enjoy!

BEEFLESS SESAME NOODLE SALAD

You can serve this summertime favorite hot or cold, at a barbecue or around the dinner table. It's the little black dress of quick and classy dishes.

MAKES 4 SERVINGS

1 batch Toasted Sesame Dressing (page 109)

1 (9-ounce) package Gardein beefless tips or beef seitan, defrosted

Olive oil cooking spray

½ teaspoon onion powder

1 (12-ounce) package whole wheat soba noodles (if you can't find any that are vegan, you can also use angel hair pasta)

2 cups broccoli slaw

1 cup raw snap pea pods

1 (14-ounce) can baby corn, drained

1 (8-ounce) can bamboo shoots, drained

1 (8-ounce) can sliced water chestnuts, drained

2 medium green onions, chopped

1 tablespoon raw sesame seeds

Make your Toasted Sesame Dressing first.

Preheat the oven to 350°F. Place your vegan beef in a glass baking dish. Spray on a light, even coating of olive oil and sprinkle with the onion powder. With a spoon, turn your vegan beef a few times to makes sure it gets a nice coating. Bake uncovered for 15 to 20 minutes and remove from the oven when your vegan beef is browned and a little crispy on the edges.

Cook your soba noodles per the instructions on the package. Just remember—they cook really fast, so keep an eye on them. When your noodles are cooked and drained but still hot, put them in a large mixing bowl and add the broccoli slaw, snap pea pods, baby corn, bamboo shoots, water chestnuts, and vegan beef, and toss. Then mix in your Toasted Sesame Dressing and gently toss with two forks. The hot noodles will heat the vegetables and dressing a little and help the flavors mix. Now, if you want to serve it cold, cover your salad and put it in the fridge for 15 to 20 minutes. Be sure to revisit your salad a few times and remix it to keep your dressing from sitting at the bottom.

Before you serve, mix in the green onions and sesame seeds.

BLACK PEPPER TOFU MACARONI SALAD

Dan brought this recipe in for a spontaneous Squirrel Appreciation Day potluck at Peta2 while he was the director there. As always, there was a pretty impressive spread ranging from spring rolls to chocolate cake from *Peta's Vegan College Cookbook*. Now, this had started as a veganized version of Betty's Macaroni Salad for the Betty Crocker Project, but as it progressed, it became more Annie Dream Lunch than anything else.

MAKES 8 TO 10 SERVINGS

1 teaspoon crushed black peppercorns	1 package extrafirm tofu, drained	¼ cup sweet pickle relish
3 tablespoons olive oil	1 package elbow macaroni	1 cup Vegenaise
3 tablespoons lemon juice	¾ cup frozen peas	2 tablespoons nutritional yeast
Dash of liquid smoke	1 red onion, diced	1 teaspoon celery seed
2 cloves garlic, minced	½ cup shredded Daiya vegan cheddar cheese or your favorite vegan cheese	2 tablespoons Tony Chachere's Creole seasoning
3 tablespoons plus 1 teaspoon Bragg's liquid aminos	4 stalks celery, diced	1 teaspoon garlic powder

In a shallow dish, combine the black pepper, olive oil, 2 tablespoons of the lemon juice, the liquid smoke, garlic, and Bragg's. Cut your tofu into pieces that are as even as possible—so they all bake evenly. Then marinate your tofu in the oil-pepper mix for 1 hour.

Preheat the oven to 400°F.

Cover a cookie sheet with foil and place your marinated tofu slices on there about an inch apart. Keep your leftover marinade. Bake your tofu for 20 minutes, then flip and bake for another 20 minutes. You want the tofu to be crispy and golden brown.

Cook the macaroni per the instructions on the package. Once you drain your cooked macaroni, gently mix in your frozen peas with the hot pasta. The steam will heat your peas. Put your macaroni and peas in a large mixing bowl, cover, and put in the fridge.

After your tofu has been baking for 20 minutes, take your macaroni and peas from the fridge and gently stir in your red onion, vegan cheese, celery, pickle relish, and leftover marinade. Once that is mixed, cover your bowl and return it to the fridge. Once your tofu is done baking, let it cool for around 10 minutes and then cut into bite-size pieces.

Then take your macaroni mixture from the fridge and gently stir in your tofu pieces. In a small bowl, whisk together the Vegenaise, the remaining 1 tablespoon lemon juice, and the nutritional yeast, celery seed, Creole seasoning, and garlic powder. Then mix the macaroni and tofu mix with your seasoned Vegenaise, cover with foil, and chill in the fridge for 45 minutes. Then you're good to go kick ass and appreciate some squirrels.

HEM'S FRUIT SALAD

When I saw the first ingredient in this recipe I admit I was immediately suspicious. Adding sugar to fruit seemed unnecessary. Fruit is sugar. But I have to admit the dressing was tasty…in particular on the mangoes and berries. It added just a touch more sweetness and a little spike of sour. The sugar and lime juice also work some kind of chemistry magic that keeps this salad fresh for hours!

MAKES 4 TO 6 SERVINGS

¾ cup sugar	1 cup cut pineapple	Handful of fresh raspberries
¼ cup water	2 Red Delicious apples, sliced	Handful of fresh blueberries
¼ cup key lime juice	1 orange, peeled and sectioned	Handful of fresh blackberries
2 tablespoons tequila	1 mango, sliced	1 teaspoon grated lime peel

Heat the sugar and water in a saucepan. Bring to a boil and then reduce the heat. Simmer uncovered for 2 minutes, stirring continually until the sugar is dissolved. Remove from the heat and add the lime juice and tequila. Let the lime juice dressing sit until it reaches room temperature. Cover and refrigerate for 2 hours—or if you are in a hurry, just until it's cool.

Mix all your fruit in a large serving bowl.

Stir the lime peel into the cooled lime juice dressing.

Pour your lime juice dressing over your fruit mix and *carefully* toss the fruit till it is evenly covered with dressing.

PEACH, PLUM, AND POMEGRANATE SALAD

One of my very favorite souvenirs from our trips to Los Angeles came from a trip to the farmers' market with my friend and fellow food blogger Anjali. They were adorable little jars of sugar-free pomegranate jam from the Sherrill Orchards booth. I had planned on using this jam to combine two of my very favorite things: pomegranates and toast (the perfect fruit and the perfect vehicle for delicious sauces and spreads). But when I came home, I found a recipe that was waiting for the perfect jam* to come around.

MAKES 4 TO 6 SERVINGS

3 fresh plums, sliced and pitted	½ cup raw walnuts, crushed	1 tablespoon apple juice
3 fresh peaches, sliced and pitted	¼ cup of your favorite jam (pomegranate or raspberry or even apple butter)	1 tablespoon lime juice
Seeds from 1 pomegranate		1 tablespoon olive oil

In a large bowl, mix the plums, peaches, pomegranate seeds, and walnuts with salad tongs. In a small bowl, whisk together the jam, apple juice, lime juice, and olive oil, and drizzle it over the top of the fruit. Then toss the fruit and dressing.

---

*You don't need pomegranate jam to make this recipe, but you do need a good jam—one with not too much sugar.

Chapter Four
DINNER ENTRÉES

SAUCES AND CONDIMENTS 282

It's ironic (actually ironic, not pop-culture, Alanis Morissette ironic) that in the original French, the word "entrée" refers to the dish served *before* the main course—what we Americans would refer to as the "appetizer" or the Brits would refer to as a "starter."

Until recently, vegan entrées in the American sense usually resembled entrées in the French sense—salads, soups, pastas, and other dishes that, while delicious, many people would view as a side rather than a main course. In November, vegans are often asked, "But what will you eat for Thanksgiving?" in a panicked tone; a common joke is to say "everything but the turkey." But unfortunately, that was often the perception of a vegan diet—an eternity of side dishes.

There's nothing wrong with making a meal out of sides. Dan has been known to make entire meals out of French fries alone. But when you are trying to be like the iconic image of Betty Crocker and serve your family a home-cooked meal, you want a *pièce de résistance*—that piping-hot, fresh-from-the-oven dish that makes everyone around the table say "whoa!" when the lid comes off. That's an entrée.

It's not to say that entrées have to be "meaty." But the advent of versatile mock meat brands like Tofurky and Gardein has made crafting traditional, hearty, vegan entrées a whole lot easier. Now we can have our own roasts, our own barbecues, our own sausages and chicken wings and hamburgers.

A bowl of Cheerios can be dinner—but it can never be an entrée. These recipes will fill that void in your vegan diet, so that you never have to make the "everything but" joke again.

MEAT, POULTRY, AND FISH

In the dying words of Spock to Kirk in *Star Trek II: The Wrath of Khan*: "I have been … and always shall be … your friend. Live long … and prosper."

That's how most vegans feel about animals. Sweet, doe-eyed cows; curious, fluttering chickens; and playful, intelligent pigs: just some of the billions of animals who are raised and slaughtered every year for food. For years, vegans have found ways around this by finding ways to substitute meat and dairy products in our meals while reaping the benefits of a healthier diet.

It's been proven for years that a meat-based diet is directly linked to the three greatest killers in the United States—heart disease, diabetes, and obesity-linked diseases. Recently, food technology finally caught up to our imaginations and created mock meats that made compassionate versions of classic dishes even closer to the originals we remember. These recipes prove that going vegan has nothing to do with sacrifice…in fact, no one needs to sacrifice at all.

Are you ready to mock?

CRABBY CAKES

Until I lived in Virginia, I wasn't aware of what can only be called the Chesapeake Bay Crab Cake Phenomenon. It's impossible to ignore all the crab-themed items littering every store along this coastline. Aprons, cereal bowls, utensils of any kind, Beanie Babies, lollipops, mechanical claws for picking up things less than 2 feet away…whatever the kitschy knickknack, you can find one with a smiling cartoon crab on it, eager to be eaten. Disturbing doesn't even begin to describe it. It's like those BBQ joints with the happy pig on the sign. In what bizarre mind does that make sense? This recipe will help you put all that aside and just enjoy this classic mid-Atlantic dish. Don't forget to make a batch of Vegan Tartar Sauce (see page 282).

MAKES 6 TO 7 CRAB CAKES

2 slices whole wheat bread

1/3 cup Vegenaise

1 tablespoon Ener-G egg replacer (just the powder, not made per the instructions on the box)

1 teaspoon ground mustard

1/4 teaspoon crushed sea salt

1/8 teaspoon lemon pepper

1/4 teaspoon Tony Chachere's Creole seasoning

2 green onions, chopped

3/4 cup Match vegan crab

1/4 cup dry bread crumbs (we used Old Bay Dip & Crisp Seasoned Bread Crumbs for a little extra flavor)

2 tablespoons olive oil

Put your slices of whole wheat bread in a blender or food processor until they're nothing but crumbs.

In a bowl, whisk together the Vegenaise and Ener-G egg replacer. Stir in the whole wheat bread crumbs you just made, ground mustard, salt, lemon pepper, Creole seasoning, green onions, and vegan crab. Shape the mixture into 6 to 7 patties about the size of your palms. Put your dry bread crumbs in a shallow bowl.

Coat each patty with dry bread crumbs.

In your infamous little cast-iron skillet or frying pan, heat the olive oil over medium heat. Once the oil is hot, place the patties in the skillet. This is important: don't crowd your patties. They'll stick together or break apart if you bump them while flipping the other patties—so give them room. Cook the patties till they are golden brown on each side.

SWEET CHILI AND CUMIN TOFURKY WITH PICO DE GALLO QUINOA STUFFING

Every vegan has her favorite way to cook Tofurky. Some of us are sentimental traditionalists, looking to re-create childhood memories of our mother's roast turkey; others of us have the spirit of Magellan in our hearts. These brave women are constantly on the lookout for something new to do with this vegan institution that used to be available only at Thanksgiving but now can be found year-round. Look no further, my adventurous friends—this is the Tofurky recipe you're looking for.

SERVES 4 TO 6 HUNGRY VEGANS

1 Tofurky or Match Premium Vegan Stuffed Holiday Roast, defrosted

2 tablespoons brown sugar

1 teaspoon smoked paprika

1 teaspoon chili powder

1 teaspoon cumin

½ teaspoon yellow mustard

1 teaspoon hot sauce

¼ teaspoon ginger paste

1 clove garlic, minced

1 teaspoon Bragg's liquid aminos

3 tablespoons olive oil or melted margarine

PICO DE GALLO QUINOA STUFFING

3 Roma tomatoes, diced

1 fresh jalapeño, diced

1 tablespoon diced red onion

2 tablespoons chopped fresh cilantro

2 teaspoons lime juice

1 teaspoon grated lime peel

½ teaspoon crushed pink Himalayan salt

¼ cup frozen corn

1 cup quinoa, cooked and still warm

Preheat the oven to 400°F.

Make sure your Tofurky is completely defrosted. Slice off one end with a seam about an inch in. You want to be able to scoop out the inside, so make sure you've cut in far enough to get at the stuffing.

Scoop out all the stuffing into a bowl. Mix all the Tofurky stuffing with the additional Pico de Gallo Quinoa Stuffing ingredients. Cover with foil so that the warm quinoa can defrost the frozen corn.

Whisk together the brown sugar, paprika, chili powder, cumin, mustard, hot sauce, ginger paste, garlic, and Bragg's in a bowl large enough to hold the Tofurky.

Restuff your Tofurky with as much quinoa stuffing as you can. There will be about ⅓ to ½ cup of stuffing that won't fit inside the Tofurky. Replace the end of the Tofurky you cut off and secure using toothpicks. Make sure

the tips of the toothpicks are still hanging outside the Tofurky so they can be removed later. Place your reconstructed Tofurky into the spice bowl. Using your hands, gently rub the Tofurky with spices until it is completely covered with an even coating.

Place your spice-rubbed Tofurky into a casserole dish, then drizzle 2 tablespoons of the olive oil or melted margarine over the top. Bake for 15 to 20 minutes, or until the outside of the Tofurky has a crispy browned crust. Then pile the rest of the stuffing around the Tofurky, and drizzle the remaining 1 tablespoon olive oil over the Tofurky.

Bake for 3 minutes, or until the stuffing is hot.

I recommend serving with some Cheezy Jalapeño Corn Bread (page 327).

CHEEZY CRUNCHY VEGAN CHICKEN STRIPS

Hope this isn't too braggy, but these vegan chicken strips are even better than squirrels and kittens hugging.

MAKES 8 TO 10 CHICKEN STRIPS

Olive oil cooking spray

2 cups Eco-Planet Non-Dairy Cheddar Crackers, slightly crushed

½ cup shredded Daiya vegan cheddar cheese or your favorite vegan cheese

¼ cup nutritional yeast

2 cups Match vegan chicken, defrosted and formed into 8 to 10 equal fingers (You can use another kind of vegan chicken, but because most other

products are already formed, the "cheesy" crackers won't stick as well or coat as evenly.)

Preheat the oven to 400°F. Spray a cookie sheet with olive oil cooking spray.

In a large resealable plastic bag, mix the crushed crackers, vegan cheese, and nutritional yeast. Add the chicken strips to the bag one at a time, seal the bag, and shake. Before removing from the bag, gently press the cracker coating into the chicken strip. Place the cracker-crusted chicken strips in a single layer on the cookie sheet. Make sure they aren't touching.

Bake uncovered for around 10 minutes. The larger the strip, the longer it will take to cook, so if you went big, give them a little longer in the oven. Remove when the crackers begin to brown.

You'll want to serve these tasty strips with a side of BBQ sauce and some fries. A basket of fries is the natural habitat for vegan chicken strips.

CHICKEN-FREE POTPIE

This is one of the first dinners I made for Dan when we moved in together. Although years have passed since then, and we've had literally hundreds of meals together, he still loves this dinner the most. Whenever I make it, it takes us back to when we were still pretty new to this whole "being more than friends" thing and had that new-love rush.[*] Ever combine a little romantic nostalgia with a solid "love of your life" situation? It's pretty great. I recommend it. I'm also pretty sure this recipe is what convinced Dan to give me a forever home.

MAKES 4 PERSONAL PIES OR 1 LARGE PIE

POTPIE FILLING
2 to 3 small red potatoes

2 tablespoons olive oil

Dash of liquid smoke

2 cups of your favorite vegan chicken, cut into bite-size pieces

1 batch All-American Vegan Gravy (page 290)

3 celery stalks, chopped

1 cup frozen green beans

1 cup frozen peas and carrots

WHOLE WHEAT PIECRUST
2 cups whole wheat flour, plus more to flour surfaces

1 teaspoon crushed pink Himalayan salt

⅔ cup plus 2 tablespoons vegetable shortening

4 to 6 tablespoons cold water

Preheat the oven to 375°F. Bake the red potatoes for 45 minutes. Once baked, cut them into small cubes. Hold them with an oven mitt so you don't burn your fingers.

Now make your dough for the crust. In a medium bowl, mix the flour and salt. Cut the shortening in; then use a pastry blender to mix. You want your dough to become little clumps that look like small peas. Sprinkle in the cold water 1 tablespoon at a time, using a large fork to mix. You want the dough to be moist but not wet.

With your hands, roll the dough into a ball inside the bowl. On a floured surface, roll your dough ball out with a floured roller. Try to keep the crust even; you don't want some areas to be thinner than others. Gently roll the flattened dough up into plastic wrap and refrigerate for 45 minutes.

Now prepare the filling. In your beloved cast-iron skillet or frying pan, heat the olive oil and liquid smoke over medium heat. Once the oil is hot, cook the vegan chicken in the skillet until it is golden brown and has crispy edges. Remove from the heat and set aside on a plate.

---

[*] Some might even call it a Potpie Time Machine.

In the same skillet, make your All-American Vegan Gravy. Heat until it thickens and starts to boil.

Stir in the celery, green beans, potato cubes, vegan chicken, and peas and carrots, and turn the heat down to a simmer.

Once your dough has chilled, remove it from the fridge and unroll it. You want the dough to be firm but still pliable, so if it's crumbly when you remove it from the fridge, press the cracks to fix them and then let it warm a little until it's more pliable.

Place your pie or casserole dishes upside down on the crust to give you a guide to cut around. Leave an extra ½ to 1 inch around the edges to seal the pies.

Once each crust top is cut, cut a small X or hole in the center. I like to use a mini heart-shaped cookie cutter.

Preheat the oven to 425°F.

Fill your casserole dishes three-quarters of the way with the vegan chicken and gravy filling mixture; then carefully place the crust on top. Gently press the dough around the edges of the dishes to seal the top. You can put a bit more vegan chicken and gravy filling mix in the dishes if you're okay with some potential overflow.

Bake for 30 to 40 minutes. You'll want to pull the pies out of the oven once the edges of your crust are a golden brown. Let your pies cool for around 10 minutes and then serve with a side of love songs. We recommend a nice Journey power ballad.

THE MOCK STARS

Newly vegan Bettys might find this list of the most common forms of meatless proteins helpful:

Seitan Also known as wheat gluten and wheat meat, seitan is made from water-processed wheat and was first developed in China by Buddhist monks looking for a substitute for meat in their diets. Since then, seitan has become a vegan institution. It holds flavors and texture better than most soy-based meat alternatives and can be used to replace beef, chicken, and duck. I've even seen vegan horse seitan in France.

Tofu Some folks call tofu "bean curd." I'm not sure why they would do that to poor tofu. I mean, have you ever heard anything that sounds less appetizing than "bean curd"? Okay, maybe "nutritional yeast." But that's just the beginning of how poor tofu has been made into a villain or a punch line over the years. Never mind that tofu can be a significant source of protein, iron, calcium, and magnesium while being easy to season and prepare. Oh no, let's just makes jokes about how it's white and squishy when raw ... hmmm. That actually sounds a lot like chicken meat. I mean, would you just pop a chicken breast in the microwave and call it delicious? No. You'd season it and cook it just right. Tofu's no different, except that it's way more versatile than chicken meat and can also used to make delicious baked goods, quiches, salads, scrambles, even a fried egg (page 23). Tofu is a vegan's BFF.

Tempeh This traditional soy product originated in Indonesia, only to become the leading ingredient in vegan Reuben sandwiches all over the world. Seriously, if I polled everyone who'd tried tempeh only once or twice, I bet 7 out of 10 of them would have had it in a Reuben sandwich. But tempeh is more than just a sandwich filling—tempeh is a pretty remarkable soy-based product made using a natural fermentation process that binds the soybeans into brick-like cakes that can be flavored or smoked. We like our tempeh in tacos (page 144), but of course you can always use it in a Reuben sandwich.

BEER-BATTERED MARINATED TOFU

Sometimes you get just what you need. The other morning I woke up and thought: "I'd love to watch a detective story that has something to do with submarines while I drink my coffee today." And you know what? I stumbled across a random episode of a CSI-type of show with Mark Harmon as a Navy FBI/police-type person who … guess what? Solved the Mystery of the Sailor Swap on a submarine! The next day I woke up and thought: "I think I need more Richard Dreyfuss movies in my life." And *Jaws* was on! Yes, I know, it's like an X-File. That night, I needed to come up with a new plan for dinner because my vegan chicken wasn't defrosted … and there she was. A forgotten little package of extrafirm tofu hiding behind some celery and a bag of baby carrots. She waved and said, "Remember me? You were going to make me into vegan fish sticks!" I smiled and thought, "I can do better than that, my little friend." Beer-Battered Marinated Tofu, you are my dream date. Don't forget the Vegan Tartar Sauce on page 282.

MAKES 6 FILLETS

- 2 packets miso soup, made per the packet instructions
- 1 package extrafirm tofu, drained and pressed
- 1¼ teaspoons vegan Worcestershire sauce
- 4 cups olive oil (you need enough to submerge your tofu fillets when you fry them)
- 3 to 4 tablespoons vegan Bisquick mix
- ½ cup stout beer
- 1 tablespoon applesauce
- ½ teaspoon lemon pepper
- ½ teaspoon Tony Chachere's Creole seasoning

Chill your prepared miso soup in the fridge until it reaches at least room temperature.

Cut your block of tofu into 6 triangle slices with a serrated knife to create a "fish" texture to the sides. These are your fillets.

Mix your chilled miso soup and vegan Worcestershire sauce in a casserole dish that's large enough to hold the fillets, but not so large you won't be able to cover the fillets with the miso marinade. Put your fillets in the marinade and let them hang out for 10 to 15 minutes, turning a few times to make sure they get an even flavor.

Heat your olive oil in a 4-quart Dutch oven or large soup pot over medium heat.

In a shallow dish, put 3 to 4 tablespoons of Bisquick mix.

In a medium-size bowl, mix the beer, applesauce, lemon pepper, and Creole seasoning with a hand mixer until smooth. If the mixture is too pasty, you can add a dash of beer, but not more than 1 tablespoon.

Once your see your oil start to bubble, it's time to deep-fry your fillets.

Breading your fillets can lead to a big mess, but here's a trick to keep your bowls from getting contaminated. Pick one hand to be powder and one to be batter. Using your powder hand, put one of the fillets into the Bisquick mix, and using only that hand, cover the fillet with Bisquick. You want to tap it a bit to get a good cover, and make sure you get the sides.

Then, still with your powder hand, remove the fillet from the Bisquick mix and put it into the beer batter. Be careful not to get any beer batter on your powder hand.

Now, using your batter hand, flip and cover the fillet with a healthy amount of beer batter. Not healthy as in good for you; healthy as in "That girl's got a healthy backside."

Now, using a slotted spoon, remove your beer-battered fillet and place it, very carefully, in the hot oil. Be careful to not let your fillet touch the side of the pot. Fry the fillet for no more than 5 minutes.

Using your slotted spoon, remove your fillet. Be careful to not break your crusty, golden-delicious batter when you're pulling your fillet out. Place on a plate with some paper towels to soak up any extra oil.

Before you fry your next fillet, use your slotted spoon to remove any bits of fried batter that have fallen off the previous fillet, so they don't stick to the next one.

Repeat this process for each fillet and enjoy the rest of your beer until you're all done.

Serve with Vegan Tartar Sauce (page 282), and maybe some corn on the cob … maybe some more beer. Just enjoy.

BIG EASY JAMBALAYA

Readers of our blog will know that we spent our honeymoon in New Orleans. While Cajun cuisine isn't known for being traditionally vegan-friendly, we ate like royalty on that trip, enjoying some of the best meals of our lives. We got the inside scoop on why New Orleans has such a wealth of vegan food from the bartender of a locals-only drinking establishment that never closes (literally—he showed us how there was no functioning lock on the front door). Apparently, it's not the tourists demanding all those vegan options at pubs and restaurants around the Big Easy—it's the new generation of young, hip service employees drawn to the city as its post-Katrina tourism industry began to develop. These "new locals" came looking to become a part of a great American city's rebirth, and they brought their love of vegan food with them. We brought ours, too. This jambalaya is inspired by that experience.

MAKES 4 TO 6 SERVINGS

3 tablespoons olive oil

Dash of liquid smoke

1 cup Match vegan Italian sausage, rolled into meatball-ish chunks, or 1 package Tofurky Italian Sausages, cut into coins

1 red onion, diced

½ cup vegan shrimp, defrosted (we recommend May Wah shrimp balls cut into fourths)

2 tomatoes, diced

1 green bell pepper, diced

½ tablespoon chopped fresh parsley

1½ cups Better Than Bouillon vegetable broth, made per the instructions on the package

1 teaspoon fresh thyme leaves

1 teaspoon Tony Chachere's Creole seasoning

¼ teaspoon Bragg's liquid aminos

2 pinches of chili powder

1 cup tomato sauce

2 splashes of your favorite beer

¼ teaspoon red wine

Louisiana hot sauce (we used 3 dashes)

2 cups cooked brown rice

In your cast-iron skillet *beaux* or frying pan, heat the olive oil and liquid smoke over medium heat. Brown the vegan Italian sausage and red onion in the heated oil. Once the sausage is crispy and the onions are tender, remove them from the heated skillet and set aside.

Then throw the vegan shrimp, tomatoes, bell pepper, parsley, broth, thyme, Cajun seasoning, Bragg's, chili powder, tomato sauce, beer, red wine, hot sauce to taste, and brown rice into your skillet, mix, and simmer until it starts to boil. While you're waiting for it to boil, stir the jambalaya to keep it from sticking to the sides. Once it starts to boil, mix in the sausage and onions. Remove from heat immediately.

Serve with a tall glass of sweet tea or a cold beer.

BUFFALO TOFU STEAKS

This classic chicken preparation is the best thing to come out of Buffalo, New York, since Mark Twain. If you grew up with those winters, you'd crave something hot and spicy too. Since classic Buffalo wings are about as far from being vegan as you can get (I mean, you've literally got a bone in your mouth), vegans seem to relish making our own Buffalo-style recipes. These Buffalo tofu "steaks" are great as snacks for the big game and demand an ice-cold beer to wash them down with.

MAKES 4 STEAKS

Olive oil cooking spray

2 tablespoons olive oil

2 teaspoons hot sauce

2 (16-ounce) packages extrafirm tofu, each block cut into 4 pieces (steaks)

BUFFALO HOT SAUCE

2 tablespoons molasses

1 teaspoon garlic powder

¼ cup margarine

1 teaspoon vegan Worcestershire sauce

½ cup hot sauce (vinegar based to get the real bite)

1 (14-ounce) can tomato sauce

1 teaspoon bourbon

2 dashes of liquid smoke

¼ teaspoon chili powder

1 tablespoon Bragg's liquid aminos

Preheat the oven to 400°F.

Spray a glass baking dish with olive oil cooking spray. In a small bowl, whisk together the olive oil and hot sauce. Brush your tofu steaks with the olive oil mixture and place in the glass baking dish so that they don't touch. Bake for 5 minutes. Flip the tofu steaks and brush them with another coating of the olive oil mixture. Put back into the oven and bake for another 5 minutes.

In a small saucepan, whisk together all the sauce ingredients and heat over medium heat. Once the sauce begins to bubble, reduce the heat to a simmer. Pour 1 cup of Buffalo Hot Sauce over the tofu steaks after they've baked for 10 minutes. Flip them a few times to make sure they get an even coating. Put the tofu steaks back in the oven and bake for another 15 minutes; then flip them over and put them back into the oven for another 10 to 20 minutes. Pull them out when they have a nice coating and crispy edges. Save the rest of the Buffalo Hot Sauce to drizzle over the top of the steaks to make them saucier.

AVOCADO AND TEQUILA STEAKLESS TACOS

Is anything better than avocado? Nothing immediately comes to mind. Avocados hold a special place in the heart of vegans everywhere—not just in California—because they hit those fatty, creamy palate notes that people generally identify with fancy cheeses. Olives can serve a similar purpose. The avocado is a great example of how while mock meats and cheeses are wonderful, sometimes you can replace the flavors and textures of meat and cheeses with other "natural" foods. Of course, these tacos have avocados *and* mock meats—the best of both worlds. Plus tequila. What more could you possibly want?

MAKES 8 TACOS

2 large Roma tomatoes, diced

½ red onion, diced

1 ripe avocado, peeled, pitted, and chopped

⅓ cup whole-kernel corn (either defrosted frozen or from a can)

8 tablespoons lime juice

½ teaspoon crushed pink Himalayan salt

1 batch Salsa Verde (page 433)

1½ teaspoons tequila

1 fresh jalapeño, chopped

1 tablespoon cumin

2 teaspoon Bragg's liquid aminos

2 teaspoons hot sauce

2 cloves garlic, minced

2 packages Gardein beefless tips or beef seitan, defrosted

8 (6-inch) corn tortillas

In a mixing bowl, mix the tomatoes, onions, avocado, corn, 4 tablespoons of the lime juice, and salt with a large spoon. Cover with foil and put in the fridge to chill out a little bit while you make the rest of your meal.

Make your Salsa Verde and put it in the fridge next to the avocado mixture to hang out with the mix above.

Put the remaining 4 tablespoons lime juice, tequila, jalapeño, cumin, Bragg's, hot sauce, and garlic in a large mixing bowl and blend with a whisk. Pour this mixture into a heavy-duty resealable plastic bag and reshake to keep it blended. Add the vegan beef to the bag, seal the bag, and shake to cover the vegan beef completely.

Turn on the broiler or set the oven to broil. Use a slotted spoon to remove the vegan beef from the marinade. Place the vegan beef on a rack in a broiler pan. Place the beef 4 to 6 inches from the heat and broil for about 10 minutes, or until the beef gets lightly crisped edges. Be sure to turn your vegan beef at least once to make sure it cooks evenly. When you pull your vegan beef from the broiler, let it cool slightly so that you can eat your tacos without burning your face off.

Warm the tortillas in the oven as directed on the package. Serve your vegan beef, avocado mixture, and Salsa Verde in separate bowls with your warm tortillas and let folks make 'em as they eat 'em.

MAPLE-PECAN-CRUSTED VEGAN CHICKEN

Sweet and nutty ... it's like wrapping your dinner in a romantic comedy.

MAKES 2 TO 4 SERVINGS

2 tablespoons margarine

¼ teaspoon crushed pink Himalayan salt

¼ teaspoon brown sugar

¼ teaspoon ground ginger

¼ teaspoon olive oil

2 tablespoons maple syrup

⅓ cup crushed pecans

2 cups of your favorite vegan chicken

In a cast-iron skillet, melt your margarine over medium heat and then blend in the salt, brown sugar, ginger, and olive oil. Stir in the maple syrup and pecan pieces and turn the heat down to low. Once your syrup begins to bubble, add your vegan chicken. Flip a few times to get an even covering and then let your vegan chicken simmer in the maple syrup mixture.

Cook for 2 to 3 minutes and then flip your vegan chicken and cook for another 2 minutes. You'll notice that your kitchen will start to smell amazing. You'll know your vegan chicken is done when you have a golden brown crust of crushed pecans. You might have to flip it a few times to brown evenly.

CAJUN BLACKENED TOFU

This recipe is freakin' hotter than the flames of Orodruin. Please don't use it to make one ring to rule them all and in the darkness bind them.

MAKES 4 SERVINGS

1 (16-ounce) package extrafirm tofu, drained and cut into 10 strips

Olive oil cooking spray

¼ teaspoon red pepper flakes

½ teaspoon freshly ground black peppercorns

1 teaspoon cumin

1 teaspoon Tony Chachere's Creole seasoning

¼ teaspoon smoked paprika

4 lemon wedges

Put your tofu in a lasagna dish and spray with olive oil cooking spray on both sides. In a shallow dish, mix the red pepper flakes, black pepper, cumin, creole seasoning and paprika. Put your tofu in the seasoning mix and flip a few times to make sure it gets a nice even coating.

Spray your cast-iron skillet or frying pan with olive oil cooking spray and heat over medium heat. Toss your tofu in the skillet and cook for a minute on each side. Then flip a few times until the edges are crispy.

Serve with lemon wedges to squeeze over the top.

VEGAN SHRIMP SCAMPI

They might not be the cutest vegan shrimp on the market, but May Wah shrimp balls are, in my opinion, the best. They're bite-size, don't get mushy, and have the perfect subtle fishy flavor and texture. Really, the only thing I'd change about this product is the name—shrimp balls.

MAKES 2 TO 4 SERVINGS

1 package whole wheat spaghetti or angel hair pasta

3 tablespoons olive oil

1 cup vegan shrimp, defrosted (we recommend May Wah shrimp balls cut in half)

1 teaspoon margarine

1 tablespoon chopped fresh parsley, plus a little extra for garnish

3 tablespoons lemon juice

¼ teaspoon crushed sea salt

2 green onions, chopped

3 cloves garlic, minced

1 tablespoon dry white wine

Vegan Parmesan, nutritional yeast, and freshly ground black peppercorns to sprinkle over the top

Make the pasta per the instructions on the package.

In your cast-iron skillet or deepest frying pan, heat the olive oil over medium heat. Add the vegan shrimp and turn it with a spatula until your vegan shrimp is completely coated. Once your vegan shrimp reaches the desired tenderness, add the margarine, parsley, lemon juice, salt, green onions, garlic, and white wine. Mix with the vegan shrimp until the green onions are caramelized and the margarine melts.

Serve the vegan shrimp and sauce over your pasta. Sprinkle vegan Parmesan and nutritional yeast over the top, followed by chopped parsley and ground black pepper.

ARTICHOKE NEWBURG

You may have never heard of Lobster Newburg, but it doesn't really matter, because Artichoke Newburg is great in a way that'll make you forget that this dish was initially intended to include those lovely crustaceans.

MAKES 6 SERVINGS

¼ cup margarine

3 tablespoons flour

1 teaspoon Bragg's liquid aminos

½ teaspoon ground mustard seed

¼ teaspoon cayenne pepper

½ teaspoon freshly ground black peppercorns

¼ teaspoon nutritional yeast

2 cups soy milk

2 (14-ounce) cans artichoke hearts, drained

1 (15-ounce) can garbanzo beans, drained and rinsed

⅓ cup raw baby spinach leaves

2 tablespoons sherry

6 cups cooked brown rice

6 lemon wedges

In a Dutch oven or large saucepan, melt your margarine over medium heat. Once your margarine is completely melted, use a whisk to blend in the flour, Bragg's, mustard seed, cayenne pepper, black pepper, and nutritional yeast. It will make a thick paste. Then whisk in the soy milk until smooth. Remove from the heat once it begins to bubble.

Add artichoke hearts, beans, spinach, and sherry and heat to a boil. Cover and simmer for no more than 1 minute.

Serve over rice with lemon wedges to squeeze over the top.

CHAMPAGNE AND HAZELNUT RISOTTO WITH VEGAN CHICKEN

This is a superfancy, supereasy dinner that anyone can use to turn any night into a romantic date night—or maybe just a *special treat for yourself* kind of night. Whatever your relationship status is, this dish also gives you an excuse to open a bottle of champagne—which in and of itself is reason to celebrate.

MAKES 4 TO 6 SERVINGS

Olive oil cooking spray

2 cups vegan chicken, defrosted and cut into strips (we recommend Gardein Chick'n Scallopini)

2 tablespoons margarine

1 red onion, diced

1 cup uncooked Arborio or risotto rice

1½ cups champagne

2 cups Better Than Bouillon vegan chicken broth, made per the instructions on the package

1 clove garlic, minced

2 teaspoons herbes de Provence

1 cup raw baby spinach leaves

1 tablespoon crushed hazelnuts

1 tablespoon nutritional yeast

½ teaspoon freshly ground black peppercorns

Chopped fresh parsley

Preheat the oven to 350°F.

Spray a glass baking dish with olive oil cooking spray. Arrange your vegan chicken in the glass dish in an even layer. Spray another coating of olive oil cooking spray over the vegan chicken. Bake for 20 minutes until golden brown and crispy.

In your favorite Dutch oven or large saucepan, melt the margarine over medium heat. Once your margarine is melted, toss in the red onion and mix. Cook until your onion is tender. Toss in the rice and mix. Pour in ½ cup of the champagne and mix. Cook uncovered, stirring frequently. Once your champagne is absorbed, add ½ cup of the broth. Continue to cook uncovered,

stirring frequently. Once the broth is absorbed, add another ½ cup of broth, continuing to cook and stir frequently. I think you see where this is going. You're going to repeat this process until you're out of broth. Then switch to the remaining champagne and continue the cooking and stirring. Be sure to use a spatula to scrape the sides of your Dutch oven a few times to keep any rice from sticking and to mix in that flavorful film that can form on the sides. In the end, your rice should be tender and creamy.

Once your rice is cooked, mix in the garlic, herbes de Provence, spinach, hazelnuts, nutritional yeast, and black pepper. Sprinkle with parsley before serving.

COCONUT VEGAN SHRIMP KEBABS

For some reason I can't help but think this would be a great date-night recipe. You could split a bottle of San Pellegrino and get all sticky fingered while you make the kebabs. Then later, after you wash your hands, you can eat the vegan shrimp off the skewers while you sit in the shade somewhere and discuss what books you're reading or movies you've seen ... all pretty good "date" things.

MAKES 2 SERVINGS

Olive oil cooking spray

¼ cup whole wheat flour

2 tablespoons brown sugar

¼ teaspoon crushed sea salt

¼ teaspoon cayenne pepper

1 tablespoon applesauce

1 tablespoon lime juice

1 cup shredded coconut

2 cups vegan shrimp, defrosted (we suggest using shrimp balls from May Wah)

2 tablespoons margarine, melted

This is a messy process.

Preheat the oven to 425°F. Spray a rack from the broiler with olive oil cooking spray.

In a shallow bowl, mix the flour, brown sugar, salt, and cayenne pepper. In another shallow bowl, whisk together the applesauce and lime juice. In a third shallow bowl, place your coconut.

Coat each vegan shrimp with the applesauce mixture, then the flour, then more applesauce mixture, and then your coconut. Thread your coated vegan shrimp onto a skewer. Once your skewer is full, place it on the oven rack and start another skewer until you're out of vegan shrimp. The applesauce will get cloudy with the flour mix, and that's okay—the last ones will actually be better than the first. Drizzle your skewers with the melted margarine.

Bake for 5 to 7 minutes, until the coconut is golden brown. Check on them often to make sure they don't burn; they cook fast!

You'll probably want to make some Herbed Lemon Butter Sauce to go with the kebabs. You can find that on page 285.

VEGAN CHICKEN WINGS

For years, one of the most sought after and beloved mock meats has been the vegan chicken drumsticks from May Wah Healthy Vegetarian Food. These are basically Chinese five-spice soy protein nuggets that have been formed around bamboo skewers so that they can be prepared and eaten like chicken wings. All over the world, these little buddies are deep-fried and buffaloed and prepared all kinds of ways. If you're not lucky enough to have access to them in your town, you can order them online, or even make your own. Just form Match vegan chicken or your own homemade seitan around a Popsicle stick in a drumstick shape. Or you can always just thread your favorite vegan chicken on a short bamboo skewer.

After all, meat on a stick is always a crowd pleaser.

ITALIAN MOCK MEATS EXTRAVAGANZA

This recipe is the vegan version of those heaping plates of meat you might see passed around giant Italian family gatherings in the movies. That's why you'll want to serve this with a nice salad or a couple of vegetable side dishes.

MAKES 6 TO 8 SERVINGS

HERB AND LEMON MARINADE

½ cup olive oil

4 tablespoons lemon juice

3 tablespoons chopped fresh parsley

1 tablespoon dried rosemary leaves, crushed

2 teaspoons fresh thyme leaves

1 teaspoon Bragg's liquid aminos

½ teaspoon freshly ground black peppercorns

2 cloves garlic, minced

2 teaspoons dry white wine

Dash of liquid smoke

MOCK MEATS

1 (14-ounce) package Tofurky Italian sausages or Field Roast Italian sausages, defrosted

2 cups of your favorite vegan chicken, defrosted

1 (9-ounce) package Gardein beefless tips or beef seitan, defrosted

1 red onion, sliced

Preheat the oven to 400°F.

In a large mixing bowl, whisk together all the ingredients for the Herb and Lemon Marinade.

Brush a large glass lasagna dish with Herb and Lemon Marinade. Place your vegan sausages, chicken, and beef in an even layer and brush with Herb and Lemon Marinade. Cover your mock meat with a layer of red onion slices and then drizzle the Herb and Lemon

Marinade over the top of the onions. Bake for 10 minutes. Pull your dish out and drizzle with more Herb and Lemon Marinade.

Bake for another 10 to 15 minutes, or until the onions are tender and the mock meat is a light golden brown with crispy edges. Drizzle a little Herb and Lemon Marinade over the mock meat before serving with a side of A.1. steak sauce.

CHERRY COLA VEGAN CHICKEN WINGS

This sauce is liquid bliss. 'Nuff said.

MAKES 8 TO 10 WINGS

CHERRY COLA BBQ SAUCE

1 cup cherry cola

¾ cup cherry preserves

⅔ teaspoon ground mustard

½ teaspoon ground ginger

3 teaspoons hot sauce

2 tablespoons brown sugar

2 tablespoons vegan Worcestershire sauce

1 teaspoon garlic powder

½ teaspoon Bragg's liquid aminos

Dash of liquid smoke

1 cup ketchup (I can't stress this enough: read your labels and use one that has actual tomatoes in it)

WINGS

2 to 3 tablespoons olive oil

Dash of liquid smoke

8 to 10 vegan chicken wings or 2 to 2 ½ cups vegan chicken on skewers, defrosted

Preheat the oven to 400°F.

Put all your Cherry Cola BBQ Sauce ingredients in one bowl and blend with a handheld electric mixer until smooth. We left a few large cherry chunks in there because they're delicious.

To prepare the wings, mix the olive oil and liquid smoke in a bowl. Brush a large glass baking dish with smoky olive oil. Place your vegan chicken wings in the dish so that they aren't touching and brush with olive oil. Bake for 20 to 30 minutes, or until your vegan chicken wings start to turn a light golden brown.

Using oven mitts so you don't burn your fingers, dip and roll your vegan chicken wings in the Cherry Cola BBQ Sauce one at a time till you get a thick, even coating on all your wings. Place back in the baking dish. Bake for 10 to 15 minutes, or until the Cherry Cola BBQ Sauce makes a nice glaze over the vegan chicken wings.

Serve with the rest of the Cherry Cola BBQ Sauce on the side to dip your wings and fingers in.

SPICY THAI VEGAN CHICKEN WINGS

Are they messy to eat? Yeah, a little bit. Are they hard to make? Not at all. Are they superspicy? Yeah, they have a kick to them. Are they amazing? Oh yes!

MAKES 10 WINGS

¼ cup sherry

¼ cup Bragg's liquid aminos

¼ cup agave nectar

3 tablespoons chopped fresh cilantro

2 tablespoons chili sauce

2 tablespoons lime juice

2 tablespoons grated lime peel

4 green onions, chopped

3 cloves garlic, minced

10 vegan chicken wings or 2 cups of vegan chicken on skewers, defrosted

Olive oil cooking spray

In a large glass dish or bowl, whisk together the sherry, Bragg's, agave nectar, cilantro, chili sauce, lime juice, lime peel, green onions, and garlic until well blended. Toss in the defrosted vegan chicken wings, and make sure the vegan chicken is completely covered in the sauce/marinade, using a spoon to turn and coat it. Marinate for 30 minutes at room temperature. Depending on how shallow your dish is, you may want to flip the vegan chicken a few times to makes sure one side doesn't get more flavor than another.

Preheat the oven to 375°F.

Spray a glass baking dish large enough to hold your wings with olive oil cooking spray. Place the marinated vegan chicken in the dish. Try to make sure the pieces aren't touching. Pour 1 tablespoon of the sauce/marinade over each wing. Bake uncovered for 30 minutes. Flip the vegan chicken wings once halfway through baking.

When you serve, put the leftover sauce/marinade in a dish for dipping your wings in. The fresh cilantro, green onions, lime juice, and spiciness are really spectacular, and the sauce adds a bit more jus. It's messy, but so worth it.

SESAME CHICKEN WINGS

This vegan version of a Chinese-food classic has a bit of a kick to it.

MAKES 10 WINGS

4 tablespoons raw sesame seeds

1 red onion, diced

2 cloves garlic, minced

Dash of liquid smoke

4 teaspoons Bragg's liquid aminos

2½ teaspoons crushed red pepper flakes

½ teaspoon ground cloves

1 teaspoon ground cardamom

½ teaspoon ginger paste

¼ cup sesame oil

2 tablespoons water

10 vegan chicken wings or 2½ cups vegan chicken on skewers, defrosted

1 batch Sesame Hoisin Sauce (page 282)

Preheat the oven to 375°F.

In a large bowl, use an electric handheld mixer to blend the sesame seeds, onion, garlic, liquid smoke, Bragg's, red pepper flakes, cloves, cardamom, ginger paste, sesame oil, and water to make your sesame coating. Coat your vegan chicken wings in the sesame coating one at a time and place them on the rack of your roasting pan. Once they are all coated, brush the extra over the top of the vegan chicken wings.

Put your rack in the oven and roast for 30 to 40 min-

utes. Baste the vegan chicken a few times while it's cooking, using the sauce that has dripped into the pan. If your sauce reduces too much, add a tablespoon or two of water to keep the sauce liquid enough to baste with. Once your vegan chicken wings are a beautiful golden brown, pull them out of the oven and let them cool until you can handle them with your fingers.

Serve warm with Sesame Hoisin Sauce and some broccoli, because everyone could eat more vegetables.

TEXAS BEEFLESS SKEWERS WITH CHIPOTLE PEACH GLAZE

What makes this particularly Texas-y? Hard to say. It's one of those mysteries that can only be answered by a journey to the Betty Crocker test kitchens in Minneapolis. Someday we'll go and visit all the little Betty Crocker elves in their natural habitat, and it will be our first question.

MAKES 4 SKEWERS

CHIPOTLE PEACH GLAZE

½ cup peach preserves

¼ cup lime juice

1 chipotle chili pepper in adobo sauce, diced (they come in a can, but you just want 1 pepper)

1 tablespoon chopped fresh cilantro

½ teaspoon cumin

SKEWERS

1 (9-ounce) package Gardein beefless tips or beef seitan, defrosted

¼ cup margarine, melted

½ teaspoon vegan Worcestershire sauce

½ teaspoon lime juice

1 teaspoon crushed black peppercorns

Olive oil cooking spray

In a saucepan, mix the Chipotle Peach Glaze ingredients with a whisk until blended and then heat over medium

heat. Remove from the heat once the preserves are melted and the glaze is smooth.

Preheat the oven to 400°F.

Thread your vegan beef onto skewers. In a shallow dish, blend the margarine, vegan Worcestershire sauce, lime juice, and black pepper. Roll your skewers over in the margarine-pepper blend until completely covered. You might need to use a brush to get in the nooks and folds.

Cut 2 (18 x 12-inch) pieces of foil. Spray one piece of foil with a light coating of olive oil cooking spray. Place your skewers in the center of the greased foil and then drizzle 2 to 4 tablespoons of Chipotle Peach Glaze over the top. Put the other piece of foil over the top and seal the edges. Fold the edges up to prevent leaking. Bake for 10 minutes.

Pull your packet out of the oven and very gently lift the top foil off. Watch out for steam that might burn your fingers. Using oven mitts so you don't burn your fingers, flip your skewers and drizzle more Chipotle Peach Glaze over the top. Put the top foil back on and seal again.

Bake for another 10 minutes. Serve with a side of Red Beans and Rice (page 218) and maybe a pie or two…you can never have enough pie.

RANCH AND CORN FLAKES CHICKEN FINGERS

Ranch dressing is the best-selling salad dressing in America, which is discouragingly unsurprising. A plate of vegetables loaded with ranch dressing is as much a "salad" as a taco salad from Chili's. Sure, it's got veggies in it—but it's also got about 300 calories and 30 grams of fat. Yikes. All that being said—it sure is delicious. These chicken fingers will give you that yummy ranch flavor without totally blowing your calorie allocation for the day on a salad dressing.

MAKE 4 TO 6 SERVINGS

½ cup soy milk

¼ teaspoon tahini

¾ cup corn flakes cereal

¾ cup Bisquick mix

½ teaspoon lemon pepper

¼ teaspoon onion powder

½ teaspoon dried dill weed

2 cups of your favorite vegan chicken,

defrosted and cut into strips the length of your index finger

Olive oil cooking spray

Preheat the oven to 400°F.

Pour the soy milk and tahini in a shallow bowl and whisk until blended. Mix the corn flakes cereal, Bisquick mix, lemon pepper, onion powder, and dill weed in a large resealable plastic bag. One piece at a time, take your vegan chicken and dip it into the soy milk mixture, flipping it a few times until it is completely covered—especially in the little nooks and folds. Then drop the coated vegan chicken into the corn flakes bag and shake. If you find that your coating isn't sticking, gently press it onto the vegan chicken. Carefully remove your vegan chicken so that the coating doesn't fall off.

Spray a glass baking dish with olive oil cooking spray. Place your vegan chicken pieces in the glass baking dish so that they don't touch. Once you've coated all your vegan chicken, spray another even coating of olive oil cooking spray over the vegan chicken in the baking dish. Bake for 5 minutes and then flip the vegan chicken. Bake for another 5 to 10 minutes, or until the vegan chicken is golden brown.

THYME AND POMEGRANATE VEGAN CHICKEN

Pomegranates were revered by many ancient and classical cultures—including the Egyptians, Greeks, and Persians—for their exotic beauty and decadent flavor. Which made the pomegranate juice fad of the early aughts all the more vexing. Is there nothing sacred that we can't package, brand, advertise, and overcharge for? But the plus side of that cultural moment was the arrival of pomegranates in grocery stores en masse. Which worked out great for us—we love pomegranates and they're great for us—and you.

You'll be unable to resist this savory-sweet chicken pomegranate dish the way Persephone was unable to resist those pomegranate seeds in Hades—but we promise you won't need to spend six months in the underworld every year.

MAKES 2 TO 4 SERVINGS

Olive oil cooking spray

2 cups vegan chicken, defrosted (we recommend Gardein Chick'n Scallopini)

½ red onion, sliced

2 tablespoons margarine

2 tablespoons whole wheat flour

1 teaspoon onion powder

1 clove garlic, minced

2 teaspoons tomato paste

½ cup dry white wine

2 teaspoon fresh thyme leaves (save a few sprigs to place on top)

½ cup Better Than Bouillon vegan chicken broth, made per the instructions on the package

½ cup pomegranate juice

2 teaspoons packed brown sugar

Preheat the oven to 400°F.

Spray a glass baking dish with olive oil cooking spray and then toss your vegan chicken in and lay the red onion in an even layer over the top. Bake for 10 to 15 minutes. You'll know it's ready when your vegan chicken is a soft golden brown.

In a saucepan, heat the margarine over medium heat until it melts. Whisk in the flour and onion powder until a smooth paste forms. Add the garlic, tomato paste, wine, thyme, broth, and pomegranate juice. Use your whisk to blend in the flour. Once your sauce begins to bubble, add the brown sugar and whisk again. The brown sugar should melt into your sauce to make it more syrupy. Cover and simmer for 2 minutes.

Serve your vegan chicken with 2 to 3 tablespoons of sauce, a few sprigs of fresh thyme over the top, and a nice glass of white wine.

HERB-ROASTED CHICKEN AND VEGETABLES

Want to hear something absurdly pretentious? I adore the French countryside. In 2005, I was taking the train from London to Paris, when I did something that could have been really stupid considering my limited French. I had just met with the gals at *Cosmo UK* about their "Nice Girls Fake It" campaign announcing that their magazine would be fur-free and was on my way to Paris. I had blocked off the day for travel and for figuring out the Metro in Paris. It was my "day off." Instead, I jumped off the train in one of those random yet charming towns on the way to Paris. I rented a locker for my stuff and walked around a town center that could fit inside any American mini-mall, with my galoshes and an umbrella. I ate a baguette and some *compote de pommes* (applesauce) with a pot of tea in a café full of mismatched chairs and chipped dishes. I know you're wondering why I'm boring you with this. Well, it's because the old guys sitting next to me at the café playing backgammon shared a small pot of something that looked just like this dish.

MAKES 4 TO 6 SERVINGS

4 red potatoes, cut into chunks about the size of the vegan chicken

1 cup sliced carrots

½ cup olive oil

1 teaspoon Bragg's liquid aminos

¼ teaspoon nutritional yeast

2 cloves garlic, minced

¼ teaspoon garlic powder

¼ teaspoon lemon pepper

1 tablespoon herbes de Provence

Pinch of celery seed

Juice and 1 teaspoon zest from 1 lemon

1 cup of your favorite vegan chicken, defrosted

1 cup green beans

Preheat the oven to 375°F.

Boil the potatoes and carrots till they are tender but not quite cooked. Drain and set aside.

In a small bowl, mix the olive oil, Bragg's, nutritional yeast, garlic, garlic powder, lemon pepper, herbes de Provence, and celery seed. Grate 1 teaspoon of fresh lemon peel into the oil mixture. Then cut the lemon and add to the oil mixture as much juice as you can get from the lemon.

In a large bowl, mix the vegan chicken, potatoes, carrots, and green beans. Pour the oil mixture over the vegan chicken and vegetables and stir gently to coat your vegetables, but be careful to not mash your potatoes.

Put the mixture in a small oven-safe casserole dish or Dutch oven. Roast uncovered for 30 to 45 minutes. You'll want to pull it out when the top is golden. When you serve it, be sure to scoop an extra spoonful of the oil mixture from the bottom of the pot and pour it over your food.

You're going to want to eat this with some bread so you can mop up the extra garlicky-lemony-herby oil. Just trust me.

TEMPEH TACOS

I never really cared for tempeh until I was in college. I think I had one too many lazy tempeh Reuben sandwiches—you know the one where they don't even cook the tempeh; they just put it in a sandwich with some mustard and call it good? That's enough to discourage even the most hopeful vegan. That's why when my college roommate Libbe told me she was making tempeh tacos for a birthday party, I was polite but disapproving... and ultimately wrong. I wish I could remember Libbe's original tempeh taco recipe to share with you all, but it's been a long time, and since then I've branched out on my own. If you're like me and weren't born with an innate love of tempeh, I hope you'll give this recipe a chance. It'll change your life forever.

MAKES 6 TO 8 TACOS

1 (8-ounce) package tempeh

2 cloves garlic, minced

1 cup Mexican-spiced diced tomatoes

1 fresh jalapeño, diced

2 to 4 teaspoons chili powder (depends on how hot you want it)

3 teaspoons cumin

2 teaspoons lime juice

2 teaspoons garlic powder

1 teaspoon onion powder

2 teaspoons dried oregano

1 teaspoon minced chipotle pepper

¼ cup Bragg's liquid aminos

½ red onion, diced

½ green bell pepper, diced

2 tablespoons water

Crushed pink Himalayan salt and freshly ground black peppercorns

Olive oil cooking spray

Dash of liquid smoke

6 to 8 hard taco shells

½ cup shredded Daiya vegan cheddar cheese or your favorite vegan cheese

1 batch Dan's Guacamole (page 432)

Chopped cilantro, sliced black olives, and salsa for toppings

Crumble your tempeh into a large mixing bowl. Then, using a large spoon, mix in the garlic, tomatoes, jalapeño, chili powder, cumin, lime juice, garlic powder, onion powder, oregano, chipotle pepper, and Bragg's. Once your tempeh is completely mixed into the spices, mix in the onion and pepper. Then drizzle the water 1 tablespoon at a time into your mix while stirring your ingredients continuously. Taste a little bit of your tempeh and add salt and pepper to taste.

Spray your favorite cast-iron skillet or frying pan with a heavy coating of olive oil cooking spray, and then heat over medium heat. Once the oil is hot, toss in the tempeh mixture and liquid smoke. Flip your tempeh-vegetable mixture a few times so that it browns evenly.

You'll know it's ready when your vegetables are tender and your tempeh has crispy edges. It should take about 10 minutes.

While your tempeh is cooking, heat your taco shells slightly in the oven following the directions on the package.

Once your taco shells are warm, fill them with the tempeh and vegetable mixture. Top with vegan cheese and set aside so your vegan cheese can melt slightly.

Dress your tacos with Dan's Guacamole, cilantro, black olives, and salsa, or personalize them with your favorite toppings, and be sure to stock up on Mexican beer and Dr Pepper.*

---

* See intro to Mexcian Stuffed Crust Pizza (page 178) for clarification.

SHRIMPY KEBABS WITH FRESH HERBS

Generally you don't think of kebabs as being particularly fancy. They're delicious and summery and barbecue-y and all sorts of wonderful things … but fancy isn't usually one of them. But it's funny how the simple act of replacing your standard bamboo skewer with a fresh sprig of rosemary will fancify an otherwise straightforward kebab significantly.

MAKES 10 KEBABS

LEMON AND ROSEMARY MARINADE

10 sprigs rosemary, cut to 6 inches long

½ cup lemon juice

3 tablespoons olive oil

2 tablespoons dry white wine

3 cloves garlic, minced

½ teaspoon freshly ground black peppercorns

¼ teaspoon onion powder

Pinch of celery seed

KEBABS

20 large whole fresh basil leaves

20 pieces vegan shrimp, defrosted (we recommend May Wah shrimp balls)

1 zucchini, sliced

10 cherry tomatoes

10 whole cloves garlic

1 (15-ounce) can artichoke hearts, drained (make sure your can has at least 10 hearts)

10 white mushrooms, cut in half

2 tablespoons olive oil

10 fresh lemon wedges

Strip the needles and leaves from your rosemary sprigs, leaving about ½ inch of leaves at the tip. Chop your rosemary leaves and toss them in a large mixing bowl. Add the remaining marinade ingredients to the mixing bowl, and blend with a whisk.

To assemble the kebabs, wrap 1 basil leaf around each piece of vegan shrimp. Using a metal skewer, poke holes all the way through your vegan shrimp, zucchini slices, cherry tomatoes, garlic cloves, artichoke hearts, and mushrooms. When you poke through your vegan shrimp, make sure to go through the basil leaves as well, so that they stay on the kebab. Thread your ingredients onto the rosemary sprigs using the holes you made with the skewers.

Place your completed kebabs in a shallow glass baking dish and pour the marinade over the top. Cover and marinate for 30 minutes at room temperature.

Brush the olive oil over your infamously awesome cast-iron grill skillet. This is one of those skillets with ridges that raise your food so that some of the juices run off and you get those cool grill lines. If you don't have one, you can use a regular old cast-iron skillet or frying pan, but I recommend getting a grill skillet—they're wonderful.

Heat your oiled skillet over medium heat. Once your oil is hot, place a few of your kebobs in the skillet at a time. Evenly space them so that they aren't touching. Let one side cook for no more than 2 minutes and then flip and cook the other side for no more than 1 minute.

Be sure to lightly brush your skillet after each batch of kebabs to keep them from sticking. Serve with lemon wedges to squeeze over the top and some white wine. Perhaps use this recipe as an excuse to dust off your ascot and monocle.

MINI POT ROAST PIES

Fact: no food is cuter than miniaturized vegan comfort-food classics. This dish combines wonderful, savory, "beefy" flavors with ""buttery"" puff pastry and one of our very favorite vegetables—peas. We've never had the luxury of living in an area with access to good fresh peas (yet), so we use frozen peas a lot. In a world where so many people don't get enough vegetables in their diet, we encourage people to eat as many vegetables as they can, even if they are frozen. This recipe is a great way to do that.

MAKES 4 PIES

- 1 tablespoon olive oil
- 1 tablespoon red wine
- 1 (9-ounce) package Gardein beefless tips or beef seitan, defrosted
- 2 shallots, diced
- 6 to 8 small red potatoes, cut into small cubes
- ¼ cup frozen peas
- ¼ cup frozen green beans
- 3 baby carrots, sliced
- ¼ cup baby portobello mushroom caps, sliced
- 1 cup Better Than Bouillon vegan beef broth, made per the instructions on the package
- ¼ teaspoon horseradish
- ½ teaspoon Bragg's liquid aminos
- 1 tablespoon nutritional yeast
- 1 tablespoon vegan Worcestershire sauce
- 1 tablespoon whole wheat flour, plus extra for flouring a surface
- 1 package puff pastry sheets
- Olive oil cooking spray

Preheat the oven to 425°F.

Heat your olive oil and red wine in your cast-iron skillet or frying pan over medium heat. Once your oil is hot, toss in your vegan beef and shallots. Cook until your vegan beef is evenly browned and has crispy edges and your shallots are tender. Then remove your vegan beef from the skillet. Toss your potatoes into the skillet to cook. Brown for a minute and then use your spatula to flip them a few times so they cook evenly.

After 3 minutes, toss in the peas, green beans, carrots, mushrooms, broth, horseradish, Bragg's, nutritional yeast, vegan Worcestershire sauce, and flour. Mix with a wooden spoon until the nutritional yeast and flour are blended and become a light gravy with the broth. Sim-mer for 10 minutes.

Fill 4 (12-ounce) ramekins ½ of the way with the vegetables and gravy. Place one-quarter of the vegan beef in the top of each ramekin.

Dust your workspace with flour and slightly roll out a sheet of puff pastry dough so that the creases and folds don't show. Then spray your puff pastry with a light coating of olive oil cooking spray and fold the pastry sheet in half. Using a 4-inch biscuit cutter, cut 4 circles out of the puff pastry. Place 1 circle on the top of each ramekin. Spray the pastry circle with another light coating of olive oil cooking spray and then bake for 10 minutes, or until the puff pastry is golden brown and fluffy.

CORNED BEEFLESS BRISKET AND CABBAGE

This traditional Irish-American meal was one of my favorites back when I was a meaty little eater. I loved this dinner. This was a classic dish that I both looked forward to and dreaded veganizing, because I had such fond memories of it from my youth. I worried it would be impossible to redo this meal vegan-style in any meaningful way. This all could have gone very wrong—but it didn't. In fact, it was a nice reminder of a dish I haven't had in like 20 years. Does it taste just like the meaty version? I would say 70 percent—which is enough to capture the spirit of the dish and make a great dinner this St. Patrick's Day.

MAKES 2 TO 4 SERVINGS

1 (9-ounce) package Gardein beefless tips or beef seitan, defrosted

1 tablespoon white wine

3 tablespoons Bragg's liquid aminos

1 tablespoon dill pickle brine (that's the juice in the pickle jar)

Dash of liquid smoke

1 clove garlic, minced

1 teaspoon onion powder

4 tablespoons pickling spices

1 teaspoon olive oil

6 cups Better Than Bouillon vegan beef broth, made per the instructions on the package

1 head cabbage, quartered

6 red potatoes, halved

1 red onion, sliced

Crushed pink Himalayan salt and freshly ground black peppercorns

Malt or balsamic vinegar to add a little bite to the cabbage and potatoes

Put the vegan beef, white wine, 1 tablespoon of the Bragg's, the dill pickle brine, liquid smoke, garlic, onion powder, 2 tablespoons of the pickling spices, and the olive oil in an airtight container and shake to mix. Then put it into the fridge and let it marinate for 2 hours.

Preheat the oven to 350°F.

Put the broth in a large stewpot and heat on high. Once it begins to boil, toss in the cabbage, potatoes, ½ of the red onion, 2 tablespoons of the pickling spices and 2 tablespoons of the Bragg's. Cover and boil until the potatoes are tender.

While they are boiling, place your pickled vegan beef in a glass dish with the marinade and put the remaining ½ red onion over the top. Bake the vegan beef and red onion for 10 minutes. Very carefully, take the glass dish from the oven and pour the marinade out of the dish. Bake for another 20 minutes. You want to remove it when the vegan beef and onions have been browned—so keep an eye on them.

Serve your potatoes and cabbage with a slotted spoon from the stewpot with salt, pepper, and vinegar to taste.

If it's St. Patrick's Day, maybe enjoy it with one of those beers with a few drops of green food coloring in it. But don't be surprised if your teeth turn green. Everything comes with a price.

VEGAN BACON CHEESE MEAT LOAFS

You maybe be wondering—what makes *Betty Goes Vegan* different from other vegan cookbooks? I think it's recipes like this one. Dinners you never knew you wanted till you gave 'em a shot one night and realized it can be fun to play the housewife. I recommend serving these with some Ranch Mashed Potatoes (page 276) and a green salad. Okay, I'm going to rephrase that. *Please* eat this recipe with a green salad. I'm begging you.

MAKES 6 SERVINGS

1 (15-ounce) can garbanzo beans, rinsed and drained

2 to 4 tablespoons Bragg's liquid aminos

2 tablespoons olive oil

3 cloves garlic, minced

¼ cup plain bread crumbs (be sure to read your label to make sure they are vegan)

½ red onion, chopped

1 teaspoon vegan bacon bits

Dash of liquid smoke

½ teaspoon finely chopped fresh basil

½ teaspoon ground mustard seed

1 teaspoon finely chopped fresh parsley

½ teaspoon chopped fresh oregano

¼ teaspoon rubbed sage

1 cup Match vegan ground beef or

Lightlife Gimme Lean vegan ground beef, defrosted

Olive oil cooking spray

3 tablespoons A.1. steak sauce

1 tablespoon brown sugar

⅓ cup shredded Daiya vegan cheddar cheese or your favorite vegan cheese

Preheat the oven to 375°F.

In your food processor, blend the garbanzo beans, 2 tablespoons of the Bragg's, the olive oil, and the garlic until smooth. Move the garbanzo bean mixture to a large mixing bowl and, using a large spoon, mix in the bread crumbs, onion, vegan bacon bits, liquid smoke, basil, mustard seed, parsley, oregano, and sage until blended. Using your hands, mix in the vegan beef until the mixture becomes a smooth paste. If it's a little dry, add more Bragg's, 1 tablespoon at a time.

Line a cookie sheet with foil and spray it with a light coating of olive oil. Separate your vegan beef mix into 6 equal loaves. Place them on the cookie sheet.

Whisk together the steak sauce and brown sugar. Brush your glaze over the tops of the loaves. Sprinkle vegan cheese over the tops of the loaves, and bake for 30 to 45 minutes, until the loaves are solid and the vegan cheese is melted.

Serve with ketchup, mustard, and a side of pickles.

MEXICAN MEAT LOAF

Throughout the history of American cuisine, there has been a long-standing tradition of making dishes that are Mexican themed but aren't really much like anything you'd ever find in Mexico. This is one of those recipes—but that doesn't make it any less delicious and wonderful.

MEAT LOAF

1 cup Match vegan ground beef or Lightlife Gimme Lean vegan ground beef, defrosted

1 (15-ounce) can black beans, drained and rinsed

¼ cup dry bread crumbs (be sure to read your label to make sure your brand is vegan)

2 cloves garlic, minced

1 fresh jalapeño, diced (half that if you don't like it spicy)

2 teaspoons Bragg's liquid aminos

Dash of liquid smoke

1 teaspoon cumin

½ red onion, diced

2 tablespoons chopped fresh cilantro

1 teaspoon chili powder

¼ cup salsa, plus extra to serve with your meat loaf

Olive oil cooking spray

GLAZE

½ cup ketchup

2 tablespoons vegan Worcestershire sauce

2 tablespoons brown sugar

Preheat the oven to 375°F.

In a large bowl, combine the vegan beef, black beans, bread crumbs, garlic, jalapeño, Bragg's, liquid smoke, cumin, onion, cilantro and chili powder. Gently mix with a large spoon until completely blended. Pour your salsa into the vegan beef mix and blend with your hands.

Cover a cookie sheet with foil and spray with a light coating of olive oil.

In another mixing bowl, whisk together all the glaze ingredients.

Separate your vegan beef into 2 equal loaves and place on your cookie sheet so that they don't touch. Brush with the glaze. Bake for 15 to 20 minutes, or until solid.

Serve with a side of salsa and some margaritas ... maybe some Apple Churros (page 332) for dessert.

VEGAN BEEF AND QUINOA-STUFFED PEPPERS

I've been making these since before I had a blog and was a Shannon. It's a timeless recipe, perfect for holiday meals—or anytime you want to sit down to dinner with five of your dearest.

MAKES 6 SERVINGS

2 tablespoons olive oil

1½ cups Match vegan ground beef or Lightlife Gimme Lean vegan ground beef, defrosted

¼ cup red onion, diced

2 teaspoons Better Than Bouillon vegetable broth, made per the instructions on the package

1 cup cooked quinoa

¼ cup raw baby spinach leaves

1 tablespoon chopped fresh parsley

2 teaspoons celery seeds

1 teaspoon fresh thyme leaves

2 teaspoons Bragg's liquid aminos

1½ teaspoons cumin

2 teaspoons crushed raw cashews

2 cloves garlic, minced

6 large green or red bell peppers, cored and seeded, tops cut off

1 jar of your favorite pasta sauce

1 cup shredded Daiya vegan mozzarella cheese or your favorite vegan cheese

Preheat the oven to 350°F.

In a cast-iron skillet or frying pan, heat the olive oil over medium heat. Once your oil is hot, toss in your

vegan beef and onion. Use a metal spatula to break your vegan beef into bite-size pieces. Cook until it is evenly browned and your onions are tender.

In a large mixing bowl, combine the broth, quinoa, spinach, parsley, celery seeds, thyme, Bragg's, cumin, cashews, and garlic. Mix in the vegan beef and onions. Make sure to try to get as much of the olive oil from the skillet as possible into the quinoa mixture to keep it from getting dry.

Place your bell peppers in an 8-inch square baking dish. Fill your bell peppers with the quinoa mixture. Pour an even layer of pasta sauce over the top of the peppers. It's okay if the sauce fills the baking dish. Sprinkle an even layer of vegan cheese over the tops of the peppers. Bake uncovered for 15 to 20 minutes, or until the vegan cheese melts.

NEW-STYLE VEGAN PORK CHOPS

I think we've taken this dish to a new level of "new style" by making it vegan. This is a classy dish that would be perfect for any special occasion but can also doll up a boring Wednesday.

MAKES 4 SERVINGS

Rice pilaf to serve with the chops

1 cup Match vegan pork, defrosted

1 cup Better than Bouillon vegetable broth, prepared using the instructions on the package

1 tablespoon lemon juice

1 tablespoon Bragg's liquid aminos

1 teaspoon agave nectar

3 tablespoons olive oil

½ cup chopped red onion

2 cloves garlic, minced

¼ teaspoon freshly ground black peppercorns

¼ cup dry white wine

½ cup kalamata olives, pitted

1 tablespoon fresh thyme leaves

1 tablespoon chopped fresh parsley

Make the rice pilaf per the instructions on the box.

Separate your vegan pork into "chops," ¼ to ½ cup per chop. Form the vegan pork with your hands into patties smaller than your hand.

In a shallow bowl, combine the broth, lemon juice, Bragg's, and agave nectar. Dip your chops into the broth mixture and count to 20. Place the dipped chops onto a dish and set them aside.

In your handy cast-iron skillet or frying pan, heat the olive oil over medium heat. Place your chops in the heated oil and brown on both sides. Once you start to have a crispy "skin" on your chops, pour the rest of the broth mixture over the chops and add the red onion, garlic, black pepper, and white wine. Continue to flip the chops and mix the other ingredients. Let the chops simmer for around 15 minutes, or until the onions are tender. Toss in the kalamata olives, thyme, and parsley. Simmer another 5 minutes.

Serve over rice pilaf with a lovely cocktail and some witty remarks.

VEGAN VENISON WITH CRANBERRY AND WINE SAUCE

When many people think of venison, they think of deer meat, but the truth is that the title "venison" is given to almost all "wild game on four legs." Venison can be caribou, or elk, or even moose, but is most commonly deer. Adorable, sweet, never-hurt-a-fly-unless-you-count-eating-the-flowers-out-of-your-yard deer. This is a special recipe for me because I got to make it for Dan's family for Christmas dinner one year.

MAKES 4 SERVINGS

1 tablespoon Dijon mustard

1 cup red wine

2 cups Gardein beefless tips or beef seitan, defrosted

½ teaspoon crushed black peppercorns

1 tablespoon olive oil

2 tablespoons Bragg's liquid aminos

½ teaspoon dried basil

½ red onion, diced

2 tablespoons chopped fresh parsley

3 tablespoons apple jelly

1 tablespoon margarine

½ cup dried cranberries

In a small bowl whisk together the Dijon mustard and ½ cup of the red wine until blended. Place the vegan beef in a shallow glass bowl and pour the wine-mustard marinade over the top. Cover the dish and place in the fridge for 1 hour. During that time go in and flip the vegan beef a few times so it gets an even coating and the marinade doesn't separate too much. If you don't like spicy food, you may not want to let it sit for the full hour.

Remove the vegan beef, place it on a plate, and sprinkle it with black pepper. Keep your wine and mustard marinade to use later. In your kindred cast-iron skillet, heat the olive oil over medium to high heat. Brown the vegan beef in the skillet till it gets nice crisp edges. It will take around 5 minutes. Remove the vegan beef and place it back on its plate.

Don't discard the oil from your skillet. Add the remaining ½ cup of red wine, the Bragg's, basil, red onion, and parsley. Cook until the red onion is tender. Mix in the apple jelly and margarine. Once the jelly melts, remove the pan from the heat and stir in the cranberries and vegan beef. When you're adding the vegan beef, try to get the drippings from the plate into the sauce. Stir it all together.

When serving, place the vegan beef on the plate first and then ladle the cranberry wine sauce over the top.

JALAPEÑO CORN DOGS

I didn't grow up in a corn-dog house. Until I was in junior high, I kind of thought they only existed on hot lunch menus at public schools. As a vegan adult I came to appreciate the campiness of mock meat on a stick, but any real affection didn't come about till we hosted an American food–themed potluck. Our friend Ben brought corn dogs made from scratch with Tofurky kielbasas, and it was one of those Moses-on-the-mountaintop moments. One of those moments when Darth Vader says "I am your father" and you can't help but be confused by how wonderfully improbable and awesome the world can be. Whether you love the prefab frozen corn dogs or are still trying to figure out the mysterious allure of mock meat on a stick … you should give this recipe a try. Search your feelings. You know it to be true …

MAKE 8 CORN DOGS

- 1 gallon vegetable frying oil
- 1 cup yellow cornmeal
- 1 cup whole wheat flour
- 2 teaspoons crushed pink Himalayan salt
- 1 teaspoon baking powder
- ½ teaspoon baking soda
- 1 teaspoon cayenne pepper (add less if you don't like things spicy)
- ¼ teaspoon freshly ground black peppercorns
- ½ teaspoon onion powder
- Dash of cumin
- 1 fresh jalapeño, diced
- 1 can cream-style corn
- 1 tablespoon diced red onion
- 1½ cups soy milk
- 4 tablespoons cornstarch
- 8 vegan sausages, defrosted (we recommend Tofurky kielbasas)

Separate 8 bamboo chopsticks and clean any slivers or rough edges off.

Pour the oil into a large stewpot or Dutch oven and heat over high heat.

In a mixing bowl, mix the cornmeal, flour, salt, baking powder, baking soda, cayenne pepper, black pepper, onion powder, and cumin with a large spoon until blended.

In a separate mixing bowl, whisk together the jalapeño, corn, onion, and soy milk. Add the cornmeal mixture to the soy milk mixture and gently blend with your spoon only enough times to make the batter. There should be lumps, so don't use the whisk. Set the batter aside and let the flavors hang out and get to know each other for about 10 minutes.

Spread the cornstarch in a shallow glass baking dish.

Roll each vegan sausage in the cornstarch. Thread each vegan sausage onto a chopstick.

Find a drinking or pint glass deep enough to dip your vegan sausage in completely. Fill your glass with enough batter to completely submerge your vegan sausage. Immediately dip your cornstarch-covered vegan sausages into the batter and then gently place them in the hot oil. Refill the glass when you need to. Fry your corn dogs until the coating is golden brown. It shouldn't take longer than 5 minutes. With tongs, move your corn dogs to a cooling rack over paper towels. Let those dogs cool till you can touch them with your fingers.

Serve with mustard, ketchup, BBQ sauce, a beer or two, and some American pride.

TOFURKY DIVAN

This recipe is one of those dishes that most people experience as a leftover makeover after Thanksgiving. But here's the thing: if you have any Tofurky left over after Thanksgiving, you're doing it wrong. We recommend starting out with a brand-new defrosted whole Tofurky and a desire for greatness.

MAKES 4 TO 6 SERVINGS

1 whole Tofurky, defrosted

Olive oil cooking spray

¼ cup raw cashews

1 cup broccoli florets

¼ cup margarine

¼ cup whole wheat flour

¼ teaspoon grated nutmeg

1 ½ cups Better Than Bouillon vegan chicken broth, made per the instructions on the package

2 tablespoons dry white wine

½ cup almond milk

¼ cup nutritional yeast

1 teaspoon onion powder

Dash of liquid smoke

½ teaspoon tahini

French-fried onions for topping

Preheat the oven to 375°F.

Cut one end off your Tofurky and use a soupspoon to remove the stuffing. Cut your Tofurky into pieces around ¼ inch thick. Spray an 11 x 7-inch glass baking dish with a light coating of olive oil cooking spray. Lay your Tofurky slices in the baking dish and spray another light coating over the top of the Tofurky. Bake for 15 minutes, or until your Tofurky is golden brown.

With a pastry blender over a cutting board, crush your cashews into small bits.

There are numerous types of steamers out there and most do a pretty good job. Steam your broccoli florets following the instructions that came with your particular kind of steamer.

In a Dutch oven or casserole dish with a lid, melt the margarine. Once it begins to bubble, whisk in the flour, cashews, and nutmeg. Once the flour and cashews begin to toast, pour in the broth, white wine, and almond milk and blend with a whisk. When your sauce is smooth, use your whisk to blend in the nutritional yeast, onion powder, liquid smoke, and tahini. Cover and simmer for 2 minutes.

Take your Tofurky out of the oven. Sprinkle your broccoli florets over the Tofurky slices, and pour your sauce evenly over the pan. Then sprinkle an even layer of French-fried onions over the top and bake for 10 minutes until the sauce is bubbly and the top of your casserole is golden brown.

QUICHE LORRAINE

The day I made this recipe, I was full of thrills and humming Doris Day songs for hours. I won't lie—this is not my first dance around the floor with quiche. I make them a lot, and Dan loves them. In fact, this quiche was completely eaten by my love in a 24-hour period.

MAKES 4 TO 6 SERVINGS

WHOLE WHEAT CRUST

2 cups whole wheat flour (you're going to want more to flour surfaces)

1 teaspoon crushed pink Himalayan salt

⅔ cup plus 2 tablespoons vegetable shortening

4 to 6 tablespoons cold water

FILLING

1 16-ounce package extrafirm tofu

1 tablespoon soy coffee creamer

2 tablespoons nutritional yeast

1 tablespoon whole wheat flour

½ teaspoon onion powder

¼ teaspoon cumin

¼ teaspoon miso paste

¼ teaspoon turmeric

¼ teaspoon Bragg's liquid aminos

¼ teaspoon paprika (you'll need a little extra to sprinkle over the top)

Crushed pink Himalayan salt and freshly ground black peppercorns

2 tablespoons olive oil

Dash of liquid smoke

1 5-ounce package vegan bacon or smoked tempeh

½ red onion, diced

½ cup shredded smoked cheddar Sheese or your favorite vegan cheese

1 tablespoon fresh thyme leaves

2 tablespoons chopped fresh parsley

1 tablespoon shredded Daiya vegan mozzarella cheese or your favorite vegan cheese

Preheat the oven to 425°F.

First make the whole wheat crust. In a medium bowl, mix the flour and salt. Cut the shortening in and use a pastry blender to mix. You want your dough to become little clumps that look like small peas. Sprinkle in the cold water 1 tablespoon at a time, and use a large fork to mix. You want the dough to be moist but not wet.

With your hands, roll the dough into a ball inside the bowl. On a floured surface, with a floured roller, roll your dough ball out into rounds 2 inches larger than a 9-inch pie dish. Try to keep the crust even. You don't want some areas to be thinner than others. Gently roll the flattened dough up into plastic wrap and refrigerate for 45 minutes. You want the dough to be firm but still pliable, so if it is crumbly when you remove it from the fridge, press any cracks to fix them and then let the dough warm a little until it is more pliable.

To make the filling, in a food processor, blend the tofu, soy coffee creamer, nutritional yeast, flour, onion powder, cumin, miso paste, turmeric, Bragg's, and paprika until you get a smooth paste. Here's where you can taste this blend and add the desired amount of salt and pepper.

In your very favorite and much-used cast-iron skillet or frying pan, heat the olive oil and a dash of liquid smoke over medium heat. Toss in your vegan bacon and cook until it is brown and crispy. Set the vegan bacon aside on a paper towel to soak up extra oil. Once it is warm enough to handle with your hands, dice your cooked vegan bacon into bits.

After your crust has chilled, unfold it into a 9-inch glass pie dish and press it firmly and evenly into the dish. Sprinkle half your vegan bacon pieces, half the red onion, and half the smoked vegan cheese into the crust. In a large bowl, mix the tofu blend, the remaining vegan bacon pieces, red onion, and smoked vegan cheese, and the thyme, parsley, and vegan mozzarella.

Gently pour it into your crust. Use a rubber spatula to scrape the side of the bowl and get all the tofu blend. Then use it to spread your tofu blend evenly into the crust so that the quiche has a flat surface.

Bake your quiche for 10 minutes and then reduce the heat to 325°F. Bake for another 30 minutes. You'll want to remove your quiche when the top is golden brown and you can insert a toothpick and remove it cleanly from the center.

When you serve, you may want to sprinkle a little extra paprika over the top … it is lovely.

CREOLE VEGAN CHICKEN AND KALE QUICHE

In every marriage, there are things that one person brings to the union that become new family traditions. In ours, I've brought *True Blood* and an unexplainable addiction to Creole and Cajun cooking. Dan has embraced this part of my nature in a way that makes me wonder if maybe he was born with the same inexplicable anomaly in his DNA. I mean, if there's one thing *The X-Files* has taught us, it's that there's more going on in this world than can be explained by science alone.

MAKES 4 TO 6 SERVINGS

WHOLE WHEAT CRUST
2 cups whole wheat flour (you're going to want more to flour surfaces)

1 teaspoon crushed pink Himalayan salt

⅔ cup plus 2 tablespoons vegetable shortening

4 to 6 tablespoons cold water

FILLING
1 package extrafirm tofu

1½ teaspoons Tony Chachere's Creole seasoning

Dash of liquid smoke

2 tablespoons soy coffee creamer

2 tablespoons nutritional yeast

1 tablespoon whole wheat flour

1 teaspoon miso paste

½ teaspoon Louisiana hot sauce

Crushed pink Himalayan salt and freshly ground black peppercorns to taste

2 tablespoons margarine

½ cup bite-size defrosted vegan chicken pieces

1 clove garlic, minced

⅓ cup raw baby kale leaves

3 teaspoons vegan bacon bits

¼ cup shredded Daiya vegan pepperjack cheese or your favorite vegan cheese

Preheat the oven to 425°F.

Prepare the crust first. In a medium bowl, mix the flour and salt. Cut the shortening in and then mix it in using a pastry blender. You want your dough to become little clumps that look like pebbles. Sprinkle in the cold water 1 tablespoon at a time, and then use a large fork to mix the dough. You want the dough to be moist but not wet.

With your hands, roll the dough into a ball inside the bowl. On a floured surface, with a floured roller, roll your dough ball out into rounds 2 inches larger than a 9-inch pie dish. Try to keep the crust even. Gently roll the flattened dough up in plastic wrap and refrigerate for 45 minutes. You want the dough to be firm but still pliable, so if it is crumbly when you remove it from the fridge, press the cracks to fix them and then let the dough warm a little till it is more pliable.

To make the filling, in a food processor, blend the tofu, Creole seasoning, liquid smoke, soy coffee creamer, nutritional yeast, flour, miso paste, and hot sauce until you get a smooth paste. Here's where you can taste this blend; if you want, add salt and pepper to taste.

In your cast-iron skillet or frying pan, melt your margarine over medium heat. Once your margarine is melted, toss in your vegan chicken and cook until the vegan chicken is golden brown and crispy. Then toss in your garlic and mix until your vegan chicken has a light coating. Toss the vegan chicken into a large mixing bowl with your kale and vegan bacon bits. Pour your tofu mixture into the bowl, and mix all your ingredients with a large wooden spoon until completely blended.

After your crust has chilled, unfold it into a 9-inch glass pie dish and press it firmly and evenly into the dish. Pour your vegan chicken and tofu blend into the crust. Use a rubber spatula to scrape the side of the bowl to get the entire tofu blend into the pie dish. Then use it to spread your tofu blend evenly into the crust. Makes sure it has a flat surface. Sprinkle your vegan cheese over the top in an even layer.

Bake your quiche for 10 minutes, and then reduce the heat to 325°F and bake for another 30 minutes. You'll want to remove your quiche when the top is golden brown and you can insert a toothpick and remove it cleanly from the center.

VEGAN BACON, WALNUT, AND SWISS CHARD QUICHE

Swiss chard is one of those vegetables I wish I ate more of. It's a great source for vitamins A, K, and C, and many folks consider it to be one of the healthiest vegetables available and necessary for a healthy diet. But mostly I just like how pretty it is and its unique bitter flavor. Mixed with smoky and "cheesy" flavors, it's pretty much fabulous.

MAKES 4 TO 6 SERVINGS

WHOLE WHEAT CRUST
2 cups whole wheat flour (you're going to want more to flour surfaces)

1 teaspoon crushed pink Himalayan salt

⅔ cup plus 2 tablespoons vegetable shortening

4 to 6 tablespoons cold water

FILLING
1 package extrafirm tofu

1 clove garlic, minced

¼ teaspoon garlic powder

¼ teaspoon onion powder

½ teaspoon cayenne pepper

¼ teaspoon dried oregano leaves

¼ teaspoon dried thyme leaves

Dash of liquid smoke

2 tablespoons soy coffee creamer

2 tablespoons nutritional yeast

1 tablespoon whole wheat flour

1 teaspoon miso paste

½ teaspoon hot sauce

Pinch of celery seed

Pinch of smoked paprika

Crushed pink Himalayan salt and freshly ground black peppercorns

¾ chopped cup Swiss chard

½ cup shredded smoked cheddar Sheese or your favorite vegan cheese (you'll want to save a little extra to sprinkle over the top)

1 tablespoon crushed raw walnuts

3 tablespoons vegan bacon bits

2 tablespoons chopped green onions

Preheat the oven to 425°F.

First make the crust. In a medium bowl, mix the flour and salt. Cut the shortening in, and then mix it in using a pastry blender. You want your dough to become little clumps that look like pebbles. Sprinkle in the cold water 1 tablespoon at a time, and then use a large fork to mix. You want the dough to be moist but not wet.

With your hands, roll the dough into a ball inside the bowl. On a floured surface, with a floured roller, roll your dough ball out into rounds 2 inches larger than a 9-inch pie dish. Try to keep the crust even. Gently roll the flattened dough up in plastic wrap and refrigerate for 45 minutes. You want the dough to be firm but still pliable. If it is crumbly when you remove it from the fridge, press the cracks to fix them and then let it warm a little till it is more pliable.

In a food processor, blend the tofu, garlic, garlic powder, onion powder, cayenne pepper, oregano, thyme, liquid smoke, soy coffee creamer, nutritional yeast, flour, miso paste, hot sauce, celery seed, and paprika until you get a smooth paste. Give it a taste test and add any salt and pepper it might need.

Pour your tofu mix into a bowl and with a large wooden spoon mix in the Swiss chard, ½ cup vegan cheese, walnuts, 2 tablespoons of the vegan bacon bits, and 1 tablespoon of the green onions until completely blended.

After your crust has chilled, unfold it into a 9-inch glass pie dish and press it firmly and evenly into the dish. Pour your tofu filling into the crust. Scrape the sides of the bowl with a rubber spatula to get all of the filling. Then use the spatula to spread your filling evenly into the crust so that it has a flat surface. Sprinkle the remaining 1 tablespoon vegan bacon bits over the top in an even layer.

Bake for 10 minutes and then reduce the heat to 325°F and bake for another 30 minutes. You'll want to remove your quiche when the top is golden brown and you can insert a toothpick and remove it cleanly from the center.

Sprinkle some shredded vegan cheese and the remaining 1 tablespoon green onions over the top and enjoy with the self-satisfaction that comes with knowing you are enjoying a nutritious dinner that tastes like it's "bacony," "cheesy," and all kinds of bad … but isn't.

A FIELD GUIDE TO MOCK MEATS

We could shake our fists in the air and curse the mock meats of the past that were pasty and weird and chased away generations of potential vegans with their broken promises—but this book is not the place for sad songs. This is where we turn Evanescence's "My Immortal" into Journey's "Don't Stop Believin'." If you're one of those unfortunate souls who was burned by spongy chick'n in the past, or even worse, had the recipe for your favorite vegan mock meat needlessly contaminated with egg whites or whey … it's time to learn to love again. This section is dedicated to you and to those countless food scientist elves who have brought us these modern-day compassionate wonders. In no particular order, here are some of our favorite products:

Gardein Here's something you might want to know about Gardein: every serving has more than twice the protein of an egg, 4 times as much protein as tofu, and even more protein than a chicken breast. It comes in convenient ready-made meals you can bring to work or reheat after a long day, but that's not what we use. We stock up on the Chick'n Scallopini (vegan chicken breasts) and beefless tips on a weekly basis. In our opinion, there is no better substitute for recipes that involve steak or chunks of beef than Gardein's beefless tips. We also can't recommend enough the importance of choosing Gardein burgers for your burger adventures.

Lightlife Lightlife is the brand that taught me how to love again. My broken heart had grown distrustful, and I had grown comfortable with a diet that relied on beans and tofu for protein. But then I had Lightlife's Smart Deli pepperoni on a pizza, and like a schoolgirl I was smitten. Next I tried their Smart Strips Chick'n in a Philly cheesesteak type of sandwich and like any good vegan immediately sent an email to everyone I knew letting them know about my new infatuation. I quickly moved on to their Gimme Lean products and then Smart Bacon and Smoked Tempeh. You are going to find a lot of Lightlife products in this book not only because are they awesome but also because you can find them in most mainstream grocery stores. These products are the *Millennium Falcon* of the mock meat world.

Tofurky It's no secret that we love Tofurky! We love the deli slices for lunch in sandwiches, baked on pizzas, and tossed in salads. We love their kielbasas with sauerkraut, Italian sausages mixed into pasta, and beer brats with, well, a lot of beer. We love the roasts with Brussels sprouts and mashed potatoes. We love the leftovers cut up into chunks in potpies. What's not to love about this vegan classic that has become a Thanksgiving tradition all over the world?

Match Match vegan meats can be a challenge to find, but you can order them online if you're not lucky enough to live in a Match vegan meats hotspot. That can seem like a little more work than you'd think you'd be into, but anyone who would say that obviously hasn't tried Match. Match is a remarkable product that doesn't have a lot of the fillers or whatever to solidify the mock meat. Because it comes in a soft form, you can make patties and fillets in whatever size you need, and all you have to do is gently press it into bread crumbs or crushed corn flakes or crackers to "bread" it. You can bake it. You can fry it. You can do anything with it, really.

It makes great burgers. Match Italian sausage would satisfy meaty eaters. Their pork can even be formed into "ribs" over Popsicle sticks. But my all-time favorite is their vegan crab. There is no other vegan crab product on the market that even comes close. Match vegan meats are the perfect blank canvas for making any meaty recipe you might ever dream up.

Field Roast If Match vegan meats are a blank canvas, Field Roast is Monet's *Water Lilies*. If you don't consider yourself a "chef" or are kitchen challenged, you can still enjoy Field Roast's numerous products that basically require heat and maybe some bread. What else can I say? They make vegan easy.

May Wah Ever wondered how in the world you would ever enjoy calamari again now that you've gone vegan? Or if there was a way you could buy vegan chicken nuggets in bulk? Well, now you can! You can order most of these mock meat marvels via Mahnahnyc.com. We recommend the Vegan shrimp balls, which despite their unfortunate and humorous name are in our opinion the best mock shrimp out there.

Boca Not all Boca products are vegan, but their vegan burger is a significant player in the world of veggie burgers and their chicken products are easy to find in most grocery stores. They're a good thing to keep in the fridge for those nights when you don't feel like making your own dinner from scratch or doing a ton of dishes.

Trader Joe's Soyrizo There are a few different vegan versions of the Mexican chorizo sausage on the market, but we think the Trader Joe's house brand is by far the best. It's got a spicy kick and is a great addition to tofu scramble or of course any Mexican-themed dish.

Beyond Meat While this book was being edited Beyond Meat became available in a limited market in California. Hopefully by the time this book is published vegans everywhere will be able to enjoy this revolutionary product.

There are new products coming out every day, though, and who knows? By the time you read this book, one of these products might not be vegan anymore, or brands like Morningstar and Gardenburger might go back to making all their products vegan again. So here's your friendly reminder to always read your labels.

CASSEROLES

Nothing says "Betty Crocker" like the tried-and-true casserole. It's easy to prepare and simple to cook, and it feeds your whole family with leftovers. A casserole can be made to satisfy any palate preference, and you can even prepare it in advance and leave it out for your husband to stick in the oven if you're not home—although this is usually the scene in the movie signaling that the marriage is in trouble.

Vegan casseroles have been around as long as vegans have. You can always throw some combination of veggies, tofu, pasta, and/or rice in a dish, bake it, and call it a casserole. And we've got nothing against that. But what we've got going on here are rock-star casseroles loaded with mock meats and vegan cheeses—in addition to a few of those old vegan standbys. Traditional vegan casseroles, along with traditional casseroles made vegan. The perfect combination.

VEGAN TUNA CASSEROLE

After years of food scientists around the world slaving away over hot plates in laboratories and spaceship kitchens, vegans now have numerous faux-fish choices—and many of them don't even come close to resembling fish. Keeping this in mind, Dan and I invited several brave friends over to sample Tuna Casserole made with fish ham—a surprisingly delicious faux fish from May Wah. Our good buddy Kim brought over the fastest vegan Caesar salad this side of the Mississippi. We ate way more than we should have ... even our friend Marta (another adamant faux-seafood dissenter) ate a big plate of it and liked it! We hope you like it too.

MAKES 6 TO 8 SERVINGS

1½ cups elbow macaroni

3 tablespoons margarine

2 tablespoons whole wheat flour

2 tablespoons Bragg's liquid aminos

2 cups soy milk

4 tablespoons nutritional yeast

1 teaspoon vegan Worcestershire sauce, optional

Dash of liquid smoke

2 teaspoons poultry seasoning (most poultry seasonings are vegan, but some aren't, so please read your label)

2 teaspoons onion powder

1 teaspoon garlic powder

Pinch of celery seed

½ teaspoon lemon pepper

2 cups frozen peas and carrots

2 cups shredded Daiya vegan cheddar cheese or your favorite vegan cheese

1½ cups vegan fish (We used fish ham from May Wah, but there are a lot to choose from. If you can't get any, baked firm tofu would be a good substitute.)

About 2 cups French-fried onions for a topping

Preheat the oven to 350°F.

Cook and drain the macaroni as directed on the package.

In a large saucepan, melt the margarine over low heat. Whisk in the flour and Bragg's until smooth. Then whisk in the soy milk until smooth. Heat to a boil and whisk in the nutritional yeast, Worcestershire sauce, if using, liquid smoke, poultry seasoning, onion powder, garlic powder, celery seed, and lemon pepper.

Add the peas and carrots. Stir in the vegan cheese.

Keep stirring slowly. You want the vegan cheese to melt and not stick to the sides. You also want to make sure the vegan cheese doesn't clump. Once you have a thick, "cheesy" sauce, add the cooked macaroni and stir until the pasta is covered completely and evenly.

Cut the vegan fish into bite-size pieces.

Put a thin layer of the pasta mixture in an ungreased 2-quart casserole dish. Add a layer of vegan fish. Alternate the pasta mixture and vegan fish until you fill the dish. You want the pasta mixture on top, so keep that in mind when making your layers.

Bake your casserole for around 5 minutes. After 5 minutes, completely cover the top of the casserole with French-fried onions. Bake uncovered for 5 to 10 minutes. Pull the casserole out when the onions have browned to a darker golden.

GREEN CHILI LASAGNA

Okay, this lasagna isn't totally green colored, per se. But it does have green vegetables in it and is a great way to recycle leftover chili into something completely new. That's green too, right?

MAKES 6 TO 8 SERVINGS

6 (8-inch) corn tortillas

¼ cup frozen corn, defrosted

2½ cups 5-Bean Chili (page 55)

2 cups shredded Daiya vegan cheddar or pepperjack cheese or your favorite vegan cheese

¼ cup chopped fresh cilantro (you might need a bit more to garnish)

¼ cup raw baby spinach leaves

¼ cup sliced white mushrooms

¼ cup Spanish green olives, pitted and sliced (save some to garnish with)

1 fresh jalapeño, diced, optional

Preheat the oven to 350°F.

Heat your cast-iron skillet or frying pan over medium heat. Add one tortilla at a time to the skillet. Let it toast until it starts to get slightly scorched edges; then flip it and do the same on the second side. Repeat with all the tortillas.

In a large mixing bowl, mix the corn and chili.

Ladle a little of the chili into the bottom of an 8 x 8-inch glass baking dish, just enough to make a light coating. Place 2 tortillas in the bottom. Top with one-third of the chili mix and then a handful of vegan cheese. Then sprinkle on a layer of cilantro and spinach. Then layer on another third of the chili mix and another handful of vegan cheese. On top of that, sprinkle an even layer of mushrooms, green olives, and jalapeño. Place another layer of 2 tortillas, then the last of your chili and vegan cheese.

Bake for 20 to 30 minutes, or until your vegan cheese melts.

Garnish with some cilantro and olives. Just because it's a leftover makeover doesn't mean it shouldn't be pretty.

VEGAN FRIED EGGS, page 23

GRAND VEGAN BREAKFAST, page 25

BANANAS FOSTER WAFFLES, page 37

BAKED VEGAN CHICKEN AND EASY WAFFLES, page 38

CREPES, page 45

BEIGNETS, page 46

SOUTH AMERICAN CORN AND QUINOA SUMMER STEW, page 63

HEARTY NEW ENGLAND CHOWDER, page 78

CREOLE-SPICED BUTTERNUT SQUASH AND SWEET POTATO SOUP (page 79) **WITH VEGAN PARMESAN CROUTONS,** page 291

SHŌYU RAMEN BOWLS FEATURING THE VEGAN HARD-BOILED EGG, page 59

TACO SALAD, page 99

ITALIAN CHOPPED SALAD (page 102) AND
RUSTIC VEGAN CRESCIA BREAD, page 321

3-BEAN SALAD, page 112

GERMAN POTATO SALAD, page 115

BUFFALO TOFU STEAKS (page 132) **AND VEGAN RANCH DRESSING,** page 110

AVOCADO AND TEQUILA STEAKLESS TACOS, page 133

CHERRY COLA VEGAN CHICKEN WINGS, page 138

SPICY THAI VEGAN CHICKEN WINGS, page 139

MINI POT ROAST PIES, page 146

CHEEZBURGER PIE

I can remember being a little eater and reading recipes on the sides of products for random things like Cornflake-Covered Pork Chops and Cheezy Corn Wiener Roast made from those mysterious "cheese food" substances that never made their way to my family's kitchen. I grew up in a home where my mother wouldn't allow us to eat food that she said "wasn't really food." So I'd read these recipes as if they were a sneak peek into what was on other dinner tables all over America, being served by non-Italian mothers who didn't think Ragu tasted like ketchup (which it does). So one of the more exciting parts of writing this book was making some of these branded, cross-promotional concoctions, such as this true classic: the impossibly easy Cheezburger Pie! I wholeheartedly suggest giving it a try. It would be a great thing to bring to a potluck or BBQ—especially one with meatier guests.

MAKES 4 SERVINGS

Olive oil cooking spray

1 tablespoon olive oil

A few dashes of liquid smoke

4 vegan burger patties, defrosted (we recommend Gardein Beefless Burger)

1 red onion, chopped

½ teaspoon Bragg's liquid aminos

⅓ cup shredded Daiya vegan cheddar cheese or your favorite vegan cheese (you'll want a little extra to sprinkle over the top)

½ cup Bisquick mix

1 cup soy milk

2 eggs' worth of Ener-G egg replacer, made per the instructions on the package

1 tablespoon nutritional yeast

Preheat the oven to 400°F.

Spray a 9-inch glass pie plate with a light coating of olive oil cooking spray.

Heat the olive oil and liquid smoke in a cast-iron skillet or frying pan over medium heat. Once your skillet is hot, brown the vegan burger patties and red onion. Using the edge of your metal spatula, cut up your vegan burgers into bite-size pieces. Mix in the Bragg's. Cook until your onion is translucent and the vegan burger clumps have crispy edges. Be sure to scrape up any vegan burger that is sticking to the skillet—those are the best parts.

Spread the vegan burger and onion in the pie plate. Sprinkle your vegan cheese over the vegan burger and onion pieces.

In a small bowl, mix the Bisquick, soy milk, and egg replacer with a wire whisk until blended. Sprinkle the nutritional yeast over the vegan burger pieces and vegan cheese, and then pour the Bisquick mix into the pie plate.

Sprinkle a little extra vegan cheese over the top. Bake for about 25 minutes, or until you can poke the center with a toothpick and have it come out clean.

I ate mine with a side of dill pickles. Dan ate his with mustard and ketchup. It is a cheeseburger, after all, and I have to admit—it was everything I always knew it would be!

THE VEGAN MEAT LOVER'S PIZZA CASSEROLE

As far as we can tell, any sort of food can be made into a pizza version of itself. Pizza burgers. Pizza tacos. Pizza soup. And so on. And if pizza casserole wasn't Americana enough for you—we went ahead and made it a meat lover's pizza casserole. Yeah. We did that.

MAKES 4 TO 6 SERVINGS

1 package rigatoni

2 tablespoons olive oil

1 (14-ounce) package Tofurky Italian sausages, Field Roast Italian sausages, or Match vegan Italian sausage, formed into small balls

½ (4-ounce) package Lightlife Smart Deli Pepperoni

2 tablespoons red wine

1 cup sliced white mushrooms

½ green bell pepper, diced

1 (2.25-ounce) can sliced black olives, drained

2 cloves garlic, minced

1 (6-ounce) can tomato paste

1 (14-ounce) can Italian-flavored diced tomatoes

1 cup shredded Daiya vegan mozzarella cheese or your favorite vegan cheese

Dried oregano, red pepper flakes, garlic powder, and vegan Parmesan for toppings

Preheat the oven to 350°F.

Prepare the pasta per the instructions on the box.

In your treasured cast-iron skillet or frying pan, heat the olive oil over medium heat. If you're using Tofurky or Field Roast sausages, slice them into coins. Once your oil is warm, toss in the vegan sausage pieces and brown them until the edges become crispy. Remove from the skillet and set aside in a large mixing bowl. Then toss in your vegan pepperoni and brown until the edges become crispy. Remove the vegan pepperoni from the skillet and toss it into the mixing bowl with your vegan sausages. Add the red wine and mushrooms to the skillet and cook. You may want to add another teaspoon of olive oil if you feel like all the oil was used up in cooking the mock meats. Frequently toss the mushrooms in the skillet and cook them until tender. Then toss the cooked mushrooms in with the cooked mock meats.

Add the green bell pepper and black olives to the mixing bowl with the mushrooms and mock meats and mix with a large spoon.

In the same cherished cast-iron skillet, add the garlic, tomato paste, and diced tomatoes to the leftover red wine and olive oil. Stir and heat until the mixture begins to bubble. In the large mixing bowl, stir together the cooked pasta and the sauce from the skillet.

Fill your mini casserole dishes or one large casserole dish with your pasta and mock meat mix. Sprinkle a good amount of vegan cheese on top. If you're like me and have a husband who doesn't like mushrooms, you can split up the toppings and keep those undesirables out of some portions. We mark ours by placing cute little mushrooms on top of the section with mushrooms.

Once you've topped your casseroles with vegan cheese and marked which ones are which, bake them for 15 to 25 minutes. Pull them out once your vegan cheese is melted.

Top with oregano, red pepper flakes, garlic powder, or vegan Parmesan, or whatever you want. It's your party.

Betty Crocker the Superhero

"You can do it—I can help you!"

No, this isn't a joke. Sometimes I write things that are a bit over the top to add a little humor, but this time I'm serious. Now, we can talk about some things that are wrong with Betty Crocker—processed foods and American corporations in general—but I'm going to focus on the positive for a second and tell you about three groups of people who were "saved" by the iconic image that Betty Crocker represents:

Working Women Many people believe that World War II and Rosie the Riveter ushered American women into the workforce. Prior to that, women stayed busy at home—locked away baking pies, sewing dresses, and changing diapers with an empty smile and a bottle of gin hidden under the sink. But the truth is that there have *always* been women in the workforce. They cleaned homes, raised other people's children, and worked on farms and in factories. Low-income and immigrant women have always been a significant presence in the agricultural, manufacturing, and service industries.

But even though many of these women worked during the day cleaning someone else's home or raising someone else's children, they still had their own homes and families to care for in the handful of hours left over. Modern conveniences like Bisquick and cake mixes made it so working women could still bake birthday cakes for their families, for less money and in less time. It might not be something we appreciate today, when most families buy cakes premade at the grocery store, but back when that would have been considered a ridiculous luxury, Betty Crocker made all the difference to working families.

Widowed, Unmarried, and Unemployed Men Yes, these days home ec. classes are coed, but they weren't always. There was a time when men who found themselves having to take over a kitchen were grossly unprepared. Their mothers hadn't typically taught them how to bake or cook, because it was considered women's work. These men found themselves tuning in to *The Betty Crocker Cooking School of the Air* radio show and writing to "her" for advice on how they could do a better job caring for their children, or asking for recipes for the dinners their wives used to make. Some of these letters are really heartbreaking when read today, and seem to talk more about loneliness than pot roasts. Betty Crocker provided an invaluable service to these men, who otherwise had nowhere else to turn.

Housewives Yes, it's a bit trite to say Betty Crocker was a superhero to America's housewives, but it doesn't make it less true. It comes down to one word—isolation. Homemaking can be pretty isolating work, and the development of suburbs that brought women even farther from the cities only made it worse. Hundreds of thousands of letters were sent in to Betty Crocker over the years asking for advice—and often, indirectly, friendship. Everyone who sent a letter to Betty Crocker would get a personalized letter in return, with a sprinkle of product placement. Both the women responding and the relationships that developed were real—one even led to a "Betty" marrying a bachelor who had written in for cooking tips. Of course, like any good hero (examples: Spider-Man, Anakin Skywalker, Jean-Luc Picard, and Wesley and Angel from *Buffy*) there was a time when Betty went "dark." For more on that, see "The Betty We Love to Hate" page 226.

It can be easy to hate on Betty Crocker, or belittle the role she's played in our culture to nothing more than a marketing gimmick. But for millions of men and women, she was a hopeful and helpful voice during the Great Depression. She was a loyal pen pal and trusted friend to many, holding their hands while they figured out how to move from using wood-burning stoves to electric kitchens or how to live without a spouse, and she brought easy-to-use mixes and products to their grocery stores. To these people, she was a hero. We can quibble over terms like "super," since as far as I can tell she couldn't fly or run faster than a locomotive—but she did have cool gadgets like Batman does. So I think she earned it.

TACO CASSEROLE

Another recipe straight from the Betty Crocker playbook: take one thing (tacos) and make it into another thing (a casserole). But the thing is—it works. You get the delicious flavor combinations that make taco night a winner in every house in this great land of ours, while making it is as easy as throwing a bunch of ingredients in a casserole dish. We do a little extra prep work in this recipe, because we want our version to be extra-delicious. But it's recipes like this that really made me understand the magic of Betty Crocker.

MAKES 4 TO 6 SERVINGS

2 tablespoons olive oil

Dash of liquid smoke

1 cup Match vegan ground beef or Lightlife Gimme Lean vegan ground beef, defrosted

1 (14-ounce) can refried beans

1 Batch DIY Salsa (page 433)

1 tablespoon cumin

2 teaspoons chili powder

1 to 2 teaspoons cayenne pepper

2½ cups tortilla chips

½ green bell pepper, chopped

5 green onions, chopped

2 ripe tomatoes, sliced

1 cup shredded Daiya vegan pepperjack cheese or your favorite vegan cheese

¼ cup black olives, pitted and sliced

1 cup romaine lettuce, shredded

Preheat the oven to 350°F.

In your dedicated cast-iron skillet or frying pan, heat the olive oil and liquid smoke over medium heat. Once your oil is hot, toss in your vegan beef in small chunks. Cook your vegan beef, stirring occasionally, until crispy on the edges and browned. Mix in the refried beans, salsa, and spices and simmer while stirring occasionally.

In an ungreased 2-quart casserole, place 2 cups of the tortilla chips. Top evenly with the vegan beef and beans mixture. Spread out your bell pepper, onions, half the tomato slices, the vegan cheese, and the olives in even layers.

Bake uncovered for 20 to 30 minutes, or until the vegan cheese melts. Pull out of the oven and cool for 5 minutes. Top the baked casserole with the lettuce and the remaining tomato slices and tortilla chips.

DIABLO BEEFLESS LENTIL CHILI MAC

If you're the kind of eater who loves our 3-Alarm Vegan Bacon Cheeseburger (page 186), then you'll love this casserole. It's all "beefy" and "cheesy" while sparing those poor cows. It also has that "smoky" and "salty" bacon flavor that makes hipsters and the hipsteresque crave it like Gollum does that evil ring—without harming any little piggies. And then on top of all that, it's also spicy. The chipotle peppers create a deep, rich, smoky, warm spiciness that will make you glad you made some Limeade to go with it. You remembered the Limeade, right?

MAKES 4 TO 6 SERVINGS

1 (16-ounce) box whole wheat macaroni

2 tablespoons olive oil

3 dashes of liquid smoke

1 cup Gardein beefless tips or beef seitan, defrosted

8 slices vegan bacon or smoked tempeh, diced

1 chipotle pepper (you can add more if you like it spicy)

1 small yellow bell pepper, diced

1 small orange bell pepper, diced

1 small red onion, diced

1 (15-ounce) can black beans, drained and rinsed

1 (15-ounce) can lentils, drained and rinsed

1 tablespoon adobo sauce (a lot of chipotle peppers come canned in this sauce, you can use that)

¼ cup beer or nonalcoholic beer

1 can Mexican-flavored diced tomatoes

1 tomato, diced

2 tablespoons Bragg's liquid aminos

1 clove garlic, minced

3 dashes of hot sauce (more if you think you can handle it)

1 teaspoon chili powder

2 teaspoons lime juice

¼ teaspoon dried oregano

2 teaspoons cumin

2 tablespoons chopped fresh cilantro

½ cup shredded Daiya vegan cheddar cheese or your favorite vegan cheese (you might want a little extra to sprinkle over the top)

1 avocado, sliced

Make your macaroni per the instructions on the package.

While the macaroni is cooking, heat the olive oil and 2 dashes of liquid smoke in your cherished cast-iron skillet over medium heat. Once the oil is hot, toss in the vegan beef. Flip it a few times so the vegan beef gets an even cover of oil and liquid smoke. Toss in your vegan bacon pieces over your vegan beef and cook. Occasionally flip the vegan beef and vegan bacon and cook them until they are a nice even brown. Use a spatula to move the mock meat out of the skillet into a bowl. You want to keep as much oil as possible in the skillet.

Add the chipotle pepper and another dash of liquid smoke to the skillet. **Warning**: it will steam, but that's why they call it "diablo." You want to make sure that steam doesn't get in your eyes. You might think I'm be-

ing sensitive, but trust me, it'll Oedipus you, and not in a Freudian way.

While the pan is still steaming, toss in the bell peppers, onion, beans, lentils, adobo sauce, beer, tomatoes, Bragg's, garlic, hot sauce, chili powder, and lime juice. Stir and cook until the peppers are tender. Then add the oregano, cumin, and cilantro. Stir and cook for no more than another minute. Remove from the heat. Stir in the vegan beef and vegan bacon.

Then, in a large bowl, combine the vegan cheese with your warm macaroni. You want the vegan cheese to start to melt slightly. To serve, put the pasta and vegan cheese mixture on a plate and ladle the chili over the pasta. Sprinkle a little vegan cheese over the top and add a few slices of fresh avocado. The avocado will mellow out the spices a bit.

THE INCREDIBLE GREEN MONSTAH CASSEROLE

So there's no Green Monstah in Betty Crocker's Big Red, but there is a spinach-bacon-chicken casserole that I started veganizing, and I just kept going. I couldn't help myself. The casserole was very good on its own, but sometimes I see opportunities to work a little more kale or broccoli into my life and I just can't stop. Call it poor impulse control. Call it leveling up. Whatever. This dish is the perfect example of Shannons Gone Wild.

MAKES 6 TO 8 SERVINGS

1 (16-ounce) package whole wheat pasta shells, macaroni, or rigatoni

6 tablespoons margarine

3 tablespoons whole wheat flour

3 tablespoons nutritional yeast

2 cups Better Than Bouillon vegetable broth, made per the directions on the package

1 tablespoon dry white wine

¾ cup almond milk

2 teaspoons Tony Chachere's Creole seasoning

1 tablespoon Bragg's liquid aminos

2 dashes of liquid smoke

¼ teaspoon freshly ground black peppercorns

1 clove garlic, minced

1 cup frozen peas

½ cup frozen green beans

2 teaspoons chopped fresh parsley

¾ cup frozen broccoli

1 cup raw chopped kale

¾ cup sliced sun-dried tomatoes

6 slices vegan bacon or smoked tempeh, chopped

2 cups bite-size defrosted vegan chicken pieces

1 cup baby spinach leaves

Olive oil cooking spray

3 tablespoons vegan Parmesan

2 green onions, chopped

Preheat the oven to 350°F.

Cook and drain the pasta per the directions on the package.

In a large saucepan, melt the margarine over low heat. Whisk in the flour and nutritional yeast until completely blended. Gradually stir in the broth. Increase the heat to medium and bring to a boil, using your whisk to mix thoroughly. Whisk in the white wine, almond milk, Creole seasoning, Bragg's, liquid smoke, black pepper, and garlic. Simmer for no longer than 1 minute.

In a large bowl, toss the pasta, peas, green beans, parsley, broccoli, kale, sun-dried tomatoes, bacon pieces, vegan chicken, and spinach. Pour in three-quarters of the sauce and gently mix with a spoon.

Spray a lasagna dish with olive oil cooking spray and fill with the vegetable-pasta mixture. Pour the remaining sauce over the top. Sprinkle the vegan Parmesan over the top and bake for 20 to 25 minutes. Remove when the top is golden brown and the sauce is bubbling.

Serve with green onions sprinkled over the top.

VEGAN BACON CHEESEBURGER POTATO PIE

Prepare to get ridiculous. Ridiculously awesome. This recipe is the perfect manifestation of the American ingenuity and resolve that turned a scrappy bunch of colonies into a superpower ... and maybe led to us becoming the chubbiest nation too. Good thing we made ours vegan—and only for special occasions.

MAKES 4 TO 6 SERVINGS

- 1½ cups Match vegan ground beef or Lightlife Gimme Lean vegan ground beef, defrosted
- ½ cup plain bread crumbs
- ½ red onion, diced
- ¼ cup A.1. steak sauce
- 2 teaspoons yellow mustard
- 1 teaspoon Bragg's liquid aminos
- Dash of liquid smoke

- 2 to 3 warm baked potatoes (enough to make 2 cups mashed)
- ½ cup Better Than Bouillon vegetable broth, made per the instructions on the package
- 3 tablespoons margarine
- 1 clove garlic, minced
- 1 tablespoon soy milk
- 1 teaspoon nutritional yeast

- 1 tablespoon vegan bacon bits
- 1 cup shredded Daiya vegan cheddar cheese or your favorite vegan cheese
- 1 small tomato, sliced
- 2 green onions, chopped
- Sliced pickles and French-fried onions for toppings, optional

Preheat the oven to 375°F.

In a medium bowl, mix the vegan beef, bread crumbs, onion, steak sauce, mustard, Bragg's, and liquid smoke. Press the mixture in the bottom and up the sides of an ungreased 9-inch glass pie plate, like a piecrust. Bake for 5 minutes.

In a bowl, mash the potatoes with their skins.

In a Dutch oven or large stewpot, mix the mashed potatoes, broth, margarine, garlic, soy milk, and nutritional yeast. Heat over medium heat while continually stirring with a large spoon. Remove from the heat. Stir in the vegan bacon bits and ½ cup of the vegan cheese.

Remove the partially baked vegan beef crust from the oven. Spoon the mashed potatoes into the crust. Use a spatula to smooth out the top and make it even. Sprinkle the remaining ½ cup vegan cheese over the top. Bake for 10 minutes longer, or until the vegan cheese is melted.

Remove the pie from the oven. Top with the tomato slices, green onions, sliced pickles, and French-friend onions, and any other fixings you like. Let cool around 10 minutes before serving.

The downside to this pie is that unless you let it cool, it doesn't serve in nice clean slices like pie. It's more like a casserole, but it's still delicious ... like crazy-good delicious.

LOVABLE JERK CASSEROLE

This casserole is named in honor of Percy, one of the feline Shannons. Sometimes he likes to cuddle on Dan's chest as he watches TV on the couch, with his little face all nuzzled up under his dad's chin. Other times he likes to bite my ankles. He's a lovable jerk cat. This is a lovable jerk casserole. Enjoy.

MAKES 4 TO 6 SERVINGS

Olive oil cooking spray

2 teaspoons Bragg's liquid aminos

½ teaspoon pumpkin pie spice

¾ teaspoon allspice

Pinch of ground cinnamon

¾ teaspoon thyme leaves

½ teaspoon cayenne pepper

2 cups vegan chicken, defrosted

1 tablespoon plus ½ teaspoon olive oil

Dash of liquid smoke

1 large sweet potato, cubed

1 (15-ounce) can black beans, drained and rinsed

¼ cup agave nectar

2 teaspoons ginger paste

½ cup lime juice

½ teaspoon cornstarch

2 tablespoons chopped green onion

3 cups cooked brown rice

Preheat the oven to 375°F.

Spray an 8-inch glass baking dish with olive oil cooking spray.

In a small bowl, mix the Bragg's, pumpkin pie spice, allspice, cinnamon, thyme, and cayenne pepper. Rub the mixture on all sides of the vegan chicken.

In everyone's favorite cast-iron skillet, heat 1 tablespoon of the olive oil and the liquid smoke over medium heat. Cook the vegan chicken in the oil until it's a light golden brown with crispy edges.

In your baking dish, lay an even layer of sweet potatoes and top with the black beans. Top that with the vegan chicken. In a small bowl, mix the agave nectar, ginger paste, lime juice, and cornstarch; then pour it into the skillet. Heat to a boil, stirring constantly. Pour the sauce over the vegan chicken in the baking dish.

Bake for 30 to 40 minutes, or until the sweet potatoes are tender. Sprinkle with green onion and serve with brown rice.

VEGAN BACON CHEESEBURGER HASH

One night, I made Vegan Bacon Cheeseburger Hash for my husband—and although we had the Hiroshima of epically passionate first kisses and our first year as an "us" was pretty dramatic, there's another kind of love story that comes from our home, and the ongoing love affair that is our life together. One that doesn't make me cry, or stay up till 3 a.m. watching cartoons and thinking of all the things I did wrong or choices I could have made differently. Yes, I'm comparing our marriage to this dinner. Somewhere in this skillet dish that combines two soul mates—bacon cheeseburgers and French fries—there's something pretty special.

MAKES 4 TO 6 SERVINGS

- 3 tablespoons olive oil
- 2 dashes of liquid smoke
- 1 cup Match vegan ground beef or Lightlife Gimme Lean vegan ground beef or Tofurky ground beef
- ½ large red onion, diced

- ½ (32-ounce) bag frozen home fries, defrosted
- 2 tablespoons Bragg's liquid aminos
- 1 (14.5-ounce) can diced tomatoes with Italian seasoning
- 2 tablespoons chopped fresh parsley

- 1 tablespoon Tony Chachere's Creole seasoning
- 1 cup shredded Daiya vegan cheddar cheese or your favorite vegan cheese
- Vegan bacon bits to sprinkle over the top

In your precious little cast-iron skillet or frying pan, heat 2 tablespoons of the olive oil and a dash of liquid smoke over medium heat. Once your oil is hot, add your vegan burger in small clumps. It's okay to have some bits fall off the clumps. You're going to want to fry your vegan burger up so that it's lightly browned and has a crispy outside. With your spatula, transfer the vegan burger from the skillet to a bowl.

To the heated skillet, add another tablespoon of olive oil and another dash of liquid smoke. Toss in the onion and home fries. Brown those for around 5 minutes. Once they start to get little crispy edges, toss the vegan burger back in. Try to make sure you don't lose too much oil in this process. Add the Bragg's, tomatoes, parsley, and Creole seasoning. You're going to want to let the mixture cook for 5 to 7 minutes, flipping it occasionally.

Turn the heat down to a simmer and toss your vegan cheese on top. Try to keep it on the vegan burger and home fries mixture and off the skillet. Don't mix it in; just let it melt on top. It should take no more than 3 minutes to melt. Sprinkle vegan bacon bits over the top and serve with some pickles. You won't need the ketchup; it's already in there!

PANZANELLA BAKE

Panzanella is a classic Tuscan dish that is traditionally vegan already, without any interference from food meddlers like us. It's a simple summer salad of tomatoes, chunks of bread, onions, and basil, with a basic oil and vinegar dressing. We've taken the concept of panzanella and fancied it up quite a bit, adding some protein and sticking it in the oven to make it a well-rounded and hearty meal. Italian traditionalists will surely scoff at us for doing this—but I doubt anyone that beholden to tradition has made it this far through this cookbook anyhow.

MAKES 4 TO 6 SERVINGS

2 cups chopped vegan chicken (we recommend Gardein Chick'n Scallopini)

1 (14.5-ounce) can diced tomatoes with Italian seasoning, extra juice drained from the can

1 clove garlic, minced

2 portobello mushroom caps, sliced into strips

¼ cup kalamata olives, pitted

⅓ cup chopped green onions

1 cup Italian-seasoned croutons

¼ cup Fresh Herb Vinaigrette (page 108)

½ cup shredded Daïya vegan mozzarella cheese or your favorite vegan cheese

½ cup fresh basil leaves, chopped

Preheat the oven to 350°F.

In an ungreased 11 x 7-inch baking dish, layer the vegan chicken, tomatoes, garlic, mushrooms, olives, green onions, and croutons. Drizzle with Fresh Herb Vinaigrette.

Cover with foil. Bake for 20 minutes. Uncover and sprinkle an even layer of vegan cheese over the top. Bake for about 10 minutes longer, or until your vegan cheese is melted. Sprinkle with basil.

For years, "vegan pizza" was basically pizza without cheese. Which, on the one hand, was totally fine. A good crust, flavorful sauce, and tons of veggies make a hearty meal in their own right. But let's face it: pizza has cheese. "Baked veggie-pile bread" is delicious—but it's not pizza.

The main obstacle to real vegan pizza was the lack of a vegan cheese that melted properly. Sure, we had our Tofutti slices for veggie burgers, and our nutritional yeast "cheese" sauces for mac and cheese. But melty, stringy, cheese that made for a great pizza? No dice. It wasn't that it was impossible—it just hadn't been discovered yet. Even though we couldn't prove it, we knew that it, like the Higgs boson particle of theoretical physics, was lurking out there somewhere—and that, once discovered, it would reveal to us the deepest secrets of the universe, like gazing into the eyes of God.

Enter Daiya vegan cheese. It 2009, it arrived in the vegan community like the Beatles on *The Ed Sullivan Show*. The appeal was simple: it melted. Like, for real. And lo: real, authentic vegan pizza was now possible. From there, the door was opened to calzones, stromboli, and all of the other melty, "cheesy" recipes we'd been missing out on. A critical element of Betty Crocker's repertoire is finally available to us—so let's make the most of it!

WHOLE WHEAT PIZZA CRUST

These days it's not hard to find premade vegan pizza dough. Trader Joe's has two different kinds for ninety-nine cents. But if you aren't lucky enough to have a vegan pizza dough hookup in your hometown, or if you're just more of a DIY type, this recipe goes out to you.

MAKES 1 PIZZA CRUST

3 cups whole wheat flour, plus extra to flour surfaces	1 teaspoon crushed pink Himalayan salt	3 tablespoons olive oil
	1 package active dry yeast	1 cup warm water
1 tablespoon sugar		

In a large bowl, mix 1 cup of the flour with the sugar, salt, and yeast. Add the olive oil and warm water. Mix with a hand mixer at medium speed for around 3 minutes. Stir in the rest of the flour, incorporating any extra stuck on the sides of the bowl. Mix until the dough is soft and doesn't stick to the bowl. Place the dough on a lightly floured surface. Knead for 5 to 8 minutes, until the dough is smooth and springy. Cover loosely with plastic wrap and let rest at room temperature for around 30 minutes.

Preheat the oven to 425°F.

On a floured surface, roll out the dough into a 13-inch round and form into a pizza crust.

Flour your beloved little pizza stone. Gently move the pizza crust to the stone; there will probably be some re-forming needed. Then build your pizza.

MOCK MEAT LOVER'S PIZZA

You know, there's really not much more to say than this: we are Mock Meat Lovers. We've both been vegan a pretty long time now and can remember when mock meat was a pasty, bland nightmare. I know a lot of vegans still hate mock meats today, because the first generation back in the day was just so very, very bad. But those days are gone. Technology has come so far, and today, with such a variety of delicious vegan products and substitutes available (even if only by mail order in some places), there's no excuse to eat animals. So if you were one of those folks burned by one of those mock meat dinosaurs, you owe it to yourself to give these new products a try. You can live a cruelty-free life and still enjoy things like a vegan meat lover's pizza.

MAKES 1 MEDIUM-SIZE PIZZA

Cornmeal for dusting your pizza stone or cookie sheet

Whole wheat flour for rolling out the dough

1 package premade whole wheat pizza dough (or you can use the recipe on page 171)

½ cup pizza sauce

Handful of chopped fresh basil

2 handfuls of shredded Daiya vegan mozzarella cheese or your favorite vegan cheese

Handful of Lightlife Smart Deli pepperoni

⅓ cup Match vegan Italian sausage

formed into flattened chunks a little smaller than your palm, or Tofurky Italian sausages cut into coins

1 Field Roast apple sage sausage, cut into coins

Handful of sliced white mushrooms

Handful of kalamata olives, pitted

Preheat the oven per the directions on the pizza crust package or to 425 °F. if you're using the Whole Wheat Pizza Crust recipe on page 171.

Dust your pizza stone or cookie sheet with cornmeal.

Flour a work surface and roll the pizza dough into a circle (around 13 inches in diameter). Move the dough very carefully to your pizza stone.

Spread the pizza sauce over the dough, leaving a

½-inch crust along the edge. Put the toppings on in this order: basil, thin layer of vegan cheese, pepperoni, thicker layer of vegan cheese, vegan sausage chunks, layer of vegan cheese, mushrooms, kalamata olives, and a final layer of vegan cheese.

Bake for 10 to 15 minutes, until the vegan cheese is melted. Let the pizza cool before you slice it up and share with the world!

EASY GREEKISH STUFFED-CRUST PIZZA

Until we made this recipe, if you had asked me about my immediate family, I would have told you all about my two loving yet willful kittens, my dashingly perfect husband, and my loyal cast-iron skillet. I might have mentioned my hand mixer: a hardworking little bee that comes out on the weekends and special occasions for cupcakes and muffins. I may even have mentioned our Xbox: always good for some Katamari or a movie. Dan and the Xbox have made the world a safer place several times over. But the weekend we first made this recipe, we welcomed into our home a new friend, a comrade that I know will grow to become a trusted and cherished member of our little clan. And now you can make it a part of yours too.

MAKES 1 MEDIUM-SIZE PIZZA

Cornmeal to dust over your pizza stone or cookie sheet and work surface

Whole wheat flour for rolling out your dough

1 package premade whole wheat pizza dough (or you can use the recipe on page 171)

2 cups shredded Daiya vegan

mozzarella cheese or your favorite vegan cheese

¼ cup pizza sauce

¼ large red onion, chopped

Fresh basil leaves

2 Tofurky Italian sausages, sliced into coins

1 (4-ounce) package Lightlife Smart Deli pepperoni

1 (14-ounce) can artichoke hearts, quartered

¼ cup kalamata olives, pitted and sliced

2 tablespoons sliced peperoncini

Nutritional yeast to sprinkle over the top

Preheat the oven as per the directions on the pizza crust package or to 425 °F if you're using the Whole Wheat Pizza Crust recipe on page 171.

Dust the pizza stone or cookie sheet with cornmeal.

Flour a work surface and roll the pizza dough into a circle (around 13 inches in diameter). Move the dough very carefully to the pizza stone. Create a little canal about the width of a finger along the outer edge of the pizza crust, about the width of one finger in from the edge of the crust. Fill the canal evenly with no more than ¾ cup of the vegan cheese. Be careful to keep the vegan cheese inside the canal. Seal the cheese in by folding over the outer edge and pressing lightly to connect the dough.

In a bowl, mix the pizza sauce and onion. Spread the pizza sauce over the dough in the center. Be careful to not get too much on the vegan cheese–stuffed crust. Sprinkle fresh basil over the sauce. Spread out a small handful of vegan cheese over the basil. Sprinkle the vegan sausage and pepperoni over the pizza. Spread another small handful of vegan cheese over the mock meat. Sprinkle the artichoke hearts, olives, and peperoncini over the pizza. Spread another small handful of vegan cheese over the top.

Bake your pizza for 15 to 20 minutes. Just wait till your crust is golden and the vegan cheese is melted.

Sprinkle with a little nutritional yeast, and repeat after me: "Meat lovers stuffed-crust deep-dish pizza commercial … *you have no power over me!*"

BBQ PIZZA

Whoever thought of using barbecue sauce for pizza sauce deserves a Nobel Prize in food sciences.

MAKES 1 MEDIUM PIZZA

Cornmeal for dusting your pizza stone or cookie sheet

Whole wheat flour for dusting your work surface

1 package premade whole wheat pizza dough (or use the recipe on page 171)

3 tablespoons of your favorite barbecue sauce

2 cups shredded Daiya vegan cheddar cheese or your favorite vegan cheese

2 cups of your favorite barbecue mock meat (we used citrus spareribs from May

Wah, but there's also Lightlife's Smart BBQ, Morningstar Farms Riblets, and Gardein's beefless tips), mixed with 5 tablespoons of your favorite barbecue sauce

½ small red onion, sliced into rings

Preheat the oven per the instructions on the pizza dough package or to 425 °F if you're using the Whole Wheat Pizza Crust recipe on page 171. Dust your pizza stone or cookie sheet with cornmeal.

Flour a work surface and roll your pizza dough out until it makes a circle around 13 inches in diameter. Very gently move your pizza dough onto your pizza stone or cookie sheet. Create a crust for your pie by pushing the dough outward about ½ inch from the edge, forming a little mound along the edge.

Brush the barbecue sauce onto the center of the pizza dough. Be careful to not get any on the crust; it'll turn a weird brown color when baking. Then lay down a thin layer of ½ your vegan cheese, followed by a layer of barbecue mock meat, then the rest of your vegan cheese, and finally the onion rings.

Bake until the vegan cheese is melted and the crust is golden brown. It should take around 20 minutes, but you'll want to check your pizza dough package to see what the manufacturer suggests. Be aware that thicker crusts will take longer. If you're unsure, use a spatula to gently check the bottom of your pizza. You'll know right away if it doesn't look and feel done. A done pizza is solid and lifts cleanly.

MARGHERITA PIZZA

We love this pizza like Jacques Cousteau loved the open ocean. I grew up watching the Jacques Cousteau specials, and I place some of the responsibility for my career in animal advocacy on that little old Frenchman and his red hat.

MAKES 1 MEDIUM PIZZA

Cornmeal to dust your pizza stone or cookie sheet

Whole wheat flour to dust your work surface

1 package premade whole wheat pizza dough (or you can use the recipe on page 171)

1 cup shredded Daiya vegan mozzarella cheese or your favorite vegan cheese

1 tablespoon vegan Parmesan or nutritional yeast, plus a little to sprinkle over the top

1 teaspoon garlic powder

2 Roma tomatoes, thinly sliced

2 teaspoons capers, drained

1 tablespoon fresh oregano leaves

¼ cup fresh basil, half chopped and half small whole leaves

A few pinches of crushed pink Himalayan salt and crushed black peppercorns

1 tablespoon olive oil

Red pepper flakes to use as a topping, optional

Preheat the oven per the instructions on the pizza dough package or to 425 °F if you're using the Whole Wheat Pizza Crust recipe on page 171. Dust your pizza stone or cookie sheet with cornmeal.

Flour a work surface and roll out your pizza dough into a 13-inch circle. Gently move your pizza dough to the pizza stone or pan, and reshape a little if it warped when you moved it. Sprinkle ¾ of your vegan cheese evenly on the dough, leaving about ½ inch clear along the edge for the crust. Sprinkle on the vegan Parmesan and garlic powder. Arrange the Roma tomatoes evenly on the pizza. Sprinkle your capers, oregano, and chopped fresh basil evenly over the top. Sprinkle on the remaining vegan cheese, salt, and pepper. Slowly drizzle your olive oil evenly over the top, and then sprinkle with a little more vegan Parmesan.

Bake for 15 to 20 minutes, or until your vegan cheese is melted.

Once you pull it out of the oven, give the pizza 3 to 5 minutes to cool, and then sprinkle with the fresh whole basil leaves and maybe some red pepper flakes right before you serve.

HAWAIIAN PIZZA

Dan was anti-Hawaiian-pizza for a long time. He can be finicky about what sorts of foods he thinks "go" with others, and pineapples and pizza was a no-no for that lovably OCD brain of his. Thankfully, this recipe caused him to see the light. Hawaiian Pizza saves!

MAKES 1 MEDIUM PIZZA

Cornmeal to dust your pizza stone or cookie sheet

Whole wheat flour for rolling out your dough

1 package premade whole wheat pizza dough (or use the recipe on page 171)

¼ cup pizza sauce

⅓ cup shredded Daiya vegan mozzarella cheese or your favorite vegan cheese

2 to 3 slices Hickory Smoked Tofurky Deli Slices, separated and cut into fourths

¼ cup pineapple chunks or rings, drained

2 slices red onion, broken into rings

½ green bell pepper, chopped

¼ teaspoon capers, drained

Red pepper flakes to sprinkle over the top, optional

Preheat the oven per the instructions on the pizza dough package or to 425 °F if you're using the Whole Wheat Pizza Crust recipe on page 171. Dust your pizza stone or cookie sheet with cornmeal.

Flour a work surface and roll out your pizza dough into a 13-inch circle. Gently move your pizza dough to the pizza stone or pan, and reshape it a little if it warped in the move.

Spread your pizza sauce over your crust, leaving a ½-inch space along the edge. Sprinkle half your vegan cheese evenly over the dough, leaving about ½ inch clear along the edge for the crust. Place your Tofurky slices, pineapple, red onion, and bell pepper in an even layer. Then sprinkle your capers and the remaining vegan cheese over the top.

Bake for 15 to 20 minutes, or until your vegan cheese is melted and your crust is golden brown.

Once you pull it out of the oven, give the pizza 3 to 5 minutes to cool, and then, if you like, sprinkle some red pepper flakes over the top right before you serve to add a little more heat to this tropical pizza.

YOUR NEW FAVORITE PIZZA

The only reason I hesitate to crown this "your new favorite pizza" is that there are a lot of really fabulous pizzas. A lot. This pizza is special; it isn't something that you can find on the menu of your local pizza joint. It's all Asian inspired and spicy and awesome. If you're looking for a fast dinner that's something new, you should try this one out.

MAKES 1 MEDIUM PIZZA

Cornmeal to dust your pizza stone or cookie sheet

Whole wheat flour for rolling out your dough

1 package whole wheat pizza dough (or use the recipe on page 171)

1 tablespoon sesame oil

2 teaspoons chili oil

½ cup vegan chicken strips (we recommend Gardein Chick'n Scallopini)

1 teaspoon ginger paste

1 cup pizza sauce

1 tablespoon chili puree with garlic (add less if you don't like it hot)

2 teaspoons Bragg's liquid aminos

1 (8-ounce) can water chestnuts, drained and sliced

5 to 6 baby corn spears

¼ cup Chinese pea pods

⅓ red onion, diced

1 cup shredded Daiya vegan mozzarella cheese or your favorite vegan cheese

1 tablespoon raw almond slivers

1 tablespoon chopped fresh cilantro

Preheat the oven per the instructions on your pizza dough package or to 425 °F if you're using the Whole Wheat Pizza Crust recipe on page 171. Dust your pizza stone or cookie sheet with cornmeal.

Flour a work surface and roll out your pizza dough into a 13-inch circle. Gently move your pizza dough to your pizza stone or cookie sheet, and reshape it a little if it got all wonky in the move.

Heat your wok over high heat. Add the sesame and chili oils and rotate the wok to coat the sides. Add the vegan chicken and ginger paste. Stir-fry for 2 to 3 min-utes, or until the vegan chicken is browned and has crispy edges. Reduce the heat to medium. Stir in the pizza sauce, chili puree, and Bragg's.

Spoon the vegan chicken mixture onto the pizza crust to within ½ inch of the edge, to create a crust. Top with the water chestnuts, baby corn, pea pods, and onion. Sprinkle with the vegan cheese and almonds.

Bake for 15 to 20 minutes, or until your vegan cheese is melted and your crust is golden brown. Sprinkle with the cilantro.

MEXICAN STUFFED-CRUST PIZZA

Dear Mexican Stuffed-Crust Pizza:

I want to thank you for combining two of our very favorite meals—tacos and pizzas—in an enchanting, seamless, ingenious way that also gave us an opportunity to eat avocados. I also want to thank you for being so easy that we could enjoy how delicious you were in less than an hour, and not have a huge stack of dishes left to do afterward. This increased our enjoyment of the evening by a factor of at least 10.* Mostly, I just want to thank you for taking our minds off the fact that the night we had you for dinner—April 19, 2011—at 8:11 p.m., the artificially intelligent Skynet global digital defense network was supposed to have become self-aware, trigger a worldwide nuclear holocaust, and then deploy legions of robot soldiers to wage genocide on the surviving humans. Having a spicy vegan stuffed-crust Mexican pizza completely distracted us from the pending robot apocalypse and, when partnered with a Dr Pepper,** made for quite a lovely night.

XO, Annie

PS: I forgot to thank you for being vegan and therefore making the world a better place.

MAKES 1 MEDIUM PIZZA

2 teaspoons olive oil

1 package vegan soyrizo

½ red onion, diced

1 teaspoon cumin

1 (15-ounce) can black beans, drained and rinsed

Cornmeal to dust your pizza stone or cookie sheet

Whole wheat flour to dust your work surface

1 package premade whole wheat pizza dough (or you can use the recipe on page 171)

2 cups shredded Daiya vegan cheddar cheese or your favorite vegan cheese

1 large tomato, sliced

1 (2.25-ounce) can black olives, sliced

(this is a topping, so you might have some left over)

1 fresh jalapeño, sliced

1 ripe avocado, sliced

1 (16-ounce) jar of your favorite salsa (this is a topping, so you'll have some left over)

Preheat the oven per the instructions on the pizza dough package or to 425 °F if you're using the Whole Wheat Pizza Crust recipe on page 171.

In your favorite cast-iron skillet or frying pan, heat the olive oil, soyrizo, red onion, cumin, and black beans over medium heat. Mix them gently with a spatula while you cook, and remove from the heat once the mixture has browned and the soyrizo has slightly crispy edges.

Dust your pizza stone or cookie sheet with cornmeal.

Flour a work surface and roll the dough into a circle around 13 inches in diameter. Move the dough very carefully to the pizza stone. Create a little canal about the width of a finger along the outer edge of the pizza crust, about ½ inch from the edge. Fill the canal evenly with no more than ⅓ of your vegan cheese. Be careful to keep the vegan cheese inside the canal. Seal the vegan cheese in by folding over the outer edge and pressing lightly to connect the dough.

---

* This is using Annie Math and pretty much estimated. We didn't actually measure anything, so there is no real data to back up this claim.
** Yes, I do believe that all Mexican food is a little better when it is served with a cold Dr Pepper. I also have no data to back up that claim except that sometimes the universe has undeniable truths that we all just know.

Make an even layer of the soyrizo mixture in the center of the pizza and cover it with a light, even layer of vegan cheese. Then place the tomato slices on the pizza so they don't overlap, and cover them with another layer of vegan cheese. Sprinkle your black olives and jalapeño over the top and cover with the rest of your vegan cheese.

Bake for 15 to 20 minutes—just until the crust is golden brown and your vegan cheese is melted. Serve with slices of avocado and some salsa on the side.

VEGAN CHICKEN CORDON BLEU PIZZA

We learned a lot of lessons while writing this book, but here's one that stands above the rest: every recipe is better when deconstructed and made into a pizza. Making a pizza based on Chicken Cordon Bleu—a relatively recent American invention masquerading as a classic French recipe—drove that lesson home for us. This is a unique, flavorful pizza recipe that feels three times as fancy as pizza ever really should.

MAKES 1 MEDIUM PIZZA

Cornmeal to dust your pizza stone or cookie sheet

Whole wheat flour to dust your work surface

1 package premade whole wheat pizza dough (or use the recipe on page 171)

1 cup shredded Daiya vegan mozzarella cheese or your favorite vegan cheese

1 tablespoon vegan Parmesan or nutritional yeast, plus a little to sprinkle over the top

1 teaspoon garlic powder

2 teaspoons fresh chives

½ teaspoon smoked paprika

1 tablespoon fresh oregano leaves

½ red bell pepper, diced

1 cup chopped vegan chicken (we recommend Gardein Chick'n Scallopini)

2 Roma tomatoes, thinly sliced

1 (5.5-ounce) package Hickory Smoked Tofurky Deli Slices

1 green onion, diced

Red pepper flakes, optional, for topping

Preheat the oven per the instructions on the pizza dough package or to 425 °F if you're using the Whole Wheat Pizza Crust recipe on page 171. Dust your pizza stone or cookie sheet with cornmeal.

Flour a work surface and roll out your pizza dough into a 13-inch circle. Gently move your pizza dough to the pizza stone or pan, and reshape it a little if it got all distorted when you moved it. Sprinkle three-quarters of your vegan cheese evenly over the dough, leaving about ½ inch clear along the edge for the crust.

Sprinkle with your vegan Parmesan, garlic powder, chives, paprika and oregano leaves. Then arrange your bell pepper, vegan chicken, tomatoes and Tofurky over your pizza so they make an even layer. Sprinkle with green onion and the remaining vegan cheese.

Bake for 15 to 20 minutes, or until your vegan cheese is melted and your crust is golden brown.

Once you pull it out of the oven, give the pizza 3 to 5 minutes to cool, and then if you like sprinkle with red pepper flakes right before you serve.

EGGPLANT PARMESAN PIZZA

Eggplant Parmesan is seen by some as a vegetarian version of the more popular Chicken Parmesan. However, the fact of the matter is that the eggplant version of this dish is actually the original, traditional southern Italian recipe—chicken and veal versions weren't developed until much later, during waves of Italian immigration to countries where having meat as the centerpiece of every meal was more common. So this vegan recipe is actually closer to the traditional Italian meal than that Chicken Parm at your local Italian sub shop—suck on that, Carmine!

MAKES 1 MEDIUM PIZZA

1 small eggplant, cut into ¼-inch slices

Olive oil cooking spray

¼ cup nutritional yeast

½ teaspoon vegan Parmesan, plus a little more to sprinkle over the top

¼ cup dry bread crumbs

2 teaspoons olive oil

2 cups shredded Daiya vegan mozzarella cheese or your favorite vegan cheese

Cornmeal to dust your pizza stone or cookie sheet

Whole wheat flour for dusting your surfaces

1 package whole wheat pizza dough (or use the recipe on page 171)

¾ cup pizza sauce

2 teaspoons capers, drained

1 handful fresh basil leaves, chopped

1 Roma tomato, sliced

Red pepper flakes, optional, and freshly ground black peppercorns to sprinkle over the top

Set the oven control to broil or turn on your broiler. Spray both sides of each slice of eggplant with a lot of cooking spray. Place on a rack in the broiler pan. Broil 4 to 5 inches from the flame for about 10 minutes, turning once, until tender and lightly golden brown.

While the eggplant is broiling, mix the nutritional yeast, vegan Parmesan, and bread crumbs. Mix in the oil to make an extremely dry paste.

Once the eggplant is out of the oven, sprinkle on 1 to 2 tablespoons of the vegan cheese. Spoon the nutritional yeast mixture over the vegan cheese. Broil for about 1 minute, or until the vegan cheese is melted and the bread crumbs are brown.

Preheat the oven per the instructions on the pizza dough package or to 425 °F if you're using the Whole Wheat Pizza Crust recipe on page 171. Dust your pizza stone or cookie sheet with cornmeal.

Flour a work surface and roll out your pizza dough into a 13-inch circle. Gently move your pizza dough to the pizza stone or cookie sheet and reshape a little if the move ruined the shape.

Evenly spread the pizza sauce over the pizza crust, leaving ½ inch along the edge to create a crust. Sprinkle a handful of vegan cheese over the pizza sauce. Sprinkle the capers and basil leaves over the vegan cheese. Then spread the broiled eggplant and tomato slices over the pizza. Sprinkle with the rest of your vegan cheese.

Bake for 15 to 20 minutes, or until your vegan cheese is melted and your crust is golden brown. Before you serve, sprinkle some red pepper flakes and black peppercorns over the top.

Betty and the Victory Veggie Burger

Although World War II may have ended the Great Depression, it didn't make things any easier for America's homemakers. Men of all ages and ethnicities were encouraged to join the military effort, even if it was by selling war bonds at home or cooking oatmeal on military bases. Women were targeted with a different message from the U.S. government—we were asked to ration foods and home goods, to repair and reuse as much as possible, and to join the workforce like Rosie the Riveter. All over America, women were making coffee filters with ruined nylons and finding new ways to feed their families without much access to sugar and meat. This might sound funny to modern-day vegans who do this every day—but when you look at what the average American family was eating at the time, and the lack of reliable nutritional information…well, let's just say that most women found this task daunting.

Armed with helpful tips on how to make more from less, Betty Crocker was there to help, via her radio show and written correspondence. Thousands and thousands of women wrote in to General Mills every week asking for advice, and each received a personal response in return. Betty's radio spots took on a patriotic theme as she spoke often of the vital role of homemaker in the war effort. Her recipes began to have names like "Yankee Doodle Macaroni," and she featured "meatless meals" on a regular basis. Now, they weren't vegan—they included plenty of cheese and eggs—but for the first time Betty deliberately encouraged American families to explore vegetable casseroles and pasta salads. Of course, the recipe that stood out to us had one of the worst names of all: the Nut Burger.

The recipe requires an egg, but even though it wasn't vegan, it was undoubtedly a veggie burger—a veggie burger developed in the Betty Crocker test kitchen in 1945 to help all of us do what we could to defeat the Nazis—and as far as I can tell, the very first veggie burger. Betty's meatless kick would pass when the war effort ended and we all went back to complete and total consumption—but my appreciation for her first attempt at veggie burgers will be eternal.

BURGERS AND MELTS

Burgers are the quintessentially American food—the culinary version of baseball, Budweiser, blue jeans, and a dog leaning out the window of a beat-up Ford pickup. Take a good burger, pair it up with some French fries (seriously, Chiquita, you're cute and all, but everyone knows that French fries are the world's most perfect food), add a chocolate milk shake, and poof: instant Americana.

Many vegans have a love-hate relationship with the veggie burger. For years, it was just about the only vegan item you could reliably find at restaurants. Some were delicious; others, not so much. So in a world with vegan chicken, mock duck, almond milk, and melty dairy-free cheese, many vegans are inclined to move on from our old relationship with the veggie burger.

This, we believe, is a mistake. There are still many discoveries left to make in the burger sciences, many burger Picassos left to paint. Just because something's been around forever doesn't mean it has nothing left to offer. Ask any married couple (like us!).

CAESAR SALAD BURGER

When making this burger, you may be tempted to try to make one big super Hulk burger, but don't. The smaller the patties are, the more crispy edges you'll get, and that's one of my favorite parts about this burger.

MAKES 4 TO 6 BURGERS

½ cup Caesar Salad Dressing (page 106)

2 to 3 cups Match vegan ground beef or Lightlife Gimme Lean vegan ground beef, defrosted

2 tablespoons chopped fresh parsley

1 tablespoon vegan Parmesan

¼ teaspoon lemon pepper

2 to 3 tablespoons olive oil

Red onion slices

4 to 6 whole wheat sandwich buns

4 to 6 tablespoons shredded Daiya vegan cheddar cheese or your favorite vegan cheese (1 tablespoon per burger)

Romaine lettuce leaves, and tomato slices for toppings

Make your Caesar Salad Dressing.

In a large bowl, mix the vegan beef, parsley, vegan Parmesan, ¼ cup of the Caesar salad dressing, and the lemon pepper. You'll want to mix this thoroughly with your hands, kneading it like bread. Form the burger mix into 4 to 6 patties and then place them in a shallow dish and pour the remaining ¼ cup dressing over the patties. Let them sit for less than 1 minute. Flip the burgers a few times to make sure they get an even coasting.

In your favorite reliable cast-iron skillet or frying pan, heat the olive oil over medium heat. Once your oil is hot, put your burgers in so they aren't touching.

You may need to do this in a few batches. Brown the burgers in the hot olive oil, flipping them a few times so they cook evenly. When the burgers look almost ready, lay the red onion rings on your burgers and let them cook until the onions are tender and your burgers are browned.

While the vegan burgers are cooking, put your burger buns on your trusted pizza stone, open and facedown, and place in the oven. Remove them when they're slightly toasted.

Build your burger inside the toasty bun in this order: burger, vegan cheese, onions, lettuce, and tomato.

Boom.

INNER BEAUTY PATTY MELT

So a while ago I was watching *Sex and the City*, and there was this itty bit of astuteness in an observation made by Sarah Jessica Parker's character that randomly pops into my head once in a while like a little good faerie. What? I'm a girl. Sometimes I like to watch stuff that has jokes from a generic ladies' point of view and doesn't discuss Jedi politics. Anyway, in some episode that I don't remember, she says something like: "She had come to terms with her looks and had decided to not just accept her body and face, but enjoy them and treat them right. Anyone who didn't appreciate her unique beauty just didn't get it." It seems trite, simple, and obvious, the kind of canned wisdom a good mom tells her little girl and which is instantly ignored. But it hovers still, like when a wedding photographer looks at me funny because I'm going to wear my glasses and not cover up my tattoos, or when my Geek Chicness is not as obvious as my social awkwardness. I think: They don't get it. I rock.

When I was taking pictures of these patty melts for the blog, it was hard not to notice that they weren't so photogenic. My heart kind of hurt for the little things. I kept thinking about how this sandwich may not have all the snazzy colors of a good old-school salad, but it has a good personality, and that's what counts! Anyone who doesn't enjoy it just doesn't get it.

MAKES 3 TO 4 SANDWICHES

2 cups Lightlife Gimme Lean vegan ground beef or Match vegan ground beef, defrosted

2 tablespoons nutritional yeast

¼ teaspoon dried thyme leaves

¼ teaspoon dried oregano leaves

2 teaspoons Dijon mustard

1 teaspoon Bragg's liquid aminos

Dash of liquid smoke

2 cloves garlic, minced

2 to 3 tablespoons plus 1 teaspoon olive oil

1 medium red onion, diced

6 to 8 slices rye bread

½ cup shredded Daiya vegan cheddar cheese or your favorite vegan cheese

In a big bowl, mix the vegan beef, nutritional yeast, thyme, oregano, Dijon mustard, Bragg's, liquid smoke, garlic, and 1 teaspoon of the olive oil. You're going to have to roll up your sleeves and do this with your hands! You'll be glad you did. Just squish the vegan beef mixture with your bare hands until you feel like it's thoroughly mixed. Form the vegan beef mixture into 3 to 4 patties.

In your trusted cast-iron skillet or frying pan, heat the remaining olive oil over medium heat. Once your oil is hot, carefully place the patties in the skillet and brown for about 1 minute. Flip the burgers and add the diced onion to the skillet. Keep flipping the patties so they brown on both sides, keeping an eye on the diced onion the whole time. If the onion starts to overcook, you can pile it on the patties. This will add extra flavor to the patties and keep your onion from burning. Remove from the heat once the patties are browned and feel firm in the center.

Preheat the oven to 350°F. Make your sandwich like so: inside your rye bread, pile the vegan beef patty, vegan cheese, and red onions. Put your sandwich in the oven and remove once your bread is toasted and your vegan cheese is melted.

PIZZA BURGER

You're going to love these burgers like the world loves Spider-Man. I think we all love Spider-Man because we love Peter Parker. He's a good friend and son (or nephew or whatever) and, like our loyal little friend the veggie burger, can always be counted on.

I have no idea how many veggie burgers I've eaten over the years. We travel a lot, and we take comfort in knowing that more and more places have a friendly neighborhood veggie burger these days. They've become a trusted friend to vegans everywhere. Saying that, if veggie burgers are Peter Parker, the Pizza Burger is Spider-Man. This burger kicks butts in a bold-faced, saucy style. It's a show-off; but who cares? *It's amazing!*

MAKES 4 BURGERS

1 to 2 tablespoons olive oil

Dash of liquid smoke

4 vegan burger patties, defrosted (we recommend Gardein Beefless Burger)

½ red onion, sliced

4 whole wheat sandwich buns

8 tablespoons pizza sauce (2 tablespoons per burger)

16 to 20 slices Lightlife Smart Deli pepperoni (4 to 5 slices per burger)

8 to 12 tablespoons shredded Daiya vegan mozzarella cheese or your favorite vegan cheese (2 to 3 tablespoons per burger)

½ small green bell pepper, chopped

8 teaspoons sliced black olives (2 teaspoons per burger)

Oregano and red pepper flakes to sprinkle over the top

Peperoncini for a little something extra

Preheat the oven to 400°F.

In your cherished little cast-iron skillet or frying pan, heat the olive oil and liquid smoke over medium heat. Add the vegan burgers. Once they start to brown, add the red onion. Flip the vegan burgers a few times, until they're brown on both sides. If the onion is done cooking before the vegan burgers are done, you can always pile it on top of the vegan burgers to add a little flavor.

While the vegan burgers and onion are cooking, put your sandwich buns on your trusted pizza stone, open and facedown. Place them in the oven and remove when they're slightly toasted.

Take the top half of the buns off the pizza stone and set aside. Flip the bottom half of the buns over and put the vegan burgers on there. Now stack the pizza toppings on the vegan burgers in this order: pizza sauce, vegan pepperoni, little bit of vegan cheese, cooked red onion, green bell pepper, more vegan cheese, black olives, and more vegan cheese. Put the pizza burgers back in the oven to bake.

It should take 10 to 20 minutes for the vegan cheese to melt, depending how much you put on. Keep an eye on it, and remove your pizza burgers from the oven once the vegan cheese is melted.

Sprinkle oregano, red pepper flakes, and pepperoncini over the vegan cheese and put the top half of the bun on.

Don't forget: with great power comes great responsibility. So don't take your pizza burger for granted. It may seem simple, but that doesn't mean it won't rock.

GREEK SLIDERS

Ever make something so good you wish you were a millionaire so you could hand it out on the street and teach the world to sing in perfect harmony? That's how I feel about these burgers. If I had my way, they'd be called World Peace Burgers, but that seemed too Hippie Miss America for us Shannons. I support the choice to stay boring with the naming of this burger because I'm sure it'll help more people find it in this book.

MAKES 8 SANDWICHES

2 cups Match vegan ground beef or Lightlife Gimme Lean vegan ground beef, defrosted

¼ cup crumbled vegan herb-flavored feta cheese (we recommend soy feta by Vegcuisine)

¼ cup diced kalamata olives

2 tablespoons Bragg's liquid aminos

2 dashes of liquid smoke

1 tablespoon fresh oregano leaves

2 teaspoons fresh thyme leaves

1 teaspoon chopped fresh mint leaves

2 teaspoons grated lemon peel

Olive oil cooking spray

4 whole wheat pitas, cut in half to form pockets

½ cucumber, diced

¼ cup diced red onion

1 Roma tomato, sliced

8 to 16 tablespoons tahini (1 to 2 tablespoons per pita)

1 batch Vegan Tzatziki Sauce (page 289)

Peperoncini, roasted red peppers, sun-dried tomatoes, pickles, and lettuce for toppings

In a large bowl, mix the vegan beef, vegan feta, olives, Bragg's, liquid smoke, oregano, thyme, mint, and lemon peel with your hands. Really get in there and knead your vegan beef to get the ingredients mixed in very well.

Form 8 small patties from the vegan beef. Spray a heavy coating of olive oil cooking spray over your cast-iron skillet with grill ridges and heat over medium heat. Once the oil is hot, cook the vegan burgers 1 or 2 at time, flipping once to get those nice grill lines on each side. You may need to spray your skillet with more cooking spray between vegan burgers.

Follow the instructions on the pita package to warm them.

Once the vegan burgers are cooked, fill the pitas with the burgers, vegetables, tahini, Vegan Tzatziki Sauce, and peperoncini, roasted red peppers, sun-dried tomatoes, pickles, and lettuce, or whatever sauces and toppings you like.

3-ALARM VEGAN BACON CHEESEBURGER

In around 20 minutes you can make a vegan bacon cheeseburger that's so hot, it's way out of your league.

MAKES 4 BURGERS

1 to 2 tablespoons olive oil

Dash of liquid smoke

4 vegan burger patties, defrosted (we recommend Gardein Beefless Burger)

8 slices vegan bacon or smoked tempeh

4 whole wheat burger buns

½ cup shredded Daiya vegan pepperjack cheese or your favorite vegan cheese

4 to 6 tomato slices

4 to 6 red leaf lettuce leaves

You still have 2 alarms left. Here are some suggestions to choose from:

Sliced peperoncini

Slices of Daiya jalapeño garlic Havarti wedge

Spicy kimchi

Any of the millions of hot sauces out there, including the beloved Sriracha

Sliced jalapeños

Chipotle peppers

Hot salsa

Wasabi

Lightlife Smart Deli pepperoni

Spicy mustard

Jerk sauce made with red Scotch bonnet pepper

Preheat the oven to 400°F.

In your cherished little cast-iron skillet or frying pan, heat the olive oil and liquid smoke over medium heat. Add your vegan burgers. Flip your vegan burgers a few times, until they're brown on both sides. Pull them out of the skillet and then use the same oil to fry up your vegan bacon. Once the vegan bacon is crispy, place it on top of the vegan burgers so any smoky flavor goes into the burger.

While the vegan burgers and bacon are cooking, put your burger buns on your trusted pizza stone, open and facedown, and place in the oven. Remove when they're slightly toasted.

To build your burger: take the top half of the buns off the pizza stone and set aside. Flip the bottom half of the buns over and stack your burger, a few pinches of vegan cheese, and the vegan bacon. Put the burgers back in the oven to bake.

It should take 10 to 15 minutes for the vegan cheese to melt. Keep an eye on it, and remove from the oven once the vegan cheese is melted.

Then stack the tomatoes, lettuce, and your favorite alarms on top and serve with a glass of something cool.

VEGAN HAWAIIAN BACON BURGER

This is going to sound weird—but here goes. Hawaii never really seems like it's actually part of the United States to me. I mean, I know that it is—I paid attention in history class. But it's this crazy little island kingdom more than two thousand miles off our shores, with a wonderful and unique blend of cultures and ethnicities that you can't find anywhere else in the United States. It's like saying the Falkland Islands are really a part of the United Kingdom, or that Greenland is really a part of Denmark. They are—but are they *really*? Final proof: these Vegan Hawaiian Bacon Burgers have a unique flavor so delicious that they should count as "ethnic cuisine." Sorry, Hawaii.

MAKES 4 BURGERS

1 to 2 tablespoons olive oil, plus more if necessary

2 dashes of liquid smoke

4 vegan burger patties, defrosted (we recommend Gardein Beefless Burgers)

1 tablespoon pineapple juice

4 to 6 slices vegan bacon or smoked tempeh

4 pineapple rings

4 whole wheat sandwich buns

½ cup teriyaki sauce

½ red onion, sliced into rings

½ green bell pepper, sliced

4 to 6 romaine lettuce leaves

1 tablespoon Vegenaise, optional

Preheat the oven to 400°F.

In your cherished little cast-iron skillet or frying pan, heat the olive oil and a dash of liquid smoke over medium heat. Add the vegan burgers. Drizzle half of your pineapple juice over your vegan burgers. Flip your vegan burgers a few times, until they're brown on both sides. While they're browning, add the vegan bacon and fry up until crispy. After you remove the vegan burgers and vegan bacon from the warm skillet, toss in another dash of liquid smoke and more oil if you need it. Then put your pineapple rings in the skillet with the rest of the pineapple juice and heat. Flip your pineapple a few times with a spatula so that it browns evenly. Be careful to not break up your pineapple rings. They will get tender as they brown.

While the vegan burgers and pineapples are cooking, put your sandwich buns on your trusted pizza stone, open and facedown, and place them in the oven. Remove when they're slightly toasted.

It's time to build your burger. Take the top half of the buns off the pizza stone and set aside. Flip the bottom half of the buns over and put your vegan burgers on them. Brush with teriyaki sauce. Then stack the pineapple rings on top and brush the pineapple and vegan burgers with more teriyaki sauce. Put back in the oven to bake.

It should take 5 to 10 minutes for the teriyaki sauce to brown and the vegan burgers to get a nice glaze.

To serve, stack your toppings—onion rings, bell pepper, and lettuce—on top of the pineapple, and then spread some Vegenaise on the top half of the bun if you like.

E 'ai ka-kou! That might be *"bon appétit"* in Hawaiian.

SMOKY PORTOBELLO MUSHROOM BURGER

Dan hates mushrooms, so I save this recipe for when he has to travel for work. You could say it's my secret boyfriend burger, except I tell everyone.

MAKES 4 SANDWICHES

4 large portobello mushroom caps

¼ cup Fresh Herb Vinaigrette (page 108)

2 dashes of liquid smoke

2 tablespoons olive oil

1 teaspoon dried oregano leaves

¼ teaspoon celery seed

2 cloves garlic, minced

1 tablespoon Bragg's liquid aminos

½ teaspoon freshly ground black peppercorns

1 cup vegetable oil, for coating the grill

4 whole wheat burger buns

¼ cup shredded Daiya vegan mozzarella cheese or your favorite vegan cheese

Handful fresh basil leaves

A.1. steak sauce, optional

Heat a gas or charcoal grill per its instructions.

Place the mushroom caps in a resealable plastic bag. In small bowl, whisk together the vinaigrette, liquid smoke, olive oil, oregano, celery seed, garlic, Bragg's, and black pepper. Pour over the mushrooms and seal the bag. Gently move your bag around to coat your mushroom caps. Marinate for 20 minutes.

Brush a clean hot grill with vegetable oil. Place the marinated mushrooms on the grill over medium heat. Save your marinade for basting. Cook the mushrooms, uncovered, for 5 to 8 minutes, frequently brushing with marinade. Turn the mushrooms over and cook for 3 to 6 minutes longer. Place the burger buns on the grill, cut side down, to toast them slightly. Once your mushrooms are tender, it's time to build your burgers. Place the mushrooms in the toasted buns, sprinkle some vegan cheese over the top, and top with fresh basil leaves.

You can put any type of condiments you want on your mushroom burger, but I can't stress enough: A.1. steak sauce is best.

INSIDE-OUT VEGAN BACON CHEESEBURGER

This burger *looks* like just a boring old hamburger—until you realize it has a dark secret it's been hiding from you all these years. Biting into this burger is like watching the episode of *Battlestar Galactica* when they reveal that Chief is actually a Cylon—mind-blowing, and a guarantee that you're hooked in for the next three episodes. Er, bites.

MAKES 4 TO 6 BURGERS

¼ cup shredded Daiya vegan cheddar cheese or your favorite vegan cheese

¼ cup vegan bacon bits

2 (14-ounce) packages Lightlife Gimme Lean burger or 3 cups Match vegan

ground beef, defrosted

Olive oil cooking spray

Dash of liquid smoke

¼ cup Bragg's liquid aminos

4 to 6 whole wheat burger buns

Hamburger fixings—sliced tomatoes, lettuce, pickles, Vegenaise, mustard, and the like

Put the vegan cheese and vegan bacon bits in two separate soup bowls.

Heat your faithful cast-iron skillet or frying pan over medium heat. Preheat the oven to 200°F.

While your skillet is heating up, mold the vegan beef into 8 to 12 patties that are a little less than ¼ inch thick and about the size of your palm. You'll need an even number—we made 12, but you might want your patties to be larger. The 12 patties will eventually be built into 6 good-size patties, so don't make them too thick. Choose six of the patties and very gently place about 2 teaspoons of the vegan cheese in the center of each, and then put 2 teaspoons of the vegan bacon bits on top of that. Then take the rest of the patties and gently place one on top of each dressed patty. Mold the patties with your fingers to seal the edges together. The vegan beef will be a little like dough, so you can use your hands to shape the burger into a patty by gently pressing and molding it. Make sure your edges are sealed up first so that none of the fixings escape.

Once your pan is hot, spray it down with olive oil cooking spray and toss in a dash of liquid smoke. Put a few patties in the hot skillet. You can cook several at the same time, but don't crowd them. Very gently pour 1 to 2 teaspoons of Bragg's over each patty, and cook. After a few minutes, flip the patties with a metal spatula. The patties should be starting to brown now, and you may want to toss another teaspoon of Bragg's on the other side. You're going to be flipping the patties a few times to evenly brown both sides. Repeat this process with all the patties, and keep the browned ones warm in a glass baking dish in the oven.

Once all your patties are cooked, place them in the buns and build your burgers with all your favorite fixings. The vegan cheese will melt inside your burger, and when you take a bite, it'll be in the center with the smoky vegan bacon bits, being delicious.

THE EVOLUTION OF VEGAN CHEESE

My first exposure to vegan "cheese" was actually a drizzle of tahini sauce over a pizza. I knew it tasted familiar, but I politely smiled and ate it up. It tasted great, and I hadn't eaten cheese in years, so it was fun to play along. The truth was that deep in my heart, I missed cheese. I grew up enjoying cheese and crackers with my mom. For years, we'd sew doll clothes and watch *Ripley's Believe It or Not* and eat cheese and crackers with a side of M&M'S. It was one of the few things we'd do together in a childhood full of her working a lot and me figure skating and taking ballet lessons. So when I went vegan, I was unintentionally declaring myself adult enough to choose my own diet. But my life was unlike all those coming-of-age movies in the eighties; I wasn't rewarded with a pink prom dress and Ducky serenading me with Otis Redding. No, I was punished with years and years of terrible oily wax called "vegan cheese."

I won't name names here. I'm a classier dame than that. But several years of my life were spent with an open heart, looking for love (by which I mean a good substitution for vegan cheese) in all the wrong places. Eventually I fell for a "cheesy" sauce made from liquid smoke and the unfortunately named but delicious nutritional yeast. For years, we mixed it with macaroni and baked it into casseroles. We'd hear rumors of revolutionary dairy-free cheeses, only to find out later that these mythical beasts were able to melt like real cheese only because they had casein (a milk protein) in them.

What's the point of dairy-free cheese that isn't even vegan?

But then something happened. In my imagination this took place in a secret bunker hidden in the side of a snowy peak in the Alps, like something from a Bond movie. Or perhaps it was in a garage, all Steve Jobs–style. Where it came from doesn't matter as much as the fact that now there are actually a few very impressive vegan cheeses on the market to choose from.

Daiya vegan cheeses You may have noticed we use Daiya a lot, and that's because it's pretty much breathtaking. I mean it's so good, I worry there was some Faustian bargain struck to make a vegan cheese so wonderfully melty and good. You can use it to replace cheese in any pizza, burger, enchilada, taco, and basically any recipe you have that requires a soft "cheesy" component. Oh, and did we forget to mention it's gluten-, soy-, and GMO-free?

Teese I wish I could tell you we use Teese from Chicago Soy Dairy just as much, but here's the truth—we can never find it. It melts pretty great and is also gluten-free. We hear from people all the time who say this is their melty vegan cheese of choice, and ya know, we're intrigued. Mostly we're just glad that we live in a world where there are two vegan cheeses that melt like the animal-based stuff and are both so good they have significant fan bases that will hopefully find a way to agree to disagree.

Tofutti slices For many of us vegans, this was our first exposure to the world of nondairy cheese. I'm going to stay classy and focus on the positive here, and say if you haven't revisited Tofutti American slices since those early years, it's time to forgive and forget. I can only in good conscience recommend the American slices, which are remarkably similar to those Velveeta slices so many

Americans swear are food. But what's great about Tofutti slices now is that they taste better than ever, and they don't have cow secretions in them. You can also toss them in a sandwich bag and bring them to a restaurant that's progressive enough to have a veggie burger but hasn't taken the leap into vegan cheese yet. I like to bring them to ball games where they have veggie dogs, to level up a night with America's favorite pastime.

Sheese Back in 1988, a group of Scotsmen followed in the footsteps of the legendary William Wallace and stood up for freedom … from dairy products. Unfortunately, it took more than twenty years for us to get some. We started with a block (yes, block) of smoked cheddar with some rosemary crackers, red grapes, and wine. It was pretty much my dream date night. Since then we've baked with it and used it in salads and pasta dishes. In a world full of shredded and spreadable vegan cheeses, this block cheese is a significant player by not just having a hard-cheese texture, but coming in specialty flavors like blue cheese, Gouda, and our favorite, the smoked cheddar. One of our favorite tricks is to let a block of the smoked cheddar dry out on a counter overnight and then use it in a parmesan cheese grater over pasta.

Dr. Cow Made from 100 percent raw organic nuts, these cheeses are soy- and gluten-free while employing the same procedures used for making traditional dairy-based cheeses to create something wonderful and vegan to spread over crackers.

Even old classics that were once horrific (sorry, just being honest) have been revamped into what they should have always been. In a world full of people who sigh and shrug and say that they would be vegan if they could find a way to give up cheese, we raise our fists in the air and say, "They can take our dairy … but they cannot take … our *freedom!*"

"Everything you see I owe to spaghetti."

—Sophia Loren

Unless you've grown up with an Italian mother, it might be impossible to explain the role pasta plays in the world. See, little Italian girls (even little half-Italian girls) grow up knowing that you can tell someone you love them a thousand times—but if you want to tell them you love them in a way that goes beyond words, you need to make them pasta.

BAKED SPINACH GNUDI

Gnudi in Italian means "naked," just like it sounds. I know, you'd think for a "Romance" language they'd have something a little classier, but no. These little dumplings are named that because they're supposed to be the filling of a ravioli without the actual ravioli. The classic gnudis are made with ricotta and eggs and boiled, but we made ours better. Better for you, and also better tasting, because when you bake them instead of boil them, the water doesn't leach out all the nutty and "cheesy" flavors that complement the spinach so well. The dark side to gnudis is that they're pretty fragile. But while you're eating them, you won't care. You'll be distracted by how tasty they are.

MAKES 2 SERVINGS

1½ cups baby spinach

1 (14-ounce) package extrafirm tofu, drained and crumbled

1 cup nutritional yeast

¼ cup shredded Daiya vegan mozzarella cheese or your favorite vegan cheese

4 tablespoons garbanzo bean flour (you might need a little extra if your tofu is too soft)

2 teaspoons dry white wine

1 teaspoon Ener-G egg replacer, just the powder, not made per the instructions on the package

1 teaspoon water

1 clove garlic, minced

1 teaspoon garlic powder

¼ teaspoon grated nutmeg

1 tablespoon diced fresh parsley

Pinches of crushed pink Himalayan salt and crushed black peppercorns

½ cup dry Italian bread crumbs

Olive oil cooking spray

1 batch Walnut, Shallot, and Sage Sauce (page 289)

Preheat the oven to 375°F.

In a large bowl, combine the spinach, tofu, nutritional yeast, vegan cheese, flour, white wine, egg replacer, and water. Very gently, use your hands to toss the ingredients. Add the garlic, garlic powder, nutmeg, parsley, and a bit of salt and pepper. Taste test some of the smaller pieces of tofu to see how much salt and pepper you need. You're going to start gently mashing the mix into dough with your hands. If it feels too loose, add more garbanzo bean flour, 1 teaspoon at a time.

Fill a shallow dish with dry Italian bread crumbs. Use your hands to gently roll 2 tablespoons of dough into little balls one at a time. Then gently roll the little balls in the bread crumbs while lightly pressing the bread crumbs into the tofu.

Spray a glass lasagna dish with olive oil cooking spray and place the gnudis in the dish so they aren't touching. You should end up with around 20 balls. Bake for 15 minutes, or until golden brown. They will lose their shape a little because the vegan cheese will melt, but they should make little mounds.

Make your Walnut, Shallot, and Sage Sauce while your gnudis are baking.

Serve hot with some bread to clean your plate, and maybe a glass or two of that white wine you were cooking with earlier.

LET'S TALK GNOCCHI

While most people think of gnocchi as being an Italian dish, you can find these little dumplings all over the world. They're popular in Croatia, parts of France, South America, and of course New York City's Little Italy. Walk down Mulberry sometime and you'll see sandwich boards advertising gnocchi lunch specials on every block. But what's the secret behind the popularity of these little buddies? Well, first of all, they're made from potatoes, and everyone loves potatoes. Second, they're easy to make and store, so you can make a few right before dinner, or make a million some Sunday night to have for lunch all week. But even though this pasta is easy, you still have to treat it right. Here are a few tips and tricks to having a successful relationship with your gnocchi:

Use the right kind of potatoes—ones that are starchy and hard. Yukon Golds make a lovely baked potato because the margarine melts right in, but they make pretty mushy gnocchi. Invest in a few good, solid russets and you won't regret it.

We use organic produce, so that might help you choose what potatoes to use in these recipes. Franken-GMO-produce can be huge, which we're not accounting for in these recipes, so keep that in mind when you're shopping.

Don't be gentle with your potatoes. You can use a food processor or an electric handheld mixer—but whatever you do, don't allow any clumps. You want your potato blend to be as fluffy and smooth as possible.

Don't get discouraged. Making gnocchi takes practice and patience. As with all Italian food, every region has its own style, and just because one recipe didn't make your heart skip a beat like the first time you visited the Tivoli Fountain in Rome … well, try and try again.

Work in only enough flour to hold the dough together while keeping it slightly sticky. If you add too much flour or overwork the dough, you'll end up with tough lumps that'll ruin your gnocchi.

Always bake your potatoes instead of boiling. The extra moisture you get from boiling the potatoes can make your gnocchi mushy.

If your gnocchi is going to fall apart, it's usually during the final boiling step. One way you can get around this if you're feeling insecure is to bake your gnocchi instead of boiling them, or even give them a quick pan-sear.

EVERYDAY GLUTEN-FREE GNOCCHI

We don't live gluten-free, but for those who do, gnocchi offer a rare opportunity to make something quite special.

MAKES 2 SERVINGS

- 4 russet potatoes
- 1 tablespoon ground flaxseeds
- 3 tablespoons water (you might need a little more)
- 3 tablespoons garbanzo bean flour (you'll need a little more to flour your surfaces)
- 3 tablespoons potato starch
- 2 tablespoons crushed pink Himalayan salt for the gnocchi water, plus more for seasoning the gnocchi
- Crushed black peppercorns

Preheat the oven to 400°F.

Bake your potatoes until they are very tender. In a small bowl, mix the flaxseeds and water and let sit while your potatoes are baking.

Your potatoes are going to be very hot, so wear an oven mitt while you use a large spoon to scrape all the white fluffy potato out of the skins into a large mixing bowl. Use an electric handheld mixer to blend up the cooked potatoes. This could take 10 minutes or so, and you'll have to stop to scrape the sides of the bowl a few times, but it's really important to get out all the lumps.

Once your potatoes are smooth and fluffy, blend in the flaxseed-water mixture, flour, and potato starch. Then give it a little taste test to see if it needs any salt or pepper and add what it needs. Keep in mind you're going to be putting sauce on it, but you still want the dumplings to have a little flavor of their own. If the dough is tough and dry, add a little more water, 1 teaspoon at a time, and keep blending until the dough is smooth.

Flour a tabletop to work on. Divide your dough into 4 equal portions. Use your hands to very gently roll 1 portion of dough into a rope about ½ inch thick. With a sharp knife, cut the rope into ¼-inch pieces. Repeat this process with the remaining 3 portions.

Then take each piece and gently press into the dough with your thumb while gently rolling your hand forward. This will create a piece of dough that looks like a little bowl or shell. Now, if you have a gnocchi board, you can use it for this step to get those little grooves to hold your favorite sauces.

Bring to a boil a large pot of water with 2 tablespoons of salt. Put the gnocchi in the boiling water a handful at a time. The little raw gnocchi will sink to the bottom of the pot, but when they rise that means they're done. Use a slotted spoon to fish 'em out and move them to a plate.

We recommend enjoying these little buddies with New Country Chunky Marinara Sauce (page 283) and Tofurky Italian sausages.

WHOLE WHEAT GNOCCHI

When Dan studied abroad in Argentina in college (before their massive economic collapse), he subsisted largely on gnocchi. Italian immigrants dominate Buenos Aires in particular, and the culture and cuisine of the city are largely Italian as a result. Neighborhood Italian kitchens each have their own proprietary gnocchi recipes—and Dan sampled them all. This recipe can go mano a mano with any of them and uses whole grains to boot. Es *super-bueno*.

MAKES 2 SERVINGS

4 large russet potatoes

4 cups whole wheat flour (you'll need a little bit more to flour your surfaces)

4 tablespoons olive oil

3 tablespoons crushed pink Himalayan salt

1 teaspoon Ener-G egg replacer, just the powder, not made per the instructions on the package

½ teaspoon water (you might need a little more)

Preheat the oven to 400°F.

Bake your potatoes until they're tender. Your potatoes are going to be very hot, so wear an oven mitt while you use a large spoon to scrape all the white fluffy awesome out of the skins into a large mixing bowl. Use an electric handheld mixer to blend up the cooked potatoes. This could take a while, and you'll need to stop a few times and scrape the sides to make sure you get it all. This can take 10 minutes, but it's important.

Once your potatoes are smooth and fluffy, blend in the flour, olive oil, 1 tablespoon of the salt, the egg replacer, and water. If the dough is tough and dry, add a little more water, 1 teaspoon at a time, and keep blending until the dough is smooth.

Flour a tabletop to work on. Divide your dough into 4 equal portions. Use your hands to very gently roll 1 portion of dough into a rope about ½ inch thick. With a sharp knife, cut the rope into ¼-inch pieces. Repeat this process with the remaining 3 portions.

Then gently press into each piece of dough with your thumb while gently rolling your hand forward. This will create a piece of dough that looks like a little bowl or shell. If you have a gnocchi board, you can use it for this step to get those little grooves to hold your favorite sauces.

Bring to a boil a large pot of water with 2 tablespoons of salt. Put a handful of gnocchi in the boiling water at a time. The little raw gnocchi will sink to the bottom of the pot, but when they rise, that means they're done. Use a slotted spoon to fish 'em out and move them to a plate.

We recommend enjoying these little buddies with Super Green Basil Pesto (page 284).

PUMPKIN GNOCCHI

Pumpkin is such a weird gourd. I think most of us probably think of *Cinderella* when we think of pumpkins, which is apt. It looks like it was imagined just for use in that fairy tale, like the weird pretend purple plants the away team always encounter on random Star Trek planets. It can't possibly be a real thing. But it is. And it makes delicious gnocchi.

MAKES 2 SERVINGS

1½ cups pumpkin puree (use a slotted spoon to remove your pumpkin from the can to cut down on the moisture a little when you measure it out)

2 tablespoons instant mashed potatoes

1 tablespoon Ener-G egg replacer, just the powder, not prepared as instructed on the package

2 tablespoons plus ½ teaspoon crushed pink Himalayan salt

¼ teaspoon ground cinnamon

¼ teaspoons grated nutmeg

2 cups all-purpose flour (you might need more to flour surfaces)

In a large bowl, combine the pumpkin, instant mashed potatoes, egg replacer, ½ teaspoon of the salt, and the cinnamon and nutmeg with an electric handheld mixer until the mixture is smooth and creamy. Mix enough of the flour into the pumpkin mixture to form a soft dough.

Flour a tabletop to work on. Divide your dough into 4 equal portions. Use your hands to very gently roll 1 portion of dough into a rope about ½ inch thick. With a sharp knife, cut the rope into ¼-inch pieces. Repeat this process with the remaining 3 portions.

Then gently press into each piece of dough with your thumb while gently rolling your hand forward.

This will create a piece of dough that looks like a little bowl or shell. If you have a gnocchi board, you can use it for this step to get those little grooves to hold your favorite sauces.

Bring to a boil a large pot of water with the remaining 2 tablespoons of salt. Put a handful of gnocchi in the boiling water at a time. The little raw gnocchi will sink to the bottom of the pot, but when they rise, that means they're done. Use a slotted spoon to fish 'em out and move them to a plate.

We recommend serving this hot with Walnut, Shallot, and Sage Sauce (page 289).

Modern-Day Betty

It's ironic that so many consider Betty Crocker to be a relic from the "good ol' days," since from the day she was created she's always been an advocate for the modern kitchen. Back in the twenties, American homes were in flux. New electric and gas appliances were making cooking and baking tips from Mom and her wood-burning stove obsolete. It wasn't just a new generation of young brides that needed help figuring out their way around these mystery machines. Women of all ages were being humbled by modern technology and needed someone to show them how to make their family's favorite meals again. Enter Betty Crocker.

Since the day they created her, Gold Medal/General Mills has had a legion of Bettys answering questions on how to fix a dry cake or how to de-lump your mashed potatoes, without judgment and without outing a local culinary hero as being lost with her new stove. Gold Medal even sent Bettys all over the country with fully functioning display kitchens. They gave crowds of all ages and genders a chance to see in person such mythical beasts as a working refrigerator. But while these Bettys were brilliant ways to promote Gold Medal products, they also were creating a level of brand loyalty that even today has few peers.

Reading through the letters sent from "Betty Crocker," it's hard not to notice that they all read more like letters from a friend (with some product placement) than like commercial circulars. That's because they weren't form letters. For generations, if you wrote to Betty Crocker, a Betty wrote you back—a practice you can see reflected today on their social networking profiles, which, while polished and professional, do have more personality and interaction than almost any other brand-based page.

Today's Bettys aren't that different from the women who came before them. We still need tips on how to work the latest wave of kitchen gadgets, and a friend to share pictures of our latest baking accomplishments with. But today we're trying to find a way to make a home while making a living. We're hoping to raise healthy children—who also enjoy their food. But with the rise of veganism and vegetarianism, and a wave of new vegan-friendly products on the market, there's another new wave of modernity sweeping over the cooking landscape—and many of us need a hand adjusting, in the way our mothers and grandmothers did in their day. Now, with some of the tips in this book, we can still look to the woman in red for guidance.

VEGAN CHICKEN TETRAZZINI

This is actually the very first recipe we made for the Betty Crocker Project, and it was kind of a bittersweet night. We loved it—but because it was the first recipe in a two-year project, we knew it would be a long time before we'd get to enjoy it again. Before you start this recipe, you should know that if you ordered this dish at a nonvegan restaurant, it would be white. This recipe is made with whole wheat flour, nutritional yeast, and Bragg's—so even though it isn't the snowy, colorless sauce you might expect, the flavor has a charming character that can class up even a casual night at home.

MAKES 4 SERVINGS

1 package whole wheat spaghetti

1 to 2 tablespoons olive oil

2 cups strips defrosted vegan chicken (we recommend Gardein Chick'n Scallopini)

6 white mushrooms, sliced

1 cup broccoli florets

¼ cup margarine

3 tablespoons whole wheat flour

½ teaspoon Bragg's liquid aminos

¼ teaspoon lemon pepper

1 cup Better Than Bouillon vegetable broth, made per the instructions on the package

½ cup soy plain coffee creamer

2 tablespoons dry sherry

½ cup nutritional yeast

Preheat the oven to 350°F. Cook and drain the spaghetti per the instructions on the package.

In your cast-iron skillet or frying pan, heat the olive oil over medium heat. Once your oil is hot, sauté your vegan chicken and mushrooms. Once your vegan chicken starts to brown, toss in the broccoli. Keep stirring to keep the broccoli from burning and make sure everything gets an even coating of the warm oil. When this has been done and the broccoli is lightly cooked, remove from the heat and set aside.

In your favorite saucepan, melt your margarine over low heat. Stir in the flour, Bragg's, and lemon pepper. Keep stirring till the mix is smooth and bubbly. Remove from the heat and stir in the broth and soy creamer. Then heat again till the mixture begins to bubble.

Mix the spaghetti, sherry, vegan chicken, broccoli, and mushrooms into the sauce. Pour the mixture into an ungreased 2-quart casserole dish. Sprinkle with the nutritional yeast.

Bake, uncovered, for 30 minutes, or until bubbly in the center.

VEGAN SHRIMP FLORENTINE ORZO

Don't be intimidated by the long list of ingredients—this is a simple, easy-to-prepare recipe for a delicious, hearty meal. It's perfect for a dinner party—your guests will think you spent hours in the kitchen preparing this modern take on a traditional Italian dish. Really, it'll take you about 20 minutes. If that's not what today's busy cooks are looking for, I don't know what is.

MAKES 4 TO 6 SERVINGS

1 tablespoon olive oil

1 red bell pepper, chopped

3 green onions, chopped

3 cloves garlic, minced

1½ cups uncooked orzo

2 teaspoons chopped fresh dill weed

2 teaspoons grated lemon peel

1 teaspoon Bragg's liquid aminos

¼ teaspoon sea kelp or seaweed flakes

¼ teaspoon dried thyme leaves

2 cups Better Than Bouillon vegetable broth, made per the instructions on the package

1 cup water

1 tablespoon dry white wine

¼ cup frozen peas

1 cup baby spinach leaves

1 cup baby kale leaves

1½ cups vegan shrimp, defrosted (we recommend May Wah shrimp balls cut in half)

Vegan Parmesan to sprinkle over the top

Heat the olive oil in your BFF Dutch oven or oven-safe casserole dish over medium heat. Cook the bell pepper, onions, and garlic until tender but still crisp.

Stir in the orzo, dill weed, lemon peel, Bragg's, sea kelp, thyme, broth, water, and white wine. Heat to a boil, and then reduce the heat. Cover and simmer for 8 to 10 minutes, or until the pasta is tender.

Stir in the peas, spinach, kale, and vegan shrimp. Cover and cook for 2 minutes, or until the vegan shrimp is hot. Sprinkle with vegan Parmesan.

LINGUINE AND VEGAN CLAM SAUCE

Yes, substituting oyster mushrooms for clams is a very old trick. I can remember making vegan fried clams with my roommate in college and thinking we were so clever, until I went to a vegetarian restaurant in San Francisco and saw them on the menu. Oh. But just because vegans are some clever and creative folks doesn't make this recipe any less delicious and amazing. Even if you don't like mushrooms, you can always replace them with vegan chicken or tofu and still have a dish that will bring the shock and awe. You need to make your vegan clams in advance, and it takes a bit of time, so you're going to need to plan ahead.

MAKES 2 TO 4 SERVINGS

VEGAN CLAMS

1 tablespoon vegan Worcestershire sauce

1 tablespoon garlic powder

1/3 cup Bragg's liquid aminos

1 can oyster mushrooms, drained, stems cut off (I recommend the canned rather than fresh ones, because they're chewier and soak up the marinade better)

LINGUINE AND SAUCE

1 package linguine

1/3 cup dry white wine

2 tablespoons olive oil

3 cloves garlic, minced

3 tablespoons margarine

1 teaspoon celery seed

2 tablespoons chopped fresh parsley (you may want a little extra to sprinkle over the top)

1 teaspoon lemon pepper

1/2 cup shredded smoked cheddar Sheese or your favorite vegan cheese

Vegan Parmesan to sprinkle over the top

In a shallow bowl, make your vegan clams. Mix the vegan Worcestershire sauce, garlic powder, and Bragg's. Add the oyster mushroom tops and marinate for 6 hours.

Prepare the linguine per the package instructions.

In your *adorato* little cast-iron skillet or deep sauté pan, add the white wine, olive oil, garlic, and margarine and heat over medium heat. Stir occasionally. Once the margarine is melted, add the vegan clams and marinade and simmer for 30 seconds to 1 minute. Stir in the celery seed, parsley, and lemon pepper. Once your vegan clams are the desired tenderness and the parsley has begun to wilt, add the vegan cheese. Keep stirring occasionally. Once the vegan cheese melts, remove the sauce from the heat.

Serve over linguine with vegan Parmesan sprinkled over the top and with some bread to really soak up this fantastic sauce … perhaps Rosemary Garlic Bread (page 271).

ZITI ALL'AMATRICIANA

You can't have a tour of Italy without a good ziti. Traditional all'Amatriciana is made with dried pork cheeks—but we're going to let those cute little piggies keep their cute little faces, and instead do this classic Italian dish vegan-style. It's so good it'll bring a smile to your own little cheeks.

MAKES 4 TO 6 SERVINGS

½ cup ziti

2 to 3 tablespoons olive oil

1 package Hickory Smoked Tofurky Deli Slices or vegan bacon, chopped

1 clove garlic, minced

¼ teaspoon red pepper flakes

1 cup finely chopped red onion

1 package extrafirm tofu, drained and mashed

3 cups diced tomatoes

8 fresh basil leaves

Dash of liquid smoke

Crushed pink Himalayan salt and crushed black peppercorns

¾ cup nutritional yeast

Cook the pasta in large pot of boiling slightly salted water until it is al dente. When you bake your ziti, the pasta will absorb some of the liquids from the sauce, so you want to make sure your pasta is a tiny bit undercooked to keep it from getting mushy. Once it is ready, drain and return your pasta to the same pot. It will get extra starch from the pot.

Heat 1 tablespoon of the olive oil in a cast-iron skillet or frying pan over medium heat. Add half of the vegan bacon and fry until crisp. It should take about 5 minutes. Transfer the vegan bacon to paper towels to drain. This is your garnish. Add the remaining 1 to 2 table-spoons olive oil to your hot skillet. Add the garlic and red pepper flakes and cook for about 2 minutes. Add the onion, tofu, and remaining vegan bacon; cook until the onion is translucent. Mix in the tomatoes, basil, and liquid smoke. Simmer for 5 to 8 minutes. Give your sauce a taste test and season with salt and pepper.

Add your tomato sauce and nutritional yeast to your pasta in the pasta pot and toss. Give it another taste test and season with salt and pepper if you need to. Transfer the pasta to a bowl. Sprinkle with the reserved vegan bacon and serve.

MACARONI AND SHEESE CUPS

This is the best recipe. No joke. Nothing more to say. The. Best. Recipe. Period.

MAKES 6 TO 8 CUPS

2 cups elbow macaroni

¼ cup margarine

¼ cup nutritional yeast

1 teaspoon Bragg's liquid aminos

¼ teaspoon crushed black peppercorns

¼ teaspoon ground mustard

½ teaspoon onion powder

Pinch of turmeric

Dash of liquid smoke

½ teaspoon vegan Worcestershire sauce

2 cups soy milk

½ teaspoon dried onion flakes

1 cup shredded smoked cheddar Sheese
or your favorite vegan cheese

1 cup shredded Daiya vegan cheddar cheese
or your favorite vegan cheddar cheese

6 to 8 tablespoons dry bread crumbs
(1 tablespoon per cup)

6 to 8 teaspoons Italian seasoning
(1 teaspoon per cup)

3 to 4 teaspoons sesame seeds
(½ teaspoon per cup)

Cook and drain the macaroni per directions on the package.

In a saucepan, melt the margarine over low heat. Stir in the nutritional yeast, Bragg's, pepper, mustard, onion powder, turmeric, liquid smoke, and vegan Worcestershire sauce. Simmer while stirring occasionally. Once the mixture is smooth, stir in the soy milk. Heat until the mixture begins to boil, and then remove from the heat. Stir in the onion flakes and vegan cheeses. Gently combine the macaroni and the vegan cheese sauce.

In a bowl, combine the bread crumbs, Italian seasoning, and sesame seeds.

Set the oven to broil or turn on your broiler. With a large spoon, fill 6 to 8 oven-safe custard or crème brûlée cups with your mac and Sheese and sprinkle around 1 tablespoon of the bread crumbs mixture over the top of each. Put the cups in the oven on the broiler pan. Shut the door and count to 10, then pull them out and check them. If they aren't brown enough to serve, put them back in for another count of 10 and then check again. Keep doing this till you like the color and crispness.

PENNE WITH VODKA SAUCE

Yeah, vodka generally isn't thought of as being traditionally Italian. We tend to get drunk on wine, and leave the potato liquor for our pals in Russia. It's cold up there, so they need to drink something with a little fire. But Italians do love their vodka sauce—and you will too once you whip up this recipe.

MAKES 4 TO 6 SERVINGS

1 package whole wheat pasta

1 (28-ounce) can fire-roasted tomatoes

¼ cup vodka

⅓ cup soy milk

2 tablespoons vegan Parmesan

1 teaspoon dried oregano

1 teaspoon chopped fresh parsley

¼ cup olive oil

3 cloves garlic, minced

½ teaspoon celery seed

1¼ teaspoons crushed black peppercorns

6 large fresh basil leaves

Make your pasta per the instructions on the package.

In a saucepan, heat the remaining ingredients over medium heat to a boil. To serve, ladle the sauce over your pasta, and don't forget some bread to clean your bowl with.

ROSEMARY VEGAN CHICKEN AND OLIVE ORZO

In addition to its use in delicious recipes like this one, rosemary offers a wide range of benefits. It's been used as an herbal remedy to improve memory, is high in antioxidants, and some believe it may be useful in treating cancers, strokes, and Alzheimer's. We just think it's delicious.

MAKES 4 TO 6 SERVINGS

Olive oil cooking spray

2 cups vegan chicken, defrosted (we recommend Gardein Chick'n Scallopini)

3 cloves garlic, minced

1¼ cups uncooked orzo

1 cup Better Than Bouillon vegetable broth, made per the instructions on the package

2 zucchinis, sliced

⅓ cup kalamata olives, pitted

3 Roma tomatoes, sliced

1 red bell pepper, sliced

1 teaspoon dried rosemary leaves, crushed

½ teaspoon chopped fresh parsley

½ teaspoon Bragg's liquid aminos

1 teaspoon olive oil

1 tablespoon chopped fresh basil leaves

Crushed pink Himalayan salt and freshly ground black peppercorns

Red pepper flakes for topping

Spray your favorite Dutch oven or saucepan with olive oil cooking spray and heat over medium heat. Once your oil is warm, toss in your vegan chicken and cook until brown and slightly crispy. Remove your vegan chicken from the pan but don't wipe out the oil.

Toss the garlic, orzo, and broth into your oily pan. Heat to a boil, and then reduce the heat, cover, and simmer until most of the liquid is absorbed.

Mix in the zucchinis, olives, tomatoes, bell pepper, rosemary, parsley, Bragg's, olive oil, and basil. Add salt and pepper to taste. Heat to a boil again, and then reduce the heat. Cover and simmer until the vegetables and orzo are tender. Mix in the vegan chicken and serve with red pepper flakes sprinkled over the top.

PENNE ALL'ARRABBIATA

I have a handful of memories from my last visit to Rome without Dan. Some delightful. Some crazy. Some kinda sad. I sent Dan a postcard from the Spanish Steps, partied at a Roman disco, and had a huge bowl of Penne all'Arrabbiata outside the Oppio Caffè overlooking the Colosseum. It was nighttime and raining and I had been wearing heels and carrying a very heavy laptop all day. And yet when I think about that trip, my favorite memory is that night, that view, and that bowl of pasta. The name of this dish literally means "angry pasta," so don't be shocked if it's pretty spicy.

MAKES 4 SERVINGS

1 package whole wheat penne

3 tablespoons olive oil

½ red onion, diced

3 cloves garlic, minced

2 to 4 fresh red chili peppers, seeded and diced (the more you add, the spicier it is)

8 to 10 fresh Roma tomatoes

6 to 8 large fresh basil leaves, chopped

Crushed pink Himalayan salt and freshly ground black peppercorns

Grated smoked cheddar Sheese or vegan Parmesan

Make your penne using the instructions on the package.

In your *adorabile* yet very large saucepan, heat your olive oil over medium heat. Once your oil is hot, toss in the onion, garlic, and peppers and sauté for around 1 minute. Then toss in the tomatoes. Stir while the mixture cooks, to help blend the flavors. Simmer for 2 minutes. During that time use your spatula to mash your tomatoes a bit.

Stir in your basil leaves, and then remove from the heat. Give the sauce a taste test to see if it needs salt or pepper, and add what you need.

Ladle your sauce over your pasta and sprinkle some grated vegan cheese over the top.

Don't forget to make some Rosemary Garlic Bread (page 271).

PAGLIA E FIENO

Also known as Straw and Hay in places like Little Italy and the Betty Crocker test kitchen, this dish is traditionally made with a combination of handmade flavored pastas. Unless you live near Little Italy, you'll probably want to make do with what you can get at the store. Even with store-bought pasta, the flavors in this dish can make you feel like you're sitting on Mulberry Street outside Pellegrino's.

MAKES 4 TO 6 SERVINGS

9 ounces plain fettuccine

9 ounces spinach fettuccine

1 tablespoon margarine

1 cup sliced white mushrooms

2 tablespoons diced red onion

8 pieces vegan bacon or smoked tempeh, chopped

2 tablespoons chopped fresh parsley

¼ cup brandy

⅓ cup almond milk

⅓ cup nutritional yeast

½ cup frozen peas

1 teaspoon Bragg's liquid aminos

Dash of liquid smoke

¼ teaspoon freshly ground black peppercorns

2 cloves garlic, minced

1 can artichoke hearts, drained

½ cup fresh baby spinach leaves

1 teaspoon olive oil

Make your pastas using the instructions on the packages.

In your much-loved and never-feared cast-iron skillet or sauté pan, melt the margarine over medium heat. Sauté the mushrooms, onion, and vegan bacon in your hot margarine. Once your mushrooms and onions are tender and your vegan bacon is crispy, toss in the parsley. Sauté for 30 seconds over medium heat.

Remove your vegetables and vegan bacon from the skillet and set aside. Pour the brandy and almond milk into your warm skillet and stir until blended. Add the nutritional yeast and blend using a whisk until smooth. Add the peas, Bragg's, liquid smoke, black pepper, and garlic and heat to a boil. Then toss in the artichoke hearts, spinach, and olive oil and remove from the heat. Mix in mushrooms, onion, and vegan bacon.

In a large mixing bowl, mix the pastas. Serve with your smoky vegan cream sauce and vegetables over the top.

Don't forget the bread to clean your plate.

EASY SESAME BEEFLESS LO MEIN BOWL

This is not a super-traditional lo mein recipe, but it's delicious and fast. You can make it in the morning, reheat it for lunch, and have leftovers for dinner. No joke, we've done it.

MAKES 4 TO 6 SERVINGS

1 (9-ounce) package Gardein beefless tips or beef seitan, defrosted

3 tablespoons plus 1 teaspoon sesame oil

1 teaspoon cornstarch

6 tablespoons Bragg's liquid aminos

1 (6-ounce) package rice stick or lo mein noodles

3 tablespoons ginger paste

2 cloves garlic, minced

1 can bamboo shoots, drained

1 can water chestnuts, drained and sliced

½ cup baby corn, drained

½ cup fresh sugar snap peas

¼ cup shredded carrots

⅓ cup baby bok choy leaves

¾ cup Better Than Bouillon vegan beef broth, prepared per the instructions on the package

⅓ cup rice vinegar

⅓ cup agave nectar

¼ teaspoon red pepper flakes, crushed

3 green onions, chopped

1 tablespoon sesame seeds

In a glass bowl, toss the vegan beef, 1 tablespoon of the sesame oil, the cornstarch, and ½ teaspoon of the Bragg's. Cover and refrigerate for 15 minutes.

Meanwhile, in a large bowl, soak the noodles in enough cold water to cover them for around 7 minutes. Read the instructions on your package, though—some may call for more or less soaking in warm or hot water. I recommend following the instructions on your noodle package.

Warm a bowl for your vegetables to go in after they are stir-fried. Heat your wok over medium heat. Add 1 tablespoon of the sesame oil and rotate the wok with your wrist to coat the inside. Add the ginger paste and garlic; mix them in the oil for 30 seconds. Add the bamboo shoots, water chestnuts, baby corn, peas, carrots, and bok choy and stir-fry until they are tender but still a little crisp. If you are planning on reheating this dish, you will want to keep them more crisp than tender. Remove the vegetables from the wok and put them in your warm bowl.

Add 1 tablespoon of the sesame oil to the wok and rotate your wok again to coat the inside. Add your vegan beef and marinade, and stir-fry for no more than 4 minutes. You want the vegan beef to have a nice browned outside. Remove the vegan beef from the wok and place it in the bowl with the vegetables. I recommend putting your vegan beef on top of your vegetables so that the oil running out of the vegan beef can flavor the vegetables.

Add the broth, rice vinegar, agave nectar, the remaining 5 tablespoons plus 2½ teaspoons Bragg's, the remaining 1 teaspoon sesame oil, and the red pepper to the wok. Stir in your soaked noodles and increase the heat slightly. Toss and cook for no more than 2 minutes. Once your noodles are tender, stir in your vegan beef and vegetables. Cook for around 1 minute. Sprinkle with green onions and sesame seeds and serve with chopsticks to keep it real.

CACIO E PEPE

This minimalist dish may seem more Spartan than Roman, but spend a day walking through Rome and you'll see this simple yet fabulous dish on every menu propped up next to a bowl of chilled oysters on the half shell or a dented Coca-Cola sign.

MAKES 2 TO 4 SERVINGS

1 package fettuccine noodles

4 tablespoons olive oil

2 teaspoons freshly ground black peppercorns

½ cup nutritional yeast or vegan Parmesan

½ cup finely grated smoked cheddar Sheese or your favorite vegan cheese

Fresh oregano leaves

Crushed pink Himalayan salt and crushed black peppercorns

Prepare your pasta per the instructions on the package—unless they recommend rinsing after you drain your pasta. Don't do that.

Once your pasta has been drained but is still steaming hot, pour it into a large serving bowl. Toss the pasta with the olive oil, black pepper, nutritional yeast, and half of your grated vegan cheese. Then sprinkle the remaining vegan cheese over the top. The heat of the pasta will melt the vegan cheese.

Serve warm with the oregano and salt and pepper so everyone can season their own plate.

SPAGHETTI ALLA CARBONARA

Spaghetti alla Carbonara is one of those dishes that you may have heard of, but no one really knows where it came from. Some claim it's been passed down from the Romans. But they say that about anything awesome in Italy. Others think it has something to do with the Carbonari, a nineteenth-century secret society that played a key role in the unification of Italy. But really, the first documentation of it was from World War II. While the United States occupied Italy, the troops sometimes traded their powdered eggs and bacon with the locals, who then used them to make this dish. Many returning troops brought their passion for this pasta back with them, and Spaghetti alla Carbonara hit menus everywhere.

MAKES 2 TO 4 SERVINGS

1 package whole wheat spaghetti

2 cloves garlic, minced

8 slices vegan bacon or smoked tempeh, diced

3 tablespoons olive oil

⅓ cup vegan Parmesan

½ cup nutritional yeast

2 teaspoons silken tofu

Dash of liquid smoke

¼ teaspoon crushed pink Himalayan salt

¼ teaspoon crushed black peppercorns (you'll want extra to sprinkle over the top)

3 tablespoons grated smoked cheddar Sheese or your favorite vegan cheese, plus extra for sprinkling

2 tablespoons chopped fresh parsley

Cook the spaghetti as directed on the package. After you drain it, put it back in the same pot because you need the little bit of the starch left in there for your dish, but make sure the pasta is away from the heat.

In your *amato* cast-iron skillet or deepest frying pan, cook the garlic and vegan bacon in 1 tablespoon of the olive oil over medium heat until the vegan bacon is crispy. Mix the vegan Parmesan, nutritional yeast, silken tofu, liquid smoke, salt, black pepper, vegan cheese, and the remaining 2 tablespoons olive oil in the cast-iron skillet and simmer over low heat for 1 minute. You're going to want to stir the sauce constantly to mix the silken tofu in with the other ingredients and make sure it's a smooth consistency. Once the sauce is smooth and beginning to bubble slightly, remove from the heat.

Add the garlic, vegan bacon, and sauce to the spaghetti in the pot and toss to evenly coat your pasta. You're going to cook and toss your spaghetti and bacon mixture for around 30 seconds to a minute while heating over low heat. Then remove from the heat.

When you serve, sprinkle some extra shredded vegan cheese, parsley, and black pepper over the top and channel your inner Sophia Loren.

FETTUCCINE WITH CANNELLINI BEANS AND ARTICHOKE HEARTS ALFREDO

When I was a little eater who had no idea what a calorie was, let alone where cheese came from, I loved cream sauces. In fourth grade I even wrote a poem that I was very proud of about my favorite food: fettuccine Alfredo. I wish I still had a copy of this literary masterpiece, or could at least remember the good parts. I have a feeling it would be comedy gold now. What I do remember is my teacher making a joke to my mom that I should enjoy it while I could, because Lord knows Italian women shouldn't be eating cream sauce after they turn eighteen unless they've completely given up on themselves. To be fair to this teacher, who was supposed to be a female role model in my life, it was the eighties, when women all over the United States unfortunately were starving themselves to be able to wear white spandex. But let's be honest: those jokes are still around today. Which is ridiculous. I mean, I'm vegan now, and I enjoy vegan Alfredo sauce all the time completely guilt-free. Is it the healthiest sauce you can pour over some pasta and clean up with some garlic toast? Not really. But as far as "guilty pleasures" go, it's pretty harmless.

MAKES 4 TO 6 SERVINGS

1 package fettuccine

1 (14-ounce) can cannellini beans, drained and rinsed (also called Great Northern beans)

1 (14-ounce) can artichoke hearts, drained

1 cup soy milk

¼ cup vegan sour cream

½ cup nutritional yeast

2 tablespoons Bragg's liquid aminos

2 tablespoons kalamata olive brine (this is the juice that kalamata olives come in)

1 teaspoon olive oil

1 tablespoon margarine

1 tablespoon lemon juice

3 cloves garlic, minced

1 tablespoon vegan cream cheese

1 teaspoon garlic powder

1 tablespoon dry white wine

Crushed pink Himalayan salt

Fresh parsley for garnish

Crushed black peppercorns

Prepare the pasta per the instructions on the package.

In your cherished food processor or overworked blender, toss in all the ingredients except the pasta, salt, pepper, and parsley and blend for over a minute. You want to liquefy your ingredients—especially the artichoke hearts—so stop blending when they are completely mixed into the sauce.

Pour your sauce into a saucepan and heat over medium heat until it begins to boil. Remove from the heat and add your desired amount of salt. We only added one dash, but you might prefer more.

When you serve your dish, toss a pinch of chopped fresh parsley and some black pepper on top and put on some white spandex. I mean—why not? You're pretty.

> **TIP:** Level up your Alfredo sauce with some steamed zucchini, asparagus, broccoli, or carrots to make it more of a pasta primavera—because vegetables are our delicious friends.

PIZZA SHELLS

In a world where vegan ravioli and tortellini can be hard to find, pasta shells can fill that vacant spot in your heart that longs for stuffed pasta. Pizza shells might sound silly, but they taste wonderful.

MAKES 4 SERVINGS

12 jumbo pasta shells

Olive oil cooking spray

1 tablespoon olive oil

1 cup diced green bell pepper

1 red onion, diced

⅓ cup sliced white mushrooms

1 (4-ounce) package Lightlife Smart Deli pepperoni, diced

3 tablespoons sliced black olives

2 teaspoons dried oregano

Pinch of crushed pink Himalayan salt

1 clove garlic, minced

3 Roma tomatoes, diced

2 cups shredded Daiya vegan mozzarella cheese or your favorite vegan cheese

2 cups pizza sauce

Cook the pasta shells using the directions on the package.

Preheat the oven to 350°F.

Spray an 11 x 7-inch glass baking dish with olive oil cooking spray.

Heat the olive oil in your favorite cast-iron skillet or frying pan over medium heat until hot. Toss in the bell pepper, onion, and mushrooms. Mix and cook until the vegetables are tender. Remove from the heat. Mix in the pepperoni, olives, oregano, salt, garlic, tomatoes, and 1½ cups of the vegan cheese. Use a wooden spoon to mix these ingredients well.

Your shells will be hot, so be careful filling them with the pepperoni filling mix. Place the filled shells in the sprayed baking dish. Any remaining filling can be spread out between the shells. Use a ladle to pour an even coating of pizza sauce over the top. Cover with foil.

Bake for 20 to 30 minutes, or until the vegan cheese is melted and the sauce is bubbling. Uncover, sprinkle with the remaining ½ cup vegan cheese, and bake for 5 to 10 minutes longer. You'll know it's done when the vegan cheese is completely melted.

TEMPEH RATATOUILLE SHELLS

Ratatouille was one of the first recipes I ever veganized. I'm not sure it really counts, though, since ratatouille is one of the most vegan-friendly dishes France has to offer. And I would just like to state for the record that I did this before the extremely popular Pixar movie came out. I was just that far ahead of the curve.

MAKES 4 SERVINGS

Olive oil cooking spray

12 jumbo pasta shells

1 tablespoon olive oil

1 green bell pepper, diced

1 red onion, diced

3 cloves garlic, minced

1 teaspoon garlic powder

2 teaspoons Bragg's liquid aminos

1 package tempeh, crumbled

1 cup cubed eggplant

1 zucchini, diced

2 tablespoons kalamata olives, pitted

⅓ cup sliced white mushrooms

½ teaspoon capers, drained

2 teaspoons herbes de Provence

1 tablespoon red wine

1 cup tomato sauce

1 cup shredded Daiya vegan mozzarella cheese or your favorite vegan cheese

Chopped fresh parsley

Preheat the oven to 350°F. Spray an 11 x 7-inch glass baking dish with nonstick cooking spray.

Cook the pasta shells per the instructions on the package.

While your shells are cooking, heat the olive oil in your cast-iron skillet over medium heat until hot. Toss in the bell pepper, onion, garlic, garlic powder, Bragg's, and tempeh. Mix and cook until your vegetables are tender and your tempeh begins to brown. Add the eggplant and zucchini. Cook for another 3 to 5 minutes. You want your vegetables to be tender and your onions translucent.

Mix in the olives, mushrooms, capers, herbes de Provence, red wine, and ¼ cup of the tomato sauce. Mix and cook until the mushrooms are tender. Stir in ½ cup of your vegan cheese.

Carefully fill each cooked pasta shell with the tempeh and vegetable mixture. Place the filled shells in the baking dish. With a ladle, pour the remaining tomato sauce over your shells. Cover with foil.

Bake for 30 minutes. Uncover and sprinkle with the remaining vegan cheese. Bake, uncovered, for 5 to 10 minutes longer, or until the dish is bubbly and the vegan cheese is melted. Sprinkle fresh parsley over the top.

VEGAN SHRIMP-STUFFED SHELLS

This recipe reads like a tongue twister but tastes like a tongue-pleaser.

MAKES 4 SERVINGS

Olive oil cooking spray

12 jumbo pasta shells

2 cups Cannellini Beans and Artichoke Hearts Alfredo Sauce (see page 207)

1 tablespoon margarine

1 red onion, diced

½ red bell pepper, diced

1½ cups 1-inch-dice fresh asparagus

½ cup frozen peas

¼ cup quartered artichoke hearts, drained

2 cups vegan shrimp, defrosted and cut into 1-inch pieces after measuring

2 cloves garlic, minced

2 teaspoons dry white wine

2 tablespoons fresh basil leaves

½ cup shredded Daiya vegan mozzarella cheese or your favorite vegan cheese

¼ cup vegan Parmesan

Preheat the oven to 350°F. Spray a 13 x 9-inch glass baking dish with olive oil cooking spray.

Cook your pasta shells as directed on your packaging.

While your pasta shells are cooking, make your Cannellini Beans and Artichoke Hearts Alfredo Sauce using the recipe on page 207. Then melt the margarine in your favorite cast-iron skillet or sauté pan over medium heat. Once your margarine is melted, toss in the onion and bell pepper and cook while mixing until your vegetables are tender. Stir in the asparagus, cover, and cook for another 3 to 5 minutes, stirring occasionally. Once your asparagus is tender, remove from the heat. Stir in the peas, artichoke hearts, vegan shrimp, garlic,

white wine, and 1 tablespoon of the basil. Once your vegan shrimp is warm, add ½ cup of your vegan Alfredo Sauce.

Spread about ¼ cup of the remaining Alfredo sauce over the bottom of the baking dish. Carefully fill each cooked pasta shell with your vegan shrimp mix. Place each filled shell in your baking dish faceup. Once the shells are all filled, sprinkle a little bit of vegan cheese over each shell. Using a ladle, pour the remaining sauce over the shells. Sprinkle each filled shell with vegan Parmesan.

Bake, uncovered, for 25 to 30 minutes, or until bubbly. Sprinkle your remaining 1 tablespoon basil over the top.

PASTA IN FRESH BASIL GREEN SAUCE WITH TOASTED WALNUTS AND VEGAN ITALIAN SAUSAGE

Avocado "cream" sauce is not a new concept in vegan cuisine. I bet hidden somewhere in a deep cave waiting out the millennia are charcoal paintings of vegan stick men eating avocado cream sauce. I've seen green sauce used as Alfredo sauce or in potato salad, but I like to think of green sauce as being its own thing. It's an institution … at least in my mind. Sharing this recipe with you all is kind of a big deal for me, to be honest. It's like the Colonel posting the secret list of eleven herbs and spices they have squirreled away in Louisville.

MAKES 4 TO 6 SERVINGS

1 package whole wheat angel hair

2 tablespoons olive oil

1 package Tofurky Italian sausage or Field Roast Italian sausage, sliced into coins

1 teaspoon red pepper flakes

¼ cup kale, chopped into big pieces

⅓ cup baby spinach leaves

¼ cup fresh basil (keep a few extra leaves to toss on top)

2 ripe avocados, peeled, pitted, and chopped

2 tablespoons nutritional yeast

¼ teaspoon onion powder

Pinch of turmeric

2 cloves garlic, minced

1 (14-ounce) can garbanzo beans, drained and rinsed

¼ cup frozen peas, defrosted

2 teaspoons Bragg's liquid aminos

⅓ cup dry white wine

Crushed pink Himalayan salt and crushed black peppercorns

Make the whole wheat pasta per the instructions on the box.

In your BFF cast-iron skillet or frying pan, heat the olive oil over medium heat. Once the oil is hot, brown your vegan sausage slices until they have crispy edges. Turn down the heat to a low simmer. Toss in the red pepper flakes, kale, and spinach and cook over low heat. Once the spinach becomes tender, remove from the heat.

While your vegan sausage is cooking, put the basil, avocados, nutritional yeast, onion powder, turmeric, garlic, beans, peas, Bragg's, and white wine in your food processor and blend into a smooth sauce.

Combine your pasta in your skillet with the sausage and vegetables. Stir a few times so the pasta gets an even coating of oil and everything gets mixed in. Pour the contents of the skillet into a large mixing bowl and toss in the avocado sauce. Give your sauce a taste test and add any needed salt and pepper. Once everything is blended, toss some extra basil on top and you're ready to eat!

I recommend getting some bread so you can clean your plate and get all the sauce … or else you'll end up licking your plate like a savage.

VEGAN CHICKEN AND PASTA WITH FRESH HERBS

Fresh herbs are the key to making this recipe sing.

MAKES 4 SERVINGS

2 cups vegan chicken, defrosted (we recommend Gardein Chick'n Scallopini)

Olive oil cooking spray

½ cup sliced white mushrooms

2 tablespoons raw pine nuts

2 teaspoons onion powder

¼ cup chopped fresh parsley

1 teaspoon diced fresh rosemary leaves

2 teaspoons diced fresh sage leaves

½ cup fresh basil leaves

1 package medium-size pasta shells, cooked and drained

¼ cup olive oil

½ teaspoon red pepper flakes

3 cloves garlic, minced

1 tablespoon capers, drained

2 tablespoons lemon juice

1 (14-ounce) can artichoke hearts, drained

1 Roma tomato, sliced

Freshly ground black peppercorns

Preheat the oven to 350°F.

In a glass baking dish, lightly spray your vegan chicken with the olive oil cooking spray. Flip your vegan chicken a few times to make sure all the pieces are lightly coated. Then toss the mushrooms and pine nuts over the top. Bake for 5 minutes. Take the dish out and with a spatula toss the vegan chicken, pine nuts, and mushrooms. Sprinkle 1 teaspoon of the onion powder over the top. Bake for another 5 to 8 minutes. Take out when everything is golden brown.

In your favorite food processor or blender, chop the parsley, rosemary, sage, and basil. In a large mixing bowl, toss the warm pasta, olive oil, red pepper flakes, garlic, the remaining 1 teaspoon onion powder, capers, lemon juice, and artichoke hearts. Then gently mix in the fresh herbs, pine nuts, mushrooms, and vegan chicken while they are still warm.

Serve with slices of Roma tomatoes and black pepper sprinkled over the top.

SKILLET-STYLE LASAGNA

This is one of those recipes that takes a classic dish and transforms it into something you can make in 30 minutes while cutting back on dishes, drama, and some of those pesky calories you find in the original version.

MAKES 4 SERVINGS

2 tablespoons olive oil

1 package Lightlife Gimme Lean vegan ground beef or Match vegan ground beef, defrosted and formed into patties smaller than your palm

1 tablespoon red wine

1 red onion, diced

3 cloves garlic, minced

2 teaspoons Italian seasoning

½ teaspoon red pepper flakes

1 teaspoon Bragg's liquid aminos

1 jar of your favorite pasta sauce

1½ cups water

¼ cup kalamata olives, pitted

¼ cup baby spinach leaves

¼ cup fresh basil leaves

3 cups mafalda pasta, uncooked (they're like mini lasagna noodles)

½ cup shredded Daiya vegan mozzarella cheese or your favorite vegan cheese

Preheat the oven to 350°F.

In your favorite cast-iron skillet or oven-safe frying pan, heat the olive oil. Once your oil is hot, cook the vegan beef, red wine, onion, and garlic over medium heat until your vegan beef is browned and has a light crust on the outside. This will help keep your vegan beef from getting spongy.

Stir in the Italian seasoning, red pepper flakes, Bragg's, pasta sauce, water, olives, spinach, basil, and pasta. Heat to a boil and then reduce the heat to low. Simmer, uncovered, for 10 to 12 minutes, stirring occasionally. Once your pasta is tender, sprinkle with vegan cheese.

Slide your skillet into the oven and bake for no more than 5 minutes. This should be long enough to melt your vegan cheese and add a nice flavor to your noodles.

FETTUCCINE WITH WILD MUSHROOMS AND ARTICHOKE HEARTS

I had my eye on this dish for a long time. Whenever we flipped through Betty Crocker's Big Red, we'd give each other a little conspiratorial nod. That's why I was heartbroken when the only fresh "wild mushroom" mix at our local grocery store was basically some sliced portobellos and white buttons with just a few cremini and oyster mushrooms mixed in. But I got over it pretty quickly when I looked in our pantry and saw a can of artichoke hearts and one of garbanzo beans. I admit in the end this recipe is 100 percent Shannon, but it was inspired by Betty Crocker and reminds me how much I love cooking with white wine.

MAKES 4 SERVINGS

- 1 package fettuccine noodles
- 2 tablespoons margarine
- 1 tablespoon olive oil
- 1 12-ounce variety pack fresh wild mushrooms
- 1 (14-ounce) can artichoke hearts, drained
- 1 (14-ounce) can garbanzo beans, rinsed and drained
- 2 cloves garlic, minced
- ¼ cup dry white wine
- 2 teaspoons Bragg's liquid aminos
- 1 teaspoon herbes de Provence
- ¼ teaspoon freshly ground black peppercorns
- ¼ teaspoon garlic powder
- 2 teaspoons chopped fresh parsley
- ½ teaspoon fresh thyme leaves
- Vegan Parmesan to sprinkle over the top

Prepare your pasta per the instructions on your package.

In *vos favoris* cast-iron skillet, heat the margarine and olive oil over medium heat until the margarine melts. Add the wild mushrooms, artichoke hearts, garbanzo beans, and garlic. Toss this mixture, and then pour the white wine and Bragg's over the top. Keep tossing until the mushrooms begin to become tender. Add the herbes de Provence, black pepper, garlic powder, parsley, and thyme and continue to cook your mushroom mixture until the mushrooms are the desired tenderness.

Add your cooked pasta to the cooked mushroom mixture and mix in the skillet. If you want a saltier, stronger flavor, put only two-thirds of your pasta in the skillet. Cook and let the flavors mingle for about 1 minute. Serve with vegan Parmesan sprinkled over the top.

TEMPEH RAGÙ ALLA BOLOGNESE

There was a lot going on in Italy during the fifth century. The Visigoths captured most of the southern peninsula. Sicily was invaded a bunch of times until the Sicilians figured out all they needed to do was bribe people to leave them alone. The Roman Empire gave up on the British Isles and, before the century came to an end, collapsed, never to rise again. Somewhere in all this the people of Bologna created their signature sauce, which is known to most Americans as "meat sauce." It's one of the most popular Italian sauces in America (even if no one knows the real name) and is made with much more tomato sauce here than in the traditional Old World recipes. Actually, the tiny bit of tomato sauce found in the traditional recipes wasn't added until after the discovery of the New World. We recommend using the Old World technique of eating this sauce with a flat noodle, which will carry more sauce than spaghetti.

MAKES 4 SERVINGS

- 1 package fettuccine
- 1 tablespoon olive oil
- Dash of liquid smoke
- 6 pieces smoked tempeh, crumbled
- 1 cup Tofurky ground beef or Match vegan ground beef
- 1 red onion, diced
- 1 (14-ounce) can garbanzo beans, drained and rinsed
- ¼ cup sliced baby portobello mushroom caps
- 3 stalks celery, chopped
- 3 cloves garlic, minced
- 1 teaspoon celery seed
- 2 teaspoons Bragg's liquid aminos
- 1¼ cups red wine
- 1 teaspoon fresh thyme leaves
- 2 teaspoons chopped fresh basil leaves
- 1 teaspoon fresh oregano leaves
- ¼ cup baby spinach leaves
- 1 (28-ounce) can crushed tomatoes
- 2 tomatoes, diced
- ½ cup Better Than Bouillon vegan beef broth, made per the instructions on the package
- 1 tablespoon vegan sour cream
- ½ teaspoon freshly ground black peppercorns
- 2 tablespoons margarine
- Crushed pink Himalayan salt and freshly ground black peppercorns
- Fresh parsley and vegan Parmesan to sprinkle over the top

Prepare your pasta per the instructions on the package.

In your favorite Dutch oven or saucepan, heat the olive oil and liquid smoke over medium heat. Add the tempeh and vegan beef and cook until browned and slightly crispy. Remove your tempeh and vegan beef from your Dutch oven and set aside in a bowl. Add your onion, garbanzo beans, mushrooms, celery, and garlic to the hot oil. Cook until your onion and celery are tender. Add the celery seed, Bragg's, ¼ cup of the red wine, the thyme, basil, oregano, and baby spinach. Cook and stir for 30 seconds. Add the remaining 1 cup red wine, the crushed tomatoes, diced tomatoes, broth, vegan sour cream, and pepper. Simmer while stirring for 1 to 2 minutes, or until the sauce begins to bubble. Add the margarine. Once the margarine is melted, stir it in and then add any salt or pepper you want to adjust the flavor. Stir in your tempeh and vegan beef. Use a rubber-tipped spatula to get all the extra oil that may have run off in the bowl.

Add your pasta to your sauce and toss inside your Dutch oven to get an even coating.

Serve your pasta topped with parsley and vegan Parmesan.

SUN-DRIED TOMATO AND WALNUT PESTO FUSILLI

Fusilli is a corkscrew-shaped pasta that's often hollow and always fun. It's great for kids, or for anyone who gets a kick out of food with a unique shape. This recipe is great for moms, or for anyone who likes a fast, easy recipe that looks and tastes a whole lot more complicated than it really is. So really, it's great for anyone.

MAKES 4 SERVINGS

- 3 cups cooked fusilli
- ½ cup shredded Daiya vegan mozzarella cheese or your favorite vegan cheese
- ⅓ cup sun-dried tomatoes
- ½ teaspoon chili oil
- ¼ cup fresh basil leaves
- 2 tablespoons fresh parsley
- 2 teaspoons fresh oregano leaves
- 2 tablespoons raw walnuts
- 2 tablespoons tomato paste
- 1 tablespoon red wine
- 1 teaspoon olive oil
- 1 teaspoon lemon juice
- ½ teaspoon grated lemon peel
- 1 teaspoon freshly ground black peppercorns
- 2 cloves garlic, minced

Prepare the pasta following the instructions on the package.

Set aside the hot pasta and the vegan cheese. In your favorite food processor or blender, blend the remaining ingredients until almost smooth. You don't want the pesto to be liquefied, just blended.

In a large bowl, toss the hot pasta, pesto, and vegan cheese.

CHIPOTLE BLACK BEAN AND PEANUT SAUCE NOODLE BOWLS

Here's an interesting thing I learned during the Betty Crocker Project: if a Betty Crocker recipe ever calls for peanut butter, they mean the processed stuff, not natural peanut butter. If you use natural peanut butter, it'll be too oily and won't have enough fillers to make the recipe work. This is our recipe, but we still used the processed creamy stuff in it. If you make it with real peanut butter, you'll need to add cornstarch and some salt to adjust the recipe. Please consider yourself warned—in writing.

MAKES 4 SERVINGS

½ cup creamy peanut butter

½ cup apple juice

2 tablespoons Bragg's liquid aminos

3 chipotle chilies in adobo sauce, diced

2 teaspoons adobo sauce (from the can of chipotle chilies)

1 (14-ounce) can black beans, drained and rinsed

¼ cup fresh chopped cilantro

1 (8-ounce) package Chinese curly noodles (they look like ramen)

1 cup shredded carrots

½ red bell pepper, thinly sliced

½ green bell pepper, thinly sliced

1 celery stalk, diced

1 (14-ounce) can baby corn, drained

2 tablespoons crushed dry-roasted peanuts

In a bowl, mix the peanut butter, apple juice, Bragg's, chilies, and adobo sauce to create a creamy sauce. Fold in the black beans and cilantro.

Prepare your noodles as instructed on the package.

Toss the noodles with the chipotle peanut sauce and beans. Divide the noodles evenly among 4 bowls. Top with the carrots, bell peppers, celery, and baby corn. Sprinkle with the peanuts.

TEXAS MACARONI BOWLS

The concept of "Texas macaroni" is something that only Betty Crocker could come up with. But the seemingly incongruous name actually makes some degree of sense. Everything's bigger in Texas—and the flavors in this dish we created are huge.

MAKES 4 TO 6 SERVINGS

1 package whole wheat macaroni

Olive oil cooking spray

½ cup beer (we recommend Dos Equis)

½ cup frozen corn

1 (14-ounce) can black beans, drained and rinsed

1 (14-ounce) can kidney beans in chili sauce, not drained or rinsed

1 (14-ounce) can garbanzo beans, drained and rinsed

1 teaspoon cumin

2 tablespoons hot sauce

1 tomato, diced

½ red onion, sliced

1 teaspoon onion powder

1 tablespoon chopped fresh cilantro

1 tablespoon Bragg's liquid aminos

Dash of liquid smoke

Nutritional yeast, black olives, fresh cilantro, and fresh avocado slices to top 'er off

Cook and drain the macaroni per the instructions on the package.

Set aside the cooked pasta, olive oil cooking spray, and toppers. In a large saucepan or cast-iron skillet, mix the remaining ingredients and bring to a boil over medium heat. Put your pasta in a large bowl and spray with olive oil cooking spray. To serve, fill a soup bowl with pasta and ladle the bean mixture on top. Sprinkle on your favorite toppers and let's party.

BEANS AND GRAINS

Once upon a time, people all over the world started combining beans and grains. Maybe it was because these little fellas were both easy to dry and easy to store. Perhaps it was because they complemented one another's flavors and textures while creating a nice canvas for spices and fresh vegetables to shine. Maybe it was because when combined, beans and grains can provide a low-fat source of protein and fiber. All of these bits of awesome combine to make the meals that built civilization—or more accurately, civilizations—as we know it.

Not sold yet? Well, how about this: beans and grains are both low in fat, so you can enjoy a decadent dessert after a meal of beans and grains, completely guilt-free.

RED BEANS AND RICE

You don't need pork rinds to have delicious smoky beans. This vegan version of a Louisiana Creole classic replicates all the flavor and texture of the original.

MAKES 4 SERVINGS

1 tablespoon vegan bacon bits or crumbled smoked tempeh

1 (14-ounce) can kidney beans, drained and rinsed

1 cup cooked brown rice

1 green bell pepper, diced

½ large red onion, diced

1 tablespoon water

½ teaspoon liquid smoke

2 tablespoons plus 1 teaspoon Bragg's liquid aminos

3 tablespoons dry white wine

2 tablespoons Tony Chachere's Creole seasoning

Set the vegan bacon bits aside.

In your sweetest Dutch oven or soup pot, toss in the remaining ingredients and turn the heat up to medium. Stir occasionally. Remove from the heat when the onions and peppers are tender but still a bit crisp. Stir in the vegan bacon bits before serving.

HOPPIN' JOHN

It's hard to say where the black-eyed-pea tradition started, but everyone knows that eating these little cuties on New Year's Day is thought to bring good luck and prosperity. The Talmud talks about eating bowls of black-eyed peas on Rosh Hashanah. In case you aren't friends with any Jews, that's in the fall. During the Civil War, these sweeties were cooked up with ham bones and collard greens, given a heavy dose of hot sauce, and served with corn bread. Legend has it when Sherman marched through the South leaving a trail of ruined farms and burned cities, he left these humble little peas alone, thinking they weren't worth the trouble. Survivors left behind came to think of these legumes as "lucky"—because they survived the burning, because they helped folks survive the aftermath, or both. This tradition is why Hoppin' John has become of one of the most popular adapted West African/soul food dishes served in the South. Our Hoppin' John skips the ham bones—but still has a lot of flavor.

MAKES 4 SERVINGS

- 1 to 2 tablespoons olive oil
- Dash of liquid smoke
- ½ green bell pepper, diced
- ¼ large red onion, diced

- 1 (14-ounce) can black-eyed peas, drained and rinsed
- 1 to 2 tablespoons Tony Chachere's Creole seasoning
- ½ teaspoon onion powder

- ¾ cup greens (collard or mustard or you can always use spinach)
- 1 cup cooked long-grain brown rice
- 2 tablespoons Bragg's liquid aminos
- Vegan bacon bits and hot sauce to dump over the top, if that's how you roll

In your trusted cast-iron skillet or deepest frying pan, heat the olive oil and liquid smoke over medium heat. Once they're hot, toss in the bell pepper, onion, and black-eyed peas and mix. Stir in the Creole seasoning, onion powder, and greens. Once the onion and bell pepper are tender, mix in the rice and Bragg's. Cook for around 5 minutes.

When you serve, toss some vegan bacon bits on top—and maybe some hot sauce—and enjoy a New Year's tradition that you won't regret the next day.

CARIBBEAN BLACK BEANS AND RICE

There are dozens of ways to make beans and rice in the Caribbean, and it has become a classic dish of the region. Now, some will say that rice isn't native to the Caribbean, and that since it was brought over by Chinese workers after slavery was abolished, it should be considered more of a hybrid. I'm not from the Caribbean, so it's not my place to say what should and shouldn't be included in that culture. But I can say that one of the things I find the most beautiful about Caribbean culture is that it combines African, Portuguese, Spanish, and Native American cultures in a beautiful way. Why draw a line and exclude Chinese imports?

MAKES 4 SERVINGS

2 tablespoons olive oil

2½ teaspoons jerk seasoning

Dash of liquid smoke

2 (14-ounce) cans black beans, drained and rinsed

1 medium papaya, peeled, seeded, and diced into bite-size pieces

½ large mango, peeled, pitted, and diced into bite-size pieces

1 red bell pepper, chopped

3 shallots, chopped

¾ cup frozen corn

½ cup orange juice with pulp

¼ cup lime juice

¼ teaspoon agave nectar

2 cloves garlic, minced

3 cups cooked brown rice

3 tablespoons diced fresh cilantro

Hot sauce, optional

In your faithful cast-iron skillet or deepest frying pan, heat the olive oil over medium heat. Once your oil is warm, add the jerk seasoning and liquid smoke and mix. Add the beans, fruit, vegetables, juices, agave nectar, and garlic. Continue to stir and heat until the red pepper is tender. Be careful not to mash your fruit.

You can either serve over the rice or mixed with it. Sprinkle a little cilantro and hot sauce over the top of each bowl and don't forget an icy ginger brew on the side.

CURRY SPINACH AND LENTIL PILAF

Dan loves curry. This has been documented in both foreign and domestic settings. As a good life partner, I felt compelled to make a decent curry pilaf in this book. This recipe started as an attempt at *aloo palak sabji* with rice replacing the potatoes, and ultimately came to have a life of its own. A delicious yet simple life that continued on in leftover heaven.

MAKES 4 SERVINGS

2 tablespoons margarine

1 red onion, diced

1 cup cooked brown rice

1 cup baby spinach leaves, chopped

1 can green lentils, drained and rinsed

2 cups Better Than Bouillon vegetable broth, made per the instructions on the package

¼ teaspoon allspice

¼ teaspoon turmeric

½ teaspoon cumin

½ teaspoon masala curry powder

Pinch of ground ginger

Pinch of coriander seeds

¼ teaspoon Bragg's liquid aminos

In your favorite stewpot with a lid, melt the margarine over medium heat. Once it begins to bubble, toss in your red onion and mix until your onion is coated. Let your onion cook, and once it begins to get tender, toss in the remaining ingredients and stir until completely mixed. Cover and simmer for 5 to 10 minutes, or until your spinach is wilted.

GREEN LENTIL AND LEEK SHEPHERD'S PIE

People have been making vegan shepherd's pies with lentils since the dawn of veganism. This recipe takes lentil shepherd's pie to the next level, packing in more complicated flavors than you could ever get from a pie made from ground meats.

MAKES 4 TO 6 SERVINGS

PIECRUST
2 cups whole wheat flour (you're going to want more to flour surfaces)

1 teaspoon crushed pink Himalayan salt

⅔ cup plus 2 tablespoons vegetable shortening

4 to 6 tablespoons cold water

POTATO TOPPING
5 large baking potatoes, cubed

2 tablespoons margarine

3 tablespoons soy milk

3 teaspoons crushed pink Himalayan salt

2 teaspoons crushed black peppercorns

FILLING
¼ cup Better Than Bouillon vegan beef broth, made per the instructions on the package

½ cup dry white wine

2 tablespoons Bragg's liquid aminos

2 teaspoons herbes de Provence

1 (14-ounce) can green lentils, drained and rinsed

1 (14-ounce) can garbanzo beans, drained and rinsed

1 large leek, sliced

1 clove garlic, minced

¼ cup baby spinach leaves

¼ cup baby kale leaves

¼ cup frozen peas

Crushed pink Himalayan salt and crushed black peppercorns

First make the piecrust. In a medium bowl, mix the flour and salt. Cut the shortening in, and then use a pastry blender to mix. You want your dough to become little clumps that look like small peas. Sprinkle in the cold water, 1 tablespoon at a time, and use a large fork to mix. You want the dough to be moist but not wet.

With your hands, roll the dough into a ball inside the bowl. On a floured surface, with a floured roller, roll your dough ball out into a flat disk on a large piece of plastic wrap. Try to keep the crust even. You don't want some areas to be thinner than others. Gently roll the flattened dough up into plastic wrap and refrigerate for 45 minutes. You want the dough to be firm but still pliable, so if it is crumbly when you remove it from the fridge, press any cracks and then let it warm a little till it is more pliable.

While your crust is in the fridge, make your topping and filling.

In a large stewpot, heat enough salted water to cover your potatoes to a boil. Once your water is bubbling, add all the potatoes and cover your pot. Once your potatoes are tender, drain them through a strainer. Don't rinse the potatoes, but return them to your original pot. Add the margarine, soy milk, salt, and black pepper and mash with a potato masher or blend with an electric handheld mixer until smooth and creamy.

While your potatoes are boiling and your crust is chilling out, make the filling. Toss the broth, white wine, Bragg's, herbes de Provence, lentils, beans, leek, and garlic in your Dutch oven or soup pot and heat over medium heat. Stir your mixture occasionally to help blend the flavors and break up your slices of leek. Once the filling begins to bubble, reduce the heat to a simmer and cover. Simmer for 5 to 8 minutes, or until the leeks and beans are tender. Then stir in the spinach, kale, and frozen peas and cover. Turn off the heat and let sit for 1 minute, then taste test your filling. Add salt and pepper till the flavor makes you swoon.

When it's ready, remove your dough from the fridge. Using a floured rolling pin, roll your dough out on your plastic wrap into a disk around 2 inches larger than your pie dish. Lift your dough by lifting the plastic wrap, and flip it over into your pie pan. Remove the plastic wrap. Gently press the dough into the curves of your dish and along the lip. Get your fingers a little wet with warm water. Use your fingers to create a wave that goes along the edge of your pie to make the crust look nice. Cut off any extra dough hanging over the edge.

Preheat the oven to 425°F. Put your crust in the oven for 5 minutes, or until it begins to look flaky but has not begun to brown.

Using a slotted spoon so you get more vegetables and beans than gravy, fill your piecrust with, well, filling. Use a large wooden spoon to pile your mashed potatoes on top in a kind of dome of "buttery" awesome. Use your spoon to smooth out the top and really press the potatoes into a nice firm mound … If right now you're thinking of Richard Dreyfuss in *Close Encounters of the Third Kind*, you're on the right track.

Bake for 25 to 30 minutes, or until your crust is golden brown and the potato topping has a light crust. Let cool in the pie pan placed on a wire rack for 20 minutes and serve with All-American Vegan Gravy (page 290).

WILD MUSHROOM BARLEY PILAF

In our home, mushrooms mean war. Dan doesn't care for fungi-related foods, but this pilaf is worth fighting for.

MAKES 4 SERVINGS

2 tablespoons margarine

1½ cups fresh wild mushroom mix

1 clove garlic, minced

1 cup Better Than Bouillon vegan beef broth, made per the instructions on the package

1 tablespoon dry white wine

1 cup cooked pearl barley

½ teaspoon dried rosemary, crushed

½ teaspoon dried thyme leaves

¼ red onion, diced

1 stalk celery, diced

1 tablespoon Bragg's liquid aminos

2 tablespoons diced fresh parsley

In your cast-iron skillet or sauté pan, heat the margarine over medium heat. Once the margarine is melted, toss in the wild mushroom mix and garlic. Sauté your mushrooms until they just begin to get tender.

Add the broth, white wine, and barley and mix with a metal spatula to make sure your mushrooms continue to cook evenly. Cook like this for 1 minute, and then add the rosemary, thyme, onion, celery, and Bragg's. Keep lightly mixing your pilaf to make sure it's cooking evenly.

Your pilaf is ready when your mushrooms are tender. Be careful to not let it cook too long or your barley can get a little pasty. No one likes a pasty pilaf.

Sprinkle with fresh parsley before serving.

CANNELLINI FAGIOLI

When I was growing up, my mom made this dish; she called it "fagioli," a term she used pretty loosely for any dish with beans. I grew up eating this on nights when no one really wanted to cook. I loved it—especially with a big piece of garlic toast. I loved it for the broccoli ... calcium-rich, high-in-fiber, and great-source-of-vitamin-C broccoli. This recipe takes about 10 minutes and tastes like home.

MAKES 4 SERVINGS

1 tablespoon olive oil

2 tablespoons chopped fresh basil (set some aside to sprinkle over the top)

2 cloves garlic, minced

2 cups chopped vegan chicken

½ cup broccoli florets

½ cup oil-packed sun-dried tomatoes (you're going to use the oil, so keep it)

½ cup kalamata olives, pitted

1 (14-ounce) can cannellini beans, drained and rinsed

Vegan Parmesan to sprinkle over the top

In your cast-iron skillet or frying pan, heat the olive oil over medium heat. Cook the basil and garlic in the oil for almost 3 minutes, stirring frequently.

Stir in your vegan chicken and broccoli, and cook for 1 minute. Toss in the sun-dried tomatoes, olives, and beans, with a tablespoon of the oil from your sun-dried tomatoes. Cook until your vegan chicken is lightly browned and your broccoli is tender. That shouldn't take more than 5 minutes, maybe 6.

Sprinkle on the vegan Parmesan and reserved chopped fresh basil.

SPANISH RICE

You can use this in burritos or as a side for something fancy, like Vegan Chicken in Mole Sauce (page 261). We didn't put it in "The Sidekicks," though, because I like it by itself with some refried beans mixed in. However you like it, this is one of those recipes you need to have around, and you'll be surprised by how often you make it.

MAKES 4 SERVINGS

2 tablespoons olive oil

1 cup cooked brown rice

1 sweet onion, diced (we recommend Walla Walla Sweet Onions)

2 teaspoons Bragg's liquid aminos

¼ teaspoon dried oregano leaves

1 teaspoon chili powder

2 cloves garlic, minced

1 teaspoon fresh parsley, diced

1 green bell pepper, diced

1 (8-ounce) can tomato paste

⅔ cup white wine

1 large beefsteak tomato, diced

In your always faithful Dutch oven or soup pot with a lid, heat the olive oil over medium heat until warm. Stir in the rice and onion. Once your onion is tender, add the Bragg's, oregano, chili powder, garlic, parsley, bell pepper, tomato paste, and white wine and reduce the heat to a simmer. Stir to mix the ingredients completely, and then cover. Cook, stirring occasionally, until your bell pepper is tender. Stir in the diced tomato, re-cover, and remove from the heat.

Let sit for another 2 minutes and serve warm.

TABBOULEH

Middle Eastern food is Dan's absolute favorite ethnic/regional/whatever cuisine. He went to college at Wesleyan University in Middletown, Connecticut—home to a branch of Mamoun's, renowned for having some of the most authentic falafel available in North America. He's eaten more falafel than just about any other single type of food in his life—so if he says this tabbouleh is delicious, you'd better listen. And he does.

MAKES 4 TO 6 SERVINGS

¾ cup uncooked bulgur

1½ cups chopped fresh parsley

3 Roma tomatoes, diced

4 green onions, diced

2 tablespoons chopped fresh mint leaves

¼ cup olive oil

½ cup lemon juice

1 clove garlic, minced

1 teaspoon crushed pink Himalayan salt

¼ teaspoon freshly ground black peppercorns

¼ teaspoon cumin

¼ teaspoon lemon zest

The first step is preparing your bulgur. If you're like us and buy your bulgur in bulk, you'll need to prepare it first. Cover your bulgur with cold water in a mixing bowl and let it stand for 30 minutes. Then press out the water with a towel. I've noticed, though, that some packaged bulgur instructs you to soak the bulgur in hot water or even to boil it. I recommend following the instructions on your package.

In a glass bowl, mix your cooked bulgur, parsley, tomatoes, green onions, and mint.

In a container that closes tightly, combine the olive oil, lemon juice, garlic, salt, pepper, cumin, and lemon zest, and shake well. Pour the dressing over the bulgur mix and toss in your glass bowl. Cover the bowl and refrigerate for around 1 hour. The longer you let the flavors mix, the better it is.

The Betty We Love To Hate

These days, I'm an unabashed "Betty-head." But it wasn't always like that. Once I was a tattooed, vegan womens' studies major with unshaved legs, a pierced nose, and a skateboard at Evergreen State College in Olympia, Washington—home of the nineties' Riot Grrrl Revolution. I worked at a domestic violence shelter and was a volunteer at the first Ladyfest in 2000. There's no doubt I said "Betty Crocker" in a derogatory way at least a few times. I'm still tattooed and vegan, but I've come to realize that the issues I had with Betty Crocker back then really stem from a woman named Marjorie Child Husted.

Husted wasn't the "Betty" you would have guessed they'd choose to hold the hand of America's homemakers. She was a married college-educated businesswoman who traveled constantly for her job. When Husted took over the Betty Crocker radio program in 1927, she began to include her own thoughts on what made a "good wife." This also happened to be the first year NBC picked up *The Betty Crocker Cooking School of the Air*, bringing Betty Crocker to millions of listeners and making Husted the most popular "Betty" ever.

Husted played off of women's insecurities and fears by talking about husbands who left their wives for women who could cook better. In a series called "Word to the Wives," men came on to talk about what they considered "wedded bliss"—and listeners were encouraged, if not passive-aggressively threatened, to become the "pretty and pleasant" women these men described. This helped create the unrealistic standard of the fifties housewife, and the feelings of inadequacy and depression that lived in every suburb—the phenomenon Friedan (another Betty) would go on to call the "the problem that has no name" in her book *The Feminine Mystique*, laying the foundation for second-wave feminism in the sixties and seventies.

Now, don't get me wrong, Husted wasn't a villain or traitor. Her attempt to glorify America's homemaker wasn't hateful—it was misguided, in the same way the Betty Crocker backlash later was too. Because the problem was never getting women excited about being in the kitchen versus driving them out into the workforce. The problem was—and still is—the idea that there's only one road to becoming a successful woman. It's just as wrong to look down on women who find fulfillment in knitting and cooking as it is to look down on women who play sports or enter the sciences—because it implies that the stereotypically male pursuits are inherently more valuable. The relegation of one activity exclusively to one gender and discouraging people to cross those lines is the true heart of the problem—and fighting this attitude is the heart of real feminism.

RAINBOW QUINOA

The fascinating pre-Columbian civilization of the Incas was sort of a mixed bag. Pro: they domesticated quinoa, a nutrition-packed superfood that remains a staple of Andean and other cuisines to this day. Con: lots and lots of human sacrifice. The two really don't cancel each other out ... but let's focus on the quinoa. It's one of the best sources of vegan protein out there, as well as being high in fiber and iron. It's also naturally gluten-free, making it a great option for our gluten-intolerant friends out there. It's such a powerful source of nutrients that NASA is actually experimenting with quinoa as part of a self-contained sustainable mini-ecosystem that would be used to provide air, water, and food for astronauts on long-range space missions. Yeah, that's right. Quinoa will conquer the universe.

MAKES 4 TO 6 SERVINGS

2 cups uncooked quinoa

4 cups Better Than Bouillon vegetable broth, made per the instructions on the package

¼ teaspoon crushed pink Himalayan salt

¼ teaspoon smoked paprika

1 tablespoons raw almond slices

1 (14-ounce) can kidney beans, rinsed and drained

¼ cup frozen shelled edamame, defrosted

¼ red bell pepper, shredded

¼ yellow bell pepper, shredded

¼ orange bell pepper, shredded

⅓ cup frozen French-cut green beans, defrosted

1 cup Greek Dressing (page 108)

In a 3-quart saucepan, heat the quinoa, broth, salt, and paprika to a boil. Reduce the heat to a simmer. Cover and simmer for 15 to 20 minutes, or until the quinoa is tender. Cool for at least 30 minutes, while mixing with a fork to keep the quinoa from getting clumpy.

In a large bowl, mix the almonds, beans, edamame, peppers, and green beans. Toss the mixture with the Greek Dressing.

In a *huge* serving bowl, toss the quinoa, beans, and vegetables. Serve immediately. The longer you wait, the more cooked and tender your peppers are going to get. That's not the end of the world, but I prefer it when they are raw and have a bit of a crunch.

NEWFANGLED BAKED BEANS

These beans are sort of a mix between Boston baked beans, which are traditionally made with molasses and salt pork, and a more Maine/Quebec-style recipe, which often uses maple syrup. We combined both sweeteners and left out the pork (obviously), replacing it with some liquid smoke to mimic that salty flavor.

MAKES 4 SERVINGS

10 to 12 cups water (you might need a little more)

1 cup India Pale Ale beer

2 cups dried cannellini beans (also called Great Northern beans)

⅓ cup brown sugar

½ cup blackstrap molasses

2 tablespoons maple syrup

1 (14-ounce) can diced tomatoes

2 teaspoons Bragg's liquid aminos

1 large red onion, diced

1 to 2 teaspoons liquid smoke (depending how smoky you like it)

Combine 9 cups of the water, the beer, and the dried beans in your cherished Dutch oven, and heat to a boil over medium heat. Don't cover your pot once it begins to bubble. Boil uncovered for no more than 2 minutes, and then add the brown sugar, molasses, syrup, tomatoes, Bragg's, and onion. With a wooden spoon, stir your pot until everything is completely blended. Put the lid on your pot, turn your heat down to a simmer, and cook for 4 to 5 hours.

That might seem like a large window, but you're re-animating those beans, and your other ingredients are cooking down into a syrupy sauce. During this time, you'll need to check on your pot a few times and add water when you notice it needs it.

Preheat the oven to 350°F.

Once your beans are tender but before they get mushy, pull your Dutch oven from the stovetop and give it a good stir and a careful taste test. It'll be hot, so watch your face. I know that technically it's impossible to watch your face per se, but seriously, be careful. After 4 hours, you get into molten-lava territory.

Stir in 2 to 3 cups of water—depending on how tender your beans are. Also mix in your liquid smoke at this time with a large spoon. Put your uncovered Dutch oven in your heated oven for 1½ to 2 hours. Take it out from time to time to stir and check on the tenderness of your beans and thickness of your sauce. Once you like the status of both those things—you're good to go!

BROOKLYN-STYLE VEGAN CHICKEN-FRIED RICE

Oh, Brooklyn … is there anywhere else like it? Almost every culture has a corner in Brooklyn—except maybe Australian Aborigines. If you ever wonder if you should move to Brooklyn, remember that besides the brownstones and hipsters, there's also a wide variety of takeout available at all hours of the day. We haven't been to China yet, so I can't tell you that this is an authentic Chinese vegan fried rice, but I can tell you that this recipe is right at home in Brooklyn.

MAKES 4 SERVINGS

½ cup tamari

4 tablespoons rice wine

½ teaspoon ginger paste

2 to 4 tablespoons sesame oil

1 cup defrosted and chopped vegan chicken

½ (16-ounce) package firm tofu

4 cups cooked rice, chilled

3 cloves garlic, minced

⅓ cup shredded carrots

¼ yellow onion, diced

2 celery stalks, chopped

1 small can water chestnuts, drained and sliced

½ cup frozen peas

½ cup fresh pea pods

3 to 4 green onions, chopped

In a small bowl, whisk together the tamari, rice wine, and ginger paste until completely blended.

Heat 1 tablespoon of the sesame oil in a wok over medium heat. Once your oil is hot, toss in your vegan chicken and stir-fry until the edges are crispy. Once your vegan chicken is a light golden brown, move it to a plate with a paper towel to soak up the extra oil.

In another bowl, use a fork to gently mash your tofu into small chunks. Make sure you don't make them too small. You don't want your tofu to become a paste or smaller than the grains of rice.

Very carefully add a few teaspoons of sesame oil to the hot wok if the vegan chicken soaked it all up. Toss your tofu bits in the hot oil to fry until the edges are crispy. Move your fried tofu over to the plate with the vegan chicken and place the tofu on top of the vegan chicken.

Again add a tablespoon of sesame oil to the hot wok—very carefully! You don't want any splattering hot oil to burn your arms and face off. Now toss the rice, garlic, carrots, onion, celery, water chestnuts, and peas into the hot wok and begin to stir-fry. Pour ½ of the tamari mixture over the rice and veggies and continue to stir-fry. Then add the pea pods, vegan chicken, and tofu and stir-fry some more. You want to really get everything mixed in there. Pour the remaining tamari mixture over the top and keep stir-frying until your carrots and pea pods are tender but still a little crisp.

Serve hot, with a sprinkling of green onions over the top, while wearing a plaid shirt, and Converse.

SWEET POTATO RISOTTO

This recipe makes a lot, which makes it great for family get-togethers, potlucks, or just rationing out sack lunches.

MAKES 6 TO 8 SERVINGS

1 large sweet potato

Olive oil cooking spray

2 tablespoons white wine

½ cup diced red onion

2 cloves garlic, minced

1 cup arborio or risotto rice

3 cups Better Than Bouillon vegan chicken broth, made per the instructions on the package

½ teaspoon Bragg's liquid aminos

½ teaspoon crushed dried rosemary

¼ teaspoon grated nutmeg

¼ teaspoon onion powder

¼ teaspoon chopped fresh parsley

Dash of liquid smoke

1 teaspoon hot sauce

Crushed pink Himalayan salt and freshly ground black peppercorns

2 tablespoons shredded Daiya vegan mozzarella cheese or your favorite vegan cheese

Preheat the oven to 400°F. Bake your sweet potato for 30 to 40 minutes, or until tender.

Spray your Dutch oven with olive oil cooking spray and add the white wine. Heat the wine to a boil over medium heat. Toss in your onion and garlic and cook until tender. Stir in the rice.

Mash 1 cup of the sweet potato into a paste and add it to the Dutch oven. Mix with a wooden spoon until blended. Stir in ½ cup of the broth. Continue to stir your rice and broth until it begins to bubble. Then stir in another ½ cup of the broth. Repeat this process until you have added all the broth. Continue to stir until your rice is tender. It should take 20 to 30 minutes.

Mix in the Bragg's, rosemary, nutmeg, onion powder, and parsley. Add liquid smoke, hot sauce, salt and pepper until you like the flavor, and then serve hot with a pinch of vegan cheese over the top.

LENTIL, KALE, AND FRESH HERB RICE

Vegan cookbooks and food blogs are full of these kinds of all-purpose lentil and vegetable recipes. We try to give you recipes you can't find anywhere else, but while writing our blog, we got a *ton* of requests for lentil recipes. Which is fine with us. I actually love lentils. So here's a recipe for a big pot of delicious lentils that you can cook up Sunday night and enjoy for your lunch all week, over rice, or just alone. I suggest eating it with some whole-wheat toast, a glass of iced tea, and a loved one—because if you really love someone, you feed them lentils.

MAKES 6 SERVINGS

1 cup baby kale leaves

1 cup dry green lentils

½ cup pearl barley

2 carrots, sliced

1 cup sliced celery

1 small yellow onion, diced

1 parsnip, sliced

1 rutabaga, cut into small cubes

¼ cup flat leaf parsley, chopped

¼ cup fresh dill, chopped

6 cups Better Than Bouillon vegetable broth, made per the instructions on the package

1 teaspoon capers, drained

Pinch of rubbed sage

3 cloves garlic, minced

½ cup frozen corn

½ cup frozen green beans

1 teaspoon celery seed

3 tablespoons Bragg's liquid aminos

½ teaspoon fresh thyme leaves

2 inches of leek, sliced

1 cup dry white wine

Set the kale aside.

Put the remaining ingredients into your handsome little slow cooker and heat on high. Mix your ingredients with a large spoon every half hour. Cook for 3 hours, and then add the kale. Mix your kale in and cook for another 3 to 4 hours. Once your lentils are tender—you're done!

INTERNATIONAL

Let's be honest here: Betty Crocker's "international cuisine" is often unlike anything actually related to its purported country of origin. I'm pretty certain they don't actually have "Mexican pizza" in Mexico.

But authenticity isn't the point. The point is that Betty Crocker exposed a generation of American cooks to the basic concepts behind a variety of different cuisines from around the world—things many of us might never have been exposed to otherwise. So, no—Betty Crocker's pad Thai doesn't taste like anything you would order in Bangkok. But now millions of us know it exists and are a bit more likely to roll the dice on that Thai place in the city the next time we're in the area. Betty Crocker is all about expanding people's horizons—even if it's incremental.

In addition to being vegan, we believe our versions of these international staples should be a lot closer to the real deal than you'd find in a Betty Crocker cookbook. Today's everywoman is a little worldlier, after all.

VEGAN RISOTTO ALLA MILANESE WITH PEAS

I think we all get a little rose-colored-glasses-y during the holidays. We recall with a warm heart our favorite childhood memories of Christmas morning surprises or piles of colorful cookies, and hope that this year will be just as memorable. That's what this dish does for me. Back in the day when I was a little eater (so small I needed to be carried), my family used to go out to an Italian restaurant that I can't recall the name of but can picture in my head perfectly. I remember white tablecloths and wooden chairs hanging on brick walls ready to be pulled down to turn a four-top into a five. I remember the tacky red, orange, and green Christmas lights, paper Santa decorations, and tables packed in so tight that you couldn't put your coat on the back of your chair. You had to give it to the hostess. Sounds fancy, but really it was just small and authentic. My parents always ordered me a bowl of Risotto alla Milanese and a ginger ale. I was pretty much the happiest kid ever. This recipe is so easy you can whip up a batch on a snowy afternoon or to serve as a side for a holiday dinner with something like our Vegan Venison with Cranberry and Wine Sauce (page 151) or the Citrus and Garlic–Basted Holiday Roast (page 443).

MAKES 2 TO 4 SERVINGS

1 tablespoon margarine

2 tablespoons olive oil

½ red onion, finely diced

1 tablespoon plus 1 teaspoon finely chopped fresh parsley

1 cup uncooked arborio or risotto rice

½ cup dry white wine

3 cups Better Than Bouillon vegan chicken broth, made per the directions on the package

½ cup nutritional yeast or vegan Parmesan

¼ teaspoon freshly ground black peppercorns, plus more if desired

¼ teaspoon dried basil leaves

Dash of grated nutmeg

1 cup frozen peas

Crushed pink Himalayan salt

In your deepest nonstick skillet, heat the margarine and olive oil over medium heat until the margarine is melted. Cook the red onion and parsley in the warm olive oil for about 5 minutes, stirring constantly, until the red onion is tender.

Stir in the rice. You're going to want to stir the rice constantly while it cooks. Once the tips of the rice are translucent, stir in the white wine. Cook and stir for about 3 minutes. You are waiting for the white wine to be absorbed by the rice. Once it is, reduce the heat to a simmer.

Stir in 1 cup of the broth. Cook uncovered for around 5 minutes while you stir constantly, making sure your rice doesn't stick to the sides. Once the rice has absorbed the broth, pour in another cup of broth. Stir the rice constantly, and when the second cup of broth has been completely absorbed, add your final cup of broth. Continue to stir the rice and scrape the sides of your skillet to make sure the rice isn't sticking anywhere. Each cup will take a little longer to absorb. Remove your skillet from the heat once your final cup of broth has been absorbed. Make sure your rice is tender and the mixture is smooth and creamy. If your rice still looks a little soupy, it's not ready.

Stir in the nutritional yeast, black pepper, basil, nutmeg, and frozen peas. At this point, check for flavor and add a few dashes of salt and pepper to taste.

BEEFLESS TIPS IN BORDELAISE

The night we first made this recipe, Hurricane Earl was at Norfolk's doorstep. Trees were waving in the wind, and the birds and squirrels who were usually up at dawn were being all crazy, hiding away in the courtyard of our apartment building waiting for it to pass. We Shannons were hiding away as well, watching the *G.I. Joe* movie and playing Xbox. Obviously that meant we had to make a fancy French dinner to go along with our evening of high culture. I mean, what goes better with a movie that literally shows the Eiffel Tower being eaten than some vegan Bordelaise? This dinner was so easy and good, I fell in love with it. We made a side of steamed green beans to go with it.

MAKES 2 SERVINGS

Olive oil cooking spray

1 (9-ounce) package Gardein beefless tips or beef seitan, defrosted

2 tablespoons margarine

1 large red onion—you'll need 1 full slice; dice the rest

2 tablespoons whole wheat flour

½ cup Better Than Bouillon vegetable broth, made per the instructions on the package

1 cup red wine

¼ teaspoon dried thyme leaves

1 teaspoon chopped fresh parsley

2 dried bay leaves

1 teaspoon Bragg's liquid aminos

¼ teaspoon olive oil

⅛ teaspoon lemon pepper

Preheat the oven to 350°F.

Coat an 8-inch glass baking dish with cooking spray. Put your vegan beef in the dish, turning the pieces a few times to make sure they have a light coating. Bake the vegan beef for no more than 10 minutes. You just want it cooked enough to be hot and have a light crispy skin. This will keep your vegan beef from getting soggy in the sauce. Making the sauce takes only around 15 minutes, so if you plan it right, you should be able to add the vegan beef right from the oven into the sauce. If not, just turn off the oven and let the vegan beef stay warm until you're ready to use it.

In your *bien-aimé* cast-iron skillet or frying pan, melt your margarine over medium heat. Cook the red onion slice in the melted margarine, stirring constantly, until tender. Remove the red onion.

Stir the flour into the melted margarine until smooth. Lower the heat to a simmer and whisk in the broth and red wine. Once the mixture is smooth, stir in the thyme, parsley, chopped onion, and bay leaves. Heat to a boil while stirring constantly for 1 minute. While you're doing this, add the Bragg's, olive oil, and lemon pepper. Mix in your hot vegan beef.

Make sure you heat up some French bread to serve with this. You need it to dip in your sauce or else you'll be stuck licking your plate to get it all. That kind of thing can ruin a date night ... or make you closer ... every relationship is different.

Bon appétit!

COQUILLES ST. JACQUES

When most people think of Betty Crocker recipes, they think of chicken-fried steaks, green bean casseroles, and impossible rainbow sprinkle layer cakes. But this just isn't the case. Much to my pleasant surprise, Betty Crocker's Big Red has quite a few fancy French dishes in there—and if you read our blog, you know how much I love being fancy and pretend French. Coquilles St. Jacques is a fancy French dish that I now have an excuse to make vegan. It was also one of Julia Child's favorite dishes—probably because it was French, and because it included loads of heavy cream, Swiss cheese, and a whole stick of butter. With artichoke hearts, white wine, a light savory sauce, hearts of palm "scallops," and of course our favorite vegan shrimp balls from May Wah, ours is still a bit rich for vegan food, but I'm sure it doesn't even come close to the real deal. So let's enjoy this more compassionate, infinitely lighter, and still super-fancy French dinner. *Bon appétit!*

MAKES 4 SERVINGS

4 tablespoons margarine

1 (14-ounce) can hearts of palm, drained

1 (14-ounce) can artichoke hearts, drained

1 cup vegan shrimp, defrosted (we recommend May Wah shrimp balls cut in half)

½ red onion, diced

1 cup sliced white mushrooms

1 cup dry white wine

2 green onions, diced

¼ cup fresh parsley, chopped

2 teaspoons herbes de Provence

3 tablespoons nutritional yeast

1 teaspoon lemon juice

½ teaspoon Bragg's liquid aminos

½ cup dry bread crumbs

1 teaspoon Italian seasoning

1 teaspoon sesame seeds

½ cup shredded smoked cheddar Sheese or Daiya vegan mozzarella cheese

In a saucepan, melt the margarine over medium heat and toss in the hearts of palm, artichoke hearts, vegan shrimp, red onion, and mushrooms. Let them brown a little. Once they're tender, add the wine, green onions, parsley, herbes de Provence, nutritional yeast, lemon juice, and Bragg's. Simmer for around 5 minutes, stirring occasionally.

Set the oven to broil or turn on your broiler.

In a small bowl, mix the bread crumbs, Italian sea-soning, and sesame seeds.

Fill 4 (4-inch) tart dishes with the vegan shrimp mixture. Sprinkle the bread crumb mixture and vegan cheese over each serving. One at a time put your dishes in the broiler for the count of 10—just enough to melt your vegan cheese a little and brown the bread crumbs.

May I suggest you enjoy this with a glass of the white wine you were using earlier … ? Um—yes, I may.

OSSO BUCCO

I've eaten a lot of Italian food in my life—probably more than most people who don't live in Italy. I still remember one of the first times I realized the world was not Italian. I was at a friend's house and saw her dad cut his spaghetti with a knife and fork and eat the tiny pieces like rice. (Insert shudder here.) But one Italian dish we never had at my house is osso bucco, and not just because it's a Milanese dish and that's basically a world away from my mother's beloved Palermo. The reason: *veal*. See, no matter how Italian my mom is, and how not down with the whole vegan thing she might be … she didn't believe in eating veal because of how the baby cows are treated. Some things just aren't right. What happens to baby cows to make veal is one of them. Ironically, this was my introduction to how awful the world can be to animals—and much to the frustration and disapproval of my mother, it's what started me on this lifelong mission to make the world a more compassionate place for animals.

MAKES 2 SERVINGS

MASHED POTATOES

6 medium red potatoes, chopped but not peeled

½ cup soy milk

¼ cup margarine, softened

¼ teaspoon freshly ground black peppercorns

VEGAN OSSO BUCCO

¼ cup whole wheat flour

¼ teaspoon freshly ground black peppercorns

1 package Gardein beefless tips or beef seitan, defrosted

2 tablespoons olive oil

2 tablespoons apple juice

⅓ cup dry white wine (you'll want to have some extra in case your sauce reduces too much)

1 clove garlic, minced

2 pinches of onion powder

1 cup Better Than Bouillon vegan beef broth, made per the instructions on the label

½ teaspoon Bragg's liquid aminos

2 dried bay leaves

Crushed pink Himalayan salt to taste

Vegan Parmesan

1 tablespoon grated lemon peel

2 tablespoons chopped fresh parsley

First make the mashed potatoes. Boil the potatoes in a 2-quart saucepan, making sure you have enough water to cover them. Once the potatoes are tender when you stab them with a fork, drain them through a colander.

Pour the cooked potatoes back into the saucepan and blend with a pastry blender. Add the soy milk, margarine, and pepper. Blend with an electric hand mixer until they are perfection. It takes less than 5 minutes. Be sure to get all the lumps out.

To make the osso bucco, in a shallow bowl or deep dish, mix the flour and pepper. Coat the vegan beef with the flour mix.

In a 4-quart Dutch oven, heat the olive oil over medium heat. Cook the vegan beef in the oil until the outside gets a crispy coasting—you need to keep the extra coating from sticking to the bottom, so scrape the bottom of the pot with a spatula a few times while cooking.

When the vegan beef is brown on all sides, stir in the apple juice, white wine, garlic, and onion powder. Reduce the heat and stir. The sauce will start to thicken in less than a minute. Once it starts to thicken, add the broth, Bragg's, and bay leaves. Simmer uncovered. If you cover it, the vegan beef will get mushy.

Once it comes to a boil, remove from the heat …

taste it really quickly to see if it needs salt or if it has reduced too much. If that has happened, add white wine 1 teaspoon at a time until the flavor mellows. Then you're ready to serve!

Place one or two scoops of mashed potatoes on a plate, and then ladle the vegan beef and gravy on top. Sprinkle with vegan Parmesan, grated lemon peel, and chopped fresh parsley. Be sure to get a lot of the gravy… it is really the best part. I was kinda-sorta licking my plate after I finished dinner to get it all.

SEITAN COQ AU VIN

Some say Coq au Vin can be traced back to ancient Gaul and Julius Caesar; others speculate that this story might be an attempt to add a little distinction and history to a rustic old French farm dish. After all, anyone who has been to Paris and seen all those statues of generals with laurel wreath halos and paintings of women in robes knows the French really love themselves some Romans. But that's not the only controversy surrounding Coq au Vin. See, *coq* is French for "rooster," and if you're making this dish with any other central ingredient, you're supposed to address it as such. So out of respect for the French, whom I adore (except that waiter in Paris who was super-rude to us when we ordered glasses of wine rather than a bottle so we could sample a bunch of different types), please enjoy our *Seitan* Coq au Vin.

MAKES 2 TO 4 SERVINGS

¼ cup whole wheat flour

½ teaspoon crushed pink Himalayan salt

¼ teaspoon freshly ground black peppercorns

2 cups defrosted large vegan chicken chunks

Olive oil cooking spray

Olive oil for cooking

8 slices vegan bacon or smoked tempeh, chopped

Dash of liquid smoke

¾ cup pearl onions

3 cups sliced white mushrooms

1⅓ cups Better Than Bouillon vegetable broth, made per the instructions on the package

1 cup red wine

2 to 3 teaspoons Bragg's liquid aminos

1 cup sliced fresh carrots

1 teaspoon onion powder

1 teaspoon garlic powder

1 teaspoon celery seed

3 cloves garlic, minced

1 bouquet garni (½ teaspoon dried thyme, 2 large sprigs fresh parsley, and 1 dried bay leaf in a small organic cloth bag or tea infuser)

Vegan Parmesan to sprinkle over the top

Chopped fresh parsley for garnish

Preheat the oven to 400°F.

In a shallow dish, mix the flour, salt, and pepper. Put your vegan chicken in a glass baking dish and spray it with olive oil. One at a time, dip your vegan chicken pieces in the flour mix and, flip a few times to coat. Once all your vegan chicken is coated, bake the coating on for 10 minutes.

In your cast-iron skillet or deepest frying pan, heat the olive oil. Cook the vegan bacon until it reaches

the desired crispiness. Place it on a plate with a paper towel to soak up extra oil. Carefully throw a dash of liquid smoke in the hot olive oil and mix it in. Add another teaspoon of olive oil to the skillet if you lost a lot of it while making your vegan bacon. Cook the vegan chicken in the smoky oil. Keep turning it till you get a crispy coating over all the vegan chicken, and then move it to the plate with the vegan bacon. The extra flour from the vegan chicken will mix with the oil to make a kind of faux roux, and that's a good thing, so don't worry about the oil getting cloudy.

Add the onions and mushrooms to the hot, smoky oil. Stir and cook until the mushrooms are tender. Add the broth, red wine, Bragg's, carrots, onion powder, garlic powder, celery seed, garlic, and bouquet garni. Bring to a boil. Simmer for around ½ hour, or until the carrots reach the desired tenderness. You can add another teaspoon of olive oil here if you want to re-create the oili-ness this dish would get from the bacon and rooster fat.

Chop up the vegan bacon. Right before you serve, add the vegan chicken and vegan bacon pieces to the onion-mushroom sauce and mix. To garnish, sprinkle with the vegan Parmesan and chopped fresh parsley. It is a stew-ish kind of dish, so it won't be pretty…but there are more important things than looks. This dish has a good personality.

VEGAN CHICKEN NIÇOISE

This dish is a spin-off of a traditional French salad made popular in the United States by none other than Julia Child herself. While a traditional Niçoise salad wouldn't contain any cooked vegetables at all, this fully cooked dish is more of a main-course meal than its traditional salad counterpart—something you can enjoy on a fancy Friday night when you want to have a pretend France stay-cation.

MAKES 4 SERVINGS

1¼ cups dry white wine

1 cup vegan chicken, defrosted (we recommend Gardein Chick'n Scallopini)

3 cloves garlic, minced

½ cup pearl onions

¼ teaspoon chopped fresh basil leaves

¼ teaspoon fresh oregano

¼ teaspoon fresh thyme leaves

¼ teaspoon celery seed

Pinch of onion powder

1 green bell pepper, diced

½ cup kalamata olives, pitted

1 warm baguette

In your *bien-aimé* cast-iron skillet or frying pan, heat the white wine over medium heat to a boil. Place the vegan chicken in the wine and cook for 3 to 4 minutes. You're going to want to flip it a few times to make sure it gets a soft golden color.

Add the garlic, onions, fresh herbs, celery seed, onion powder, bell pepper, and olives and cook for another 3 to 4 minutes. You're going to want to keep flipping and stirring it a bit to make sure everything gets evenly cooked.

Don't forget the bread. You'll need that bread to get all that sauce.

HEARTY PAELLA

When Dan's sister Lisa was studying abroad in Spain, Dan visited her and had authentic Spanish paella for the first time—and it blew his mind. At least, we think it was authentic. To hear Dan tell it, the restaurant had a heavily designed brand logo and a menu that was all bright, bold colors and cutesy names, and the whole place seemed just a little too "neat." It's possible he ate at the Spanish version of, like, Chili's. Either way, Dan fell in love with the vegetarian paella—the kind of dish that leaves you pining after it for years like an old flame. That is, until this recipe!

MAKES 4 SERVINGS

Olive oil cooking spray

1 cup vegan shrimp, defrosted (we recommend May Wah shrimp balls cut in half)

2 Tofurky Italian sausages or Field Roast Italian sausages, cut into coins

½ cup hearts of palm, drained

1 (14-ounce) can artichoke hearts, drained

2 tablespoons olive oil

2 teaspoons saffron threads

2 tablespoons dry white wine

4 cups Better Than Bouillon vegan chicken broth, made per the instructions on the package

¼ teaspoon turmeric

1 teaspoon paprika

2 bay leaves

6 cloves garlic, minced

3 shallots, diced

1 red bell pepper, chopped

1 cup fresh green beans

2 Roma tomatoes, diced

2 cups cooked jasmine rice

1 cup frozen peas

2 tablespoons chopped fresh parsley

Preheat the oven to 375°F.

Spray a glass lasagna dish with olive oil cooking spray. In a medium bowl, toss the vegan shrimp and Italian sausage together, and then put them in your baking dish. Spray on another coating of olive oil cooking spray and bake for 10 minutes. You want a light, crispy coating to form on your mock meats so that they don't get spongy later.

In another mixing bowl, toss the hearts of palm and artichoke hearts with 1 tablespoon of the olive oil and a pinch of the saffron threads. Cover and refrigerate.

In a saucepan, heat the wine, broth, turmeric, paprika, bay leaves, and remaining saffron threads to a boil over medium heat. Take out the bay leaves.

In your very favorite Dutch oven or stewpot, heat the remaining 1 tablespoon olive oil over medium heat. Toss in the garlic and shallots and cook while mixing from time to time until your shallots are tender. Stir in the red bell pepper, green beans, tomatoes, and artichokes–hearts of palm mixture. Cook for 2 minutes while stirring frequently. Mix in the rice. Spread half of the artichoke-rice mixture evenly in the hot lasagna dish you cooked your vegan shrimp and Italian sausage in. Spread an even layer of vegan shrimp and Italian sausage over the artichoke-rice mixture, and then sprinkle your frozen peas over the top of that. Spread the remaining artichoke-rice mixture over the top. Pour the broth mixture over the top of the rice.

Cover with foil and bake for 10 minutes. Remove the foil and bake for another 30 to 40 minutes. Your paella should have a light, crispy crust on the top.

Serve with fresh parsley over the top and maybe a glass or two of that white wine you were cooking with.

ROASTED RED PEPPER LASAGNA

This is one of the recipes I brought with me to the great merger that was our marriage. I'm pretty sure it was part of my allure. I debated calling it Siren Song Lasagna, but I thought that might sound a little like I had led Dan to his doom or something. And if that were the case I'd just go all in and call it Temple of Doom Lasagna. This recipe makes a huge fancy lasagna that will fit in perfectly on any holiday table or schmancy dinner party.

MAKES 6 TO 8 SERVINGS

1 package whole wheat lasagna noodles (the kind you need to boil)

1 package extrafirm tofu

2 cloves garlic, minced

1 teaspoon garlic powder

2 teaspoons Italian seasonings

2 tablespoons olive oil

1 teaspoon Bragg's liquid aminos

2 tablespoons roasted red peppers in oil

1 teaspoon red pepper flakes (save a little extra to sprinkle over the top)

2 teaspoons vegan Parmesan

2 (24-ounce) jars of your favorite pasta sauce

½ cup red wine

3 Tofurky Italian sausages or Field Roast Italian sausages, cut into coins

½ cup sliced white mushrooms

½ cup baby spinach leaves

½ cup fresh basil leaves

¼ cup kalamata olives, pitted

1 Roma tomato, sliced

2 teaspoons capers, drained

1 cup shredded Daiya vegan mozzarella cheese or your favorite vegan cheese

Cook your lasagna noodles per the instructions on the package.

In a large bowl, use a fork to mash your tofu. Mix your mashed tofu with the garlic, garlic powder, Italian seasonings, 1 tablespoon of the olive oil, the Bragg's, roasted red peppers, red pepper flakes, and vegan Parmesan.

In a saucepan, heat your pasta sauce.

In a large cast-iron skillet or frying pan, heat the remaining 1 tablespoon olive oil and the red wine over medium heat. Once your oil is warm, toss in the vegan Italian sausage and mushrooms. You'll want to cook them evenly in the red wine. As they cook, you'll notice a deep red coating form on the vegan Italian sausage and mushrooms from the red wine reducing. Remove them when they are browned and have a heavy, even coating.

Preheat the oven to 375°F.

Build your lasagna by ladling a thin layer of a quarter of the sauce across the bottom of a glass baking dish, followed by a layer of a third of the lasagna noodles and all of the tofu ricotta. Add another layer of a third of the lasagna noodles. Ladle on another quarter of the pasta sauce, followed by the spinach and basil leaves. Top that with the vegan Italian sausages and mushrooms, the olives, tomato slices, and capers. Ladle another quarter of the pasta sauce over the top. Sprinkle half the vegan mozzarella cheese over the sauce. Then place your last layer of lasagna noodles. Ladle more pasta sauce over the top and the rest of your vegan cheese over the top of that.

Bake for 30 to 40 minutes, or until your vegan cheese is melted. Sprinkle some red pepper flakes over the top of your lasagna.

BEEFLESS WELLINGTON POTPIE

This is a nice date-night recipe. These savory little pies seem really impressive and hard to make, even, though they are super-simple and will give you a ton of time to clean your apartment. Recipes like this are today's busy cook's best friend.

MAKES 2 PIES

1 tablespoon olive oil

1 (9-ounce) package Gardein beefless tips or beef seitan, defrosted

2 tablespoons Dijon mustard

½ cup sliced baby portobello mushrooms

½ cup frozen peas

1 tablespoon Bragg's liquid aminos

2 teaspoons red wine

1 clove garlic, minced

½ teaspoon onion powder

¼ teaspoon freshly ground black peppercorns

1 teaspoon vegan Worcestershire sauce

1 teaspoon chopped fresh parsley

⅓ cup chopped spinach leaves

1 puff pastry sheet, defrosted

¼ cup apple juice

Preheat the oven to 400°F.

In a saucepan, heat the olive oil over a medium heat. Once your oil is hot, sear the outside of your vegan beef until it turns golden brown and has a light crust. When you remove your vegan beef from the skillet, place it on a plate, but don't dab off any oil. Brush a light, even coating of Dijon mustard over your vegan beef.

In a large bowl, mix the mushrooms, peas, Bragg's, red wine, garlic, onion powder, black pepper, vegan Worcestershire sauce, parsley, and spinach. Gently mix in your vegan beef. Fill 2 (32-ounce) ramekins with your beef and vegetable mix.

Fold your puff pastry sheet in the middle and then cut it in half. Gently fold the corners of your puff pastry under so that each piece fits into the top of a ramekin. Use a butter knife to tuck any edges into your ramekins. Gently cut a tiny X in the top and brush with apple juice. Bake for 10 to 15 minutes, or until the tops of your pies are golden brown and hard.

Let cool for 2 to 3 minutes before serving or you might burn your face off.

BASQUE VEGAN CHICKEN

This pretty, fancy, wonderful dinner is a mock meat lover's dream come true! It has it all. Beautiful colors, rich, unique flavors … and olives. This dinner makes enough for two people, with leftovers for a few days—but there weren't any in our house, because it was too good to stop eating. No regrets. Well, one regret: that we didn't have any leftovers to eat the next day.

MAKES 4 SERVINGS

2 cups vegan chicken (we recommend Gardein Chick'n Scallopini)

Olive oil cooking spray

2 tablespoons olive oil

1 package Tofurky Italian sausages or Field Roast Italian sausages

2 tablespoons red wine

1 large red bell pepper, sliced

4 cloves garlic, minced

1 (14-ounce) can diced tomatoes

2 teaspoons dried oregano

1 tablespoon Bragg's liquid aminos

2 teaspoons cumin

1 (14-ounce) can artichoke hearts, drained

½ cup Spanish green olives, pitted and sliced

½ teaspoon red pepper flakes

3 cups cooked brown rice

Preheat the oven to 400°F.

Put your vegan chicken in a glass baking dish and spray with a light, even coating of olive oil cooking spray. Bake for 15 to 20 minutes. Halfway through, flip your vegan chicken once to make sure it bakes evenly. Remove the vegan chicken from the oven once it is golden brown.

In your loyal cast-iron skillet or frying pan, heat your olive oil over medium heat. Once your oil is hot, add the vegan sausages and red wine. You'll want to cook your vegan sausages evenly in the red wine. As they cook, you'll notice a deep red coating form on the vegan sausages from the red wine reducing. Remove your vegan sausages when they are browned and have a heavy, even coating. Add your red bell pepper, garlic, diced tomatoes, oregano, Bragg's, and cumin to the olive oil and what is left of the red wine. Stir constantly. Once your sauce begins to bubble, add the artichoke hearts, olives, and red pepper flakes and then cover and cook for another minute.

To serve, place the vegan chicken and vegan sausages over your rice and cover with your sauce.

MANICOTTI WITH KALAMATA OLIVE PESTO TOFU RICOTTA FILLING

In our house at Christmas, manicotti might be as popular as Santa Claus. It's a fancy centerpiece dish that pulls off that rare combination of being both impressive and simple. People who know me know I am a slave to olives. I love them all and try to work them into every meal. I like olives in my tofu scramble just as much as I love them in a salad, tossed with pasta, or in a taco. Is there anything an olive can't do? Maybe geometry. Olives seem bad at math.

MAKES 6 TO 8 SERVINGS

PASTA AND SAUCE

1 package (10 to 12) manicotti tubes

1 jar of your favorite pasta sauce

3 tomatoes, diced

2 cloves garlic, minced

2 tablespoons Bragg's liquid aminos

⅓ cup red wine

1 teaspoon olive oil

1 teaspoon garlic powder

2 teaspoons dried oregano

⅓ cup chopped fresh basil

⅓ cup baby spinach leaves

2 tablespoons chopped fresh parsley

Crushed pink Himalayan salt and crushed black peppercorns to taste

KALAMATA PESTO TOFU FILLING

1 package extrafirm tofu, drained

½ cup baby spinach leaves

¼ cup fresh basil leaves

15 kalamata olives, pitted

5 to 6 white mushrooms

1 ½ teaspoons toasted pine nuts

2 teaspoons sun-dried tomatoes

2 cloves garlic, minced

1 tablespoon nutritional yeast

EXTRAS

Olive oil cooking spray

½ cup shredded Daiya vegan mozzarella cheese or your favorite vegan cheese

2 tablespoons vegan Parmesan

Red pepper flakes and dried oregano to sprinkle over the top

Cook your manicotti per the directions on the package. You want them to be a little firmer than al dente so they don't get mushy when baked with the sauce and to keep them from tearing while you're filling them.

Preheat the oven to 350°F.

Put all the sauce ingredients in a large pot and heat over medium heat. Stir periodically.

Put the ingredients for the tofu ricotta in a food processor or blender one at a time, and blend each one into a smooth paste. Don't worry about wiping out the machine after each ingredient—you'll be mixing them anyway. Put all the processed ingredients in a large bowl and mix with a rubber-tipped spatula so you can scrape the sides until blended. If you have a pastry bag set or decorating gun, fill that with the tofu filling and set it up with the largest tip.

Spray a lasagna dish with olive oil cooking spray. Fill your cooked manicotti tubes with the tofu ricotta—either with your pastry bag or a decorating gun, or just use a spoon and be gentle. After you fill each one, place it in the lasagna dish. You should end up with just the right amount of tofu ricotta to fill your manicotti tubes.

Pour 2 ladles of the sauce over the top and sprinkle with vegan cheese and vegan Parmesan. Bake for 20 to 25 minutes. You'll know it's done when your vegan cheese is melted and your sauce is bubbly. Sprinkle red pepper flakes and dried oregano and more sauce if you'd like over the top when you serve. We put at least another ladleful of sauce on each plate.

BABY SOUR CREAM AND CHIVE SOUFFLÉS

Given that the key ingredients in a traditional soufflé are egg yolks and egg whites, this has been without question one of the more difficult dishes to veganize. But we never back down from a challenge. It took many attempts and many rounds of kitchen cleaning and dish doing, but we finally got these bad boys down. The Mount Everest of veganizing has been ascended—and we stuck a big fat SHANNON flag at the summit.

MAKES 4 SOUFFLÉS

Margarine to grease your ramekins

6 tablespoons all-purpose flour (you'll need a little more to coat your ramekins)

2 tablespoons soy milk

2 teaspoons cornstarch

2 tablespoons vegan sour cream

2 tablespoons nutritional yeast

3 teaspoons chopped fresh chives

¼ teaspoon crushed pink Himalayan salt

¼ teaspoon crushed black peppercorns

½ cup baby spinach leaves

2 tablespoons Ener-G egg replacer, just the powder, not prepared as instructed on the package

4 teaspoons cream of tartar

Preheat the oven to 350°F.

Grease 4 (10-ounce) ramekins with margarine and then lightly dust with all-purpose flour.

In your newfangled food processor, blend all the ingredients to create the batter. Fill your ramekins to the lip and slide them into the oven directly on the rack.

Bake for 15 to 25 minutes, or until the tops of the soufflés are a light golden brown.

BEEFLESS STROGANOFF

I have so many fond memories of Beef Stroganoff. For nights when my dad was in charge of dinner, this was one of the most impressive recipes he knew how to make. He actually had a few "secret" recipes he picked up from his bachelor days in college. They all involved cans of soup—but this one was the best. Of course, he had enough Eastern European in his blood to know how to doll up a simple Stroganoff recipe and make it exceptional. A few years ago, I hosted a ladies' night dinner party where we randomly picked "Russian" as the theme for the food and booze. We drank an improvised cocktail I made with apple juice and paprika vodka we'd brought back from Budapest. I veganized my dad's Stroganoff. And after a few cocktails, we spoke in pretty terrible accents that made us sound like villains in a Rocky and Bullwinkle cartoon. Eeet vas da vunderfal night …

MAKES 4 TO 6 SERVINGS

- 1 package whole wheat farfalle (bow-tie pasta)
- 2 tablespoons margarine
- 2½ cups sliced baby portobello mushrooms
- 1 large red onion, diced
- 2 cloves garlic, minced
- ½ cup sliced black olives
- 2 teaspoons Bragg's liquid aminos, plus more if desired
- 2 teaspoons freshly ground black peppercorns
- 1 cup Better Than Bouillon vegan beef broth, made per the instructions on the package
- 1 teaspoon olive oil
- ½ cup red wine
- ¾ cup vegan sour cream, plus more if desired
- 3 tablespoons chopped fresh parsley

Make your pasta per the instructions on the package.

In a your much loved cast-iron skillet or saucepan, melt your margarine over medium heat. Once your skillet is hot, toss in your mushrooms and onions and mix. Cook while tossing repeatedly till your vegetables are tender. Add the garlic, olives, Bragg's, and black pepper and mix.

In a Dutch oven or soup pot, mix the broth, olive oil, red wine, and vegan sour cream and heat over medium heat. Stir continually. Once the broth begins to thicken a bit and bubble, pour in the mushroom mix. Try to get as much oil and garlic and all those little flavorful parts in there as possible. Stir and reduce the heat to low. Simmer for no more than a minute, and then give it a taste test. If the sauce is too salty for you, add 1 teaspoon of vegan sour cream; if you want more flavor, add 1 teaspoon of Bragg's.

Serve your sauce over the top of your pasta and with some fresh parsley sprinkled over the top.

Приятного аппетита!

HUNGARIAN GOULASH

In the spring of 2008, Dan and I spent a week in Budapest. One of our many quests on this trip was to track down a legendary restaurant rumored to have the best vegan pizza in Eastern Europe. You might think that's a dubious claim to fame, but Budapest is an extremely vegan-friendly city. We trekked for what felt like miles, through a biblical downpour ... until we finally found the restaurant, Napfenyes Izek, on the darkest, most random street possible. We got there right as they were supposed to be closing—but taking pity on these weary travelers, they agreed to serve us. While we waited for the famous pizza, we had two bowls of vegan Hungarian goulash and some cups of tea to warm us up a little. This was the night I found a new appreciation for paprika. Not all paprika is the same. It's one of those spices that is very regional. If you've never been impressed with paprika in the past, we recommend picking up some Hungarian or smoked paprika. The sweet and subtly hot flavors of these spices will change your mind about this red powder forever. You'll need that positive attitude toward paprika to truly appreciate this wonderful stew. Oh, and the pizza was amazing.

MAKES 4 TO 6 SERVINGS

Olive oil cooking spray

5 red potatoes, cubed

2 carrots, thinly sliced

1 (14-ounce) can garbanzo beans, drained and rinsed

¼ cup pearl onions, defrosted

1 tablespoon Hungarian paprika

1 teaspoon smoked paprika

2 cloves garlic, minced

¼ teaspoon caraway seeds

¼ teaspoon marjoram

¼ teaspoon onion powder

1 teaspoon nutritional yeast

1 tablespoon chopped fresh parsley

¼ cup whole wheat flour

2 cups Better Than Bouillon vegan beef broth, made per the instructions on the package

1 package Gardein beefless tips or beef seitan, defrosted

½ red onion, sliced

1 cup frozen peas

¼ cup baby spinach leaves

4 to 6 tablespoons vegan sour cream (1 tablespoon per bowl)

2 to 3 teaspoons chopped fresh chives (½ teaspoon per bowl)

Crushed pink Himalayan salt and freshly ground black peppercorns

Preheat the oven to 400°F.

Spray your beloved slow cooker with a light coating of olive oil cooking spray. Toss the potatoes, carrots, beans, pearl onions, both paprikas, garlic, caraway seeds, marjoram, onion powder, nutritional yeast, parsley, whole wheat flour, and broth in the cooker and stir until well mixed.

Cover and cook on medium heat for 3 hours.

While your slow cooker is, well, cooking, spray a glass baking dish with olive oil cooking spray and arrange your vegan beef in the dish. Spray another coating of olive oil cooking spray over the top, and then layer on the red on-

ion. Roast for 20 minutes. Check on it to make sure your vegan beef is cooking evenly.

After your stew has been in the slow cooker for 3 hours, stir the peas and spinach into it, cover, and cook for another 20 minutes. You'll be cooking your vegan beef while your peas and spinach are in the slow cooker.

Give your goulash a taste test and add any needed salt and pepper. To serve it, first ladle in the stew, add the vegan beef and onions, and then top with a tablespoon of vegan sour cream and some chives.

Jó étvágyat!

VEGAN CHICKEN AND KALE SCALOPPINE

A scaloppine is a basic, traditional Italian dish consisting of thinly sliced meat covered in flour, sautéed, and served with sauce. This dish uses vegan chicken for the meat base and incorporates a superfood (kale) to healthy it up a bit and also add some extra flavors. All in all, this is a fairly simple but still impressive recipe that'll make for a great family dinner.

MAKES 4 SERVINGS

1 package whole wheat spaghetti

3 slices stale baguette

¼ teaspoon lemon pepper

¼ teaspoon crushed pink Himalayan salt

1 teaspoon nutritional yeast

2 cups vegan chicken, defrosted (we recommend Gardein Chick'n Scallopini)

Olive oil cooking spray

1 to 2 lemons, cut into slices

1 cup Better Than Bouillon vegan chicken broth, made per the instructions on the package

¼ cup lemon juice

1 (14-ounce) can cannellini beans, drained and rinsed

1 cup kale, chopped

¼ teaspoon chopped fresh parsley

2 teaspoons capers, drained

¼ teaspoon red pepper flakes

Freshly ground black peppercorns to taste

Preheat the oven to 400°F.

Cook the spaghetti according to the directions on the package.

In a blender, blend the baguette slices into crumbs. Dump into a bowl and mix with the lemon pepper, salt, and nutritional yeast.

Spread your vegan chicken out in a glass baking dish and spray with olive oil cooking spray. One piece at a time, dip your vegan chicken in the bread crumbs and flip a few times until lightly breaded. Place the vegan chicken back in the baking dish. Once all your vegan chicken is coated, spray your glass baking dish with a light, even coating of olive oil cooking spray again. Place a lemon slice on top of each piece of vegan chicken. Bake for 20 to 30 minutes, or until the vegan chicken is a light golden brown.

In a saucepan, heat the broth, lemon juice, beans, kale, parsley, capers, and red pepper flakes over low heat. Once the broth begins to bubble, remove from the heat.

Serve your spaghetti with the vegan chicken on top. Ladle some lemon sauce over your vegan chicken and spaghetti and dash some black pepper over the top of that.

VEGAN CHICKEN MARSALA

Not to be confused with chicken masala, a traditional Indian dish, this classic Italian recipe is extremely popular with vegans and nonvegans alike, due to how easy it is to make and how tasty the end product is. This recipe kicks it up a notch (sorry, Emeril) with some extra flavors and ingredients—without making it any more complicated or sacrificing any of its classic simplicity.

MAKES 2 TO 4 SERVINGS

1 package whole wheat spaghetti

½ cup garbanzo bean flour

¼ teaspoon crushed pink Himalayan salt

¼ teaspoon freshly ground black peppercorns

2 cups vegan chicken, defrosted (we recommend Gardein Chick'n Scallopini)

Olive oil cooking spray

2 tablespoons olive oil

3 cloves garlic, minced

2 shallots, thinly sliced

1 cup sliced baby portobello caps

¼ cup fresh parsley, chopped

Pinch of fresh oregano leaves

½ cup Marsala wine

¼ cup Better Than Bouillon vegan chicken broth, made per the instructions on the package

¼ teaspoon nutritional yeast

Prepare the pasta per the instructions on the package.

In a shallow dish, mix the flour, salt, and pepper. Spray the vegan chicken with a heavy coating of olive oil cooking spray and then drop it into the flour mixture. Flip your vegan chicken a few times to get a good coating. Shake off excess flour.

In your cast-iron skillet or sauté pan, heat the olive oil over medium heat. Once your oil is hot, toss in the garlic, shallots, mushrooms, parsley, and oregano. Cook while stirring frequently.

Add the coated vegan chicken to your hot skillet. Cook for 5 to 8 minutes, turning only once, until golden brown. Remove the vegan chicken from the skillet and set aside. Add the wine, broth, and nutritional yeast. Mix until your sauce is smooth, and heat until it begins to boil.

To serve, place your vegan chicken on top of your spaghetti and ladle sauce over the top.

GAZPACHO

Chilled soup is one of those things you're either into or not. I was never a big fan until I had a spicy Spanish gazpacho with cucumbers in it. It's a combo I never would have thought I'd like, but this recipe has taken my heart.

MAKES 2 SERVINGS

8 to 10 baguette slices

Crushed pink Himalayan salt and freshly ground black peppercorns

1 (28-ounce) can diced tomatoes

1 large fresh tomato, diced

1 cup Better Than Bouillon vegetable broth, made per the instructions on the package

2 tablespoons white wine

3 cloves garlic, minced

2 tablespoons lemon juice

2 teaspoons cumin

2 teaspoons hot sauce

1 teaspoon fresh thyme leaves

2 tablespoons olive oil

1 tablespoon Bragg's liquid aminos

1 large fresh cucumber, diced

½ green bell pepper, chopped

½ red onion, diced

Set aside the baguette slices, salt, and pepper. In your favorite food processor or blender, mix the remaining ingredients on medium speed. Pour your blended ingredients into a nonmetallic bowl, cover with foil, and refrigerate for at least an hour. Do a taste test and add any salt or pepper it might need.

Serve chilled with slices of baguette and a little limoncello!

BORSCHT FOR VEGANS WHO DON'T LIKE BEETS

When I first saw this recipe in Betty Crocker's Big Red, I made an unpretty face because I'm just not a beet fan. But when we took on the Betty Crocker Project, we both knew that there would be some recipes we wouldn't want to make. Then I looked at the recipe and realized I could make it taste like all the good things about borscht without being heavy on actual beets or making your teeth pink. There are still beets in there, and you can still taste them, but just the right amount to make you say, "Whoa. I might not hate beets." In fact, speaking as a reformed semipro beet hater and grumpasaurus: this soup is a fall classic that I would eat every day.

MAKES 4 TO 6 SERVINGS

Olive oil cooking spray

2 packages Gardein beefless tips or beef seitan, defrosted

1 large red onion, sliced

4 cups Better Than Bouillon vegan beef broth, made per the instructions on the package

⅓ cup red wine

3 tablespoons Bragg's liquid aminos

¼ teaspoon freshly ground black peppercorns

5 red potatoes, cubed

3 cloves garlic, minced

3 cups fresh cabbage, shredded

1 (14-ounce) can garbanzo beans, drained and rinsed

2 teaspoons dried dill weed

1 teaspoon fresh thyme leaves

1½ teaspoons onion powder

1 tablespoon pickling spices

1 (14-ounce) can shoestring sliced beets,* drained

1 tablespoon olive oil

Vegan sour cream and chopped chives for toppings

Some great bread for dipping

Preheat the oven to 400°F.

Spray a glass baking dish with olive oil cooking spray. Arrange your vegan beef in the dish so none is touching, and then place the red onion in a layer over the vegan beef. Bake for 5 to 8 minutes. Remove when the onions are tender and golden brown.

In your favorite Dutch oven or stewpot, add the broth, wine, Bragg's, pepper, potatoes, garlic, cabbage, garbanzo beans, dill weed, thyme, onion powder, and pickling spices.** Cook over medium heat until your soup begins to boil; then turn heat down to a simmer. Add the beets and olive oil. Simmer for around an hour. To serve, top with vegan sour cream, chopped chives, and the vegan beef.

Don't forget the bread because you're going to want to clean your bowl.

---

* If you love beets and pink teeth, you can use 4 medium-size fresh beets that have been sliced, and you'll need to add an extra 30 minutes to your simmer time.
** Let's say you hate actually eating spices. You can also take the pickling spices and put them in a tea diffuser all bouquet garni–style—like we did in the Seitan Coq au Vin recipe (page 236) instead of mixing them in the soup.

FAUX CASSOULET

Traditional French cassoulet is a slow-cooking white bean stew made with a whole zoo of animals and their second cousins. It takes all day to make, and sometimes people let it simmer on the stove overnight. This one takes less than ½ hour to make and really captures the spirit of this French classic.

MAKES 4 TO 6 SERVINGS

1 (15-ounce) can cannellini beans, rinsed and drained

1 (15-ounce) can garbanzo beans, rinsed and drained

2 tablespoons pearl barley

5 cups Better Than Bouillon vegan beef broth, made per the instructions on the package

1 tablespoon olive oil

1 tablespoon dry white wine

Dash of liquid smoke

1 tablespoon Bragg's liquid aminos

1 teaspoon dried oregano

1 teaspoon dried thyme

2 cloves garlic, minced

2 bay leaves

1 (28-ounce) can fire-roasted whole tomatoes

1 green bell pepper, diced

1 red onion, diced

2 celery stalks, diced

Olive oil cooking spray

1 package Tofurky Italian sausages or Field Roast Italian sausages, sliced into coins

1 cup chopped vegan chicken

Chopped fresh parsley to sprinkle over the top

Pinch of dry bread crumbs per bowl

Toss the beans, barley, broth, olive oil, wine, liquid smoke, Bragg's, herbs, and vegetables in a slow cooker and set it to high. Cook for 2 hours.

About 15 minutes before you are ready to serve your dinner, spray your favorite cast-iron skillet or frying pan with olive oil cooking spray and heat over a medium heat. Once your oil is hot, toss in the vegan sausages and vegan chicken. Flip a few times to makes sure your mock meats cook evenly. Set your hot skillet aside once your mock meats are golden brown and have crispy edges.

Sprinkle your mock meat over the top of your stew. Ladle into bowls and sprinkle chopped parsley and dry bread crumbs over the top. Don't forget the bread. I mean, it's a French dish. It's not complete without a little bread.

MINI TEMPEH POT STICKERS WITH TAMARI AND SESAME DIPPING SAUCE

You might look through this recipe and think, "Wow, that's a lot of steps. What can I skip over to make this go faster?" Sorry to have to be the one to break this to you, but you have to follow all the steps. There are no shortcuts to Mordor—or pot stickers. But if it makes you feel any better, the steps actually go very quickly. This recipe also makes a lot. It would be perfect for a party or potluck, especially since you serve the pot stickers at room temperature or chilled, and they aren't terribly expensive for how cool they are.

MAKES 6 TO 8 SERVINGS

FILLING

1 cup crumbled tempeh

1½ cups broccoli slaw

2 tablespoons white wine

1 tablespoon cornstarch

3 tablespoons Bragg's liquid aminos

1 teaspoon sesame oil

¼ teaspoon chopped lemongrass

2 cloves garlic, minced

3 green onions, chopped

Pinch of freshly ground black peppercorns

DUMPLINGS

2 cups whole wheat flour

2 cups all-purpose flour (you'll need a little extra to flour your surfaces)

2 cups boiling water

¼ cup sesame oil

3 cups water (for steaming)

SAUCE

3 tablespoons agave nectar

3 tablespoons tamari

3 tablespoons rice vinegar

3 tablespoons Sriracha sauce

2 tablespoons water

1½ teaspoons lime juice

1½ teaspoons sesame oil

Raw sesame seeds to sprinkle over the top

In a large bowl, mix all the filling ingredients with a large spoon.

Next make the dumplings. In another large bowl, mix the whole wheat flour, all-purpose flour, and boiling water with a handheld mixer. Once the mixture makes small pebbles and cools a little bit, use your hands to knead the dough into one large ball. Knead your dough inside the bowl for 5 minutes to make sure it is completely blended. The dough will be warm while you do this. Divide your dough into 4 equal segments.

Roll each of those segments into a 12-inch-long rope. You want them to be evenly rolled, like a cigar. You don't want "tails" at the end like Jabba the Hutt. I mean, I find, as a good rule of thumb, that if your food looks anything like Jabba the Hutt—something has gone wrong. Slice each of these ropes into 24 pieces about

½ inch thick. They will look like little marshmallows.

One at a time, form each piece of dough into a small, rounded pancake shape. You want to keep them a little smaller than your palm. Gently fill each of them with about 1 teaspoon of filling, and then fold over the dough and pinch the edges together to seal it. You want them to be seamless and smooth but with a slight rolled/pleated edge. They will make little pockets and look a lot like oyster shells. Once they are sealed, place them on a plate, seam up. Gently press them onto the plate to flatten the bottoms.

Set up your steamer. Now, we used a traditional Chinese bamboo steamer that fits over a pot of boiling water—and, as a side note, makes your home smell really amazing when you use it. I know a lot of you have fancy electric steamers, and you'll need to read your instruction manuals before starting this part. You want to follow the instructions that will keep your dumplings from getting wet. Most electric steamers have baskets or racks to do this. It's important that the dumplings be raised above the water.

Heat your wok over high heat. Add 2 tablespoons sesame oil to the wok for each batch of pot stickers. Place about 10 pot stickers into the wok in a single layer, with the flat surface down. Fry for 2 minutes, or until the bottom is golden brown.

Move your fried dumplings into the steamer and steam for 5 to 7 minutes, or until the dough feels solid. You're going to be doing this in batches for about 20 minutes, and you'll want to keep an eye on your steamer and wok, because the longer you cook, the hotter everything gets and the faster the dumplings cook.

Once they are solid, place the dumplings on a plate and set aside. You're going to serve them at room temperature, so don't worry about keeping them warm. If you prefer them chilled, place your dumplings in the fridge.

To make your dipping sauce, mix all the sauce ingredients except the sesame seeds until the agave nectar dissolves. After you pour the sauce into a small serving bowl or ramekin, sprinkle with the sesame seeds.

Once your dumplings are cool, serve on a platter with the sauce on the side.

DRUNKEN VEGAN DUCK STIR-FRY

Mock duck is kinda weird. You can usually find it in a can at Asian markets and Asian grocery stores. Yeah, a can. I told you it was weird. But it's got a great flavor and texture—softer and juicer than a lot of mock meats, like I'm told real duck is compared to chicken. It takes on a nice crispy texture on the outside when pan-fried—hey, like we're going to do in this recipe!

MAKES 4 SERVINGS

MARINADE

3 teaspoons Bragg's liquid aminos

1 teaspoon tamari

1/3 cup sherry or rice wine

1 teaspoon Chinese five-spice powder

1/4 teaspoon ginger paste

1 teaspoon hot sauce

1 1/4 teaspoons sesame oil

STIR-FRY

1 cup vegan duck pieces

1/4 cup sliced mushrooms

3 cloves garlic, minced

2 cups rice wine

2 tablespoons Bragg's liquid aminos

2 teaspoons ginger paste

1 teaspoon Chinese five-spice powder

2 tablespoons hoisin sauce (read your label to make sure your brand is vegan)

2 tablespoons sesame oil

1 cup Chinese string beans

1 red bell pepper, thinly sliced

1 (8-ounce) can sliced water chestnuts, drained

1/3 cup dry-roasted cashews

2 cups cooked brown rice

4 green onions, diced

Whisk together all the marinade ingredients in a bowl. Place your vegan duck and sliced mushrooms in a deep bowl and pour the marinade over the top. Cover and marinate for 30 minutes. Toss the vegan duck and the mushrooms in the marinade a few times during that period to make sure all your vegan duck gets evenly coated with the marinade.

While your drunken duck hangs out, make your stir-fry sauce. In the same bowl you made your marinade in, whisk together the garlic, rice wine, Bragg's, ginger paste, Chinese five-spice powder, and hoisin sauce and set aside.

Heat your sesame oil in your always-helpful wok over a high heat. Once your oil is hot, toss in your string beans and stir-fry until they start to become tender. Then add the vegan duck, mushrooms, bell pepper, water chestnuts, and cashews and toss to combine. Carefully pour the stir-fry sauce over the top of the vegetables and stir-fry until your string beans are the desired tenderness. It shouldn't take more than 1 to 2 minutes.

Serve hot over the brown rice with diced green onions over the top.

PAD THAI

I still remember the first time I had Pad Thai. I was going to school in Olympia, Washington, and I was out to dinner with my friend Amanda from San Francisco. I can still remember how hilarious she found it that I'd never had Pad Thai before. I mean, I'd eaten Chinese and Japanese food before. I enjoyed years of eating smelly kimchi and even had Vegan Tempeh Mongolian Stew once. But I never had Thai food until I was twenty-one, and I had no idea that the Pad Thai I thoroughly enjoyed that night wasn't even very good. Since then I've come to love Thai food—all that basil, coconut milk, peanut, and spice. And now, as a self-proclaimed Thai food expert, I hope it's not too braggy to say that this is the good stuff. Plus I got to use one of my very favorite tricks for replacing the fried egg bits in fried rice, chow mein, and egg drop soup.

MAKES 4 TO 6 SERVINGS

1 package flat stir-fry rice noodles

⅓ cup lime juice

⅓ cup water

3 tablespoons brown sugar

⅓ cup stir-fry sauce*

3 tablespoons Bragg's liquid aminos

1 tablespoon white wine vinegar

6 tablespoons sesame oil

¼ to ¾ teaspoon cayenne pepper

3 cloves garlic, minced

1 package extrafirm tofu, mashed into smallish clumps

1 package vegan chicken, cut into bite-size pieces

1 (14-ounce) can baby corn, drained

2 cups fresh pea pods

¼ cup dry-roasted peanuts

2 cups fresh mung bean sprouts

¼ cup fresh cilantro, chopped

4 to 6 fresh green onions, chopped (1 per serving)

Lime wedges

Make up your noodles per the instructions on the package. The noodles we used were ready in 5 minutes, so we didn't make them until we'd made the rest of the dish, but some take longer, and you need to boil the water. Please use your best multitasking/time-management skills.

In a bowl, mix the lime juice, water, brown sugar, stir-fry sauce, Bragg's, vinegar, and 1 tablespoon of the sesame oil.

So you know on the menus for Thai restaurants where they let you choose how spicy you want something to be by choosing the number of little chili peppers or stars? We're at that part of the recipe. If you're not a fan of heat, I would go with ¼ teaspoon cayenne pepper; if you like it hot, I'd max it out at ¾ teaspoon cayenne

pepper—¾ teaspoon cayenne pepper will make it seriously spicy, and you always have the option of tossing some Tabasco on the finished dish if you want it so hot your eyelashes fall out. Some people don't like eyelashes, so go crazy.

In your favorite little wok, heat 3 teaspoons of the sesame oil over medium heat. Cook the garlic in the warm oil for less than a minute. Add the mashed tofu and fry for about 2 minutes. Remove your tofu from the wok when it turns golden brown and has a crispy skin. Put your tofu in a bowl on the side; don't dab off any of the oil.

Add the remaining 2 tablespoons sesame oil to the warm wok. Be careful; it may steam or splatter. Toss in

---

* You're replacing the fish sauce you usually find in pad Thai, so please read your labels, because some stir-fry sauce has fish or oyster sauce in it, or is actually just fish sauce relabeled. Vegan stir-fry sauce is more like a thinner hoisin sauce—which might also work, but will cost you a dollar more.

the vegan chicken, baby corn, and pea pods and cook. Stir frequently, so the vegan chicken and vegetables cook evenly. Once the vegan chicken begins to brown and the vegetables become tender, pour the lime sauce in. Add the tofu and mix. Next, mix in the cooked noodles. Stir in the peanuts, bean sprouts, and half the cilantro. You're going to let this cook for 3 to 6 minutes; it depends on how saucy you want your dish to be. The longer you cook it, the more liquid evaporates and soaks into the noodles.

Serve with green onions and cilantro sprinkled on and a lime wedge to squeeze over the top.

ASIAN TOFU STEAKS WITH WASABI AIOLI

"Tofu steaks" are a perfect example of those old-school vegan recipes that, sadly, probably turned a lot of people off veganism back in the day. They undoubtedly took a bite out of poorly cooked, underseasoned tofu and were left to believe that vegan cuisine was all mushy white goop. You can't just take some tofu, grill it, put it on a plate, and call it a steak, people. Of course, the irony is that tofu steaks can actually be a delicious meal when cooked and seasoned properly—and this recipe will allow you to do just that.

MAKES 3 TO 6 SERVINGS

TOFU STEAK
2 packages extrafirm tofu, drained
½ cup olive oil
½ cup Bragg's liquid aminos
2 tablespoons brown sugar
½ teaspoon vegan Worcestershire sauce
2 teaspoons sesame oil
3 teaspoons ginger paste
3 cloves garlic, minced
1 sheet nori (dried seaweed), crushed
6 teaspoons sesame seeds (1 teaspoon per tofu steak)

WASABI AIOLI
½ cup Vegenaise
2 teaspoons wasabi
2 teaspoons lemon juice

Cut your tofu into 6 pieces, or steaks, with a serrated knife to give it the "fish" texture on the sides. Place the tofu steaks in a casserole dish that will fit all the tofu steaks but isn't so large that when you pour the marinade mix in you won't completely cover the tofu steaks. Mix the olive oil, Bragg's, brown sugar, vegan Worcestershire sauce, sesame oil, and ginger paste in a bowl with a hand mixer until the sugar is dissolved. Add the garlic and crushed nori. Pour the marinade over the tofu steaks. Let your tofu steaks marinate for 2 hours.

While the tofu steaks are marinating, make the wasabi aioli. Mix the Vegenaise, wasabi, and lemon juice with a hand mixer. Put in the refrigerator for later.

Preheat the oven to 400°F.

On a lined cookie sheet, place the tofu steaks so they're close but not touching. Pour ½ teaspoon of the marinade over each tofu steak. Bake for 15 minutes. Then take them out, flip them, and pour another ½ teaspoon of the marinade over each tofu steak. Bake for 20 to 25 minutes. Pull the tofu steaks out when they are baked to a golden brown.

Serve with the wasabi aioli on the side and sprinkled with sesame seeds.

VEGAN CHICKEN CHOW MEIN

This recipe makes a lot of food, and there's none of the MSG you get from those fabulous Chinese takeout spots that fry their tofu "chicken" into little nuggets. You know, the ones that have disgusting bags of chicken wings and a huge selection of Mexican sodas. I love those places. They're usually really sweet about leaving out the fish and oyster sauces, you can watch them make your food, and they're eager to make vegan spring rolls and serve mock meat as long as you promise to tell your friends. Alas, without the MSG there's a bit of blandness, but that's easy to fix with some Bragg's liquid aminos.

MAKES 4 SERVINGS

1 tablespoon olive oil

2 cups vegan chicken, defrosted and cut into bite-size pieces

1 cup sliced carrots

1 cup chopped celery

½ red onion, chopped

2 cloves garlic, minced

1 (8-ounce) can sliced water chestnuts, drained

1 cup halved white mushrooms

½ cup raw cashews

½ cup baby corn, drained

1 (8-ounce) can bamboo shoots, drained

1 cup raw pea pods

1 cup Better Than Bouillon vegetable broth, prepared using the directions on the package

4 tablespoons Bragg's liquid aminos

2 tablespoons cornstarch

½ teaspoon ginger paste

4 cups cooked brown rice

Chow mein noodles

In everyone's favorite wok, heat the olive oil over medium heat. Add your vegan chicken and cook until both sides are golden brown and have crispy edges. Remove the vegan chicken and set aside on a plate with a paper towel to soak up any extra oil.

Throw the carrots, celery, onion, garlic, water chestnuts, mushrooms, cashews, baby corn, bamboo shoots, and pea pods into the oil and cook. Keep turning the vegetables so they cook evenly.

In a bowl, whisk together the vegetable broth, Bragg's, cornstarch, and ginger paste until smooth.

Add the vegan chicken to the bowl and mix until it is coated. Add the vegan chicken mixture to the cooking vegetables, being sure to pour all your broth mixture into the vegetables. Keep mixing to make sure everything gets coated.

This is when you want to test the flavor to see if you want more ginger or Bragg's. If the sauce has reduced too much and gotten too thick or salty during the cooking, you can add 1 or 2 teaspoons of water.

Serve over rice and chow mein noodles.

PEKING TOFURKY WITH DRUMSTICKS AND EMPEROR'S RICE STUFFING

While we were writing this book, a string of unfortunate events led to me spending Thanksgiving 2011 alone in our apartment in Brooklyn, baking away with Indiana Jones and Superman movies in the background, while Dan was in Boston with the original Shannon Crew enjoying his dad's epic Thanksgiving feast. In some ways it really sucked. But there was a lot to do to get this book to you, and my inner jerk reminded me of our looming deadline and how much this project means to me. The good news is that I got to make and enjoy an entire Tofurky dinner all by myself. Although I hope you get to share this recipe with your loved ones.

MAKES 4 TO 6 SERVINGS

PEKING TOFURKY

1 Tofurky or vegan holiday roast, defrosted

2 cloves garlic, minced

1 tablespoon dry white wine

3 tablespoons Bragg's liquid aminos

1 teaspoon sugar

1 teaspoon ginger paste

1 tablespoon sesame oil

3 green onions, diced

1 cup apple juice

½ cup agave nectar

¼ cup rice vinegar

2 to 4 vegan drumsticks, defrosted (see "Vegan Chicken Wings," page 137)

½ cup hoisin sauce (be sure to read your label to make sure your brand is vegan)

2 tablespoons sesame seeds

EMPEROR'S RICE STUFFING

1 cup emperor's or black rice

½ cup long-grain jasmine rice

1 (8-ounce) can bamboo shoots, drained

1 (8-ounce) can sliced water chestnuts, drained

2 tablespoons shredded carrots

¼ cup chopped baby corn spears

⅓ cup chopped celery

Olive oil cooking spray

½ teaspoon chopped lemongrass

1 teaspoon grated lemon peel

2 cloves garlic, minced

2 green onions, chopped

1 cup Better Than Bouillon vegetable broth, made per the instructions on the package

2 tablespoons Bragg's liquid aminos

Preheat the oven to 400°F.

Make sure your Tofurky is completely defrosted. Cut off one end that has a seam about an inch in. Using a soupspoon, remove the stuffing that comes with the Tofurky. Make your Peking marinade by mixing the garlic, white wine, Bragg's, sugar, ginger paste, sesame oil, and green onions.

Prepare your emperor's rice and jasmine rice separately and per the instructions on the packages. Once both kinds of rice are cooked, mix in the bamboo shoots, water chestnuts, carrots, baby corn, celery, and the stuffing you removed from your Tofurky earlier.

Spray your favorite wok with a heavy coating of olive oil cooking spray and heat over high heat. Once your oil is hot, toss in half the rice and vegetable mix. Add ¼ teaspoon of the lemongrass, ½ teaspoon of the lemon peel, 1 clove of the garlic, 1 of the green onions, ½ cup of the broth, and 1 tablespoon of the Bragg's. Stir-fry your mixture until your vegetables are tender. Repeat this step with the other half of your ingredients.

While it's still warm, restuff your Tofurky with the Emperor's Rice Stuffing. It's okay if your Emperor's Rice Stuffing is moist. The extra flavors will only add to the Tofurky. You really want to get as much stuffing as possible in the Tofurky, so really press it in there. You'll have some left over, and that's good because there is really room for only one serving of stuffing in the Tofurky. Place the end you cut off back on and secure with bamboo skewers.

In your warm wok, heat the apple juice and agave nectar. Bring to a boil and then blend in the rice vinegar with a whisk. Once your agave nectar has completely dissolved into your sauce, stir in your Peking marinade mix. Boil for 2 minutes.

Place your restuffed Tofurky and the defrosted drumsticks in a deep casserole dish and ladle ½ to 1 cup of the Peking marinade over the top. Bake for 20 minutes and then spoon more marinade over the top

to baste your Tofurky and drumsticks. Bake for another 10 to 15 minutes, or until your Peking Tofurky is golden brown and has a light, crisp crust on it. Pull it out of the oven, brush with the hoisin sauce, and bake for another 10 to 15 minutes, or until the glaze on your Peking Tofurky is set.

When you serve, place the Peking Tofurky and drumsticks over your Emperor's Rice Stuffing and sprinkle with sesame seeds. You can mix any extra marinade in with the hoisin sauce in the warm casserole dish to make a dipping sauce for your drumsticks.

LENTIL DHANSAAK

Betty Crocker describes this flavorful Indian dish as follows: "What apple pie is to an American, this stew is to a Parsee from the city of Mumbai." I haven't been to India yet, but I'd love to think she knows what's she's talking about—not just because of my undying affection for Betty Crocker, but because this dish is delicious and I want to think of it being enjoyed everywhere. I won't even try to pretend that our recipe is 100 percent authentic, but I can tell you that this recipe is easy and makes a lot, and the leftovers are even better than the first day's dish. Those things alone make this dish very special and one of my favorite things to make on a Sunday.

MAKES 6 TO 8 SERVINGS

1 cup margarine, cut into slices

½ cup dried yellow split peas, rinsed and drained

½ cup dried red lentils, rinsed and drained

3 tablespoons dried green lentils, rinsed and drained

3 tablespoons dried green split peas, rinsed and drained

1 large carrot, sliced into coins

1 yellow onion, diced

1 (14-ounce) can diced tomatoes

2 fresh jalapeños or serrano chilies, cut in half

6½ cups water (you might need more)

2 cups baby spinach leaves

1 tablespoon olive oil

1 tablespoon ginger paste

6 cloves garlic, minced

3 teaspoons ground coriander seeds

1 tablespoon Bragg's liquid aminos

1 teaspoon red pepper flakes

½ teaspoon ground cinnamon

¼ teaspoon ground cloves

2 whole cardamom pods

Pinch of turmeric

½ teaspoon garam masala

1 tablespoon chopped fresh cilantro

Lime wedges on the side

Toss the margarine, yellow peas, red lentils, green lentils, green peas, carrot, onion, tomatoes, chilies, and water into your slow cooker, cover, and set on high. Your margarine is going to melt and the water will

start to get absorbed into the dried lentils and peas after about 30 minutes. So it's okay to start mixing with a wooden spoon every once in a while after that, but make sure you keep covering the cooker back up.

It should take around an hour for your lentils and peas to become tender, but every cooker is a little different, so don't lose hope if it takes longer. Once your lentils and peas are tender, mix in the spinach, olive oil, ginger paste, garlic, coriander seeds, Bragg's, red pepper flakes, cinnamon, cloves, cardamom pods, and turmeric. Cover and simmer for 20 minutes, and then stir in the garam masala. If during that time your stew has become too thick, add 1 tablespoon water—maybe 2. Cover and simmer for another 5 minutes, and then serve with fresh cilantro over the top and some lime wedges to squeeze over the top.

KUNG PAO PORK WITH SESAME RICE NOODLES

This recipe is a twist on the classic Americanized Chinese dish you'll find at every Sichuan-style restaurant in North America, substituting pork—well, vegan pork—for the traditional chicken. So it's sort of a double substitution. If you can't find Match vegan meats in your area, you can substitute with your favorite vegan chicken or even tofu. Go crazy!

MAKES 2 TO 4 SERVINGS

1 package flat rice noodles

5 tablespoons sesame oil (you may need a bit more or less)

1 (1-pound) bag broccoli slaw mix

1 package Match vegan pork, formed into bite-size pieces

½ cup water

½ cup stir-fry sauce (read label to make sure your brand is vegan)

1 tablespoon agave nectar

1 to 2 tablespoons Sriracha sauce (depends how spicy you want it to be)

Dash of red pepper oil

1 tablespoon Bragg's liquid aminos

1 red bell pepper, sliced

4 stalks celery, sliced

1 (8-ounce) can water chestnuts, drained

4 to 8 tablespoons dry-roasted peanuts (2 tablespoons per serving)

Make your rice noodles per the instructions on the package. Once they're done and drained, toss them with 2 teaspoons of the sesame oil.

Heat around 1 tablespoon of the sesame oil in your favorite wok over medium heat. Once your oil is hot, toss in the broccoli slaw and cook, stirring frequently. Remove from the heat when your slaw is tender. Move the slaw into a bowl and cover with foil to keep warm.

Add your vegan pork and another tablespoon of sesame oil. Cook for 5 to 6 minutes, gently flipping and stirring, until your vegan pork browns on all sides. Small pieces of your vegan pork may fall off, but that's a good thing—you want that. The pieces will make your sauce thicker.

In a bowl, mix the water, stir-fry sauce, agave nec-tar, Sriracha sauce, red pepper oil, and Bragg's.

Now toss another tablespoon of sesame oil into your wok if you think you need it. Add the red bell pepper, celery, and water chestnuts. Cook for around a minute. Once your vegetables are tender, add your sauce. Mix your sauce in thoroughly and simmer for 1 to 3 minutes. You're cooking the vegetables, so keep stirring and mixing in the sauce. If your sauce gets too thick, add more sesame oil, ¼ teaspoon at a time. You're done when the vegetables are the desired tenderness.

To serve, put the rice noodles on your plate first, then the broccoli slaw, then the vegan pork with sauce, and finally sprinkle with the peanuts.

THAI VEGAN CHICKEN WITH BASIL

Thai food is one of Dan's favorite ethnic/regional cuisines, and he loves this dish. It's full of flavor but doesn't take a long time to make. You can adjust the level of spiciness to your own personal taste preference based on how much chili you choose to use. Making it the traditional Thai way would probably burn out all of our wimpy Americanized palates, but you can push it as far as you feel up to.

MAKES 4 SERVINGS

2 tablespoons olive oil

2 teaspoons sesame oil

2 cups vegan chicken strips

1 cup fresh pea pods

3 cloves garlic, minced

1 fresh jalapeño, diced (add as much as you need to get the desired heat)

2 tablespoons Bragg's liquid aminos

2 teaspoons agave nectar

1 (14-ounce) can baby corn, drained

1 (8-ounce) can sliced water chestnuts, drained

1 (8-ounce) can bamboo shoots, drained

2 teaspoons lemon juice

¼ teaspoon grated lemon peel

½ cup chopped fresh basil leaves

2 tablespoons chopped fresh mint leaves

2 to 3 cups cooked brown rice

2 tablespoons dry-roasted peanuts

In your favorite wok, heat the olive and sesame oils over medium heat. Once your oil is hot, toss in the vegan chicken and pea pods, and continue to toss. When your vegan chicken begins to brown and the pea pods begin to get tender, toss in the garlic and jalapeño and cook for about 5 minutes. Stir in the Bragg's, agave nectar, corn, water chestnuts, bamboo shoots, lemon juice, and lemon peel and cook for another 5 minutes, or until your vegan chicken is a golden brown. It's called stir-fry because you keep stirring it, so keep tossing the mixture while it's cooking to get an even sauce and coating on your vegan chicken and vegetables. Stir in the basil and mint. Sprinkle the peanuts on top, and serve with the brown rice.

VEGAN CHICKEN IN MOLE SAUCE

Now, I know what some of you are thinking. Chicken in chocolate sauce sounds about as enjoyable as a Skittles and Tootsie Roll omelet. But mole [pronounced "moe-lay"] is a traditional Mexican sauce that can differ greatly from region to region, and it does have dark chocolate powder in it—but the flavor is more like coffee than the sweet Easter-basket stuff. Really, in this version the cumin is the star—especially once you squeeze the lime over the top. *¡Vamos a comer!*

MAKES 4 SERVINGS

Olive oil cooking spray

3 cups vegan chicken (we recommend Gardein Chick'n Scallopini)

1 clove garlic, minced

½ red onion, diced

1 teaspoon sesame seeds

½ teaspoon Bragg's liquid aminos

¼ teaspoon cayenne pepper

1 teaspoon cumin

¼ teaspoon ground cinnamon

1 (14-ounce) can Mexican-flavored diced tomatoes

½ cup dry white wine

1 teaspoon olive oil

2½ teaspoons cocoa powder

¼ to ½ teaspoon Sriracha sauce

1 tablespoon chopped fresh cilantro, plus more for garnish

1 cup cooked brown rice

Toasted pumpkin seeds to sprinkle over the top

Lime wedges to squeeze over the top

Preheat the oven to 250°F.

Pull out your favorite cast-iron skillet or deepest frying pan for this very special occasion. Spray it down with olive oil cooking spray and heat your skillet over medium heat. Once your oil is hot, add your vegan chicken. Flip it a few times, and when you begin to see the edges brown, toss the garlic, onion, sesame seeds, and Bragg's into the skillet with your vegan chicken. Cook, flipping your vegan chicken and stirring your red onion a few times, until the red onion is tender. Mix in the cayenne pepper, ½ teaspoon of the cumin, and the cinnamon.

Put your vegan chicken in a glass casserole dish in the oven to keep warm while you make your sauce.

Add the diced tomatoes, white wine, remaining ½ teaspoon cumin, olive oil, cocoa powder, Sriracha sauce, and cilantro to the skillet with the cooked red onion mixture. Stir your sauce to make sure your cocoa powder doesn't clump. Then place your vegan chicken in the sauce and gently mix.

Serve over the brown rice with the cilantro and pumpkin seeds sprinkled on and lime wedges to squeeze over the top.

FAJITAS

Most fajitas you'll find in American restaurants inhabit that very thin demilitarized zone between authentic Mexican cuisine (think mole sauce) and Taco Bell–ized American bastardizations (think "gorditas"). Yes, they eat fajitas in Mexico. No, they don't look much like what you get at Applebee's. We hope this version is a bit closer to being authentic than what you're used to—but either way, they're delicious.

MAKES 4 FAJITAS

MARINADE
⅓ cup olive oil

2 tablespoons tequila

⅓ cup lemon juice

1½ teaspoons agave nectar

1 teaspoon dried oregano

1 teaspoon cumin

1 teaspoon chili powder

½ teaspoon garlic powder

½ teaspoon Bragg's liquid aminos

¼ teaspoon lemon pepper

Dash of liquid smoke

FAJITAS
2 cups vegan chicken

4 (8-inch) flour tortillas

2 tablespoons olive oil

Dash of liquid smoke

½ red bell pepper, sliced

½ green bell pepper, sliced

½ yellow bell pepper, sliced

½ large red onion, sliced

1 cup sliced white mushrooms

2 cups shredded Daiya vegan cheddar cheese or your favorite vegan cheese

1 ripe avocado, peeled, pitted, and sliced

1 cup pico de gallo

Combine all your marinade ingredients in a shallow dish.

Slice your vegan chicken into pieces about the size of the pepper and onion slices. Submerge your vegan chicken in the marinade dish. Keep an eye on it; different mock meats behave differently. You'll know it's ready when you squeeze it and 1 or 2 drops come out. You want to keep the marinade in the vegan chicken, so don't dab or squeeze out the marinade. Don't dump the marinade when you're done with this step! You'll need it.

Preheat the oven to 250°F.

Put a stack of tortillas in the oven to warm as your vegan chicken and vegetables cook.

In your magic little cast-iron skillet or frying pan, heat the olive oil and liquid smoke. Once your oil is hot, toss in your vegan chicken. Let it cook, moving and flipping it to make sure it evenly cooks. Once it starts to brown, add your peppers, onion, mushrooms, and the rest of the marinade. Remove from the heat when the vegetables are tender and your vegan chicken is golden brown.

To build your fajitas, place a warm tortilla on a plate, and put a fourth of the vegan chicken and vegetable mixture on one side. Top with vegan cheese, avocado slices, and pico de gallo.

BEAN AND CHEESE ENCHILADAS

This recipe from the Betty Crocker Project is a bit more heavy and rich than the recipes we usually enjoy, but as far as guilty pleasures go, this one shouldn't make you feel too bad. It's awesome and cruelty-free, and you can share it with people. We had a big enchilada party the first time we made this and fed eight professional vegans with this epically "cheesy" recipe.

MAKES 4 TO 6 SERVINGS

2 cups shredded Daiya vegan pepperjack cheese or your favorite vegan cheese

1 cup shredded Daiya vegan cheddar cheese or your favorite vegan cheddar

¾ cup corn

1 (14-ounce) can black beans, rinsed and drained

½ cup vegan sour cream

1 red onion, diced

¾ cup baby spinach leaves

3 tablespoons chopped fresh cilantro, plus more for garnish

½ teaspoon freshly ground black peppercorns

1 (15-ounce) can tomato sauce

1 can Mexican-flavored diced tomatoes

1 small green bell pepper, diced

1 (4.5-ounce) can chopped green

chilies, drained

2 cloves garlic, minced

1 tablespoon chili powder

½ teaspoon dried oregano

½ teaspoon cumin

¼ teaspoon onion powder

8 to 10 flour tortillas

Sliced green onion for topping

8 to 10 lime wedges

Preheat the oven to 350°F.

In a large bowl, mix 1 cup of the vegan cheese, ½ cup of the vegan cheddar, the corn, beans, sour cream, onion, spinach, cilantro, and black pepper and set aside.

In a saucepan, heat the tomato sauce, diced tomatoes, bell pepper, chilies, garlic, chili powder, oregano, cumin and onion powder to a boil. Stir the pot occasionally to make sure the ingredients are mixed. Once the mixture is boiling, reduce the heat to a simmer. Let cook for 4 minutes before pouring the mixture into an ungreased pie pan or other shallow dish.

In an ungreased 11 x 7-inch glass baking dish, use a ladle to pour ⅓ cup of the enchilada sauce in an even, very shallow layer, completely covering the bottom. Dip each tortilla into the sauce to coat both sides.

Spoon about ¼ cup of the cheese mixture into each dipped tortilla. Again, this depends on the size of your tortilla. You really want to fill it, but you also need to be able to wrap it into a cigar with open ends.

Place each dipped, filled, and wrapped tortilla, seam down, in the baking dish as you go. Pour the remaining enchilada sauce over the top.

Sprinkle the remaining vegan cheese over the top and bake uncovered for about 20 minutes, or until bubbly. Let sit for about 5 minutes to cool—it will make the enchiladas easier to serve. Serve with green onions or cilantro over the top and at least one lime wedge to squeeze over the whole thing before you dig in. The acid from the lime wedge really helps break up this pretty heavy dish and make it a little brighter.

CEVICHE

Anyone who's ever watched *Top Chef* knows that there isn't a classy dish in the world that can be made faster than ceviche. It's a quick-fire standard that shows up in episodes as often as an instrumental of "My Funny Valentine" does in a Manhattan cigar bar. Ceviche is very popular in Central and South America and is typically made with fresh raw fish and citrus juice mixed with chili peppers. This simple, elegant, exotic dish makes a quick dinner on a night you don't feel much like cooking, or during the summer when the heat chases you out of the kitchen.

MAKES 4 TO 6 SERVINGS

1½ cups vegan shrimp, defrosted (we recommend May Wah shrimp balls cut in half)

¼ cup white wine

½ red onion, diced

1 (14-ounce) can quartered artichoke hearts, drained

¼ cup julienned carrots

½ cup lime juice

1 clove garlic, minced

1 fresh jalapeño, sliced (the more you add, the hotter it will be)

1 teaspoon crushed pink Himalayan salt

2 tablespoons chopped fresh cilantro

½ teaspoon sea kelp or seaweed granules, optional

1 ripe avocado, peeled, pitted, and sliced

Dash of hot sauce

6 lime wedges

Heat your favorite wok over medium heat. Once your wok is hot, add the vegan shrimp and white wine. Toss and cook for around 30 seconds. The food will steam a bit, but this process will kind of "flash cook" your vegan shrimp. After 30 seconds, remove your wok from the heat and toss in your onion, artichoke hearts, carrots, lime juice, garlic, jalapeño slices, salt, and cilantro. Mix your vegan shrimp and vegetables.

Sea kelp will add a bit of a "fishy" flavor to your dish that will make your ceviche have a more genuine taste. I know that a lot of vegans kind of lost their desire for a "fishy" flavor after a while, so the vegan shrimp might be enough. I recommend giving your dish a taste test before adding the sea kelp.

Move your ceviche into a mixing bowl, and then toss with the avocado slices and hot sauce.

Serve at room temperature with lime wedges to squeeze over the top.

THE SIDEKICKS

Every good hero needs a sidekick. Batman had Robin. Sherlock had Watson. Han had Chewbacca. Harry had Ron (although we all know Hermione is the *real* hero).

Narratively, the role of the sidekick is critical. The sidekick highlights the hero's strengths but also makes it possible for the hero to have weaknesses. The hero can save the day by rescuing the sidekick, but the hero can lose one every once in a while with someone there to bail them out. The sidekick provides insight into the hero's character through dialogue and friendship. The hero's strength, skills, and courage make the hero heroic; the hero's sidekick makes the hero human.

The same goes for food. No single dish stands alone. The perfect meal includes a main course along with a side that complements it—accentuating the main flavors and supplementing them with its own. Burgers need fries like Kirk needs Spock. Pasta needs garlic bread like Frodo needs Sam. The side dish makes the main course a meal.

FRIED OKRA

When we think of okra in the United States, we tend to think of Paula Deen–style southern food. But okra is actually a staple of cuisines from around the world, from the Middle East and Mediterranean to the Indian subcontinent to Japan to Malaysia to the Caribbean. But this recipe is definitely southern-style. Sorry for all that exciting buildup just to lead you back to Paula Deen.

MAKES 2 TO 4 SERVINGS

1 cup cornmeal

2 tablespoons Tony Chachere's Creole seasoning

5 to 7 tablespoons unsweetened applesauce

½ pound fresh okra, washed and sliced into coins

2 to 3 tablespoons olive oil

Dash of liquid smoke

In a shallow bowl, mix the cornmeal and Creole seasoning. Put your applesauce into another shallow bowl.

Cover your okra slices in applesauce, and then cover them in the cornmeal mix. You'll get a dusty batter covering the okra if you do it right. Once the okra is covered, set it aside on a plate. Keep doing this with all your sliced okra.

In your little cast-iron skillet buddy or frying pan, heat the olive oil and a dash of liquid smoke over medium heat. Pour your coated okra into the skillet. Keep flipping your okra to make sure it doesn't burn. It should take 5 to 10 minutes to fry completely. Remove from the heat when you have a nice golden coating.

We served ours up with some farmers' market artichoke sweet relish we got on the drive home from Savannah to Norfolk. Fried okra and sweet relish are BFFs; like red beans and rice, and like eating southern food and drinking icy beers while you walk along the Savannah River.

24-HOUR PICKLES

I love pickles. I always have. When I was little, my grandfather used to buy me one of those big barrel pickles from the shop on the corner to keep me busy for a while after school while I watched cartoons. When I think of any kind of pickle—garlicky gourmet ones to crappy ballpark chips—my mouth begins to water. No joke. I'm not trying to be poetic here. I adore them all. Sweet, kosher, tsukemono, half-sour, gherkin…whatever! They will always be welcome on my plate. These pickles are not the traditional wait-a-month pickles. Anyone who knows me knows I can't wait a month for anything. This recipe takes only 24 hours and makes a crisp pickle with the old-school *zayern* flavor. They aren't exactly like those wait-a-month pickles—that would take magic—but they're pretty darn close. *Ess gezunterhait!!*

MAKES 6 TO 8 SERVINGS

2 to 4 large pickle cucumbers, sliced into thin chips (around 4½ cups)

1 large red onion, diced

1 small red bell pepper, diced

1 large carrot, cut into coins

1 cup apple cider vinegar

2 tablespoons kosher salt

1½ cups sugar

2½ teaspoons dried dill weed

3 cloves garlic, minced

½ teaspoon slightly crushed black peppercorns

1 teaspoon celery seed

1 teaspoon whole mustard seeds

In a 2½- or 3-quart glass jar with a lid that can seal air-tight, layer the cut vegetables. You might not fill the jar to the top—it depends on how wide and tall your jar is. It's okay to have space at the top.

In a mixing bowl, stir the vinegar, salt, and sugar until the sugar is dissolved. Add the dill weed, garlic, pepper, celery seed, and mustard seeds and mix thoroughly. Be sure the sugar is dissolved. That's really important.

Pour your herb-vinegar mixture over the vegetables in the jar. Seal your lid on as tight as you can. Your brine might not initially cover the vegetables, and this is okay. Just shake the jar to get some brine on the top vegetables. Put your sealed jar in the fridge.

Over the next 24 hours, take out the jar and shake it every once in a while. You'll see that the vegetables will sink and eventually be covered by the brine. In 24 hours, they are ready to be eaten! They last only 2 weeks, so share with friends and eat many and often!

GARLICKY LEMONY GREENS CORPS OF JUSTICE

This dish combines a whole lotta greens and flavor without adding a lot of salt or fat. It's basically a green superhero that is actually a little better because it can't be defeated.

MAKES 2 TO 4 SERVINGS

1 cup chopped Swiss chard

½ cup chopped spinach

½ cup chopped kale

1⅓ cups green beans, stems removed

1 leek, sliced

½ cup olive oil

2 shallots, chopped

3 cloves garlic, minced

1 cup lemon juice

2 tablespoons Bragg's liquid aminos

½ teaspoon freshly ground black peppercorns

½ teaspoon grated lemon peel

½ cup dry white wine

Set aside the Swiss chard, spinach, and kale. Toss the remaining ingredients into your Dutch oven or soup pot and heat to a boil while mixing with a wooden spoon. Cover and simmer for 5 minutes.

Toss in the Swiss chard, spinach, and kale and mix. Cover and simmer another 15 minutes, or until your green beans are tender.

MEXICAN MASHED SWEET POTATOES

This recipe levels up mashed potatoes twice—once by using sweet potatoes instead of traditional white potatoes, and twice by giving it a kick of spicy Mexican flavors!

MAKES 4 TO 6 SERVINGS

Olive oil cooking spray

5 to 6 large sweet potatoes, cubed

1 (14-ounce) can Mexican-flavored diced tomatoes

1 fresh jalapeño, sliced (remember: the more you add, the hotter it will be)

2 teaspoons hot sauce

2 tablespoons chopped fresh cilantro

¼ red onion, diced

1 green bell pepper, diced

2 teaspoons chili powder

2 cloves garlic, minced

1 tablespoon margarine

1 teaspoon cumin

Dash of liquid smoke

¼ cup vegan sour cream

⅓ cup frozen whole-kernel corn

Crushed pink Himalayan salt and crushed black peppercorns to taste

1¼ cups shredded Daiya vegan pepperjack cheese or your favorite vegan cheese

Preheat the oven to 400°F.

Spray your 9 x 9-inch baking dish with olive oil cooking spray, and then spread your sweet potato cubes in the dish and coat them with a light layer of olive oil cooking spray. Bake for 40 minutes, or until the sweet potatoes are tender.

While those little orange lovies are baking, mix the diced tomatoes, jalapeño slices, hot sauce, cilantro, onion, bell pepper, chili powder, and garlic in a large mixing bowl with a large spoon.

In another large mixing bowl, blend the margarine, cumin, liquid smoke, and vegan sour cream with an electric handheld mixer until it's creamy. Once your sweet potatoes are tender, move them to the bowl with the sour cream mixture. Mash with a pastry blender into a paste. Use your electric handheld mixer to blend your sweet potatoes until they are creamy and smooth.

Respray your glass baking dish with olive oil cooking spray.

Mix your tomato mixture and corn into your sweet potato mixture with a large spoon. Give it a taste test and add any needed salt and pepper. Move your mash to the baking dish. Sprinkle your vegan cheese over the top in an even layer. Bake for 30 minutes, or until your vegan cheese is melted.

You'll want to let your baked sweet potatoes cool a little bit before you serve.

GARLIC SHIITAKE MUSHROOMS AND GREEN BEANS

In a marriage, you have to overlook a lot of imperfections in your mate. Maybe they have a bit of a bossy streak. Maybe they like the Elvis Christmas album a little too much. Maybe they spend more time playing fantasy basketball than they do cleaning the apartment. But this hypothetical person brings a lot of good things to the table too—so you overlook these other things to make it work. But the closest thing to an honest-to-God deal breaker in the Shannon marriage is this: Dan hates mushrooms. And he of course refuses to eat them. But … after much soul-searching, and much reflection on all the good things he brings to our relationship (like a relentless positivity), I've found a way to look past this shortcoming. I'm still putting this recipe in the cookbook, though. Why should you have to suffer like I do?

MAKES 2 TO 4 SERVINGS

- 1½ pounds fresh green beans, with their ends removed
- ¼ cup almond slivers
- 1½ tablespoons olive oil
- 1 tablespoon sesame oil
- 2 cups shiitake mushroom caps
- 3 cloves garlic, minced
- 2 shallots, thinly sliced
- 3 tablespoons Bragg's liquid aminos
- Pinch of freshly ground black peppercorns

Steam your green beans. Please follow the directions on your steamer—they are all different. We use a bamboo steamer, but people have electric ones, some have baskets—it's a big world with a lot of steamers out there. In the spirit of inclusiveness, I accept you all.

In your handy cast-iron skillet, heat the almonds over low heat until they start to turn a golden brown and have a lovely smell. Stir them constantly to make sure they brown evenly.

Add the olive and sesame oils. Turn the heat up slightly. Once you feel that the oil mixture has started to heat, add the mushrooms, garlic, shallots, and green beans. Keep stirring, making sure to cover the mushrooms and green beans evenly with the oil mixture. Add the Bragg's and remove from the heat when the mushrooms are the desired tenderness.

Toss a pinch of pepper over the top before you serve.

CITRUS, BLACK PEPPER, AND CHEESE CAULIFLOWER

The cauliflower is admired in fractal geometry for its unique fractal dimension—a measure of how completely its basic shape replicates itself in order to fill space. What does this mean? I'm honestly not 100 percent sure. But what I do know for sure is that this recipe will make you never look at cauliflower the same way again—just like a fractal geometer.

MAKES 2 TO 4 SERVINGS

1 cup cauliflower florets

3 tablespoons olive oil

½ teaspoon crushed pink Himalayan salt

2 teaspoons grated orange peel

1 teaspoon grated lemon peel

½ teaspoon Italian seasoning

1 teaspoon crushed black peppercorns

½ cup shredded Daiya vegan mozzarella cheese or your favorite vegan cheese

1 tablespoon chopped fresh basil

2 teaspoons vegan parmesan or nutritional yeast

Preheat the oven to 450°F.

In your largest mixing bowl, toss the cauliflower florets, olive oil, salt, orange peel, lemon peel, Italian seasoning, and black pepper.

Put the seasoned cauliflower in an even layer in an ungreased baking dish. Use a rubber-tipped spatula to get all the oil and seasonings from inside the bowl and drizzle them over the top.

Sprinkle your vegan cheese over the top and roast for about 20 minutes. You're ready to take it out when your cauliflower is tender and your vegan cheese is melted.

Serve hot with the fresh basil and vegan parmesan sprinkled over the top.

SMOKY PEAS WITH VEGAN BACON AND MUSHROOMS

Hipsters seem to think that everything is better off with bacon. We would argue that many things are better with vegan bacon—as well as liquid smoke and almonds.

MAKES 2 TO 4 SERVINGS

2 tablespoons olive oil

Dash of liquid smoke

¼ cup sliced white mushrooms

¼ large red onion, diced

¼ cup raw almond slivers

3½ cups frozen peas, defrosted

1 teaspoon onion powder

1 teaspoon Bragg's liquid aminos

1 teaspoon chopped fresh parsley

2 tablespoons vegan bacon bits or crumbled smoked tempeh

In your favorite and largest cast-iron skillet or frying pan, heat the olive oil and liquid smoke over low heat. Once your oil is warm, toss in the mushrooms, onion, and almonds. Mix your vegetables into the hot oil to make sure they get an even coating. Once your mush-rooms and onions start to get tender, mix in the peas, onion powder, Bragg's, and parsley.

Once your peas are tender, stir in your vegan bacon bits and you're ready to eat!

SESAME BUTTERED BROCCOLI

This broccoli side takes about 10 minutes to make, and we usually serve it with the Asian Tofu Steaks with Wasabi Aioli (page 255). Two great tastes that go great together.

MAKES 4 SERVINGS

1½ pounds fresh broccoli florets

2 tablespoons margarine, melted

2 tablespoons Bragg's liquid aminos

1 teaspoon sesame seeds

½ teaspoon sesame oil

¼ teaspoon onion powder

Steam your broccoli following the directions on your steamer. They're all different. We got a really lovely traditional bamboo steamer as a wedding present that I think works perfectly, but I know a lot of you are in love with technology. Oh, sweet electric technology that can also steam your veggies while flying to the moon.

In a small bowl, stir the remaining ingredients until they are completely mixed. Pour the margarine sauce over your steamed broccoli once it's been served.

OLD BAY COLESLAW

Old Bay seasoning is obscenely popular in the mid-Atlantic region, where Dan and I spent the first five years of our lives together. This distinctive blend of spices was traditionally used to season seafood, but expanded out into everything from potato chips to Bloody Marys. Here, we've turned it into coleslaw that'll give you that Chesapeake Bay crab cake flavor.

MAKES 4 TO 6 SERVINGS

4½ cups thinly chopped cabbage

½ cup julienned carrots

½ red onion, chopped

½ cup Vegenaise

¼ cup vegan sour cream

1 tablespoon sugar

3 teaspoons lemon juice

3 teaspoons Dijon mustard

2 teaspoons Old Bay seasoning

1 teaspoon celery seed

½ teaspoon Bragg's liquid aminos

¾ teaspoon lemon pepper

Set aside the cabbage, carrots, and red onion. In a very large bowl, mix the remaining ingredients with a hand mixer until completely blended. Add the cabbage, carrots, and onion and toss until the vegetables are evenly coated. Cover and store in the fridge for at least an hour. Stir again before serving.

EASY OLIVE OIL GARLIC TOAST

I grew up eating many different versions of authentic Sicilian garlic bread, because you know every *zia* (auntie) had her own. I've had it with fresh Parmesan mixed with oregano, and with melted mozzarella over butter and basil. Garlic bread is one of those dishes where Italian cooks can really leave their signature. This is probably my favorite.

MAKES 4 SERVINGS

4 tablespoons olive oil	4 cloves garlic, minced	1 baguette, sliced in half lengthwise and then sliced in half again vertically, making 4 pieces

Preheat the oven to 425°F.

Mix your olive oil and garlic in a small bowl. Drizzle the garlic oil over the top of the baguette and bake for 5 minutes, or until it has toasted the desired amount.

ROSEMARY GARLIC BREAD

A classic Italian spice incorporated into a classic Italian side dish. Just throw on your *Godfather* Blu-ray set and you're in pretty good shape.

MAKES 4 TO 8 SERVINGS

1 baguette	⅓ cup margarine 2 cloves garlic, minced	2½ teaspoons dried rosemary, crushed

Preheat the oven to 350°F.

Slice the bread in half horizontally. Spread margarine on both sides. Brush on the minced garlic and sprinkle the rosemary over the top.

Pop the bread in the oven with the dressed side up, and bake until it reaches the desired golden color. Keep an eye on the bottom as well. It always sucks to have a perfectly golden brown top and a burned crust.

LEMON PEPPER GARLIC BREAD

Lemon pepper tofu is a classic, delicious vegan dish dating back to the pre–mock meat days. This recipe is sort of like a blast from the flavor past and takes a classic Italian side dish in an entirely new direction.

MAKES 4 TO 8 SERVINGS

1 baguette

⅓ cup margarine

2 cloves garlic, minced

2 teaspoons lemon pepper

1 fresh lemon, cut into wedges

½ teaspoon chopped fresh chives

Preheat the oven to 350°F.

Slice your bread horizontally. Spread margarine on both sides. Brush on the minced garlic and sprinkle the lemon pepper over the garlic. Squeeze your lemon wedges over your bread.

Bake for 5 to 10 minutes, or until the edges of your bread are golden brown and crispy. Sprinkle with chives before servings.

BROILED TEXAS GARLIC TOAST

The Lone Star State's answer to garlic bread. Of all the states, it's pretty fitting that Texas is the only one to lay claim to its own toast. It just seems like a pretty Texas thing to do.

MAKES 8 TO 10 SERVINGS

½ cup margarine, softened

4 cloves garlic, minced

2 tablespoons chopped fresh parsley

Crushed pink Himalayan salt and freshly ground black peppercorns to taste

1 loaf high-quality white bread, sliced into 1-inch slices

Set the oven to broil or turn on your broiler.

Mix together the margarine, garlic, and parsley in a bowl with an electric handheld mixer, and season with salt and pepper to taste. Brush both sides of the bread slices with the garlic butter and place on the rack of a broiler pan. Broil the bread for 1 to 2 minutes per side until lightly golden brown.

TWICE-BAKED POTATOES WITH THE WORKS

In college, we used to eat brunch every Sunday (or basically whenever) at this rundown diner off campus. The shortcut there was this random road through the woods, but it was off the highway, so all the logging trucks could stop by there on their way to and from the Olympic Mountains. The diner was pretty famous locally for its Potato Boats—these huge twice-baked potatoes with the "works." They obviously weren't organic; I mean, these potatoes were like Cadillacs. Okay, maybe they were more like the size of a shoe … but that's still pretty big. They were the perfect hangover cure and one of my favorite memories from my years in Olympia, Washington. When we hit twice-baked potatoes in Betty Crocker's Big Red, I thought about those long-lost boats and smiled.

MAKES 4 SERVINGS

4 large baking potatoes

¼ cup margarine

2 tablespoons plus 2 teaspoons nutritional yeast

½ teaspoon crushed pink Himalayan salt

½ teaspoon freshly ground black peppercorns

⅓ cup vegan bacon bits or crumbled smoked tempeh

1 tablespoon chopped fresh chives

1 ⅓ cups shredded Daiya vegan cheddar cheese or your favorite vegan cheddar

Preheat the oven to 375°F. Pierce the top of each potato a few times with a fork. Try to poke the potatoes where you will later be splitting them. It looks nicer and helps them keep their shape better.

Bake the potatoes for 1 to 1½ hours—just until the potatoes are tender when you stick a fork into the holes you poked before. You can also tell by how soft the potatoes are when you lift them with an oven mitt.

Place the potatoes aside to cool. Once they are cool enough to handle, cut them in half lengthwise and then gently scoop out the center of each—leaving some potato along the edges to help the skin keep its form. Scoop the potato into a large bowl and blend with an electric mixer until fluffy.

Increase the oven temperature to 400°F.

Add the margarine, nutritional yeast, salt, and black pepper and blend until your potatoes are smooth. At this point you can taste them to see if they need more salt or pepper. Once you like the flavor, stir in the vegan bacon bits, chives, and 1 cup of the vegan cheese with a large spoon until completely blended. Then gently fill each potato shell with the mashed potato mix. You want them to be completely full and overflowing a bit. Take your spoon and gently push the mashed potato mix in there to really seal it in. Sprinkle the remaining ⅓ cup vegan cheese over the tops of the potatoes.

Gently place the potatoes in the oven—I put mine directly on the rack so they won't fall over. Bake your potatoes for another 20 to 25 minutes. Once the vegan cheese is melted, pull them out and let cool a little before you serve.

VEGAN BACON AND KALE SCALLOPED POTATOES

I love scalloped potatoes. They combine potatoes and cheese to become pretty much the perfect comfort food. This recipe takes your old friend scalloped potatoes to a new place by adding a smoky flavor and the wonderfood kale. I might have just swooned a little.

MAKES 6 SERVINGS

Olive oil cooking spray

6 pieces vegan bacon or smoked tempeh

½ red onion, chopped

½ cup margarine (you'll need more to grease your casserole dish)

½ cup whole wheat flour

3½ cups Better Than Bouillon vegetable broth, made per the instructions on the package

4 teaspoons Bragg's liquid aminos

A few dashes of liquid smoke

1 teaspoon onion powder

2 cloves garlic, minced

Pinch of turmeric

Pinch of smoked paprika

Crushed pink Himalyan salt and freshly ground black peppercorns

1½ cups nutritional yeast

2 cups Yukon gold potatoes cut into ⅛-inch slices

3 green onions, chopped

½ teaspoon fresh thyme leaves

1 cup raw kale

1 cup shredded Daiya vegan cheddar cheese or your favorite vegan cheddar cheese

Preheat the oven to 350°F.

Lightly grease a large casserole dish with margarine.

Spray a light coating of olive oil cooking spray over your cast-iron skillet or frying pan and then heat over medium heat. Toss your vegan bacon and red onion in the skillet once it's hot. Use your spatula to flip them a few times so they cook evenly. They're ready when your vegan bacon is crispy and your onion is tender.

In a saucepan, melt the margarine over low heat. Whisk in the flour until smooth and bubbly. Then add the broth, Bragg's, liquid smoke, onion powder, garlic, turmeric, and paprika. Add a few dashes of salt and black pepper to taste. Continue whisking until incorporated. Once your sauce is thick and bubbling, whisk in the nutritional yeast. Add salt and pepper to taste.

Put your potatoes, green onions, and thyme in a large mixing bowl and pour your sauce over them. Use a spoon to fold the sauce into the potatoes. Chop up your bacon. Mix the bacon, red onions, and kale into your saucy potatoes. Pour into your greased casserole dish and top with vegan cheese.

Bake for 15 to 20 minutes, until your potatoes are tender. Then broil for a few minutes until the top is crispy.

ROASTED ROSEMARY POTATOES

This quick and easy side dish packs a ton of flavor and goes with just about everything.

MAKES 4 TO 6 SERVINGS

Olive oil cooking spray

½ red onion, chopped

2 tablespoons olive oil

2 teaspoons dried rosemary, lightly crushed

¼ teaspoon celery seed

¼ teaspoon dried thyme

¼ teaspoon onion powder

¼ teaspoon Bragg's liquid aminos

¼ teaspoon lemon pepper

Dash of liquid smoke

6 to 8 medium-size red potatoes, cubed

Preheat the oven to 450°F. Spray a 15 x 10-inch glass baking dish with cooking spray.

In a large bowl, mix the remaining ingredients, adding the potatoes last. Toss the potatoes to coat. Spread your herb-coated potatoes in a single even layer in the baking dish.

Roast uncovered for 20 minutes. Pull out the dish and flip the potatoes with a metal spatula. Return to the oven to bake for another 5 to 10 minutes; remove when the potatoes are golden brown and tender.

NOTE: The smaller you cut your cubes, the faster they bake, so please keep an eye on them. Yours might take less time to cook because they were cut smaller or your potatoes weren't as large.

CREOLE POTATO WEDGES

Stemming from our honeymoon in New Orleans, Dan and I have a special love for Cajun and Creole flavors. They remind us of those first few days of our marriage and that postwedding high that's a combination of excitement for the rest of our lives together and relief that the wedding itself is finally over. To us, these potato wedges taste like true love conquering all. To you, they might just taste spicy. But spicy is still pretty good on its own.

MAKES 4 TO 6 SERVINGS

5 to 7 red potatoes, quartered

3 tablespoons olive oil

1½ teaspoons Tony Chachere's Original Creole seasoning

Preheat the oven to 450°F.

In a casserole dish, with a large spoon, mix the potatoes, olive oil, and Creole seasoning until the potatoes are evenly covered with the olive oil and Creole seasoning. Turn your potatoes so that their skin is down and their white insides are on top. This will make them brown better.

Bake for 20 to 30 minutes. Remove from the oven when the potatoes are tender and the desired crispiness.

RANCH MASHED POTATOES

If you're looking for an easy recipe to make your dinner a little more special, you've found it. The vegan sour cream makes your potatoes a bit creamier, and I recommend getting some vegan bacon bits to toss over the top because the smokiness and ranch really work together. And if you're one of those folks who don't live off just potatoes … I recommend making some Ranch and Corn Flakes Chicken Fingers (page 141) or Buffalo Tofu Steaks (page 132) and a pot of Smoky Collard Greens with Vegan Bacon (page 281) too. And if you're an overachiever who really loves food and your friends, you'll toss all that on a toasted baguette and pour a little gravy over the two. You'll have an open-face sandwich that will win over the heart of even the meatiest loved one.

MAKES 4 TO 6 SERVINGS

6 medium red potatoes

2 tablespoons soy milk

⅓ cup Vegan Ranch Dressing (page 110)

Margarine and vegan bacon bits for toppings

Boil the potatoes in a 2-quart saucepan; make sure you have enough water to cover the potatoes. Once the potatoes are tender when you stab them with a fork, drain them through a colander. While they're still steaming hot, pour the cooked potatoes back into a large mixing bowl and blend with a pastry blender. Add the soy milk and ranch dressing. Blend with an electric hand mixer until it is perfection! It takes less than 5 minutes; be sure to get all the lumps out. Serve hot enough that your margarine will melt nicely over the top of your mashed potato bowl but not so hot it's like you're serving lava. If for some reason your potatoes cooled while you were blending them, you can always microwave them for 30 seconds and then do a quick blend to distribute the warmer potatoes throughout the bowl. Sprinkle some vegan bacon bits over the top and enjoy!

BEER-BATTERED ONION RINGS

The combination of salty and fried in this recipe is exactly what you're looking for when you're drinking or just hanging out … breathing.

MAKES 4 TO 6 SERVINGS

Vegetable oil for frying

3 to 4 large sweet onions (we recommend Walla Walla Sweet Onions)

½ cup whole wheat flour

½ cup all-purpose flour

¼ teaspoon baking soda

¼ teaspoon baking powder

1 teaspoon sugar

¾ teaspoon Tony Chachere's Creole seasoning

1 tablespoon Ener-G egg replacer, just the powder, not prepared as described on the package

1 12-ounce bottle India Pale Ale beer

2 teaspoons olive oil

Put your vegetable oil in your largest stockpot or Dutch oven. You'll need enough oil to completely submerge your onion rings.

Cut your onions into ½-inch slices. Break up your slices into rings.

In a bowl, mix the whole wheat flour, all-purpose flour, baking soda, baking powder, sugar, Creole seasoning, and egg replacer with a whisk. Add the beer and olive oil. Blend your batter with your whisk until smooth.

Once your oil is hot enough to fry a small test drop of batter, dip the onion rings into the batter. Then place them gently into the hot vegetable oil.

Fry until golden brown and crispy. When you remove your onion rings, place them on a plate with a paper towel to absorb the extra oil.

HUSH PUPPIES

If you're looking for something to go with these handsome fellows, we recommend trying one of the vegan po'boys on pages 84 and 85.

MAKES 2 TO 4 SERVINGS

2 cups cornmeal

1 tablespoon all-purpose flour

½ teaspoon Bragg's liquid aminos

1 teaspoon baking powder

½ teaspoon baking soda

1 teaspoon sugar

½ cup chopped green onions

1 tablespoon Ener-G egg replacer, just the powder, not made per the instructions on the package

2 tablespoons applesauce

1 cup soy coffee creamer

1 teaspoon Tony Chachere's Creole seasoning

1 tablespoon nutritional yeast

3 to 5 tablespoons olive oil

In a large bowl, mix the cornmeal, flour, Bragg's, baking powder, baking soda, and sugar. Stir in the green onion, egg replacer, applesauce, creamer, Creole seasoning, and nutritional yeast. Once you have a nice smooth paste, form the batter into small balls that are about the size of a tablespoon.

Grab your darling cast-iron skillet or frying pan.

Heat the olive oil over medium heat. Once your skillet is hot, drop your hush puppies in to fry. Use a spatula to roll them around once in a while to make sure they cook evenly. They're going to take about 10 minutes, tops, to fry. Take them out when they're golden brown and put them on a plate with a paper towel to soak up the extra oil.

VEGAN CHICKEN–FRIED GREEN BEANS

You know those green bean French fries you find at TGIF-ish establishments that always sound intriguing, but you never find yourself in those kinds of places so you never have an excuse to eat them? That's what this recipe is for. It's so you don't have to go to a place that humiliates its staff with silly birthday songs or riddles them with flair. This recipe would go great with any of the burgers in our "Burgers and Melts" section on page 181 and some techno-colored margaritas.

MAKES 4 TO 6 SERVINGS

Vegetable oil for frying

1 cup whole wheat flour

¼ teaspoon dried parsley

¼ teaspoon hot sauce

¼ teaspoon garlic powder

2½ teaspoons Tony Chachere's Creole seasoning

Pinch of freshly ground black peppercorns

1 cup India Pale Ale beer

1 cup panko crumbs (you can usually find these in the Asian food aisle of the grocery store)

1 pound raw green beans, stems removed

Heat the oil on high in a large stewpot.

In a very large bowl, whisk together the whole wheat flour, parsley, hot sauce, garlic powder, Creole seasoning, black pepper, and beer until smooth.

Put your panko crumbs in a shallow dish.

Drop a little bit of batter into your oil to see if it's hot enough to fry. If it is, dip one green bean in the batter and then immediately lightly roll it in the panko to get a light coating. Place the bean carefully into the hot oil. Use a slotted spoon to make sure your green bean doesn't stick to the sides or bottom of the pot.

Once your coating is light golden brown, use your slotted spoon to remove your green bean from the hot oil. Place it on a paper towel on a plate to help drain off some of the extra oil. Now you can fry a few of your green beans at a time, but use your slotted spoon to make sure they don't stick together.

Serve hot with barbecue sauce, yellow mustard, or ketchup; whatever your favorite dipping sauce is.

"It all started with a lobster..."

Lorraine Eaton opened her feature article about the Betty Crocker Project in the lifestyle section of the *Virginian-Pilot* on March 11, 2011, with that line, and it's been kicking around in my head ever since. When I try to slow down all the highlights and memories from our little project, they always seem to speed up like whirling dervishes. They wink and flirt and spin away to the other side of the room. But there are a few that can't escape—like the night Lorraine came over for dinner.

Cooking for a food writer is an odd experience. Your better judgment reminds you that you're not having a friend over for dinner and that everything has to be perfect—but there's this little part of you that knows you're meeting someone who shares one of your great passions … well, if you love food like we do, anyway. Dan and I found it impossible not to crack jokes about the struggles we faced going vegan in the nineties, like terrible mock meat selections and giving up Pepperidge Farm goldfish crackers. We couldn't help but be ourselves, and our love of food and excitement about advocating for animals worked itself into every conversation—and Lorraine seemed genuinely interested.

There was one moment in particular that I'll save for rainy days when things aren't going according to plan. It was right after Lorraine took her first bite of vegan crab cake with our homemade dairy-free tartar sauce. She stopped, smiled, and said, "This tastes just like a crab cake. A really good one."

Inside my chest I felt something that I can describe in two words: Gold. Medal. Yes, the band began to play the national anthem, the Stars and Stripes rose over my head, and somewhere doves were released. Having a mainstream professional food writer for the largest newspaper in a state pretty famous for Chesapeake Bay Crab Cakes tell me our meatless version was just as good as the "real" thing—well, it really was like winning a gold medal in vegan cooking.

No, the fishermen didn't all go out the next day and dump their traps, and all those billboards featuring dancing crabs inviting tourists to come eat them weren't pulled down overnight. But thanks to Google alerts and Facebook, the Betty Crocker Project was introduced to vegans and soon-to-be-vegans all over the country who also weren't charmed by Julie Powell's ability to overcome her own conscience and boil those lobsters. Our Facebook page got more than a thousand new followers in forty-eight hours, and emails asking for everything from egg replacers to dating advice started to pour in faster than I could answer them.

The Betty Crocker Project was pretty popular before Lorraine came to dinner, but it leveled up to downright notable after that. Later there would be a little mention in the *New York Times* and a book deal … but in the beginning it really did all start with a lobster.

SMOKY COLLARD GREENS WITH VEGAN BACON

This is a vegan version of a classic southern dish that would make even Paula Deen proud.

MAKES 4 SERVINGS

6 cups chopped collard greens

3 tablespoons olive oil

Dash of liquid smoke

½ red onion, chopped

½ teaspoon dried thyme

½ teaspoon Tony Chachere's Creole seasoning

½ teaspoon lemon juice

½ teaspoon white wine

¼ cup vegan bacon bits or crumbled smoked tempeh

Crushed pink Himalayan salt and freshly ground black peppercorns

In a 4-quart Dutch oven or soup pot, heat 4 cups water to a boil. Add the collard greens. You're going to need a slotted spoon to push them down to fit them all in there. Boil for 30 minutes.

Meanwhile, in your handy cast-iron skillet or frying pan, heat the olive oil and liquid smoke over medium heat. Once the collard greens have changed color and are soft, move them into the skillet. Add the remaining ingredients one at a time, and mix to get an even, smooth coating over the greens. If the seasoning is too salty for you, just add more olive oil, ½ teaspoon at a time. Not salty enough? Add salt a few dashes at a time. Cook for 3 to 5 minutes.

SAUCES AND CONDIMENTS

Coco Chanel is credited for tactfully pointing out that most women wear too much junk when they go out. It didn't save the world or anything, but it needed to be said. Just take a look at photos of those flappers in the twenties, with the hats, strings of pearls, earrings, gloves, bracelets, furs with faces, little dogs, brooches, shoes with brooches on them, scarves, and beauty marks ... I could go on, but I think I've made my point.

Accessorizing is key. But it's got to be done right. This is a collection of a few of our favorite food accessories (aka sauces) that we use all the time over vegetables, rice, pasta, whatever. We're both avid fans of sauces—as long as you don't overdo it.

VEGAN TARTAR SAUCE

Vegan tartar sauce will make you look forward to faux fish in a way you never thought possible. There are a few recipes for vegan shrimp or fish that go great with this sauce, but if you're wondering where to start: Crabby Cakes on page 126 will challenge your concept of reality in a way you thought was only possible on *Doctor Who*.

MAKES 4 SERVINGS

1 cup Vegenaise	1 tablespoon chopped fresh parsley	¼ teaspoon onion powder
2 tablespoons sweet pickle relish	2 teaspoons chopped pimientos	¼ teaspoon nutritional yeast
	1 teaspoon Dijon mustard	

Mix all the ingredients and eat up!

SESAME HOISIN SAUCE

Despite deriving its name from the Cantonese word for "seafood," hoisin sauce is traditionally vegan already. This is a recipe to level up that sauce and make it something truly special.

MAKES 4 SERVINGS

3 tablespoons hoisin sauce	1 tablespoon plus 2 teaspoons water	2 tablespoons sesame oil
1 tablespoon brown sugar	½ teaspoon rice wine	2 teaspoons sesame seeds

Blend all the ingredients with your electric handheld mixer using the whisk attachments until completely combined.

LEMON AIOLI

Aioli is traditionally made using garlic, olive oil, and egg. Our version leaves out the egg, but none of the flavor.

MAKES 4 SERVINGS

1 cup Vegenaise

1 teaspoon grated lemon peel

2 tablespoons lemon juice

3 cloves garlic, minced

1 teaspoon freshly ground black peppercorns

In a small bowl, blend all the aioli ingredients with an electric handheld mixer until well mixed. Cover and refrigerate at least 1 hour before serving.

NEW COUNTRY CHUNKY MARINARA SAUCE

Old Country "gravy" with a new spin.

MAKES 6 SERVINGS

2 tablespoons olive oil

1 large red onion, diced

6 cloves garlic, minced

8 to 10 large ripe tomatoes, diced (around 10 cups)

1 teaspoon agave nectar

⅓ cup fresh basil leaves, chopped

¼ cup baby spinach leaves

2 teaspoons capers, drained

2 tablespoons Bragg's liquid aminos

1 tablespoon chopped fresh parsley

1½ teaspoons celery seed

1 can quartered artichoke hearts, drained

2 teaspoons red pepper flakes

¼ teaspoon freshly ground black peppercorns

1 tablespoon fresh oregano leaves

⅓ cup red wine

¼ cup Better Than Bouillon vegetable broth, made per the instructions on the package

In a large Dutch oven or saucepan, heat the olive oil over medium heat. Once your oil is warm, toss in the onion. Use a wooden spoon to mix the onion into the warm oil, and cook until tender. Toss in the garlic and tomatoes and mix so that your vegetables get covered with warm oil. Turn down the heat, cover, and simmer for 30 seconds. Uncover and toss in the agave nectar, basil, spinach, capers, Bragg's, parsley, celery seed, artichoke hearts, red pepper flakes, pepper, oregano, red wine, and broth. Continue to simmer and stir occasionally. The tomatoes should start to fall apart once the broth and red wine start to boil.

Simmer over low heat for around an hour, or until the tomatoes dissolve into the sauce.

SUPER GREEN BASIL PESTO

You can use this recipe with pastas, sandwiches, and crostini, over steamed vegetables … all kinds of awesome.

MAKES 4 SERVINGS

4½ cups fresh basil leaves

½ cup fresh parsley

½ cup raw baby spinach leaves

¼ cup artichoke hearts, drained

2 tablespoons nutritional yeast

½ teaspoon white wine

⅓ cup raw pine nuts

2 cups olive oil

4 cloves garlic, minced

2 teaspoons freshly ground black peppercorns

Put all your ingredients into a food processor or blender and puree on medium speed until completely blended.

NACHO STEVE SAUCE

In Norfolk lives a man named Steve. He's a pleasant sort of chap with a winning smile and a love for animals and good times. We both adore Steve. Everyone does. I wanted to make something really special for his 2008 birthday party, and Nacho Steve Sauce was born!

We make this sauce and dip every time we want to rock.

MAKES 6 TO 8 SERVINGS

½ cup margarine

½ cup whole wheat flour

1 cup water

2½ cups soy milk

½ teaspoon crushed pink Himalayan salt, plus more as desired

3 tablespoons Bragg's liquid aminos

1½ teaspoons garlic powder

1 teaspoon onion powder

1 cup nutritional yeast

¼ teaspoon cumin

Dash of cayenne pepper

Dash of liquid smoke

Pinch of turmeric

1 (15-ounce) jar of your favorite salsa

Crushed black peppercorns, diced fresh jalapeños, and Texas Pete, or other hot sauce to taste

½ cup shredded Daiya vegan pepperjack cheese or your favorite vegan cheese

In a Dutch oven or saucepan, melt the margarine over the lowest heat. Whisk in the flour over medium heat until smooth. Then whisk in the water, soy milk, salt, Bragg's, and garlic and onion powders. Once your sauce is smooth, whisk in the nutritional yeast, cumin, cayenne pepper, liquid smoke, and turmeric. Cook the sauce until it thickens, whisking it occasionally until all the clumps are gone. Remove from the heat. Add the entire jar of salsa and stir with a wooden spoon.

Taste test with a tortilla chip, and then add crushed black pepper, jalapeños, and Texas Pete until you love it. Put your sauce into a serving dish and spread your vegan cheese over the top. It will melt slightly.

Nacho Steve Sauce will thicken up as it cools. So serve warm for more of a sauce or cool for more of a soft cheese spread. It is also good on burgers and mixed in chili.

HERBED LEMON BUTTER SAUCE

This sauce is easy and good on everything. Seriously everything.

MAKES 4 SERVINGS

⅓ cup margarine

½ cup lemon juice

2 cloves garlic, minced

1 teaspoon garlic powder

2 teaspoons freshly ground black peppercorns

¼ teaspoon grated lemon peel

2 teaspoons herbes de Provence

Put your margarine in a saucepan and cook over low heat. Once your margarine melts, remove your pan from the heat and blend in the remaining ingredients with a large spoon until smooth. You'll have to keep this sauce warm to keep it beautiful.

WHITE DILL SAUCE

There is this versatile sauce, called béchamel that is kind of a base, or "mother sauce," for several other sauces. This sauce works over pasta and vegetables, and goes wonderfully with mashed potatoes. This is our vegan béchamel with some fresh dill and garlic to personalize it a bit.

MAKES 4 SERVINGS

2 tablespoons margarine

2 tablespoons all-purpose flour

¼ teaspoon Bragg's liquid aminos

1¼ teaspoons chopped fresh dill weed

¼ teaspoon freshly ground black peppercorns

1 clove garlic, minced

1 cup soy milk

In a saucepan, melt the margarine over low heat. Stir in the flour, Bragg's, dill weed, pepper, and garlic until blended. Add the soy milk while stirring constantly until the mixture is smooth and bubbly. Remove from the heat.

CHEEZY SAUCE

The night Dan made me this sauce, I fell in love with him … well, started to. It still took a few more bad relationships, long phone calls, and years of being best friends. But this sauce may have started it all.

MAKES 6 TO 8 SERVINGS

½ cup margarine

3½ cups boiling water

½ cup all-purpose flour

1½ teaspoon crushed pink Himalayan salt

2 tablespoons Bragg's liquid aminos

1½ teaspoon garlic powder

1 teaspoon onion powder

A few dashes of liquid smoke

Pinch of turmeric

Paprika and crushed black peppercorns to taste

1½ cup nutritional yeast

In a saucepan, melt the margarine over low heat. While the margarine melts, bring the water to a boil in a separate pot. Once your margarine has completely melted, whisk in your flour. Continue whisking over medium heat until smooth and bubbly.

Next, whisk in the boiling water, salt, Braggs, garlic powder, onion powder, liquid smoke, and turmeric. Add parika and pepper to taste.

Continue whisking until dissolved. Once thick and bubbling, whisk in the nutritional yeast flakes until your sauce is creamy. If it gets too thick, add more water.

ALMOND MORNAY SAUCE

Yeah, we're pretty fancy. This is a cheesier béchamel sauce that is wonderful with pasta and vegetables. You can even pour it over a Vegan Fried Egg (page 23) and some toast to be pretend French some Sunday morning.

MAKES 4 SERVINGS

2 tablespoons margarine

2 tablespoons all-purpose flour

½ cup almond milk

½ cup Better Than Bouillon vegan chicken broth, made per the instructions on the package

¼ cup shredded Daiya vegan mozzarella cheese or your favorite vegan cheese

1¼ teaspoons vegan Parmesan

½ teaspoon dry white wine

¼ teaspoon crushed pink Himalayan salt

¼ teaspoon cayenne pepper

In a saucepan, melt the margarine over low heat. Stir in the flour. Continue to stir your sauce while you add the remaining ingredients. Use a whisk to blend your sauce until it is smooth and creamy.

ORANGE BEURRE BLANC SAUCE

Beurre Blanc is a fancy French sauce based on a reduction of shallots combined with an acid such as vinegar or citrus and then mixed with cold butter. Julia Child's Beurre Blanc is one of her most famous sauces, probably because it's one of her easiest. I'd like to think she'd be excited about how creatively we substituted the "fish juice" in this simple sauce that goes great over any vegetable or mock meat. But I might just have to accept that she'd probably be annoyed that we messed around with this sauce she adored. The original Beurre Blanc is known for its creamy tanginess and is intended to go with fish like trout, shad, haddock, or shellfish. We enjoyed our tangy, creamy sauce with vegan lobster from May Wah and drank a toast to Julia.

MAKES 4 TO 6 SERVINGS

¼ cup orange juice with pulp

2 tablespoons grated orange peel

1 tablespoon lemon juice

½ cup dry white wine

3 shallots, minced

½ cup margarine

¼ teaspoon cornstarch

Crushed pink Himalayan salt, crushed black peppercorns, and red pepper flakes

With a whisk, blend the orange juice, orange peel, lemon juice, white wine, and shallots in a saucepan, and heat over medium heat. Cook until the sauce is syrupy. Reduce the heat to a simmer and whisk in the margarine and cornstarch until the margarine melts, but don't let it get to a boil. Remove the sauce once it is smooth. If it reduces too much, add white wine 1 teaspoon at a time until it is smooth again. Then give it a taste test and add salt and whatever pepper you need until you fall madly in love with the taste.

Then marry this sauce. Just kidding. I don't think this sauce is the commitment type.

SWEET AND SOUR SAUCE

In China, sweet and sour sauce is commonly used as a dipping sauce, rather than as a cooking sauce as it traditionally is in Westernized "Chinese" cuisine. You can use this recipe as either. You can drink it from a bottle for all we care. It's that good. We won't judge.

MAKES 4 TO 6 SERVINGS

½ cup brown sugar

1 tablespoon cornstarch

½ cup crushed pineapple

1 tablespoon pineapple juice

1 tablespoon orange juice

1 tablespoon agave nectar

1 teaspoon Sriracha sauce

2 tablespoons Bragg's liquid aminos

¼ cup rice vinegar

¼ cup green bell pepper, diced

In your cast-iron skillet, mix the brown sugar and cornstarch. Add the pineapple, pineapple juice, orange juice, agave nectar, and Sriracha sauce and heat over medium heat. Once the sauce begins to bubble, add the Bragg's, vinegar, and bell pepper.

You'll want to use this immediately and serve warm.

CREOLE VEGANAISE

This veganaise was invented for our vegan po'boys (pages 84 and 85) but really it classes up even the most humble of everyday Tofurky sandwiches.

MAKES 4 TO 6 SERVINGS

8 to 10 tablespoons Vegenaise

1 tablespoon Tony Chachere's Creole seasoning

2 teaspoons Louisiana hot sauce

¼ teaspoon cumin

¼ teaspoon chopped fresh thyme leaves

1½ teaspoons lemon juice

Pinch of celery seed

Dash of liquid smoke

In a large bowl, mix all the ingredients. Put in the fridge to chill until ready to use.

CHIMICHURRI SAUCE

This is the sauce that will make you believe in love. This Argentinian sauce is delicious over any mock meat. It's lovely over vegetables and baked potatoes and pretty much anything you're looking to level up.

MAKES 4 TO 6 SERVINGS

1 teaspoon lemon juice

½ teaspoon grated lemon peel

1 cup fresh parsley

2 cloves garlic, minced

¾ cup olive oil

¼ cup white wine

1 teaspoon Bragg's liquid aminos

¼ teaspoon freshly ground black peppercorns

¼ teaspoon garlic powder

In a blender or food processor, puree all your ingredients on high speed until the sauce is well blended. Cover and chill in the fridge for at least an hour.

VEGAN TZATZIKI SAUCE

You'll be tempted to use soy yogurt. It'll give you a bit more of that bitter yogurt taste, but it will also be much thinner. This sauce goes great with a Roasted Vegan Chicken Gyro (page 96) or falafels. If you're feeling a bit lazy, just grab a bag of baby carrots.

MAKES 6 TO 8 SERVINGS

1 large cucumber, cut into very small pieces

1 package silken tofu

3 tablespoons Bragg's liquid aminos

2 tablespoons chopped fresh dill

1 teaspoon chopped fresh mint

Pinch of celery seed

2 teaspoons lemon juice

½ teaspoon grated lemon peel

3 cloves garlic, minced

2 tablespoons olive oil

2 tablespoons chopped fresh parsley

Set aside the cucumber. Blend the remaining ingredients in a food processor or blender until the sauce is smooth. Pour your sauce into a bowl and mix in your cucumber with a spoon.

WALNUT, SHALLOT, AND SAGE SAUCE

This is the sauce that, when partnered with our Pumpkin Gnocchi (Page 195), will make you understand what's going on in all those power ballads. You don't have to serve it with gnocchi, though; you can pour this thin but flavorful sauce over vegetables, or your favorite vegan chicken, or whatever. It's pretty versatile stuff.

MAKES 2 TO 4 SERVINGS

2 tablespoons margarine

2 tablespoons raw crushed walnuts

3 shallots, thinly sliced

2 tablespoons chopped fresh sage

2 teaspoons fresh thyme leaves

1 cup dry white wine

½ cup Better Than Bouillon vegan chicken broth, made per the instructions on the package

In your deepest cast-iron skillet or saucepan, melt your margarine over medium heat. Add the walnuts and shallots. Mix them in with a metal spatula and let them simmer in the melted margarine for 30 seconds before adding the sage, thyme, white wine, and broth.

Mix all your ingredients with your spatula until completely blended, and simmer for 2 minutes while stirring occasionally.

You want to serve this sauce warm. Once it begins to cool, the margarine might separate. It will still taste great, but it won't look as nice.

ALL-AMERICAN VEGAN GRAVY

Everyone needs a good vegan gravy recipe. It's one of the most requested recipes on our blog. People want it for themselves, for Thanksgiving, or for when their son brings home his new vegan grrrlfriend. My only regret with this recipe is that we named it "gravy." If we had come up with some clever way to name it soup, it would be socially acceptable to eat big bowls of this with a spoon—which is all I want to do.

MAKES 4 TO 6 SERVINGS

½ cup whole wheat flour

½ cup nutritional yeast

2 tablespoons olive oil

4 cups Better Than Bouillon vegan chicken broth, made per the instructions on the package

2 tablespoons Bragg's liquid aminos

3½ teaspoons poultry seasoning (most poultry seasonings are vegan, but some aren't, so be sure to read the label)

2 teaspoons onion powder

1 teaspoon garlic powder

¼ teaspoon celery seed

3 tablespoons chopped fresh parsley

¼ teaspoon freshly ground black peppercorns

In your Dutch oven or deepest saucepan, toast your flour and nutritional yeast over medium heat. Add the olive oil and cook until the mixture starts to brown. Gently whisk in the broth until there are no lumps. Stir in the Bragg's, poultry seasoning, onion powder, garlic powder, garlic powder, celery seed, parsley, and black pepper. Heat until the gravy thickens and starts to boil.

VEGAN HOLLANDAISE SAUCE

Try on our Benedict Omelet (page 31) or with a steamed artichoke. Just try it.

MAKES 4 SERVINGS

½ cup vegan sour cream

3 tablespoons nutritional yeast

3 tablespoons lemon juice (may need a little more to thin out sauce)

1 teaspoon margarine

¼ teaspoon turmeric

1 teaspoon Bragg's liquid aminos

In a small saucepan, mix all your ingredients with a whisk over a low heat. This sauce will thicken pretty fast so don't start to prepare it until you're almost ready to use. If it gets too thick, you can thin out your sauce by adding small amounts of lemon juice until you like the consistency.

VEGAN PARMESAN CROUTONS

These are the larger "French-style" croutons you find in schmancy restaurants and on the pages of gourmet food magazines. Good with soups or salads—but exceptional with both!

MAKES 6 TO 8 CROUTONS

½ baguette, cut into slices

⅓ cup olive oil

6 to 8 tablespoons vegan Parmesan (1 tablespoon per slice)

Preheat the oven to 400°F.

Brush one side of each slice of bread with olive oil, and then sprinkle 1 tablespoon of vegan Parmesan over the top. Place the bread on your loyal pizza stone or cookie sheet and put it into the oven.

Pull the croutons out when they are light golden brown. It shouldn't take more than 10 minutes.

The ancient Greeks had a collection of gods and goddesses that played very important roles in the lives of those struggling to survive in the Mediterranean. Hera watched over your mother when you were born and followed you throughout your childhood protecting you from dangers. Poseidon kept the seas calm and full of fish. Ares either brought war to your doorstep or kept you alive while you brought war to someone else.

Here's where I wax poetic about the role that baked goods play in our lives. How they're present when we celebrate our birth, our unions, our holidays, our accomplishments, and our retirements. We get baked goods in the morning when we want to make it special or share them with loved ones at parties. We bring them to someone's house to express our sympathy when they lose a loved one. Whenever you see a movie when some character talks about how his life passed before his eyes, ten bucks says half of those highlighted moments include a baked good playing the role it was baked to play.

This chapter contains the recipes you'd want and need to live a full vegan life—and then some. They range in difficulty from the extremely simple to the somewhat challenging, but we really tried to create a chapter that could grow with a newly vegan baker or provide even the most experienced one a simple treat.

Because unlike those fickle and overly emotional Greek gods, we actually care. We want you to enjoy being vegan as much as possible, and we're here to help you do that!

COOKIES, BROWNIES, AND BARS

There's a reason why home economics classes start off with cookies, brownies, and bars. These baked treats are easy to make and fun to share. You won't have to buy a ton of fancy pans, worry about weaving latticework out of piecrust, or make identical frosting peaks. Cookies, brownies, and bars are a great first step to becoming a vegan baking god and/or goddess.

CHOCOLATE CHIP COOKIES

These little fellas are like the Cadillac of cookies. Show me someone who hates chocolate chip cookies and I'll show you a robot. Yes—I'm saying you would have to have a cold, clockwork heart to hate chocolate chip cookies.

MAKES 2 DOZEN COOKIES

2¼ cups all-purpose flour

1 teaspoon baking soda

½ teaspoon crushed pink Himalayan salt

½ cup granulated sugar

¼ cup brown sugar

½ cup margarine, softened

½ cup hazelnut or olive oil

3 tablespoons water

1½ teaspoons vanilla extract

1 cup vanilla soy milk

½ cup vegan chocolate chips

Preheat the oven to 375°F.

In one bowl, mix the flour, baking soda, and salt. In another bowl, mix the sugars, margarine, oil, water, vanilla extract, and soy milk until smooth. Add the flour mixture to the oil mixture and stir until smooth. Add the vegan chocolate chips. Drop by the teaspoonful onto a greased cookie sheet. Bake for 8 to 10 minutes, or until the cookies are a light golden brown.

HAZELNUT MOCHA COOKIES

There's a running joke in our family that I don't really drink coffee; I drink coffee-flavored almond milk. I'll admit it; I like my coffee to taste like mocha almond ice cream. But who wouldn't want that? That's one of the best flavors of ice cream there is, and if you can find a way to have more of it in your life in any form, why not enjoy it? You only get one life.

That's what I love about these cookies. They have a lot of what I like, and when I go to schmancy coffeehouses for personalized caffeine, hazelnut lattes are my personal favorite.

MAKES 2 DOZEN COOKIES

1 tablespoon hazelnut-flavored syrup for beverages

½ cup toasted whole hazelnuts

1 cup powdered sugar

½ cup brown sugar

½ cup margarine, softened

1¼ cups vanilla soy coffee creamer

1½ teaspoons vanilla extract

2½ cups all-purpose flour

1 tablespoon cornstarch

1 teaspoon baking soda

1 teaspoon cream of tartar

½ cup vegan chocolate chips

⅓ cup unsweetened baking cocoa

2 tablespoons instant coffee granules

Preheat the oven to 350°F.

Set aside the syrup and hazelnuts. In large bowl, blend together all the remaining ingredients to create a soft dough. Stir in the syrup and hazelnuts with a spoon.

Use an ice cream scoop to drop the dough in rounded clumps about the size of one tablespoon onto an ungreased cookie sheet. Keep your cookies 2 inches apart. With your palm, gently flatten the dough into cookies.

Bake for 5 to 7 minutes, or until set. Cool on the sheet for 3 minutes and then move to a wire rack to cool completely.

SHORTBREAD COOKIES

I have very fond memories of shortbread cookies. My grandfather and I used to eat them with chocolate milk while we watched *Perry Mason*, *Twilight Zone*, and *Dick Van Dyke Show* reruns when he babysat me in the afternoons. I remember my grandfather—or as I called him, "Great Dad"—opening a big red tin and explaining to me that they were special. They came from Scotland. So we could only have three at a time. These aren't that exotic, but they are vegan, and you can eat as many as you want.

MAKES 2 DOZEN COOKIES

¾ cup plus 3 tablespoons margarine, softened (you may need a little more)	¼ cup sugar	2 cups all-purpose flour

Preheat the oven to 350°F.

In a large bowl, stir the margarine and sugar together until well mixed. I used a pastry hand blender; I think it worked perfectly. Stir in the flour with a large spoon. Then use your hands to make the dough into a large ball. Really work it. If it's too crumbly, use the hand blender to work in 1 to 2 more tablespoons margarine.

Fill cookie cutters that are at least 1 inch tall with shortbread dough, making sure you get in the corners and the cookie is ½ to ¾ inch thick. Gently push them out. You're forming little biscuits.

Put your little biscuits on a cookie sheet covered in foil and bake them for 10 to 15 minutes. You want them to be just a little golden. Immediately put them on a wire rack to cool. Use a spatula, and be careful, because they're flaky and crumbly, and also are kind of soft and will dent.

I suggest storing them in a tin and eating them with tea and some *Perry Mason*.

LEMON CHAMOMILE SHORTBREAD

Tea parties aren't just for little girls. These cookies will make any morning fancy and proper.

MAKES 2 DOZEN COOKIES

1 cup margarine, softened	¼ teaspoon crushed pink Himalayan salt	1 teaspoon brewed chamomile tea
½ cup sugar	2 teaspoons grated lemon peel	2¼ cups all-purpose flour

Preheat the oven to 325°F.

In a large bowl, combine the margarine, sugar, and salt with an electric handheld mixer until smooth. Blend in the lemon peel, tea, and flour until smooth. Press into an 8-inch-square cake pan.

Bake for 30 minutes, or until light golden brown.

Cut into 9 squares. Then cut each square in half into 2 triangles. Use a fork to poke 3 little dots in the top of each cookie.

Remove the shortbread cookies from the pan. Be careful—these cookies are a bit crumbly, and the edges and corners can "shatter." Cool completely on a wire rack.

BROWN SUGAR, OATMEAL, AND APPLE COOKIES

It is an indisputable fact that autumn is the best season.* In no small part, it's because of the flavors. These cookies take your favorite fall flavors and pull them all together into one magical cookie, like USA's Cartoon Express from the eighties.

MAKES 2 DOZEN COOKIES

2 cups packed brown sugar

1 cup margarine, softened

1 teaspoon vanilla extract

1 tablespoon applesauce

1 cup all-purpose flour

1 cup whole wheat flour

1 teaspoon baking powder

½ teaspoon ground cinnamon

Pinch of grated nutmeg

Pinch of crushed pink Himalayan salt

2 cups old-fashioned oats

⅓ cup crushed walnuts

⅓ cup dried apple pieces

¼ cup water

Preheat the oven to 350°F.

In a large mixing bowl, blend the brown sugar and margarine with an electric handheld mixer until creamy. Mix in the vanilla and applesauce until well blended.

On low speed, beat in the flours, baking powder, cinnamon, nutmeg, salt, and 1 cup of the oats until blended. Using your hands, mix in the remaining oats, the walnuts, apple pieces, and water.

Use an ice cream scoop to drop heaping balls that are a little less than 2 tablespoons of dough 2 inches apart from each other on an ungreased cookie sheet. Use your palm to gently flatten your dough into cookies that are about ½ inch thick.

Bake for 15 to 20 minutes, or until light golden brown. Cool for 1 minute on the cookie sheet and then move to a wire rack to continue cooling.

NEAPOLITAN COOKIES

Chocolate, vanilla, cherry, and coconut all in one cookie.

MAKES 1 TO 1½ DOZEN COOKIES

1 ounce unsweetened baking chocolate (1 square)

1 cup margarine, softened

1½ cups powdered sugar

1 teaspoon vanilla extract

¼ cup coconut milk

1 tablespoon cornstarch

1 teaspoon baking soda

1 teaspoon cream of tartar

1¼ cups all-purpose flour

1 cup coconut flour

½ teaspoon crushed pink Himalayan salt

2 tablespoons drained, chopped maraschino cherries

2 tablespoons shredded coconut

Melt and cool your baking chocolate.

In a bowl, blend the margarine, powdered sugar, vanilla, coconut milk, cornstarch, baking soda, and

cream of tartar with an electric handheld mixer until smooth. Stir in the flour, coconut flour, and salt to create a dough. You might need to scrape the sides of

---

* Not an indisputable fact.

your bowl a few times.

Divide the dough into 3 equal portions and place them in separate bowls. Into the first portion mix the melted chocolate with an electric handheld mixer. Mix the cherries into the next portion with a large spoon. Mix the coconut into the last portion with an electric handheld mixer.

Line a 9 x 5-inch loaf pan with plastic wrap, leaving enough plastic wrap overhanging at 2 opposite sides of the pan to easily overlap and cover the entire pan. Gently press the chocolate dough into the bottom of the pan. Then press the cherry dough over the top of the chocolate dough in an even layer. Spread the co-conut dough over the cherry dough in an even layer. Fold the overhanging plastic wrap over to cover and refrigerate for at least 2 hours, until chilled.

Preheat the oven to 375°F.

Lift your dough from the pan by grabbing the plastic wrap. Very gently unwrap your dough to make sure it stays in the log shape. Cut the dough in half length-wise. Use a serrated knife to cut your dough crosswise into ¼-inch-thick slices. On ungreased cookie sheets, place your cookies 1 inch apart.

Bake for about 10 minutes, or until your coconut section is a light brown. Immediately remove from cookie sheets and place on a wire rack.

Betty Crocker and the Baked Goods Gods

I've heard it said that in the culinary world, bakers are considered the mad scientists. Which I love. I admit that I love popping my creations in the oven and then pulling out something different from what went in. I love the chemistry and tinkering, the measuring and testing, and how it really has to be just right or it's just a disaster. That sounds weird, huh? But the world is a messy, chaotic place, and I just need to rule it… through baking.

Enter Betty Crocker.

All over America there are cabinets with tiny red spoons in them. But Betty Crocker has brought us so much more than just cake mixes and plastic jars of frosting. In a world where grocery store delis and fast-food joints can easily cater our lives, some folks these days find it challenging to justify cooking their own meals… let alone baking their own bread. Betty Crocker doesn't just offer a mix for every kind of cake you could need and a plastic jar of (often vegan) frosting to go with it—she also makes baking seem easy and fun. She holds your hand through those first nerve-wracking steps from hopeless bakery customer to domestic goddess.

I grew up baking, and by the time the Betty Crocker cookbooks inspired me, I'd already become a full-blown baking addict. But even then, the iconic Betty Crocker found a way to encourage me to strive for more. When I threw down the oven mitt and accepted the challenge of creating vegan recipes for culinary classics… I pushed myself to try things that seemed impossible. But there was no greater feeling than seeing my first vegan soufflé rise or pulling the ring off my first New York–style cheesecake. Sometimes all any of us need is just to be encouraged to strive for greatness.

SOFT MOLASSES COOKIES

Molasses cookies are one of my favorite fall treats. I'm not sure what makes them seasonal in my head, except that they just are. I made a few different versions of this cookie to find the "right" one, and actually had two versions that I loved equally…but I'm sharing the one closest to Betty Crocker's, because this is a book about how Betty Crocker inspires us all, and that's how we roll here!

MAKES 1 TO 1½ DOZEN COOKIES

1 cup sugar

¾ cup vegan sour cream

½ cup margarine, softened

½ cup vegetable shortening

½ cup blackstrap molasses

1 ripe banana

3 cups whole wheat flour

1½ teaspoons baking soda

1 teaspoon ground cinnamon

1 teaspoon ground ginger

½ teaspoon crushed pink Himalayan salt

Preheat the oven to 375°F.

In a large bowl, mix the sugar, sour cream, margarine, shortening, molasses, and banana with a handheld mixer until smooth. Gradually stir in the flour, baking soda, cinnamon, ginger, and salt with a large spoon. Blend with a handheld mixer for around 2 minutes, until the dough is completely blended and smooth.

Use a soupspoon to drop little balls of dough onto an ungreased cookie sheet—make sure they are about 2 inches apart. These guys need their space.

Bake for 5 to 7 minutes. You'll know they're ready when the center isn't sticky when you touch it. Let them cool on a wire rack for 2 minutes.

BANANA, PEANUT BUTTER, AND CHOCOLATE CHIP COOKIES

This is a pretty simple recipe, and the cookies are still chewy even a day later.

MAKES 2 DOZEN COOKIES

1 cup brown sugar

½ cup chunky peanut butter (sorry, not the good made-from-real-peanuts kind; it's too oily)

½ cup margarine, softened

1 large ripe banana

1¼ cups whole wheat flour

¾ teaspoon baking soda

½ teaspoon baking powder

¼ teaspoon crushed pink Himalayan salt

1 cup vegan chocolate chips

Preheat the oven to 350°F.

In a bowl, mix the brown sugar, peanut butter, margarine, and banana with a handheld mixer. Then mix in the flour, baking soda, baking powder, and salt. Stir in vegan chocolate chips with a spoon.

Shape the cookies into balls about the size of a melon ball. Place on an ungreased cookie sheet about 3 inches apart.

Bake for about 10 minutes, or until your cookies are a light golden brown. They do a bit better if they cool on a wire rack.

SNICKERDOODLES

I won't bore you (or possibly offend you) with some of the Snickerdoodle jokes we made while baking this recipe. Let's just be honest here—the name Snickerdoodle is begging for some filthy fifth-grade humor. There are multiple theories on where this "whimsical name" comes from, but this little cookie that might have originated in New England or maybe Germany has been around since at least the 1800s and has remained a popular cookie to pair with coffee and tea since the days of Gibson Girls and when "Official Bathing-Suit Checker" was actually a job. That pretty much makes them popular with us Shannons too. I mean, who doesn't love a nice little cookie with a big mug of their favorite warm beverage?

MAKES 2 DOZEN COOKIES

1½ cups sugar

½ cup margarine, softened

½ cup vegetable shortening

2 tablespoons applesauce

1 teaspoon Ener-G egg replacer, just the powder, not made per the instructions on the package

2¾ cups all-purpose flour

2 teaspoons cream of tartar

1 teaspoon baking soda

¼ teaspoon crushed pink Himalayan salt

¼ cup raw sugar

2 teaspoons ground cinnamon

Preheat the oven to 400°F.

In a large bowl, mix the sugar, margarine, shortening, applesauce, and egg replacer with a handheld mixer until smooth. Blend in the flour, cream of tartar, baking soda, and salt with the mixer until the dough is completely blended. The dough will form little balls like pebbles, but that's okay.

Shape the dough into 1¼-inch balls. In a small bowl, mix the raw sugar and cinnamon. Roll the dough balls in the cinnamon sugar. Place on an ungreased cookie sheet about 2 inches apart.

Bake for 8 to 10 minutes, but start checking on them after around 5. Some of the smaller cookies we made were done after baking for 5 minutes.

RUSSIAN PEPPERMINT TEA CAKES

A lot like Mexican wedding cookies, these are the perfect potluck cookie. They're easy, inexpensive, and supergood.

MAKES 2 DOZEN COOKIES

1 cup margarine, softened

2½ cups powdered sugar

1 teaspoon vanilla extract

3 vegan candy canes, crushed

½ cup crushed walnuts

2¼ cups all-purpose flour

¼ teaspoon crushed pink Himalayan salt

Preheat the oven to 350°F.

In a large bowl, using an electric handheld mixer, combine the margarine, ½ cup of the powdered sugar, the vanilla, and the candy cane pieces until blended. Blend in the walnuts, flour, and salt. You're going to get crumbly dough.

Roll the dough into balls, each about 1 tablespoon. Place them on an ungreased cookie sheet about 1 inch apart.

Bake your cookies for 5 to 10 minutes. Start keeping an eye on them at 5 minutes. Check the bottom to see if they are ready. Remove them from the oven when the bottoms are golden brown. Place on a wire rack to cool.

Put the remaining 2 cups powdered sugar in a shallow bowl. When the cookies are still warm but not so soft they dent when you touch them, roll the cookies in the powdered sugar one at a time. Right before you serve them, roll them in the powdered sugar again and sprinkle a little bit over the top.

RASPBERRY WALNUT THUMBPRINT COOKIES

These cookies are delicious, without having to rely on chocolate or peanut butter to make you swoon. They also have those omega-3-packed walnuts in them, which give you yet another reason to enjoy these cookies guilt-free.

MAKES 1 TO 1½ DOZEN COOKIES

¼ cup packed brown sugar	½ teaspoon almond extract	¼ teaspoon crushed pink Himalayan salt
¼ cup vegetable shortening	1 tablespoon applesauce	1½ cups walnuts, crushed
¼ cup margarine, softened	1 cup whole wheat flour	6 to 9 tablespoons raspberry jam (1½ teaspoons per cookie)

Preheat the oven to 350°F.

In a mixing bowl, combine the brown sugar, shortening, margarine, almond extract, and applesauce with an electric mixer. Once the mixture is smooth, blend in the flour and salt. You're going to have little pebbly crumbles.

Put your walnuts in a small bowl. Shape the dough into balls about the size of a melon ball. Very gently roll the dough balls in the walnuts. You want to get a nice light coating of the dust and at least some chips on each cookie. Place the dough balls on an ungreased cookie sheet about 1 inch apart. Gently push your thumb into the center to make a little cup for your jam. Don't push so hard you go through the dough. You want a shallow bowl. After you're done, you can gently put more walnuts on your cookies. Just take the bigger pieces and gently push them into the edges.

Bake for 5 to 10 minutes. Most of our batches were ready at around 6 minutes, so you'll want to start checking on them at around 5 minutes. Once the cookies are a nice golden brown, remove them from the oven. With a soupspoon, gently press any cookies that have lost their jam cup. Cool on a wire rack and then fill with 1½ teaspoons raspberry jam each.

PB AND J THUMBPRINT COOKIES

You can't pack these cookies for lunch—they're still just cookies. But their flavor will definitely bring you back to your bag-lunch days. Best of all, they won't force you to take sides in the bitter crunchy-versus-creamy war. Although, full disclosure: the Shannons are officially Team Creamy.

MAKES 1 TO 1½ DOZEN COOKIES

½ cup granulated sugar

⅓ cup brown sugar

½ cup creamy peanut butter (not the organic kind made from real peanuts—too oily)

½ cup margarine, softened

1 tablespoon applesauce

1 teaspoon Ener-G egg replacer, just the powder, not prepared per the instructions on the package

1¼ cups all-purpose flour

1 teaspoon baking soda

½ teaspoon baking powder

¼ teaspoon crushed pink Himalayan salt

⅓ cup real fruit jam (we recommend strawberry or raspberry)

In a large cool bowl, mix the sugars, peanut butter, margarine, applesauce, and egg replacer with an electric handheld mixer until smooth. Then blend in the flour, baking soda, baking powder, and salt. Cover and refrigerate for 3 hours.

Preheat the oven to 375°F.

Shape the dough into 1¼-inch balls. Place the dough balls about 3 inches apart on an ungreased cookie sheet. Bake for 7 to 10 minutes, or until the cookies are light golden brown. Immediately remove your cookies from the oven and press the back of a spoon into each one to make an indentation. Cool for 2 minutes; remove from the cookie sheet and very gently place on a wire rack. Let the cookies cool for 20 minutes on the rack.

Fill your frosting gun with jam and gently fill the cup in each cookie. If you don't have a frosting gun, you can always just use a spoon. Let cool for another 10 minutes.

BROWN SUGAR PUMPKIN COOKIES WITH MAPLE FROSTING

Ta-da! This is a soft, sweet, and delicious cookie that is pretty much wonderful. I know a lot of us overdose on pumpkin every fall, but these little buddies aren't so pumpkiny that they'll put you over the edge into Mia Wallace territory.

MAKES 2 TO 2½ DOZEN COOKIES

⅔ cup packed brown sugar

⅔ cup granulated sugar

¾ cup margarine, softened

1 teaspoon vanilla extract

½ cup pumpkin puree

2 tablespoons applesauce

2 cups all-purpose flour

1 teaspoon baking soda

½ teaspoon crushed pink Himalayan salt

1 teaspoon pumpkin pie spice

1 batch Soft Maple Frosting (page 401)

Preheat the oven to 375°F.

With a handheld electric blender, mix the sugars and margarine until smooth. Add the vanilla, pumpkin, and applesauce and blend until smooth. Then add the flour, baking soda, salt, and pumpkin pie spice and blend for 2 minutes. You want the cookie dough to be smooth and all the margarine to be completely blended into the dough.

We used our frosting gun as a cookie press to get perfectly round cookies. All you have to do is fill your frosting gun with cookie dough and place the tip very close to the cookie sheet. When you squirt the dough onto the cookie sheet, you'll see it spread out from the tip in an even circle around the center. You'll want to make sure your cookies are bigger than a silver dollar.

You're going to want to press out your cookies onto an ungreased cookies sheet. Bake for 10 to 15 minutes. Pull your cookies out of the oven when they are slightly brown along the edges and any little ridges on the top.

While your cookies are baking and cooling, make your Soft Maple Frosting (page 401). Cool your baked cookies on a wire rack.

Once your cookies have cooled to the point that they are only warm to the touch, use your whisk to drizzle your Soft Maple Frosting over the tops of your cookies. You can eat them then or let them cool to room temperature...go crazy!

APRICOT COOKIES WITH A DARK CHOCOLATE DRIZZLE

Apricots dipped in dark chocolate are a classic fancy candy. These cookies capture all the flavor of that combination, in convenient cookie form.

MAKES 2 DOZEN COOKIES

1 ½ cups powdered sugar

1 cup margarine, softened

¼ cup almond milk

¼ teaspoon grated orange peel

1 ¼ teaspoons vanilla extract

¼ teaspoon orange extract

2 ½ cups all-purpose flour

2 tablespoons cornstarch

1 teaspoon baking soda

1 teaspoon cream of tartar

¾ cup diced dried apricots

1 ½ cups vegan dark chocolate chips

In a large bowl, blend the powdered sugar, margarine, almond milk, orange peel, and vanilla and orange extracts with an electric handheld mixer until smooth. Gradually mix in the flour, cornstarch, baking soda, and cream of tartar and blend until the dough is soft. It will first become small pebbles, but if you continue to blend it will become a soft dough. Be patient.

With a large spoon, mix in the dried apricot until it is evenly spread though out the dough. Cover the bowl with foil and chill in the fridge for 1 hour.

Preheat the oven to 375°F.

After the dough has chilled, pull it out and use a soupspoon to scoop out your cookies. Use your hands to form them into coins smaller than your palm and place them on an unlined cookie sheet. Bake the cookies for 5 to 7 minutes, or until they are light golden brown.

Cool them on a wire rack. Once your cookies are cooled, melt your vegan chocolate chips following the instructions on the package. With a whisk, drizzle chocolate on top of each cookie.

Place your cookies back on the wire rack to cool. Once your chocolate has hardened, they are ready to eat!

BUTTERSCOTCH BROWNIES

These brownies take around 5 minutes to mix…I made them during the credits of an episode of *Supernatural* if that helps give you some context. They were also amazing with vanilla soy ice cream—maybe too good. These brownies went fast.

MAKES 1 DOZEN BROWNIES

¼ cup margarine, softened, plus extra to grease the pan

1 cup packed brown sugar

1 teaspoon vanilla extract

2 tablespoons vanilla soy milk

1 large ripe banana

1 cup whole wheat flour

1 teaspoon baking powder

½ teaspoon crushed pink Himalayan salt

½ cup raw whole cashews

Preheat the oven to 350°F.

Grease the sides and bottom of an 8-inch-square pan with margarine. Make sure you are pretty liberal with the margarine. Don't be stingy.

In a saucepan, melt ¼ cup margarine over a low heat. Remove from the heat and stir in the brown sugar, vanilla, soy milk, and banana. Mix with a hand mixer until smooth. Stir in the flour, baking powder, salt, and nuts, and then pour into the greased pan. Spread out to make sure the batter lies in an even layer.

Bake for 15 to 25 minutes. Take these babies from the oven when they have a golden crust across the top, don't slide when the pan is turned very slightly to the side, and you can insert a toothpick in the center and remove it cleanly. After they cool for 5 minutes, you can eat them without burning your face off.

BROWNIE BITES

We've found a way to increase the enjoyment allotment of brownies by figuring out what we've been calling "the edge constant." What's that, you ask? Well, in every square or rectangle pan of brownies there is a finite number of edges and corners. The brownies that include these edges and corners are considered more desirable by the general population of brownie eaters. By making your brownies in a cupcake pan, you can objectively increase the enjoyment of your brownies by increasing the edge constant. These brownies are also small, so they're easy to give out to friends and squirrels and various other friendly folks.

MAKES 2 DOZEN BROWNIES

Baking spray

4 ounces baking chocolate (4 squares)

2 cups plus ½ teaspoon sugar

½ cup water

1 cup soy milk

1 teaspoon apple cider vinegar

2¼ cups all-purpose flour

1 teaspoon baking soda

1 teaspoon crushed pink Himalayan salt

1 cup margarine, softened

4 tablespoons applesauce

1 teaspoon vanilla extract

Preheat the oven to 350°F.

Spray a regular-sized cupcake pan with baking spray for supersize brownie bites. Use a mini cupcake pan if you are going for an actual bite-size brownie.

In a saucepan, heat the baking chocolate, ½ teaspoon of the sugar, and the water over medium heat until the chocolate is melted. Remove from the heat and whisk until smooth.

In a small bowl, mix the soy milk and apple cider vinegar. Let sit for around a minute.

In a large bowl, combine the flour, the remaining 2 cups of sugar, baking soda, salt, margarine, applesauce, and vanilla with a handheld mixer. Add the soy milk mixture and melted chocolate. You want to blend your batter for around 5 minutes, until it's smooth and creamy. You will be tempted to give up when the margarine is just little clumps, but don't. It will become a smooth and perfect batter that you will fall on one knee and pledge to spend the rest of your life with…if you are patient.

Using an ice cream scoop, fill the sprayed cups about half full. Be careful and don't overfill; if you do, they'll bake over and not get those perfect little caps on them. Bake the brownie bites for 15 to 20 minutes. Pull them out when you can stick them with a toothpick and remove it cleanly.

When you take them out of the oven, let them cool in the pan for 15 minutes.

MINI ROCKY ROAD BROWNIE BITES

I feel like these brownies should be renamed: justice.

MAKES 2 DOZEN BROWNIES

Baking spray

4 ounces baking chocolate (4 squares)

2 cups plus ½ teaspoon sugar

½ cup water

1 cup soy milk

1 teaspoon apple cider vinegar

2¼ cups all-purpose flour

1 teaspoon baking soda

1 teaspoon crushed pink Himalayan salt

1 cup margarine, softened

4 tablespoons applesauce

1 teaspoon vanilla extract

½ cup vegan chocolate chips

½ cup vegan mini marshmallows

¾ cup dry roasted peanuts, crushed

Preheat the oven to 350°F.

Spray a regular-size cupcake pan with baking spray for supersize brownie bites. Use a mini cupcake pan if you are going for an actual bite-size brownie.

In a saucepan, heat the baking chocolate, ½ teaspoon of the sugar, and the water over medium heat until the chocolate is melted. Remove from the heat and whisk until smooth.

In a small bowl, mix the soy milk and apple cider vinegar. Let sit for around a minute.

In a large bowl, mix the flour, 2 cups of sugar, baking soda, salt, margarine, applesauce, and vanilla. Add the soy milk mixture and melted chocolate. You want to blend your batter for around 5 minutes, until it is smooth and creamy. You will be tempted to give up when the margarine is tiny clumps, but don't. It will become a smooth and perfect batter that you'll consider naming your firstborn after…if you are patient.

In a bowl, toss the vegan chocolate chips, marshmallows, and peanuts.

Using an ice cream scoop, fill the sprayed cups about half-full. Be careful and don't overfill; if you do, they'll bake over and not get those perfect little caps on them. Put a pinch of vegan chocolate chips, marshmallows, and peanuts in the middle of each brownie, and very gently press them into the uncooked batter. Bake for 15 to 20 minutes. Pull them out when you can stick them with a toothpick and remove it cleanly; when you do the toothpick test, try to avoid the toppings, because melted vegan chocolate chips can make it seem like your brownie is not fully baked. When you take them out of the oven, let them cool in the pan for 15 minutes.

CREAM CHEESE BROWNIE BITES

What more can I say here? They're mini brownies made with cream cheese, and they're vegan. Do you need me to draw you a diagram?

MAKES 2 DOZEN BROWNIES

Baking spray

2 cups plus 3 tablespoons sugar

1 (8-ounce) package vegan cream cheese

1 tablespoon applesauce

¾ cup vegan chocolate chips

2¼ cups all-purpose flour

¼ cup baking cocoa powder

1¼ cups warm water

½ cup olive oil

2 tablespoons apple cider vinegar

2 teaspoons baking soda

1 teaspoon vanilla extract

1 teaspoon crushed pink Himalayan salt

Preheat the oven to 350°F.

Spray a cupcake pan with baking spray.

In a bowl, mix ½ cup of the sugar and the vegan cream cheese with an electric handheld mixer until smooth. Blend in the applesauce. Once your mixture is smooth and creamy, use a large spoon to mix in the vegan chocolate chips.

In a large mixing bowl, mix the remaining 1½ cups plus 3 tablespoons sugar with the flour, cocoa powder, water, olive oil, vinegar, baking soda, vanilla, and salt with an electric handheld mixer until completely blended.

Fill the cups in your cupcake pan one-third of the way with your brownie batter. Top with a tablespoon of cream cheese batter. Then drop 1 to 2 teaspoons of brownie batter on top of that.

Once all your cups are filled, use a bamboo skewer to gently stir just once the top of each brownie. You don't want to completely blend the cream cheese into the brownie or anything like that—just create a swirl with the cream cheese.

Bake for 30 to 40 minutes, or until you can stick a bamboo skewer into the brownie and have it come out cleanly. To make sure you get an accurate reading on your brownie, try to avoid hitting any cream cheese when you do the test. That part will remain creamy and soft until the brownies cool.

When you remove the brownies from the oven, let them cool in the pan for 15 minutes.

TOFFEE BARS

It's hard to imagine where toffee bars were invented. I imagine they were whispered in Moses's ear by a certain burning bush and the original recipe smolders away in a crate in some warehouse in North Dakota. A quick Internet search will reveal a dozen or so recipes for this "buttery" treat, but ours is special. Ours has all the salty and chocolaty sweetness with a lot less fat than the ones you'll find on the butter company websites.

MAKES 6 BARS

1 cup plus 2 tablespoons brown sugar	1 tablespoon applesauce	¼ teaspoon crushed pink Himalayan salt
¾ cup margarine, softened	2 tablespoons creamy peanut butter	1 cup vegan dark chocolate chips
1 teaspoon vanilla extract	2 cups all-purpose flour	⅓ cup dry roasted peanuts

Preheat the oven to 350°F.

In large bowl, mix the brown sugar, margarine, vanilla, applesauce, and peanut butter with an electric handheld mixer until smooth. Blend in the flour and salt. Press the dough into an 8 x 8-inch glass baking dish.

Bake for 30 minutes, or until the top is lightly browned. Pull out of the oven and sprinkle the vegan chocolate chips over the top of the bars. Wait until the vegan chocolate chips melt, and then with a spatula spread the chocolate out evenly. Sprinkle with the peanuts.

Let your bars cool for 45 minutes in the dish and then cut into bars.

MOJITO BARS

This was my last post to our blog before I turned thirty-six. I might have been a little fragile and distracted at the time. The year I turned thirty-six, a televangelist decided my birthday was going to be the rapture. So just in case this was my last post before I was sucked away to paradise, I wanted to make sure that all our blog readers would have what they needed to celebrate in style. That means vegan Mojito Bars. They're perfect for bringing to farewell potlucks or to just enjoy at home with some real mojitos—which was our plan.

MAKES 6 BARS

3 tablespoons rum

16 large mint leaves, chopped

¾ cup margarine, softened

½ cup powdered sugar, plus more to dust the tops of your bars

2¼ cups all-purpose flour

Baking spray

2 tablespoons applesauce

1¾ cups granulated sugar

3 tablespoons Ener-G egg replacer, just the powder, not prepared per the instructions on the package

¼ teaspoon crushed pink Himalayan salt

3 teaspoons grated lime peel

⅔ cup lime juice

1 tablespoon soy milk

In a small bowl, mix the rum and mint. Let soak for 1 hour. While the mint is soaking, continue to prepare the bars.

Preheat the oven to 350°F.

In a large bowl, blend the margarine and powdered sugar with an electric handheld mixer until smooth. Blend in 2 cups of the flour with the electric handheld mixer until the mixture looks like fine sand.

Evenly coat a 13 x 9-inch glass baking dish with baking spray. Press the flour blend into the dish in an even layer to make your crust. Bake your crust for 20 to 25 minutes. Pull out of the oven once the crust is a very light golden brown .

While your crust is baking, in another bowl blend the applesauce, granulated sugar, and egg replacer with a whisk. Once the mixture is smooth, blend in the remaining ¼ cup flour and salt. Mix in the lime peel, lime juice, and soy milk.

Place a strainer over the bowl containing the lime filling and pour the rum-mint mixture over the strainer. Then, with a spatula, press the mint into the strainer to get the last drops of mint and rum flavor out of the leaves. You'll get a few stray leaves in the filling, and that's okay. Use a whisk to blend the filling until it is smooth and creamy.

Evenly pour the lime filling over the slightly browned crust and return it to the oven. Bake for 20 to 30 minutes, until the top is golden and doesn't move when you tilt the baking dish slightly to the left and right. You want the top layer to have the firmness of a cheesecake. Remove from the oven and let cool for 30 minutes, then cut into bars.

If you have one, use a sifter to dust powdered sugar over the top. You can also use a large spoon but it won't have that fallen-snow look.

FRENCH TOAST BISCOTTI

Biscotti and French toast are two perfect treats to enjoy with coffee. Why not enjoy them both together? With coffee, of course.

MAKES 2 DOZEN BISCOTTI

2 cups all-purpose flour

2 teaspoons ground cinnamon

Pinch of grated nutmeg

1 teaspoon baking powder

¼ teaspoon crushed pink Himalayan salt

6 tablespoons margarine, softened

1 cup sugar

1 tablespoon Ener-G egg replacer, just the powder, not prepared per the instructions on the package

1 tablespoon applesauce

1 teaspoon vanilla extract

2 teaspoons maple syrup

TOPPING

3 teaspoons ground cinnamon

1 cup pure maple sugar

Preheat the oven to 325°F.

Line a cookie sheet with parchment paper.

In a medium bowl, whisk together the flour, cinnamon, nutmeg, baking powder, and salt.

In another mixing bowl, blend your margarine and sugar together with an electric handheld mixer on a high setting to get it light and fluffy. Slightly turning the bowl on its side and slowly rolling the bowl while you blend it will help make the mixture fluffy. Add the egg replacer, applesauce, vanilla, and maple syrup while still blending and turning your bowl to help keep your mixture fluffy. Once your mixture is smooth and completely blended, reduce your handheld mixer to low and blend in the flour mixture 1 cup at time. Once your flour mixture is blended and your batter is smooth, divide your dough in half. Gently shape each half into a rectangular loaf on the prepared sheet. Be sure to space the biscotti loaves at least 4 inches apart. In a small bowl, make the topping by combining the cinnamon and maple sugar. Sprinkle about half of it over the loaves.

Bake for 20 minutes and then sprinkle half the remaining topping over the loaves and return the loaves to the oven to bake for another 20 minutes. Remove the cookie sheet from the oven but don't turn off the oven.

Let the loaves cool on the cookie sheet. Once the logs are cool enough to comfortably handle, use a serrated knife to diagonally slice the loaves into ½-inch-wide pieces. Place the biscotti cut-side down on the baking sheet and sprinkle with the remaining cinnamon-sugar topping. Bake the biscotti again until pale golden, 10 to 15 minutes. Remove and cool on wire racks.

BREADS, BISCUITS, ROLLS, AND SO MUCH MORE

Welcome to the section that could have been named "A List of Some of the Shannons' Favorite Things to Bake on Sundays." This section does have an extensive selection of breads, but it also has cinnamon rolls, scones, and pretzels—it's pretty much a collection of baked goods you may have always meant to bake but lacked a vegan recipe for. Whatever the reason, this section has a lot of bready treats to bake for friends and family—or to keep greedily to yourself. Some aren't much harder than a macaroni and cheese recipe—others have more steps than Chichén Itzá. We tried to include something for every level of baking god or goddess, so that you won't ever outgrow our book all *Velveteen Rabbit*–style.

CARAMEL AND CRANBERRY STICKY ROLLS

You will be thinking about this caramel sauce when you fall asleep tonight. This sauce will be dancing through your head like a Caramel Sauce Revolution. A special thank-you goes out to our friend and professional Cinnaholic Shannon Radke for her expert cinnamon roll tips, which have helped make these beauties so pretty.

MAKES 1 DOZEN ROLLS

ROLLS
4 cups whole wheat or all-purpose flour (you'll want some extra to cover surfaces)

⅓ cup granulated sugar

⅓ teaspoon crushed pink Himalayan salt

2 packages quick active dry yeast

1 cup warm soy milk

¼ cup margarine, softened (you will want some extra to grease the rising bowl)

1 egg's worth of Ener-G egg replacer, made per the instructions on the package

CARAMEL SAUCE
1 cup packed brown sugar

1 cup margarine, softened

¼ cup corn syrup

1 tablespoon powdered sugar

FILLING
3 tablespoons margarine, softened

¼ cup dried cranberries

¼ cup sliced almonds

¼ cup packed brown sugar

1 teaspoon ground cinnamon

Begin by making the rolls. In a large bowl, mix 2 cups of the flour the granulated sugar, salt, and yeast. Add the warm soy milk, margarine, and egg replacer, blending with a hand mixer on a low speed until completely combined. Be sure to scrape the sides of the bowl to get all the ingredients. Mix in the remaining 2 cups flour.

Place the dough on a lightly floured surface and knead for about 5 minutes, until it becomes springy. Grease a large bowl with margarine. Place the dough in the bowl and turn it slowly to make sure it gets greased on all sides. Cover the bowl loosely with plastic wrap and let the dough rise in a warm place for about 1½ hours, or until the dough has doubled in size.

Make your caramel sauce while the dough rises. In a 2-quart saucepan, heat the brown sugar and margarine to a boil, stirring constantly. Remove from the heat. Stir in the corn syrup and powdered sugar until completely blended. Let cool.

Now make the filling. First set aside the margarine. In another bowl, combine the remaining filling ingredients.

Once the dough has doubled in size, place it back on the floured surface. Gently push your fist into the dough to deflate it. With a floured rolling pin, flatten the dough into a rectangle around 15 x 10 inches. Spread the reserved margarine over the dough. Sprinkle with the filling. Roll the dough up tightly starting with the long side, like a giant cigar. Pinch the edge of the dough into the roll to seal the filling in.

You can cut the dough into 1-inch slices using a serrated knife, or you can cut it with a piece of heavy thread. Just place the thread under the dough roll, bring the ends up, and crisscross them over the top of the dough roll; then pull the ends in opposite directions. We invested in a wire cheese garrote to do the cutting, and it worked perfectly.

Place the slices of dough at least 1 inch from each other on a cookie sheet, making sure the ends are securely tucked or pinched in. You will also want to reshape them into circles and tuck in any extra cranberries or almonds in that may have sneaked out in the cutting process. Go through and one at a time, *very slightly* push the centers up using your thumb—just the tiniest bit. *Seriously* just the tiniest. It should help make the bottoms more secure so the cranberries and brown sugar don't sneak out when you bake. Cover loosely with plastic wrap and let rise in a warm place for 30 minutes.

Preheat the oven to 350°F.

Bake for 20 to 30 minutes, or until golden brown. Place the roll slices on a heatproof serving plate. Let stand for around 5 minutes. Drizzle as much caramel as your heart can take over the top.

Warning: You will have a lot of caramel left over for ice cream and other such delicious treats. I hope that news isn't too heartbreaking.

THE TRANS-AM CINNAMON ROLL

This is the cinnamon roll you could find at the mall flirting with you in the food court. The cinnamon roll that waves at you from your cloudy brain when you think back to when you fell in love with one of the most beloved of all baked goods. The way some car-aholics never forget the first time the saw a Trans-Am…this cinnamon roll will remind you why you bought a house with an oven to begin with.

MAKES 1 DOZEN ROLLS

ROLLS
4½ cups all-purpose flour (you'll need more to flour your surfaces)

⅓ cup sugar

½ teaspoon crushed pink Himalayan salt

2 packages active dry yeast

1 cup soy milk

⅓ cup margarine, softened

2 tablespoons applesauce

1 tablespoon ground flaxseed

Olive oil cooking spray

1 batch Apple Vanilla Glaze (page 398)

FILLING
1 cup brown sugar

¼ cup coconut flour

2 tablespoons ground cinnamon

1 tablespoon coconut milk

½ cup margarine, softened

Olive oil cooking spray

½ cup raisins

¼ cup crushed walnuts

This might take a while, but it will be so worth it! Just stay with me…

To make the rolls, in your largest mixing bowl, stir 2 cups of the flour and the sugar, salt, and yeast with a wooden spoon until well mixed.

In a saucepan, heat the soy milk over medium heat until it's warm but not bubbling too much. Add the warm soy milk, margarine, applesauce, and flaxseed to the flour mixture. Blend with an electric handheld mixer using the dough hook attachments for 2 minutes. Add the remaining flour ½ cup at a time and stir in using a wooden spoon. The dough will be sticky. You'll know you have added enough flour when the dough is easy to handle and isn't sticking to the sides of the bowl.

Flour your workspace and hands. Using your hands, move the dough to your workspace. Knead your dough in a rocking motion for about 5 minutes. If your dough starts to stick, add more flour to your workspace and hands. Knead your dough until it's springy.

Spray a mixing bowl with olive oil cooking spray and place your dough in the bowl. Roll the dough a few times to make sure it gets a nice coating. Place a clean dish towel over the top and let your dough rise in a warm place for an hour. You'll know your dough is ready if you can gently poke it with your finger and the dent remains.

In another bowl, mix the brown sugar, half of your coconut flour, and the cinnamon for the filling. In a separate bowl, blend the coconut milk, remaining coconut flour, and margarine with an electric handheld mixer until smooth and creamy.

Spray the bottom and sides of a lasagna pan with olive oil cooking spray. Reflour your workspace, rolling pin, and hands. Gently push your fist into the dough to deflate it, and then place it on the floured surface.

Use your rolling pin to flatten your dough into a rectangle. You will probably have to use your hands to shape it a little, but in the end you want a rectangle that is 15 x 10 inches and is an even thickness.

Use a knife to spread your coconut mixture over your dough, leaving ½ inch around the edges. Sprinkle your brown sugar and cinnamon mixture over the coconut mixture. Then sprinkle on the raisins and walnuts. Starting at your longest side, gently roll up the dough as tightly as you can. Once you get to the end, pinch the edge of dough into the roll to seal the edge.

Okay, now that all that drama is done, let's get to the fun part!

You can cut the dough into 1-inch slices using a serrated knife or you can use a piece of heavy thread. We invested in a wire cheese garrote and it really made a huge difference! Just place the wire under the dough roll, bring the ends up, and crisscross them over the top of the dough roll. Then pull the ends in opposite directions. It will slice right through, and *boom*—raw cinnamon roll!

At this point you will want to make sure the ends are securely tucked or pinched in. You will also want to reshape the slices into circles and tuck in any extra raisins or walnuts that may have sneaked out in the cutting process. One at a time, use your thumbs to *very gently* push the centers up, just the tiniest bit. Seriously don't get crazy; you'll unroll your rolls. You just want the center raised *slightly*. It should help make the bottoms more secure so the filling goods don't sneak out when you bake. Place your roll slices in the greased pan. Cover loosely with plastic wrap and let rise in a warm place for 30 to 40 minutes. They should pretty much double in size. You're ready to remove your plastic wrap.

Preheat the oven to 350°F.

Bake for 20 to 30 minutes, or until golden brown. While your rolls are baking, make your Apple Vanilla Glaze. Place your rolls on a heatproof serving plate. Let stand for around 5 minutes before drizzling the glaze over the top.

MARKET SPICE TEA ROLL

Living on the Puget Sound is really a treasured memory for me. Gray skies that looked like smudged glass and lush trees and ferns overtaking the suburbs... they made everything seem special. One of my favorite memories was finding a tea shop in Pike Place Market with warm, exposed beams made from trees that were so large they were ancient when they were logged more than a hundred years ago. It's a tourist shop now, but that doesn't make it any less special, because this is the shop where the best tea in the world comes from. Okay there might be shops in India or China that can compete, but I haven't been to those places yet, so after acknowledging my ignorance I stand by the statement. If you're not lucky enough to live in Seattle, you can order your own cinnamon-orange black tea from MarketSpice.com and see for yourself. These rolls combine all things awesome about this tea from my memories.

MAKES 1 DOZEN ROLLS

ROLLS

4 cups all-purpose flour (you'll need more to dust your surfaces)

⅓ cup sugar

1 teaspoon crushed pink Himalayan salt

2 packages active dry yeast

1 cup warm brewed orange spice tea

1 tablespoon almond milk

⅓ cup margarine, melted

2 tablespoons applesauce

2½ teaspoons grated orange peel

1 tablespoon ground flaxseed

Olive oil cooking spray

1 batch Sweet Orange Spice Glaze (page 400)

FILLING

¾ cup brown sugar

1 tablespoon plus 2 teaspoons ground cinnamon

3 tablespoons margarine, softened

2 tablespoons coconut flour

3 tablespoons grated orange peel

1 tablespoon orange juice with pulp

Olive oil cooking spray

¼ cup crushed walnuts

Baking your own cinnamon rolls can seem intimidating when you see all the steps, but once you do it, you'll see it's really not that much more complicated than baking a layer cake or playing with Legos. It's all about construction, and you can do it!

To make the rolls, in your largest mixing bowl, stir 2 cups of the flour and the sugar, salt, and yeast with a wooden spoon until well mixed. Add the warm tea, almond milk, margarine, applesauce, orange peel, and flaxseed to the flour mix. Beat with an electric handheld mixer using the dough hook attachments for 3 minutes. Then stir in the remaining flour, ½ cup at a time, using a wooden spoon. The dough will be sticky. You'll know you have added enough flour when the dough is easy to handle and isn't sticking to the sides of the bowl.

Flour your workspace and hands. Using your hands, move the dough to your workspace. Knead your dough in a rocking motion for about 5 minutes. If your dough starts to stick, add more flour to your workspace and hands. Knead your dough until it's springy.

Spray a mixing bowl with olive oil cooking spray and place your dough in the bowl. Gently roll the dough a few times to make sure it gets a nice coating. Place a clean dish towel over the top and let your dough rise in a warm place for an hour. You'll know your dough is ready if you can gently poke it with your finger and the dent remains. If your dough giggles when you poke it and the dent disappears, that's totally creepy and means your dough isn't ready.

In another bowl, mix the brown sugar and cinnamon

for the filling.

In yet another bowl, mix the margarine, coconut flour, orange peel, and orange juice with an electric handheld mixer until smooth.

Spray the bottom and sides of a lasagna pan with olive oil cooking spray. Reflour your workspace, rolling pin, and hands. Gently push your fist into the dough to deflate it, and then place it on the floured surface.

Use your rolling pin to flatten your dough into a rectangle. You will probably have to use your hands to shape it a little, but in the end you want a rectangle that is 15 x 10 inches and is an even thickness and doesn't taper at the ends.

Use a knife to spread your orange-coconut mixture over your dough, leaving ½ inch around the edges. Sprinkle your brown sugar and cinnamon mixture over the margarine. Then sprinkle the walnuts over the top. Starting at your longest side, gently roll up the dough as tightly as you can. Once you get to the end, pinch the edge of the dough into the roll to seal the edge.

Now, stop! Take a breath and smile. The hardest and messiest parts are over! Give yourself a round of applause and then get over it. There is more to do.

It's time to cut your rolls. You can cut the dough into 1-inch slices using a serrated knife, or you can use a piece of heavy thread. We recommend investing in a wire cheese garrote. It worked perfectly! Just place the wire or thread under your dough roll, bring the ends up, crisscross them over the top of the dough roll, and then pull the ends in opposite directions. It will slice right through, and ta-da! Raw cinnamon roll!

At this point you will want to make sure the ends are securely tucked or pinched in. You can use your hands to very gingerly reshape the slices into circles and tuck any extra walnuts in that may have sneaked out in the cutting process. One at a time, use your thumb to ever so slightly push the centers up, just the tiniest bit. Seriously don't put your shoulder into this, or you'll unroll your rolls. You just want the center raised slightly. Place your roll slices in the greased pan. Cover loosely with plastic wrap and let rise in a warm place for 30 to 40 minutes. They should pretty much double in size.

Preheat the oven to 350°F.

Remove the plastic wrap and pop your rolls in the oven. Bake for 20 to 30 minutes, or until golden brown. While your rolls are baking, make your Sweet Orange Spice Glaze. Place your rolls on a heatproof serving plate. Let stand for around 5 minutes before drizzling the glaze over the top.

DIY BISQUICK

If you love Bisquick mix but you can't find one of the vegan Bisquicks or you're just more of a DIY type, this recipe is for you. It can be used as a substitute for Bisquick mix in any of the recipes in this book.

2 cups all-purpose flour

3 teaspoons baking powder

1 teaspoon crushed pink Himalayan salt

2 tablespoons vegetable shortening

In your favorite food processor, blend all the ingredients and substitute in any recipe calling for 2 cups Bisquick mix.

We've Got a Mix for That...

There once was a man named Carl Smith, who had what could be considered a pretty normal job. He was an executive at General Mills and was one of those dedicated employees always looking for new opportunities for his company. On a train trip from Portland to San Francisco, he ordered a late dinner and found one of those opportunities sitting on his plate in the form of a fresh, hot biscuit. He realized that the train company had pulled off one of those impossible kitchen miracles men in his line of work were always hoping to find. They had found a way to keep shortening fresh and the leavening agent active for several hours after being combined. Not long after that, General Mills created Bisquick mix—and Carl Smith would earn his place in culinary history.

Boxes of Bisquick mix hit the shelves of supermarkets in 1931 and became a wild success. At the time, the Great Depression had been ravaging the United States for years. Traditional gender roles had taken a backseat to making a living, and more men found themselves out of work, stuck at home with the housework and children while their wives took jobs doing other people's laundry, cleaning strangers' houses, and in factories making half what their husbands had made doing the same jobs years earlier. These unemployed men didn't grow up learning how to work an electric stove, let alone how to bake from scratch, and found themselves further discouraged at an already frustrating time in their lives. Working women who weren't lucky enough to have a husband willing or able to share the burdens of homemaking oftentimes had to come home and catch up with the chores of their own homes. It wasn't just a hard time for the American economy; it was a hard time for the American family. Is it any wonder that a product that came with pretty simple instructions for almost instant biscuits, pancakes, and waffles did so well?

Soon you could find mixes for pretty much everything. During World War II, when everything from sugar to pantyhose was being rationed, mixes reached a new level of "handy" by helping Americans make their pantry goods stretch a little further. But as the war came to an end and rationing gave way to postwar consumerism, the convenience that came from baking with mixes remained.

The 1950 release of *Betty Crocker's Picture Cook Book*—or, as it would come to be known, Big Red—actually documents this shift in the American diet by including several recipes that require mixes. Of course this wasn't an accident; the release of Betty Crocker's Big Red was timed perfectly to coincide with the release of several new mixes by General Mills, although by then, several other companies had already become deeply invested in mixes. The Betty Crocker brand had waited, though. "She" wanted hers to be perfect, and that required a lot of trial runs in the ol' test kitchens. Betty Crocker mixes quickly became known as the best.

These days you can find the Betty Crocker red spoon logo on boxes all over the world. There are mixes for every cake, biscuit, brownie, and cookie you'd ever want. And here's some great news—many are already vegan!

GARLIC AND CHEESE BISCUITS

I made these on a Saturday morning, thinking we could eat them all weekend…but they never saw another sunrise. Yes, we ate the whole batch in one day, and not because we didn't have any other food. Since we started this project, our pantry and fridge have never looked so healthy and big-boned. We ate them all because these biscuits are that good.

MAKES 1 TO 1½ DOZEN BISCUITS

2 cups Bisquick mix

⅔ cup soy milk

2 tablespoons nutritional yeast

½ cup shredded Daiya vegan cheddar cheese or your favorite vegan cheddar

¼ cup olive oil

¼ teaspoon garlic powder

1 clove garlic, minced

¼ teaspoon dried dill weed

¼ teaspoon dried thyme leaves

¼ teaspoon dried rosemary, crushed

Preheat the oven to 450°F.

In a bowl, combine the Bisquick mix, soy milk, and nutritional yeast with a handheld mixer until completely mixed. Stir in the vegan cheese with a spoon.

On an ungreased cookie sheet, drop spoon-size clumps. They won't be pretty, but it's important that they don't get too thick or they won't bake all the way through.

Bake for 8 to 10 minutes, but keep an eye on them. They bake *fast*. Pull them out once they're golden.

In a bowl, mix the olive oil, garlic powder, garlic, dill weed, thyme, and rosemary. Brush the warm biscuits with the herbed olive oil. Once they've cooled, eat them.

SOUR CREAM, BLACK PEPPER, AND CHIVE BISCUITS

The vegan sour cream in these biscuits makes them so smooth, they're like the Billy Dee Williams of biscuits.

MAKES 1 TO 1½ DOZEN BISCUITS

2 cups Bisquick mix

¾ cup vegan sour cream

2 tablespoons chopped fresh chives

1 tablespoon freshly ground black peppercorns

1 tablespoon nutritional yeast

¼ teaspoon baking soda

½ teaspoon water

All-purpose flour, for rolling out the dough

Preheat the oven to 400°F.

In a large bowl, mix all the ingredients with an electric handheld mixer until there are no clumps and a soft dough forms. Knead the dough for 30 seconds on a floured surface, and then roll it out to ½ inch thickness.

Use a biscuit cutter or metal cookie cutter to cut your biscuits from the dough. Place them on an ungreased cookie sheet about 2 inches apart.

Bake for 5 to 7 minutes, or until golden brown. Serve warm.

BEER, BACON, AND PEPPERJACK BISCUITS

This is one of those recipes that are often labeled a "Man Treat" in home journal types of magazines. The kinds of recipes someone has decided will curl the hair on your chest and make your mustache thicker. I hope that's not true, because I love these little fellas and would happily eat a whole a plate of 'em for breakfast.

MAKES 1 TO 1½ DOZEN BISCUITS

2 cups Bisquick mix

½ cup shredded Daiya vegan pepperjack cheese or your favorite vegan cheese

½ cup beer

¼ cup vegan bacon bits

1 tablespoon nutritional yeast

¼ teaspoon baking soda

¼ teaspoon water

All-purpose flour, for rolling out the dough

Preheat the oven to 400°F.

In a large bowl, mix all the ingredients with an electric handheld mixer until there are no clumps and a soft dough forms. Knead the dough for a minute on a floured surface, and then roll it out to ½ inch thickness. Use a biscuit cutter or metal cookie cutter to cut your biscuits from the dough. Place them on an ungreased cookie sheet about 2 inches apart.

Bake for 5 to 7 minutes, or until golden brown. Serve warm with margarine.

RASPBERRY CHOCOLATE CHIP SCONES

Friday morning is a good time to just chill, think about the weekend that lies just a few hours away, drink some coffee, and listen to French pop music or take a walk. Whatever your mood, set aside half an hour to enjoy these scones with some coffee or tea and some of your favorite time wasters, and it can make any day feel like a Friday.

MAKES 8 SCONES

1¾ cups all-purpose flour

3 tablespoons sugar

2½ teaspoons baking powder

½ teaspoon salt

⅓ cup margarine, softened

1 tablespoon Ener-G egg replacer (just the powder, not made per the instructions on the package)

1 tablespoon applesauce

½ teaspoon vanilla extract

¾ cup frozen raspberries

1 dark chocolate candy bar, crushed

¼ cup plus 2 tablespoons soy coffee creamer, plus more for brushing the dough

Baking spray

Raw sugar to sprinkle over the top

Preheat the oven to 400°F.

In a large bowl, mix the flour, sugar, baking powder, and salt. Then with a hand pastry blender, mix in the margarine. Mix until your ingredients look like fine crumbs. With a large spoon, stir in the egg replacer, applesauce, vanilla, frozen raspberries, and crushed chocolate. Then stir in the soy coffee creamer 1 tablespoon at a time.

Spray a glass pie pan or dish with baking spray. Gently press the dough into the pie pan. Make sure it's even and that there are no pockets or holes. Brush with soy coffee creamer and sprinkle with raw sugar.

Bake for 15 to 20 minutes. Start checking on it after 10, and remove it from the oven once you can stick a toothpick in the center and remove it cleanly. When you remove it from the oven, move it onto a rack to cool. Once it's cool, move it to a cutting board and use a pizza cutter to cut it into 8 pieces.

WHOLE WHEAT SUNFLOWER HERB BREAD

When people think of vegan baked goods, they might think of healthy brown breads full of seeds. Which is okay with me. This bread has a really nice flavor and texture. It makes great sandwiches and toast and is great dipped in Greek Dressing (page 108). This is one cliché we embrace with our whole heart.

MAKES 2 LOAVES

- 5 cups whole wheat flour, plus more for flouring surfaces
- ⅓ cup agave nectar
- ¼ cup vegetable shortening
- 3 teaspoons crushed pink Himalayan salt
- 2 packages bread yeast
- 1 cup sunflower seeds
- Pinch of celery seeds
- 1 tablespoon dried basil
- 1 teaspoon dried thyme leaves
- 1 teaspoon dried dill weed
- 2¼ cups warm water
- Margarine for greasing the rising bowl
- Olive oil to brush each loaf with

In a large bowl, beat 3 cups of the whole wheat flour and the agave nectar, shortening, salt, yeast, sunflower seeds, celery seeds, and dried herbs with an electric mixer on low speed with dough hook attachments until it's well mixed. Add the warm water and beat with the electric mixer using the dough hooks on low speed until thoroughly mixed. Be sure to scrape the sides.

You're going to want to start mixing in the rest of whole wheat flour 1 cup at a time to make the dough easier to handle.

Place the dough on a lightly floured surface. Knead the dough for around 10 minutes, or until it's smooth. Grease a large bowl with margarine. Place the dough in the bowl and wrap the top with plastic wrap. Let it rise in a warm place for about an hour.

Once it has risen, gently push your fist into the cen-ter of the dough. This will deflate the dough a little. Then take a knife and cut the dough in half. Flatten each half with a floured rolling pin. Roll the dough into 2 rectangles. Try to get 90-degree angles on your rectangle. Take one of the shorter sides of one of the rectangles and roll up the dough tight. Press your thumbs into the dough gently to seal the dough as you roll. Pinch the ends when finish rolling. Fold the ends under and use your hands to form the bread into a loaf. Pinch the edges in to seal them. Brush with olive oil and place on your handy little pizza stone or in a greased bread pan. Cover and let rise another hour. Do that with both rectangles.

Preheat the oven to 375°F.

Bake each loaf separately for 40 to 45 minutes, or un-til the bread makes a hollow noise when you thump it and it is deep golden brown.

VEGAN CHICKEN CORDON BLEU PIZZA, page 179

CAESAR SALAD BURGER, page 182

3-ALARM VEGAN BACON CHEESEBURGER, page 186

EVERYDAY GLUTEN-FREE GNOCCHI, page 193

FETTUCCINE WITH CANNELLINI BEANS AND ARTICHOKE HEARTS ALFREDO, page 207

CARIBBEAN BLACK BEANS AND RICE, page 220

SWEET POTATO RISOTTO, page 230

BORSCHT FOR VEGANS WHO DON'T LIKE BEETS, page 249

MINI TEMPEH POT STICKERS WITH TAMARI AND SESAME DIPPING SAUCE, page 251

PEKING TOFURKY WITH DRUMSTICKS AND
EMPEROR'S RICE STUFFING, page 257

CEVICHE, page 264

24-HOUR PICKLES, page 266

SNICKERDOODLES, page 302

BROWN SUGAR PUMPKIN COOKIES WITH MAPLE FROSTING, page 304

TOFFEE BARS, page 309

CHEEZY JALAPEÑO CORN BREAD (page 327)
AND 5-BEAN CHILI, page 55

MINI CHOCOLATE COPACABANA DOUGHNUTS, page 334

MINI STRAWBERRY SHORTCAKE DOUGHNUTS, page 335

MINI PUMPKIN SPICE DOUGHNUTS, page 336

WILLIAMSBURG, page 336

BABY BLUTHS, page 337

MARIE ANTOINETTE, page 338

TIRAMISU WHOOPIE PIES, page 346

SALTED CARAMEL APPLE WHOOPIE PIES, page 348

MEXICAN HOT CHOCOLATE CUPCAKES, page 355

NEW YORK CHEESECAKE, page 362

PUMPKIN PIE SOUFFLE, page 366

PEANUT BUTTER AND PRETZEL–SWIRLED
CHOCOLATE ICE CREAM, page 373

FROZEN COCONUT CREAM PIE, page 388

MIXED BERRY CRUMBLE TART
WITH CITRUS CRUMBLE, page 390

MINI PUMPKIN CHEESECAKES, page 454

SOY NOG CHEESECAKE WITH BUTTERY RUM SAUCE, page 457

PEANUT BUTTER EGGS, page 470

RUSTIC VEGAN CRESCIA BREAD

Many people know that Dan and I live in a house divided. He grew up in the Red Sox Nation and I'm from Yankee stock. I love TV that is so bad it is amazing, and Dan would prefer to spend his TV time with nobler pursuits like killing Xbox mutants. When it comes to one of the most heated debates in the Nerd Nation, my husband, the Love of My Life, thinks Jean-Luc Picard is the baddest cat to wear a Federation Starfleet uniform. It's not like we're Trekkies or anything. This is just one of those things that comes up. This is one of my very favorite breads to bake. I love it. You may love some breads more than others, but with breads, unlike with Star Trek captains, you don't have to have a favorite. You can love them all equally.

MAKES 1 LOAF

3¼ cups bread flour (you'll need more to flour your surfaces)

1 teaspoon sugar

1 package active dry yeast

1¼ cups very warm water

2 tablespoons olive oil (you'll want some extra to brush over the bread)

2 tablespoons dried rosemary, crushed

½ teaspoon dried thyme leaves

1 teaspoon crushed pink Himalayan salt

1 package smoked cheddar Sheese or Daiya jack-style wedge, cut into tiny cubes

Margarine for greasing a bowl

½ cup shredded Daiya vegan mozzarella cheese or your favorite vegan mozzarella cheese

In a large bowl with high sides, mix the flour, sugar, and yeast. Add the warm water. Mix with an electric mixer with the dough hook attachments. **Warning**: This dough gets really sticky! I know I may sound like I'm being silly, but I'm not. Don't touch this stuff, and watch out for your mixer, and just be careful. *It is very sticky!*

Once it's completely mixed, put some plastic wrap over the top and let stand in a warm place for about an hour, or until bubbly.

Stir in the olive oil, herbs, and salt. Cover and let stand another 15 minutes.

On a floured surface, gently knead the bread for 5 to 15 minutes. You're going to be working in more flour, so the dough should start to lose its stickiness. Knead in your Sheese. Grease a large bowl with margarine. Place your dough in the bowl, roll it a bit to coat it with the margarine, and then cover the bowl tightly with plastic wrap and let the dough rise in a warm place for another hour.

Place the dough on your pizza stone dusted with flour or on a slightly greased cookie sheet. Gently shape the dough into a sort of football-shaped loaf. Cover with plastic wrap and let rise another hour. The dough should (sorta) double in size.

Preheat the oven to 450°F.

Brush the outside of the bread with olive oil. Put the bread in the oven for 5 to 10 minutes. The outside of the bread should start to harden, but not really bake. Cut a slit down the middle, and gently open the cut with your knife to create a little canal. Sprinkle your vegan mozzarella in the canal. Bake for another 20 to 25 minutes, until your bread turns golden brown and sounds hollow when tapped. Cool on a wire rack.

PIZZA BREAD

What can I say about pizza bread? It may sound like something you'd find in a Lunchable, but really it's a pretty delicious loaf of bread that finds a nice way to combine all the key flavors of your favorite pizzas. We made ours with some of our favorite pizza toppings, but it's not hard to substitute in what you'd want instead. Just remember, if you add a lot of raw veggies, you're adding moisture to your mix—so try not to overload, because your bread won't bake properly.

MAKES 1 LOAF

1 tablespoon ground flaxseeds

2 tablespoons water

1¼ cups soy milk

¼ cup olive oil

2 tablespoons chopped fresh basil

¼ teaspoon red pepper flakes

2¼ cups all-purpose flour

¾ cup shredded Daiya vegan mozzarella cheese or your favorite vegan mozzarella

1 Tofurky Italian sausage or Field Roast

Italian sausage, diced into small pieces

¼ cup sliced black olives

2 tablespoons nutritional yeast

2 teaspoons chopped sun-dried tomatoes

3 teaspoons baking powder

Vegetable shortening for greasing your pan

Preheat the oven to 350°F.

In a small bowl, mix the flaxseeds and water.

In a large bowl, mix the soy milk, olive oil, basil, red pepper flakes, and flaxseed with a handheld electric mixer until smooth and completely blended. Mix in the flour 1 cup at a time using the dough hook attachments on your electric mixer. Then mix in the vegan cheese, vegan sausage, olives, nutritional yeast, sun-dried tomatoes, and baking powder.

Grease a bread pan with vegetable shortening. Using a spatula, scrape the sides of your bowl and pour your dough into the bread pan. Use your spatula to gently press the dough into the pan so there aren't any air pockets in the corners and the top is even.

Bake for 45 to 50 minutes, or until you can stick a bamboo skewer into your bread and have it come out clean. Remember that you have vegan cheese in your bread, so you should do the bamboo test a few times to make sure that anything on your skewer isn't just melted cheese.

Once your bread is baked, move it to a wire rack to cool.

PEPPERJACK BREAD

If you really want some physical proof of how far veganism has come in the past twenty-some years… we have pepperjack cheese that not only has the spot-on spiciness of its dairy peer, but also melts. This recipe combines that vegan cheese with a soft, chewy bread that is supereasy to make and great with a bowl of chili or just toasted for breakfast.

1 tablespoon ground flaxseed

2 tablespoons water

Vegetable shortening to grease your bread pan

2 cups all-purpose flour

1 cup shredded Daiya vegan pepperjack cheese or your favorite vegan pepperjack cheese

1 teaspoon sugar

1 teaspoon baking powder

½ teaspoon baking soda

½ teaspoon crushed pink Himalayan salt

½ cup margarine, softened

1 teaspoon grated lemon peel

1 teaspoon nutritional yeast

1¼ cups soy milk

1 teaspoon diced green chilies

½ teaspoon red pepper flakes

Preheat the oven 350°F.

In a small bowl, mix the flaxseed and water. Grease your bread pan with shortening.

In a large bowl, mix the flour, vegan cheese, sugar, baking powder, baking soda, and salt with a large spoon. Then mix in the margarine, lemon peel, flaxseed mixture, nutritional yeast, 1 cup of the soy milk, the chilies, and the red pepper flakes with a handheld mixer with dough hook attachments until smooth. If your dough is dry, add more soy milk 1 tablespoon at a time until it is smooth and sticky.

Using a spatula, scrape the sides of your bowl and move your dough into the greased bread pan. Use your spatula to gently press the dough into the pan so there aren't any air pockets in the corners and the top is even.

Bake for 45 to 50 minutes, or until you can stick a bamboo skewer into your bread and have it come out clean. There is vegan cheese in this bread, so do your bamboo skewer test a few times to make sure you don't mistake melted vegan cheese for raw dough.

Once your bread is baked, move it to a wire rack to cool.

EGG REPLACERS

You can scramble your tofu and have a nice morning. You can easily skip the bits of egg in pad Thai, or change your brand of pasta. But then one day it happens—someone you love has a birthday, or maybe you just want to bake some brownies. You stop and look into your heart and ask, "What the heck am I going to do about that egg?"

At first, you might think the problem is figuring out how to replace the egg. But in reality, it's figuring out which of the numerous ways to replace eggs is right for you and what you're making. Here are just some of the suggestions we have:

- 1 large ripe banana = 1 egg
- 2 tablespoons applesauce = 1 egg
- 1 tablespoon ground flaxseeds plus 2 tablespoons water = 1 egg
- ¼ cup canned pumpkin puree = 1 egg
- 1 tablespoon agar-agar flakes plus 1 tablespoon warm water = 1 egg

In this book we use applesauce a lot. In our opinion it's one of the most versatile egg replacers, and you can find it at any grocery store. Heck, you can find it at some gas stations. We also use a product called Ener-G egg replacer quite a bit. This product can be found at most Whole Foods or health food stores and is primarily potato starch, tapioca starch, flour, and some leavening agents. It's a clever and versatile product that every vegan baker finds herself falling back on from time to time. Of course, if you can't find it where you live, it might be just the excuse you need to order from the vegan shops you can find online, like Food Fight! in Portland, Oregon, or Pangea Vegan Store in Rockville, Maryland.

CHEEZY FOCACCIA BREAD

This is one of those memorable breads that are surprisingly uncomplicated. What is memorable bread? Well, if you have to ask, you haven't had it yet. Memorable bread comes into your life all sneaky-like. Maybe it was part of your favorite sandwich; or maybe it was something more significant, like that toast that had the face of Jesus in it. Your memorable bread is a personal choice that no one can make for you. You just have to know yourself and what you value. This is what I value in bread.

MAKES 2 LOAVES

2½ cups whole wheat flour, plus more to flour surfaces

1 tablespoon dried rosemary, crushed

1 tablespoon sugar

1 teaspoon crushed pink Himalayan salt

¼ cup nutritional yeast

1 package active dry yeast

5 tablespoons olive oil (you might want a little extra to dip your bread in after it's baked)

1 cup very warm water

Vegetable shortening for greasing your bowl

2 to 4 tablespoons shredded Daiya vegan mozzarella cheese or your favorite vegan mozzarella cheese

In a large bowl, mix 1 cup of the flour, the rosemary, sugar, salt, 2 tablespoons of the nutritional yeast, and the active dry yeast. Add 3 tablespoons of the olive oil and the warm water. Mix with a handheld electric mixer with dough hook attachments for 3 minutes. Then slowly mix in enough of the whole wheat flour that your dough is soft and pulls from the sides of the bowl.

Place the dough on a lightly floured surface and knead for 6 minutes. You want the dough to be springy and smooth. Grease a large bowl with shortening. When you put your dough in the greased bowl, turn it a few times to makes sure it gets greased on all sides. Loosely cover with plastic wrap and set aside to rise in a warm place for ½ hour. Once the dough has grown to twice its size and an indentation remains when you touch it, you're ready to move on to the next step.

You can bake this bread on a lightly floured pizza stone or a cookie sheet that has been lightly coated with olive oil cooking spray.

Gently push your fist into the dough to deflate. Divide the dough into 2 equal portions. Shape each half into a flattened 10-inch round loaf. Cover the dough loosely again with plastic wrap and let it rise in a warm place for another 30 minutes.

Preheat the oven to 400°F.

Once your dough has risen, gently make shallow impressions about 2 inches apart in the dough with your fingers.

Brush each loaf with the remaining 2 tablespoons olive oil and sprinkle with 2 tablespoons nutritional yeast and 2 to 4 tablespoons vegan cheese. If you don't want your bread so "cheesy," you might want to use a little less nutritional yeast and vegan cheese.

Bake for 15 to 20 minutes, or until golden brown.

GREEN GREEK OLIVE CIABATTA

Funny thing about this recipe: there are more steps than there are ingredients. Although it looks like a lot of work, this bread is definitely worth it. In a world of instant everything, this bread might seem Old World, but in actuality ciabatta bread is the new kid in Italian baking. What we know as ciabatta, or "slipper," bread came about in the eighties, and in the nineties it became the "it" bread for schmancy sandwiches and crostini. We like it by itself with a little dish of olive oil. So while you're making this bread, remember: once this bread goes in the oven, it becomes a "simple pleasure."

MAKES 2 LOAVES

2 packages active dry yeast

2 cups warm water

4½ cups bread flour (you'll need more to flour your surfaces)

2 teaspoons crushed pink Himalayan salt

1 teaspoon sugar

1 tablespoon olive oil

¼ cup sliced green Greek olives

2 teaspoons chopped fresh parsley

Vegetable shortening for greasing your bowls and hands

Olive oil cooking spray

In a small bowl, dissolve the yeast in the warm water. Let stand until the yeast dissolves and the excess starts to rise to the top. It should take no more than 5 minutes.

Meanwhile, in large bowl, mix the flour, salt, and sugar.

Fold the dissolved yeast into your flour mixture using a wooden spoon. Once your flour is moist, fold in the olive oil, olives, and parsley. This dough is sticky, so we recommend greasing your hands with vegetable shortening before reaching in to shape the dough into a ball.

Place the dough on a lightly floured surface and knead for 10 minutes, or until the dough is smooth and springs back when gently pressed. Grease a very large bowl with shortening, place the dough in the bowl, and turn the dough so that the shortening coats it. Cover with plastic wrap and let rise in a warm place for about 40 minutes, or until the dough has doubled in size. You'll know the dough is ready when you gently poke it and the indentation remains.

Gently push your fist into the center of the dough so that it deflates. Place the dough on a lightly floured surface, divide the dough in half, and shape it into round balls. Loosely cover with a tea towel and let rise for about 40 minutes, or until the dough has doubled in size.

Spray a cookie sheet with olive oil cooking spray, and move your dough balls to the cookie sheet so that they are about 2 inches apart. Gently pull your dough into flat rectangles that are about ½ inch thick. The more you handle your dough, the stickier it gets. Very lightly flour your dough as you handle it to keep it from getting too sticky. Re-cover with your tea towel and let rise about 30 minutes, or until the dough has doubled in size. Don't worry if your dough is all lumpy and weird looking. If it looks bumpy, you're doing it right.

Preheat the oven to 400°F.

Dust the loaves lightly with flour and put your bread in the oven. Bake for 25 to 35 minutes, or until the loaves are golden brown and sound hollow when tapped. Immediately remove from the cookie sheet and place on wire racks to cool.

ZUCCHINI APPLE BREAD

The cloves and ginger in this bread really accentuate the cinnamon and add a warm flavor to each and every slice. It's perfect for rainy fall days, when you realize Halloween isn't really that far away and all the good pumpkins are already gone.

MAKES 2 LOAVES

Olive oil cooking spray

3 medium-size fresh zucchinis, shredded

1 small Granny Smith apple, cored and diced pretty small

1⅔ cups sugar

⅔ cup olive oil

2 teaspoons vanilla extract

4 tablespoons applesauce

3 cups whole wheat flour

2 teaspoons baking soda

1 teaspoon crushed pink Himalayan salt

1 teaspoon ground cinnamon

½ teaspoon ground cloves

Pinch of ground ginger

½ teaspoon baking powder

½ cup walnuts, crushed

Preheat the oven to 350°F.

Spray 2 (8 x 4-inch) glass baking dishes or loaf pans with olive oil cooking spray.

In a large bowl, stir the zucchini, apple, sugar, olive oil, vanilla, and applesauce until well mixed. Then stir in the flour, baking soda, salt, cinnamon, cloves, ginger, baking powder, and walnuts. Divide the batter into two equal parts and pour into the pans.

Bake for around 1 hour. Start checking on them after 45 minutes. Take them out of the oven when you can insert a bamboo skewer or toothpick in the center and remove it cleanly. Cool for 15 minutes in the pan on a wire rack. The loaves should come out of the pans easily, but if they don't, gently use a metal spatula to loosen the sides.

You're going to want to wrap the loaves tightly in foil and store them in the fridge. And don't be stingy. Even if you don't have a potluck to contribute to, you have 2 loaves. Bring one to work if for no other reason than to show how good vegan baked goods are.

CHEEZY JALAPEÑO CORN BREAD

Whenever I bake this bread, I feel like the woman who played Betty Crocker in the old commercials. There is just something about pulling the skillet from the oven and seeing this sunny yellow bread that makes me want to confidently smile at the imaginary camera so the shine from my pearls sparkles off my straight white teeth as I glide in my heels across a spotless floor. Now you can do it too!

MAKES 1 LOAF

Vegetable shortening to grease your skillet

1½ cups yellow cornmeal

½ cup all-purpose flour

1 cup soy milk

⅓ cup olive oil

2 teaspoons baking powder

1 teaspoon sugar

1 teaspoon crushed pink Himalayan salt

½ teaspoon baking soda

1 tablespoon applesauce

1 can cream-style corn

2 fresh jalapeños, seeded and chopped

½ cup shredded Daiya vegan cheddar cheese or your favorite vegan cheddar

1 teaspoon chili powder

1 teaspoon cumin

1 tablespoon nutritional yeast

Preheat the oven to 450°F.

Grease your darling cast-iron skillet with vegetable shortening. Put the skillet in the oven to heat up.

In a large bowl, stir together all the ingredients until well mixed. Then use a handheld mixer and blend for another 30 seconds on the highest setting. Carefully pour the batter into your preheated skillet. As it hits the hot skillet, it will sizzle and bubble. With a wooden spoon or spatula, spread the corn bread batter out to make an even layer.

Bake for 20 minutes in the skillet, or until the top is golden brown and you can remove a toothpick cleanly. You want to serve it warm, but it'll still be good at room temperature the next day with some leftover chili.

MUSTARD-FILLED SOFT PRETZEL BITES

Why put mustard *on* a pretzel when you can put it *in* one?

MAKES 2 DOZEN PRETZEL BITES

1 package active dry yeast

1½ cups warm water

1 tablespoon granulated sugar

½ teaspoon brown sugar

3½ cups all-purpose flour (you'll need more to flour your surfaces)

1 cup bread flour

1 teaspoon baking soda

1 teaspoon crushed pink Himalayan salt

1 teaspoon apple juice

1 tablespoon applesauce

¼ cup coarse sea salt (you're sprinkling this over the top, so you may need more or less; it's up to you)

¼ cup yellow mustard

4 tablespoons margarine, melted

Preheat the oven to 425°F.

Line your cookie sheet with parchment paper.

In your largest mixing bowl, combine the yeast and warm water. Let the mixture hang out for a while until your yeast dissolves. After 2 to 3 minutes, stir the granulated sugar and brown sugar into the yeast mixture until they also dissolve.

Add the flours, baking soda, and salt to the yeast mixture. Blend with an electric handheld mixer using dough hooks. The dough will be crumbly and not really as sticky as you thought it would be.

Flour your workspace and hands. Move your dough to the floured workspace and knead until it's springy and firm. It should take no more than 3 minutes.

Divide the dough into 3 equal portions. One at a time, roll the dough segments into ropes that are about 1 inch in diameter. These ropes should be an even thickness throughout, like a cigar. Use a serrated knife or wire to cut the rope into 1-inch segments. They should look kind of like little cubes with rounded edges.

In a shallow dish, whisk together the apple juice and applesauce to make a thin wash.

Drop each of the dough pieces into the apple wash and immediately place them on the cookie sheet. Sprinkle with coarse sea salt.

Put your bitty pretzels in the oven and bake for 8 to 10 minutes, or until golden brown. You'll have to repeat this process a few times to make all the pretzel bites.

But that's okay—while one batch is baking, you can put the final touches on another.

To finish your pretzels, put your yellow mustard in a bowl. Rinse out your frightening yet fabulous flavor injector and, using it like syringe, fill it with yellow mustard by dipping the needle in the mustard. Inject ¼ to ½ teaspoon yellow mustard into each pretzel bite while still warm.

After they are all filled, brush your bites with melted margarine, and then sprinkle a little more sea salt over the top.

This recipe will make enough to serve at some kind of Super Bowl party, or just enjoy with your sweetheart over a *Battlestar Galactica* marathon.

"CHEESY" JALAPEÑO PRETZEL KNOTS

These seem like something you'd order at a Chili's or somewhere equally ridiculous, and let's face it, they're not exactly haute cuisine. But here's what they are: (1) undeniably delicious; (2) easy to make; and (3) a great treat for kids or for anyone who loves fun and flavorful food they can eat with their hands.

MAKES 10 KNOTS

1 package active dry yeast

1½ cups warm water

1 tablespoon granulated sugar

½ teaspoon brown sugar

3 cups all-purpose flour (you'll need more to flour your surfaces)

1 cup bread flour

1 teaspoon baking soda

½ teaspoon crushed pink Himalayan salt

1 tablespoon applesauce

1 teaspoon apple juice

¼ cup coarse sea salt (you're sprinkling this over the top, so you may need more or less; your call)

⅓ cup shredded Daiya vegan cheddar cheese or your favorite vegan cheddar

2 fresh jalapeños, sliced

Preheat the oven to 425°F. Line a cookie sheet with parchment paper.

In your largest mixing bowl, combine your yeast and warm water. Let the mixture hang out so your yeast can dissolve. After 2 to 3 minutes, stir the granulated sugar and brown sugar into the yeast mixture until they dissolve too.

Blend the flours, baking soda, and salt into the yeast mixture with an electric handheld mixer using dough hooks. The dough will be crumbly, not really sticky.

Flour your workspace and hands. Move your dough to the floured workspace and knead until it's springy and firm. It should take no more than 3 minutes.

Divide the dough into 10 equal portions. One at a time, roll the dough segments into small ropes that are about 1 inch in diameter. These ropes should be an even thickness throughout, like a cigar. After you roll each rope, very gently tie it into a loose knot that doesn't have any gaps but isn't so tight it creases the rope.

In a shallow dish, whisk together the apple juice and applesauce to make a thin wash.

Drop each of the dough pieces into the apple wash and immediately place them on the cookie sheet. Sprinkle with coarse salt.

Put your pretzel knots in the oven and bake for 4 to 6 minutes, or until they start to get a light golden, almost sunny brown color. After you pull your pretzels out of the oven, sprinkle a few pinches of vegan cheese over each knot and gently place a few jalapeño pieces over the cheese. The knot will have little pockets or creases that you can fill with vegan cheese, so try to get the vegan cheese in those spots rather than sweating getting every inch of the knot covered. Put the knots back in the oven and bake them for another 5 to 8 minutes. You'll know they are done when your pretzels have reached a golden brown and your vegan cheese is melted.

Serve these pretzel knots warm with some napkins and lemonade.

DOUGHNUTS AND TURNOVERS

I don't have a lot in common with Homer Simpson. Dan doesn't have blue hair and we haven't rescued a greyhound or spider-pig yet. What I do share with this animated icon is an appreciation for doughnuts. Mmmm. Doughnuts. I love them and I'm pretty sure they love me back.

As a doughnut enthusiast, I've invested in a few things required to make a variety of doughnuts. First, of course, came the mini doughnut pan. Everyone should get one of these—it's like an adorable little dollhouse doughnut pan. These doughnuts are much faster to make and bake than people who responded to my informal Twitter poll seemed to believe. With a little planning, you'll be able to make a batch of baked mini doughnuts before work one day. Once you get the hang of those minis, you'll want to spend the extra eight dollars and get the full-size doughnut pan. It's the same concept…the doughnuts are just bigger. The next tool I recommend investing in is a good cookie press or frosting gun to fill your doughnut pan. The gun helps you fill your pans faster and give them a smooth top that will make your doughnuts appear more polished and professional.

But not everyone likes baked doughnuts. In fact, in an uncontrolled Facebook poll that may easily have been fixed, most vegans preferred the raised and fried doughnuts to their baked counterparts—but also didn't like the mess that comes with pots of hot oil. If you're one of those (like me), you'll want to invest in a deep fryer. These little guys can tell you what temperature your oil is, to keep your churros from getting too *crujiente* or your beignets from getting too *ramolli*. They also have tips for how to reuse oils and for keeping the oil clean.

If you're going to all the trouble to get a deep fryer, you'll want to invest in one of those two-dollar aluminum doughnut cutters. I mean, you can always use the top of a pint glass or a soup can…but they're two dollars, and they make the perfect holes in the center. And if you divide the price of your doughnut cutter by how many doughnuts you make…a baker's dozen comes out to only seventeen cents per doughnut. And that's if you only ever make one batch of pretty, perfect doughnuts.

Now that you know your tools…let's make some doughnuts.

HOMER

"Doughnuts. Is there anything they can't do?" —Homer Simpson
No, good sir. No, there is not. Not when they're this delicious.

MAKES 1 TO 1½ DOZEN DOUGHNUTS

2 packages active dry yeast

¼ cup warm water

1⅓ cups almond milk

½ cup sugar

½ teaspoon crushed pink Himalayan salt

1 tablespoon applesauce

2 teaspoons Ener-G egg replacer, just the powder, not prepared using the instructions on the package

⅓ cup vegetable shortening

5 cups all-purpose flour, plus extra to flour

your surfaces

3 to 4 cups vegetable oil for frying

1 batch Cherry Glaze (page 399)

Sprinkles to doll up your doughnut

In one of your largest mixing bowls, mix the active dry yeast and warm water with a whisk. Let sit for a while so your yeast can dissolve. Once your yeast is bubbly, you're ready to move on to the next step.

Mix in the almond milk, sugar, salt, applesauce, egg replacer, vegetable shortening, and flour using your electric handheld mixer with dough hooks. This is sticky stuff, so don't get it on you or anything or anyone you love. Once the dough is completely blended, place a cloth over the top of the bowl and put the bowl in a cozy spot to let the dough rise. It should take a few hours. I usually make mine before bed and then move on to these next steps in the morning. You'll know your dough is ready when it's doubled in size.

Heat your vegetable oil on high in your largest stockpot or Dutch oven.

Use your fist to deflate the dough. Then move your dough to a floured workspace to roll it out with your floured rolling pin until it's about ½ inch thick. Use a doughnut cutter to cut out your doughnuts. You can also use a biscuit cutter or the top of a pint glass if you don't care about having that signature hole in the center. Flip the raw doughnuts a few times in the flour. Use one of the doughnut holes to see if your oil is hot enough to fry your doughnuts yet. Once your test pilot doughnut hole is frying, place your doughnuts gingerly into the hot oil one at a time. Once your doughnuts are golden brown, use a slotted spoon to move them onto a plate with a paper towel to drain off any extra oil.

While your doughnuts are frying and cooling, make your Cherry Glaze.

Once your doughnuts are cool enough to handle, dip the tops in the Cherry Glaze and move them to a wire rack to cool. Once they're all glazed, sprinkle your sprinkles over the top to make them all fancy.

APPLE CHURROS

The origin of churros is one of mystery and controversy. There are some who believe they were developed by Spanish shepherds and that recipes were developed and handed down from generation to generation. Others claim to have proof that this delicious treat was first made by monks in the thirteenth century and then shared with the people in an act of great charity. We may never know the truth without the plot to *Bill and Ted's Excellent Adventure* coming true. What we can do is make a batch of these historically enjoyable little guys.

MAKES 2 DOZEN CHURROS

3 to 4 cups vegetable oil for frying

1 cup apple juice

½ teaspoon crushed pink Himalayan salt

½ cup plus 2¼ tablespoons sugar

2 tablespoons olive oil

1 cup all-purpose flour

1 teaspoon ground cinnamon

In a large pot or Dutch oven, heat your vegetable oil over high heat.

In a small saucepan, combine the apple juice, salt, 2¼ tablespoons of the sugar, and the olive oil and heat over medium heat. Once the mixture begins to boil slightly, mix in the flour with a large wooden spoon and remove from the heat. Once the batter is thoroughly mixed and has formed a paste, spoon your dough into either a pastry bag or a frosting gun and attach the largest star-shaped tip.

Once your oil is hot, gently pipe strips of dough about the length of your index finger into the oil. I recommend doing this 1 or 2 at a time so they don't end up sticking together. Fry until the churros turn a light golden brown. They will cook a little once you remove them from the oil, so you want to pull them out before they get too brown. Place them on a plate with a paper towel to soak up the extra oil.

In a shallow bowl, mix the cinnamon and the remaining ½ cup sugar.

While the churros are still warm but cool enough to handle, drop them in the cinnamon-sugar mixture and coat heavily. You want to make sure they have cooled and a lot of the oil has drained out so you don't end up getting too much oil in the cinnamon sugar.

APPLE FRITTERS

For some reason, a "fritter" sounds so much healthier and fancier than a "doughnut," doesn't it? But don't be fooled. These apple fritters are just as a much of treat.

MAKES 1 TO 1½ DOZEN FRITTERS

1 cup olive oil

1 tablespoon applesauce

1 teaspoon ground flaxseeds

½ cup vanilla soy milk

3 teaspoons sugar

1¼ teaspoons ground cinnamon

Pinch of grated nutmeg

1 cup vegan sour cream

2 cups all-purpose flour

2 Granny Smith apples, peeled, cored, and diced

1 batch Apple Vanilla Glaze (page 398)

Heat the olive oil on a high heat in a large stockpot or Dutch oven.

In your favorite mixing bowl, combine the applesauce, flaxseeds, soy milk, sugar, cinnamon, nutmeg, and vegan sour cream with an electric handheld mixer. Once the batter is smooth, add the flour, ½ cup at a time. Once the flour is all mixed in and the batter is creamy, use a spoon to mix your apples into the batter.

Gently place your batter into the hot oil using your spoon and being careful not to splash yourself. Use your spoon to drizzle hot oil over your fritters and to turn your fritters over a few times in the hot oil. Once your fritters are completely golden brown and fried, move them to a wire rack to cool. I recommend placing a paper towel under the rack to catch any extra oil.

While you're frying your fritters, make your Apple Vanilla Glaze.

Once your fritters are all fried and cool enough to handle, dip the tops into your glaze and put the fritters back on the rack.

Serve at room temperature with a hug.

MINI CHOCOLATE COPACABANA DOUGHNUTS

Please forgive me boring you with my "I survived the NYC Earthquake of 2011" story, but I think that I might have learned something about myself that day. And don't worry; this isn't a story about surviving a traumatic event as much as a story that gives me a chance to laugh at myself. There I was, typing away on the sofa. Our beloved kitten Agatha was under the sofa playing. Then I started to feel like there were thirty cats under the sofa. The screen on my laptop seemed to be swaying. My mind tried to figure out why I felt seasick, and then it hit me. I hadn't eaten breakfast or lunch…hadn't even finished my coffee that day. So like a good New Yorker, I began neurotically Googling symptoms for low blood sugar, because I had this tiny fear I was going to pass out. I mean, what would happen if I passed out? Then I spotted a Tweet about an earthquake near D.C. Yay! We're saved! Back to work! Now, the moral of this little tale is this, my friends—eat these doughnuts for breakfast.

MAKES 2 DOZEN DOUGHNUTS

1 cup all-purpose flour

⅓ cup coconut flour

½ cup sugar

1¼ teaspoons baking powder

1 teaspoon baking cocoa

¾ teaspoon crushed pink Himalayan salt

¾ cup coconut milk, from a carton, not a can

1 tablespoon applesauce

1½ tablespoons margarine, softened

Baking spray

1 batch Chocolate Agave Glaze (page 398)

½ cup raw shredded coconut

Preheat the oven to 425°F.

In a large mixing bowl, whisk the flours, sugar, baking powder, and baking cocoa until blended. With an electric mixer, blend in the salt, coconut milk, applesauce, and margarine until the dough is smooth. Once your dough is thoroughly mixed and has formed a paste, spoon it into either a pastry bag or a cupcake-decorating gun and attach the largest tip.

Spray your doughnut pan with baking spray. Fill your doughnut rings halfway with dough.

Bake for 4 to 6 minutes, or until the tops of the doughnuts spring back when you touch them.

Keep in mind that the bottom of the doughnuts will be more golden than the top and there might be little air bubbles in them, but you can hide them with the Chocolate Agave Glaze. Put the doughnuts on a wire rack to cool.

While your doughnuts cool, make your Chocolate Agave Glaze.

While you make your glaze, you can toast your coconut. Sprinkle your coconut on a cookie sheet and put in your still warm oven for 1 to 2 minutes, or until the edges are a golden brown and your house smells like what suntan oils would like you to believe the tropics smell like. Then pull the pan out and let your coconut cool. Once your coconut is cool enough to touch, lightly crumble it with your fingers.

Brush the tops (or the less attractive side) of your doughnuts with warm Chocolate Agave Glaze, and then sprinkle the toasted coconut over the top. If you are having problems with the coconut sticking, you can press it lightly into the glaze. Now, the not-so-secret drama behind mini things is keeping them cute. The hole in your bitty doughnut might get filled with chocolate and coconut. If you want to open up your doughnut hole without losing too much of the toppings, just poke a bamboo skewer into the bottom of the doughnut and through the toppings, and gently push the toppings back onto the doughnut. Repeat this process on all the other dough-nuts. I admit that this part of the recipe took longer than any other step.

I recommend having 2 or 3 with a coffee on a Thursday morning when you're feeling like you need a little more summer or chocolate in your life.

MINI STRAWBERRY SHORTCAKE DOUGHNUTS

Like many women in my generation, I was a Strawberry Shortcake doll fanatic. I could make it sound more socially acceptable by using that gentrifying term "fan," but the truth is I was bananas for those smelly little dolls. Seriously, there are several photos of me from my childhood where I have a doll stuck to my nose like some little doll-huffing addict. Ironically, I didn't have actual strawberry shortcake until I was in college. It was a Tuesday night dessert on my meal plan and was actually accidentally vegan. It was one of the highlights in a meal plan that relied heavily on the salad bar. So when I think of strawberry shortcake in any of its forms, I have nothing but fond memories. That's why it was really important to me that these doughnuts turned out just right and included actual strawberries. It took a few times, but in the end they were lovely. It can be challenging baking with real fruit, but so rewarding.

MAKES 2 DOZEN DOUGHNUTS

Baking spray

1 tablespoon applesauce

¾ cup sugar

¼ teaspoon baking soda

¼ teaspoon lemon juice

1½ cups all-purpose flour

2 teaspoons baking powder

¼ teaspoon crushed pink Himalayan salt

¼ cup olive oil

1 teaspoon soy milk

1 teaspoon vanilla extract

1 cup frozen strawberries, defrosted (try to not get too much juice in there)

1 batch Apple Vanilla Glaze (page 398)

Vegan sprinkles, optional

Preheat the oven to 425°F. Spray your mini doughnut pan with baking spray.

In your always-faithful food processor, mix the applesauce, sugar, baking soda, lemon juice, flour, baking powder, salt, olive oil, soy milk, vanilla, and strawberries until smooth and completely blended. Fill a frosting gun with batter. Fill the doughnut rings three-quarters of the way full.

Bake for 5 to 8 minutes, or until the doughnuts are light golden brown. You'll have to bake your doughnuts in batches. Quickly move your doughnuts from the pan onto a wire rack to cool. Spray your pan with another coating of baking spray and refill your pan immediately. The second batch will bake slightly faster since your pan is already hot. Pull them out when they are light golden brown and repeat the process till you are out of batter.

Once all your doughnuts have completely cooled to room temperature, glaze them with the Apple Vanilla Glaze by dipping the ugliest side of your doughnut in a bowl of the glaze. Decorate with sprinkles, if using. Let the glaze dry on the doughnuts before you serve.

MINI PUMPKIN SPICE DOUGHNUTS

These doughnuts were made for a lovely vegan baby shower brunch I went to for the beautiful Leinana Two Moons. You might know her as the talented veganista behind *Vegan Good Things*.

MAKES 2 DOZEN DOUGHNUTS

2 cups all-purpose flour

1 cup brown sugar

2 teaspoons pumpkin pie spice

1¼ teaspoons ground cinnamon

½ teaspoon crushed pink Himalayan salt

1½ teaspoons baking powder

½ teaspoon baking soda

2 tablespoons arrowroot powder

1 cup almond milk

¼ cup applesauce

1 teaspoon vanilla extract

¾ teaspoon apple cider vinegar

6 tablespoons margarine, softened

1 can pumpkin puree

Baking spray

1 batch Apple Vanilla Glaze (page 398)

Preheat the oven to 400°F.

In a large bowl, blend the flour, brown sugar, pumpkin pie spice, cinnamon, salt, baking powder, baking soda, and arrowroot powder. Add the milk, applesauce, vanilla, vinegar, margarine, and pumpkin and blend with an electric handheld mixer until smooth.

Once your dough is thoroughly mixed and has formed a paste, spoon your dough into either a pastry bag or a cupcake-decorating gun and attach the largest tip.

Spray your mini doughnut pan with a light coating of baking spray. Fill your doughnut rings halfway with dough.

Bake for 4 to 6 minutes, or until the tops of the doughnuts spring back when you touch them.

Keep in mind that the bottoms of the doughnuts will be more golden than the tops, and there might be little air bubbles in them, but you can hide them with the glaze. Put them on a wire rack to cool.

This is when you make your Apple Vanilla Glaze. Make sure your doughnuts are cool before you try to glaze them or they will get all melty and not work out. But if you can wait… they'll be perfect!

WILLIAMSBURG

Oh, Williamsburg, you are such a vintage wonderland of beards, flannel, black-rimmed glasses, and scarves. This is our tribute to you! With the bourbon, a Pabst Blue Ribbon chaser, and some vegan bacon to top it off.

MAKES 1 DOZEN DOUGHNUTS

Baking spray

⅓ cup soy milk

3 ounces dark chocolate

2 cups all-purpose flour

1 tablespoon baking chocolate

1½ teaspoons baking powder

½ teaspoon crushed pink Himalayan salt

1 tablespoon applesauce

1 teaspoon vanilla extract

3 tablespoons margarine, softened

1 cup sugar

½ cup Pabst Blue Ribbon or your favorite microbrewed pale ale

1 batch Maple Bourbon Glaze (page 400)

⅓ cup vegan bacon bits

Preheat the oven to 425°F. Spray your mini doughnut pan with baking spray.

In a saucepan, heat the soy milk and dark chocolate over medium heat. As your soy milk begins to bubble and the chocolate melts, use a whisk to blend them thoroughly. Keep mixing with a whisk until completely blended. Remove from the heat.

In a large mixing bowl, combine the flour, baking chocolate, baking powder, and salt. Then with an electric handheld mixer, blend in the applesauce, vanilla, margarine, and sugar. Pour in the warm soy milk–chocolate mixture and keep blending with the mixer while pouring in your ale.

Fill your frosting gun with batter. Fill the doughnut rings in the pan three-quarters of the way with batter. Bake for 8 to 10 minutes, or until you can see that the doughnuts are set. As soon as they are completely baked, move your doughnuts to a wire rack to cool.

Make a batch of Maple Bourbon Glaze. Dip the ugliest side of the doughnuts in the Maple Bourbon Glaze and then sprinkle with vegan bacon bits. Let the glaze set before serving.

BABY BLUTHS

"There's always money in the banana stand." —George Bluth Sr.
If you didn't watch *Arrested Development*, then I have nothing more to say to you.

MAKES 2 DOZEN DOUGHNUTS

Baking spray

1 cup all-purpose flour

½ teaspoon baking soda

½ teaspoon baking powder

2 ripe bananas

1 teaspoon vanilla extract

2 tablespoons almond milk

6 tablespoons margarine, softened

½ cup sugar

1 batch Chocolate Agave Glaze (page 398)

Betty Crocker Parlor Perfect Ice Cream Praline Crunch ice cream toppings to sprinkle over the top

Preheat the oven to 350°F. Spray your mini doughnut pan with baking spray.

In a bowl, combine the flour, baking soda, and baking powder with a whisk.

In a food processor, mix the bananas, vanilla, almond milk, and flour mixture until completely blended.

In a large bowl, mix the margarine and sugar together with an electric handheld mixer until it's fluffy and creamy. Then gradually blend in the banana mixture 1 cup at a time until it is all mixed in and your batter is smooth.

Fill your frosting gun with your doughnut batter and fill the rings in your doughnut pan three-quarters of the way. Bake for 5 to 8 minutes, until the doughnuts are light golden brown. Once they are ready, move them to a wire rack. While your doughnuts are cooling, make your Chocolate Agave Glaze.

Once your doughnuts reach room temperature, dip the uglier sides in Chocolate Agave Glaze and sprinkle some Praline Crunch over the top. Let the glaze set before serving.

MARIE ANTOINETTE

Marie Antoinette was known for her blond hair and powdered wig. These yellow cake doughnuts with powdered sugar are so delicious that they'll be doomed to meet a similarly early demise. Let them eat cake doughnuts!

MAKES 2 DOZEN DOUGHNUTS

Baking spray

1¾ cups all-purpose flour

¼ cup coconut flour

2 teaspoons baking powder

1 teaspoon crushed pink Himalayan salt

¼ teaspoon ground cinnamon

Pinch of grated nutmeg

2 tablespoons margarine, softened

¾ cup granulated sugar

2 tablespoons applesauce

1 teaspoon ground flaxseeds

¾ cup coconut milk, from a carton, not a can

1 teaspoon vanilla extract

4 cups powdered sugar

Preheat the oven to 325°F. Coat your mini doughnut pan with baking spray.

In a large mixing bowl, combine your flour, coconut flour, baking powder, salt, cinnamon, and nutmeg.

In another mixing bowl, blend your margarine and sugar until creamy. Then mix in the applesauce and flaxseeds and blend. Once that's completely mixed, gradually add the coconut milk and vanilla. Once your margarine mixture is smooth and creamy, blend in your flour mixture, ½ cup at a time. Once your batter is completely blended, you're ready to bake your little doughnut friends.

Fill each doughnut ring about three-quarters full. Bake for 8 to 10 minutes, or until the doughnuts are lightly golden brown. Allow the doughnuts to cool in the pan for about 10 minutes before moving them to a wire rack to cool.

Pour your powdered sugar into a deep bowl. Once your doughnuts are cool enough to handle, dip them into the powdered sugar and roll 'em around to get them thoroughly coated.

MASALA SPICED DOUGHNUTS

Since the day we moved to New York City, we've been eating a lot of curry. To quote my handsome husband: "I am now more curry than man." Thai, Indian, Chinese, Jamaican…you name a curry, and we've enjoyed it. So you can imagine what happened in the Shannon Homestead when we combined the sweet and warm flavors of curry spices with doughnuts…Yeah. I admit one of us might have passed out.

MAKES 2 DOZEN DOUGHNUTS

DOUGHNUTS
⅓ cup margarine, softened

½ cup sugar

1 tablespoon applesauce

1½ cups all-purpose flour

1½ teaspoons baking powder

½ teaspoon crushed pink Himalayan salt

¼ teaspoon grated nutmeg

¼ teaspoon cumin

¼ teaspoon ground ginger

½ cup almond milk

Baking spray

SPICE COATING
1 cup sugar

1 teaspoon ground cinnamon

1 teaspoon garam masala

¼ teaspoon ground cardamom

½ cup margarine, melted

Preheat the oven to 350°F.

First make the doughnuts. In a large bowl, mix the margarine, sugar, and applesauce with an electric mixer till blended and fluffy like a thick frosting. In another bowl, mix the flour, baking powder, salt, nutmeg, cumin, and ginger. Pour half the flour mixture into the bowl with the margarine mixture and blend with your electric mixer until smooth. Add the almond milk and blend until smooth. Add the rest of the flour and again blend until smooth.

Spray your beloved mini doughnut pan with baking spray. Fill your doughnut pan three-quarters of the way with doughnut batter, and bake for 10 to 15 minutes. You'll want to pull the doughnuts out when they are a *very* light golden brown and you can stick a bamboo skewer in the largest one and remove it cleanly.

Put the sugar, cinnamon, masala, and cardamom in a large food storage bag, seal, and shake to mix. Roll your warm doughnuts in the melted margarine one at a time. Pop the doughnuts into the plastic bag one at a time, seal the bag, and shake to cover with the spice coating.

CHERRY AND BERRY TURNOVERS

These turnovers are a great combination of sweet and tart, with a dash of delicious thrown in just for kicks.

MAKES 4 TURNOVERS

All-purpose flour to dust your surfaces

1 box vegan puff pastry sheets, defrosted (we recommend Pepperidge Farm)

1 cup frozen cherries, defrosted

1 cup frozen mixed berries, defrosted

½ cup sugar

2 tablespoons lemon juice

1 teaspoon grated lemon peel

1 tablespoon whole wheat flour

1¼ teaspoons cornstarch

¼ cup apple juice

4 tablespoons raw sugar

Preheat the oven to 375°F.

Lightly flour your workspace and use a rolling pin to very gently flatten your puff pastry sheets while still folded in a rectangle. Using a pizza cutter, cut the rectangle into 4 equal squares.

In a mixing bowl, use a spoon to mix your cherries, berries, sugar, lemon juice, lemon peel, flour, and cornstarch. Once your sugar has dissolved in the juices, you're ready to fill your turnovers.

Spoon a mound of filling into the center of each piece of puff pastry, making sure to leave ½ inch margin along the edge.

Gently brush the edges with apple juice and get your fingers wet with the apple juice too. Gently fold one corner to the opposite corner, making a triangle. Using your wet fingers, gently seal the edges. If you don't trust your seal, use a fork to gently crimp the edges.

Carefully move your turnovers to a baking sheet. With a sharp knife, cut 3 to 4 slits in the top of each turnover. Brush each turnover with apple juice and sprinkle with raw sugar.

Bake until turnovers are a golden brown and puffy. It should take 30 to 40 minutes.

PEACH MELBA TURNOVERS

Peach Melba was a "new classic" dessert invented in the 1890s by a French chef in London to honor the Australian opera singer Nellie Melba. This recipe brings that peach, almond, and raspberry flavor combination into a turnover. You can eat it on January 13—National Peach Melba Day in the United States—or any other day you like.

MAKES 4 TURNOVERS

All-purpose flour to dust your surfaces

1 box vegan puff pastry sheets, defrosted (we recommend Pepperidge Farm)

2 cups frozen peaches, defrosted

2 tablespoons fresh raspberries

½ cup sugar

2 tablespoons lemon juice

1 teaspoon grated lemon peel

1 tablespoon whole wheat flour

1¼ teaspoons cornstarch

¼ cup apple juice

4 tablespoons raw sugar

Preheat the oven to 375°F.

Lightly flour your workspace and use a rolling pin to very gently flatten your puff pastry sheets while still folded in a rectangle. Using a pizza cutter, cut the rectangle into 4 equal squares.

In a mixing bowl, use a spoon to mix your peaches, raspberries, sugar, lemon juice, lemon peel, flour, and cornstarch. Once your juices have dissolved the sugar, you're ready to fill your turnovers.

Spoon a mound of filling into the center of each piece of puff pastry, making sure to leave ½ inch margin along the edge.

Gently brush the edges with apple juice and get your fingers wet with the apple juice too. Gently fold one corner to the opposite corner, making a triangle. Using your wet fingers, gently seal the edges. If you don't trust your seal, just use a fork to crimp the edges.

Carefully move your turnovers to a baking sheet. With a sharp knife, cut 3 to 4 slits in the top of each turnover. Brush each turnover with apple juice and sprinkle with raw sugar.

Bake until the turnovers are golden brown and puffy. It should take 30 to 40 minutes.

BAKLAVA TURNOVERS

One of the few remaining legacies of the erstwhile Ottoman Empire, baklava is a classic Turkish dessert enjoyed the world over, and normally laden with lots and lots of butter. This turnover made with classic baklava flavors maintains that flaky, "buttery" texture.

MAKES 4 TURNOVERS

All-purpose flour to dust your surfaces

1 box vegan puff pastry sheets, defrosted (we recommend Pepperidge Farm)

1 cup crushed walnuts

½ cup crushed pistachios

½ cup almond slivers

½ cup brown sugar

¼ cup margarine, softened

3 teaspoons ground cinnamon

¼ teaspoon vanilla extract

¼ teaspoon agave nectar

Pinch of crushed pink Himalayan salt

2 tablespoons hazelnut oil

1 teaspoon whole wheat flour

1¼ teaspoons cornstarch

¼ cup apple juice

4 tablespoons raw sugar

Preheat the oven to 375°F.

Lightly flour your workspace and use a rolling pin to very gently flatten your puff pastry sheets while still folded in a rectangle. Using a pizza cutter, cut the rectangle into 4 equal squares.

In a mixing bowl, use a spoon to mix your walnuts, pistachios, and almonds.

In a different mixing bowl, blend the brown sugar, margarine, 1 teaspoon cinnamon, vanilla, agave nectar, salt, hazelnut oil, flour, and cornstarch with an electric handheld mixer until smooth and creamy. Then use your spoon to mix the nuts in. Once your spiced nut filling is completely blended, you can fill your turnovers.

Spoon a mound of spiced nut filling in the center of each piece of puff pastry, making sure to leave ½ inch margin around the edge.

In a small bowl mix the remaining 2 teaspoons of cinnamon and the raw sugar.

Gently brush the turnover edges with apple juice and get your fingers wet with the apple juice too. Gently fold one corner to the opposite corner, making a triangle. Using your wet fingers, gently seal the edges. If you don't trust your seal, just use a fork to crimp the edges.

Carefully move your turnovers to a baking sheet. With a sharp knife, cut 3 to 4 slits in the top of each turnover. Brush each turnover with apple juice and sprinkle with the cinnamon-sugar. Bake until the turnovers are golden brown and puffy. It should take 30 to 40 minutes.

WHOOPIE PIES

Whoopie pies are a cross between sandwich cookie and cupcake that ultimately becomes a soft and chewy thing that's all its own. They are the future of baking in the Shannon Homestead, and not just because they have the right amount of frosting and are easy to personalize. It's not even because you don't have to worry about making perfect symmetrical frosting tops or because there's a lot less to clean up after baking them. What's truly great about them is that they're freaking adorable—without being time-consuming. Much like our beloved doughnuts, you can whip up an impressive batch of whoopie pies in less than half an hour, and all you need is a whoopie pie pan.

Yes. I bought a pan just for making whoopie pies. It was a onetime investment of ten dollars that will never require paper liners, and so even if I forget someone's birthday or a potluck…I still have what I need to be a Baking Goddess.

If you're not sure what a whoopie pie pan looks like, it is kind of like a combo of a cookie sheet and cupcake pan with much shallower cups. A whoopie pan can also be used for cookies—but who wants that when you can have tender cakey cookies filled with frosting? I mean, seriously.

IRISH COFFEE WHOOPIE PIES

Around St. Patrick's Day 2010, we made a batch of Irish Coffee cupcakes that I was extremely proud of. I planned on posting the recipe, which used coffee and Bushmills whiskey, but then all of a sudden there were Irish-y cupcake posts all over the Internet! It made us want to reevaluate our plans a little—and that's a big deal. I like sticking to the plan. But ever the voice of reason, Dan said, "It's not our readers' fault that there are a bunch of Irish-y cupcakes out there. So why are they going to be punished and denied these cupcakes that are really amazing?" So the cupcakes were posted. But there was an epilogue to this story that was actually even more remarkable than tasty cupcakes. We made Irish Coffee whoopie pies next. And here they are.

MAKES 2 DOZEN WHOOPIE PIES

Baking spray

2 cups all-purpose flour

1 teaspoon baking powder

½ teaspoon baking soda

¼ teaspoon crushed pink Himalayan salt

2 teaspoons cocoa powder

½ teaspoon Ener-G egg replacer, just the powder, not prepared per the instructions on the package

½ cup boiling water

2 tablespoons instant espresso powder

¼ cup almond milk

½ cup margarine, softened

½ cup granulated sugar

½ cup packed brown sugar

2 tablespoons applesauce

1 Batch Whiskey Frosting (page 397)

Preheat the oven to 350°F. Spray your whoopie pie pan with baking spray.

In a large mixing bowl, whisk together the flour, baking powder, baking soda, salt, cocoa powder, and egg replacer.

Pour the water over the espresso powder. Then combine the espresso with the almond milk.

Mix the margarine and sugars with an electric handheld mixer on medium speed until the mixture is completely blended and looks like small pebbles. It should take 2 to 3 minutes. Add the applesauce to the margarine mixture and blend for another 5 minutes. Add the margarine-applesauce mixture and the espresso almond milk to the flour mixture and blend for another 5 minutes.

Fill your frosting gun or pastry bag with your coffee dough. Gently fill the cups of your whoopie pie pan three-quarters of the way. Make sure your cups are evenly filled.

Bake for 8 to 10 minutes. They are soft cookies, so you don't want them too crispy. Let them cool on a wire rack with the bottom side down so you don't mess up the pretty side.

While your cookies are baking, make your frosting.

Once your cookies reach room temperature, put your frosting in your frosting gun or pastry bag. Cover one cookie's underside with frosting, and then put another cookie on top. Gently press the cookies to make the frosting peek out.

DREAMSICLES WHOOPIE PIES

These whoopie pies were inspired by a Betty Crocker ad I saw from 1969 of a teenage girl baking a birthday cake for her steady—but I've added a little kick to that inspiration. So if you're looking for something fun for an office potluck, birthday party, or maybe something to make for your not-yet-vegan sweetheart…I think you can count on these being just as popular as those frozen treats we all loved so much we would've chased an ice cream truck through an asteroid field.

MAKES 1 DOZEN WHOOPIE PIES

Baking spray

2¼ cups all-purpose flour

1½ cups sugar

½ cup margarine, softened

1¼ cups soy milk

3½ teaspoons baking powder

1 teaspoon salt

1 teaspoon vanilla extract

¼ teaspoon orange extract

3 tablespoons applesauce

1 tablespoon plus ½ teaspoon orange zest

Red and yellow food coloring if you want that bright Creamsicle color

1 batch Just Like Buttercream Frosting (page 392)

Preheat the oven to 350°F. Spray your whoopie pan with baking spray.

In large bowl, mix the flour, sugar, margarine, soy milk, baking powder, salt, vanilla and orange extracts, and applesauce with an electric mixer on a low speed for about 3 minutes, until it's smooth. If you tilt your bowl a little you can get a nicer, creamier batter. With a large spoon, stir in the orange zest. In a clear glass cup, mix 8 drops of red food coloring with 25 to 30 drops of yellow food coloring to make orange. After you mix it, hold it up to a sunny window or light and roll your wrist with the glass so some of the food coloring goes up on the sides. Your whoopie pies will be a little lighter than the color on the sides. Add a little more red or yellow based on your preference. Once you have the desired shade of orange, stir the color in with a large spoon or blend until the batter is a uniform orange color and not streaky.

Fill your frosting gun or pastry bag with your orange dough. Gently fill the cups of your whoopie pie pan three-quarters of the way. It's important to try to keep your cookies the same size.

Bake for 8 to 10 minutes. They are soft cookies, so you want to make sure you pull them out of the oven before they become little poker chips. Let them cool on a wire rack with the bottom side down so you don't mess up the pretty side.

While your cookies are baking, make your frosting.

Let the cookies cool on a wire rack for around 10 minutes before filling with frosting. Fill your frosting gun or pastry bag with your frosting. Cover one cookie's underside with frosting and then put another cookie on top. Gently press the cookies to make the frosting peek out.

GERMAN CHOCOLATE WHOOPIE PIES

If you'd asked me a while ago why a dessert with so much coconut was called German chocolate cake, I would have grasped at straws. I mean, Bavaria isn't really known for its coconut trees. (Insert shrug here.) The truth is that an English immigrant named Samuel German developed a certain type of sweet chocolate for the Baker's chocolate factory in 1852 that became quite popular, so the company named it after him. More than one hundred years later, a homemaker in Dallas, Texas, used Mr. German's signature chocolate to create this baking masterpiece, and shared her recipe with the world in the local newspaper. The rest is cake history! I'm really excited to add our version of vegan German chocolate whoopie pies to our Pantheon of Baked Treats. Even though we didn't use Mr. German's chocolate to make it, I feel like these whoopie pies really capture the spirit of this classic American dessert. And when you make it, please give a little tip of your hat to all those generations of creative and talented women who shared their recipes with us in newspapers and home journals. Here's to the first food bloggers!

MAKES 1 DOZEN WHOOPIE PIES

Baking spray

¼ cup margarine, softened

1 cup brown sugar

1 tablespoon applesauce

½ teaspoon French vanilla extract

¼ cup vegetable shortening

1 cup all-purpose flour

1 cup whole wheat flour

1 cup sugar

¼ cup baking cocoa powder

1 teaspoon baking soda

½ teaspoon crushed pink Himalayan salt

¼ cup hazelnut or vegetable oil

1 teaspoon apple cider vinegar

½ cup cold water

1 batch Coconut Pecan Frosting (page 396)

Preheat the oven to 350°F. Spray your whoopie pie pan with baking spray.

In a large bowl, blend the margarine, brown sugar, applesauce, vanilla, and shortening with a handheld electric mixer until smooth.

In a separate bowl, mix the flours, sugar, cocoa powder, baking soda, and salt with a whisk to break up any large clumps. In another bowl, mix the oil and vinegar with a whisk. Pour your oil mixture into your cocoa-flour mixture and blend with an electric handheld mixer until smooth. Then blend in the margarine mixture. Once the ingredients are completely mixed, add the water and blend with an electric hand mixer on low for 5 minutes.

Fill your frosting gun or pastry bag with your chocolate dough, and fill the cups of the whoopie pie pan three-quarters of the way. The dough will expand when it cooks, but you want to make sure your cups are evenly filled.

Bake for 8 to 10 minutes. They are soft cookies, so you don't want them too crispy. Let them cool on a wire rack with the bottom side down so you don't mess up the pretty side.

While your cookies are baking, make your Coconut Pecan Frosting.

Once your cookies are room temperature, put your frosting in your frosting gun or pastry bag. Cover one cookie's underside with frosting and put another cookie on top. Then gently press the cookies to make the frosting peek out.

TIRAMISU WHOOPIE PIES

While a classic Italian chef might turn up her nose at the idea of a tiramisu whoopie pie, personally I think it's a great shortcut to some really delicious flavors that are admittedly pretty difficult to make—vegan or not.

MAKES 1 DOZEN WHOOPIE PIES

Baking spray

2 cups all-purpose flour

2 teaspoons baking powder

¼ teaspoon grated nutmeg

¼ teaspoon ground cinnamon

1 teaspoon crushed pink Himalayan salt

1 tablespoon margarine, softened

¾ cup sugar

1 tablespoon applesauce

1 teaspoon ground flaxseeds

1 teaspoon vanilla extract

¾ cup almond milk

2 teaspoons ground hazelnuts

2 cups strongly brewed espresso

1 tablespoon amaretto

1 batch Cream Cheese Frosting (page 393)

Cocoa powder for dusting over the top

Preheat the oven to 375°F. Spray your whoopie pie pan with a light coating of baking spray.

In a medium bowl, blend your flour, baking powder, nutmeg, cinnamon, and salt together with a whisk.

In another bowl, blend your margarine and sugar together with an electric handheld mixer until it's creamy. Then mix in the applesauce, flaxseeds, and vanilla until smooth.

Gradually add your flour mixture to the margarine mixture and blend until smooth. Then pour in your almond milk and ground hazelnuts and blend until you have a smooth batter.

Fill a cookie press or frosting gun with the batter and then fill the cups of your whoopie pie pan three-quarters of the way full. Bake for 20 to 25 minutes, or until the edges are golden brown.

While your cookies are baking, make your Cream Cheese Frosting.

Once your cookies are done, move them immediately to a wire rack to cool with the less adorable side down.

In a small bowl, mix the espresso and amaretto with a whisk. Once your cookies are cool enough to handle, dip the less adorable side of each cookie into your amaretto coffee blend for just a second, and then move the cookies back to the wire rack with the coffee side down. Once the cookies are dry, you're ready to build your whoopie pie.

Pipe frosting onto the side of a cookie that has amaretto coffee on it. Then take another cookie and make a sandwich with the amaretto coffee side on the inside. Sprinkle some cocoa powder over the top. Repeat with all your cookies until you have a bunch of little tiramisu cookie sandwiches.

RED VELVET WHOOPIE PIES

Fun fact: the reddish color of red velvet cake originally came from a chemical reaction between the cocoa powder and the buttermilk. Now most recipes just use food coloring. We're skipping the buttermilk here, so we'll have to get our red color from cherry juice.

MAKES 1 DOZEN WHOOPIE PIES

Baking spray

2¾ cups all-purpose flour

½ cup cocoa powder

1½ teaspoons baking powder

¼ teaspoon crushed pink Himalayan salt

1 cup margarine, softened

1½ cups sugar

2 tablespoons applesauce

¾ cup soy milk

1 teaspoon apple cider vinegar

1 teaspoon baking soda

1½ teaspoons vanilla extract

2 teaspoons cherry juice from a bag of frozen cherries or red food coloring

1 batch Cream Cheese Frosting (page 393)

¼ cup crushed walnuts

Preheat the oven to 375°F. Spray your whoopie pie pan with baking spray.

In a medium bowl, whisk together your flour, cocoa powder, baking powder, and salt.

In another bowl, blend your margarine and sugar together with an electric handheld mixer until fluffy and smooth. Mix in the applesauce until it's creamy.

In a small bowl, whisk together the soy milk and apple cider vinegar. Let sit for 30 seconds.

Gradually add the flour mixture to the margarine mixture and blend thoroughly. Then pour in the soy milk mixture, baking soda, vanilla, and cherry juice or food coloring and blend until your batter is creamy.

Fill a cookie press or frosting gun with the batter, and then fill the cups of your whoopie pie pan three-quarters of the way full. Bake for 15 to 20 minutes, or until the edges are golden brown.

While your cookies are baking, make your Cream Cheese Frosting.

Once your cookies are done, move them immediately to a wire rack to cool with the less adorable side down.

Pour your walnuts into a shallow bowl.

Pipe frosting onto the less cute side of one cookie. Top with another cookie to make a sandwich. Then roll the edge of your cookie sandwich in the walnuts so that the frosting gets coated. Repeat with all your cookies until you have a bunch of little red velvet cookie monsters—I mean sandwiches.

SALTED CARAMEL APPLE WHOOPIE PIES

The mystery behind the "whoopie pie" is not whether or not they were really invented by the Amish, or why they're the official baked treat of Maine, but this: why is it that you never see a photo of one that looks as delicious as the actual "pie"? I think it might be one of those things you just have to live through to really understand, because unlike old-school caramel apples, it can be hard to see all the stuff inside the whoopie pie that makes it special. This recipe is particularly elusive. See, in this one golden-brown baked treat, you have sweet and slightly spiced apples, "buttery" and salted caramel frosting, and roasted peanuts.

MAKES 1 DOZEN WHOOPIE PIES

SPICED APPLE COOKIES
Baking spray

¼ cup margarine, softened

1 cup brown sugar

1¼ cups applesauce

½ teaspoon vanilla extract

¼ cup vegetable shortening

1 cup all-purpose flour

1 cup whole wheat flour

½ teaspoon ground cinnamon

½ teaspoon allspice

¼ teaspoon ground ginger

1 teaspoon baking soda

SALTED CARAMEL FROSTING
½ cup margarine, softened

1 cup packed brown sugar

½ teaspoon crushed pink Himalayan salt

¼ cup vanilla soy milk

1 cup powdered sugar (you may want to add more if you want a thicker frosting)

½ cup dry-roasted peanuts, crushed

Preheat the oven to 375°F. Spray your whoopie pie pan with a light coating of baking spray.

In a large bowl, blend the margarine, brown sugar, applesauce, vanilla, and shortening with a handheld electric mixer until smooth.

In another large bowl, whisk together the flours, cinnamon, allspice, and ginger until blended. Add the margarine mixture to the flour mixture and blend with an electric mixer until smooth. Watch out for any clumps of margarine. Add the baking soda and blend on medium speed for a little more than 1 minute.

Fill your frosting gun or pastry bag with your apple dough and fill the cups in your whoopie pie pan three-quarters of the way. Make sure your cups are evenly filled.

If you are using a cookie sheet, still use the frosting gun or pastry bag because it will give you nice smooth edges. Make even "coins" or cookies evenly spaced on your sheet. Don't go too big, like monster-cookie size,

because the cookies get bigger when you bake them. It's really important to try to keep all your cookies the same size and to have an even number.

Bake for 8 to 10 minutes, or until they are golden brown. Make sure you pull them out while they are still soft. Let them cool on a wire rack with the bottom side down so you don't mess up the pretty side.

While your cookies are baking, make your Salted Caramel Frosting.

In a 2-quart saucepan, melt your margarine over medium heat. Stir in your brown sugar and salt. Heat the mixture to a very light boil, stirring constantly. Once the sugar and salt have dissolved, stir in your soy milk. Let it boil for about 1 minute while stirring constantly. Remove from the heat and let your caramel sauce cool until it's lukewarm, which should take about ½ hour.

After your caramel sauce has cooled to room temperature, gradually whisk in your powdered sugar. It's important to mix in a little at a time and repeat, until it's all in there in a smooth mixture. If the frosting is too stiff, you can add in a little extra soy milk a few drops at a time. Add more powdered sugar if you want it thicker.

Crush your peanuts with a potato masher and spread them out on your cutting board.

Once your cookies reach room temperature, put your frosting in your frosting gun or pastry bag. Cover one cookie's underside with frosting and then put another cookie on top. Gently press the cookies to make the frosting peek out. Then roll the cookies in the crushed peanuts to cover the frosting. You can brush off the salt and peanut dust if you like your treats more polished...but I liked the ones with it on the most.

INSIDE-OUT PEANUT BUTTER CUP WHOOPIE PIES

In our society, I think we have been conditioned to crave the combination of chocolate and peanut butter daily. Put those things in a whoopie pie and you've just figured out a secret to an amazing treat.

MAKES 1 DOZEN WHOOPIE PIES

Baking spray

2¼ cups whole wheat flour

1½ cups sugar

⅓ cup creamy peanut butter (sorry, we can't recommend using natural peanut butter—too oily)

1¼ cups vanilla soy milk

3½ teaspoons baking powder

1 teaspoon crushed pink Himalayan salt

3 teaspoons Ener-G egg replacer, just the powder, not made using the instructions on the package

1 batch Chocolate Basically Buttercream Frosting (page 393)

Preheat the oven to 350°F. Spray your whoopie pie pan with a light coating of baking spray.

In a large bowl, mix the flour, sugar, peanut butter, soy milk, baking powder, salt, and egg replacer with an electric handheld mixer until smooth and creamy. You're going to want to do this for about 5 minutes. Make sure you get all the ingredients off the sides of the bowl and that the dough is thoroughly mixed.

Fill your frosting gun or pastry bag with your peanut butter dough, and if you're using a whoopie pie pan, gently fill the cups three-quarters of the way. Make sure your cups are evenly filled.

Bake for 8 to 10 minutes. They are soft cookies, so you don't want them to bake so long that they get crunchy. Let them cool on a wire rack with the bottom side down so you don't mess up the pretty side.

While your cookies are baking or cooling, make your Chocolate Basically Buttercream Frosting.

Once your cookies reach room temperature, put your frosting in your frosting gun or pastry bag. Cover one cookie's underside with frosting and then put another cookie on top. Gently press the cookies to make the frosting peek out. Done!

When it comes to the epic "cake versus cupcakes" debate, we live in a house divided. Dan is a traditional cake guy; Annie is a straight-up cupcake gal. Although since one of us does the vast majority of the baking (hint: it's not Dan), it's a bit of a moot point. Of course, since one of us does the vast majority of the dishes (hint: it's not Annie), only one of us gets stuck washing out all of those tiny little holes in the mini cupcake pans. But that's not the point. The point is that these recipes can be made either way, to suit your mood, your personal preference, or the amount of dishes you feel up to doing on any particular evening.

BANANA SPLIT BUNDT CAKE

There are a lot of flavors going on in a traditional banana split—banana, chocolate, vanilla, strawberry, and cherry. We tried to cram as many of them as possible into this cake recipe. And you can have a slice regardless of whether or not you won your Little League game.

MAKES 1 BUNDT CAKE

Vegetable shortening for greasing your cake pan

3½ cups all-purpose flour (you'll need a little more to dust your cake pan)

½ teaspoon crushed pink Himalayan salt

1 cup margarine, softened

2½ cups sugar

3 tablespoons applesauce

3 ripe bananas, 1 whole and 2 sliced

2 teaspoons Ener-G egg replacer, just the powder, not prepared per the instructions on the package

1 cup coconut milk

2 teaspoons vanilla extract

¼ teaspoon red food coloring or cherry juice from frozen cherries

½ cup strawberry preserves

¾ cup vegan chocolate sauce

1 batch Apple Vanilla Glaze (page 398)

1 batch Chocolate Agave Glaze (page 398)

½ cup fresh cherries, pitted

⅓ cup crushed peanuts

Preheat the oven to 350°F. Generously grease and flour a 12-cup fluted tube cake pan.

Start by making your cake batter. Blend your flour, salt, margarine, sugar, applesauce, 1 banana, egg replacer, coconut milk, and vanilla until smooth and creamy.

Pour about 1 cup of your batter into your greased pan. In small bowl, mix 1 cup of the batter with the cherry juice/food coloring and strawberry preserves. Carefully pour pink batter over the white batter in the pan, and then very gently spread it out with a spatula so that you can't see any white batter. This will create your pink color ribbon. In another bowl, blend your re-maining cup of batter with the vegan chocolate sauce. Carefully pour your chocolate batter over your pink batter. With a clean spatula, spread the chocolate batter over the pink batter. It might start to blend a little, but try to avoid this. It will bake into a marbled effect if you don't blend the two batters too much.

Bake for 30 to 45 minutes. Different cake pans have different patterns and depths, so some will take longer than others. You'll know your cake is ready when the top has browned and you can stick a bamboo skewer in the cake and remove it cleanly. Using the bamboo skewer, make a dozen or so little stabs into the top of the cake. You're releasing moisture from the cake to help it cool and also to help release it from the pan. Let your cake cool for 10 minutes and then turn your cake pan upside down on a large serving dish.

While your cake is baking, make your glazes. Once your cake has cooled completely, drizzle your Apple Vanilla Glaze and then your Chocolate Agave Glaze over the top. Top the cake with sliced bananas and cherries and crushed peanuts.

LIMONCELLO BUNDT CAKE

Every Italian-American woman I know (who is, ya know, into being an Italian-American) has a special-occasion lemon cake recipe. They can make them in less than an hour and always have the ingredients stocked in their kitchen just in case one of those special occasions sneaks up on them. You can find these cakes at baby showers, and they're given to neighbors who have just lost a loved one. They're at PTA meetings, church potlucks, and office parties. I would bet cash money that there is at least one sitting in a Knights of Columbus hall right now. But I think you've figured out by now that these cakes aren't the headliners like those four-story wedding monuments to buttercream. They're like the universal cake soldiers. They're around to feed nervous bridesmaids before the wedding. They're something to pick at while you're staying up to go to Midnight Mass at Christmas, and they are always around for those folks who gave up chocolate for Lent or just to be enjoyed with coffee after church. I have always loved these simple lemon cakes. I've been playing around with them for years… This one combines the rich texture of pudding cakes with the signature flavor of southern Italy's second favorite alcoholic beverage.

MAKES 1 BUNDT CAKE

CAKE
Baking spray

1½ cups sugar

½ cup margarine, softened

1 tablespoon applesauce

1 tablespoon Ener-G egg replacer, just the powder, not made per the instructions on the package

2½ cups all-purpose flour

1 teaspoon baking soda

1 teaspoon crushed pink Himalayan salt

1 (14-ounce) can coconut milk

2 tablespoons lemon zest

3 tablespoons limoncello

GLAZE
¼ cup margarine, softened

2 cups powdered sugar

2 tablespoons lemon zest

¼ cup limoncello

Preheat the oven to 325°F. Spray a fluted tube cake pan with baking spray.

In a large bowl, blend your sugar and margarine with a handheld electric mixer on a high setting until it is smooth and fluffy. Blend in the applesauce and egg replacer.

In another bowl, whisk together the flour, baking soda, and salt until completely blended. Add the flour mixture to the margarine mixture a little at a time, alternating with the coconut milk. Each time you add flour or coconut milk, use your mixer to blend it in completely. Once your flour and coconut milk are completely blended in, add your lemon zest and limoncello and blend on a medium setting for 2 to 3 minutes. You want your batter to be fluffy and smooth.

Pour your batter into the pan evenly. Use a spatula to

spread it out to make a nice even layer. It's important to make sure the batter is even because the cake will be sitting with the rimmed ring on top. If you see any ridges or clumps, be sure to smooth them out now.

Bake for 45 to 50 minutes. Now, not every fluted cake pan is the same, and some are deeper than others. So start checking on your cake at around 30 minutes. Use a bamboo skewer to test if your cake is done. If you can poke the bamboo skewer in a few times and remove it cleanly, you're done. Once you've pulled the cake out of the oven, immediately poke it several more times—like 15 times—with the bamboo skewer. You only want to go in about as deep as a fork would go. You're releasing moisture from the cake to help it cool and also to help release it from the pan. Let your cake cool for 20 minutes and then turn your cake pan upside down on a large serving dish to cool to room temperature.

While your cake is baking, make your glaze. In a saucepan, melt your margarine over low heat. Once your margarine is melted, use a whisk to blend in your powdered sugar. Then blend in the lemon zest and limoncello. The glaze is pretty sweet. If you taste it and are, like, "This is too sweet," just add a little more melted margarine and lemon zest until you get the flavor you like. You're going to want to keep your glaze warm till you drizzle it over the top of the cake.

Once your cake is cool, drizzle your glaze over the top. In the springtime, it's really nice to decorate these lemon cakes with edible flowers and completely worth hunting them down.

ORANGE GINGER POUND CAKE

A traditional pound cake is made from a pound each of four things: flour, butter, eggs, and sugar. Which clearly is ridiculous. Our recipe is a little more complex, a lot less gigantic, and infinitely more delicious.

MAKES 1 CAKE

1½ cups margarine (you'll need more to grease your pan)

2 tablespoons olive oil

1½ cups sugar

1 tablespoon silken tofu

2 tablespoons applesauce

¼ teaspoon crushed pink Himalayan salt

1½ teaspoons vanilla extract

1½ cups all-purpose flour

½ cup coconut flour

1 teaspoon ginger paste

½ teaspoon cardamom

1 teaspoon lemon zest

1 tablespoon orange zest

5 tablespoons orange juice

¼ cup coconut milk, from a carton, not a can

1 batch Whipped Coconut Cream (page 403)

Fresh berries and fruit to serve over the top of your cake

Preheat the oven to 350°F. Grease your glass 9 x 3-inch loaf pan.

In a large bowl, blend the margarine, olive oil, and sugar until creamy. Blend in the tofu, applesauce, salt, and vanilla until smooth. Mix in the flours, ½ cup at a time, until completely blended. Then add your ginger paste, cardamom, lemon zest, orange zest, orange juice, and coconut milk and blend until creamy.

Pour your batter into your pan and use a spatula to smooth out the top to makes sure it's even. Bake for an hour, or until you can poke a bamboo skewer into your cake and remove it cleanly.

Allow to cool for 10 minutes in the pan, and then use a metal spatula around the edges to loosen the cake from your pan. Using an oven mitt, flip your cake out of the pan into your hand, and then let it cool on a wire rack until it reaches room temperature.

While your cake cools, make your Whipped Coconut Cream.

Serve your cake with some Whipped Coconut Cream on top and some fresh berries and fruit.

MINI BUTTERFINGER CUPCAKES

The third Sunday of every month, around 1 p.m., Dan and I have a huge lunch at Foodswings in Williamsburg with anybody who wants to come and eat some good old-fashioned vegan diner food and hang out with the Shannons. If you ever find yourself in Brooklyn, you need to stop by and check out their very impressive menu; it will make you believe that really anything can be vegan. We recommend the Butterfinger milkshake.

MAKES 2½ DOZEN CUPCAKES

Baking spray

2¼ cups all-purpose flour

1½ cups sugar

½ cup margarine, softened

1¼ cups soy milk

3½ teaspoons baking powder

1 teaspoon crushed pink Himalayan salt

1 teaspoon vanilla extract

2 tablespoons applesauce

½ teaspoon Ener-G egg replacer, just the powder, not prepared per the instructions on the package

7 Chick-O-Sticks, crushed

1 batch Chocolate Ganache (page 400)

Preheat the oven to 350°F. Spray the cups in your favorite mini cupcake pan with baking spray.

In a large bowl, mix the flour, sugar, margarine, soy milk, baking powder, salt, vanilla, applesauce, and egg replacer with an electric mixer on low speed for about 3 minutes, until the batter is smooth. If you tilt your bowl a little, you can get a creamier batter. Fold in half of your crushed Chick-O-Sticks with a large spoon.

Fill the cups in your mini cupcake pan halfway with your batter. Bake for 8 to 10 minutes, until the tops start to turn a nice light sunny cream color. Immediately

move to a wire rack to cool.

Make your Chocolate Ganache while your cupcakes bake. Once your cupcakes have cooled, dip the tops into the ganache and put them back on the wire rack. Let the extra ganache run down the sides. Once they are all coated, sprinkle the remaining crushed Chick-O-Sticks evenly over the top. Let your cupcakes sit for about 5 minutes to let the ganache set before serving. The ganache will never really get hard, but you'll see that it gets kinda waxy looking.

MINI DALMATIAN CUPCAKES

Aggie, our bittiest Shannon, likes to bring me presents. She does it all day, every day. She brings me plastic bags, toy mice, dirty socks from the hamper…once she even brought me a shoe. And, if you've ever seen how small she is, you know that took real willpower—and, like, five minutes to drag it from the living room closet. I appreciate Agatha's determination, creativity, and of course her thoughtfulness. The morning after I made these, I woke up to Aggie sitting next to me in bed with one of these cupcakes on my pillow. What a nice way to start a day.

MAKES 2½ DOZEN MINI CUPCAKES

Baking spray

2¼ cups all-purpose flour

1⅓ cups sugar

⅔ cup vegetable shortening

1¼ cup soy milk

¼ teaspoon apple cider vinegar

3¼ teaspoons baking powder

1 teaspoon crushed pink Himalayan salt

2 teaspoons vanilla extract

4 tablespoons Ener-G egg replacer, just the powder, not prepared using the instructions on the package

½ cup vegan chocolate chips, crushed

1 Batch Chocolate Ganache (page 400)

Preheat the oven to 350°F. Spray your mini cupcake pan with a light coating of baking spray.

In a large bowl, mix the flour, sugar, shortening, soy milk, vinegar, baking powder, salt, and vanilla. Blend with a handheld mixer for about 3 minutes. Add the egg replacer and blend for another minute. Fold the vegan chocolate chips into the batter.

With a soup ladle, fill the mini cupcake pan cups halfway. Keep an eye on those vegan chocolate chips to make sure every cupcake gets some. Bake for 8 to 10 minutes, or until the cupcakes are golden on top and you can insert a bamboo skewer in the top and remove it cleanly from the largest cupcake. While your cupcakes bake, make your Chocolate Ganache.

Let your cupcakes cool on a rack until they reach room temperature. Dip the tops of the cupcakes in your ganache. Put them back on the wire rack, glazed side up, to let the ganache set.

MEXICAN HOT CHOCOLATE CUPCAKES

A certain portion of my life has been dedicated to searching out and locating ways to eat chocolate with chili pepper. They're uninteresting stories about mixing soy chocolate ice cream with Tabasco, or baking dozens of chocolate cookies till I figured out how much chili powder to add to get that kick at the end. Some flavors just really speak to certain palates, and mine loves dark chocolate with a dash of cayenne. If someone ever made a master list or database of Annie's favorite foods, Mexican hot chocolate would have its own category/folder/color code, depending on how they chose to record this data. Because really, there's so much you can do with Mexican hot chocolate: beverages, frozen treats, baked goods, candy. I love them all.

MAKES 1 DOZEN CUPCAKES

1 cup cocoa powder

2 cups all-purpose flour

1 tablespoon baking soda

1 tablespoon baking powder

Pinch of crushed pink Himalayan salt

2 teaspoons chili powder

Pinch of grated nutmeg

1 teaspoon ground cinnamon

1¼ cups soy milk

1 teaspoon apple cider vinegar

1 cup maple syrup

1 teaspoon orange juice

1 teaspoon vanilla extract

¾ cup sugar

12 vegan marshmallows (1 for each cupcake)

Preheat the oven to 350°F. Fill your cupcake pan with cupcake liners.

Sift the cocoa powder, flour, baking soda, baking powder, salt, chili powder, nutmeg, and cinnamon into a large bowl.

In another bowl, mix the soy milk and vinegar. Let sit for around a minute.

With an electric hand mixer, blend the maple syrup, orange juice, vanilla, and sugar into the flour mixture until smooth. Blend in the soy milk and vinegar. Mix your batter on medium speed for around 2 minutes, turning the bowl gently to get some air into the mix and getting any ingredients that are stuck to the sides.

With a ladle, fill each cupcake liner about three-quarters of the way. Press a vegan marshmallow into the top of each cupcake. Now, this is important: the marshmallows will melt. So make sure the marshmallows are in the cupcakes deep enough that only one side is exposed. That way, when they melt, they'll make a little pool of marshmallow that will cool and harden again rather than melt down the sides of the cupcake.

Bake the cupcakes for 20 to 25 minutes. Check on them often. Remove from the oven when you can remove a toothpick without any chocolate batter on it. Set the oven to broil or turn on your broiler. Move your cupcake pan to the broiler for 20 to 30 seconds to "roast" your marshmallows. Once they have a nice golden coating, they're ready to cool and enjoy.

TIN ROOF SUNDAE CUPCAKES

The tin roof is a somewhat suburban sundae concoction, consisting of vanilla ice cream topped with chocolate syrup and Spanish peanuts, that is often overlooked because it's awesomly simple. It would be a shame to skip over these cupcakes simply because they're a classic cupcake version of a classic sundae.

MAKES 1 DOZEN CUPCAKES

2¼ cups all-purpose flour

1½ cups sugar

½ cup margarine, softened

1¼ cups soy milk

3½ teaspoons baking powder

1 teaspoon crushed pink Himalayan salt

1 teaspoon vanilla extract

2 tablespoons applesauce

½ teaspoon Ener-G egg replacer, just the powder, not prepared per the instructions on the package

1 batch Chocolate Ganache (page 400)

¼ cup Spanish peanuts

Preheat the oven to 350°F. Fill your cupcake pan with cupcake liners.

In large bowl, mix the flour, sugar, margarine, soy milk, baking powder, salt, vanilla extract, applesauce, and egg replacer with an electric mixer on low speed for about 3 minutes, until the batter is smooth and creamy. If you tilt your bowl a little, you can get your batter even creamier.

Fill your cupcake liners halfway with your batter. Bake for 8 to 10 minutes, until the tops start to turn a nice light sunny cream color.

While your cupcakes bake, make your ganache and pour it into a shallow bowl.

Let your cupcakes cool on a wire rack until they reach room temperature. Dip the tops of your cupcakes in the ganache to get a nice light coating. Sprinkle a few peanuts on top of each coated cupcake. You may have to gently press your peanuts into the ganache to make sure they stick.

JEAN LUC'S CUPCAKES

Those of you who read our blog and are big Trekkies (most of you, I hope) will know that Captain Picard and I share a love of Earl Grey tea. I hope he'd also enjoy these Earl Grey cupcakes with an orange frosting—and I hope you do to. Make it so!

MAKES 1 DOZEN CUPCAKES

½ cup almond milk

6 bags Earl Grey tea

½ cup margarine, softened

1 cup sugar

2 tablespoons applesauce

1 teaspoon ground flaxseeds

¼ teaspoon vanilla extract or orange extract

¼ teaspoon grated orange peel

1½ cups all-purpose flour

2 teaspoons baking powder

¼ teaspoon crushed pink Himalayan salt

1 batch Ginger Orange Frosting (page 395)

Preheat the oven to 350°F. Place liners in your cupcake pan.

In a saucepan, simmer your almond milk over medium heat. Once it begins to bubble, add your bags of Earl Grey tea, remove your saucepan from the stove top, and let steep.

In a large bowl, blend the margarine and sugar until creamy and fluffy. Mix in the applesauce, flaxseeds, vanilla, and orange peel.

In another bowl, whisk together your flour, baking powder, and salt. Add the flour mixture to the creamed margarine ½ cup at a time. Squeeze your tea bags to get the most flavor you can into the almond milk, and then blend the tea-infused almond milk into your batter until it's smooth.

Fill your cupcake liners about three-quarters of the way full. Bake for 20 to 25 minutes, or until you can remove a bamboo skewer inserted into the largest cupcake cleanly.

While your cupcakes are baking, make your Orange Ginger Frosting.

Once your cupcakes have cooled, frost with your frosting and *engage*.

BABY PIÑA COLADA CUPCAKES

There is always something you have to watch out for when you make piña colada anything, and that's making sure your little piece of tropical-themed sweetness doesn't end up tasting like suntan lotion. I tried to keep the flavors subtle and natural where I could. We also kept these mini because they're easier to give away like that and you can enjoy a little cupcake at lunchtime without risking a potential sugar coma. They also look much cuter with a little drink umbrella.

MAKES 2½ DOZEN CUPCAKES

2⅓ cups all-purpose flour	1 teaspoon crushed pink Himalayan salt	1 teaspoon coconut milk, from a carton, not a can
1½ cups sugar	1¼ teaspoons rum or rum extract	
½ cup margarine, softened	3 tablespoons applesauce	1 batch Coconut Rum Frosting (page 397)
3½ teaspoons baking powder	1 cup crushed pineapple in juice	4 cups shredded raw coconut

Preheat the oven to 350°F. Line your cupcake pan with paper liners.

Mix the flour, sugar, margarine, baking powder, salt, rum, applesauce, pineapple, and coconut milk in a large bowl with a handheld electric mixer for 5 minutes on medium speed. You want the batter to be smooth and fluffy. Turn your bowl at a slight angle to make your batter a little fluffier.

Fill your cupcake liners three-quarters of the way and bake for 10 to 15 minutes. Remove the cupcakes from the oven when you can stick a toothpick in the center of one and remove it cleanly.

While your cupcakes are baking, make your Coconut Rum Frosting. Pour your shredded coconut into a shallow dish.

When your cupcakes are cool, frost with your Coconut Rum Frosting, roll the tops in your shredded coconut, and maybe add little paper umbrellas if you're feeling sunny.

LITTLE DEVIL'S FOOD CUPCAKES

Now, if you're not familiar with devil's food cake, it is light, fluffy chocolate cake that has a hint of coffee to it. Some brands and recipes don't add the coffee, but the fancy ones do, and who doesn't want to be fancy? We usually use this recipe as the base for those intricate, holiday-themed cupcakes because it goes so well with so many different types of frostings. You can find several different frostings in this book that work with this recipe that keeps it simple and classic—like the blue jeans of cupcake recipes.

MAKES 3 DOZEN CUPCAKES

2¼ cups all-purpose flour

1⅔ cups granulated sugar

¾ cup margarine, softened

⅔ cup baking cocoa

1¼ cups brewed coffee, at room temperature

1¼ teaspoons baking soda

1 teaspoon crushed pink Himalayan salt

1 teaspoon vanilla extract

¼ teaspoon baking powder

1 tablespoon plus 1 teaspoon applesauce

2 teaspoons Ener-G egg replacer, just the powder, not prepared as instructed on the package

¼ cup powdered sugar, optional

Preheat the oven to 350°F. Put your cupcake liners in your mini cupcake pan.

In a large bowl, blend all ingredients except the powdered sugar with an electric hand mixer for 2 to 3 minutes. You want your batter to be light and airy. I find it helpful to tilt the bowl slightly to help the batter get more fluffy.

Fill each cupcake liner two-thirds of the way, and bake for 5 to 8 minutes. You'll know they are ready when you can remove a bamboo skewer or toothpick inserted into the center of the largest cupcake cleanly.

Let the cupcakes cool on a wire rack before decorating with either powdered sugar dusted over the top or your favorite frosting.

MINI PEANUT BRITTLE CUPCAKES

We made them mini because they're easier to share that way—even if they're a little sticky…but that's kinda part of their charm. These little guys are the perfect breakfast cupcakes! They aren't your mama's cupcakes.

MAKES 2 TO 2½ DOZEN MINI CUPCAKES

1 batch Peanut Brittle Sauce (page 403)

2¼ cups all-purpose flour

1½ cups sugar

½ cup margarine, softened

1¼ cups soy milk

3½ teaspoons baking powder

1 teaspoon crushed pink Himalayan salt

1 teaspoon vanilla extract

2 tablespoons applesauce

½ teaspoon Ener-G egg replacer, the powder, not prepared as instructed on the package

Make your Peanut Brittle Sauce first. While your Peanut Brittle Sauce cools, make your cupcakes.

Preheat the oven to 350°F. Fill your cupcake pan with liners.

In a large bowl, mix the remaining ingredients with an electric mixer on low speed for about 3 minutes, until the batter is smooth. If you tilt your bowl a little, you can get a creamier batter.

Fill your cupcake liners halfway with your batter.

Use a small spoon to create a small bowl in the batter. Put 1 to 1½ teaspoons Peanut Brittle Sauce in the center of each small bowl. You'll want to make sure you get some peanuts in there. Try to keep the sauce in the center and keep it from spilling over the sides because it is pretty sticky.

Bake for 8 to 10 minutes, until the tops start to turn a nice light sunny cream color. Put the cupcakes on a rack to cool.

CARROT CAKE CUPCAKES

Fabulous. Cupcakes. Period.

MAKES 1 TO 1½ DOZEN CUPCAKES

Baking spray

1¼ cups granulated sugar

¼ cup brown sugar

1 cup olive oil

3 tablespoons applesauce

1 teaspoon Ener-G egg replacer, just

the powder, not prepared per the instructions on the package

2⅓ cups all-purpose flour

2 teaspoons ground cinnamon

1 teaspoon baking soda

1 teaspoon vanilla extract

½ teaspoon crushed pink Himalayan salt

3 cups shredded carrots

½ cup raw walnuts, chopped (you may want a little more to sprinkle over your frosting)

1 batch Cream Cheese Frosting (page 393)

Preheat the oven to 350°F. Spray a cupcake pan with baking spray.

In a large bowl, mix the sugars, oil, applesauce, and egg replacer with an electric hand mixer until smooth. Add the flour, cinnamon, baking soda, vanilla, and salt and blend until smooth.

If you bought preshredded carrots, you're going to want to crush them a little more with a pastry hand blender, or chop them up a bit more using a food processor. You don't want paste, just fine shavings or chips.

Stir your carrots and nuts into your cake batter.

Using a soupspoon, make small balls about the size of your cupcake pan cup. Place one batter ball in each

cup in the pan and bake for 20 to 25 minutes. Once you can insert a toothpick into the center of a cupcake and pull it out clean, remove the cupcakes from the oven and let them cool on a wire rack out of the pan.

While your cupcakes are baking, make your Cream Cheese Frosting.

Make sure the cupcakes are cool before you start frosting them. One of the best things about frosting is how it melts in your mouth, but it melts on hot cake too—especially vegan Cream Cheese Frosting. After you frost your cupcakes, sprinkle some crushed walnuts over the top.

CHEESECAKES, PUDDING, ICE CREAM, AND A FEW SURPRISES

Ever want to ruin a perfectly good afternoon? Do a Google image search of "cheesecake in space." The idea was that I wanted to see if astronauts were given dehydrated cheesecake on their missions. I mean, it's creamy and sweet—much like ice cream, though definitely thicker. I never did find an answer to this question. Perhaps someone at NASA will buy this book and write me with the answer. Hint, hint.

Nevertheless, cheesecake was one of the first desserts vegans successfully conquered. We looked cheesecake in the eyes and said, "You better get vegan if you know what's good for you," and cheesecake obliged. The downside to there being remarkable vegan cheesecakes all over the world now is that it can be easy to take an exceptional vegan cheesecake for granted.

Being ever the ambitious dreamers, we decided that

meant that we needed to make sure this section included the vegan cheesecakes that were more than just good... they were extraordinarily enjoyable while still being easy to make.

Now, I've heard it said that using vegan cream cheese is the "cheater's method," but if you weren't vegan and were making a cheesecake, you wouldn't make your cream cheese from scratch using milk, so why do you *have* to make your own vegan cream cheese? It doesn't have to be harder to be vegan if you don't want it to be. If you were the kind of not-yet-vegan who made your own cheese before you became vegan, that's cool, I guess, but most of us just got our cheese already made from the grocery store, and dramatic lifestyle changes can be hard to maintain. Working a healthy and compassionate lifestyle into your life doesn't mean you have to become a whole other person.

Having said all that, we have included a cashew cheesecake for those who want to really make a cheesecake from scratch. It's creamy and lovely too.

TURTLE CHEESECAKE

Vegan fudge sauce, pecans, chocolate cookie crust, and cheesecake, and wait for it ... *caramel!*

MAKES 1 CHEESECAKE

2 (8-ounce) packages vegan cream cheese (we recommend Tofutti Better Than Cream Cheese)

2 cups vegan sour cream

¾ cup sugar

2 teaspoons vanilla extract

¼ cup whole wheat flour

1 tablespoon ground flaxseeds

1 vegan chocolate cookie piecrust (we recommend Keebler Ready Crust

chocolate piecrust)

¼ cup toasted pecans

1 batch Hot Fudge Sauce (page 402)

1 batch Caramel Sauce (page 402)

Preheat the oven to 300°F.

In your largest mixing bowl, blend the vegan cream cheese, vegan sour cream, and sugar using an electric handheld mixer until smooth. Add the vanilla, flour, and flaxseeds and mix for about a minute. It's important to make sure there aren't any lumps. Pour your creamy filling into the chocolate crust.

Bake for 40 to 45 minutes. Check the center with a toothpick to make sure it's solid. Pull the cheesecake out of the oven when it is solid to the touch and passes the toothpick test or when the top starts to crack a little and begins pulling from the sides.

Cool on a wire rack for around an hour and then top with pecans, Hot Fudge Sauce, and Caramel Sauce.

Refrigerate overnight and then enjoy this wonderful treat!

NEW YORK CHEESECAKE

I grew up with New York cheesecake. Big, thick, virtually crustless slices of dreamy, creamy cheesecake. I could never finish a slice alone and suspect they were always secretly intended to share. I've always had these romantic ideas of this dream date: two people splitting a huge slice of New York cheesecake in a place like the Carnegie Deli at 3 a.m., after seeing a show or after a night of wandering the city. I've never done that, but I have walked through New York City at 3 a.m. and seen this scene a dozen times at numerous shops. By the time I was wandering the city with the love of my life, I was vegan. This isn't Carnegie cheesecake, but to be honest, it's been so long since I've had it that I don't think even the Carnegie Deli cheesecake is really what I remember it to be. But this "cheesecake" is better. It's vegan, and I can share it with the love of my life anywhere I want. I didn't even realize how much I missed this cheesecake until I tackled this recipe. Funny, I finally had my childhood dream date at thirty-five after I married the most amazing man I'd ever met.

MAKES 1 CHEESECAKE

CRUST
Vegetable shortening to grease your springform pan

1 cup all-purpose flour

½ cup margarine

¼ cup sugar

1 tablespoon applesauce

CHEESECAKE
5 (8-ounce) packages vegan cream cheese (we recommend Tofutti Better Than Cream Cheese)

1¾ cups sugar

3 tablespoons flour

1 tablespoon grated orange peel

1 tablespoon grated lemon peel

¼ teaspoon crushed pink Himalayan salt

4 tablespoons applesauce

2 tablespoons Ener-G egg replacer, just the powder, not made per the instructions on the package

½ cup vegan sour cream

½ to ¾ cup of your favorite berries for a topping

Preheat the oven to 400°F. Lightly grease a 9-inch springform pan with vegetable shortening.

In a bowl, mix the flour, margarine, sugar, and applesauce with a fork until a dough forms; gather into a ball. Press your dough into your springform pan in an even layer with some of the dough going up the sides to create a shallow bowl. Bake for 5 minutes and then set your crust aside to cool while you make your cheesecake filling.

Preheat the oven to 475°F.

In a bowl, blend the vegan cream cheese, sugar, flour, orange peel, lemon peel, and salt with an electric mixer on medium speed until smooth. Beat in the applesauce, egg replacer, and vegan sour cream on a low speed until well blended. Pour your cheesecake filling over your crust and use a spatula to make sure the top is smooth and level.

Bake for 15 minutes and then reduce the oven temperature to 200°F. Bake for an additional hour—no longer. The cheesecake may not appear done, but if a small area in the center seems soft, it will become solid when it cools. Don't do the toothpick test. Turn off the oven and leave the cheesecake in there 30 minutes longer. Remove from the oven and let it cool in the springform pan on a wire rack for 30 minutes.

Without releasing or removing the sides of the pan, run a metal spatula or a butter knife carefully along the sides of the cheesecake to loosen it. Refrigerate uncovered overnight for at least 9 hours but no longer than 48 hours.

Run a metal spatula or butter knife carefully around the sides of the cheesecake to loosen it again before unclasping the side of the pan. Leave your cheesecake on the bottom to serve, and don't forget your berries.

MINT CHOCOLATE CHIP CHEESECAKE

Yet another one of Dan's eating idiosyncrasies is that he hates the mint/chocolate flavor combination. He inherited this from his father—along with a number of other, more positive qualities. The Shannon clan still repeats the story of a late-night trip to the local ice cream shop for a hand-packed pint of chocolate chip ice cream, only to discover too late that it was in fact the dreaded *mint* chocolate chip! The horror! Anyway, I hope you like mint and chocolate paired together more than he does—because this is one delicious cheesecake. I adore it.

MAKES 1 CHEESECAKE

CRUST
Vegetable shortening to grease the springform pan

2 cups crushed vegan chocolate cookies (we recommend Oreo cookie wafers)

1/3 cup sugar

1/2 cup margarine, melted

CHEESECAKE
5 (8-ounce) packages vegan cream cheese (we recommend Tofutti Better Than Cream Cheese)

1 3/4 cups sugar

3 tablespoons flour

1 tablespoon pureed fresh mint leaves, or 1 teaspoon peppermint extract

1/4 teaspoon crushed pink Himalayan salt

4 tablespoons applesauce

2 tablespoons Ener-G egg replacer, just the powder, not made per the instructions on the package

1/2 cup vegan sour cream

2 to 3 drops green food coloring, optional

2 tablespoons vegan chocolate chips

Preheat the oven to 400°F. Lightly grease a 9-inch springform pan with vegetable shortening.

In a bowl, mix the vegan chocolate cookies, sugar, and margarine with a fork until a dough forms; gather into a ball. Press the dough into the springform pan in a very shallow bowl, with some dough going up the sides. Bake for 5 to 6 minutes, or until your crust is slightly browned. Set it aside to cool while you make your filling.

Preheat the oven to 475°F.

In a bowl, beat the vegan cream cheese, sugar, flour, mint, and salt with an electric mixer on medium speed for about 1 minute, or until smooth. Mix in the applesauce, egg replacer, vegan sour cream, and food coloring, if you want, on low speed until well blended. Then, with a large spoon, fold in your vegan chocolate chips. Pour your cheesecake filling over your crust in a nice even layer and bake for 15 minutes.

Reduce the oven temperature to 200°F. Bake for an additional hour. The cheesecake may not appear done. The small area in the center might seem soft, but it will become solid when it cools. Turn the oven off but leave your cheesecake in the oven for another 30 minutes. Then remove your cheesecake from the oven and let it cool in the springform pan on a wire rack for 30 minutes.

Without releasing the sides of your pan, run a metal spatula or a butter knife carefully along the sides of the cheesecake to loosen. Refrigerate uncovered overnight at least 9 hours but no longer than 48 hours.

Run a metal spatula or butter knife carefully around the sides of your cheesecake to loosen it again before unclasping the side of the pan. Leave the cheesecake on the bottom to serve.

SALTED CARAMEL LATTE CHEESECAKE

I'm a big fan of fancy sugary coffees. Dan's more of a "regular" coffee guy. This cheesecake takes one of my favorite latte flavors and rolls it into a cheesecake that even a gas-station-coffee aficionado will enjoy.

MAKES 1 CHEESECAKE

CRUST
Vegetable shortening to grease the
    springform pan
2 cups crushed vegan chocolate cookies
    (we recommend Oreo wafers)
⅓ cup sugar
½ cup margarine, melted

CHEESECAKE
1 tablespoon very strongly brewed espresso
5 (8-ounce) packages vegan cream cheese

(we recommend Tofutti Better Than
    Cream Cheese)
1 cup granulated sugar
1 cup brown sugar
4 tablespoons flour
1 tablespoon grated orange peel
1 tablespoon ground almond meal
½ teaspoon crushed pink Himalayan salt
4 tablespoons applesauce

2 tablespoons Ener-G egg replacer,
    just the powder, not made per the
    instructions on the package
1 tablespoon vegan sour cream

TOPPING
1 batch Caramel Sauce (page 402)
1½ teaspoons flaked sea salt

Preheat the oven to 400°F. Lightly grease a 9-inch springform pan with vegetable shortening.

In a bowl, mix the vegan chocolate cookies, sugar, and margarine with a fork until a sandy dough forms. Press your dough into your springform pan in an even layer, with some going up the sides lightly—making a shallow bowl. Bake your crust for 5 minutes, or until lightly browned. Set it aside to cool while you make your cheesecake filling.

Preheat the oven to 475°F.

In a bowl, beat your espresso, vegan cream cheese, sugar, brown sugar, flour, orange peel, almond meal, and salt with an electric handheld mixer on medium speed for about 1 minute, or until smooth. Blend in the applesauce, egg replacer, and vegan sour cream on low speed until well blended. Pour your cheesecake filling over the crust and smooth out the top with a spatula. Bake for 15 minutes.

Reduce the oven temperature to 200°F. Bake for an

additional hour. The cheesecake may not appear done, but it will become solid after your cheesecake cools. Turn off the oven and leave your cheesecake in the oven 30 minutes longer. Remove from the oven and cool in the pan on a wire rack away from drafts for 30 minutes.

Without releasing the side of the springform pan, run a metal spatula or a butter knife carefully along the sides of your cheesecake to loosen. Refrigerate uncovered overnight at least 9 hours but no longer than 48 hours.

While your cheesecake is cooling, make your Caramel Sauce.

Run a metal spatula or butter knife carefully around the side of the cheesecake to loosen again before removing the side of the pan. Leave the cheesecake on the bottom of the pan to serve. Drizzle Caramel Sauce and sprinkle some sea salt over each piece of cheesecake before serving.

CHOCOLATE ORANGE CASHEW CHEESECAKE

Cashew-based vegan cheeses, while sounding kinda granola-y, are actually often quite delicious and decadent. This cheesecake takes the idea of cashew cheese to a whole other level. Throw in a classic orange-chocolate flavor combination, and you've got yourself a winner.

MAKES 1 CHEESECAKE

CRUST
1 cup crushed raw walnuts

1 cup dried apricots

¼ teaspoon crushed pink Himalayan salt

FILLING
⅓ cup coconut oil

⅓ cup agave nectar

¼ teaspoon cornstarch

2 cups raw cashews, soaked in water overnight

1 tablespoon orange juice with pulp

1 teaspoon vanilla extract

1 cup vegan chocolate sauce

In your favorite food processor, blend the walnuts, apricots, and salt until they are completely mixed and sticking together to form a dough.

Gently press your dough into a 9-inch glass pie pan in an even layer. Make sure that the edges are well packed and that the base is relatively even throughout. Be sure to scrape the sides of your food processor so you get all the dough.

In a saucepan, heat the coconut oil and agave nectar over low heat until the oil becomes liquid and begins to bubble. Use a whisk to blend the oil and agave nectar. Once the mixture is smooth, whisk in the cornstarch. In your food processor, blend the agave nectar mixture with the cashews, orange juice, and vanilla until the filling is very smooth and creamy.

Pour your filling onto the crust and smooth it out with a spatula. Drizzle 2 to 3 tablespoons of chocolate sauce over the top in either a decorative pattern or randomly. Try to keep the sauce from getting within ½ inch of the edge. Cover your cheesecake and place in the freezer overnight.

To serve, remove from the freezer about 30 minutes before serving and have the remaining chocolate sauce slightly warmed to drizzle over each piece as you serve.

PUMPKIN PIE SOUFFLÉ

Everyone loves pumpkin pie. And its creamy texture lends itself extremely well to being reinvented as a soufflé. You can enjoy this recipe as a fancy dessert with a fall-flavors meal, or just any old time you're craving something cinnamony and sweet.

MAKES 2 SOUFFLÉS

½ cup pumpkin puree

1 tablespoon agave nectar

½ cup sugar (you'll need more to coat your ramekins)

3 tablespoons plus 2 teaspoons all-purpose flour

½ teaspoon vanilla extract

2 tablespoons Ener-G egg replacer, just the powder, not made per the instructions on the package

1 ½ teaspoons pumpkin pie spice

Pinch of crushed pink Himalayan salt

2 teaspoons cream of tartar

Olive oil cooking spray

Preheat the oven to 375°F.

In a large mixing bowl, blend the pumpkin puree, agave nectar, sugar, flour, vanilla, egg replacer, pumpkin pie spice, salt, and cream of tartar until smooth. Spray 2 small ramekins with olive oil cooking spray and then coat with sugar. I find the 6-ounce tall ramekins work best.

Fill each ramekin three-quarters of the way with batter and bake for 30 to 35 minutes.

TIP: If you take your puffed-up soufflé from a warm kitchen into a cold room, it's guaranteed to fall, so keep in mind room temperature when serving. It'll make a huge difference and will also keep you from thinking you did something wrong in the preparation if your soufflé does fall. It can be heartbreaking to see a soufflé fall, but it happens, and they still taste just as sweet and lovely.

Soufflés

Throughout the late eighties and nineties, soufflés played a key role in American cinema. In cartoons and comedies, deflated soufflés were the punch line for jokes and the embodiment of disappointment in the kitchen. The thing is that any banana head with a whisk and a dozen eggs can make a soufflé with eggs. If you really want to be a kitchen superstar—make one of these things vegan.

I know my role as a cookbook author, food blogger, and vegan advocate is to tell you how easy and fun it was figuring out how to beat the egg conspiracy that surrounds this French dessert—but here's the truth. The first time I made a vegan soufflé that rose like a pillar of chocolate from its little ramekin home,

I was shocked that it worked. I couldn't stop giggling and called Dan into the small, ancient kitchen in Virginia to witness this wonder before it fell. I was terrified it would fall. I couldn't stop talking his face off about how when you bake this strange batter at just the right temperature, all those little trapped air bubbles expand, and next thing you know you have a soufflé. A fluffy pudding that will make you feel like you can do anything.

Some experiments during this project were more successful than others. Figuring out soufflés…well, that was a victory for us all! You can find the Baby Sour Cream and Chive Soufflés in Chapter 4, "Dinner Entrées" on page 243.

BANANA CRÉME BRÛLÉE

This crème brûlée recipe replaces the massive amounts of eggs in a traditional recipe with bananas—which not only make it vegan but give it a unique flavor as well.

MAKES 4 CRÈMES BRÛLÉES

3 large ripe bananas

⅓ cup sugar

1 package silken tofu

¼ teaspoon cornstarch

¼ teaspoon Ener-G egg replacer, just the powder, not prepared the way the package instructs

¼ teaspoon nutritional yeast

1½ teaspoons vanilla extract

Preheat the oven to 300°°F.

Cut one of the bananas into thin slices and toss it into a bowl with 2 tablespoons of the sugar.

In your favorite food processor, blend the remaining 2 bananas, the remaining 3 tablespoons plus 1 teaspoon sugar, the silken tofu, cornstarch, egg replacer, nutritional yeast, and vanilla until they're smooth and creamy. Pour the custard into 4 (4-ounce) ramekins

and then top with a layer of sliced sugared bananas. Bake for 10 minutes, or until the top is golden brown.

Then, if you have a crème brûlée torch, you can go over the top of the bananas again to make sure they get a crispy crust, but most of us don't have one of those, so we can quickly broil them for 30 seconds with the ramekins close to the flames.

VANILLA BEAN PUDDING

Some foodies think you need a few eggs to make a nice vanilla pudding and ironically never learn that you can make this classic treat healthier and easier by thickening it with cornstarch and skipping the dairy. This recipe is not only better for you than those rich custardy things…it's supereasy.

MAKES 4 TO 6 SERVINGS

⅓ cup sugar

2 tablespoons cornstarch

2 tablespoons Ener-G egg replacer, just the powder, not prepared the way you're instructed to on the package

⅛ teaspoon crushed pink Himalayan salt

2 cups vanilla soy milk (you may need a little more if your pudding reduces too much)

Seeds scraped from ½ vanilla bean

2 tablespoons margarine, softened

1 teaspoon vanilla extract

In a saucepan, mix the sugar, cornstarch, egg replacer, and salt. Stir the mixture while pouring in the soy milk and heating the saucepan over medium heat. Add the vanilla seeds to your pot. Stir constantly. The pudding will start to thicken as it boils. Boil and stir for about a minute.

Remove from the heat and pour your pudding-thus-far into a large mixing bowl with high sides. Add the margarine and vanilla. Blend with a hand mixer at the highest setting with the whisk attachments. One thing I like to do is turn the bowl slightly to the side; I think it makes the mixer whip a little more air in there and the pudding comes out a little lighter. Do that for about a minute; then cover the bowl and put it in the fridge for about an hour, or until chilled.

CHOCOLATE HAZELNUT PUDDING

Chocolate has become the ultimate decadent treat. All over the world people have found ways to bake, liquefy, and soufflé what was once a simple treat into a guilty pleasure. When we were in Belgium in 2012, we enjoyed several different types of vegan dark chocolate and hands down found the toasted hazelnut dark chocolate bark at Elisabeth the best. It inspired us to level up our simple chocolate pudding into something really special.

MAKES 4 TO 6 SERVINGS

½ cup sugar

2 tablespoons cornstarch

2 tablespoons Ener-G egg replacer, just the powder, not prepared per the instructions on the package

⅛ teaspoon crushed pink Himalayan salt

1 teaspoon ground hazelnuts

½ cup baking chocolate

2 cups vanilla soy milk (you may need a little more if your pudding reduces too much)

2 tablespoons margarine, softened

1 teaspoon vanilla extract

In a saucepan, mix the sugar, cornstarch, egg replacer, and salt. Add the hazelnuts and chocolate and stir the mixture while pouring in the soy milk and heating the saucepan over medium heat. The mix will start to thicken as it boils. Boil and stir for about a minute.

Remove from heat and pour your pudding-thus-far into a large mixing bowl with high sides and add margarine and vanilla. Blend with a hand mixer at the highest setting with the flat beater attachments. Make sure all the chocolate gets blended in. Turn your bowl slightly to the side while you whip the pudding to get a little more air in there and make it a little lighter. Blend for about a minute; then cover the bowl and put it in the fridge for about an hour, or until chilled.

BUTTERSCOTCH PUDDING

This is my very favorite of the puddings.

MAKES 4 TO 6 SERVINGS

⅔ cup plus 4 tablespoons packed brown sugar

2 tablespoons cornstarch

2 tablespoons Ener-G egg replacer, just the powder, not prepared per the instructions on the package

⅛ teaspoon crushed pink Himalayan salt

2 cups vanilla soy milk (you may need a little more if your pudding reduces too much)

4 tablespoons margarine, softened

2 teaspoons vanilla extract

2 to 4 drops yellow food coloring, optional

In a saucepan, mix the brown sugar, cornstarch, egg replacer, and salt. Stir the mixture while pouring in the soy milk and heating the saucepan over medium heat. Stir constantly. The mixture will start to thicken as it boils. Boil and stir for about a minute.

Remove from the heat and pour your pudding-thus-far into a large mixing bowl with high sides. Add the margarine and vanilla. This pudding will not naturally have that golden brown color of old-school butter-scotch Jell-O pudding. If you want that kind of mythical beast, you can add a little yellow food coloring at this point. Then blend with a hand mixer at the highest setting with the whisk attachments. Try turning your bowl slightly to the side. I think it makes the mixer whip a little more air in there and your pudding comes out a little lighter. Do that for about a minute; then cover the bowl and put it in the fridge about an hour, or until chilled.

COCONUT TAPIOCA PUDDING

For years I avoided tapioca pudding because no one could tell me what tapioca really was. I figured if no one knew, it had to be really bad. But I was wrong. Tapioca pearls are just a starch from cassava roots that's been made into itty bitty balls. They're actually really lovely—especially in this coconut and vanilla pudding. This recipe requires you to start the night before you want to serve it.

MAKES 4 TO 6 SERVINGS

2 cups coconut milk, from a carton, not a can

½ cup small-pearl tapioca

⅓ cup sugar

2 tablespoons cornstarch

2 tablespoons Ener-G egg replacer, just use the powder, not prepared per the instructions on the package

⅛ teaspoon crushed pink Himalayan salt

2 tablespoons margarine, softened

2 teaspoons vanilla extract

In a large bowl, pour 1 cup of the coconut milk over your tapioca pearls and cover with foil. Put in the fridge and let chill overnight.

The next day, in a saucepan, mix the sugar, cornstarch, egg replacer, and salt. Stir while pouring in the remaining 1 cup coconut milk. Heat your saucepan over medium heat, stirring constantly. The mix will start to thicken as it boils. Boil and stir for about a minute.

Remove from the heat and mix in the margarine, vanilla, and coconut milk–tapioca pearls mixture. Pour the mixture into a large mixing bowl with high sides and gently blend with a whisk until smooth. Turn your bowl slightly to the side to get a little more air in there. It will help your pudding come out a little lighter. Whisk for about 3 minutes; then cover the bowl with foil and put in the fridge for about an hour, or until chilled.

COCONUT KEY LIME PIE PUDDING

This is a combination of a few different recipes to make a creamy, summery treat. You'll need to start this recipe the night before you want to serve it.

MAKES 4 TO 6 SERVINGS

KEY LIME PUDDING
½ cup sugar

3 tablespoons cornstarch

¼ teaspoon crushed pink Himalayan salt

⅔ cup water

1 tablespoon margarine, softened

1 teaspoon lime juice

2 teaspoons lime zest

2 drops green food coloring, optional

COCONUT CREAM
1 (14-ounce) can coconut milk

2 tablespoons tapioca flour

1 tablespoon vanilla extract

1 teaspoon cornstarch

¼ teaspoon agave nectar

¼ to ⅓ cup powdered sugar

GRAHAM CRACKER TOPPING
1 sheet graham cracker

1 teaspoon agave nectar

Put your can of coconut milk in the fridge to chill overnight.

To make the pudding, mix the sugar, cornstarch, and salt in a large saucepan. Gradually stir in the water and heat over medium heat. You want to whisk it constantly, until the mixture thickens and begins to bubble. Boil and stir for around a minute and then remove from the heat.

Whisk in the margarine, lime juice, and lime zest until the margarine melts and the pudding is smooth. Now, here's where you can decide if you want to add the food coloring. If you do add it, add 1 drop at a time and whisk it in thoroughly before adding the second drop.

Cover with plastic wrap and put in the fridge for 2 hours, or until your pudding has set.

While your Key Lime Pudding is chilling, make the Coconut Cream. Combine the coconut milk, tapioca flour, vanilla, cornstarch, and agave nectar in a large mixing bowl, and blend with your hand mixer on medium for 30 seconds. Gradually add the powdered sugar and blend on the highest setting for at least 3 minutes. You want to stop adding the powdered sugar when the mix begins to get fluffy and smooth, almost like whipped cream. Cover with plastic wrap and put in the fridge for ½ hour to thicken.

In your busy little food processor or blender, mix the graham crackers and agave nectar until they form little pebbles and crumbs.

To serve, spoon equal amounts of Key Lime Pudding and Coconut Cream into a dish, and top with the Graham Cracker Topping. Don't forget to invite a few friends over to enjoy this with you! Dessert loves company.

S'MORES PUDDING

Campfire fun in your kitchen.

MAKES 4 TO 6 SERVINGS

1 batch Chocolate Hazelnut Pudding (page 368)

⅓ cup vegan marshmallows

1 batch Graham Cracker Topping (page 370)

While your Chocolate Hazelnut Pudding is cooling, lightly roast your marshmallows on bamboo skewers over one of the burners on your stovetop.

Once your Chocolate Hazelnut Pudding is firm and ready to serve, spoon it into a dish and top with roasted marshmallows and Graham Cracker Topping.

CHAI TEA CASHEW ICE CREAM

Many people don't know this about me, but my uncle Wendall used to work for Baskin-Robbins. I'm not sure exactly what his job title was, but basically he worked in marketing and invented ice cream flavors. All I really remember about him was that he was very kind, that he died when I was young (long before his wife), and that he wore ties with ice cream cones and sundaes on them. He also played some role in the original marketing of Tofutti, though I'm not really sure what. I'd like to think if he were still around today, he would read our blog and at least enjoy the creativity. I'd also like to think he would approve of what we did with the maiden run of our new ice cream maker. This recipe has all the warm flavor and spice of our almond chai drink recipe, and complements the flavor of the cashews rather than trying to hide it, sort of like a good friendship. It brings out the best in everyone.

You're going to need to soak your cashews and prep your ice cream maker (see below) the night before you make your ice cream.

MAKES 4 TO 6 SERVINGS

2 cups raw cashews	⅛ teaspoon ground cinnamon	1 ripe banana
1¼ cups water	⅛ teaspoon ground cardamom	4 tablespoons pumpkin puree
3 bags organic Darjeeling tea	⅛ teaspoon ground cloves	1 tablespoon vanilla extract
¼ cup agave nectar	2 pinches of crushed black peppercorns	1 tablespoon coconut milk

Follow the instructions for your ice cream maker. You might need ice and salt or you might need to freeze a gel core overnight, so it's important to know what you need to get or do before you start.

Soak your raw cashews for 10 to 12 hours in a deep bowl.

In your food processor, blend your cashews for 5 to 8 minutes, until they become a smooth paste. Stop the machine a few times to scrape the sides. I know it's hard to be patient, and it will seem like it takes forever, but it's worth it to get the right texture.

In a saucepan, heat the water to a rapid boil over medium heat. Add the tea bags and reduce the heat to a simmer. Simmer for 5 minutes. Remove the tea bags.

Stir in the agave nectar, cinnamon, cardamom, cloves, and pepper and heat to a boil. Once the tea starts to boil, remove the saucepan from the heat.

Pour your tea into the blended cashews. Add the banana, pumpkin puree, vanilla, and coconut milk to the food processor and blend for another 2 minutes, until the mixture is completely combined.

Pour the mixture into your ice cream maker and turn it on. Ours took 30 minutes to make, but I know some others take longer. You're going to have to check your ice cream maker instructions.

The one serving tip I will share is to stress the importance of investing in a good ice cream scoop. You'll be happy you did.

PEANUT BUTTER AND PRETZEL-SWIRLED CHOCOLATE ICE CREAM

Yes, we could have come up with some clever quippy name for this—but then you may have skipped over this recipe, not realizing it was the one that'll make your summer as magical as those soda commercials always promise. If you're skeptical, remember: if you use salt correctly, it can level up your desserts into a whole new stage of sweet awesomeness. The timeless combination of peanut butter and chocolate is beloved in America, but when you add the bits of pretzel…you create something that goes beyond the classic. You have a masterpiece.

Heads up: you'll need to start this recipe the night before you make your ice cream and then let your ice cream chill out overnight.

MAKES 4 TO 6 SERVINGS

2 tablespoons Hot Fudge Sauce (page 402)

1½ cups raw cashews

1 ripe banana

1 teaspoon vanilla extract

3 tablespoons vegan chocolate chips

5 teaspoons baking chocolate

¼ teaspoon crushed pink Himalayan salt

1 teaspoon arrowroot

¾ cup sugar

1 cup coconut milk, from a can

2 tablespoons coconut oil

⅓ cup creamy peanut butter

¼ cup broken pretzels with salt (try to avoid the dust)

Follow the instructions for your ice cream maker. You might need ice and salt or you might need to freeze a gel core overnight, so it's important to know what you need to get or do before you start.

Make your Hot Fudge Sauce the night before so it's at room temperature by the time you start making your ice cream.

In your favorite food processor, blend the cashews, banana, vanilla, vegan chocolate chips, baking chocolate, salt, arrowroot, sugar, coconut milk, and coconut oil until you get a smooth and creamy mix. Blend for at least 4 minutes, though, to make it as smooth as you can.

Pour your mixture into your ice cream machine and turn it on. Let it mix for around an hour. Right before it is solid and set, add your peanut butter and Hot Fudge Sauce into the ice cream while it's still churning. Sprinkle the large pretzel bits in.

Stop your machine and transfer your ice cream to an airtight container. Put your ice cream in the freezer and freeze overnight.

Reheat your remaining Hot Fudge Sauce the next day so you can serve it drizzled over your ice cream.

COOKIES AND CREAM ICE CREAM

Like most Americans in my generation, I can relate cookies and an innate desire to eat all the cookies ever with a lovable blue monster that spoke baby talk. I was tempted to tell you to add blue food coloring to this recipe for just that reason, but the truth is, if you really want to pay homage to our azure friend, I suggest you wear blue while you enjoy this ice cream.

You may need to prep your ice cream maker the night before you make your ice cream (see below).

MAKES 4 TO 6 SERVINGS

4 cups coconut milk

2 tablespoons coconut flour

1 teaspoon cornstarch

1 cup sugar

1 tablespoon coconut oil

¼ teaspoon crushed pink Himalayan salt

1 tablespoon vanilla extract

⅓ cup crushed vegan chocolate cookies (we recommend Oreo wafers)

Follow the instructions on your ice cream maker to prep your machine. We have to freeze the core of our machine overnight, but I know some machines require ice. Every machine is different, so it's important to know what your machine needs.

Blend the coconut milk, coconut flour, cornstarch, sugar, coconut oil, salt, and vanilla with an electric handheld mixer until the sugar melts and the mixture is completely blended. Pour your coconut milk mixture into your ice cream machine and turn it on. Let it mix for around an hour. Right before your ice cream is set, sprinkle your crushed cookies into the ice cream while it's still churning.

Once your cookie bits are blended in, stop your machine and transfer your ice cream to an airtight container. Put your ice cream in the freezer and freeze overnight.

Leaving Your Signature...

For almost one hundred years, there has been a debate in American homes…is Betty Crocker a real person? One of the strongest arguments for her physical existence was the hundreds and hundreds of letters sent in response to inquiries on topics ranging from flour storage to dinner party tips that were sent out to aspiring bakers, chefs, and hostesses. These letters were typed, they name-dropped Gold Medal flour, and later General Mills products, in bold type, but they were always personalized with responses that actually answered the questions these (mostly) women had. They also included a signature.

We all know this signature—even if we don't know we do.

Betty Crocker's signature is curly and feminine while being more legible than any other signature I've ever seen. Really, this should have been the first tip that Betty wasn't real.

That signature came about after Samuel Gale, the department manager who was the mastermind behind Betty Crocker, held an impromptu contest among the female employees. The winning script was humble while still being pretty and distinct. Of course, I think what put the submission of the winning secretary, Florence Lindeberg, over the top was that it could be clearly read.

Shortly after Florence's win, that signature would grace hundreds of letters and countless products and become one of the most famous trademarks in America.

CRISPS AND COBBLERS

Ever hear the term "humble pie"? Well, that's what crisps and cobblers are all about. They aren't as showy and complicated as those elusive diva pies with their frilly latticework, but they have all the warm spices and sweet fruit... and they come with a lot less drama.

Everyone can make a crisp or cobbler, and really they should. They're incredibly easy and go great with a scoop of soy or coconut ice cream. If you ever find yourself wondering what to make for a party or get-together full of not-yet-vegans... well, this is a dessert that will get a ton of praise for tasting just like its non-vegan peers.

APPLE, PEAR, AND WALNUT CRISP

Every autumn should include an apple crisp... correction—this apple crisp. If you find it's November and you haven't had an apple crisp yet... you're doing it wrong.

MAKES 8 TO 10 SERVINGS

5 Granny Smith apples, cored and sliced

3 firm pears, cored and sliced

4 tablespoons lemon juice

2 tablespoons granulated sugar

1 cup brown sugar

½ cup whole wheat flour

4 tablespoons crushed raw walnuts

½ cup old-fashioned oats

1 teaspoon ground cinnamon

¼ teaspoon ground ginger

½ teaspoon grated nutmeg

¼ teaspoon crushed pink Himalayan salt

⅓ cup margarine, plus more to grease your baking dish

Preheat the oven to 350°F. Lightly grease a 7 x 11-inch baking dish with margarine.

In a large mixing bowl, toss the apples, pears, lemon juice, and sugar. Spoon the apples and pears into the prepared dish and set aside.

In another bowl, mix the brown sugar, flour, walnuts, oats, cinnamon, ginger, nutmeg, and salt with a large spoon until combined. Add the margarine and blend with an electric handheld mixer until there are no clumps.

Spread the oat mixture evenly over the apples and pears. Bake for 45 to 50 minutes, or until the juices are bubbling and the topping is, ya know, crisp.

POMEGRANATE, CRANBERRY, AND CHERRY CRISP

This is the crisp that has saved more Christmases than Bruce Willis and Mel Gibson combined. Now, you might be wondering why it's not in the "Holiday Favorites" chapter…and that's because pomegranates are at their best in October (at least in my neck of the woods), so this recipe is also a nice gooey red treat for a Halloween party. It's also a sweet way to start a day with a large hot cocoa. The point being that this crisp transcends its holiday-ness and is a wonderful recipe meant for the world to enjoy whether "Jingle Bells" is playing in the background or not.

MAKES 6 SERVINGS

2 cups frozen cherries, defrosted

1 cup Can-Free Cranberry Sauce (page 447)

½ cup granulated sugar

½ cup plus 2 tablespoons brown sugar

1 ½ teaspoons ground cinnamon

¼ cup cornstarch

½ teaspoon ground ginger

1 cup whole raw pomegranate seeds

½ cup whole wheat flour

½ cup old-fashioned oats

¼ cup margarine, softened

Vegetable shortening for greasing your baking dish

Preheat the oven to 375°F. Grease the bottom and sides of an 8 x 8-inch glass baking dish with vegetable shortening.

In your saucepan, mix the cherries in their juice, Can-Free Cranberry sauce, sugar, 2 tablespoons of the brown sugar, 1 teaspoon of the cinnamon, and the cornstarch and ginger. Cook over medium heat while stirring constantly. Once your fruit mixture begins to bubble and thicken, gently stir in the pomegranate seeds and remove from the heat. Pour the fruit mix-

ture into the baking dish. Use a spatula to spread out your fruit in an even layer.

In a mixing bowl, blend the flour, the remaining ½ cup brown sugar, the oats, margarine, and the remaining ½ teaspoon cinnamon with an electric handheld mixer until the mixture forms large crumbs. Sprinkle over your fruit.

Bake for 30 to 35 minutes, or until the topping is golden brown and your fruit is bubbling.

BLUEBERRY CRISP

Sometimes you just need to be alone with some blueberries. The cinnamon and sugar can add ambiance, but really…this crisp is all about you and some blueberries.

MAKES 8 TO 10 SERVINGS

5 cups frozen blueberries, defrosted

1 tablespoon lemon juice

1 teaspoon lemon peel, grated

2 tablespoons granulated sugar

¾ cup brown sugar

½ cup whole wheat flour

½ cup old-fashioned oats

¾ teaspoon ground cinnamon

¾ teaspoon grated nutmeg

Pinch of crushed pink Himalayan salt

⅓ cup margarine (you'll need more to grease your baking dish)

Preheat the oven to 350°F. Lightly grease a 7 x 11-inch baking dish with margarine.

In a large mixing bowl, toss the blueberries in their juice, lemon juice, lemon peel, and granulated sugar. Spoon the dressed blueberries into the prepared dish and set aside.

In another bowl, mix the brown sugar, flour, oats, cinnamon, nutmeg, and salt with a large spoon until combined. Add the margarine and blend with an electric handheld mixer until there are no clumps.

Spread the sugared oat mixture evenly over the blueberries. Bake for 45 to 50 minutes, until the juices are bubbling and the topping is golden brown.

SPICED PEACH AND WALNUT CRISP

I lived in Georgia and thought I knew everything about peaches. I drove on multiple streets dedicated to peach trees, and I think they had their own mall. They definitely had local vendors on the side of the road that sold pretty rosy peaches the size of softballs.

It's easy to get a little peach crazy when you have access to that kind of peach supply; you can build up an impressive arsenal of peachy recipes. This is one of those recipes.

MAKES 6 TO 8 SERVINGS

Vegetable shortening for greasing your baking dish

4½ cups fresh peaches (5 to 6 peaches, pitted and sliced)

1 Granny Smith apple, cored and sliced

⅓ cup granulated sugar

¼ teaspoon ground ginger

1 teaspoon ground cinnamon

¼ teaspoon grated nutmeg

2 pinches ground cloves

½ cup old-fashioned oats

½ cup brown sugar

¼ cup whole wheat flour

¼ cup margarine, softened

⅓ cup crushed walnuts

Preheat the oven to 375°F.

Grease a 2-quart glass baking dish with vegetable shortening.

In a large bowl, very gently mix the peaches, apple slices, sugar, ginger, ½ teaspoon of the cinnamon, the nutmeg, and cloves with a large spoon. Pour your spiced peaches and apples into your greased baking dish and use a spatula to make the fruit level and even.

In the same bowl, mix the oats, brown sugar, flour, and remaining ½ teaspoon cinnamon with an electric handheld mixer. Blend in the margarine with a pastry blender so that you get large crumbs. If you use your electric mixer, it won't turn out right—so don't do that. Using a large spoon, mix in the crushed walnuts. Sprinkle your walnut crumbs over the spiced peach mix.

Bake for 30 minutes, or until your walnut topping is golden brown and your peaches are tender.

You'll want to serve it warm, but you'll need to let it cool. Crisps can turn into little dishes of molten lava—and that's no fun to eat.

POMEGRANATE AND PEACH COBBLER

From pomegranate-peach Popsicles to smoothies to salads, the combo is popping up all over. This cobbler brings these powerful flavors together in a way that accentuates their strengths—like any good relationship should.

MAKES 6 TO 8 SERVINGS

- ½ cup plus 1 tablespoon granulated sugar
- 1 tablespoon cornstarch
- 5 to 6 fresh peaches, pitted and sliced
- ¼ cup pomegranate seeds
- 2 teaspoons pomegranate juice
- ¼ cup whole wheat flour
- 1 ½ teaspoons baking powder
- ½ teaspoon crushed pink Himalayan salt
- 3 tablespoons margarine, softened
- ½ cup vanilla soy milk
- 2 tablespoons raw sugar

Preheat the oven to 400°F.

In a saucepan, mix ½ cup of the sugar and the cornstarch. Stir the peaches, pomegranate seeds, and juice into your sugar. Cook over medium heat while stirring constantly for 5 minutes. Once the sugared fruit begins to bubble, remove it from the heat and pour it into an ungreased glass casserole dish. Use your spoon to make sure the fruit is in an even layer.

In a mixing bowl, blend the flour, remaining 1 tablespoon sugar, the baking powder, and salt with a whisk.

With a pastry blender, mix the margarine into the flour until it begins to look like little clumps the size of peas. Using an electric handheld mixer, blend in the soy milk until the dough is smooth and has no lumps.

Drop spoonfuls of the dough onto the fruit in little clumps. Once you have dropped in all the dough, sprinkle your raw sugar over the top.

Bake for 30 minutes, or until your dough is golden brown.

BLACKBERRY, RASPBERRY, AND ALMOND COBBLER

If you've ever spent any time in the Pacific Northwest, you've probably seen the hillsides overgrown with creeping blackberry bushes. These lush little berries were all over my college campus and were a great way to snack or stain your clothes after a long run or a trip to the library. Over the years, the combination of adoration and college poverty led to several recipes including these black beauties. This is one of the best ones.

MAKES 6 SERVINGS

1 cup frozen blackberries, defrosted (keep the juice)

1 cup frozen raspberries, defrosted (keep the juice)

1 large ripe pear, cored and diced very small

1 teaspoon lemon juice

1 cup sugar

¾ cup all-purpose flour

¼ cup almond flour

2 teaspoons baking powder

½ teaspoon crushed pink Himalayan salt

1 cup almond milk

½ cup margarine, melted

2 pints vanilla soy ice cream

Preheat the oven to 375°F.

In a large mixing bowl, stir together the blackberries, raspberries, diced pear, lemon juice, and sugar. Cover and refrigerate for 20 to 25 minutes.

In a separate large bowl, blend the flours, baking powder, salt, and almond milk. Stir in the melted butter until blended. Spread your batter evenly into an ungreased 8 x 8-inch glass baking dish. Gently pour your mixed berries over the batter.

Bake for 40 to 55 minutes, or until the dough rises and turns a golden brown. Serve warm, spooned into little dishes with some vanilla soy ice cream on top.

PIES AND TARTS—WHEN BAD PIES GET GOOD

There's nothing I love more than eating a nice piece of pie, and for years there was nothing I hated more than making them. Seriously, all those steps, and you had to make sure everything was just right. I'm exhausted even typing about it. *Gah.* It can be hard to even see the point.

But in a way, it's a lot like those colorful Magic Eye posters that used to clutter up the malls with promises of sailboats and views of the Grand Canyon... once you just relax and stop trying so hard, it just kind of comes together. Well, maybe it's not that easy. But it happens. Unlike that idiot you dated in college—you can make bad pies go good.

I actually love baking pies now. And you can't have a great pie without a great crust. Here are a few tips for how to make a crust worthy of all those ripe blueberries, tangy cherries, and sweet apples.

You need the right pan. I recommend investing in a good glass pie pan, not only because it won't give you a soggy crust like a shiny metal one, but also because you can see what's going on with your crust while you're baking. Beginning pie bakers can appreciate that.

Don't grease your pie pans. There's already enough fat in your crust. Adding more will only make a gooey mess.

To prevent your crust edges from getting too brown, you'll need to mold 2-inch strips of foil to make a ring around the edge of the pie. Remove the foil 15 minutes before your pie is done baking so that the edges can catch up with the rest of the crust.

Rolling your dough out on plastic wrap can save you a step and lots of cracks and drama. You want your dough to be firm but still pliable when you pull it out of the fridge. If it's crumbly, though, that's okay. Just press the cracks with moist fingers to fix any imperfections and then let your dough warm a little till it's more pliable.

BASIC PIECRUST

The little black dress of piecrusts.

MAKES 2 CRUSTS—ENOUGH FOR 1 REGULAR PIE OR 2 OPEN-FACED PIES

1 cup all-purpose flour (you're going to want more to flour surfaces)

1 cup whole wheat flour

¾ teaspoon crushed pink Himalayan salt

⅔ cup plus 2 tablespoons vegetable shortening

3 to 6 tablespoons cold water

Refrigerate your water for 2 hours before making your crust.

In a medium bowl, mix the flours and salt with a whisk. Cut the shortening into your flour, and then use a pastry blender to mix your dough until it becomes little clumps that look like small peas. Sprinkle in the cold water, 1 tablespoon at a time, and then use a large fork to mix. You want the dough to be moist but not wet, so you have to use your judgment about how much to use.

With your hands, roll the dough into a ball inside the bowl and then separate it into 2 equal portions. On two large pieces of plastic wrap, roll your dough out with a floured roller into two round disks. Try to keep the crust's thickness even. You don't want some areas to be thinner than others. Gently roll the flattened dough up into plastic wrap and refrigerate for 45 minutes.

Now you're ready to build your pie.

SWEET "BUTTERY" PIECRUST

If you're looking for a crust that's more like the ones in those sticky, "buttery" pies you find at your local grocery store, this is the crust for you.

MAKES 2 CRUSTS—ENOUGH FOR 1 REGULAR PIE OR 2 OPEN-FACED PIES

2 cups all-purpose flour (you may need a little more)

1 teaspoon crushed pink Himalayan salt

¾ teaspoon sugar

1 cup margarine, very cold

¼ to ½ cup cold water

Put your margarine in the freezer and your water and mixing bowl in the fridge for an hour before starting to make your piecrust.

In a very large, chilled mixing bowl, mix the flour, salt, and sugar with a whisk until blended. Cut in your margarine and blend with an electric handheld mixer until it becomes little pebbly balls. Gradually add your chilled water a few tablespoons at a time while you continue to blend your dough. As soon as your dough becomes moist, stop adding water. If you add too much, add more flour, 1 tablespoon at a time.

Use your hands to gently roll the dough into a ball inside the bowl and then move it to a large piece of plastic wrap. Use your hand to gently flatten the dough on the plastic wrap and then wrap and refrigerate for 3 hours. After your dough has had time to chill out, you're ready to build your pie.

CHOCOLATE CHIP CRUST

Level up any pie in a way only chocolate can.

MAKES 1 PIECRUST

2 cups all-purpose flour (you'll need extra to flour surfaces)

1 teaspoon crushed pink Himalayan salt

⅔ cup plus 2 tablespoons vegetable shortening

2 tablespoons shredded vegan dark chocolate

4 to 6 tablespoons cold water

In a large bowl, mix the flour and salt. Blend in your shortening using a pastry blender until the dough looks like small pebbles or peas. Sprinkle with the chocolate and the water, 1 tablespoon at a time. Between tablespoons of water, use your hands to press the dough into a ball. Stop adding water when the dough is moist but not pasty and leaves the side of the bowl easily.

With your hands, gather your dough into a ball inside the bowl and then separate the dough into 2 equal portions. Move your dough balls to two large pieces of plastic wrap and flatten them slightly. Wrap your dough and refrigerate for 30 minutes. Once your dough is chilled, remove it from the fridge and let it soften slightly. Roll out your dough on a floured surface using a floured roller. You're going to have to be really careful when you move your dough—like Tom-Cruise-hanging-from-the-ceiling-spy careful—because it's not on the plastic wrap, but it's okay. It'll be worth it. Now you're ready to buid your pie!

COCONUT OIL PIECRUST

Despite what we've been led to believe for years, it turns out coconut oil is actually pretty good for you. Yes, it has a lot of saturated fat, but it's not the same kind of fat you find in animal-based products and is a significant plant source of lauric acid. This fatty acid has been known to help speed up metabolism and is good for your hair and nails. It will give you that good-looking flaky piecrust you have been striving for all along.

MAKES 2 CRUSTS—ENOUGH FOR 1 PIE OR 2 OPEN-FACED PIES

2½ cups all-purpose flour

1 teaspoon crushed pink Himalayan salt

1 cup virgin coconut oil

½ cup cold water

In a bowl, mix your flour and salt. Add your coconut oil and blend with a pastry blender until your dough becomes tiny pea-size bits.

Slowly add the water a little at a time and mix by hand until a dough is formed. Divide into 2 equal parts, wrap in plastic wrap, and refrigerate for about 30 minutes. Remove from the fridge and roll out between 2 pieces of plastic wrap. Now you're ready to build your pie!

GRAHAM CRACKER CRUST

There are few things that are fair in this world. Here's one of them: there are several brands of vegan graham cracker crusts on the market. As of this moment, my favorite ones are made by Keebler and Wholly Wholesome, but if for some reason you find yourself in a vegan graham cracker desert…this recipe is for you and the cheesecake or cream pie you're making.

MAKES 1 PIECRUST

2 cups crushed vegan graham crackers

⅓ cup margarine

2 tablespoons granulated sugar

1 tablespoon brown sugar

Preheat the oven to 350°F.

In your food processor, blend all your ingredients until well mixed. Gently press your crumb batter into the bottom and onto the sides of your pie pan.

Bake for 8 to 10 minutes, or until lightly brown. Let cool completely before filling your crust so that your filling doesn't melt. Once you can touch your pan with your bare hands, you should be ready to party.

BROWN SUGAR TART CRUST

This recipe is just as provocative and edgy as the Rolling Stones song of the same name, but not nearly as problematic.

MAKES 1 TART CRUST

1 ½ cups all-purpose flour

1 ¼ cups margarine, softened

⅓ cup powdered sugar

2 teaspoons lemon zest

2 teaspoons brown sugar

Preheat the oven to 350°F.

In a food processor, blend all the ingredients until a dough forms. Press the dough firmly and evenly into an 11-inch tart pan. You'll want to press the dough into the sides, creating a little piecrust well in the center.

Bake for 10 to 15 minutes, or until your crust is a light golden brown. Remove from the oven and let cool to room temperature. Now you're ready to fill your tart.

EARL GREY TEA TART CRUST

This is the most English recipe in this whole cookbook. Nothing says England like Earl Grey tea and fancy tarts. Put whatever kind of filling you like in this crust and drink it with a nice, steaming cup of the Earl—it'll be a jolly good show.

MAKES 2 TO 4 MEDIUM-SIZE TARTS

1 cup all-purpose flour (you will need more to flour your surfaces)

½ teaspoon crushed pink Himalayan salt

⅓ cup plus 1 tablespoon vegetable shortening

2 to 3 tablespoons Earl Grey tea, prepared using the instructions on the package and chilled

Preheat the oven to 450°F.

In a large bowl, mix the flour, salt, and shortening with a pastry blender. Once your mixture is blended and looks like pebbles, sprinkle with the chilled Earl Grey tea, 1 tablespoon at a time. Continue to blend with the pastry blender, and once your dough is moist and pulls away from the sides of the bowl, gather it into a ball in the center.

Flour your surface and rolling pin for rolling out your dough. Roll out your dough and then wrap in plastic wrap and refrigerate for about 45 minutes. You want your dough to be firm but still pliable. Chilling your dough will make your crust flakier.

After your dough has chilled, roll it out again to make sure it has stayed even, and fix any cracks or splits. Divide your dough into segments to fit your tart dishes. Press your dough into your tart dishes. If there are any cracks or splits that come up, just take some extra dough and press it into the spots that need a little help. If you smooth out your edges with moist fingers, no one will ever know!

Be sure to cut off any extra dough that might hang over the edges. Now you're ready to fill your tarts and bake.

AMERICA'S FAVORITE APPLE PIE

This recipe is so American, they'll carve it on Mount Rushmore. They'll put it on the million-dollar bill. It'll win the World Series and the Super Bowl and *American Idol* and get elected president all in the same year. Or maybe it'll just wow all your friends and family at your next Fourth of July cookout. That's still a pretty amazing accomplishment.

MAKES 1 PIE

1 Basic Piecrust (page 381)

½ cup plus 1 tablespoon sugar

¼ cup coconut flour

½ teaspoon ground cinnamon

½ teaspoon grated nutmeg

¼ teaspoon ground ginger

Pinch of crushed pink Himalayan salt

6 Granny Smith apples, cored and thinly sliced

1 tablespoon margarine, softened

2 teaspoons apple juice

Preheat the oven to 425°F.

Make your Basic Piecrust. Gently press one of the rolled-out piecrusts into your glass pie plate.

In a large mixing bowl, mix ½ cup of the sugar, the coconut flour, cinnamon, nutmeg, ginger, salt, and apples. Very gently pour your apple mixture into your piecrust. Your apple mixture will be taller than the edge of your pie plate. With your spoon, gently shape the apple mixture so that it makes a peak in the center of the pie.

In another bowl, use a pastry blender to break up the margarine. Sprinkle the small pieces over the apples.

Roll out the other half of your Basic Piecrust dough and cut it into strips to make a lattice top—see "Making a Lattice Top for Your Pie" on page 386 for tips on making a lattice top for your pies.

In a small bowl, blend the apple juice and remaining 1 tablespoon sugar with a whisk until the sugar dissolves. Brush the top of the pie with the apple juice glaze.

Bake for 45 minutes, or until the top of your pie is golden brown.

Cool on a rack for at least an hour before serving.

BLUEBERRY AND PEACH PIE

Two of summer's favorite fruits working together make one amazing pie.

MAKES 1 PIE

1 Sweet "Buttery" Piecrust (page 382)

¾ cup sugar

⅓ cup coconut flour

½ teaspoon ground cinnamon

5 cups fresh blueberries

1 cup fresh peach slices

3 teaspoons lemon juice

1 teaspoon grated lemon peel

1 tablespoon margarine, softened

Preheat the oven to 425°F.

Make your Sweet "Buttery" Piecrust. Gently press one of the rolled out piecrusts into your glass pie plate.

In a large mixing bowl, very gently mix the sugar, coconut flour, cinnamon, blueberries, and peaches. Pour your berry and peaches mixture into your piecrust. Your fruit mix will be taller than the edge of your pie plate. With your spoon, gently shape your fruit mix so that it makes a peak in the center of the pie. Sprinkle the lemon juice and lemon peel over the top of your pie.

In another bowl, use a pastry blender to break up the margarine. Sprinkle the small pieces over the fruit.

Roll out the other half of your piecrust dough on the plastic wrap. Use a small cookie cutter to cut a small hole in the center of your dough. Then flip the dough over on top of the fruit so that the small hole is centered on the pie. Get your fingers wet and gently go around the edge of the pie, sealing the crusts together by gently pinching them into a little wave.

Bake for 45 minutes, or until the top of your pie is golden brown.

Cool on a rack for at least 2 hours before serving.

MAKING A LATTICE TOP FOR YOUR PIE

After you've made your crusts, gently pressed one into your pie pan, and filled it with your favorite stuff…you're ready to get fancy-pants. There are a lot of fancy things you can do with your top crust, and a trip to any Williams-Sonoma can send you home with cutters and kits to get all artsy with. But if you want to keep your fancy simple, there is always the traditional lattice top. It might seem like more work, but really if you're worried about your top crust being pretty, the easiest way to guarantee a pretty pie is to lattice-top it. Here are the five steps you need for a pie makeover.

Make your piecrust and press it into your pan. Don't trim off any of the extra dough overhanging on the edge. Fill your pie with yummy stuff before moving on to the next step.

Roll out the top crust and cut it into strips that are ½ inch thick. You'll need 10 to 15 strips, so keep that in mind.

Your piecrust strips can be kind of fragile, so be very gentle with them. Place 5 to 8 strips of piecrust over the filling about an inch apart, leaving a little bit of an overhang on the ends.

Now take your remaining piecrust strips and gently weave them into the first 5 to 8 strips in a crisscross pattern, leaving gaps. Start at the center with the longest strip first.

Fold the edges of the bottom crust over the ends of the lattice-top strips using moist fingers to seal up the crust by gently pinching.

Now, go out and bake pies, you magnificent vegans.

STRAWBERRY AND RHUBARB PIE

When Dan was growing up in suburban Boston, the next-door neighbor grew rhubarb in the backyard. Being a punk kid, Dan would always steal the little rhubarb plants and eat them—despite the fact that rhubarb is pretty much disgusting when eaten raw. But that didn't stop the love of my life from doing it anyway, just for the thrill of the chase. Neither did the fact that the leaves actually contain a strong toxin—which his neighbors and parents both warned him about. Luckily, you'd need to eat more than 10 pounds of them to actually poison yourself, and Dan wasn't that good a thief. You won't need to steal anything to enjoy this delicious summer recipe—although it tastes so good it's criminal.

MAKES 1 PIE

1 Basic Piecrust (page 381)

2 cups plus 1 tablespoon granulated sugar

1 tablespoon brown sugar

⅔ cup all-purpose flour

2 teaspoons grated orange peel

1 tablespoon orange juice with pulp

3 cups ½-inch pieces fresh rhubarb

3 cups sliced fresh strawberries

½ teaspoon ground cinnamon

1 tablespoon margarine, softened

2 teaspoons apple juice

Preheat the oven to 425°F.

Make your Basic Piecrust. Gently press one of the rolled-out piecrusts into your glass pie plate.

In a large mixing bowl, very gently mix 2 cups of the granulated sugar and the brown sugar, flour, orange peel, orange juice, rhubarb, strawberries, and cinnamon. Pour your strawberry-rhubarb mixture into your piecrust.

In another bowl, use a pastry blender to break up the margarine and then sprinkle the small pieces over your fruit.

Roll out the other half of the piecrust dough and cut it into strips to make a lattice top—see page 386 for tips on how to make an awesome lattice top for your pie.

In a small bowl, whisk together the apple juice and remaining 1 tablespoon sugar until the sugar dissolves. Brush the top of the pie with the apple juice glaze.

Bake for 45 minutes, or until the top of your pie is golden brown.

Cool on a rack for at least an hour before serving.

FROZEN COCONUT CREAM PIE

It's 798 miles to Chicago, we've got a full tank of gas and half a pack of chilled San Pellegrinos, it's sunny out, and we're wearing sunglasses. Let's make some pie!

Hit it.

MAKES 1 PIE

1 cup shredded raw coconut

⅔ cup sugar

¾ cup coconut oil spread

1¼ teaspoons vanilla extract or coconut extract

1 tablespoon coconut milk, from a can

1 tablespoon coconut flour or cornstarch

Pinch of crushed pink Himalayan salt

¼ teaspoon agave nectar

1 package silken tofu

1 vegan chocolate cookie piecrust (we recommend Keebler Ready Crust chocolate piecrust)

Preheat the oven to 350°F. Spread ¾ cup of the raw shredded coconut evenly over a cookie sheet. Place in the oven for 5 to 7 minutes. Remove when the coconut is lightly browned and toasted.

In your food processor, puree the remaining ¼ cup shredded raw coconut. Add the sugar, coconut oil spread, vanilla, coconut milk, coconut flour, salt, agave nectar, and silken tofu to your food processor. Blend until smooth and creamy. Pour into your piecrust and evenly sprinkle toasted coconut over the top. Put in the freezer for 8 hours.

FROZEN MOCHA FRENCH SILK PIE

I started to make the cream filling for this pie, and it was so lovely and sweet… It felt like it needed a dark side… like how Wesley in *Buffy* was a pale shadow of the dreamboat Dark Wesley in *Angel*. So I went back to our Little Devil's Food Cupcakes recipe for inspiration and added a little coffee. We now have a supereasy and creamy and awesome pie that will make you swoon. I hope you have someone around to fetch you those smelling salts…

MAKES 1 PIE

½ cup granulated sugar

½ cup brown sugar

¾ cup coconut oil spread

1½ teaspoons vanilla extract

3 ounces (3 squares) unsweetened baking chocolate, melted and cooled to room temperature

1½ teaspoons instant coffee

½ teaspoon agave nectar

1 package silken tofu, drained

1 vegan chocolate cookie piecrust (we recommend Keebler Ready Crust chocolate piecrust)

Shredded dark chocolate

Blend the sugar, brown sugar, coconut oil spread, vanilla, baking chocolate, instant coffee, agave nectar and silken tofu in your food processor, until blended and smooth. Pour into your piecrust and sprinkle dark chocolate over the top. Put in the freezer for 4 hours.

VÉGÉTALIEN TARTE AUX FRUITS FRAIS (VEGAN FRENCH FRESH FRUIT TART)

I've always noticed these bright, cheerful little tarts outshining all the creamy éclairs and frosty rose-petaled cakes in bakeries, but have never actually had one. There were always eggs and cream to avoid, or a lack of events to justify making one. But that doesn't mean I never thought about it. If you've ever been to Paris, you'll know that these tarts are in every coffee shop and patisserie widow, flirting with you like only a Parisian can. Those tarts are so polished and flawless, they could grace the cover of a magazine. Even the humblest café serves supermodel-caliber tarts. These beautiful baked goods combine fresh colorful fruit and a "buttery" shortbread-ish crust into the perfect storm of desserts that will melt in your mouth in a combination of sweet vanilla cream, tangy fruit, and a slightly savory crust. A storm that you can now make in your very own home!

MAKES 1 TART

1 Brown Sugar Tart Crust (page 384)

1 (8-ounce) package vegan cream cheese (we recommend Tofutti Better Than Cream Cheese)

¾ teaspoon vanilla extract

¼ teaspoon bourbon (you can just use more vanilla extract if alcohol isn't your thing)

½ cup sugar

Slices of your favorite fresh fruit (we recommend 2 white peaches, 2 kiwifruit, 1 apricot, blueberries, and boysenberries, but some other popular choices are strawberries, raspberries, melons, and mangos)

Make your Brown Sugar Tart Crust in an 11-inch tart pan.

In a bowl, blend the vegan cream cheese, vanilla, bourbon, and sugar with a handheld electric mixer until smooth and creamy.

Once your crust reaches room temperature, use a spatula to spread your vanilla filling evenly into the crust. Then arrange your rinsed, dried, and sliced fruit on top of the vanilla filling very slowly and deliberately to create your pattern. You're going to want to have an idea going into your tart as to what fruit you want where because it will be messy and troublesome to move a slice of fruit once it goes into the vanilla filling. We suggest fanning and layering your fruit like a flower so you can get the most fruit possible on there. I also like the rosebud look it creates.

Once your toppings are arranged, cover your tart with plastic wrap and cool for 20 minutes to firm up your filling before serving. When you serve, be sure to remove your tart cover (the ring on the outside of the pan) first if your tart pan comes in 2 pieces. It will make it easier to serve and cut. You do this by gently lifting the tart from the ring from underneath. The plate holding the tart should separate from the ring. Again, this is only if your tart pan comes in 2 pieces. I recommend practicing a bit before you start your tart.

MIXED BERRY CRUMBLE TART WITH CITRUS CRUMBLE

These tarts are just…lovely. The bright, flavorful berries kind of steal the show, but I have to mention that the crust and crumble for this tart are pretty exceptional as well. We used the Earl Grey Tea Tart Crust and then we topped the tart with an orange zest crumble to bring out the bergamot flavors in the tea.

MAKES 2 TARTS

2 Earl Grey Tea Tart Crusts (page 384)

1½ cups fresh strawberries, sliced

1½ cups fresh raspberries

1½ cups fresh blueberries

⅔ cup sugar

2 tablespoons cornstarch

CITRUS CRUMBLE TOPPING

¾ cup all-purpose flour

¼ cup granulated sugar

¼ cup brown sugar

2 teaspoons orange zest

⅓ cup margarine

Preheat the oven to 450°F. Make your 2 Earl Grey Tea Tart Crusts.

In a large bowl, gently toss the berries with the sugar and cornstarch. Spoon into your pastry-lined tart dishes.

In another bowl, mix the crumble topping ingredients with a fork until they're crumbly. Sprinkle an even amount over the berries in each tart. You want some berries to peak through, so don't get too heavy-handed with the crumble topping.

Bake for around 30 minutes, or until the berries are bubbling and your crust has a light golden color. Let them cool until they aren't too hot to touch but are still warm. Keep in mind also that the crust will continue to brown a little bit as it cools because your dishes are still hot. So be sure to pull them out before they are too brown.

CHOCOLATE ORANGE TEA TARTS

It can be easy to forget how nicely the tangy sweetness of orange can mellow out even the bitterest of chocolate and create something quite wonderful and special. I mean, everyone can make an orange cake or chocolate pie…but bring out a Chocolate Orange Tea Tart at a dinner party, and there is bound to be one person who is impressed enough to post a photo on Facebook.*

MAKES 4 TARTS

CANDIED ORANGE SLICES

1 cup sugar

1 cup water

1 navel orange, cut into ¼-inch-thick slices with the peel on

2 cinnamon sticks

TARTS

4 Earl Grey Tea Tart Crusts (page 384)

1 (8-ounce) package vegan cream cheese (we recommend Tofutti Better Than Cream Cheese)

¾ teaspoon vanilla extract

½ teaspoon orange liqueur

½ cup sugar

1 tablespoon cornstarch

1 cup vegan chocolate chips

Start with the candied orange slices! Line a cookie sheet with parchment paper.

Bring the sugar and water to a boil in a saucepan over medium heat. Stir constantly until the sugar dissolves. Add the orange slices and cinnamon sticks and reduce the heat to a simmer. Use your spoon to flip the orange slices a few times. Once the rinds become soft, you'll notice a syrup beginning to form. Heat your orange slices for 40 minutes.

Move your soft orange slices to the cookie sheet and arrange them in a single layer so none of them are touching. Keep your syrup to drizzle over the tart later.

Preheat the oven to 450°F. Make your 4 Earl Grey Tea Tart Crusts.

In a bowl, blend the vegan cream cheese, vanilla, orange liqueur, sugar, and cornstarch with a handheld mixer until your orange cream is smooth and creamy.

In a small saucepan, melt your vegan chocolate chips following the instructions on the package.

Use a spatula to spread your orange cream evenly into the crusts. With a whisk, drizzle the desired amount of chocolate over the top of your orange cream.

Bake for around 20 minutes, or until your crust has a light golden color. Don't let your tarts bake for too long; the crust will continue to brown a little bit as it cools because your dishes are still hot. So be sure to pull them out just as they begin to brown, then let them cool until you can touch them but they are still warm.

Once they're cool, arrange 1 to 2 of the prettiest candied orange slices on top and drizzle a little of the orange syrup over the top.

---

* Little-known fact: it is the aspiration of every baked good to be forever memorialized on Facebook—to be enjoyed by everyone for years and years.

FROSTINGS, GLAZES, AND SAUCES

Frostings, glazes, and sauces are often thought of as the supporting cast of a dessert. I mean, we say we baked a birthday cake, not a birthday frosting. But I think this shows how much we take these dessert wonders for granted. These little extras add the color and punch to our desserts and can be the difference between a chocolate cake being German and a chocolate cake hailing from the Black Forest. Without frosting, our cupcakes couldn't wish us a "happy birthday," or become little snowmen, turkeys, or sunshines. They'd just be little handfuls of cake.

Although these recipes are rarely "baked," they still have their place in the Pantheon of Baked Goods: much like Aphrodite's little cherubs, Athena's owl, or Poseidon's dolphins. We kept them separate in the book so that you can mix and match them in whoopie pies and on cupcakes to create your own baked wonders.

JUST LIKE BUTTERCREAM FROSTING

Classic buttercream is made by creaming butter with powdered sugar, but we know you're a little more advanced than that. This recipe has all the delicious simplicity of the traditional recipe, with 10 percent more fancy.

MAKES ENOUGH FOR 1 DOZEN CUPCAKES

6 cups powdered sugar (you may need a little more)

⅔ cup margarine, softened

4 teaspoons vanilla extract

5 tablespoons almond milk (you may need a little more)

In a large mixing bowl, blend the powdered sugar and margarine with an electric handheld mixer until it becomes little pebbly clumps. Blend in the vanilla and almond milk. If your frosting is too thin, add more powdered sugar. If it's not fluffy and soft enough, add a tiny bit more almond milk, 1 teaspoon at a time.

CHOCOLATE BASICALLY BUTTERCREAM FROSTING

What could make buttercream frosting more delicious? Making it chocolate. Duh. And for the record, that is *always* the correct answer when the question is "What could make something more delicious?"

MAKES ENOUGH FOR 1 DOZEN CUPCAKES

6 cups powdered sugar (you may need a little more)

⅔ cup margarine, softened

4 teaspoons vanilla extract

3 ounces unsweetened baking chocolate, melted and cooled

5 tablespoons almond milk (you may need a little more)

In a large mixing bowl, mix the powdered sugar and margarine with an electric handheld mixer until it looks like little peas. Blend in the vanilla and chocolate. Gradually beat in the almond milk. If your frosting is too runny, add more powdered sugar. If it is too dry, add a tiny bit more almond milk, 1 teaspoon at a time.

CREAM CHEESE FROSTING

This frosting is perfect for carrot cake, or really anything that you want to become more delicious.

MAKES ENOUGH FOR 1 DOZEN CUPCAKES

1 package plain vegan cream cheese (we recommend Tofutti Better Than Cream Cheese)

¼ cup margarine

2 teaspoons vanilla soy milk

1 teaspoon vanilla extract

4 cups powdered sugar

In a mixing bowl, beat the cream cheese, margarine, soy milk, and vanilla with an electric mixer on low until smooth.

Gradually mix in the powdered sugar, 1 cup at a time, on a low speed to prevent one of those messy blowbacks. Mix till smooth.

CHERRY FROSTING

This recipe goes equally well with a chocolate- or vanilla-based cake recipe.

MAKES ENOUGH FOR 1 DOZEN CUPCAKES

6 cups powdered sugar (you may need a little more)

⅔ cup margarine, softened

4 teaspoons grenadine or cherry-flavored extract

5 tablespoons almond milk (you may need a little more)

In a large mixing bowl, blend the powdered sugar and margarine with an electric handheld mixer until it becomes little pebbly clumps. Blend in the grenadine and almond milk. If your frosting is too thin, add more powdered sugar. If it's not fluffy and soft enough, add a tiny bit more almond milk, 1 teaspoon at a time.

CARAMEL FROSTING

This is the kind of soft frosting you'll want for filling a whoopie pie or a layer cake.

MAKES ENOUGH FOR 1 DOZEN CUPCAKES

½ cup margarine

1 cup packed brown sugar

¼ cup soy milk (you may need a little more)

2 cups powdered sugar

In a 2-quart saucepan, melt the margarine over medium heat. Stir in your brown sugar once your margarine is melted. Heat the mixture to a boil while whisking constantly. Once it's boiling, reduce the heat to low, and let it boil for 2 minutes, stirring constantly. After 2 minutes, stir in the soy milk. Heat the mixture back up to boiling, stirring constantly, and then remove from the heat. Let it cool until it's lukewarm. This should take about ½ hour.

After it's cooled, gradually stir in the powdered sugar. It's important to add it a little at a time, stir it up, and repeat, until it's all in there in a smooth mixture. Take the whole saucepan and submerge the base of it in a big bowl of cold water to cool down the frosting—but don't let the water get in the pan! Remove the pan from the water and mix the frosting with an electric mixer until it becomes smooth and spreadable. If it's too stiff, you can add in a little extra soy milk, a few drops at a time.

MINT CHOCOLATE CHIP FROSTING

Yes. This is really happening. You're welcome.

MAKES ENOUGH FOR 1 DOZEN CUPCAKES

3½ cups powdered sugar (you might need a little extra)

⅓ cup margarine

1½ teaspoons vanilla extract

¼ teaspoon peppermint extract

3 tablespoons vanilla soy milk (you may need a little more)

1 to 2 drops green food coloring, optional

⅓ cup vegan chocolate chips, crushed

Blend the powdered sugar and margarine with an electric handheld mixer until creamy. Mix in the vanilla and peppermint extracts and soy milk. If your frosting is too soft, add more powdered sugar, 1 tablespoon at a time. If it is too dry, add a tiny bit more soy milk, ½ teaspoon at a time.

Once you like the consistency of your frosting, you can mix in your food coloring, if using, and then your crushed vegan chocolate chips.

LEMON FROSTING

This is a simple recipe that's packed with flavor, and a great counterpart to any number of recipes in this book.

MAKES ENOUGH FOR 1 DOZEN CUPCAKES

3 cups powdered sugar

⅓ cup margarine

2 to 3 tablespoons lemon juice

3 teaspoons grated lemon peel

In a medium mixing bowl, mix the powdered sugar and margarine together using an electric handheld mixer on low speed. It'll still be really powdery and look nothing like frosting. It will look more like little pebbles. Add in 1 tablespoon of the lemon juice and mix again. Add a second tablespoon of the lemon juice and mix again. From here you have to use your judgment, and add as much of the remaining lemon juice as you need, a couple of drops at a time, mixing together each time, until the frosting becomes smooth and spreadable. Once you like the consistency, blend in your lemon peel.

GINGER ORANGE FROSTING

This is pretty much the same recipe as the Lemon Frosting, but with oranges.

MAKES ENOUGH FOR 1 DOZEN CUPCAKES

3 cups powdered sugar

⅓ cup margarine, softened

½ teaspoon ginger paste

2 to 3 tablespoons orange juice

1 teaspoon grated orange peel

2 teaspoons grated lemon peel

In a medium mixing bowl, mix the powdered sugar, margarine, and ginger paste together using an electric handheld mixer on low speed until the mixture becomes little pebbles. Add in 1 tablespoon of the orange juice and mix again. Then add a second tablespoon of the orange juice and mix again. It should look more like frosting now. Start adding the remaining orange juice a couple of drops at a time, mixing each time, until the frosting becomes smooth and spreadable. You might not use all the orange juice. Once you have a lovely frosting, blend in the orange and lemon peel.

PEANUT BUTTER FROSTING

This is a soft frosting that is perfect as a filling for a layer cake or whoopie pie.

MAKES ENOUGH FOR 1 DOZEN CUPCAKES

3 cups powdered sugar (you may need a little more)

⅓ cup creamy peanut butter (sorry, you can't use the all-natural brands— they're too oily)

⅓ cup margarine, softened

In a large bowl, mix the powdered sugar, peanut butter, and margarine together using a hand mixer on low speed until your frosting is completely blended and smooth. If your peanut butter is too oily, it might make your frosting too soft. You'll have to add more powdered sugar, a tablespoon at a time, until it has a smooth yet firm consistency.

COCONUT PECAN FROSTING

This is that signature frosting that makes those German Chocolate Whoopie Pies on page 345 into something to cheer about.

MAKES ENOUGH FOR 1 DOZEN WHOOPIE PIES

½ cup margarine, softened

1 cup packed brown sugar

1 (14-ounce) can coconut milk

1 teaspoon French vanilla extract

2 tablespoons arrowroot

2 tablespoons Ener-G egg replacer, just the powder, not prepared per the instructions on the package

2 cups shredded raw coconut

1⅓ cups raw pecans, chopped

In a saucepan, melt the margarine. Mix in the brown sugar, coconut milk, and vanilla. Heat over low heat while stirring. Once the mixture is blended and begins to bubble, stir in the arrowroot, egg replacer, coconut, and pecans. Remove from the heat. Let the frosting cool for 1 hour to thicken up before using.

Keep in mind that this is a soft frosting intended for a whoopie pie, so it will always have that sticky-sweet wonderful you want in a cookie sandwich.

WHISKEY FROSTING

We treated ourselves to some Bushmills when we made this one and we're happy we did. When I say "we," I mean Dan.

MAKES ENOUGH FOR 1 DOZEN CUPCAKES

3 cups powdered sugar

⅓ margarine, softened

2 to 3 tablespoons whiskey

In a medium mixing bowl, mix the powdered sugar and margarine together using a hand mixer on low speed. Add in 1 tablespoon of the whiskey and mix. Add a second tablespoon of the whiskey and mix again. Now, if the frosting is still a little thick, you might want to add a little more whiskey, a few drops at a time, until the frosting is the consistency and flavor you want.

COCONUT RUM FROSTING

This frosting brings a little bit of an island kick to your desserts.

MAKES ENOUGH FOR 1 DOZEN CUPCAKES

2½ cups powdered sugar (you may need a little more)

½ cup margarine, softened

2 teaspoons rum or rum extract

2 teaspoons coconut milk, from a carton, not a can (you may need a little more)

4 cups shredded raw coconut

Blend the powdered sugar, margarine, rum, and coconut milk in a large bowl with a handheld electric mixer on medium speed for 5 minutes using the beater attachments first. When the margarine is soft, switch to the whisk attachments and blend for another 5 minutes. You want to stop when the frosting gets fluffy.

If you want your frosting to be thicker, add more powdered sugar, a tablespoon at a time. If you want your frosting softer, add more coconut milk, a teaspoon at a time.

Put your shredded coconut in a bowl. Once you have frosted your cupcakes or whoopie pies, gently dip the frosted treat into the bowl of coconut and very gently press down. You'll want to roll your cupcake tops or whoopie pie sides in the coconut a little to make sure they get a lot. You're pressing the coconut into the frosting, but make sure you don't press so hard the frosting comes off into the bowl.

If you're using this frosting on a cake, just sprinkle the coconut over the top.

CHOCOLATE AGAVE GLAZE

Perfect for doughnuts and other decadent treats.

MAKES ENOUGH FOR 2 DOZEN DOUGHNUTS

½ cup vegan chocolate chips

2 tablespoons agave nectar

2 tablespoons margarine, softened

1 to 2 teaspoons hot water

Heat your vegan chocolate chips in your favorite saucepan over medium heat. Once they begin to get glossy, add the agave nectar and margarine and whisk until everything is melted and smooth. Set aside and let cool. Once the glaze is cool, whisk until it is smooth. Add 1 teaspoon water and whisk until blended. If you want your glaze thinner, just add another teaspoon of water.

Once you like the consistency, dip your baked goods in your glaze while it's still warm.

APPLE VANILLA GLAZE

This glaze is great for vanilla or fruit-flavored cakes and cupcakes.

MAKES ENOUGH FOR 2 DOZEN DOUGHNUTS

1 cup powdered sugar

1 tablespoon almond milk

½ teaspoon vanilla extract

1 to 2 teaspoons apple juice

In a small bowl, whisk the powdered sugar, almond milk, and vanilla until blended. Add 1 teaspoon apple juice and blend with your whisk.

Keep whisking the glaze to break up any clumps. If the glaze seems too thick, add a tiny bit more apple juice till you like the consistency. Remember: you want to be able to brush the glaze over your baked goods, but you don't want it to be so liquefied that it won't dry to create a nice "shell."

CHERRY GLAZE

Cherry glaze will go equally well with a vanilla- or chocolate-based cake. It's fair like that.

MAKES ENOUGH FOR 3 DOZEN DOUGHNUTS

2 eggs' worth of Ener-G egg replacer, made per the instructions on the box

¼ cup maraschino cherries with juice

½ cup granulated sugar

½ teaspoon agave nectar

2 tablespoons water

1 teaspoon vanilla extract

⅓ cup vegetable shortening

3 to 4 cups powdered sugar

Prepare the egg replacer in a large bowl.

Blend your cherries with their juice in your food processor until the mixture becomes a paste.

In a saucepan, stir the sugar, agave nectar, and water until well mixed. Cover and heat to a boil over medium heat, stirring often. Remove from the heat and pour into a bowl over the prepared egg replacer. Blend with an electric mixer using the whisk attachments until smooth. Add the vanilla, shortening, and powdered sugar gradually and beat on high speed for around 10 minutes. Once you like the consistency, stop adding powdered sugar.

PEPPERMINT GLAZE

Everyone knows that mint and chocolate go great together. So try this glaze on a chocolate cake or cupcake and prepare to be amazed.

MAKES ENOUGH FOR 2 DOZEN DOUGHNUTS

1 cup powdered sugar

2 cups almond milk

¼ teaspoon peppermint extract

¼ teaspoon vanilla extract

In a bowl, whisk all the ingredients until they are smooth and creamy.

SWEET ORANGE SPICE GLAZE

This glaze is great for cinnamon rolls or other breakfast-y treats.

MAKES ENOUGH FOR 1 DOZEN CINNAMON ROLLS

1¼ cups powdered sugar (you may need a little more)

¼ cup margarine

½ teaspoon ground cinnamon

1 teaspoon orange cinnamon tea, strongly brewed and cooled to room temperature

2 tablespoons orange juice with pulp (you may need a little more)

1 tablespoon grated orange peel

In a bowl, whisk all the ingredients until the glaze is smooth and you like its consistency. If you want your glaze thicker, add more powdered sugar, 1 teaspoon at a time. If the glaze is too thick, add more orange juice, 1 teaspoon at a time.

MAPLE BOURBON GLAZE

Just like with bourbon, enjoy this glaze in moderation.

MAKES ENOUGH FOR 2 DOZEN DOUGHNUTS

2 cups powdered sugar

2 tablespoons bourbon, or apple juice if you aren't into booze

2 tablespoons maple syrup

2 tablespoons water

Whisk all the ingredients together until you have a nice, smooth glaze.

CHOCOLATE GANACHE

Traditional ganache is typically made by pouring heated cream over dark or semisweet chocolate; we're going to make ours by heating everything up together to spare you having to clean up an extra pan. See? We care about you and want your life to be better.

MAKES ENOUGH FOR 2 DOZEN CUPCAKES

1 cup vegan chocolate chips

4 tablespoons margarine, softened

4 tablespoons corn syrup

2 teaspoons water

Grab your sweetest little saucepan—you know, that little one that looks like it was meant for a dollhouse. If you don't have a tiny one, use a regular-size saucepan; just watch out for scorching, because the glaze will be spread out thin. Toss in all the ingredients, heat over a medium heat, and stir while they melt. Once they're melted and blended, use your whisk to thoroughly blend your ganache into a light paste.

SOFT MAPLE FROSTING

Goes great drizzled over soft cookies and doughnuts.

MAKES ENOUGH FOR 2 DOZEN COOKIES

| 1 cup powdered sugar | 3 tablespoons maple syrup | 1 tablespoon plus 1 teaspoon water |

Blend all your frosting ingredients with a whisk until completely blended. Let sit for 1 minute so the sugar has a chance to dissolve. Blend with your whisk again before drizzling over the top of your still warm but not hot baked goods.

LEMON FILLING

This is a great filling for doughnuts or cupcakes alike. We do not recommend eating it plain. It's delicious—but once you've gone there, there's no turning back.

MAKES ENOUGH FOR 2 DOZEN DOUGHNUTS

¾ cup sugar	¼ teaspoon crushed pink Himalayan salt	1 tablespoon margarine, softened
3 tablespoons cornstarch	⅔ cup lemonade (the kind made with real lemons works best)	1¼ teaspoons grated lemon peel
		¼ cup lemon juice

In a saucepan, mix the sugar, cornstarch, and salt. Gradually stir in the lemonade. Cook over medium heat, stirring constantly, until the mixture thickens and boils. Boil and stir for 1 minute, and then remove from the heat.

Stir in the margarine and lemon peel. Stir until the margarine melts. Gradually stir in the lemon juice.

Remove the filling from the heat and blend with a whisk until it's smooth. Cover the saucepan tightly with plastic wrap. Refrigerate for 2 hours.

RASPBERRY FILLING

This raspberry sauce over vanilla cheesecake is pure heaven. It's also great as a doughnut filling.

MAKES ENOUGH FOR 2 DOZEN DOUGHNUTS

2 cups frozen raspberries, defrosted

3 tablespoons sugar

4 tablespoons cornstarch

⅓ cup water

3 tablespoons lemon juice

In a saucepan, heat the raspberries, sugar, cornstarch, water, and lemon juice over medium heat, mixing with a large spoon. As the mixture begins to bubble, it should start to thicken. Let it boil and thicken for more than a minute.

Set aside and let cool to room temperature for 30 minutes.

HOT FUDGE SAUCE

It's hot fudge sauce. I think you know what to do with it.

MAKES ENOUGH FOR 1 CHEESECAKE

½ cup vanilla coffee creamer

¾ cup vegan chocolate chips

½ cup sugar

1 tablespoon margarine, softened

1 teaspoon vanilla extract

In a saucepan, heat the creamer, vegan chocolate chips, and sugar over medium heat, stirring till the mixture starts to boil.

Remove from the heat and whisk in the margarine and vanilla until the sauce is smooth and creamy. Cool for 30 minutes.

Interesting fact: If you put it in the fridge, it gets firm—like fudge.

CARAMEL SAUCE

This is critically important: It's "ca-ra-mel," not "car-mel." Three syllables. *Three*. That is all.*

MAKES ENOUGH FOR 1 DOZEN CINNAMON ROLLS

1 cup light corn syrup

1¼ cups brown sugar

¼ cup margarine, softened

½ cup vanilla coffee creamer

In a saucepan, heat the corn syrup, brown sugar, and margarine to a boil over low heat while stirring constantly. Boil for 5 minutes, stirring occasionally. Stir in the creamer. Remove from the heat and let cool.

* For the record, this intro was written by Dan.

PEANUT BRITTLE SAUCE

It's like melty peanut brittle you can put on ice cream or a cheesecake!

MAKES ENOUGH FOR SEVERAL BOWLS OF ICE CREAM

1½ cups sugar

1 cup plus 1 teaspoon water

1 cup agave nectar

3 tablespoons margarine (you'll want extra to grease your cookie pan)

1 teaspoon vanilla extract

1 teaspoon hazelnut syrup used in beverages

3 cups roasted Spanish peanuts

1½ teaspoons baking soda

Preheat the oven to 350°F. In the oven, warm your cookie pan that has sides. Once it is warm to the touch, grease the pan with margarine.

In a saucepan, mix the sugar, water, and agave nectar. Cook over medium heat for 25 minutes, stirring occasionally. Stir in the margarine, vanilla, hazelnut syrup, and peanuts. Cook over medium heat for about 10 minutes, stirring constantly. Make sure the sauce doesn't burn. If it starts to burn before the 10 minutes are up, decrease the heat to low. Quickly stir in the baking soda. The sauce will get light and foamy, and that's good!

Pour your Peanut Brittle Sauce into your greased pan and let it cool into a thick syrup before using.

WHIPPED COCONUT CREAM

A delicious and natural vegan alterative to whipped cream that's supereasy to make. But remember to start your preparations the night before (see below).

MAKES ENOUGH FOR 1 PIE

2 (14-ounce) cans coconut milk (not low-fat or no-fat)

¾ cup powdered sugar

4 tablespoons coconut flour

2 teaspoons cornstarch

2 teaspoons vanilla extract

Chill your cans of coconut milk and a mixing bowl overnight in the fridge. Open the cans and spoon the thick cream that has separated and risen to the top into the chilled mixing bowl. Try to avoid getting any of the clear liquid in the bowl.

Use your electric handheld mixer with the whisk attachments to blend in your powdered sugar, coconut flour, cornstarch, and vanilla until fluffy. It should take 2 to 3 minutes.

Use your rubber spatula to move your Whipped Coconut Cream to an airtight storage container, and chill for 2 to 3 hours, until firm. Serve cold with a side of smug, self-satisfied joy in knowing you rock.

VEGAN MARSHMALLOW FILLING

I could candy-coat* this recipe and tell you a bunch of half-truths and bury you in rainbows, but the truth is that this recipe is kind of hard and may take a few tries to get right. Making your own vegan marshmallow fluff at home is a lot like finding your soul mate—it takes a few bad dates before you find the "one," but when you do, it all becomes worth it!

MAKES ENOUGH FOR 1 PIE

¾ cup water

Olive oil cooking spray

4½ teaspoons agar-agar powder

2 cups sugar

¾ cup corn syrup

¼ teaspoon crushed pink Himalayan salt

1 tablespoon vanilla extract

1 teaspoon baking soda

Chill ½ cup of the water in the refrigerator for 2 hours. You want to make sure it's good and cold.

Line your baking pan with plastic wrap and lightly spray a coating of olive oil cooking spray over your plastic wrap.

In your largest mixing bowl, mix the agar-agar with your ½ cup cold water with an electric handheld mixer until completely blended.

In your sauciest saucepan, mix the sugar, corn syrup, and the remaining ¼ cup water with a whisk, and heat over a high heat. Once the mixture begins to boil, stop stirring and let it boil for 1 minute. Make sure you don't burn your syrup, though. If it begins to scald turn down the heat, but keep it bubbling.

Pour your bubbling syrup into your agar-agar and blend it with your electric handheld mixer until smooth and creamy. Add the salt, vanilla, and baking soda and blend for 10 minutes on high. You'll have to stop a few times to scrape the sides of your bowl to make sure you get everything. If your filling is super-sticky, you'll want to spray your rubber-tipped spatula with olive oil cooking spray before using it.

Once your filling is fluffy but still soft like a cream, use your rubber-tipped spatula to pour it into the plastic-lined pan and spread it out evenly. You'll want to scrape the sides of the bowl to make sure you get all of the filling.

Spray another piece of plastic wrap with olive oil cooking spray and gently lay it on top of the filling. Seal the plastic wrap around the edges of the pan. Let your mix sit for 3 to 5 hours, or until it becomes a firm but creamy fluff.

Use a spoon or butter knife to spread your filling. You can put it into a frosting gun or pastry bag too, but expect it to be a little gummy and like the original Marshmallow Fluff.

---

* Yep—terrible baking humor.

Chapter Six
APPETIZERS AND SNACKS

There might be a few things vegans aren't good at…like hunting boar and eating those five-pound hamburgers designed as dares. But for every "all-you-can-eat ribs" contest vegans skip, there are five vegan parties or potlucks being held on any given day with spreads so impressive they'd put any gourmet buffet to shame. The best part is that every one of these cruelty-free events offers a great opportunity to prove that vegan food is not only better for you, for the animals, and for the planet— but it's also frakking delicious.

That's why it's always important to invite not-yet-vegans to your potlucks and parties and maybe even include some suggestions on what they can bring. It's also a great excuse to share some of your favorite recipes too.

This chapter is full of appetizers, starters, and snacks that that will level up any get-together from forgettable to fabulous!

DIPS AND APPETIZERS

Appetizers really shine when you're entertaining— when they put on their fancy clothes and insist that you call them "hors d'oeuvres." Nothing sparks good conversation like sharing great food—and nothing shows off one's culinary skills better than plate after plate of delicious finger foods. Everyone gets a bite or two, remarks on how wonderful they are, and starts fantasizing about how delicious dinner is going to be.

Thankfully, many traditional dips and appetizers are already vegan. From the holy trinity of chips/salsa/guacamole to your classic bean dip, most hosts are already serving vegan appetizers without even thinking about it. But we're here to expand your repertoire. Who doesn't want to throw a great party? These recipes can help make your next one even greater.

CASHEW ONION DIP

This dip is heavy on the onions, so vegan Bettys on hot dates might want to skip it. But it's fine for those of us who are married and don't have to worry about avoiding bad breath because of that unconditional love thing. Life's too short to not eat what you love.

You're going to want to start making this recipe the night before your party. So plan ahead.

MAKES 6 TO 8 SERVINGS

1 cup raw cashews	1 tablespoon diced red onion	1 teaspoon onion powder
½ cup white wine	4 green onions, sliced	¼ teaspoon smoked paprika
2 tablespoons lemon juice	1 tablespoon chopped fresh chives	2 teaspoons Bragg's liquid aminos
1 clove garlic, minced	1 tablespoon chopped fresh basil	Crushed pink Himalayan salt and freshly ground black peppercorns
	1 tablespoon chopped fresh dill weed	

Soak your cashews overnight in enough water to cover them. Drain any extra water out in the morning and pat dry.

Use a food processor to blend all the ingredients until smooth. Scrape the sides of the food processor with a spatula to make sure there aren't any clumps. Pour the dip into a serving bowl and cover with foil. Chill for 3 hours and serve with baby carrots and celery sticks and all kinds of raw vegetable awesomeness.

SMOKY 2-BEAN AND CHILIES DIP

This is one of those recipes that make you RSVP to parties you don't actually want to go to so that you have an excuse to make this dip. If you're reading this and recognize this recipe as something I brought to a potluck you held…I wasn't talking about your potluck. Of course I wanted to go to your potluck.

MAKES 6 TO 8 SERVINGS

1 (14-ounce) can black beans, drained and rinsed

1 (14-ounce) can kidney beans, drained and rinsed

2 chipotle chilies in adobo sauce

¼ teaspoon liquid smoke

1 teaspoon Bragg's liquid aminos

2 cloves garlic, minced

1 cup fresh salsa

3 tablespoons chopped fresh cilantro

1 green bell pepper, diced

2 cups shredded Daiya vegan

pepperjack cheese or your favorite vegan cheese

2 tomatoes, diced

2 green onions, diced

2 tablespoons black olives, sliced

Preheat the oven to 350°F.

In your favorite food processor or blender, mix the black beans, kidney beans, chilies, liquid smoke, Bragg's, and garlic. Move your bean mixture to a large mixing bowl and use a spoon to mix in the salsa, cilantro, bell pepper, and 1 cup of the vegan cheese. Spoon into a shallow ovenproof dish and spread an even layer of the remaining 1 cup vegan cheese over the top. Bake for 15 to 20 minutes, or until your vegan cheese is melted.

Serve warm with fresh tomatoes, green onions, and black olives over the top and with a side of tortilla chips and some limeade…seriously, it's kinda hot but in the right way.

SUN-DRIED TOMATO AND LEMON HUMMUS

Vegans and not-yet-vegans all love hummus. It's the great equalizer.

MAKES ENOUGH FOR 4 TO 6 SERVINGS

3 (14-ounce) cans garbanzo beans, rinsed and drained

¾ cup olive oil (you'll want another 1 to 2 tablespoons to pour over the top)

5 cloves garlic, minced

5 tablespoons lemon juice

3 teaspoons lemon zest

1½ teaspoons Bragg's liquid aminos

3 tablespoons sun-dried tomatoes in oil

1½ teaspoons tahini

Put all your ingredients in a food processor or blender and puree on the highest setting. You'll want to stop the machine a few times to scrape the sides and then blend some more. Your hummus is done once you have a nice, smooth paste.

Spoon into a serving dish and pour 1 to 2 tablespoons of olive oil over the top. Serve with pita and fresh vegetables.

ARTICHOKE DIP

This recipe headlines one of my very favorite vegetables: a charming fellow known to all as the artichoke. It's a delicious, spiky flower that I would eat every day if I could. I'll be honest: this is kind of a rich dip. But if you have had the non-vegan version of this classic, you know it's even richer. Actually, our vegan Artichoke Dip isn't even close to being as rich as Betty Crocker's "lighter" version, but put this on a thin cracker or pita ... this dip is pretty much divine.

MAKES 6 TO 8 SERVINGS

1 cup Vegenaise

1 cup nutritional yeast

1 cup shredded Daiya vegan

mozzarella cheese

4 green onions, diced

1 can artichoke hearts, drained

1 cup chopped raw spinach

1 tablespoon lemon pepper

½ teaspoon onion powder

Preheat the oven to 350°F.

In a bowl, blend the Vegenaise and nutritional yeast with an electric handheld mixer. Stir in ½ cup of the vegan cheese and the green onions, artichoke hearts, spinach, lemon pepper, and onion powder. Spoon into an ungreased glass baking dish or ceramic casserole dish.

Cover with the remaining ½ cup vegan cheese. Bake for 15 to 20 minutes, or until the top begins to brown and the vegan cheese is melted. Serve warm or at room temperature with crackers or bread.

HOT 10-LAYER DIP

For when 7 layers just aren't enough.

MAKES 6 TO 8 SERVINGS

Olive oil cooking spray

1 can vegan refried black beans (most are labeled "vegetarian" but when you read the label you'll see they are actually vegan)

Dash of liquid smoke

Dash of hot sauce

1 teaspoon Bragg's liquid aminos

1 (8-ounce) package vegan cream cheese (we recommend Tofutti Better Than Cream Cheese)

1 teaspoon nutritional yeast

1 (4.5-ounce) can jalapeños, diced

1 cup frozen corn, defrosted

¼ green bell pepper, diced

2 cups shredded Daiya vegan cheddar or pepperjack cheese or your favorite vegan cheese

½ cup Salsa Verde (page 433)

½ cup pico de gallo

1 large tomato, diced

1 cup chopped fresh cilantro

½ cup sliced black olives

1 fresh jalapeño, sliced

Preheat the oven to 350°F.

Coat an oven-safe platter with olive oil cooking spray.

In a mixing bowl, blend the beans, liquid smoke, hot sauce, and Bragg's with an electric handheld mixer until smooth.

In another mixing bowl, blend the vegan cream cheese, nutritional yeast, and canned jalapeños until smooth.

Drain any excess water from your defrosted corn and mix with the green bell pepper in a bowl with a spoon. Now you're ready to build your dip!

Spread your beans evenly over your coated oven-safe platter. Spread the vegan cream cheese over the beans in an even layer. This part can be tricky to do without messing up the beans. We recommend gently spreading one-third of your vegan cream cheese at a time and starting at one end of the plate and then the other. The last third of your vegan cream cheese goes in the middle. Use a butter knife to gently spread the vegan cream cheese until it meets and you have one even layer.

Using a slotted spoon, sprinkle your corn and pepper mixture over the cream cheese in an even layer. Sprinkle the vegan cheese over the top. Bake for 20 minutes, or until your vegan cheese melts.

Pour your Salsa Verde over one half of pan the and pico de gallo over the other half. Top with tomatoes, cilantro, black olives, and fresh jalapeño.

You're going to want to invest in some good tortilla chips and Mexican beer. This recipe makes a lot of food and is like the Swiss army knife of dips. Good for any occasion and has something for everyone.

AVOCADO ZUCCHINI CRAB DIP

Once I figured out how to get a seafood-y taste by using seaweed and kelp (also a great source of iron, vitamin C, and iodine), I was thrilled. It expanded our universe of food exponentially.

MAKES 4 TO 6 SERVINGS

2 to 3 ripe avocados, dark patches removed, peeled, pitted, and mashed

½ cup vegan sour cream

½ teaspoon prepared horseradish

1 clove garlic, minced

1½ teaspoons lemon juice

¼ teaspoon crushed black peppercorns

1½ teaspoons nutritional yeast

1 teaspoon sea kelp or seaweed granules

2 small fresh zucchinis, shredded (about 1 cup)

Crushed sea salt

2 teaspoons Old Bay seasoning

1 tablespoon vegan bacon bits

3 green onions, diced

In a large bowl, whip your avocados, vegan sour cream, horseradish, garlic, lemon juice, black pepper, nutritional yeast, and sea kelp with an electric handheld mixer until smooth. Using a large spoon, fold in the zucchini. At this point give your dip a taste test and add the needed salt and Old Bay seasoning.

Once you like the flavor, pour your dip into a serving bowl and sprinkle vegan bacon bits and green onions over the top. Serve with toasted baguette slices or schmancy crackers.

PIZZA DIP

The first time we made this recipe we started a fire. Even with blurry burned photos, it remained one of the most popular recipes on our blog from the day we posted it. We get emails all the time from people who love this campy, "cheesy" dip and have welcomed it into their Friday night movie dates and birthday parties with open arms.

MAKES 6 SERVINGS

1 (8-ounce) package vegan cream cheese (we recommend Tofutti Better Than Cream Cheese)

1 cup pizza sauce

2 cloves garlic, minced

1 teaspoon garlic powder

2 tablespoons nutritional yeast

1 teaspoon fresh oregano leaves

½ cup shredded Daiya vegan mozzarella cheese or your favorite vegan mozzarella

10 slices Lightlife Smart Deli pepperoni

⅓ cup diced red pepper

⅓ cup diced green bell pepper

⅓ cup diced red onion

Handful of black olives, sliced

Handful of fresh basil

Set the oven to broil or turn on your broiler.

In a bowl, mix the vegan cream cheese, pizza sauce, garlic, garlic powder, nutritional yeast, and oregano with an electric handheld mixer. Spread into a 9-inch glass pie dish. Then layer your dip in this order on top of the cheese mixture: small handful (about one-quarter) of vegan cheese, vegan pepperoni, another small hand-ful of vegan cheese, peppers and onions, more vegan cheese, olives and basil, and then the last of your vegan cheese.

Put in the broiler until your vegan cheese is melted. This should take 1 to 2 minutes.

Serve immediately with slices of baguette or vegan breadsticks.

GREEN OLIVE SALAD

This is basically a recipe for Creole tabbouleh—which combines two of our favorite flavor profiles in one amazing dish.

MAKES 4 TO 6 SERVINGS

2 cups large green Spanish olives, pitted, drained, and diced

1 cup large kalamata olives, pitted, drained, and diced

¼ cup roasted red peppers in oil, drained

2 tablespoons capers, drained

3 cloves garlic, minced

4 celery stalks, diced

¼ red onion, diced

2 tablespoons chopped fresh parsley

3 teaspoons fresh oregano leaves

2 teaspoons crushed red pepper flakes

2 tablespoons chopped pimientos

2 green onions, diced

3 tablespoons Bragg's liquid aminos

1 tablespoon crushed black peppercorns

1 cup olive oil

3 tablespoons red wine vinegar

Combine all your ingredients in a bowl and toss thor-oughly. Pour your salad into a large container with a resealable lid. Refrigerate overnight.

You can serve your salad chilled over a bed of mixed greens or with some crackers or pita.

FRESH HERB SPINACH DIP

Ah, spinach dip. A potluck classic. We jazzed this dish up a bit with some fresh herbs—everything's better with fresh herbs.

MAKES 6 TO 8 SERVINGS

1 round loaf of bread (we recommend vegan sourdough bread if you can find it)

1 cup chopped baby spinach

2 stalks celery, diced

4 green onions, diced

1 (8-ounce) can water chestnuts, drained and chopped

1 (8-ounce) package vegan sour cream

1½ cups Vegenaise

2 teaspoons lemon juice

2½ teaspoons grated lemon peel

1 teaspoon celery seed

2 teaspoons fresh dill weed, diced

2 teaspoons chopped fresh basil

1 teaspoon fresh thyme leaves

½ teaspoon capers, drained

½ teaspoon onion powder

2 teaspoons nutritional yeast

1 diced tablespoon pimientos, drained

Crushed pink Himalayan salt and crushed black peppercorns to taste

Olive oil cooking spray

Cut and hollow out to within 1 inch of the bottom a 3-inch-wide ring on top of the bread loaf, leaving the center of the loaf intact.

Combine the vegetables, vegan sour cream, Vegenaise, lemon juice, lemon peel, celery seed, fresh herbs, capers, onion powder, nutritional yeast, and pimientos in a large bowl and give it a taste test. Add whatever salt and pepper you feel like it's missing. Cover your bowl with foil and refrigerate for 2 hours to blend the flavors.

Use your hands to gently break off the center of the bread loaf that you cut out with your knife. You don't want to dig out the loaf. Just remove the center part that was cut out with the knife. Then use a bread knife to cut the top part of the bread so that it makes a little cap.

You want the bread to look like a little pot with a lid.

Preheat the oven to 350°F.

Cut the bread you removed from the loaf into bite-size cubes. Spread them out in a glass baking dish and lightly spray with olive oil cooking spray. Put them in the oven for 5 minutes, or until your bread cubes are lightly toasted.

Fill the little bread pot with your spinach dip and serve with the toasted bread cubes and maybe some extra crackers. You can't dip the bread cubes in the dip and get all the good green stuff, so make sure you have a small dull knife out to spread the dip on your bread and crackers.

CURRIED COCONUT CASHEW SPREAD

For a brief time on my road to the vegan I am today, I flirted with a raw diet. This favorite from those days would come out at parties and times when I craved a warm, spicy, nutty flavor. It will always remind me of long afternoons reading feminist literature and discussing topics like ethical fashion and body-image issues with the ladies at the domestic violence shelter I worked at. Yes. I was a cliché.

You'll want to soak your cashews overnight, so start this recipe the night before you want to serve it.

MAKES 6 TO 8 SERVINGS

1 cup raw cashews

½ cup shredded raw coconut

1 teaspoon agave nectar

Dash of hot sauce

¼ teaspoon crushed pink Himalayan salt

1½ cups carrot juice

2 teaspoons lime juice

2 tablespoons curry powder

1 teaspoon cumin

1 tablespoon flaxseed oil

2 tablespoons chopped fresh cilantro

Soak your cashews overnight in enough water to cover them.

The next day, blend all your ingredients except the cilantro in your food processor or blender until smooth. The shredded coconut will take forever to blend in completely, so don't worry about that too much. You really just want to make sure your cashews become a creamy paste similar to hummus.

Cover and chill for 2 hours to let the flavors blend. Serve chilled with cilantro over the top and warm pita bread on the side.

OPEN-FACED CUCUMBER TEA SANDWICHES

When I was very small, I fell in love with *My Fair Lady*. I loved the story about the pompous and impossibly tan Professor Higgins, who realized he was a hopeless curmudgeon and needed this rough-around-the-edges Eliza to find happiness. I loved the songs and the clothes, and of course Audrey Hepburn. I mean, I'm hardly the first little girl who wished she would grow up to be one of those dazzling Hepburns. One memory that really stood out for me is when poor Eliza was trying to get her delicate little hands on a cucumber sandwich and some tea but was forced instead to practice her vowels or something. I asked my mom if cucumber sandwiches were any good. She did that Sicilian shrug and said, "British seem to like them. I bet they're really bland." It was a fair observation, but when I got older and finally had a vegan cucumber sandwich at Moby's Teany in New York City, I realized that I actually adore these cute, fresh-flavored sandwiches, which are perfect for bridal and baby showers or really any ladylike event—like a tea party.

MAKES 30 OPEN-FACED SANDWICHES

- 1 (8-ounce) package vegan cream cheese (we recommend Tofutti Better Than Cream Cheese)
- 2 teaspoons Dijon mustard
- ½ teaspoon grated lemon peel
- ¼ teaspoon crushed black peppercorns (you'll want more to dash over the top)
- 2 to 3 large cucumbers
- 10 thin slices rye bread
- 10 thin slices whole wheat bread
- 10 thin slices pumpernickel bread
- Edible flowers, fresh dill weed, diced chives, diced green onions, and shredded carrots for garnish, optional

In a small mixing bowl, blend half of your package of vegan cream cheese and the Dijon mustard with a hand-held electric mixer.

In a different small mixing bowl, blend the remaining half of your vegan cream cheese with the lemon peel and black pepper.

Using a vegetable peeler or mandoline, thinly slice your cucumbers. Slice one lengthwise and one horizontally into coins. Try to get your slices so thin, you can see light through them.

Spread your Dijon cream cheese over half of your rye, wheat, and pumpernickel bread slices in even layers that go all the way to the crust. Then do the same thing with your lemon pepper cream cheese.

Now here's where it gets fun! Are you ready for adventure?

Gently lay your cucumbers across the bread so they overlap and make a pretty pattern. Then use a very sharp knife to cut the crust off your bread and the ends of the sliced cucumbers, making a clean edge. Then cut each piece of bread into 4 equal triangles.

Or if you're feeling a little crazy, use large, sharp metal cookie or biscuit cutters to cut shapes out of your bread. I recommend keeping to stars, hearts, and circles. If you get too complicated, it distracts from the pretty cucumbers.

Decorate your cucumber sandwiches with edible garnishes such as flowers, carrots, fresh herbs, and a dash of freshly ground black pepper.

NOTE: I didn't care for the combination of edible flowers and the Dijon vegan cream cheese, but the flowers were absolutely amazing with the lemon pepper vegan cream cheese.

SHEVILED SHEGGS

I'd like to think that if Betty Crocker was a real person, she'd smile when she saw our tray of vegan deviled eggs come out at any party. They have the whimsical look of a deviled egg, minus the cholesterol and cruelty that comes with eggs. I mean, win-win, right?

MAKES 16 "EGGS"

4 16-ounce packages extrafirm tofu (drain as much water out of your tofu as you can)

¾ cup nutritional yeast

1 tablespoon plus 1 teaspoon cumin

2 teaspoons onion powder

1 teaspoon turmeric

1 teaspoon Dijon mustard

2 green onions, diced

Olive oil cooking spray

Paprika to dash over the top

Preheat the oven to 300°F.

Cut each block of tofu into 4 rectangular pieces. You should have 16 pieces for 16 "eggs."

With your 1-teaspoon measuring spoon, scoop a half-circle cup out of each tofu piece. This is what you are going to fill with your "yolk," so make sure it isn't too shallow—but you want to make sure it isn't too deep either, because it'll make your "egg" fall apart. Try to make it about the same size and depth as the measuring spoon.

Then, with a soupspoon, form the outside shape of the "egg." Just gently cut the corners off your rectangular "egg."

Put in a small bowl the extra tofu you scooped out of and cut off your "egg." Mash it into a paste, and mix in the nutritional yeast, cumin, onion powder, turmeric, Dijon, and green onions to make your "yolk." Fit your frosting gun or pastry bag with the largest tip and fill it with the "yolk" mixture. Fill the cups you made in your "eggs" with the "yolk" mixture. You are going to have some "yolk" left over, so it's okay to overfill the "eggs."

Coat a glass baking dish with olive oil cooking spray. Place the eggs in the baking dish and into the oven for 10 minutes. Remove from the oven and refrigerate for 1 hour, or until chilled.

Serve with a dash of paprika over the top and maybe a gin and tonic. Sounds odd, but I've seen it in old movies and *Mad Men*, and it actually looks like a party I'd want to go to.

VEGAN BACON RANCH SHEVILED SHEGGS

This recipe is a perfect combination of two Betty Crocker Project all-stars. Creamy ranch flavor in a cute deviled "egg" package. You could say … we've given her all we've got, Captain!

MAKES 16 "EGGS"

4 16-ounce packages extrafirm tofu (drain as much water out of your tofu as you can)

¾ cup nutritional yeast

1 tablespoon Vegan Ranch Dressing (page 110)

2 teaspoons vegan bacon bits

2 teaspoons onion powder

1 teaspoon turmeric

1 teaspoon Dijon mustard

2 teaspoons chopped fresh dill weed

Olive oil cooking spray

2 tablespoons chopped fresh chives

Preheat the oven to 300°F.

Cut each block of tofu into 4 rectangular pieces. You should have 16 pieces for 16 "eggs."

With your 1-teaspoon measuring spoon, scoop a half-circle cup out of each tofu piece. This is what you are going to fill with your "yolk," so make sure it isn't too shallow—but you want to make sure it isn't too deep either, because it'll make your "egg" fall apart. Try to make it about the same size and depth as the measuring spoon.

Then, with a soupspoon, form the outside shape of the "egg." Just gently cut the corners off your rectangular "egg."

Put in a small bowl the extra tofu you scooped out of and cut off your "egg." Mash it into a paste, and mix in the nutritional yeast, Vegan Ranch Dressing, vegan bacon bits, onion powder, turmeric, Dijon, and dill weed to make your "yolk." Fit your frosting gun or pastry bag with the largest tip and use it to fill the cups you made in your "eggs" with the "yolk" mixture. You are going to have some "yolk" left over, so it's okay to overfill the "eggs."

Coat a glass baking dish with olive oil cooking spray. Place the eggs in the baking dish and into the oven for 10 minutes. Remove from the oven and refrigerate for 1 hour, or until chilled.

Serve with a pinch of chopped fresh chives over the top of each "egg."

ANTIPASTO PLATTER

The term "antipasto" always confused me as a kid. I got that it *wasn't* pasta, but what does it have *against* pasta? Why can't cured meats, cheeses, olives, and pasta all just be friends?

MAKES 6 TO 8 SERVINGS

⅓ cup olive oil

3 tablespoons balsamic vinegar

1 whole wheat baguette, sliced

12 to 15 slices hickory smoked Tofurky Deli slices

12 to 15 slices Lightlife Smart Deli Pepperoni slices

12 to 15 slices smoked cheddar Sheese or Daiya jalapeño garlic wedge

⅓ cup marinated artichoke hearts, drained

¼ cup marinated mushrooms, drained

¼ cup marinated sun-dried tomatoes, drained

⅓ cup kalamata olives, pitted

¼ cup stuffed Spanish olives

¼ cup peperoncini, drained

4 tablespoons roasted red peppers, drained

1 fresh lemon, cut into wedges

Set aside the olive oil, vinegar, and bread slices. Arrange your remaining ingredients on a serving platter in a pleasing style, cover with plastic wrap, and chill in the fridge for about an hour.

Pour your olive oil into a little dish and drizzle the vinegar over the top. If your vinegar just forms a giant blob in the center of your olive oil, use a fork to swirl it around a few times before serving, to make it look a little more interesting.

Serve your antipasto chilled with the slices of bread in a basket on the side and the olive oil and vinegar in the center. You'll need bamboo skewers or serving forks so your guests can build their plates, and a small spoon in the olive oil and vinegar so guests can drizzle the mixture over their food. Some prefer squeezing the fresh lemons instead. That's part of what makes this appetizer so wonderful. Everyone gets what they want.

BIG BABY HOT WINGS

When I married an Irish-Italian boy from Boston, I knew what I was getting into…unlike the Miami Heat the week we made this recipe for the first time during the 2010 NBA play-offs. They might have thought that since Kevin Garnett was suspended, they had a chance against the Celtics. Even the die-hard Boston fans were like, "How will we live without him?" What they didn't count on was Glen "Big Baby" Davis stepping up and proving to us all that just because someone or something is a substitute doesn't mean they can't bring it! Just like these faux chicken wings that we have renamed *Big Baby Hot Wings*…because even the Heat have nothing on how hot they are! Sadly, since we made this recipe, Big Baby was traded to the Orlando Magic…but the name lives on.

MAKES 8 TO 10 WINGS

2 tablespoons margarine

½ cup whole wheat flour

½ teaspoon crushed pink Himalayan salt

¼ teaspoon crushed black peppercorns

8 to 10 vegan chicken wings (see "Vegan Chicken Wings" on page 137 for substitutions)

1 cup of your favorite barbecue sauce

2 tablespoons hot sauce

1 teaspoon Tony Chachere's Creole seasoning

¼ teaspoon liquid smoke

½ teaspoon cumin

1 batch Vegan Ranch Dressing (page 110)

Celery sticks, carrots, or other raw vegetables

Preheat the oven to 425°F.

In a 13 x 9-inch pan, melt the margarine in the oven. In a large ziplock bag, mix the flour, salt, and pepper. Put the vegan chicken in the bag, 2 pieces at a time, and shake until your vegan chicken gets a nice even coating. Place the coated vegan chicken in the pan.

Bake uncovered for 3 to 5 minutes and then flip your vegan chicken to make sure it gets completely covered with your margarine. It should take 5 to 10 minutes for the vegan chicken to become a golden color and have a crispy coating.

While your vegan chicken bakes, mix the barbecue sauce, hot sauce, Creole seasoning, liquid smoke, and cumin in a bowl.

Once your vegan chicken has a golden crispy coating, pull it out of the oven and pour the barbecue mixture over the entire dish. Flip your vegan chicken a few times to make sure it gets completely coated.

Bake uncovered for 10 to 12 minutes, or until your barbecue sauce makes a sticky glaze. Some folks like their vegan chicken wings more sticky than saucy, so this is kind of your call.

Serve with Vegan Ranch Dressing on the side to dip your vegan chicken in and some raw vegetables to cool your palate once in a while. Also because vegetables are good for you and you should eat them every day.

BAKED JALAPEÑOS STUFFED WITH AWESOME

Imagine some of the most popular savory "guilty pleasure" foods stuffed in a jalapeño and then baked.

MAKES 24 JALAPEÑOS

½ cup vegan cream cheese (we recommend Tofutti Better Than Cream Cheese)

1 tablespoon vegan sour cream

3 tablespoons vegan bacon bits

3 green onions, diced

2 cloves garlic, minced

½ cup shredded Daiya vegan mozzarella cheese or your favorite vegan mozzarella

2 tablespoons chopped fresh cilantro

1½ teaspoons cumin

1 teaspoon dried oregano

Dash of liquid smoke

12 large jalapeño peppers, cut in half lengthwise and seeded

Nutritional yeast (a pinch per pepper)

Preheat the oven to 375°F. Line a baking sheet with foil.

In a large mixing bowl, blend all ingredients except the jalapeños and nutritional yeast.

Pack each jalapeño half with vegan cream cheese filling and arrange them on the baking sheet. Bake for 20 minutes, or until your vegan cheese is bubbly and lightly browned and the jalapeños have crispy edges.

Allow to cool to the point that you can touch them, and sprinkle with a pinch of nutritional yeast before serving.

FAUX FONDUE

Here's one of my many, many freak flags: sometimes I like to be "French." I love French music. I like French movies. I wear black a lot. I like bike rides and wearing hats all year round. I've even been known to wear a scarf with a T-shirt or sundress. I *love* vegan French food! I know this sounds obnoxious. I guess if we're being honest, I am a *Frenchie* (I am also the most mixed-up nondelinquent on the block). So really, it only makes sense that I'd get so excited about Betty Crocker's fondue—even though technically it's a Swiss dish. But if you've ever been to France, you know that the French take pride in getting creative with cheese. Our fondue might not be "real" cheese, but we're not really French or Swiss—so what's the harm in enjoying something that's better for you and the cows? *Bon appétit!*

MAKES 10 TO 12 SERVINGS

½ cup margarine

2 tablespoons whole wheat flour

2½ cups nutritional yeast

1½ cups water

3 teaspoons Bragg's liquid aminos

Dash of liquid smoke

1½ teaspoons garlic powder

1 teaspoon onion powder

1 cup dry white wine

1 tablespoon lemon juice

2 cloves garlic, minced

1 teaspoon dry sherry

2 cups shredded Daiya vegan mozzarella cheese or your favorite vegan mozzarella

2 whole wheat baguettes, sliced and slightly toasted

Apple and pear slices for dipping

Melt the margarine in a Dutch oven or soup pot over low heat. Blend in the flour and nutritional yeast with a whisk a little at a time until smooth. Then whisk in the following ingredients in this order: water, Bragg's, liquid smoke, garlic powder, onion powder, white wine, lemon juice, garlic, and sherry. Simmer till the mixture starts to bubble. Using a spoon, stir in your vegan cheese. Turn the heat up a little and let your vegan cheese melt. Stir the mixture occasionally to keep the vegan cheese from sticking to the bottom.

Serve warm with the toasted slices of baguette and fruit. You'll have a lot—so invite over some friends and make sure you have enough skewers for everyone.

> **TIP:** The pear slices were particularly delicious with the Faux Fondue.

FAUX FONDUE AU BEURRE D'ARACHIDE

Remember those old commercials where folks tried to figure out how they thought up putting peanut butter in the chocolate? Well, I'm not sure who thought of that, but I can tell you that this peanut butter fondue is a really good dessert dish that is kind of fun over chocolate or even with some celery sticks.

MAKES 8 TO 10 SERVINGS

1 teaspoon margarine
½ cup brown sugar
¼ cup almond milk

1 tablespoon tahini
1 tablespoon agave nectar
1½ cups creamy peanut butter

Chilled dark chocolate, broken into pieces
1 baguette, sliced and slightly toasted
Celery sticks and apple slices for dipping

Heat the margarine, brown sugar, almond milk, tahini, and agave nectar to a boil in your Dutch oven or soup pot over medium heat. Once your margarine melts, use a whisk to blend in the brown sugar and prevent clumping.

Once your ingredients begin to bubble, whisk in the peanut butter until smooth.

Serve warm with the chocolate, toasted slices of baguette, fruit, and veggies for dipping. Don't forget the skewers!

> **TIP:** Most Oreos on the market are vegan and are delicious with this sauce.

SKILLET NACHOS

Every fall, there are literally millions of folks who are focused on two things: football and basketball. Our home includes all the above. Dan is addicted to sports and fantasy sports and all that's included. It's slowly spreading. I find myself knowing players' names and taking a genuine interest in things that I never had any interest in before. Maybe this is what it means to really be a life partner. If you find yourself in the same spot, you may need these nachos. They're a full meal for two or a great party dish, and the bean chili dip is so good, I was eating it with a spoon. Once we put these down on the coffee table, it was on till the break of dawn...or really, until halftime. We ate them pretty fast.

MAKES 4 TO 6 SERVINGS

Olive oil cooking spray

½ red onion, diced

1 green bell pepper, diced

1 (14-ounce) can black beans, drained and rinsed

1 (14-ounce) can pinto beans in chili sauce

1 cup DIY Salsa (page 433)

1 teaspoon cumin

Dash of liquid smoke

1 tablespoon Bragg's liquid aminos

1 tablespoon smoked chipotle peppers, diced

Dash of hot sauce

½ to ¾ 9-ounce bag tortilla chips

1 cup shredded Daiya vegan cheddar cheese or your favorite vegan cheddar

¼ cup sliced black olives

1 batch Dan's Guacamole (page 432), optional

Spray your cast-iron skillet with olive oil cooking spray and heat over medium heat. Add the red onion and green pepper and cook for around 2 minutes, or until tender. Add the black beans, pinto beans with chili sauce, salsa, cumin, liquid smoke, Bragg's, chipotle peppers, and hot sauce and stir until completely mixed. Stir frequently, remove from the heat when your bean mixture begins to boil, and place in a bowl.

Turn the heat down to low. Spray your skillet with olive oil again. Make an even layer of tortilla chips in the warm skillet. Be careful not to touch the sides of the hot skillet. You want to also make sure there aren't any big holes or tall piles of chips in the layer. Spoon an even layer of 1 to 1½ cups of your bean mixture over the chips. Spread your vegan cheese over the beans and chips.

Cover and cook for around 5 minutes, or until your vegan cheese melts. Be careful to not wait too long, though, because you don't want your chips to burn. Sprinkle your olives on top and serve in the skillet with the remaining bean mixture on the side to dip your chips in...We also had guacamole with ours, and it was pretty much the best thing ever.

BBQ CHICKEN NACHOS

The hardest thing about this recipe was trying to figure out how to put something green in there. When I closed my eyes and imagined all the parts of a barbecue that we could combine to make a plate of nachos—all Zoltron style—well, all the greens were too wilty. Basically what I'm saying is…enjoy these nachos with a salad.

MAKES 8 TO 10 SERVINGS

Olive oil cooking spray

Dash of liquid smoke

2 cups diced vegan chicken (we recommend Lightlife Smart Strips, Chick'n)

½ red onion, diced

1 (14-ounce) can pinto beans, drained and rinsed

½ cup frozen corn, defrosted

1 cup of your favorite barbecue sauce

1 bag tortilla chips

1½ cups shredded Daiya vegan cheddar cheese or your favorite vegan cheddar

1 large tomato, diced

1 fresh jalapeño, diced

Preheat the oven to 325°F. Cover a rimmed cookie sheet with foil.

Spray your favorite cast-iron skillet with olive oil cooking spray and throw in a dash of liquid smoke. Heat your skillet over medium heat. Once your skillet is hot, toss in your vegan chicken, onion, and pinto beans and use your spatula to mix. Once your onion is tender, mix in your corn and barbecue sauce. Turn the heat down to a simmer. Once your barbecue sauce starts to bubble, remove your skillet from the heat and set aside.

Arrange your chips on the cookie sheet in an even layer. Sprinkle the vegan cheese in an even layer over the top of your chips and put your cookie sheet in the oven to bake for 5 to 8 minutes, or until your vegan cheese melts.

Serve your chips and vegan cheese with your barbecue chicken mixture over the top and the tomato and jalapeño sprinkled over that.

BAKED SPICY QUESADILLAS

Sometimes we come across one of Betty Crocker's recipes that makes us ask ourselves, "Does this really need a recipe?" The thing is, we don't make the rules, and if the Betty Crocker brand believes this needs a recipe, well, it does. Also, some people are beginners…so if our version is helpful to you, that's good enough for us!

MAKES 12 TO 18 QUESADILLA SLICES

2 cups shredded Daiya vegan cheddar cheese or your favorite vegan cheddar

6 flour tortillas

4 medium green onions, chopped

2 tablespoons diced fresh jalapeños

¾ cup chopped raw spinach

Fresh cilantro, a batch of DIY Salsa (page 433), and ripe avocado slices for topping

Preheat the oven to 350°F.

Spread ⅓ cup of the vegan cheese evenly over half of each tortilla. Sprinkle the green onions, jalapeños, and spinach over your vegan cheese. Fold the tortilla over your filling and place on your pizza stone or cookie sheet.

Bake for about 5 minutes, or until your vegan cheese is melted and your tortilla is golden brown. Cut each tortilla into 2 to 3 wedges and top with cilantro, salsa, and avocado.

BAKED GREEK QUESADILLAS

A blend of Mediterranean cultural traditions that'll leave you confused about which language you should butcher trying to describe how delicious it is.

MAKES 12 TO 18 QUESADILLA SLICES

2 cups shredded Daiya vegan mozzarella cheese or your favorite vegan mozzarella

6 flour tortillas

2 tablespoons crumbled vegan feta cheese

2 Roma tomatoes, sliced

½ cup pitted diced kalamata olives

½ cup baby spinach leaves

⅓ cup sliced white mushrooms

3 tablespoons diced peperoncini

½ teaspoon capers, drained

Vegan Tzatziki Sauce (page 289)

Preheat the oven to 350°F.

Spread ⅓ cup vegan cheese evenly over half of each tortilla. Sprinkle the vegan feta, tomatoes, olives, spinach, mushrooms, peperoncini, and capers over your vegan cheese and fold your tortilla over. Place on your pizza stone or cookie sheet.

Bake for about 5 minutes, or until your vegan cheese melts and your tortilla is golden brown. Cut each tortilla into 2 to 3 wedges and serve with a side of Vegan Tzatziki Sauce.

POTATO SKINS WITH THE WORKS

A classic recipe for bar food, served in the comfort of your own home. Pair with your favorite microbrew, put a game on TV, and try to act interested as your husband explains what a zone defense is. Maybe that's just me.

MAKES 16 TO 24 SKINS

4 to 6 medium to large russet potatoes

½ cup margarine

¾ cup shredded Daiya vegan cheddar cheese or your favorite vegan cheddar

⅓ cup vegan sour cream

4 to 6 tablespoons vegan bacon bits (1 tablespoon per potato skin)

8 green onions, diced

Preheat the oven to 375°F.

Prick your potatoes with a fork and bake for around 1 hour, or until tender. Remove your tender potatoes from the oven and let cool for 10 minutes. Then cut into fourths lengthwise. Carefully use a spoon to scoop out a little of the soft pulp in the center. You want to leave most of the soft potato on the skin but also create a little bowl or cup for your toppings. Save the pulp to eat later as mashed potatoes or in soup.

Set your oven to broil or turn on your broiler.

Place your potato skins, skin down, on a covered broiler pan. With a butter knife, spread the margarine over them. You might not need to use all the margarine.

Broil your potato skins for 8 minutes, until the edges are crispy. Then sprinkle the vegan cheese over each buttered skin. Put your skins back in the broiler and broil for 30 seconds, or until your vegan cheese melts.

Serve hot with the vegan sour cream, vegan bacon bits, and green onions over the top and a cooler of your favorite beer!

MEXICAN CROSTINI

As far as I know, there has never been a Betty Crocker recipe for an appetizer like this, which is the hybrid of two of the most popular types of food out there. But we decided to make this one anyway—and not just to have another excuse to eat avocados.

MAKES 10 TO 12 CROSTINI

¼ cup olive oil

4 teaspoons hot sauce

10 to 12 (½-inch-thick) slices of baguette

2 ripe avocados, peeled and pitted

½ red onion, diced

½ cup black beans, cooked, drained, and rinsed

2 plum tomatoes, diced

2 tablespoons chopped fresh cilantro

2 tablespoons lime juice

2 cloves garlic, minced

1 teaspoon cumin

½ teaspoon cayenne pepper

⅓ cup black olives, sliced

1 fresh jalapeño, diced

Preheat the oven to 375°F. Cover a cookie sheet with foil.

In a small bowl, blend the olive oil and hot sauce with a whisk. Lay your slices of baguette out in an even layer on your cookie sheet. Brush your baguette slices with the olive oil and hot sauce blend. The vinegar in the hot sauce is going to make the two ingredients separate, so watch out for that. You might need to whisk the oil and hot sauce a few times to keep them from separating. Put your bread slices in the oven and let them brown for around 1½ minutes. Once the edges of your bread are lightly toasted, pull the bread from the oven and let cool on the pan.

In a large bowl, mash your avocados with a handheld pastry blender. Then use a large spoon to gently mix in the onion, beans, tomatoes, cilantro, lime juice, garlic, cumin, and cayenne pepper. Spread your avocado mixture over the baguette slices. Garnish with olives and jalapeños.

Olé!

CANNELLINI, KALE, AND BASIL CROSTINI

I've heard that a fear of commitment is one of the most popular self-diagnosed phobias in our society. I understand it, but it's not really a phobia I have. I mean, I'm not perfect. Needles can send me into a panic attack, and sandwiches with wet bread give me the chills. I also might have a mild case of social anxiety issues that I should Google more about. Though I'm pretty sure it's just run-of-the-mill shyness. Don't worry, I'm getting to my point: I want to marry these crostini.

MAKES 10 TO 12 CROSTINI

¼ cup olive oil

2 cloves garlic, minced

10 to 12 (½-inch-thick) slices of baguette

¾ cup baby kale leaves, steamed

1 (14-ounce) can cannellini beans, drained and rinsed

4 tablespoons chopped fresh basil

1 tablespoon dry white wine

1 teaspoon Bragg's liquid aminos

⅓ cup shredded Daiya vegan mozzarella cheese or your favorite vegan mozzarella

½ teaspoon crushed black peppercorns

Preheat the oven to 375°F. Cover a cookie sheet with foil.

Whisk together the olive oil and garlic in a mixing bowl. Place your slices of baguette on your cookie sheet. Brush your garlicky olive oil over your slices of bread and put them in the oven for no longer than 1½ minutes. You want the bread slices to be very lightly toasted.

In another mixing bowl, toss the kale, beans, basil, wine, and Bragg's. Spoon enough kale and bean mixture over each slice of bread to cover it. Then sprinkle about a tablespoon of vegan mozzarella over the top and put the bread back in the oven.

Let the crostini bake for about 10 minutes, or until your vegan mozzarella melts and the crusts are golden. Serve warm with some freshly ground black peppercorns over the top and with the leftover garlicky oil in a little bowl on the side to dip the crusts in. Yeah, it's kind of messy, so remember the napkins.

MON CHER MUFFULETTA CROSTINI

A muffuletta is a classic New Orleans sandwich made of about a million different deli meats and an olive spread. This recipe takes those flavors and makes them snackable—and vegan, of course.

MAKES 10 TO 12 CROSTINI

....

10 to 12 (½-inch-thick) slices of baguette

1½ cups Green Olive Salad (page 410)

¼ cup olive oil

⅓ cup shredded Daiya vegan mozzarella cheese or your favorite vegan mozzarella

8 slices Peppered Tofurky Deli Slices, separated and chopped

8 slices Field Roast Lentil Sage Deli Slices, separated and chopped

Grated smoked cheddar Sheese (a pinch per crostini)

½ teaspoon crushed black peppercorns

Sliced peperoncini for garnish

....

Preheat the oven to 375°F.

On an uncovered cookie pan, place the bread slices and toast lightly in the oven for no more than 1½ minutes.

In a large bowl, make your Green Olive Salad (page 410). When you remove the bread slices from the oven, flip them over in the same spot and drizzle 1 teaspoon of olive oil over each slice.

Then put 1 to 2 pinches of vegan mozzarella on your bread. Try to spread it out a little to cover the bread. Put an even amount of Tofurky and Field Roast on each slice of bread and then a pinch of Sheese followed by another pinch of vegan mozzarella and sprinkle with the crushed black peppercorn. Once all your crostini are built, put your pan back in the oven.

Bake for no more than 10 minutes—just long enough for your vegan cheese to melt. Check on them often. After your crostini are toasted, top each with a large spoon of Green Olive Salad and a slice of peperoncini. Serve warm, and remember the napkins because this is one of the best things to eat in the world…and that means it's gotta be messy.

GOOD FELLAS CROSTINI

This is a recipe for those classic crispy and garlicky crostini you find on restaurant menus. I won't insult you by pretending my Sicilian grandmother made these before Sunday dinner or something. These are the perfect homemade happy hour or party appetizers. They're easy and quick, and best of all they have capers in them. No, not the mysteries … the flower buds of *Capparis spinosa*, a prickly, perennial plant native to the Mediterranean and some parts of Asia. They come in little jars and are extremely cute.

MAKES 10 TO 12 CROSTINI

10 to 12 (½-inch-thick) slices of baguette

1 tomato, diced

4 tablespoons chopped fresh basil

1 tablespoon capers, drained

1 teaspoon Bragg's liquid aminos

½ teaspoon crushed black peppercorns

¼ cup olive oil

Shredded Daiya vegan mozzarella cheese or your favorite vegan mozzarella (a pinch per crostini)

Preheat the oven to 375°F.

Place your bread slices on an uncovered cookie sheet and toast lightly in the oven for no more than 1½ minutes.

In a large bowl, combine the tomato, basil, capers, Bragg's, and pepper. When you remove your toasted bread slices from the oven, just flip them over in the same spot and drizzle 1 teaspoon of the olive oil over each toasted slice of bread.

Then spoon just enough of your tomato mixture over each toasted slice of bread to cover it evenly. You will have some left over, but that's okay. Just put it in a cup for dipping crusts later. Top your tomato mixture with a pinch of vegan mozzarella and put the pan back in the oven.

Bake for no more than 10 minutes. Check on the crostini often. You want to remove them when the crusts are golden brown and your vegan mozzarella is melted. Serve warm, and remember the napkins—these crostini can be messy.

BLT CROSTINI

Keep an open mind: this is actually a pretty remarkable appetizer. See, if you were one of the folks who followed the Betty Crocker Project on our blog, you know that some of the Betty Crocker recipes seem kinda random, but that's how our little project meets its quotas for danger and adventure. Our recipe ended up looking a lot different from the Betty Crocker recipe, but I actually love these crostini in a way that I've never really loved BLT sandwiches. I hope you'll give them a chance and add some kitschy style to your next party.

MAKES 10 TO 12 CROSTINI

10 to 12 (½-inch-thick) slices of baguette

3 tablespoons olive oil

3 tablespoons vegan cream cheese (we recommend Tofutti Better Than Cream Cheese)

3 tablespoons shredded Daiya vegan mozzarella cheese or your favorite vegan cheese

2 teaspoons capers, drained

1 teaspoon garlic powder

1 teaspoon finely chopped fresh parsley

2 small Roma tomatoes, sliced

3 teaspoons vegan bacon bits or crumbled smoked tempeh

Freshly ground black peppercorns (a few dashes per crostini)

4 to 6 leaves red leaf lettuce, chopped

Preheat the oven to 400°F.

Brush one side of your slices of baguette with olive oil and place on your pizza stone to bake with the olive oil side up. You want your bread to get just slightly crispy, so pull the pizza stone from the oven as soon as you see the bread even begin to slightly brown. It should take no more than a minute. Depending on how large your pizza stone is, you might have to toast your baguette in batches.

While you are toasting your baguette, you can make your vegan cheese mixture. Mix your vegan cream cheese, vegan cheese, capers, garlic powder, and parsley in a large bowl with an electric handheld mixer until smooth. Spread each toasted slice of baguette with your vegan cheese mixture on the side that was brushed with olive oil. Place one slice of tomato and sprinkle some vegan bacon bits over the top, and then gently press them down to secure your toppings in your vegan cheese mix. Put your crostini back in the oven to bake.

It should take about 15 minutes for your vegan cheese to melt and get slightly golden brown. Remove the crostini from the oven and let cool on a wire rack until they can be handled but are still warm. Dash some black pepper over the top of your crostini while they cool. Put a pinch of red leaf lettuce on top right before you serve.

Happy eating!

ROASTED GARLIC

Sometimes I think roasted garlic looks good; sometimes not so much. But even when it's ugly, it's *delicious!*

MAKES 4 TO 6 SERVINGS

4 bulbs raw garlic

16 teaspoons olive oil (4 teaspoons per bulb)

Crushed pink Himalayan salt and crushed black peppercorns

Sliced French bread

Preheat the oven to 350°F.

Cut about ¼ inch down from the tip of the garlic bulb to expose the cloves. Carefully peel the paper skin off each bulb, being sure to leave just enough to hold the bulbs together. Then place the bulbs, exposed cloves up, in a small oven-safe dish and drizzle your olive oil over the bulbs. Add salt and pepper to taste. Cover with foil and put in the oven. Bake for 45 minutes, or until your garlic is tender when you poke it with a toothpick. Let the garlic cool and then serve by gently squeezing the soft paste out of the roasted cloves onto the slices of bread.

GREEN OLIVE TAPENADE

If you're looking for more ways to level up your olives, may I suggest this recipe that combines green olives and awesome into a spread that's good on everything from toasted baguette slices to vegan chicken sandwiches? I recommend this tapenade on warm pita with a side of red grapes.

MAKES 6 TO 8 SERVINGS

1¼ cups green Spanish olives, pitted

¼ cup marinated artichoke hearts

2 tablespoons raw pine nuts

2 teaspoons lemon juice

1 tablespoon capers, drained

2 cloves garlic, minced

¼ cup olive oil

1 tablespoon chopped fresh cilantro

Freshly ground black peppercorns

Toasted baguette slices

Blend the olives, artichoke hearts, pine nuts, lemon juice, capers, garlic, and olive oil in your food processor or blender.

Transfer the tapenade to a bowl. Stir in the cilantro and season to taste with pepper. Serve the tapenade with the toasted baguette slices.

GRILLED ANTIPASTO PLATTER WITH LEMON AIOLI

The citrusy zest in the lemon aioli really brings out the savory flavors of the antipasto in this recipe. Enjoy it with a nice glass of red wine.

MAKES 8 TO 10 SERVINGS

1 zucchini, cut into 4-inch sticks

1 yellow summer squash, cut into 4-inch sticks

1 red bell pepper, cut into 2-inch pieces

1 (14.75-ounce) can whole artichoke hearts

½ cup marinated asparagus spears

1 cup cherry tomatoes

1 cup whole white mushrooms

½ cup whole kalamata olives, pitted

½ cup large Sicilian green olives, pitted

½ cup peperoncini

6 to 8 whole cloves garlic

3 tablespoons olive oil

2 teaspoons fresh oregano leaves

1 package peppered Tofurky Deli Slices, separated

½ cup cubed smoked cheddar Sheese or Daiya jalapeño garlic wedge

1 tablespoon chopped fresh basil

1 batch Lemon Aioli (page 283)

Heat your coals or gas grill for direct heat. Combine the vegetables, olives, pepperoncini, garlic, olive oil, and oregano in a large bowl and toss until all the ingredients are lightly coated in oil and oregano. Heat your grill basket until hot. Toss your coated vegetables into your grill basket. Cover and grill the vegetables for 5 to 10 minutes, shaking your basket to stir your vegetables occasionally.

Roll your Tofurky into little tubes and arrange them around the edge of a large serving platter. Once your vegetables are tender and lightly charred, pour them into the center of your serving platter. Sprinkle vegan cheese cubes over the vegetables. Sprinkle the fresh basil over the top and serve with a side of the Lemon Aioli for dipping.

VEGAN CHICKEN LETTUCE ROLLS

These lettuce wraps require very little cooking and eased our suffering during Brooklyn's 2011 heat wave—known in the local media as the Heat Dome. If you're wondering if that's worse than the Thunderdome...it seriously is. We're not big on air-conditioning, so the Heat Dome was pretty much a nightmare for us. You'd think we'd be used to heat after years in Virginia. Back then, the sadistic humidity gave us an excuse to drive to the beach. On nights when we were feeling kinda fancy, we'd stop by P.F. Chang's on the way back. Their vegan lettuce wrap appetizers are pretty spectacular and always went perfectly with sunburned shoulders and large lemonades. We made ours with Gardein Crispy Tenders and enjoyed them with some beers from Brooklyn's Sixpoint Brewery,[*] a game of Civilization, and a giant fan pointed directly at us. It was like hanging out in a wind tunnel.

MAKES 8 TO 10 SERVINGS

Olive oil cooking spray

1 (9-ounce) package Gardein Crispy Tenders vegan chicken or your favorite vegan breaded chicken nuggets, defrosted

1 (8-ounce) can water chestnuts, sliced

2½ teaspoons minced fresh ginger

1 tablespoon sliced raw almonds

2 tablespoons Bragg's liquid aminos

2 cloves garlic, minced

1 tablespoon lime juice

2 teaspoons agave nectar

2 tablespoons teriyaki sauce

3 celery stalks, chopped

½ cup shredded carrots

¼ cup cilantro, chopped

½ head of iceberg or Bibb lettuce

Spray your wok with olive oil cooking spray and heat over high heat. Once your oil is hot, toss in your defrosted vegan chicken. Begin to cook your vegan chicken while flipping occasionally. Once the breading begins to get crispy, add the water chestnuts, 1½ teaspoons of the ginger, the almonds, Bragg's, and garlic. Reduce the heat to medium. Don't worry if the breading begins to come off your vegan chicken. It will become little crunchy bits in the mixture. Continue to stir-fry your vegan chicken and other ingredients until your vegan chicken gets a nice golden brown. Then transfer your mixture to a large bowl and set it aside to cool.

In another large bowl, whisk together the remaining 1 teaspoon ginger, the lime juice, agave nectar, and teriyaki sauce. Add the celery, carrots, and cilantro and toss. Let sit for 10 to 15 minutes so your vegetables can marinate a little in the sauce. While that's happening, dump your vegan chicken mixture onto a cutting board and lightly chop into large chunks. Scrape your vegan chicken mixture into your vegetable mixture and toss to combine.

Serve with fresh lettuce leaves and some napkins...it can be messy. You're going to be spooning the vegan chicken and vegetables into your lettuce leaves and then folding the leaves over like little tacos. Be careful—lettuce isn't as durable a good tortilla.

---

[*] Go local or go home—right?

CLEMENTINE AND OLIVE-STUFFED ENDIVE LEAVES

"Clementines and olives—together?" you're thinking. "This lady is *crazy*." I'm telling you—this flavor combination, and this guaranteed-to-impress party recipe, is delicious. As for whether or not I'm crazy, well, that's another matter entirely.

MAKES 14 TO 16 SERVINGS

2 to 3 pounds Belgian endives (this should be enough for you to have 14 to 16 good-size leaves to stuff)

1½ teaspoons grated orange peel

2 teaspoons lemon juice

¼ cup olive oil

8 to 9 ripe clementine oranges, peeled, skinned, seeded, and segmented

1 cup kalamata olives, pitted and drained

4 celery stalks, chopped

2 tablespoons chopped fresh parsley

1½ teaspoons capers, drained

¼ cup shredded Daiya vegan mozzarella cheese or your favorite vegan cheese

Crushed pink Himalayan salt and crushed black peppercorns to taste

Separate your endive leaves and spread them out onto your serving plate or plates to see how many you have. Cover with plastic wrap.

In your smallest mixing bowl, whisk together your orange peel, lemon juice, and olive oil.

In your largest mixing bowl, toss your orange segments, olives, celery, parsley, capers, and vegan cheese. Give it one last taste test and add any needed salt and pepper. Remove the plastic wrap from the endive leaves. Using a spoon, fill your endive leaves with the orange and olive mix. Try to get an even amount of orange segments and olives in each leaf. Drizzle no more than ½ teaspoon of your olive oil blend over the top of each endive leaf.

Re-cover with plastic wrap until serving.

DAN'S GUACAMOLE

Is anything better than guacamole? (Thinks.) Nope, can't think of anything. This classic Mexican dish, and its name, dates back to the pre-Columbian Aztecs—which makes guacamole even cooler, something I never would have thought possible.

MAKES 4 TO 6 SERVINGS

2 large ripe avocados

2 tablespoons lime juice

1 clove garlic, minced

1 tablespoon chopped cilantro

1 teaspoon onion powder

1 fresh jalapeño, diced

1 teaspoon hot sauce

Crushed pink Himalayan salt and crushed black peppercorns

Mash your avocados into a paste and mix in the rest of the ingredients. Then eat—eat—eat.

CHIPOTLE BLACK BEAN SALSA

This flavorful take on salsa is incredibly easy to make—especially if you have a partner who specializes in chopping vegetables. It's guaranteed to impress at any get-together, and guaranteed to disappear in under 5 minutes flat.

MAKES 4 TO 6 SERVINGS

1 (14-ounce) can black beans, drained and rinsed

1 tomato, diced

1 green bell pepper, diced

1 chipotle pepper, diced

2 tablespoons India Pale Ale beer

1 tablespoon olive oil

1 tablespoon Bragg's liquid aminos

½ teaspoon fresh oregano leaves

1 tablespoon fresh cilantro, diced

2 tablespoons lime juice

Mix all the ingredients in an airtight container and refrigerate for 2 hours before serving.

DIY SALSA

This is a simple recipe for classic salsa that'll blow any of that store-bought nonsense out of the water. Once you've made your own, you'll never go back.

MAKES 6 SERVINGS

3 large tomatoes

1 green bell pepper, diced

8 green onions, diced

3 cloves garlic, minced

2 tablespoons chopped fresh cilantro

1 tablespoon diced fresh jalapeños

3 tablespoons lime juice

½ teaspoon crushed pink Himalayan salt

Mix everything together in a large mixing bowl. Cover the bowl and refrigerate it for at least an hour.

SALSA VERDE

This is my favorite salsa of all the salsas to ever salsa.

MAKES 4 TO 6 SERVINGS

2 pounds whole tomatillos, husked

2 tablespoons sliced fresh jalapeños

2 cloves garlic, minced

1 teaspoon cumin

Pinch of cayenne pepper (more if you like it spicy)

2 tablespoons lime juice

1 tablespoon chopped fresh cilantro

1½ cups water

Place all the ingredients in your *chiquitita* cast-iron skillet, cover, and heat on medium heat for 10 minutes. Check on your salsa often and stir it to blend the flavors.

Pour into your food processor and blend until it is a smooth liquid. Put the salsa in an airtight container and chill in the fridge for 20 minutes.

SNACKS

It's not hard to find vegan snacks these days. I've been on road trips through Texas barbecue country where gas stations were where locals went on date night and found hummus and baby carrots. I've been on trains in countries where I didn't speak the language and still found bags of vegan peanut-butter-flavored puffed corn yummies that were actually really good. So this section is more for the DIY type. These snacks are as fun to make as they are to eat.

HOMEMADE POTATO CHIPS

Here are a few fun facts about our Homemade Potato Chips before we start: These chips are baked, not fried. The key to a great homemade potato chip is slicing your chips as thin and as even as possible. You may want to have a few practice potatoes to play around with. The reject chips can be used in the Ultimate Corn Chowder Experience recipe (page 60) to replace the hash browns. If you have a mandoline (see "Where Do They Get Those Wonderful Toys?" on page 16), I would recommend using it to get the thinnest and most even slices.

Shall we begin?

MAKES 4 TO 6 SERVINGS

Olive oil cooking spray

6 medium to large russet or sweet potatoes

1 teaspoon crushed black peppercorns

3 teaspoons crushed pink Himalayan salt

½ teaspoon garlic powder

Preheat the oven to 425°F. Line a cookie sheet with foil and coat with an even, heavy layer of olive oil cooking spray.

With a very sharp knife or mandoline, thinly slice your potatoes diagonally to get the largest yet thinnest chips possible. You want them to be around ⅛ inch thick.

Arrange your potato slices on the cookie sheet so none of them are touching. Spray another even layer of cooking spray over the top. We had to make ours in 3 batches. If you have to do that, don't worry. They actually bake quickly.

Bake your chips for 5 to 8 minutes and then flip them. Put them back in the oven to bake for another 8 to 10 minutes. Pull them out of the oven when the chips are a light golden brown and crispy. Keep in mind that the thinner your chips are sliced, the quicker they will brown.

In a bowl, mix the black pepper, salt, and garlic powder. When you pull the chips from the oven, they are really hot but they are also kind of fragile, like store-bought potato chips, so very gently move them to a wire rack to cool. Using a slotted spoon, sprinkle the salt and pepper mixture over the top of the warm chips before the oil cools, to help attach the mixture to the chips.

Let them cool to room temperature before gobbling them up by the handful!

SEA SALT AND VINEGAR CHIPS

This is one of my favorite potato chip flavors, but it's usually not vegan, which pisses me off because it's not necessary to put animals in there. But now we can make our own.

MAKES 4 TO 6 SERVINGS

4 cups malt vinegar

2 tablespoons water

2 cloves garlic, minced

6 medium to large russet potatoes

Olive oil cooking spray

1 teaspoon crushed black peppercorns

4 teaspoons crushed sea salt

½ teaspoon garlic powder

Fill a large glass lasagna dish with the vinegar, water, and garlic and blend with a whisk.

With a very sharp knife or mandoline, thinly slice your potatoes diagonally to get the largest and thinnest chips possible. You want them to be around ⅛ inch thick. Place each slice immediately into the vinegar mix. Once all your potato slices are in the vinegar, cover your dish with foil and refrigerate for 1½ hours. Then pull out the dish and rotate your potato slices so that the ones that were at the bottom of the dish are now at the top. Put the dish back in the fridge for another 1½ hours. You'll notice that some of the slices have started to curl, and that's okay.

Preheat the oven to 425°F.

Line a cookie sheet with foil and coat with an even layer of olive oil cooking spray. Arrange your marinated potato slices on the cookie sheet in an even layer so none of them are touching. Spray another even layer of cooking spray over the top.

We had to make ours in 3 batches. If you have to do that, don't worry. They actually bake quickly and the ones that have to wait in the vinegar longer are only slightly more flavorful.

Bake your chips for 5 to 8 minutes and then flip them. Put them back in the oven to bake for another 8 to 10 minutes. Pull them out of the oven when the chips are a light golden brown and they are crispy. Keep in mind that the thinner your chips are sliced, the quicker they will brown.

In a bowl, mix the black pepper, sea salt, and garlic powder. When you pull the chips from the oven, they are really hot but they are also kind of fragile, like store-bought potato chips, so very gently move them to a wire rack to cool. Using a slotted spoon, sprinkle the pepper and salt mixture over the top of the warm chips before the oil cools, to help attach the mixture to the chips.

While your chips cool to room temperature, you'll have more than enough time to make yourself a Tofurky Reuben sandwich (page 81) to go with them.

LITTLE BIT CHEEZY POPCORN

Betty Crocker has convinced me to never buy microwave popcorn again, and now you don't have to either.

MAKES 6 TO 8 SERVINGS

½ cup uncooked popcorn

¼ cup olive oil

2 tablespoons nutritional yeast

In a 4-quart Dutch oven or soup pot with a lid, put the popcorn and olive oil. Rotate the Dutch oven so your popcorn and oil spread out evenly. Cover and cook over medium heat until the first kernel pops. Remove from the heat and let stand while you count to 45. Return to the heat.

Cook, shaking the pan occasionally, until the popcorn stops popping. Immediately pour the popcorn into a serving bowl. Sprinkle your bowl of popcorn with nutritional yeast.

CARAMEL CORN

Now you can make your own version of this classic ballpark snack in your very own friendly confines. Spending three hours watching grown men scratch themselves: optional.

MAKES 6 TO 8 SERVINGS

½ cup uncooked popcorn

¼ cup olive oil

½ cup brown sugar

2 tablespoons apple juice

2 tablespoons water

1 tablespoon margarine

1 tablespoon agave nectar

¼ teaspoon crushed pink Himalayan salt

¼ teaspoon arrowroot

1 teaspoon vanilla extract

In a 4-quart Dutch oven or a soup pot with a lid, put the popcorn and olive oil. Rotate the Dutch oven so your popcorn and oil spread out evenly. Cover and cook over medium heat until the first kernel pops. Remove from the heat and let stand while you count to 45. Return to the heat.

Cook, shaking the pan occasionally, until the popcorn stops popping. Immediately pour it into a serving bowl. Separate out any unpopped kernels and discard those bad seeds.

In your warm Dutch oven, heat the brown sugar, apple juice, water, margarine, agave nectar, salt, and arrowroot over medium heat. Use a whisk to blend your caramel sauce until it is smooth and your brown sugar dissolves and margarine melts. Once the sauce begins to bubble, reduce the heat to a simmer. Let your sauce simmer for about 3 minutes to thicken. Remove from the heat and whisk in your vanilla. Continue to stir and blend until the sauce cools to a warm temperature and thickens more.

Pour your caramel sauce over your popcorn and very gently mix with a slotted spoon. You don't want to crush or break up your popcorn too much. Once your popcorn is evenly coated, let chill for at least 30 minutes before serving.

COOKIES AND CREAM POPCORN

This is a great, kid-friendly recipe for a holiday potluck, or any gathering during any season. It's fun, unique, and guaranteed to have everyone asking you for the recipe.

MAKES 6 TO 8 SERVINGS

½ cup uncooked popcorn

¼ cup olive oil

1 Batch Apple Vanilla Glaze (page 398)

12 Oreos or your favorite vegan chocolate cookie sandwiches, crushed

In a 4-quart Dutch oven or soup pot with a lid, put the popcorn and olive oil. Rotate the Dutch oven so the popcorn and oil spread out evenly. Cover and cook over medium heat until the first kernel pops. Remove from the heat and let stand while you count to 45. Return to the heat.

Cook, shaking the pan occasionally, until the popcorn stops popping. Immediately pour it into a serving bowl. Separate out any unpopped kernels and discard the duds.

While your popcorn is popping, make your Apple Vanilla Glaze and mix your crushed chocolate sandwich cookies into the glaze using a large spoon.

Pour your cookies and Apple Vanilla Glaze over your popcorn and very gently mix with a slotted spoon. You don't want to crush or break up your popcorn and cookies too much. Once your popcorn is evenly coated, let it chill for at least 30 minutes before serving.

KALE CHIP PARTY MIX

We made this fun holiday-themed recipe during our very first live cooking demonstration, at an event held by the great animal advocacy organization Mercy for Animals with the ladies of Our Hen House at the Jivamukti yoga studio in Manhattan. It's possible that I was just the tiniest bit nervous. But the party mix turned out great anyway.

MAKES 8 TO 10 SERVINGS

1 cup baby kale leaves

Olive oil cooking spray

1 (14-ounce) can garbanzo beans, drained and rinsed

5 teaspoons Bragg's liquid aminos

2 teaspoons red pepper flakes

¼ cup uncooked popcorn

¼ cup olive oil

3 tablespoons nutritional yeast

¼ cup sun-dried tomatoes, diced

1 teaspoon garlic powder

Preheat the oven to 350°F. Line a cookie sheet with foil.

Start with your kale chips. Spread out your little leaves on your cookie sheet and spray very lightly with olive oil cooking spray. Bake for 20 minutes. Keep an eye on them, though—there is very small window when kale becomes the perfect chip. It can be easy to miss it and end up with singed edges.

While your kale chips are baking, toss the beans, Bragg's, and 1 teaspoon of the red pepper flakes and let sit for 20 minutes.

While your beans are marinating and your kale chips are baking, you can start your popcorn. Put your uncooked popcorn and olive oil in a Dutch oven or soup pot with a lid and roll your Dutch oven slowly so that the kernels are coated in oil. Heat over medium heat uncovered until you hear the first pop. Then cover and roll the pot again to make sure the popcorn continues to heat evenly.

Your popcorn will probably be completely popped by the time you need to pull your kale chips out of the oven, but don't forget about those kale chips while your popcorn pops. Once you hear the pops slow down, almost stopping completely, remove your popcorn from the heat to keep it from burning.

While your popcorn is still hot, pour half of it into an enormous serving or mixing bowl and sprinkle 1 tablespoon of the nutritional yeast over the top.

It will probably be time to pull your kale chips out now. Immediately lift your foil lining from the cookie sheet and transfer your kale chips on the foil to a wire rack to cool. Then while still wearing the oven mitts, reline your hot cookie sheet with foil and pour your garbanzo beans out over the cookie sheet in an even layer. Spray with olive oil cooking spray and bake for 45 minutes. They'll be ready to come out of the oven when they're roasted but still a little chewy.

Add your kale chips to your nutritional yeast–covered popcorn and sprinkle another tablespoon of nutritional yeast over the top. Toss in the sun-dried tomatoes and the rest of the popcorn. Add the garbanzo beans while they are still hot. Sprinkle the garlic powder, your last tablespoon of nutritional yeast, and the last of the red pepper flakes over the top. They should slowly shift down through the popcorn mix when people start serving themselves, but you can gently toss it all if you want. Just be careful not to break up your kale chips too much.

TOASTED GINGER AND TAMARI PUMPKIN SEEDS

This snack features bold Asian flavors and makes enough for your whole party to share.

MAKES 8 TO 10 SERVINGS

1 tablespoon olive oil	¼ teaspoon ginger paste	1 pound raw pumpkin seeds, shelled
1 tablespoon tamari	1 teaspoon brown sugar	

Use a whisk to blend the olive oil, tamari, ginger paste, and brown sugar in your Dutch oven or sauté pan. Heat the blend over medium heat. Once it begins to bubble, mix in the pumpkin seeds with a metal spoon and sauté for 2 to 3 minutes, until they start to pop and turn golden brown. Transfer to a lined cookie sheet and carefully spread out in a single layer. Set aside to cool before enjoying by the handful.

CAJUN BBQ ALMONDS

These spicy almonds have just the kick you're looking for when you've got a cold beer in your hand. Perfect as a snack for a group watching a game.

MAKES 8 TO 10 SERVINGS

- 4 cups raw whole almonds
- ⅓ cup Bragg's liquid aminos
- ⅓ cup whiskey
- 1 teaspoon hot sauce
- 1 teaspoon liquid smoke
- 3 tablespoons vegan Worcestershire sauce
- 2 teaspoons Tony Chachere's Cajun seasoning
- ¼ teaspoon cumin
- 1 teaspoon garlic powder
- ¼ cup margarine, melted

Preheat the oven to 275°F. Line a cookie sheet with parchment paper.

Set aside your almonds. In your best mixing bowl, whisk together all your remaining ingredients until smooth and well blended. Toss in the almonds and mix with a slotted spoon to give them a nice, even coating.

Use your slotted spoon to transfer your coated almonds to the lined cookie sheet. Bake for 15 minutes.

Pull out your cookie sheet and use a metal spatula to move your almonds around a little so they can brown evenly. Put them back in to brown for another 20 to 30 minutes. Once your almonds are golden brown, move them to room-temperature dishes to cool. The almonds are pretty great warm but I prefer them at room temperature with a beer and my old man.

MAPLE ROASTED ALMONDS

This recipe is bursting with great fall flavors—although feel free to enjoy it any time of year.

MAKES 8 TO 10 SERVINGS

- 3 tablespoons margarine, melted
- ⅓ cup maple syrup
- ¼ teaspoon arrowroot
- 1 teaspoon brown sugar
- 1 teaspoon crushed pink Himalayan salt
- 4 cups raw whole almonds

Preheat the oven to 300°F. Line a cookie sheet with parchment paper.

In the luckiest mixing bowl in the world, blend the margarine, maple syrup, arrowroot, brown sugar, and salt until the mixture is smooth and the sugar and salt have dissolved. Use a slotted spoon to mix in your almonds. Once your almonds have a nice even coating, use the spoon to transfer them to the cookie sheet.

Use a spatula to spread your almonds out evenly over the cookie sheet. Bake for 15 minutes. Then pull out your cookie sheet and use a metal spatula to move your almonds around a little so they can brown evenly and to keep them from sticking to the parchment paper. Put them back in to brown for another 20 to 30 minutes. Once your almonds are golden brown, move them to room-temperature dishes to cool.

Chapter Seven

HOLIDAY FAVORITES

The holidays can be a little rough on all of us. With parties to plan, presents to get, relatives to see, and meals to prepare, it can sometimes feel less like a holiday and more like a marathon. And for vegans, it can be even more difficult. Given that most holiday meals involve an animal at the center of the table—whether it's a Thanksgiving turkey, a Christmas ham, or a Hanukkah brisket—it's hard not to feel a little excluded from the festivities.

Food has a special resonance during the holidays. We often return to the same tables we sat around as kids, preparing and eating the same meals our mothers and grandmothers prepared and ate before us, spending time with those we've known and loved our whole lives. Italians like to say that "food is love"—never is that more true than during the holiday season.

For many of us, going vegan may have thrown a wrench into all that—separating us from some of our most cherished holiday traditions. But never fear! There is a whole range of vegan meals to choose from that'll help spread holiday cheer far and wide.

These recipes will make even your meat-loving uncle reach across the table for seconds. Now you can start your own holiday tradition that'll have your great-granddaughter telling her own family, "This is my great-grandma Betty's Tofurky recipe," as they sit down to share a traditional holiday meal.

THANKSGIVING

If you ever need something to measure how far our civilization has advanced, just take a look at vegan Thanksgivings. First came an extra pasta dish for the vegans. Then came mashed potatoes with margarine. Then, in the eighties, a breakthrough: Tofurky! Tofurky has been a loyal friend, leading the way in cruelty-free holiday feasts for vegan Bettys everywhere. But these days, we've got a number of vegan holiday roasts to choose from.

The Match vegan meats holiday roast is a perfect canvas for experimenting with glazes and marinades because it's not a formed product—you make it yourself, like a meatball, so it can hold toppings and breading better than its smooth-skinned comrades. It's all "white meat," with Match's signature sausage stuffing, and can be either grilled or baked.

Field Roast's Hazelnut Cranberry Roast en Croute combines herbed seitan, tart cranberries, sweet curry powder, and candied ginger and wraps them all up in a butter-flavored puff pastry crust. It's all comes in a box, ready to bake—so it's perfect for Bettys who don't want to meddle much. Whenever someone tells me it's too hard to be vegan, I think of this holiday roast, which is an instant and impressive centerpiece.

Gardein Savory Stuffed Turk'y is perfect for vegan Bettys spending the holidays with not-yet-vegan families, or with a special not-yet-vegan someone. They come two to a package and are prepared perfectly. You just need to roast 'em up and focus on your sides.

But even if these vegan holiday roasts don't rock your holiday world, don't worry: there seems to be a new holiday roast every year. Such is the continual progress of our civilization.

CITRUS AND GARLIC-BASTED HOLIDAY ROAST

No doubt this recipe will be a scene-stealer on any holiday table. It's tangy and savory, with a black pepper kick. I think this baste would be great over any kind of mock meat or tofu in a fajita or burrito, and I plan on testing that hypothesis soon.

MAKES A ROAST THAT SERVES 4 TO 6

1 Tofurky or other vegan holiday roast, defrosted

2 limes, cut into wedges

1 lemon, cut into wedges

⅓ cup Better Than Bouillon vegetable broth, made per the instructions on the package

2 tablespoons olive oil

3 tablespoons lemon juice

2 teaspoons lime juice

1 tablespoon dry white wine

¼ cup whole fresh basil leaves

¼ cup whole fresh cilantro

1 teaspoon Bragg's liquid aminos

¼ teaspoon crushed black peppercorns

2 cloves garlic, minced

¼ teaspoon celery seed

Preheat the oven to 400°F.

Set aside the roast and lemon and lime wedges. In a large bowl, mix all the remaining ingredients. Add the roast and turn it a few times in the bowl so it gets a good coating. Put your roast in a glass loaf pan, and then pour ¼ to ⅓ cup of the citrus-garlic baste over the top. Using a fork, remove the basil and cilantro leaves from the sauce in the baking dish. Gently lay the basil and cilantro leaves on the roast in an even coating that covers the roast completely. Press your leaves into the basted roast if you need to; they'll stick to some roasts better than others.

Bake for 15 minutes. Then spoon another ¼ cup of baste over the top. Bake for another 15 minutes. Check the roast a few times to make sure the herbs aren't getting too crispy and your roast is cooking evenly. Don't worry if there's still some baste in the dish when you pull the roast out of the oven. When you transfer your roast to the serving dish, pour some of the leftover baste from the baking dish over the top. Serve with lemon and lime wedges on the side—squeeze those over the top for extra flavor.

BEER CAN TOFURKY

Beer can chicken is an American tradition. I mean, I never made one, or even ate one, before going vegan…but apparently people all over the country have. The second we saw this recipe, we began plotting our strategy for this ambitious grilling project. We discussed the challenges, such as stabilizing the Tofurky, and the differences between mock meat and, well, meat. We also developed a plan of attack for our "beer can rub," and which brand of beer to use. A Shannon Offensive, if you will. The results speak for themselves. It has flavor and texture, and a unique smokiness. This recipe turned Tofurky—something we've eaten a million times—into something completely new and different.

MAKES 4 SERVINGS

TOFURKY
1 Tofurky roast, defrosted

1 can beer (use ginger ale or lemon-lime soda if beer isn't your thing)

BEER CAN RUB
3 tablespoons Tony Chachere's Creole seasoning

1 tablespoon Bragg's liquid aminos

½ teaspoon onion powder

1 to 2 tablespoons olive oil

Preheat the oven to 200°F. Start your grill per the instructions that came with it.

Find the end of your Tofurky roast where a bit of stuffing is peeking out; cut that end off about 2 inches from the seam. Using a spoon, remove the stuffing from your Tofurky. Make sure you don't carve away any of the actual Tofurky, and be careful you don't squeeze the Tofurky too hard and crack the side.[*] Take your time and be gentle.

After you've removed all the stuffing, gently place the open end of the Tofurky on top of the unopened can of beer to measure how much you'll need to widen the opening to get the can to fit. Very gently, press the Tofurky down to make a slight indentation around the open end; this will be your guide to widen the opening. With a small, sharp knife, cut away the Tofurky along the indentation from the can, going about 1½ inches deep into the Tofurky. Cut a little at time, and test the Tofurky on the top of the beer can between cuts to see if it's wide enough. You want it to be just wide enough

to fit the can snuggly and form a seal.

Place the Tofurky in the oven, hollowed-out end down, for 5 minutes to harden it a bit.

In a bowl, mix the ingredients for the beer can rub with a whisk, making sure there are no clumps.

Remove the Tofurky from the oven and let it sit. Once it's cool enough to touch, brush with the beer can rub, inside and outside.

Once your coals are ready to start grilling, open the can of beer, pour ½ cup beer into the bowl with the rub, and mix with a whisk. Gently push your Tofurky onto the top of the beer can.

Place the beer can with the Tofurky on top of it onto the grill upright. While the Tofurky is on the grill, periodically baste it with the beer can rub to keep it moist and add flavor. Be careful not to tip it over! The hole in Tofurky isn't centered; one side will be heavier than another. We suggest using a pair of barbecue tongs to hold the can while you baste.

Drips of beer will start to roll down the sides of the

---

[*] If you get a tear in the side of your Tofurky, you can still lay it on the beer can. It's not ideal, but if this happens you can still make your Tofurky work.

can; this is good sign. You want the beer to vaporize and steam up inside your Tofurky. Eventually, you'll see beer steam come through the top of the Tofurky.

Once you have steam coming out of the top, and the outside of the Tofurky is golden brown, use the barbecue tongs to remove your Tofurky from the grill. It should take between 30 and 45 minutes, depending on how hot your grill is. When you move your Tofurky, be careful not to spill the beer inside of it. The can and Tofurky are both very hot, so don't touch them with your bare hands. While keeping the beer can upright with your tongs, use an oven mitt to pull the Tofurky off and into a large bowl.

To serve, cut the Tofurky into chunks, and maybe dip them in your favorite BBQ sauce. But to be honest, we loved it as is.

CAJUN DEEP-FRIED TOFURKY WITH OKRA GIBLET GRAVY

Every year people all over the country burn down their homes, patios, and sports-themed gazebos trying to deep-fry turkeys for Thanksgiving. Something so dangerous and reckless seemed like a great way to launch our Thanksgiving Parade of Food on our blog! So we kicked things off with a southern tradition that's been called more dangerous than a fistful of illegal firecrackers and tastier than a house made of pie. Before you start, check out our tips for deep-frying Tofurky on page 446.

MAKES 4 TO 6 SERVINGS

TOFURKY

6 to 7 cups oil

1 Tofurky or vegan holiday roast (make sure it is completely defrosted)

CAJUN MARINADE

½ cup olive oil

1 teaspoon Bragg's liquid aminos

2 teaspoons Tony Chachere's Creole seasoning

1 teaspoon garlic powder

Dash of liquid smoke

Dash of hot sauce

CAJUN RUB

2 teaspoons crushed black peppercorns

1 tablespoon Tony Chachere's Creole seasoning

1 tablespoon cumin

1 tablespoon grated nutmeg

1 tablespoon olive oil

1 teaspoon Bragg's liquid aminos

OKRA GIBLET GRAVY

1 (14-ounce) package Tofurky gravy (it comes in the Tofurky dinner set or can be bought separately)

1 cup dry white wine

¾ cup nutritional yeast

½ cup sliced okra

2 teaspoons Tony Chachere's Creole seasoning

½ teaspoon poultry seasoning (most poultry seasonings are vegan, but some aren't, so be sure to read the label)

Pinch of crushed black peppercorns

2 cloves garlic, minced

½ teaspoon onion powder

½ teaspoon celery seed

1 tablespoon chopped fresh parsley

1 ½ teaspoons Bragg's liquid aminos

Fill a large stock or soup pot with the oil and turn on high. Leave it uncovered. I know—crazy, right? But that's what to do.

In a small bowl, mix all the Cajun marinade ingredients with a fork until thoroughly blended. Let it sit for a bit.

For the Cajun rub, in a large bowl mix the pepper, Creole seasoning, cumin, and nutmeg. Put the defrosted roast in the bowl and pour the oil and Bragg's over it. Roll the roast around in the rub and use a brush to give it a nice even coating. Let it sit for 5 minutes, turning it every once in a while.

Now it's time to grab your handy flavor injector. Fill the injector with marinade, stick it into the roast all the way to the hilt, and then remove it halfway before injecting—you're making a little tunnel to fill with marinade. When you inject the marinade, stop when it starts to leak out of the injection spot. Repeat this process numerous times, using different injection sites, until you feel good about how much marinade you've injected into your roast. We used about ¼ cup to get a really juicy roast and flavorful stuffing. Something to watch out for: your needle can get clogged by spices or chunks of roast. If this happens, just use a clean safety pin or warm water to clean your needle, and keep going.

Check on your pot of oil. If you see bubbles forming, you're ready. Using oven mitts and barbecue tongs, slowly lower your roast into the hot oil. Leave the roast in there for around 20 minutes, but if it the oil starts bubbling too high and showing signs that it might overflow, you have to abort: remove the roast, turn off the burner, let the oil cool, remove the excess oil, and start over. But if there are no signs of overflowing, let the roast hang out in the pot for around 20 minutes, 30 if you want it extra-crispy. When you remove the Tofurky, place it on a plate with some paper towels to suck up excess oil.

In a saucepan, mix all your okra giblet gravy ingredients and bring to a boil while stirring continually. Serve the Tofurky cut into slices with gravy on top. Enjoy!

Here are some tips to keep in mind when deep-frying your Tofurky or other vegan holiday roast:

Make sure your roast is completely defrosted. This is absolutely critical—because it's melting water from frozen turkeys that makes the frying oil splash out of the pot and cause fires.

Tofurkys are small enough to fry in your kitchen, but make sure you have the proper equipment. You need barbecue tongs and a grilling fork to pull your holiday roast out of the pot; a pot large enough so the oil won't spill over when the roast is lowered in; baking soda to put out any fires (because you never use water on a grease fire); and really good oven mitts and long sleeves to protect yourself.

If you're using a vegan roast that's not pre-formed, you should bake the roast first for 20 to 30 minutes at 300°F to makes sure you get a nice "skin" on it, so that it won't fall apart in the pot of oil.

Don't ever leave anything frying unattended—especially if it's a holiday roast.

Please, please, please be careful. I have to add that although we'd feel terrible if anyone was hurt while attempting to deep-fry their Tofurky this Thanksgiving, we aren't responsible for any damages or injuries that may happen. So make sure your roast is defrosted and your pot doesn't overflow.

LEMON PEPPER TOFURKY WITH CORN BREAD AND CRANBERRY STUFFING

Even if you don't have time to spend all day cooking an enormous feast, you can use this shortcut to Thanksgiving that takes only 2 hours and ain't too shabby.

MAKES 4 TO 6 SERVINGS

2 teaspoons poultry seasoning (most poultry seasonings are vegan, but some aren't, so be sure to read the label)

2 teaspoons lemon pepper

2 teaspoons grated lemon peel

1 Tofurky, defrosted to the point that you can stick a skewer all the way through

Olive oil cooking spray

3 cups dried corn bread stuffing (make sure it isn't instant, and check for any special instructions like presoaking)

¼ cup dried cranberries

2 tablespoons crushed raw walnuts

2 tablespoons chopped dry-roasted cashews

½ Granny Smith apple, cored and chopped

1 cup Better Than Bouillon vegetable broth, made per the instructions on the package

2 tablespoons apple juice

⅓ cup margarine

In a small bowl, blend the poultry seasoning, lemon pepper, and lemon peel. Place the defrosted Tofurky in a large mixing bowl and rub with the lemon poultry seasoning blend.

Spray your cherished slow cooker with olive oil cooking spray. In the cooker, mix the remaining ingredients. Gently press the Tofurky into the stuffing, but not hard or deep enough that it touches the bottom of the cooker.

Cover and cook on a medium setting for 2 to 3 hours. Your Tofurky will be much moister than if you baked it, but the flavor is wonderful—and this recipe is supereasy.

CAN-FREE CRANBERRY SAUCE

Just about every single food that comes in a can is better when made fresh. But the difference is maybe the most obvious when it comes to cranberry sauce. Seriously—is anything more unappetizing than that cylindrical mound of goo, complete with ridgelines? Next Thanksgiving, make your cranberry sauce from scratch—you'll never go back to the can.

MAKES 6 TO 8 SERVINGS

1 cup packed brown sugar

1 cup orange juice with pulp

Pinch of cloves

1 teaspoon lemon juice

2 cups fresh cranberries

2 teaspoons grated orange peel

In your Dutch oven or saucepan, heat the brown sugar, orange juice, cloves, and lemon juice to a boil over medium heat. Stir in the cranberries and boil for 5 minutes—the cranberries will start popping open, and your sauce will begin to thicken, so keep stirring. Once all your cranberries have popped, stir in the orange peel and remove from the heat. Cover and refrigerate for 4 hours.

Meet Beatrice!

Our first summer living in Brooklyn, Dan and I loaded up our little black car and drove up into the tie-dyed wilderness past Albany to visit the Woodstock Farm Animal Sanctuary. The first thing we did upon arriving at the beautiful farm in the woods was pick up two overloaded plates of vegan burgers and corn on the cob. We found a spot on a bale of hay, began to eat and chat…when this little pink head popped around my arm, scaring the bejesus out of me.

Her name is Beatrice, she's a turkey, and she has no fear. She apparently loves corn so much she's willing to talk to strangers to get it—something I'm hardly even willing to do. She helped herself to some of our corn and hung out with us for a long time, curiously looking into Dan's bag when he went to get our camera and nibbling on my hair when I wasn't paying her enough attention.

Beatrice was born on a factory farm but was spared this cruel life when she was purchased as a gift for a kind man in Staten Island, New York, on Thanksgiving. But it was Staten Island—there was no way he could give this little girl the home she needed. Beatrice needed a forever home, and in the end was welcomed to the Woodstock Farm Animal Sanctuary with open arms.

The Woodstock staff describes Beatrice as charming and curious. "She loves to be around people and often sits to have her beautiful, white feathers stroked or follows our caretakers around as they try to feed the other animals." After spending some time with Beatrice, one of the Woodstock volunteers proclaimed, "I'll never eat turkey again. I'll probably become vegan after this experience."

POMEGRANATE AND CRANBERRY SAUCE

I love the flavor of this sauce on Tofurky sandwiches, on biscuits, and on my sticky fingers. It's so good it'll make you understand how cranberry sauce earned its spot on the table during one of the high holy days of food. It also has so much vitamin C and antioxidants in it, I'm pretty sure it'll make you live forever. Okay, maybe I'm not so sure.

MAKES 6 TO 8 SERVINGS

1 (12-ounce) bag fresh whole cranberries
Seeds from ½ fresh pomegranate
1 cup sugar

½ cup water
¼ cup lemon juice

¼ cup orange juice with pulp
1 tablespoon grated orange peel

Wash the cranberries and get your seeds from your pomegranate.

In a large saucepan or Dutch oven, heat the sugar, water, lemon juice, and orange juice over medium heat until it starts to bubble slightly. Add the cranberries and mix until blended. Boil for 5 minutes. Then toss in the pomegranate seeds and orange peel. Your cranberries will begin to pop. Keep stirring while the sauce boils for 5 more minutes. Cover and let cool for another 5 minutes. Move into another container and refrigerate for 30 minutes, or until chilled.

GREEN BEAN AND LEEK CASSEROLE

We weren't big on Thanksgiving at my house. To quote my mom: "Do we look like we came from Pilgrims?" (Insert a Sicilian shrug in there.) So my affection for this longtime American holiday classic didn't actually develop till much later in life, after I was vegan and had a new appreciation for food. I'm glad it did, though, because I can say with complete confidence that I have never taken a green bean casserole for granted.

MAKES 6 TO 8 SERVINGS

¼ cup margarine

¼ cup whole wheat flour

1½ cups Better Than Bouillon vegan chicken broth, made per the instructions on the package (you may need a little more)

2 tablespoons Bragg's liquid aminos

Dash of liquid smoke

2 cloves garlic, minced

2 tablespoons olive oil

½ cup nutritional yeast (you may need a little more)

4 (14-ounce) cans green beans

2 leeks, sliced

1 (2.8-ounce) can French-fried onions

Preheat the oven to 350°F.

In a saucepan, melt the margarine over low heat. Add the flour and whisk until it forms a roux. Whisk in the broth, Bragg's, liquid smoke, and garlic until thick and bubbly. Add the olive oil and nutritional yeast. Continue whisking the mixture. Make sure it's like gravy: if it's too dry, add more broth; if it's too wet, add more nutritional yeast. Pour into a small casserole dish. Mix in the green beans and leeks. Be gentle so the green beans stay intact. Bake the casserole for 10 minutes, top with French-fried onions, and bake for 10 more minutes, or until brown and bubbly.

CANDIED ORANGE SWEET POTATOES

We usually like a savory sweet potato around these parts, but we tried these babies out because we trust Betty Crocker—and because this is an American holiday classic, and no one messes with that. We ended up loving them, and now I make them all the time.

MAKES 4 TO 6 SERVINGS

4 large sweet potatoes, cubed

⅓ cup brown sugar

3 tablespoons margarine

2 tablespoons orange juice with pulp

2 tablespoons orange peel

½ teaspoon crushed pink Himalayan salt

Olive oil cooking spray

1 to 2 cups vegan marshmallows

In a large pot, boil the sweet potato cubes in water for 15 minutes, or until they begin to get tender. Drain. In your festive cast-iron skillet or saucepan, heat the brown sugar, margarine, orange juice, orange peel, and salt over medium heat until bubbling. Add the sweet potatoes and stir gently until glazed.

Set the oven to broil.

Coat your 8-inch glass baking dish with cooking spray and fill with sweet potatoes. Spread the vegan marshmallows over the top in an even layer. Slide the baking dish into the roaster for the count of 10. This will give you a nice browned layer of marshmallows, as well as some crispy edges on top.

Is this the healthiest way to enjoy your veggies? Hell no. Is it an age-old American classic that you can enjoy once a year or so? Hell yes! And if you were missing these since you went vegan, I hope they take you back. My mission will be complete.

MAPLE GINGER SWEET POTATO MASH

We enjoy this recipe year-round. Sweet potatoes are a great source of beta-carotene, and they also taste great with margarine. Why is that important? Studies suggest that a minimum of 3 grams of fat per serving of sweet potatoes significantly increases your intake of beta-carotene. What a great excuse to enjoy some "buttery" orange mashed potatoes.

MAKES 8 TO 10 SERVINGS

8 to 10 sweet potatoes

2 tablespoons maple syrup, plus a little more to drizzle over the top

2 teaspoons ginger paste

¼ cup margarine

2 teaspoons crushed pink Himalayan salt (you may want to add more)

¼ teaspoon hot sauce (you may want to add more of this too)

¼ teaspoon grated nutmeg

Olive oil cooking spray

Preheat the oven to 350°F.

Pierce the sweet potatoes with a fork. Place the potatoes in a glass baking dish and bake until tender. It should take around an hour.

Chop up your baked sweet potatoes, skins and all, and place them in a large bowl. Blend the potatoes with an electric handheld mixer on medium until no lumps remain. You'll need to scrape pieces of potato skin off the beater, but it's worth it. Add all the remaining ingredients and continue beating until everything is blended in. Taste test it to see if you'd like more salt or hot sauce. Keep in mind, you're going to drizzle a little more maple syrup over the top. Once you like the flavor, you're ready to serve.

APPLE-STUFFED ACORN SQUASH

These good-looking fellas aren't just eye candy: they're a sweet, tangy, "buttery," and filling Thanksgiving side. If you're trying to work some vegan items into a nonvegan holiday meal, you can absolutely slip these guys in unnoticed. They're this weird combination of obviously and secretly awesome at the same time.

MAKES 2 SERVINGS

1 acorn squash

1 Red Delicious apple, diced

2 tablespoons dried cranberries

2 tablespoons crushed walnuts

2 tablespoons brown sugar

1 tablespoon margarine

Preheat the oven to 350°F.

Cut your squash in half lengthwise and remove the seeds and fibers. Cut 2 to 3 little slits in the inside of the hollowed-out squash. Bake the squash halves for 30 minutes.

In a bowl, mix the apple, cranberries, walnuts, brown sugar, and margarine. Make sure you break up any clumps of brown sugar.

After 30 minutes, remove the squash and use a large spoon to fill it with the apple mixture. You'll need to really pack it in there, and it'll still be overflowing a bit. Once the squash halves are full, put them back in the oven for another 30 to 40 minutes. You'll know they're ready to take out when the squash is a nice golden brown and has crispy edges.

MAPLE CASHEW PUMPKIN PIE

No matter where you live, you know that summer is over and it's time to start planning your Thanksgiving dinner when you see "pumpkin spice" flavored things showing up at every chain restaurant and coffee shop. Pumpkin starts showing up in everything from lattes and pancakes to frozen yogurt. Thanks, corporate America, for giving us a universal symbol of fall! Don't forget to make a batch of Whipped Coconut Cream (page 403)—no pumpkin pie is complete without it. Please note, you'll have to prep the whipped cream the night before you want to serve the pie.

MAKES 1 PIE

CRUST

2 to 3 tablespoons chilled water

1 cup all-purpose flour, plus more to flour your workspaces

1 teaspoon crushed pink Himalayan salt

⅓ cup plus 1 tablespoon vegetable shortening

FILLING

1 (15-ounce) can pumpkin puree (not pumpkin pie filling)

1¼ cups raw cashews, soaked overnight

1 teaspoon arrowroot

1 cup maple syrup

2½ teaspoons pumpkin pie spice

Pinch of crystalized ginger

Pinch of crushed pink Himalayan salt

Refrigerate the water for your crust for 20 minutes. In a mixing bowl, sift together the flour and salt. Cut in the shortening using a pastry blender until your dough looks like small pebbles. Sprinkle with cold water, 1 tablespoon at a time, tossing with a fork until all your flour is moist and you have a solid dough that doesn't stick to the sides of the bowl. You can add 1 to 2 teaspoons more water if your dough is too dry.

Using your hands, form the dough into a ball. Shape the dough into a flattened round on a floured surface. Wrap in plastic wrap and refrigerate for 45 minutes, or until the dough is firm and cold, yet still pliable.

Preheat the oven to 425°F.

With a floured rolling pin, roll the dough into a round flat disk that is 2 inches larger than your glass pie plate.

Fold the dough into fourths and transfer it to the pie plate; then unfold and press it gently into the plate. Use wet fingers to seal any cracks that appear in the crust. Trim any overhanging edges of crust to 1 inch from the rim of your pie plate. Use your fingers to pinch the edge of the pie to create a nice rolling wave along the crust's edge.

In your favorite food processer or blender, mix all the filling ingredients until smooth. Pour into the crust and use a spatula to smooth out the top. Bake for 15 minutes.

Reduce the oven temperature to 350°F. and bake the pie for 45 minutes longer, until a knife inserted in the center comes out clean.

Cover and refrigerate for at least 4 hours.

GEORGIA-STYLE PUMPKIN PIE

I actually never had a pumpkin pie like this when I lived in Georgia, but I did enjoy making vegan pralines. The candied pecan topping on this pie is something any southern baker would be proud to have on his or her Thanksgiving table. We added a little heat to our topping for more of a Savannah-style praline, making this pie unique.

MAKES 1 PIE

CRUST

2 to 3 tablespoons chilled water

1 cup all-purpose flour, plus more to flour your workspaces

1 teaspoon crushed pink Himalayan salt

⅓ cup plus 1 tablespoon vegetable shortening

FILLING

1 (14-ounce) package silken tofu

1¼ cup packed brown sugar

1½ cups pumpkin puree (not pumpkin pie filling)

1 teaspoon arrowroot

½ teaspoon ground ginger

Pinch of crushed pink Himalayan salt

4 teaspoons pumpkin pie spice

PRALINE TOPPING

⅓ cup packed brown sugar

⅓ cup chopped pecans

½ teaspoon cayenne pepper

1 tablespoon margarine, softened

½ teaspoon ground cinnamon

Put the water for your crust in the refrigerator for 20 minutes. In a mixing bowl, sift together the flour and salt. Cut in the shortening using a pastry blender until the dough looks like small peas. Sprinkle with cold water, 1 tablespoon at a time, tossing with a fork until all the flour is moist and you have a solid dough that doesn't stick to the sides of the bowl. You can add 1 to 2 more teaspoons of water if your dough is too dry.

Using your hands, form the dough into a ball. Flatten your dough ball on a floured surface. Wrap in plastic wrap and refrigerate for 45 minutes, or until the dough is firm and cold, yet still pliable.

Preheat the oven to 425°F.

With a floured rolling pin, roll the dough into a round flat disk 2 inches larger than your glass pie plate. Fold the dough into fourths and transfer it to the pie plate; then unfold and press it gently into the plate.

Use wet fingers to seal any cracks that appear in the crust. Trim any overhanging edges of crust to 1 inch from the rim of your pie plate. Use your fingers to create a nice rolling wave along the crust edge.

In your food processer or blender, mix all the filling ingredients until smooth. Pour into the crust and use a spatula to smooth out the top. Bake for 15 minutes.

Meanwhile, in small bowl, mix all the praline topping ingredients until crumbly.

Reduce the oven temperature to 350°F. and bake the pie for 35 minutes longer. Sprinkle the praline topping over the pie. Bake for about 10 more minutes, or until a bamboo skewer inserted in the center comes out with only a little pumpkin and praline topping on it. This pie will be a little softer than store-bought pumpkin pies because of the topping.

Cover and refrigerate for at least 4 hours.

MINI PUMPKIN CHEESECAKES

Vegan pumpkin cheesecake is actually one of the first recipes I ever tried out on nonvegans. This recipe has evolved a lot since that first Thanksgiving cheesecake, and while I have fond memories of that one, I'm willing to admit that it was a pale shadow of this version of the recipe. This is a firm and creamy pie, which means you can make the always impressive New York–style cheesecake (with no crust). We made ours mini by using four 4.5-inch springform pans, but you can also just make one standard-size cheesecake by using a 9-inch pan. If you are making the large cheesecake, you'll want to check out the baking instructions in our original New York Cheesecake recipe on page 362. Or you can put this filling in a regular old piecrust and not sweat the springform pan. Either way, it's delicious.

These little fellows need to chill out in the fridge for at least 7 hours before serving so you might want to keep that in mind when you make them.

MAKES 1 LARGE CHEESECAKE OR 4 MINI CHEESECAKES

CRUST
Vegetable shortening to grease your springform pans

1 cup whole wheat flour

½ cup margarine

¼ cup sugar

1 tablespoon applesauce

PUMPKIN CHEESECAKE FILLING
3 (8-ounce) packages vegan cream cheese (we recommend Tofutti Better Than Cream Cheese)

1¼ cups sugar

3 tablespoons whole wheat flour

1 tablespoon grated orange peel

1½ teaspoons pumpkin pie spice

¼ teaspoon ground ginger

Pinch of crushed black peppercorn

¼ teaspoon crushed pink Himalayan salt

3 tablespoons applesauce

2 tablespoons Ener-G egg replacer, just the powder, not made per the instructions on the package

¾ cup pumpkin puree

VEGAN SPICED CREAM CHEESE FROSTING TOPPING
½ (8-ounce) package vegan cream cheese (we recommend Tofutti Better Than Cream Cheese)

⅛ cup margarine

¼ teaspoon ground cinnamon

¼ teaspoon brown sugar

2 teaspoons vanilla almond milk

¼ teaspoon vanilla extract

1½ cups powdered sugar

Preheat the oven to 400°F. Lightly grease your 4 mini springform pans with vegetable shortening.

In a bowl, mix the flour margarine, sugar, and applesauce with a fork until a dough forms, and then gather it into a ball. Separate the dough into 4 equal portions. One at a time, press two-thirds of a portion of dough into the bottom of a springform pan. Then press the remaining third up the sides of the pan to create a shallow cup. Once you've done that for all the springform pans, place all the pans on a cookie sheet. Bake for 3 to 5 minutes, or until the crusts are a light golden brown; remove from the oven and let them cool while you make the filling.

Preheat the oven to 475°F.

In a bowl, mix all filling ingredients on low speed until blended. Using a ladle, fill the pans a little more than three-quarters of the way to the top. Don't fill to the brim, because your cakes will bake over.

Bake for 15 minutes. Reduce the oven temperature to 200°F. Bake for an additional 30 minutes. The cheesecakes may not appear done, but if a small area in the center seems soft, it'll become solid as it cools.

Don't do the toothpick test. Turn off the oven; leave the cheesecake in the oven 30 minutes longer. Remove from the oven and cool in the springform pans on a wire rack. Without releasing or removing the sides of the pans, run a small metal spatula or a butter knife carefully along the sides of the cheesecakes to loosen.

In a mixing bowl, beat the vegan cream cheese, margarine, cinnamon, brown sugar, almond milk, and vanilla extract with an electric mixer on low until smooth. Gradually mix in the powdered sugar, ½ cup at a time, on low speed to prevent one of those messy blowbacks. Mix until smooth. This is really soft frosting, so I recommend using a frosting gun to make an even layer over the top of the cheesecake while it's still in the pan.

Refrigerate the frosted cheesecakes uncovered for at least 7 hours.

Run a metal spatula or butter knife carefully around the side of the cheesecake to loosen again. Remove the sides of the springform pans. Leave your cute little cheesecakes on the bottom disk when you serve them.

MAPLE SWEET POTATO WHOOPIE PIES WITH MARSHMALLOW FILLING

This recipe takes everything that's great about your standard sweet potato casserole—sweet potatoes, marshmallows, and fall spices—and makes them even better by turning them into a whoopie pie.

The marshmallow filling takes a few hours to make so keep that in mind when making this recipe.

MAKES 2 DOZEN WHOOPIE PIES

1 Batch Vegan Marshmallow Filling (page 404), or you can use Ricemellow

3 cups all-purpose flour

½ cup whole wheat flour

2 teaspoons ground cinnamon

1½ teaspoons baking powder

1½ teaspoons baking soda

6 tablespoons margarine

½ teaspoon crushed pink Himalayan salt

½ teaspoon vanilla extract

1 teaspoon maple syrup

1 cup brown sugar

⅓ cup granulated sugar

⅓ cup olive oil

2 tablespoons applesauce

2 teaspoons Ener-G egg replacer, just the powder, not made per the instructions on the package

1⅓ cups baked, peeled, and mashed sweet potatoes

½ cup soy milk

Baking spray

Prepare your Vegan Marshmallow Filling 3 to 5 hours before you make your pies.

Preheat the oven to 350°F.

In your favorite mixing bowl, mix the flours, cinnamon, baking powder, and baking soda with a whisk until blended.

In a separate bowl, use an electric handheld mixer to blend the margarine, salt, vanilla, maple syrup, and sugars until creamy and smooth. Gradually blend the oil, applesauce, and egg replacer into the margarine mixture. Once your mixture is creamy, mix in the sweet potatoes ⅓ cup at a time. Blend in your potatoes for at least 5 minutes to get all the clumps out—this is really important.

Once the sweet potato mixture is smooth, blend it into the flour mixture; then add the soy milk. Cover and chill the batter for 45 minutes so that it gets firmer.

Spray your always-perfect whoopie pie pan with baking spray. Once the batter has chilled out, fill your frosting gun or pastry bag with the sweet potato batter and put the largest tip on there.

Fill the cups on the whoopie pie pan three-quarters of the way full. It's important to make your whoopie pie cookies the same size and to have an equal number.

Bake for 10 to 15 minutes, or until lightly browned. You'll know they're done when they're firm but soft to the touch. Immediately transfer the cookies to a cooling rack, putting the ugliest part of the cookie on the rack. Make sure the cookies cool completely before building your whoopie pies.

To build your whoopie pies, put 2 to 3 tablespoons of Vegan Marshmallow Filling on one cookie, then take another cookie and put it on top to make a cookie sandwich. Gently squeeze your whoopie pies before serving so the marshmallow peeks out a bit.

CHRISTMAS

When most people think of Christmas food, they're thinking of the steady stream of cookies, pies, and other baked goods that are always up for grabs at family get-togethers. Hence why most New Year's resolutions involve losing that holiday weight.

It used to be that vegan Bettys didn't need to worry about this holiday gluttony like their nonvegan counterparts did—most of those goodies weren't vegan. But now all that's changed. For better or for worse, now you have all the vegan recipes you'll need to crank out enough Christmas treats to fatten up an entire family in that one-month period between Thanksgiving and New Year's. And we've got some delicious roasts to replace that ham at Christmas dinner as well.

You're thanking us now…but let us know how you feel on January 1 when it's time to get started on that resolution. Don't worry—we've got some salads in this book too. Somewhere…

SOY NOG CHEESECAKE WITH "BUTTERY" RUM SAUCE

Christmas is a magical season. We get to give each other thoughtful gifts. People host parties centered around cookies. People donate and volunteer more. There's random mistletoe everywhere to kiss your loved one under. You get to drink hot chocolate. And the *retour au sommet*…soy nog hits the shelves! Every year we find a new way to level up our vegan nog. This recipe is one of our very favorites. Bring this treat to any holiday party and watch it disappear, plate by plate. I personally guarantee at least one "Hmmm. This is vegan?"

You'll need to make this recipe the night before you want to serve it. It needs time to set in the fridge.

MAKES 1 LARGE CHEESECAKE WITH SAUCE

CRUST

Vegetable shortening to grease your springform pan

1 cup all-purpose flour

½ cup margarine

¼ cup sugar

1 tablespoon applesauce

¼ teaspoon ground ginger

¼ teaspoon ground cinnamon

Pinch of grated nutmeg

CHEESECAKE

3 (8-ounce) packages vegan cream cheese (we recommend Tofutti Better Than Cream Cheese)

1 tablespoon coconut flour

1 cup sugar

3 tablespoons all-purpose flour

1 tablespoon grated orange peel

¼ teaspoon crushed pink Himalayan salt

¾ cup soy nog

1 teaspoon rum or rum extract

1 teaspoon ground cinnamon

¼ teaspoon grated nutmeg

2 tablespoons applesauce

3 tablespoons Ener-G egg replacer, just the powder, not prepared per the instructions on the package

2 tablespoons vegan sour cream

"BUTTERY" RUM SAUCE

1 tablespoon cornstarch

1 cup water

2 tablespoons margarine

⅓ cup brown sugar

1 teaspoon rum or rum extract

Preheat the oven to 400°F. Lightly grease your springform pan with vegetable shortening.

In a bowl, mix the flour, margarine, sugar, applesauce, ginger, cinnamon, and nutmeg with a fork until a dough forms; gather into a ball. Press two-thirds of the dough into the bottom of the springform pan. Then press the remaining dough 2 inches up the sides of the pan to create a shallow cup. Bake for 5 to 6 minutes, or until light golden brown; cool.

Preheat the oven to 475°F.

In a bowl, beat the vegan cream cheese, coconut flour, sugar, all-purpose flour, orange peel, and salt with an electric handheld mixer on medium speed for 2 minutes, or until smooth. Beat in the soy nog, rum, cinnamon, nutmeg, applesauce, egg replacer, and vegan sour cream on low speed until blended. Make sure you don't have any lumps. Pour the cheesecake filling into your pan, over the crust. Use your spatula to scrape the sides of the bowl and smooth out the top of the filling.

Bake for 15 minutes. Reduce the oven temperature to 200°F. Bake for an additional 60 minutes. The cheesecake may not appear done, but if a small area in the center seems soft, it'll become solid when it cools. Don't do the toothpick test. Turn off the oven and leave your cheesecake in the oven 30 minutes longer. Remove from the oven and cool in the pan on a wire rack for 30 minutes.

Without releasing the sides of your pan, run a metal spatula or a butter knife carefully along the sides of the cheesecake to loosen it. Refrigerate uncovered overnight for at least 9 hours but no longer than 48.

Run a metal spatula or butter knife carefully around the sides of the cheesecake to loosen it again. Remove the side of the pan.

Leave the cheesecake on the bottom of the springform pan when you serve.

This cheesecake is pretty fabulous, but there is one thing that might actually make it better…warm "Buttery" Rum Sauce. *Gasp!*

To make your sauce, heat all the "Buttery" Rum Sauce ingredients in a saucepan over a medium heat. Once the sauce begins to bubble, remove from the heat. Let it cool until warm to the touch, but not so hot it'll burn your face off. It'll take about 3 minutes.

PEAR AND CRANBERRY COBBLER

We made this cobbler during the Great East Coast Blizzard of 2010—aka Snowmageddon. We were literally snowed in under 20 inches of snow in a town that doesn't own a snowplow. Everything was closed and no one delivered. At one point, Dan had to hike through the snow to get us some juice, coffee, tortilla chips, and salsa from a 7-Eleven that was open. *Sigh.* But this cobbler made everything right.

MAKES 6 SERVINGS

½ cup plus 1 tablespoon sugar

1 tablespoon cornstarch

½ teaspoon pumpkin pie spice

4 large Bosc pears, cored and cubed

½ cup dried cranberries

Juice from ½ a large lemon

3 tablespoons vegetable shortening

1 cup all-purpose flour

1½ teaspoons baking powder

½ teaspoon crushed pink Himalayan salt

½ cup vanilla soy milk

Preheat the oven to 400°F.

Mix ½ cup of the sugar, cornstarch, and pumpkin pie spice in a 2-quart saucepan. Stir in the pears, cranberries, and lemon juice. Cook over medium heat, stirring constantly, until the mixture thickens and boils. Boil and stir for 1 minute. Pour into an ungreased 2-quart casserole and keep the pear mixture hot in the oven.

Mix the shortening, flour, remaining 1 tablespoon sugar, the baking powder and salt in a medium bowl, using a pastry blender until the mixture becomes crumbs. Stir in the soy milk. Drop the dough in six big spoonfuls onto the hot pear mixture.

Bake for 25 to 30 minutes. Remove when the top is golden brown.

ROASTED CHERRY AND POMEGRANATE TOFURKY AND TEA STUFFING

Why is this holiday roast recipe more Christmasy than Thanksgiving-y? Well, because it's red and because I said so. Any other questions? Though, in all seriousness, this dish would be equally at home at either holiday—or any other family dinner, for that matter.

MAKES ENOUGH TO SERVE 4 TO 6

1 tablespoon chopped fresh sage leaves

2 tablespoons Bragg's liquid aminos

1½ teaspoons crushed black peppercorns

1 Tofurky or vegan holiday roast, defrosted

½ cup pomegranate-flavored black tea, brewed per the instructions on the package

Olive oil cooking spray

GLAZE
½ cup whole cherry jam

2 teaspoons grated orange peel

1 teaspoon brown sugar

½ cup pomegranate juice

½ cup Better Than Bouillon vegan chicken broth, made per the instructions on the package

Preheat the oven to 350°F.

In a small bowl, mix the sage, Bragg's, and black pepper. Place the Tofurky in a large bowl and rub the sage mixture into it.

Fill your frightening yet fabulous flavor injector (see "Where Do They Get Those Wonderful Toys?" on page 16 for more details) with tea. Stick the flavor injector at an upward angle at the seam in one end of your Tofurky and inject the tea. You're flavoring the stuffing, so try to keep the tea in the stuffing but high enough so that while the Tofurky is baking, the tea will trickle down into the stuffing.

Place the Tofurky on the rack of your much-loved shallow roasting pan. Spray a light coating of olive oil cooking spray over the top. Place the Tofurky in the oven and roast for 20 minutes.

Meanwhile, in small bowl, mix the glaze ingredients with an electric handheld mixer and set aside.

Once the Tofurky has a light golden crust on the outside, pull it out and brush on the glaze. Roast for 1 hour, brushing periodically with more glaze.

I recommend serving with Pomegranate and Cranberry Sauce (page 448) and some green beans to add a little more color to your holiday feast.

GINGERBREAD COOKIES

These cookies are soft vegan versions of those traditional Christmas treats from your childhood. The week we made these, we ate them with our morning coffee every day. Cookie breakfasts are one of the best things about the holidays.

MAKES 4 DOZEN LARGE COOKIES

1 cup packed brown sugar

1½ cups dark molasses

⅓ cup vegetable shortening

⅔ cup plus 4 tablespoons cold water

7 cups all-purpose flour, plus more for flouring surfaces and your rolling pin

2 teaspoons baking powder

2 teaspoons ground ginger

1 teaspoon allspice

1 teaspoon ground cinnamon

1 teaspoon ground cloves

½ teaspoon crushed pink Himalayan salt

Baking spray

Preheat the oven to 350°F.

In a bowl, mix the brown sugar, molasses, shortening, and ⅔ cup of the water with an electric mixer until completely blended. Mix in the flour, baking powder, ginger, allspice, cinnamon, cloves, and salt with the electric mixer and blend completely. The dough will be pasty and sticky—it's the molasses. Once your dough is completely blended, cover it and put in the fridge for at least 2 hours.

Spray your cookie sheet with baking spray. Roll the dough out to ¼-inch thickness on a floured surface with a floured rolling pin. Use cookie cutters to cut out your cookies. Place them on the cookie sheet, making sure they're at least 1 to 2 inches apart.

Bake for 5 to 10 minutes; it depends on how big your cookies are. Immediately move them to a wire rack to cool for at least an hour. Then decorate! You can use the Apple Vanilla Glaze on page 398, but there are also a lot of vegan-friendly frosting kits that come out around the holidays with all those fun sprinkles and sparkles.

GINGERBREAD WHOOPIE PIES

We made these whoopie pies at our very first live cooking demonstration, at an event held by the great group Mercy for Animals in Manhattan. They were a huge crowd-pleaser—and they will be at your next holiday party, too.

MAKES 1 ½ DOZEN WHOOPIE PIES

Baking spray

1 batch Just Like Buttercream Frosting (page 392)

Christmasy sprinkles

3 cups all-purpose flour

2 teaspoons ground ginger

1 teaspoon ground cinnamon

1 teaspoon baking soda

¼ teaspoon grated nutmeg

¼ teaspoon crushed pink Himalayan salt

¾ cup margarine

1 cup brown sugar

½ cup blackstrap molasses

2 tablespoons applesauce

1 teaspoon vanilla extract

Set aside the baking spray, Just Like Buttercream Frosting, and sprinkles.

In a large bowl, mix all the remaining ingredients with an electric handheld mixer until you get a paste. Cover your bowl with foil and refrigerate for 3 hours.

Preheat the oven to 350°F. Spray a light coating of baking spray over your whoopie pie pan or cookie sheet.

Use your hands to roll your dough into small balls and then flatten them with your palms. Place the flattened balls in the cups of your whoopie pie pan. Make sure you make an even number of equally sized cookies.

Bake for 8 to 10 minutes, or until the cookies are somewhat springy. Use an oven-mitted hand to poke one of the cookies to test it out. You might ruin this cookie if you poke it too soon—so think of this one as your sacrificial cookie.

Once your cookies are done, move them to a wire rack to cool. You need to make sure your cookies reach room temperature before you start building your whoopie pies. Pour a few tablespoons of Christmasy sprinkles in a shallow dish.

To build your whoopie pies, put 2 to 3 tablespoons of frosting on 1 cookie; then take another cookie and put it on top to make a cookie sandwich. Gently squeeze your whoopie pies so the frosting peeks out. Roll the frosting edge in the Christmasy sprinkles.

HANUKKAH AND PASSOVER

Don't worry; I'm not going to get all Talmudic scholar on you. But I will tell you what Hanukkah means to the Shannons.

Hanukkah—which isn't even a high holiday in the Jewish calendar—is one of the best holidays of the year. It's a holiday about heroism and the importance of hope. It's about a guy named Judah and his band of merry Maccabees defeating one of the most powerful armies in the world and standing up to tyranny. As activists, it's inspiring to celebrate a holiday about standing up to bullies—and as vegans, it's fun to celebrate a holiday so easy to veganize.

Unfortunately, Hanukkah is put in the impossible position of having to compete with Christmas every winter. Jewish families—or half-Jewish ones, like mine growing up—can find themselves struggling to get their kids as excited about playing dreidel, eating chocolate gelt, and lighting candles as their Santa-loving peers are about candy canes and decorating trees. But maybe rather than trying to make Hanukkah into "Jewish Christmas," we just need to take it as an opportunity to reflect on the importance of fighting the good fight, and enjoy some baked latkes and beefless brisket.

CHALLAH

I had never baked challah bread before, so it was a huge thrill for me to find this recipe in Betty Crocker's Big Red. Finally I had an excuse to come up with a vegan recipe for this traditional treat. It was a wonderful way for Dan and me to celebrate our first Hanukkah together, and introduce my *goyish* husband to my family's traditions. We exchanged presents, lit candles, spun a dreidel, and watched basketball—you know, just like Judah and the rest of those badass Maccabees did back in the day.

This bread is dedicated to Captain Kirk and Mr. Spock—both Jewish!

MAKES 1 LOAF OF BREAD

3 cups all-purpose flour, plus more for flouring your surfaces

4 tablespoons maple syrup

1½ teaspoons crushed pink Himalayan salt

1 teaspoon nutritional yeast

1 package dry active yeast

1 cup very warm water

2 tablespoons olive oil, plus more to brush on the bread

1 tablespoon applesauce

Vegetable shortening, for greasing your bowl

Olive oil cooking spray

VEGAN "EGG" WASH

1 tablespoon water

½ teaspoon olive oil

½ teaspoon maple syrup

1 teaspoon apple juice

¼ teaspoon nutritional yeast

In a large bowl, mix 1½ cups of the flour with the maple syrup, salt, nutritional yeast, and yeast. Add the water and olive oil and blend with an electric mixer for 2 minutes. Be sure to scrape the sides of the bowl often to make sure all the ingredients are mixed in. Blend in the applesauce and remaining flour until your dough is smooth.

Place the dough on a lightly floured surface and knead for 10 minutes. Grease a large bowl with vegetable shortening. Place the dough in your greased bowl and spin it around a few times to get a light coating. Loosely seal the bowl with plastic wrap and place in a warm place to rise for 1 hour, or until it doubles in size. We let ours sit overnight.

Preheat the oven to 375°F. Spray a light coating of olive oil cooking spray over a cookie sheet.

Once your dough has doubled in size and is springy to the touch, remove it from the bowl and divide it into three equal segments. Roll each segment into a long rope. Try to keep the ropes about the same size. Don't stretch your dough, though. It'll cause the bread to have a pulled, stretched, not-smooth appearance. Just roll it out.

Lay the 3 ropes in a row and braid them loosely from the center out. Pinch the ends under to secure them. Brush a light coating of olive oil over the bread and place the loaf on the greased cooking sheet. Cover loosely with plastic wrap and let rise in a warm place for another hour.

In a small bowl, mix all the ingredients for the vegan "egg" wash with a whisk. Once your loaf has risen, brush it with the vegan "egg" wash.

Bake for 20 to 30 minutes. Remove from the oven once the loaf is golden brown. Thicker braids may take longer to bake.

MARBLE BUNDT CAKE

Marble cake is pretty common at the Hanukkah tables of many Ashkenazi Jews, although it's hard to really explain why. There isn't a specific cultural relevance that I'm aware of, or some historical connection to this dish. Maybe it's as simple as this: it's delicious. Why *wouldn't* you want to eat it for Hanukkah? Or any other time of the year?

MAKES 1 CAKE

2½ cups sugar	2 teaspoons baking powder	1 cup almond milk
¾ cup baking cocoa powder	½ teaspoon crushed pink Himalayan salt	½ teaspoon almond extract
¼ cup agave nectar	1 cup margarine	Baking spray
½ cup hot water	3 tablespoons applesauce	1 batch Chocolate Agave Glaze (page 398)
2 teaspoons vanilla extract	2 teaspoons Ener-G egg replacer, just the powder, not prepared per the instructions on the package	
3 cups all-purpose flour		

Preheat the oven to 350°F.

In your favorite saucepan, whisk together ½ cup of the sugar and the cocoa powder, agave nectar, and water, and heat over medium heat. Bring to a simmer while constantly whisking. Once you have smooth syrup, remove your saucepan from the heat and whisk in ½ teaspoon of the vanilla. Once your syrup is smooth, wash off your whisk.

In a large mixing bowl, mix the flour, baking powder, and salt with a whisk until blended.

In another bowl, using an electric hand mixer, blend the margarine and remaining 2 cups of sugar into a fluffy cream. Tilting your bowl while you blend will help make your blend fluffier by getting more air in there. Mix in the applesauce, egg replacer, almond milk, and remaining 1½ teaspoons vanilla. Once your margarine blend is smooth and creamy, add your flour mixture 1 cup at a time, blending with your handheld mixer until you have a smooth cake batter.

Move a third of the cake batter to a separate bowl and

blend in your chocolate syrup until thoroughly mixed. You want your chocolate batter not to have any marbling or pockets of white in it. Be sure to clean your mixer attachment before you move from one batter to another. This will keep the swirls of flavor and color distinct in your marbling. Blend your almond extract into the remaining batter.

Coat your Bundt cake pan with a heavy layer of baking spray.

Using a ladle, pour half of your white cake batter into your Bundt cake pan. Use a spatula to spread the batter out evenly. Pour your chocolate cake batter over your white cake batter and gently spread it out with your spatula. Then pour the remaining white cake batter over the top. Using a bamboo skewer, *very* slightly swirl the cake batter only once in a small wave. Use your spatula to make sure the top of the cake batter is flat. This will be the bottom of the cake, so make sure it's even.

Bake until you can stick a bamboo skewer in the cake and have it come out cleanly. It should take 30 to 45 minutes. There are a lot of different types of Bundt cake pans, though, so yours might take a little more or less time.

Before you remove your cake from the pan, use the bamboo skewer to make a dozen or so little stabs into the top of it. You're releasing moisture from the cake to help it cool and also releasing the cake from the pan. Let the cake cool for 10 minutes in the pan, and then turn the pan upside down on a large serving dish.

While the cake is baking and cooling, make your Chocolate Agave Glaze in a small bowl. Once the cake is completely cooled, drizzle the glaze over it.

Mazel tov! You've just made a cake that would make your bubbe verklempt!

BAKED LATKES

In a world of latke recipes, here's what makes this one special: (1) It's vegan. (2) It's baked, not fried. (3) It's extra-super tasty. We enjoyed these little *bubelas* during Hanukkah with some vegan sour cream while we watched basketball and played board games and tried to stay alive under three layers of blankets.

MAKES 12 TO 15 LATKES

5 to 6 Yukon Gold potatoes

1 red onion, diced

¼ cup whole wheat flour

1 teaspoon crushed pink Himalayan salt

½ teaspoon Bragg's liquid aminos

1 teaspoon applesauce

1 tablespoon nutritional yeast

1 tablespoon olive oil

¼ teaspoon crushed black peppercorns

1 tablespoon Ener-G egg replacer, just the powder, not prepared as instructed on the package

Olive oil cooking spray

Vegan sour cream and applesauce for toppings

Preheat the oven to 450°F.

Shred enough potatoes with either a cheese grater or food processor to make 4 cups. In a large bowl, combine the onion, flour, salt, Bragg's, applesauce, nutritional yeast, olive oil, pepper, and egg replacer with the shredded potatoes. Spray a baking sheet with olive oil cooking spray.

Place rounded tablespoons of the batter on the baking sheet and flatten with a spatula. Pop the latkes in the oven, bake for around 5 minutes, flip them, and put them back in the oven to bake for another 5 minutes. Check them and keep flipping them every 5 minutes till they reach the desired crispiness.

Serve warm with vegan sour cream and applesauce.

PINCH OF CHUTZPAH MATZO BALL SOUP

Before we moved to Brooklyn, every spring Dan and I hosted some of the best Secular Passover Potluck Seders in Virginia. We lived in PETA-ville (also known as Norfolk, Virginia: HQ for People for the Ethical Treatment of Animals), where most people we knew were transplants from elsewhere, and maybe that's why we all grew so close. You find yourself within walking distance of people who share your view of the world and your love of vegan food, and it's impossible not to find a family—a *mishpocha*—in this home away from home. Modern technology will still keep us close now that we've moved away, but I'm not sure when we'll ever be able to sit down at a table to share bowls of this soup together. I guess that's what airplanes are for.

Your matzo dough will need to hang out in the fridge overnight so you're going to need to start this recipe the night before you're going to serve your soup.

MAKES 6 TO 8 SERVINGS

- 1 (14-ounce) package firm silken tofu
- 9 cups Better Than Bouillon vegetable broth, made per the instructions on the package
- ½ cup olive oil
- 1 cup matzo meal
- ½ cup nutritional yeast
- ¾ teaspoon Bragg's liquid aminos
- ¾ teaspoon crushed black peppercorns
- 2 tablespoons dry white wine
- 3 carrots, sliced into coins
- ¼ teaspoon celery seed
- ½ large red onion, diced
- 1 tablespoon chopped fresh parsley
- 1 teaspoon chopped fresh dill
- 2 pinches of onion powder

Blend your tofu, 1 tablespoon of the broth, and the olive oil in your food processor or blender. In a bowl, mix the matzo meal, nutritional yeast, Bragg's, and black pepper. Then combine the matzo and broth mixtures in the bowl until everything is moist, and ta-da—you have dough! Cover the bowl and put in the fridge overnight. You can visit your matzo a few times throughout the evening and give it a good mix with a spoon, but always put it back in the fridge.

It'll take about an hour to cook your matzo balls, so 1½ to 2 hours before you want to serve your soup, fill your pot with the rest of your vegetable broth, the white wine, carrots, celery seed, onion, parsley, dill, and onion powder and bring to a boil.

Line a casserole dish with parchment paper. Remove your matzo dough from the fridge. Form extremely tightly packed balls about the size of a melon ball, and place them on the parchment paper so they don't touch. Once they're all made, you can start dropping them in the boiling soup one at a time. Give yourself time so you don't need to rush. After they're all in your broth, put the lid on and leave it on for around ½ hour. Don't lift the lid. I know you'll want to, but it's okay. Just give them time. Sometimes you just have to let things do their thing and have faith.

After that ½ hour, lift the lid and watch your matzo balls rise to the top.

Now you're ready to *nosh all night!*

BAKED BEET AND CARROT LATKES

For the non-Jewish among you: latkes are potato pancakes traditionally eaten during Hanukkah. Yep. Pancakes. Made out of potatoes. Yep. Being Jewish pretty much rules.

MAKES 8 TO 10 LATKES

2 raw beets

3 large raw carrots

1 large raw Yukon Gold potato

1 red onion, diced

¼ cup whole wheat flour

1 teaspoon crushed pink Himalayan salt

½ teaspoon Bragg's liquid aminos

1 teaspoon applesauce

1 tablespoon nutritional yeast

2 tablespoons olive oil

¼ teaspoon crushed black peppercorns

1 tablespoon Ener-G egg replacer, just the powder, not prepared as instructed on the package

Olive oil cooking spray

1 (12-ounce) package vegan sour cream for topping

1 tablespoon chopped fresh chives for toppings

Preheat the oven to 450°F.

Use a cheese grater or food processor to shred your beets, carrots, and potato. Move the vegetables to a large bowl. Mix in the onion, flour, salt, Bragg's, applesauce, nutritional yeast, olive oil, pepper, and egg replacer with a large spoon. Spray your foil-lined cookie sheet with olive oil cooking spray.

Place rounded small mounds of the latke batter on the baking sheet and flatten with a spatula. Pop them in the oven, bake for 5 minutes, flip them, and put them back in the oven to bake for another 5 minutes. Check them and keep flipping them every 5 minutes till they reach the desired crispiness.

Serve warm with the vegan sour cream and chives.

SUFGANIYOT (JELLY DOUGHNUTS)

These deep-fried doughnut-y treats are traditionally served in Israel in the weeks leading up to Hanukkah and during the holiday itself. Ours are filled with jelly, although they can also be filled with chocolate or vanilla custard. They're generally eaten warm—so no slacking!

Your dough will need to chill out overnight so you're going to need to start this recipe the night before you're going to make your doughnuts.

MAKES 1½ DOZEN DOUGHNUTS

1¼ cups vanilla soy milk

2 tablespoons brown sugar

2 tablespoons margarine

1 package active dry yeast

½ teaspoon crushed pink Himalayan salt

¾ teaspoon grated nutmeg

2 cups all-purpose flour (you'll need more to flour your surfaces)

1 tablespoon Ener-G egg replacer, just the powder, not prepared as instructed on the package

1 tablespoon applesauce

1 batch of Raspberry Filling (page 402) or Lemon Filling (page 401)

Vegetable oil for frying

Powdered sugar for topping

In a small saucepan, heat the soy milk until it begins to steam. Stir in the brown sugar and margarine and turn the heat down to a simmer. Once your margarine is melted, remove from the heat and cool to room temperature. Transfer the sweetened soy milk to a large bowl, and stir in the yeast, salt, nutmeg, and flour. Stir in the egg replacer and applesauce with a large spoon, and then blend with a hand mixer using dough hooks for about 2 minutes. You want the batter to be smooth. It's very sticky, though, so be careful to not get it on yourself or anyone you care about...it'll cause unhappiness. Cover your bowl with foil and allow your batter to chill in the fridge overnight.

The next morning, gently knead your batter on a heavily floured surface and roll it out with a floured rolling pin. Use a biscuit cutter or the top of a pint glass to cut out your doughnuts. Try to plan out your strategy beforehand to make sure you get as many doughnuts from your dough as possible. You can toss the little bits of extra in the hot oil too at the end and have bitty doughnut bites.

Lay your raw doughnuts out on a piece of wax paper and cover with a fabric napkin or towel. Let them chill out and rise for another 35 minutes.

During this time, make your filling. You can choose between the Raspberry Filling and the Lemon Filling, or you can use real fruit jam.

Fill your Dutch oven or soup pot halfway with vegetable oil and heat at a high temperature until it starts to bubble.

Carefully place a piece of leftover doughnut dough in your hot oil to see if it's ready to fry. Once your oil is hot enough, start placing the doughnuts in one at time. Let them fry for 30 to 45 seconds on each side, or until they turn golden brown. Use a slotted spoon to remove them, and place them on a plate with a paper towel to soak up extra oil. Once they're cool enough to handle—but not cold—fill your favorite frosting gun with filling and, using the smallest tip, gently fill each doughnut by poking the tip into the side and pressing in 1 to 2 tablespoons filling. Sprinkle a lot of powdered sugar over each doughnut and enjoy!

The Vegan Seder Plate

We all know the classic movie with Charlton Heston, and the lyrics to "Swing Low, Sweet Chariot." But you may not know what those things have to do with Passover. See, Passover is the Jewish celebration of God sparing the Jews from the curse of the firstborn, and freeing them from slavery in Egypt. The traditions behind this seven-day celebration of freedom go back thousands of years and are meant to remind us that God doesn't approve of oppression and exploitation. So it's about time we celebrated, vegan-style!

The traditional Seder plate includes an egg (*beitzah*). Some say this represents a sacrifice; others say it represents a new beginning. I like to replace the *beitzah* with an avocado. Not only does it replace the egg aesthetically, but the seed inside represents the idea of rebirth in the same way the egg is meant to.

Then there's the roasted shank bone (*z'roa*). This represents both the lamb sacrificed at the Temple of Jerusalem and the blood used to mark the doors of the Israelites. I use a piece of TVP to replace the *z'roa* on my plate, but I've also heard of people using a beet (which gets a big thumbs-up from the Talmud).

Just as Jews have come to embrace technology like airplanes and running water, embracing modern, compassionate alternatives to meat truly reflects the spirit of Passover. It's never been easier to have a Seder that reflects the ideals of freedom and liberation behind this celebration, and that's what makes this one of my favorite holidays.

Shalom!

EASTER

Vegan Easter has many fine qualities, including Sweet and Sara's Peepers and Skippers (vegan peeps) and dark chocolate bunnies. But what most of us look forward to the most is the big dinner or brunch parties full of springtime vegetable dishes. See, Easter can have a bad reputation of being the unhealthiest holiday from all that cheap, colorful candy, chocolate, and of course those eggs. But it doesn't have to be like that. Around Easter a new wave of fresh vegetables hits the grocery stores, and farmers' markets open. Beautiful avocados, asparagus, and artichokes pop up to encourage us to add more green to our diet. Fresh berries add more than just some color and flavor to our breakfasts. They're full of antioxidants that can curb the growth of some cancers.

Throughout this book you can find recipes like Fresh Lemon and Asparagus Soup (page 58), Carrot Cake Cupcakes (page 360), and Végétalien Tarte aux Fruits Frais (Vegan French Fresh Fruit Tart) (page 389) to complete your Easter feast. In this section you'll find recipes to help you create a few of those signature Easter treats you see in magazines.

MAPLE GLAZE HOLIDAY ROAST

Every dinner party has a centerpiece, whether they know it or not, and from what I gather, when it comes to Easter the traditional superstars are ham, lasagna, and manicotti. We used a Tofurky to replace the less compassionate ham but still played around with the whole cloves and baked it with a smoky maple and brown sugar glaze to create a vegan dish that will feel right at home being the center of attention.

MAKES 4 TO 6 SERVINGS

1 Tofurky or vegan holiday roast, completely defrosted

20 to 25 whole cloves

⅓ cup brown sugar

¼ cup dry white wine or apple juice

1 tablespoon applesauce

2 to 3 dashes of liquid smoke

¼ teaspoon ground mustard seed

¼ cup plus 2 tablespoons maple syrup

Pinch of crushed pink Himalayan salt

Pinch of crushed black peppercorns

Preheat the oven to 350°F.

Once your roast is completely defrosted, gently press a long knife in a shallow crisscross pattern across the top of it. Take a bamboo skewer and gently poke a hole in the center of each diamond created on the roast by the pattern. Cloves can be a little brittle, so this will help you insert them into your roast without crumbling them. Very gently press your cloves into the holes in your roast until the stem is completely inserted and just the little bud is showing. Place your roast in a glass baking dish.

In your favorite mixing bowl, whisk together the brown sugar, white wine, applesauce, liquid smoke, mustard seed, ¼ cup of the maple syrup, salt, and pepper until the brown sugar dissolves. Brush a layer of this glaze over your entire roast. You want to make

sure you get the glaze on the ends and into all the folds and cuts. Lift your roast in the dish so that any glaze that has collected in the dish can cover the bottom. Put your roast in the oven to bake for 10 minutes.

Pull your roast out of the oven and brush another layer of glaze over the top. Bake for another 10 minutes. Brush yet another layer of glaze over the top and bake for another 10 minutes. Let your roast cool for 5 to 8 minutes, and then drizzle the remaining 2 tablespoons maple syrup over the top.

Before you begin slicing, you might want to remove your cloves using a fork. It not only makes it easier to slice, but have you ever eaten a whole clove? I'm pretty sure humankind wasn't meant to. Don't worry, you'll keep the spice flavor of the clove in the roast even without the actual clove.

PEANUT BUTTER EGGS

VegNews magazine featured our veganized Girl Scout cookies in February 2012. We took our veganized Tagalongs and made them into a perfect Easter cookie that combines chocolate with a soft peanut butter filling and a crunchy, "buttery" cookie.

MAKES 1 ½ TO 2 DOZEN COOKIES

COOKIES

1 cup vegan margarine

½ cup granulated sugar

2¼ cups all-purpose flour

¼ teaspoon ground flaxseed

1 teaspoon vanilla extract

½ teaspoon salt

1 tablespoon applesauce

2 tablespoons vanilla soy milk

PEANUT BUTTER FILLING

1 cup powdered sugar

½ cup chunky natural peanut butter

⅛ teaspoon salt

CHOCOLATE COATING

1 (10-ounce) bag vegan chocolate chips

Preheat the oven to 400°F. Line a cookie sheet with foil.

In a large bowl, blend the margarine and sugar until creamy with an electric handheld mixer. Add the flour, flaxseed, vanilla, salt, applesauce, and soy milk, and blend until the dough is smooth.

In a cookie press without a form, or with your hands, roll the dough into a uniform tube. Slice into ¼-inch wafers. Use your thumb to gently press one side of your wafer to create an oblong or egg shape. On your lined cookie sheet, bake your wafers for 6 to 8 minutes, or until the edges are golden brown. Remove and place on wire cooling rack.

While your cookies are baking, make your peanut butter filling. In a large bowl, mix the powdered sugar, peanut butter, and salt. With your hands, use roughly 1 tablespoon of peanut butter filling each to form small balls, and gently press one on top of each cooled cookie.

Once your cookies are built, make your chocolate coating. Follow the directions on the vegan chocolate chips package on how to melt them. Once your chocolate is fully melted, drop the cookies into your chocolate one at a time, using a spoon to pour chocolate over the top and coat evenly.

Place the dipped cookies on a piece of parchment. When all your cookies are coated, place the parchment paper on a cookie sheet and chill the cookies in the refrigerator for 2 hours, or until the chocolate is fully dry.

SWEET POTATO HOT CROSS BUNS

Baking special sweet buns in the springtime is a practice that goes back to the ancient Greeks and Saxons. Some did it to "bless" their baking for the rest of the year; some believed if you took them on an ocean voyage it would keep your ship safe. When these buns got sweet crosses painted on them and became a Good Friday tradition is hard to say. We added brightly colored sweet potatoes packed with beta-carotene to our dough to add flavor and natural sweetness.

MAKES 2 DOZEN ROLLS

¾ cup warm water

1 package active dry yeast

1 sweet potato, baked and cooled to room temperature

1 cup soy milk

¼ cup margarine

2 tablespoons brown sugar

1 teaspoon grated orange peel

½ teaspoon ground cinnamon

½ teaspoon cardamom

¼ teaspoon grated nutmeg

2 teaspoons crushed pink Himalayan salt

3 cups all-purpose flour (you'll need more to flour your surfaces)

1 cup whole wheat flour

1½ cups raisins

1 batch Apple Vanilla Glaze (page 398)

In a large bowl, mix your water and yeast and let stand until the yeast is dissolved. Then scrape the soft inside of your baked sweet potato into your mixing bowl and blend. Add the soy milk, margarine, brown sugar, orange peel, cinnamon, cardamom, nutmeg, and salt. Use your handheld mixer to blend all your ingredients until they're creamy. Change your attachments on your handheld mixer to your dough hooks and blend in your flours, 1 cup at a time. Your dough is going to be ridiculously sticky—so avoid getting it on yourself or anyone you love. Use a large spoon to fold in your raisins.

Cover your bowl loosely with foil and let stand in a warm spot until the dough doubles in size. It should take about 45 minutes. Line a cookie sheet with parchment paper.

Use floured hands to form your dough into 24 buns that are about the size of your palm. Place your raw buns about 5 inches apart on your parchment-lined cookie sheet. Cover loosely with plastic wrap and allow your buns to rise until they double in size. This should take another 30 minutes.

Preheat the oven to 400°F.

Once your buns have risen, remove the plastic wrap and bake the buns for 20 to 25 minutes, until they are puffed and toasted brown.

While your buns are baking, make your Apple Vanilla Glaze.

Let your buns cool to room temperature before crossing your buns with your Apple Vanilla Glaze. Let the glazed buns sit for another 10 minutes so your glaze can set before serving.

MAPLE BUNNIES

These tasty treats are a great recipe to make with kids. They're simple to make, don't take so long the little ones lose interest, and end up in fun shapes they'll love. You'll love them because they're delicious, with a maple sweetness that isn't too overpowering or saccharine.

MAKES 2 DOZEN BUNNIES

2 packages active dry yeast

¼ cup warm water

1⅓ cups almond milk

½ cup sugar

½ teaspoon crushed pink Himalayan salt

1 tablespoon applesauce

2 teaspoons Ener-G egg replacer, just the powder, not prepared per the instructions on the package

⅓ cup vegetable shortening

5 cups all-purpose flour (you'll need some extra to flour your surfaces)

3 to 4 cups vegetable oil for frying

1 batch Maple Bourbon Glaze (page 400; you can make it without the bourbon for kids)

Sprinkles to doll up your doughnut

In one of your largest mixing bowls, mix the yeast and warm water with a whisk. Let sit for a while so your yeast can dissolve. Once it's bubbly, you're ready to move on to the next step.

Mix in the almond milk, sugar, salt, applesauce, egg replacer, vegetable shortening, and flour using your electric handheld mixer with dough hooks. This is sticky stuff, so don't get it on you or anything or anyone you love. Once the dough is completely blended, place a cloth over the top of the bowl and put the bowl in a cozy spot to let the dough rise. It should take a few hours. You'll know your dough is ready when it's doubled in size.

Heat your vegetable oil on high in your largest stockpot or Dutch oven.

Use your fist to deflate the dough. Then move your dough to a floured workspace to roll it out with your floured rolling pin until it's about ½ inch thick. Use a bunny cookie cutter to cut out your doughnuts. You can also just use a biscuit cutter or the top of a pint glass if you hate bunnies.[*] Flip the raw doughnuts a few times in the flour. Use some of the extra dough between the bunnies to see if your oil is hot enough to fry your doughnuts yet. Once your sacrificial tester dough clump is frying carefully place your doughnuts in the hot oil one at a time. Once they're golden brown, use a slotted spoon to move them onto a plate with a paper towel to drain off any extra oil.

While your doughnuts are frying and cooling, make your Maple Bourbon Glaze.

Once your bunnies have cooled enough that you can handle them, dip the tops in the Maple Bourbon Glaze and move them to a wire rack to cool. Once they're all glazed, sprinkle your sprinkles over the top.

---

[*] What kind of monster hates bunnies?

AFTERWORD

If you were to stop a hundred people on the street and ask them who Martha Gellhorn was, the sad fact is that the very small percentage of people who did know would say, "Wasn't she married to Ernest Hemingway?"

The thing is, they wouldn't be wrong. But before she was Mrs. Hemingway, she was an American war correspondent and author who did some amazing things—including covering the rise of Adolf Hitler in Germany. She had an exceptional career full of extraordinary moments, such as when she impersonated a stretcher bearer to cover the D-Day landings because she lacked the penis required to get press credentials. She was one of the first reporters on the scene at the Dachau concentration camp after it was liberated. She was even a close friend of Eleanor Roosevelt. But sadly, to much of the world, she will always be one of Hem's old ladies.

When I started the Betty Crocker Project, I wasn't nearly as accomplished as Martha—but I could relate. After years and years in the animal rights movement, I often felt that I was known in the animal rights world more for whom I'd married and dated and what I brought to potlucks than for the projects, campaigns, and victories I'd worked on. The year I started this book was also the year Dan and I found out that becoming parents was going to be more challenging than we had ever expected—which was especially hard because it was also the year some of our closest friends became parents. We had friends move away and get promotions that kept them on the road or in the office constantly. For me, it seemed like despite all my personal success in my marriage, my professional life was stuck in a rut…tracking down animal abusers online and working from home in boxer shorts and hoodies. But it all changed with the Betty Crocker Project and this book.

Two years, several meltdowns, experimental casseroles, hundreds of recipes, first-degree burns, and a very dramatic move to Brooklyn later: we have this book. I had the hardest time writing it—not because of those things I listed or my impossible expectations of myself, but because I never wanted to be finished with it. From that first day, with that first lobster, I have found a way to meet amazingly creative and compassionate people and be shamelessly nerdy in a socially acceptable way, and have become downright obsessed with challenging the myth that being vegan is anything less than fabulous.

This book doesn't mean we'll stop writing the blog, of course; there will always be more whoopie pies to bake and casseroles to veganize. There are still billions of animals needlessly being killed each year for food, and countless not-yet-vegans out there who still have no idea that vegans don't just live off raw tofu and quinoa salads. That's where we come in.

One of our dear friends gave me a huge cherry red box of circa 1970 Betty Crocker recipe cards to inspire the next generation of *Betty Goes Vegan*. I won't lie—there are some real challenges in there that have already gotten me thinking. We're also taking a pilgrimage to the Betty Crocker test kitchens in Minnesota to see the real "Bettys" in their natural habitat…and who knows what could happen after that? Maybe it'll be like Narnia, and I won't come back until after I've already lived a lifetime of culinary adventures. I guess we'll never know until I show up at her door.

But I can tell you this. I was soul sick when I brought home my copy of the *Betty Crocker Cookbook*. But I'm better now. In the end, Betty Crocker did encourage me to "Bake Someone Happy"—me. I know that sounds unbelievably trite, but sometimes the most sincere statements just do.

INDEX

ACKNOWLEDGMENTS

We just want to say thank you to some of the folks who helped turn our little project into this book: Ed and Linda Shannon, Laura Dail (our rainmaker), Diana Baroni (for her patience with my typos), Amanda Englander, Rory Freedman, Libbe Blain, Alka Chandna, Sarah Kramer, Lisa Lange, Jasmin Singer, Mariann Sullivan, Anjali Prasertong, John McDevitt (for being the first reader of our blog), Chloe Jo Davis, Quarry Girl, Kathy Patalsky, Marisa Miller Wolfson, Melisser Elliot, Erik Marcus, Shannon Radke, Sarah Fitch Posey, Joel Bartlett, Jack Shepherd, Stephanie Corrigan, Ben Gould, Marta Holmberg, Ben Peterson, Josh Hooten, Michelle Schwegmann, Cassandra Cusack Curbelo, Erin Edwards, Lorriane Eaton, Tareth Mitch, Melissa Chang, Lisa Shapiro, Allison Burgess, Sara Sohn, Greg Rekas, Kristin Treat, Chris Overton, Leinana Two Moons, Royale Ziegler, Anne Kingston, Gretchen Tseng, Eric Hopf, and the folks over at *VegNews* magazine.

And of course a big thank you to anyone who has ever decided that going vegan—even one day a week—is a good idea. I bet the animals would thank you too if they could!

ABOUT THE AUTHORS

Annie and Dan Shannon have lived all over the United States but now have a real home with two spoiled cats and a growing graphic novel collection in Brooklyn, New York. During her years as an activist Annie has worked in a wide variety of roles ranging from sexual assault counselor to fashion industry liaison promoting animal-friendly fashion, and playing a key role in Project Runway winner Jay McCarroll's fur-free fashion show at New York Fashion Week in 2006. In college, Dan served as president of the Wesleyan Animal Rights Network—the first campus animal rights organization to successfully lobby their school administration to use only cage-free eggs on campus, setting a precedent for many more to follow. Since college, Dan has worked for People for the Ethical Treatment of Animals, where he was the director of youth outreach and campaigns. These days Annie gets to focus full-time on veganizing everything and has completely given in to her inner nerd, which she likes to think of as "Geek Chic." Dan is the director of strategy at the social movement consulting firm Purpose and enjoys the wide range of superpowers this solar system's yellow sun gives him. You can follow their adventures at MeetTheShannons.com.